The Origins of the American High School

WILLIAM J. REESE

Yale University Press
New Haven
and
London

Designed by Christopher Harris/Summer Hill Books.
Set in Janson type by Marathon Typography Services, Inc., Durham, North Carolina.
Printed by Vail-Ballou Press, Binghamton, New York.

Library of Congress Cataloging-in-Publication Data

Reese, William J., 1951–
    The origins of the American high school / William J. Reese.
        p.   cm.
    Includes bibliographical references and index.
    ISBN 0-300-06384-9 (cloth : alk. paper)
    ISBN 0-300-07943-5 (pbk. : alk. paper)
    1. High schools—United States—History—19th century.
2. Education, Secondary—Social aspects—United States—
History—19th century.   I. Title.
LA222.R39   1995
373.73—dc20   94-24975
                                                        CIP

A catalogue record for this book is available from the
British Library.

The paper in this book meets the guidelines for permanence
 and durability of the Committee on Production Guidelines for
Book Longevity of the Council on Library Resources.

10 9 8 7 6 5 4 3 2

To Carl F. Kaestle, mentor and friend

Contents

Acknowledgments

During the past several years, many friends and colleagues have provided constructive criticisms of my research and writing on the nineteenth-century high school. My oldest debt, however, extends further back in time, before I began this project in the mid-eighties. This book is dedicated with affection to Carl F. Kaestle, my mentor in graduate school, who shepherded me through some wonderful years in Madison. My interest in social history flourished under his guidance, and I hope that this book approaches his high standards of scholarship. Despite his many professional obligations, Carl characteristically found the time to read the penultimate draft of this study and offer suggestions for improvement.

Through her love and encouragement, Carole Blemker made my years of research and writing possible. Ronald D. Cohen of Indiana University Northwest has encouraged me throughout this project, asking the right questions and sharing his vast knowledge about American history. Ron's own superb scholarship served as a model as I tried to make some sense out of my research notes. During an era when capitalism and communism literally appeared bankrupt, I have been spared the unemployment lines and been fortunate to get a regular paycheck from Indiana University at Bloomington, home to many supportive colleagues. B. Edward McClellan has been a special friend who stole time from his own research and administrative responsibilities to offer helpful comments. I've also benefited from the outstanding research assistance of several graduate students. Dina Stephens helped me gather materials on graduation ceremonies and other topics early in the study. Diana Bush was an invaluable research assistant, diligent in her work and wise in her judgments. Laurie Moses Hines was especially helpful in the time-consuming task of locating and preparing illustrations for this volume.

Over the past several years, members of the History of Education Colloquium at Bloomington criticized early drafts of my work. It is impossible to
say enough kind things about the graduate students and faculty members who
corrected my prose, questioned my logic, and encouraged me still. At different
points in the completion of the study, I've benefited from their wise counsel.
Many thanks to Ed Beauchamp, Don Cunningham, Alex Duke, Ben Eklof,
Jesus Garcia, Betty Hanson, Steve Harp, Alison Packwood Henry, Laurie
Moses Hines, Frank Lester, David Martin, Don Moore, Dan Mueller, Mark
Olesh, Joanne Passett, Dick Rubinger, Amy Schutt, Bob Schwartz, Liz
Spaulding, Ted Stahly, Charlie Titus, Greg True, Alex Urbiel, Don Warren,
and Scott Walter. Don Hossler, my department chair, graciously provided
steadfast financial support for the Colloquium. An early version of the chapter
on the English Classical School received constructive criticisms from members of the Colloquium on Religious History at Indiana; I am especially
grateful to Paul Lucas, Richard Miller, Bob Orsi, and Steve Stein.

Several secretaries also contributed enormously to this book, typing
numerous drafts with expert skill. Kathleen Chadwick prepared the early
chapters with incredible speed and accuracy. Laura Rogers somehow found
time in her busy schedule to type the rest of the book and its innumerable
revisions. I am very grateful to both Kathleen and Laura for their kindness.
The book has also benefited from generous research grants provided by the
Graduate School of Indiana University and by the Spencer Foundation and
Proffitt Foundation administered through the I.U. School of Education.
These funds enabled me to travel to many research collections and archives to
explore some remarkable materials essential to this study. My colleague Rick
Pugh has continually supported my research efforts, for which I remain very
grateful.

Several friends outside of Bloomington kindly offered constructive com-
ments on my work or encouraged me in other ways. Richard Aldrich of the
University of London became a steadfast friend during the course of this project, and our conversations on the state of the field proved invaluable. Mary
Ann Dzuback of Washington University, David Adams of Cleveland State
University, and Maris Vinovskis of the University of Michigan also provided
incisive commentaries on my manuscript. David Labaree of Michigan State
University and Larry Cuban of Stanford University provided encouragement
when it was especially needed and offered helpful suggestions for revision. So
did John Rury of DePaul University, who also offered chapter-by-chapter
constructive criticisms, and Jurgen Herbst, who gave me sound advice as I
brought this project to a close.

Barry Franklin of the University of Michigan-Flint read my chapters on the
high school curriculum and textbooks, offering cogent criticisms at every turn.
Ken Teitelbaum of SUNY-Binghamton kindly directed me toward valuable
studies on the history of the curriculum. I am also grateful to Herbert
Kliebard and the late Edward Krug, whose teaching and writing about secondary education kindled my interest in the subject. Gladys Topkis, senior

editor at Yale University Press, consistently extended welcome doses of encouragement and thoughtfully wielded her masterful pen. To her a special thank you. My manuscript editor, Dan Heaton, has been unfailingly helpful, a master of his craft.

The contributions of many other scholars who helped me try to understand high schools before the 1880s remain buried in the notes. Without their dissertations, articles, and books, however, I could not have attempted to write a comprehensive history of the early high school. They and all of the wonderful friends whose help I've acknowledged could not save me from my mistakes of judgment and interpretation. Without them, however, the final product would have suffered.

Librarians and archivists were unfailingly helpful in my research, which led me to a few dozen university libraries and state and local historical societies. The reference librarians at Indiana University, especially Fred Musto, deserve special praise. He and his colleagues amazed me with their ability to locate even the most obscure documents, as they cheerfully responded to my constant stream of requests.

Midway through the completion of this project, I searched for illustrations for my prospective book, which led me to the photography collections of the Library of Congress. As I fumbled through the card catalogue, searching for materials on the American high school before the 1880s, an employee asked me what I was looking for. When I told him, he replied that my efforts were in vain: "There weren't any high schools before the 1880s." I hope he was wrong. Still, our knowledge of early secondary education is in its infancy. What I have said will require revision. As Walt Whitman wrote in 1855 in *Leaves of Grass*, "All I mark as my own you shall offset it with your own, / Else it were time lost listening to me."

Introduction

> It has always seemed to me that a large school like this of ours resembles a kingdom. The Principal is the King, the two head assistants his prime ministers, the rest officers of state, the Board of Committee is the Parliament; the special High School Committee representing the House of Lords, the rest the House of Commons. We the scholars are the subjects of higher or lower rank according to our intellectual capacities, for wealth and noble birth are of no consideration. The aristocracy is only in intellect. Many a one in the lowest ranks may reach the highest.
>
> Student, Girls' High School, Portland, Maine, 1863

The American high school was born in the nineteenth century. It hardly resembled any modern secondary school, but its appearance heralded the coming of a new educational order. Adolescents and their families faced the unsettling consequences of the early commercial and industrial revolution, urban growth, and immigration, which rendered familiar strategies for personal mobility and family security obsolete. In response, political activists and school reformers redefined the educational experiences of a minority of young men and women. The rise of an increasingly commercial, market-oriented society intensified social class divisions, providing the backdrop to the birth of America's public school system.[1]

Western nations everywhere invested more money in educating the young and reshaped existing secondary schools or invented new ones to confront the dilemmas of this new age. Without an established church or a powerful tradition of endowed Latin grammar schools, Americans embraced social innovation, inventing an institution that proved controversial in many communities. By the 1820s and 1830s, a few cities and towns along the eastern seaboard had built high schools for a small but crucial segment of American youth—those whose parents believed that access to the higher branches of study was essential for personal advancement in a volatile social order.

By the 1880s, especially in the North, public high schools stood triumphant.

Social reformers had eliminated most alternative forms of secondary instruction, as tuition academies and seminaries increasingly disappeared or were converted into free public high schools. By wedding the native bourgeoisie in particular to the new system, activists had won a stunning political victory. How and why this occurred—in an age of democratic, commercial, and later industrial revolutions—remains a fascinating historical puzzle.[2]

The Origins of the American High School is a history of the genesis and nature of American high schools from the establishment of the first public high school in 1821: Boston's English Classical School. Soon known as English High, the school restricted admission to boys and thus reinforced age-old ideas about gender and higher learning. Major urban areas along the East Coast also later built separate public high schools for boys and girls, despite the spread of coeducation in the majority of northern secondary schools. Boston's decision to teach some teenage boys the higher subjects nevertheless illuminated one of the responses of community leaders to social crises and class concerns in the early nineteenth century. Indeed, English High epitomized utilitarian reform and the growing equation of secondary education with nonclassical subjects and bourgeois values.

Without a national ministry of education to dictate policy and implement reform, Americans built high schools through local initiative. Educators and activists shared ideas across state boundaries about how to create, shape, and administer high schools, producing some common features to educational systems across the nation. But "high schools" still varied enormously. Most pupils studied the higher branches in modest, ungraded country schools, others in more elaborate "union graded" schools in villages and towns, and a privileged minority in ostentatious facilities that critics called palaces.

To understand the origins and social life of nineteenth-century high schools requires searching for clues in an array of sources: in local political debates, in the speeches and memoirs of school activists, and in the writings of students, teachers, principals, superintendents, and school board leaders in diverse times and places. Readers will travel from mighty commercial centers on the Atlantic seaboard to towns and cities along the middle border, agricultural villages, and various southern communities.

I have written *The Origins of the American High School* for several reasons: because Americans seem perpetually attracted to the sirens of school reform, because of my fascination with the ideological and political dimensions of formal education, and because although people base their appeals for change on the past, few understand the origins of high schools. Why were high schools first created? Whose political and economic values determined their mission? What constituted the academic culture and what characterized the lives of students and teachers?

The founders of America's high schools saw themselves as acting in the public interest and for the common good. Many of them were brilliant politicians, cloaking themselves in the mantle of good intentions while simultaneously distorting the ideological tenets of their opponents. What follows briefly attempts to place my work within a larger body of historical scholarship and to introduce the major concerns of the text. Readers deserve a lamp to help light the way.

In the early 1960s such scholars as Bernard Bailyn and Lawrence Cremin properly reproached historians of education for exaggerating the importance of schooling in the past and for underestimating the myriad influences upon children's learning. They also appropriately chastised many scholars for their uncritical historical interpretations, views that dominated teacher-preparation textbooks. As a field of study, history of education largely helped to prepare novices for their place in that noble, democratic enterprise: the public school.[3]

My own ideological perspective on America's past is more critical than Bailyn's or Cremin's, and my focus on schools is likewise at odds with their seminal works. This book is explicitly about schools, not about other sources of learning. Like many historians of education, I believe that understanding the deliberate and formal ways a society educates illuminates one's picture of the wider society. Schooling rose in importance across the course of the nineteenth century. To what degree various social classes would participate in state-financed educational systems was one of the burning questions of the period.

Power and its distribution inform all educational debate. When reformers seemed less than truthful or deceived themselves or others, I've tried to say so. When individuals used schools for their own purposes, I've tried to let them speak, too. Often I describe the opponents of public high schools sympathetically, suggesting that their dissident sounds are worth hearing and remembering. Public school activists largely defeated their critics, however, and the consequences of their victory loom largest in this volume.

Education can be vital to individual enlightenment and human dignity, but believing this does not necessarily demand uncritical support for any school system, past or present. In the very decade when Bailyn and Cremin urged scholars to shift their focus from formal education, the role of schools in American culture increasingly received extensive and critical examination. By the late 1960s and early 1970s, writers from diverse political perspectives argued that schools were often racist, inhumane, undemocratic institutions, that they were imbued with the values of the middle classes, and that they were never centrally concerned with helping or liberating the dispossessed. Whether these so-called revisionist scholars were political radicals or liberal Democrats, they raised troubling questions about America's public schools.[4]

By providing not-always-pleasant interpretations of the past, these writers enlivened scholarship but infuriated some historians of education. A few scholars such as Michael B. Katz found their motives questioned by critics who reaffirmed an older faith in the democratic mission and potential of the nation's schools. Educational reformers in the nineteenth century often proclaimed that high schools represented the triumph of democracy and republican virtue, a gateway to social mobility for the poor. They believed as a corollary that such alternative forms of secondary schooling as academies were unworthy and aristocratic. Katz angered some readers and fellow scholars by arguing that public school systems were imposed upon working populations and the poor and deeply stained by class prejudice and racial and gender discrimination. The criticism stung because it questioned prevailing myths about the origins of public schools.[5]

All modern professions have been built upon founding myths: as education has its democracy and learning, so law has justice and medicine health. To deny the mythic origins of the history of the high school may especially offend militant defenders of the public schools. Nevertheless, I share with earlier "revisionist" writers a critical perspective on the public schools and the society that produced them. This book depicts schools as deeply embedded in political struggles that frequently strengthened the power of the white middle and upper classes at the expense of the less fortunate. It asks why school children not from dominant social classes have in the past (and by implication the present) always competed with dice loaded against them.[6]

The nineteenth century was preeminently the age of the bourgeoisie. The earlier collapse of feudal systems in Europe and of mercantile systems throughout the trans-Atlantic world signaled the origins of modern society, and schools became an important and controversial public concern. Establishing and making legitimate new ways to educate and socialize particular adolescents was often politically complicated.

Uneasily poised at times between the obscenely rich and the desperately poor, many members of the American bourgeoisie turned to new state school systems to help direct their most academically talented children to adulthood. They demonstrably shaped such new institutions as public high schools, opening the doors of opportunity to the few and elevating the symbolic and cash value of their formal education.

The history of the American high school—itself never a monolithic institution—surfaces in many places. It is found in the dreams of antebellum reformers who promoted a common school system but lived in a society where slavery and wage labor ensured wide gulfs between rich and poor. It is also located in the lives of teachers trying to pay the rent, superintendents building better careers, and students wondering what learning algebra had to do with getting a job or becoming a parent. This book incorporates the histories of dozens of communities and institutions across the land, little villages as well as major cities, all confronting irresistible social changes that helped alter the nature of education and the shape of young people's lives. I've tried to capture local nuances and regional differences as well as to isolate the common characteristics of secondary schools as they evolved over time.

The first four chapters trace the broad social and intellectual changes that laid the foundation for the creation of America's earliest high schools. After examining the political and ideological struggles that led to the creation of English High in 1821, I explore the dynamics of antebellum politics, the ideology of educational reform, and the clashes between friends and foes of tax-supported secondary schools. At stake were competing visions of the place of education and the state in redefining republican values in a century of rapid change.

The next three chapters move the reader from the larger society to the schools themselves. They highlight the values and knowledge most prized in the emerging high schools, as revealed in school architecture, the curriculum, textbooks, and the ways teachers taught and interacted with students.

How students experienced the phenomenon of going to high school is the focus of the final five chapters. After passing their entrance examinations, a wide range of middle-class youths—and some poor ones—officially became high school scholars, subject to the discipline of teachers, textbooks, and still more tests. An array of documentary evidence, including student diaries, helps bring to life how boys and girls, whites and blacks, and young people in the countryside, village, and city encountered the "higher branches" and reveals the great diversity of student life and the steep path to commencement.

Because very few pupils could hope to reach the senior class in the nineteenth century, those who did knew that they were special, worthy of society's approbation. Some leading citizens even called these remarkable youths the embodiment of modern republicanism. In an age marked by crass materialism, deepening poverty, and ultimately civil war, these scholars reaped the fruits of hard work, self-discipline, and careful study.

The principal of the Girls' High School in Portland, Maine, allowed these rays of sunlight to shine splendidly every Saturday morning, when the senior girls presented original poems, essays, and other original materials before their peers. One day in 1863, as a bloody war raged to the south, one young scholar dispensed with the usual rhetoric about republicanism and education. Instead, she shifted the metaphors slightly, likening her institution to a kingdom. This scholar explained that schools were hierarchical institutions that rewarded individual merit, a concept central to bourgeois school reform. She called the principal "the king" and the teachers "his prime ministers." She and her friends held an honorable place in this republican kingdom, part of an aristocracy of intellect.[7]

That the public schools prevented the hardening of social classes, fostered the mobility of the poor, and rewarded only those with the most intellect and knowledge became cardinal principles among many reform-minded citizens by the middle of the nineteenth century. And high schools became an increasingly important segment of the public schools, drawing the native middle classes away from private academies to these new centers of learning.

No one could have predicted the outcome when a handful of elite reformers built America's first public high school in 1821. No one knew that by the 1880s high schools would be common on the educational and social landscape. No one realized that a story that began in a famous city on the eastern seaboard would conclude in diverse systems of public secondary schools that stretched across the land.

The Origins of the American High School

Boston's Legacy

In the history of popular education in the
United States, Boston has been before all
others the city set on a hill.

–WILLIAM T. HARRIS, 1887

The gavel sounded at 10 A.M.
at Faneuil Hall on January 15, 1821, for the "Freeholders & Other Inhabitants
of . . . Boston, qualified to vote in Town Affairs." The town meeting soon disappeared as Boston became a city, but on this fateful day a minority of
townsmen shared a unique civic communion with a remarkable past. Created
in a simpler time, the town meeting was still an important public ritual in a
commercial center whose population had soared from twenty-four thousand
to forty-three thousand since 1800. On the eve of settlement nearly two centuries earlier, John Winthrop, drawing inspiration from the Gospel of
Matthew, implored his countrymen to found a model Christian commonwealth, a "city upon a hill." Religious controversies, wars, revolution, and
social transformations had not shattered this sense of mission. Boston's
leaders prided themselves on their Christian benevolence, civic enlightenment, and commitment to learning. In 1821, leading citizens faithfully honored their history.[1]

The meeting began inauspiciously, with disappointing attendance. Citizens
discussed first the paving of Water Street, then sewer improvements, then
snow removal. Finally, the moderator, Francis J. Oliver, introduced members
of a school subcommittee who favored the creation of a new institution: a
public high school. In June 1820 the Boston School Committee had considered a resolution by one of its members, Samuel A. Wells, who advocated an

"English Classical School." Wells was appointed to head a subcommittee to study the feasibility of such an institution. After some debate in the following months, the School Committee approved the idea of a new school. The matter then went before the town meeting for a final vote.

The juxtaposition of *English* and *Classical* was somewhat confusing: English schools taught modern subjects and nonclassical languages, whereas classical schools, like Boston's venerable Latin Grammar School, taught such college preparatory subjects as Latin and Greek. Indeed, the nomenclature disguised Wells's preference for an English high school for boys, not another classical training school, though the name was a matter of debate into the 1830s. After some discussion, those present at the town meeting approved Wells's plan with only three dissenting votes. Later that year, on the upper floor of the Derne Street Grammar School, 102 students commenced their "high school" studies.[2]

The all-male English Classical School earned acclaim among educators but never became a blueprint for most secondary schools. Other eastern port cities eventually created separate male and female secondary schools, but "high schools" in most villages, towns, and cities educated boys and girls together. English High was also unusual because it never taught any ancient languages. Finally, most high schools grew up from the bottom of the system, as elementary enrollments swelled, grammar level enrollments grew, and then some youth studied the "higher branches" together in separate classes or buildings.

Boston's new high school was emulated mostly in other large coastal cities that had begun to encounter the problems and possibilities accompanying commercial development and the rise of a market economy. Economic change generated new questions about social relations and the place of schools in society. Whether girls should have access to the same publicly financed schools, whether communities owed anything to academically talented youth beyond the grammar grades, whether those who attended secondary schools should pay for the privilege were issues that first raged in the seaboard cities. Wells and his peers had few models to guide them, and the questions they debated, rather than the institution they built per se, remained central to high school development everywhere for many decades.

A prominent merchant on Boston's India Wharf and the grandson of a famous revolutionary leader, Samuel Adams Wells played a seminal role in early school reform by pressing for new kinds of advanced studies in public schools. The high school ultimately became the capstone to an emerging educational system across the nation. Other communities might modify their high schools somewhat to fit indigenous conditions, but concerns about public responsibility for secondary education first heard in Boston in 1821 soon echoed elsewhere.

Exactly why did Boston cast its lot with innovation? Did the high school mark a momentous break from tradition and Boston's educational past?

The social changes so dramatically encountered in Boston in the early 1800s ultimately affected the rest of the nation. Economic, social, and political upheavals transformed everyday life, challenging urban leaders to redefine the nature of private and public responsibility for education and schooling.[3]

Boston's role in secondary school reform confirmed its reputation for education, culture, and learning. Understanding the creation of the nation's first public high school, however, requires more than reconstructing the immediate historical context: deepening urban poverty, the transformation of Boston's maritime economy, and the response of business leaders, Unitarian ministers, and Federalist politicians to social change.

The commitment of Boston's first white citizens to schooling remains a staple of educational historiography. An inordinate number of the Puritan settlers had received grammar school and college educations in England, often at Cambridge. The nuclear family, the church, and the neighborhood and town shared responsibility for educating youth in colonial Boston; even this largely oral culture, however, was shaped by printed matter, religious as well as secular. By 1636 the "richer inhabitants," including John Winthrop and the Rev. John Cotton of First Church, had also pledged support for a Latin grammar school. After their newly founded college on the banks of the Charles, Boston Latin was perhaps the most famous school in colonial America.[4]

Those who built and sustained Boston's schools were men of wealth, property, and learning. That Boston Latin was established by the "richer inhabitants" reflected the unequal distribution of power in the Anglo-American world of the seventeenth century. John Winthrop articulated the elite view of the social order in the Bay Colony: "God Almighty in his most holy and wise providence hath so disposed of the Condition of mankind, as in all times some must be rich some poor, some high and eminent in power and dignity; others meane and in subjection." The propertied elite who prized order and stability in civil society were influential beyond their numbers in town meetings and in the Congregational churches. Access to formal education confirmed their power in the community, as the Latin grammar school sent a small, steady stream of classically trained, privileged boys to Harvard to help replenish the supply of educated leaders.[5]

Boston's Puritan fathers, therefore, aligned formal schooling with the needs of their own social group. Admission to Boston Latin, the only tax-supported school until the 1680s, required the ability to read and write, usually acquired through private tutors, literate parents, or dame schools, in which women taught in their homes. The core of the classical curriculum, which remained virtually unchanged until the early 1800s, was Latin and Greek, the prerequisites for college admission. Most Boston Latin pupils never attended college because business and the professions didn't require collegiate training. Boston's ruling citizens had thus invested in the education of the town's children—but only a small number, as befit an elitist world where changes in social rank were unlikely. Boston's schools excluded girls until 1789, most boys remained outside the pale, and the parents of the most degraded class, black children, hardly fretted about a son's chances for classical education or admission to Harvard.[6]

Throughout the seventeenth century, the champions of Zion confronted the power of Mammon. The religious impulse central to Puritanism favored literacy, learning, reason, and respect for the classics. It also promoted among its middle- and upper-class adherents the idea of civic responsibility, not retreat from the world, and made one's calling a religious and practical obligation. The clash between godly goals and worldly desires fractured the community from the start. Boston's Protestant ministers continued to exert considerable power and authority, but over time another social group, Puritan merchants, became more powerful and noticeably altered Boston's approach to formal education.[7]

By the 1680s mercantile leaders had slowly expanded Boston's conception of town schooling. Classical education remained the gateway to Harvard, and it hardly disqualified anyone for the counting house. But an important segment of the town wanted to offer children a more practical education. A writing school soon opened, followed by a second one at the turn of the century. The writing schools provided practical skills for the world of commerce. Courses in penmanship, writing, reading, and arithmetic introduced middle- and upper-class boys to the serious business of trade, in which Latin verbs seemed less valuable than a clear hand and a crafty mind.[8]

By 1690 Boston had approximately six thousand residents, making it the largest colonial center and a leader in regional inland trade and Atlantic shipping. Heaven may have beckoned the first settlers to cross the sea, but the Atlantic trade loosened Boston's religious moorings. The new writing schools enabled some merchants to leave their mark on basic social institutions. At the same time, these schools were largely irrelevant to the many families whose children never attended any school. Boston's tax lists for 1687 demonstrated serious inequalities. Property ownership had consolidated into the hands of a minority. Merchants held 66 percent "of the town's wealth," while the top 15 percent of Boston's property owners possessed 52 percent of the town's "taxable assets."[9]

The Rev. Cotton Mather, a graduate of Boston Latin and Harvard, lamented late in the century that beggars walked the city streets. The free market had weakened religious bonds within the community. Moreover, northern port communities greatly influenced the entire colonial economy. Long before Adam Smith extolled the invisible hand and free trade, a market culture within the English mercantile system supplanted barter exchange in these overgrown towns. Customary protection for the poor often disappeared with the rise of individualistic, competitive economic values. The process seemed to strengthen the powerful and to impoverish the powerless, and within a half-century of settlement Boston's leaders had selectively adapted their schools to a changing economic order.[10]

The town schools never fully satisfied the growing demand for a nonclassical education in this more secular market culture. Many taxpayers probably preferred market solutions to educational needs. Still, Boston had five public schools by 1720: three writing schools, Boston Latin, and a smaller classical grammar school founded in the North End in 1713. Although some ministers foresaw irretrievable educational decline and the erosion of spiritual faith, the town schools flourished throughout the eighteenth century, except during wars. What had declined was Boston Latin's monopoly; it still sent its few graduates to college or to other esteemed positions in provincial life, but classical schools provided only a fraction of the community's educational needs. In fact, the colony's famous laws that required towns to establish classical grammar schools were essentially dead letters.[11]

Public schools had not declined so much as responded to key mercantile leaders who wanted their economic behavior subject to fewer religious restrictions—including traditional ideas of a fair wage and a just price. Writing schools offered business what Latin grammar schools could not. By the early 1700s, private schools for boys abounded as the market provided the merchant classes with alternatives to classical education. The *Boston News-Letter* ran numerous advertisements by masters who promised to teach a variety of subjects and social accomplishments. Profits from trade and commerce helped finance the public schools and other educational investments.[12]

Owen Harris, for example, opened a school in a room near the Mitre Tavern, on Fish Street near Scarlets-Wharf in 1709. Mathematics, writing, navigation, and astronomy were taught by a master "Who Teaches at as easie Rates, and as speedy as may be." Benjamin Franklin, after some unhappy days as a student at Boston Latin, enrolled in Mr. George Brownell's school, which offered classes in subjects from writing to treble violin. Enterprising Ben, who later epitomized middle-class practicality and respectability, recalled learning to write very well but never quite succeeding in math. Throughout the century, advertisements described other subjects of great utility in a seaport town: bookkeeping, stenography, accounting, and even "the General Rules of Fortification and Gunnery."[13]

The private sector thus offered many educational opportunities absent from Boston's town schools. Even women, widely viewed by men as intellectually inferior, sometimes attended private classes. These fortunate pupils improved their reading skills and studied more polite accomplishments such as painting, singing, and dancing. The schools varied enormously in longevity, quality, and relative importance, but their existence revealed the gaps that still separated the public schools and a changing economic system. When public high schools emerged in the nineteenth century, they would embrace many of the pedagogical practices and subjects first taught in private schools and academies.[14]

The private sector was the real educational innovator in eighteenth-century Boston. The town schools had a restricted orientation, either toward the classics at Boston Latin, or toward rudimentary writing and reading at the three nonclassical schools. Private schools taught many of the higher branches of learning that attracted middle- and upper-class families seeking a more practical education. Allowing their daughters a broader range of accomplishments and their sons an edge in a more competitive economy through the mastery of mathematics, bookkeeping, or navigation must have seemed like a reasonable filial investment.

And so there was no educational decline in Boston or in colonial Massachusetts in the early eighteenth century. Towns and villages often enjoyed an assortment of private schools, public writing and reading schools, and dame schools. In spite of laws that mandated the establishment of secondary schools, communities that had nonclassical public schools and various private alternatives often refused to establish Latin schools that nobody wanted; the General Court simply accepted this reality and refused to fine the many lawbreakers. The tension between distant and local political authority over education continued in the next century. Like the colonial grammar schools, higher schools in the nineteenth century appeared only when local leaders perceived sufficient demand and a practical need for them.[15]

Men of property, learning, and wealth had built Boston's schools. As instruction in modern subjects grew increasingly popular among the middle classes, merchant capitalists advanced a more secularized understanding of one's calling, emphasizing the intimate bonds between schools and the commercial world.[16]

But colonial public schools were not created as potential avenues of opportunity for poorer boys or *any* girls or people of color. Education largely confirmed one's status or enabled young men with family advantages to gain the skills to compete more favorably in a world of supply and demand. Boston's merchant classes supported a handful of schools that offered some privileged boys a classical education and more still a practical, nonclassical alternative useful in a commercial society. The expansion of a market culture reinforced Boston's deep economic divisions.

Who will rule the world of public schools and who will benefit from them cannot be completely determined by one generation for the next. Ruling elites, however, bequeath powerful traditions that help shape the destiny of future generations. By the mid-eighteenth century, Boston's leading citizens had demonstrably connected the educational experiences of the favored few with the community's future growth and prosperity. After the Revolution, wealthy citizens continued to try to couple schooling with cultural authority.

"Society in seaboard New England was carefully stratified" in the eighteenth century, wrote historian Samuel Eliot Morison, "and the Revolution brought little change save in personnel." The revolutionary struggle began, of course, in Boston. Its merchant class had profited from the mercantile system, helped finance the war after imperial power tightened in the 1760s and 1770s, and then struggled to reassert its authority after the victory at Yorktown. Many members of the professional classes as well as shopkeepers and artisans contributed to the revolutionary cause, though various social groups interpreted the meaning of the Revolution differently. Poverty remained a terrible affliction throughout the eighteenth century, and the war did nothing to redistribute wealth and power.[17]

The schools inherited from the colonial period seemed somewhat archaic to Boston's new leaders in the 1780s, who prized their inheritance but reshaped educational configurations in the light of changing conditions. Leaders came from well-known merchant and professional families, though some new men like Sam Adams rose to fame and fortune on the wave of revolution. Once again Boston was the crucible for change.

Influential citizens everywhere called for a new education for the new republic. Educating girls took on heightened importance, as political theorists emphasized the role of mothers in instructing children in republican values. Similarly, Massachusetts legislators reaffirmed the importance of public schools in 1789 by requiring towns to establish primary schools and, to a lesser extent, grammar schools that taught English subjects. Classical education still attracted a small number of college-bound boys in large towns like Boston, but the new law reflected popular sentiment by weakening the requirement to maintain Latin grammar schools. As the population dispersed to rural areas, local residents and then lawmakers embraced another controversial idea: district control of education. Cries of educational decline again arose, but legislators furthered the spread of learning and especially an English education by aiding nonclassical academies through land grants later in the century.[18]

Even Sam Adams, a Boston Latin alumnus, clamored in the 1780s and 1790s for the expansion of the town schools to counter the appeal of private instruction among the local middle and upper classes. What Boston's poor thought of these educational problems is unclear. In keeping with tradition, however, elites debated the issues and imposed their views at the town meeting. While schools in the hinterland increasingly came under district control, Boston's schools remained under more centralized authority. In October of 1789 Adams headed a delegation of twelve distinguished citizens that aimed to reorganize the schools of Boston. Some 140 citizens heard their proposal for a "System of Public Education" at the town meeting.[19]

The local initiatives of 1789 confirmed the allegiance of Boston's merchant and professional leaders to the local public schools. Previously, the selectmen and other town notables invested leisure time overseeing Boston's various schools. The new law provided for the election of a special School Committee. Together with the selectmen, this committee would administer and supervise public education, inspect the schools, hire teachers, and set the school curriculum and schedule. It hoped to stimulate all scholars "to excel in a virtuous, amiable deportment, and in every branch of useful knowledge."[20]

This specialized committee, the first formal school board in an American city, persuaded the voters at the annual meeting to establish several new schools. The North End Latin grammar school closed, but three reading schools and three writing schools opened. Momentously, girls were welcomed to their own grammar schools. These English grammar schools underscored the attractiveness of nonclassical education among Boston's middle and upper classes. They were not schools for the poor. Admission was set at age seven and thus, like admission to the all-male Latin school, required previous instruction through private tutors or dame schools. Boston Latin raised the age for admission from seven to ten and shortened the course of study. A network of primary schools did not appear until 1818, so Boston's system remained uncoordinated, controlled by the rich, and restricted to relatively prosperous families.[21]

Even though girls attended the English grammar schools for fewer hours daily and for fewer months annually than boys, their inclusion demonstrated the power of republican themes in shaping women's education after the Revolution. But these improvements failed to trickle down to the poorest citizens. Access to schools had expanded only for advantaged citizens.

In the 1780s and 1790s, Boston's merchant and professional classes, alarmed by the dislocations of the economy during the war and antifederalist agitation against centralized power afterward, overwhelmingly supported the Federalist Party. This so-called revolutionary generation of leaders firmly opposed the expansion of male suffrage and the ideals of liberty, equality, and fraternity that found expression in the French Revolution. Confirmed Anglophiles, these merchant capitalists were appalled by the election of Thomas Jefferson in 1800 and the successes of the Republicans.[22]

In the last decades of the eighteenth century, elites continued to dominate the city's major political offices. The selectmen, the Overseers of the Poor, and those in other powerful positions—including now the School Committee—resisted changes that threatened their authority. The 1789 school reorganization, for example, did little for anyone lacking access to dame schools. And whereas earlier in the century, rich, middling, and poor residents had lived fairly close to one another, neighborhoods now became more stratified by income. The richest citizens often served in office together, voted for each other, formed private corporations together, and lived on the same fashionable streets close to the center of the city. Their lives became increasingly separate from the laboring classes.[23]

Boston's ruling classes in 1800 found themselves in a much-changed historical context from that of their predecessors who had in the 1630s seized influence from the Puritan ministers. Intermarriage among the children of the merchant princes increased during the eighteenth century, adding stability in this increasingly market-oriented society. However, to preserve control and forge dependable new links between schools and society remained a challenge.[24]

The question of how to prevent anarchy, revolution, and challenges to the special privileges of wealth consumed enormous amounts of the time and energy of Boston's leaders. Boston's original notables had viewed poverty as a natural condition, sanctioned by an inscrutable God; but Winthrop's generation had been spared the egalitarianism of even so wealthy a man as Sam Adams. In addition, they had the comfort of Biblical support and largely unquestioned patriarchal authority. Some poor folk, on the other hand, even thought the Revolution raised serious questions about who should rule at home as well as from abroad.

Boston's school reforms of 1789 hardly threatened the class system, but other threats to order surfaced. In the 1790s, disorder seemed endemic, exemplified by Shays's Rebellion in Western Massachusetts. Moreover, the violence of the French Revolution horrified Federalists. Boston's leaders wanted schools and other institutions to adapt to change in socially agreeable ways.[25]

By the early 1800s, the Republicans assumed power in Washington. Still, Boston and seaboard Massachusetts remained heavily Federalist, and Federalist merchants and their political representatives opposed Jefferson's embargo and later the War of 1812, which they feared would destroy New England's maritime economy. Jefferson's Republican ideology, which praised freedom, liberty, and agrarian life (for white men), often horrified many Federalists whose commercial interests benefited more, they thought, from the safe and steady rule of a George Washington. Although their party declined in power, upper-class Bostonians strengthened their influence over such social institutions as the public schools.[26]

The vast majority of these merchant and professional leaders in the early nineteenth century were Federalists, and some were also Unitarians. Federalism was a dying national force and Unitarianism was still almost indistinguishable from liberal, nonpredestinarian Congregationalism; yet both influenced the political thought of important upper-class leaders. Federalist thinking, of course, was compatible with many time-tested beliefs of Boston's merchant princes: cultural authority, hierarchical rule, political stability, and centralized power. Preserving centralized control over schools and preventing the dispersal of power to smaller districts guaranteed that the best would rule.

New religious currents that shaped Boston Unitarianism also influenced political ideals. By the late 1700s, the merchant classes had gradually abandoned the harshest forms of Calvinism, especially the tenet of predestination. By the 1730s members of the prominent First Church heard sermons that emphasized a loving, benevolent God who held out the promise of universal salvation. Arminianism slowly congealed into Unitarianism, a type of Christian humanism that emphasized man's goodness and human reason. In the early 1800s, many Unitarians were still Biblical Christians and political conservatives. Still, by 1820 Boston Protestantism had changed significantly, for Unitarians headed all but one of the Congregational churches founded before the American Revolution.[27]

The cultural authority of the merchant class and its professional allies was never stronger than in the early 1800s. Unitarians dominated Harvard by 1805. The sons of leading Federalists often attended boarding schools like Phillips Academy or exclusive public schools like Boston Latin before enrolling at Harvard and ultimately assuming a place in the family business or in the professions. The leading merchants engaged in widespread public service, whether as selectmen, fire wardens, school committeemen, or members of Harvard's Board of Overseers. They financed charitable endeavors as well as scientific organizations, libraries, and other philanthropic activities. Federalism declined as a visible, coherent political entity, but elite control by the merchant leaders remained potent.[28]

Like every dominant class before them, turn-of-the-century leaders had to adapt schools to an ever-changing, unpredictable future. Poverty remained an explosive issue. Elites in other northern port cities had responded to rising levels of pauperism by opening charity schools to teach basic literacy skills and Protestant morality to children of the unchurched poor. Significantly, these "free" schools were only for the poor, and they were sponsored by a diverse range of philanthropic Protestants, whose own children attended private schools. Boston's town schools, of course, were quite different: they were run by the well-to-do for relatively prosperous families. The problems of poverty terrified many local Federalists, uncertain how best to respond to this perennial, worsening malady.[29]

Only children who could already read and write well could enter any of the public schools, which effectively excluded most poor children. After the War of 1812, however, the elites who made up the School Committee, like town notables across the eastern seaboard, debated whether taxpayers should educate the poor by creating primary schools. Should the children of all social classes attend Boston's system of schools?[30]

Evangelical Protestants, especially Baptists, became central figures in debating these issues. Christian benevolence ran deep in Boston's evangelical past, and the terrors of poverty, the prevalence of rowdy youth, and faith in the power of conversion moved local evangelical women to open a charity school for poor children in 1814. But many indigent parents, too embarrassed to admit that they were paupers, kept their children out of school. Evangelical Protestants pressed the town for a solution. The activists, though strongly opposed to the deistic beliefs of some of their allies, cooperated with elite Republicans and even some Federalists to establish public primary schools.[31]

Boston's Baptists first established Sunday schools to teach basic literacy and Christian morality to the local poor. They ran five schools by 1817, quickly finding that their means were insufficient to reach the many urchins who ran wild in the streets, loafing or hustling, endangering themselves and the larger community. Although some of the poor and certainly some Republicans viewed education as a potential lever for social mobility, most primary school advocates stressed moral training and basic reading. Some hoped that Christian charity might promote a better republic. "All should be taught to read," claimed an upper-class attorney from an established family: "The poor and the rich should have an equal chance to understand the nature and principles of our republican government."[32]

Federalists also favored keeping children off the streets and teaching them proper behavior, but a few feared that free education would reduce individual responsibility and bankrupt the town. Famous Boston Latin alumni and such Federalists as the architect Charles Bulfinch and the wealthy politician Harrison Gray Otis confirmed their elitist reputation by opposing public primary schools.[33]

The town meeting in 1818 nevertheless approved the establishment of primary schools for children under the age of seven. A permanent Primary School Committee governed these schools. Many Federalists, hardly egalitarians and perhaps amused by the idea that education could promote social mobility for the poor, did not block the reformers but rather concentrated their efforts elsewhere. Federalist school committeemen labored to improve Boston Latin. In 1814 Benjamin Gould, a Harvard senior, was paid an attractive salary to become the new Latin master and was empowered to strengthen educational quality and the links between Latin and Harvard. By the time primary schools for the poor opened, Gould had extended the course of study from four to five years and had increased the standards, enrollments, and reputation of the old school. The institution that had educated Cotton Mather, John Hancock, and Samuel Adams would again produce a new cavalcade of stars.[34]

The addition of primary schools never threatened the class privileges of Boston's leading citizens. Even the Primary School Committee was a bastion of the upper classes, so there seemed little to fear from educating the poor at public expense. Yet a handful of Boston's leaders still thought the schools inadequately addressed the needs of a commercial city. Boston Latin provided excellent preparation for college or business life, but many middle-class families doubted that their sons needed Latin and Greek to take advantage of expanding commercial opportunities. Linking past and present, the town meeting provided a perfect forum for the reform minded.

The subcommittee that proposed the creation of America's first public high school in 1821 represented a microcosm of a leadership class. Several were direct descendants of powerful men in colonial New England. They were also remarkable individuals with a keen sense of moral duty and cultural authority. Samuel A. Wells, chairman of the special subcommittee and the driving force behind the high school, was, like all the other members, a Federalist. Born in Boston in 1787, the son of a former army major and patriot, he was baptized in the prestigious Brattle Square Congregational Church. Wells's family had deep roots in the Bay Colony, and Samuel Adams was his grandfather. Like other upper-class boys, young Wells received private instruction to prepare for Boston Latin. With a more practical than bookish inclination, he eschewed college and used his family position to enter commerce. By 1812 he had married into an elite family; soon he held a variety of public offices, including that of school committeeman. He confirmed his prominence in Boston by delivering the prestigious Fourth of July oration at Faneuil Hall in 1819.[35]

By 1820 Wells was an extremely successful Federalist merchant whose star grew more lustrous. That year, only thirty-three years old, he not only continued his service on the School Committee but also became a member of the State Constitutional Convention. He owned a prosperous business on the India Wharf, where one could purchase anything from "indigo to opium."

Like many merchants before him, he was committed to elite support for and control over the public schools, although he fought for an alternative to classical education for ambitious and talented middle- and upper-class boys.[36]

John Pierpont and Nathaniel L. Frothingham, who also served on the subcommittee, demonstrated the continuing civic influence of Protestant ministers. Just as Wells highlighted the commanding public role of merchants, these fellow Federalists represented an emerging religious elite. Pierpont and Frothingham were studies in contrast, yet both men cooperated with Wells in 1821 in the cause of reform.

The Rev. John Pierpont had strong claims to stewardship. His distant forebears had been major property owners in Derbyshire, England. Pierpont was born in 1785 in Litchfield, Connecticut, a Calvinist and Federalist stronghold and also the home of a major Federalist law school. His father was a successful clothier. A famous evangelical Calvinist, Lyman Beecher, was the family minister, and family tradition led Pierpont to orthodox, Federalist Yale College.[37]

Pierpont nevertheless was a restless soul who struggled to find his proper niche. After graduating from Yale in 1804, he taught school in Connecticut, then served as a tutor on a South Carolina plantation, and by 1809 had enrolled in the Litchfield Law School. In 1812 he married. After failing miserably as an attorney, Pierpont opened a dry goods store in Boston. He tried to expand his business to Baltimore and Charleston but was soon bankrupt. While in Baltimore, however, he attended a Unitarian Church, where he found solace in a time of despair. Rejecting the Calvinism of his youth but not his Federalism, he enrolled at Harvard, the great Unitarian nursery, to study for the ministry.

Falling under the sway of the leading Unitarians at Harvard and in Boston, Pierpont became minister of the prestigious Hollis Street Church in 1819. Although he had failed as a businessman, prosperous merchants and professionals filled his church, which, like Boston's other Unitarian congregations, gradually lost most of its working-class members. Pierpont became an inveterate reformer, "a man addicted to causes." He championed the English Classical School and an ill-fated girls' high school in 1825 and later embraced an array of causes, including phrenology, abolitionism, and temperance.[38]

The Rev. Nathaniel L. Frothingham also traveled the road from Congregationalism to Unitarianism. Born in Boston in 1793, Frothingham traced his lineage to early Massachusetts. One ancestor was a selectman in Charlestown in 1634. Frothingham's father, a very successful "crockery merchant and appraiser of taxes," built a "brick mansion" in a fashionable neighborhood. Young Nathaniel attended Boston Latin and Harvard and became a Unitarian. At the age of twenty-two he was ordained minister in historic First Church. The founders of First Church—including John Winthrop and John Cotton—had helped establish the Boston Latin School. Frothingham remained the minister at First Church until 1850.[39]

Like most contemporary Unitarians, Frothingham was a political and social conservative. Less socially active than Pierpont, he criticized abolitionists and women's rights advocates. Not surprisingly, he was remembered not as an incurable joiner of causes but as "a scholar, a poet of no mean gifts, and the master of a prose diction of rare and faultless elegance." He was a man of learning and social position, related by marriage to distinguished families with names like Adams, Brooks, and Everett.[40]

A fourth member of the subcommittee was Lemuel Shaw. Born in 1781 in Barnstable, a small village on Cape Cod, Shaw traced his ancestry to Dedham in 1636. Like other committee members, he counted many ministers in the family, including his father and grandfather. Without access to a village school, young Shaw learned Latin and Greek from his father, then lived with a wealthy uncle in Boston who arranged for the tutoring necessary to pass Harvard's admission exam. Like Frothingham, he fell under the spell of Unitarianism there and also retained a rather conservative, reserved bearing.[41]

By 1810 Shaw had rapidly established himself as a rising Federalist attorney. In 1811 he was elected to the General Court, where he attacked efforts to disestablish the Congregational Church and pilloried Republicans, Francophiles, and supporters of the War of 1812. He soon became town orator, a Federalist activist, a bank director, a fire warden and, like Samuel Wells, a member of the State Constitutional Convention and the School Committee. In 1830 he became chief justice of the Massachusetts Supreme Court, issuing 2,200 opinions over the next thirty years.[42]

The fifth member of the subcommittee was Benjamin Russell, one of the nation's most prominent newspapermen. Born in Boston in 1761, he was the oldest member and the most colorful. Related maternally to the most famous schoolmaster in colonial America, Ezekiel Cheever of Boston Latin, Russell came from respectable but hardly distinguished lineage. His father was a mason. Destiny did not lead him to Boston Latin and Harvard. His brief attendance at one of Boston's writing schools suggests that he had previous access to a dame school or private tuition, but compared with most civic leaders in turn-of-the-century Boston, he was guided by talent, drive, and luck without benefit of a truly privileged heritage.[43]

Russell's education in the town schools ended with the outbreak of the Revolution. Apprenticed in Worcester to Isaiah Thomas, the revolutionary printer, Russell was released early from his apprenticeship for serving his master's military stint. He soon helped establish what ultimately became the *Columbian Centinel*, America's foremost Federalist newspaper. He championed the ratification of the Constitution, applauded the suppression of Shays's Rebellion, idolized George Washington, viciously attacked Jefferson and the Republicans, and later denounced the War of 1812.[44]

Russell demonstrated that the collapse of the Federalist party as a national force did not curtail its local influence. With other elites in the early 1800s he helped direct the course of social, economic, and political life by becoming a compulsive joiner and civic activist. Besides terms in the legislature, Russell served on the Board of Health and the town council, and in other municipal offices. He was nearly sixty years old when he helped found the English Classical School.[45]

These five men, drawn from the elite membership of the School Committee, believed deeply in the importance of Boston's public schools. By 1820, primary schools, English grammar schools, a much improved Boston Latin, and even a "colored school" for the most impoverished children testified to the growth of the system. Although they left little record of their individual thoughts on the new high school, these school leaders fostered another creative educational response to change.

For months before the town meeting approved the establishment of the English Classical School, Samuel Wells endeavored to popularize the idea of an alternative to Boston Latin. "Till recently," Wells told his listeners at one town gathering, "our system occupied a middle station: it neither commenced with the rudiments of education, nor extended to the higher branches of knowledge." He argued that attendance at the grammar schools, which currently admitted children at age seven and permitted them to remain until age fourteen, should be restricted to five years. These were important years of maturation, "that interesting and critical period of life, when the habits and inclinations are forming by which the future character will be fixed & determined." Boston needed a special school, a high school, to teach young boys not destined for college "those early habits of industry . . . so essential in leading to a future life of Virtue and usefulness." The English grammar schools simply did not teach the many useful and advanced "branches of knowledge" now necessary for commercial success. Only by "enlarging the present system" of schools, said Wells, could Boston "give a Child an education that shall fit him for Active life, and . . . serve as a foundation for eminence in his profession, whether Mercantile or Mechanical."[46]

Wells and his colleagues advocated a distinctive seminary of learning. Admission to the English Classical School was to be restricted to boys at least twelve years of age who could pass a "strict examination" in reading, writing, English grammar, and basic arithmetic. The three-year course of study, taught by well-paid, college-educated teachers, included advanced work in English literature, science, mathematics, and ancient and American history. Nothing could better preserve the "tranquility and order" of the community, "perpetuate" the republic, or "promote the happiness and prosperity of a people" than the "general diffusion of knowledge." The English Classical School, Wells concluded, "would raise the literary and scientific character of the Town, would incite our Youth to a laudable ambition of distinguishing themselves in the pursuit and acquisition of knowledge, and would give strength and stability to the civil and religious institutions of our Country."[47]

Strength for some and stability for all: these might have served as the watchwords of the American high school wherever it was found in the nineteenth century. By establishing the English High School, at a time when the poor of the city first received some public education—directed more toward their morals than to their minds—some of the city's middle and upper classes came to value the "higher branches." Boston's school reformers led the assault on private academies, popularized the modern subjects in free secondary schools, and persuaded their fellow citizens to provide special educational opportunities for certain academically talented children.

Many of the arguments heard on behalf of the English Classical School in the early 1820s remained staples of school reform, including the idea that the higher schools helped centralize authority, perfect a sequenced, graded curriculum, reward talent, and, most importantly, retain support from the right families for the public school system. Samuel Adams Wells and his colleagues persuaded the townsmen to vote for progress. In the process they showed respect for the elite traditions of a revered past.

The name of the new institution, the English Classical School, confused some people, but its significance was beyond debate. As the author of a local pamphlet wrote, "The establishment of this school forms an era in the history of free Education in Boston. Its present high reputation and growing importance, while they render it an object of increasing interest, promise extensive and lasting utility; and furnish a gratifying proof of the wisdom of that policy which brings forward to places of high responsibility *young men* of talents and learning, who have a reputation and fortune to gain." In the coming decades, public school educators across the nation would applaud Boston's citizens for their foresight and wisdom.[48]

Schools of a Higher Order

I look with sorrow on the gradual demoli-
tion of the old country schools, and the
rise of high, eclectic, collegiate, and other
academies and institutes. . . . If I thought
there was any part of the land safe from
the sophisticating invasion of steamboats
and railroads, newspapers and orators, I
would retire thither, establish a school on
the old plan, and thus live over my early
days. But "the age of chivalry is gone," and
that of high-schools, seminaries, and institutes is come.

New-York Mirror, 1833

"The subject of Education has,
for some time past, occupied no inconsiderable share of the public attention in
the United States," wrote the editor of the *North American Review* in 1819. From
the early days of independence, citizens had often debated the role of education
and schools in the new republic, and renewed discussions in the 1820s and 1830s
laid the foundations for free secondary schools. By opening schools to girls, to
the poor, and finally to the sons of the mercantile middle classes at the English
Classical School—all within the span of a generation—Boston exemplified
growing municipal responsibility for youth in a time of rapid change. One typical observer wrote in 1824 that concern for education was "a striking characteristic of the age" and reflected a "greater willingness to regard moral and
intellectual good, as more valuable than anything beside."[1]

The spread of market economies after the War of 1812 rekindled debates
about public responsibility for the young in many northern communities. "No
subjects engage public attention more at the present time than the diffusion of
knowledge, and the instruction of youth," noted the editor of a middle-class magazine in 1830. One heard "a never ceasing ding-dong about reform and change
in our public schools." From this public clamor emerged an array of secondary
schools and some of the earliest free public high schools. No single system of secondary schools existed before the 1840s, but a broad range of middle-class parents and educational reformers increasingly supported the higher learning.[2]

Public high schools ultimately became the predominant form of secondary instruction in the North after the 1880s. Few citizens earlier in the century, however, could have confidently predicted this outcome. For decades after the Revolution, America remained largely an agrarian nation without an elaborate system of formal education. Many articulate citizens—educators, politicians, journalists, and other community notables—nevertheless sensed a rising demand for advanced instruction.

The "higher branches of learning" grew in popularity, even though the phrase remained ill-defined, describing a domain somewhere above the elementary subjects and below collegiate instruction. Scholars studied these branches in a variety of institutions, as they had since the mid-eighteenth century. By the 1820s and 1830s, however, a growing network of reformers sought to discredit past and current practices and to lobby for a common system of tax-supported public high schools.

Following Boston's lead, some coastal cities soon opened free secondary schools. Enthusiasm for the higher branches long preceded the creation of the English Classical School, but the effort to build a single system of secondary instruction was an important break from the past. When free public high schools first opened in the 1820s, students still studied advanced subjects in an array of settings. Since the mid-eighteenth century some youth had often sought the higher learning in institutions that were neither solely tax supported nor free. Before the Revolution a handful of boys in the mid-eighteenth century still studied Latin and some Greek in the local classical grammar schools; afterward an equally small number of boys and even some girls pursued some higher English subjects in tax-supported, rural district schools. However, most of the demand after the 1750s for postelementary instruction—beyond reading, writing, basic arithmetic, and religious education—was met by nonclassical pay schools, seminaries, and academies.

Between the 1820s and 1840s, social changes transformed the nation, deepening concerns about the nature, control, and purposes of elementary and secondary education. America had entered an exciting era of social development and educational discourse. Early common school reformers in particular praised the educational aspirations of those who sought the higher learning while disparaging the institutions—both district schools and academies—that had taught ambitious youth an occasional course in algebra, literature, or advanced geography or grammar. While the demand for secondary education grew by the 1820s, a rising generation of school reformers began to argue that public high schools alone should provide advanced instruction for the talented few.

Most citizens continued to live on farms or in agricultural villages in the 1820s and 1830s. But social change everywhere challenged time-tested ways of educating boys as well as girls. Apprenticeships for young men, for example, increasingly disappeared with the advent of mechanization. By the 1820s, teenage boys in eastern towns and cities faced an economy in which unskilled laborers would soon outnumber craftsmen, aggravating social tensions. As a result, urban leaders reexamined the links between education, secondary schools, and the changing marketplace. New England's handful of public Latin grammar schools seemed insufficient to the higher educational needs of ambitious, talented young men, who struggled for survival and preferment in an individualistic and competitive commercial world.

Economic changes were not restricted to cities, whose growth was tightly bound to agricultural communities. Until they began to limit family size by the early 1800s, New England farmers produced too many sons in proportion to available land, so thousands of young men with slim prospects of inheriting property sought their fortunes in urban areas. The opening of rich western lands also weakened the economic competitiveness of older farming communities, further endangering the independence and security of those left behind.[3]

Young girls, too, faced a new social world that made their passage to adulthood complicated. Home and family responsibilities still circumscribed women's lives, and even reform-minded champions of educational expansion—echoing the views of Benjamin Rush and other earlier theorists—linked women's education with heightened domestic roles in the new republic. Bourgeois parents in particular worried about how well education prepared their sons and daughters for a commercial society, as the demise of an older economic order eroded familiar patterns of social relationships.[4]

During the antebellum period, cities grew faster than ever again in American history, and ideas about educational innovation correspondingly accelerated. Based principally upon commerce and upon the labors of artisans and small shopkeepers, cities both on the East Coast and on inland waterways became financial centers of merchant capitalism by the 1820s. Here lived the merchants and middlemen who bought and sold raw materials, finished products, and a growing surplus of agricultural goods for domestic and international consumption. Here lived the bankers whose control of money and credit allowed commerce to flourish in town and countryside. America remained predominately a land of farmers, but Thomas Jefferson's dream of a nation of independent, yeoman agrarians slowly faded.

Transportation after the War of 1812 improved dramatically through public and private investment in canals, steamboats, plank roads, and, later in the antebellum period, railroads. There were, of course, still many subsistence farmers, and most farm products in 1820 were consumed locally. But the expansion of the market and new transportation systems cemented closer ties between rural and urban economies, and with each passing decade wage laborers increasingly replaced craftsmen in the production of consumer goods. All of these trends had ominous implications for education.[5]

Indeed, the education of children and youth provoked many anxious conversations among parents in the 1820s and 1830s and spawned numerous voluntary associations dedicated to social and educational improvement. Community leaders and ordinary citizens in urban areas wondered whether tax-supported schools should embrace all social classes and whether they could solve pressing economic and civic ills. Southern slaveholders tightened their restrictions on black education in the 1830s, but northerners especially believed that all white youths should become literate to promote economic productivity and good citizenship.

In the northern countryside, where most people lived, girls as well as boys after the 1780s had increasingly attended locally controlled district schools, where rudimentary subjects and basic Protestant morality constituted the marrow of learning. By the 1820s, however, middle-class citizens in Boston and other areas believed that economic changes made advanced learning imperative for some teenagers. Proudly noting the creation of primary and grammar schools and the English Classical School, the secretary of Boston's School Committee claimed in 1823 that they "are intended to form a system of education, advancing from the lowest to the highest degree of improvement, which can be derived from any literary seminaries inferior to colleges and universities." Higher schools varied considerably, and most were not tax-supported or free before the 1840s. Still, their increased visibility reflected a growing bourgeois demand for more formal education for certain pupils.[6]

"This age is said, and said truly to be marked by nothing more distinctly, than by its wide and earnest diffusion of knowledge," claimed a literary journal in 1825. Exactly what did this mean? Throughout the decade, middle-class writers applauded the age's preoccupation with schooling, whether as a solution for grave social ills or as a gateway to opportunities in the free market. The rise of more distinctive social classes in towns and cities created a market for specialized women's and children's magazines, particularly for the bourgeoisie. These magazines described for nervous readers the profound changes altering contemporary life: the separation of home and work, the enhanced importance of mothers, the collapse of male apprenticeships and hence traditional forms of discipline and instruction, and the centrality of moral education for all children and higher education for the most talented youth.[7]

"An industrious and virtuous education of children is a better inheritance for them than a great estate," the editor of *The Casket* told middle-class Philadelphians in 1826. The editor subsequently wrote, with some hyperbole, that "our cities are filled with seminaries of a high order; every species of literary instruction is open to girls equally to boys." The writer failed to mention that, as access to the higher learning widened for some youth, the children of the urban poor in the coastal cities still remained largely uneducated and filled the city streets, grubbing for subsistence for themselves and their families. Pauper children in the City of Brotherly Love and most urban areas who received a "free" or "public" elementary education swallowed their pride and attended charity schools.[8]

In a society racked by deepening levels of social inequality, combative political parties, and high-pitched debates about southern slaves and northern wage slaves, "seminaries of a high order" offered something comforting and elevating for those in a position to benefit from them. A typical writer in the *New York Mirror* in 1828 praised the teaching of modern as well as ancient foreign languages in "all schools of a higher order." Samuel Wells would have smiled with approval. Indeed, most bourgeois writers realized that education had captivated the imagination of many leading citizens.[9]

Popular journals and magazines in the 1830s published numerous essays on the new economic order and the spread of all types of elementary and secondary schools throughout the developing nation. Anticipating the core values of high school textbooks, *The Lady's Book*, a famous bourgeois magazine, asserted that industry, temperance, diligent study, and hard work enabled the ambitious to rise to riches, while slovenly habits, drink, and laziness caused the mighty to fall. Schools certainly seemed like a solution to the era's profound social changes, and, according to the *Illinois Monthly Magazine* in 1832, the United States led the world in building educational institutions, whether primary schools or "high schools and academies."[10]

If the magazines they read reflected widespread social beliefs, the comfortable classes felt anxious as well as exhilarated about the future. America lacked the family-based aristocracies of the Old World, abundant educational opportunities enabled youth to avoid poverty, and family advantage rarely determined one's place in society. A Unitarian on the urban frontier caught the spirit, arguing in the *Western Messenger* that Christianity and republican values would shape the new educational order. Intellectual and material riches awaited those whose individual talents sparkled like the brightest stars: "The great Idea—as Coleridge would call it—the great *reforming idea* of Republicanism, is not that distinctions, and ranks, and privileges, are to be abolished; but that MERIT shall take the place of BIRTH, WEALTH, and PROWESS, and become the basis of an Aristocracy. . . . What is merit? It is genius, learning, experience, and above all character." To counter socialists and agrarians who wanted to level all human distinctions or to redistribute property, warned the author, schools would accept youth of unequal talents but reward the best. "Republicanism does not oppose differences of rank; it does not teach that men are born equal, or are ever equal."[11]

Such civic cautionary tales portrayed America as a place where an individual's contribution to society, not family background, determined everything, where formal education uplifted the poor and rewarded the talented. Was the refrain so common because it reflected reality or wishful thinking? Why were these apparently self-evident truths publicized so frequently?

Those infected with nostalgia or simply skeptical looked critically upon the prophets of the coming educational order. One writer in New York looked "with sorrow on the gradual abolition of the old country schools, and the rise of high, eclectic, collegiate and other academies and institutes." A world filled with steamboats and railroads, he feared in 1833, had destroyed the familiar contours of an older way of life. The " 'age of chivalry is gone,' and that of high-schools, seminaries, and institutes is come." A radical workingman writing in the *North American Magazine* was less nostalgic but agreed that "nothing is so much talked about as Education; and every scribbler who can eke out an Essay, thinks himself qualified to broach to the world, a grave and solemn diatribe upon the utility of *Education*."[12]

Unlike those who praised the higher schools, this radical claimed that republicans should embrace equality, not a different form of aristocracy. A European aristocracy based on wealth or an American one based on intellect or academic achievement: both spelled doom for equal rights. Was this why revolutionaries had shed their blood in 1776 and 1789?

> The unequal distribution of property is the great cause of the unequal distribution of knowledge; and he will yet prove the greatest benefactor of mankind, who shall so reduce the price of Education, that every citizen's son, however poor, can acquire it without expense. . . . *Education* will never spread over the great mass of the people of Europe. Here, it is possible, and barely possible—for fortunes are too unequal, luxury too swollen, vice too prevalent, pride too formidable, hypocrisy too fashionable, and ambition too corrupt.[13]

A kindred spirit on the western frontier, who favored more tax-supported schools for the poor, similarly doubted the need for more higher schools until first helping the destitute. "The wealthy send their children to high schools and colleges; but very few are wealthy enough for that," he insisted.[14]

Neither rural romantics nor urban radicals could deny that the age of the high school and academy had arrived in the 1820s and 1830s. "[O]urs is peculiarly the age of schools, colleges, and seminaries," said the *Western Messenger* in 1836, and the belief spread that an aristocracy of intellect was necessary in these unsettling times. Reform-minded activists who sought a common system of free public schools for all white children, with access to the elementary and the higher branches, attacked diversity and campaigned against all rivals. The age of Latin grammar schools soon faded into the historical mists, but controversies over the place of secondary schools in local communities never disappeared.[15]

Enterprising Americans who built so many kinds of schools between the 1780s and early 1840s generally disappointed common school activists such as Henry F. Barnard and Horace Mann. To reformers who favored a single system of public schools—with age-graded classrooms, a uniform curriculum, and hierarchical authority in the hands of men like themselves—this was an era of neglect and decline. Everywhere the Horace Manns of the world saw retrogression from the much sounder practices of the colonial school.

According to common school reformers in the 1820s and 1830s, Americans after the victory at Yorktown committed two major sins: they undermined town control of public education by creating district schools, and they actively supported countless private schools and academies that taught both elementary and higher subjects. Common school reformers rightly complained that these developments challenged their efforts to centralize political control over a system of tax-supported education. After the Revolution, for example, Massachusetts and Connecticut responded to the dispersal of population from villages and towns by permitting the establishment of autonomous, self-governing district schools in the hinterland. Decentralized control also became common in the old northwest territories and new western states in the early 1800s. School reformers who sought to enhance state power assailed local rule and lamented the collapse of centralized town control.[16]

The rise of an array of private academies and seminaries in both urban and rural settings after the 1780s horrified Mann's generation of reformers. Even though most antebellum common school leaders were alumni of district schools and academies, they claimed that private schools undermined the public interest. The eclipse of town control by districts was bad enough; that states often nurtured many private academies seemed almost heretical. Since the 1780s most states stimulated the growth of academies through gifts of money, acts of incorporation, and land grants, as legislators helped grease America's steep educational slide.

Theories of educational decline, of course, had precedents in colonial America. After Bostonians in the late seventeenth century established reading and writing schools for boys and after pay schools became popular, ministers and other public servants lamented the "decline" of local education. The passage of time allows a different vantage point. The creation of nonclassical schools and the subsequent admission of girls, the poor, or middle-class "high school" boys to the town schools hardly reduced the luster of Boston Latin. Nor did the rise of the rural district system and the appearance of thousands of academies constitute the dark ages. To many contemporaries, the spread of common district schools and private academies after the 1780s signified enlightenment and learning.

James G. Carter helped popularize attacks on district schools and the private sector in the 1820s. Sam Adams and others decades before had warned that town influence diminished as private schools expanded. Now, however, an educator and self-appointed reformer made a more elaborate inquiry into the past and present state of American schools. Indeed, in a eulogy in the *American Journal of Education*, Henry Barnard praised Carter for providing the first comprehensive account of the precipitous fall of education after the Revolution. Carter's became a story repeated by Barnard, Mann, and countless reformers who favored uniform schools. Those who wanted a single system of public education to triumph naturally saw the past through a glass darkly.[17]

Born on a Massachusetts farm in 1795, Carter attended local district schools, then advanced to Groton Academy and to Harvard College, graduating in 1820. Like most common school reformers, he thus had benefited from the mix of schools that citizens supported after the Revolution. Carter taught in district schools to help finance college; after graduation, he opened an academy. Articulate and ambitious, Carter shared the federalist faith in centralized authority. Most Yankee schoolmen—like Carter, Barnard, and Mann—typically became Whigs and not antimonopoly Jacksonian Democrats.[18]

In the very year that Boston's Federalists and Unitarians built America's first public high school, Carter condemned the serious erosion of public school traditions in some celebrated newspaper articles. Soon after he bitterly opposed the emasculation of state laws that mandated Latin grammar schools; his view of educational history became received wisdom among school reformers. According to Carter, the "original school policy" of colonial Massachusetts "contemplated the establishment in every large town of at least one school of a higher grade of studies than the district school, with a teacher of college qualifications, so as to bring the means of preparing for college within the reach of the poor, and, at the same time, of qualifying teachers for the district schools."[19]

Carter and those who quoted him had a fanciful but politically strategic view of the past, aimed at rallying support for the common schools. In fact, the original purpose of Latin grammar schools was to train a handful of boys, often college bound, in classical subjects; and the poor, lacking surplus capital, could ill afford the dame schools or private tutoring to prepare for admission to these institutions. Moreover, although many Latin school alumni in Boston and elsewhere became teachers, preparing district schoolmasters was hardly an original intent—district schools did not exist when the Latin grammar schools were founded. When district schools did emerge, their teachers were mostly alumni of English-oriented seminaries and academies, not classical scholars.

For nearly two centuries citizens in Massachusetts, Connecticut, and other colonies realized that classical schools educated only a select few children, all boys, and that these schools existed only when conditions allowed and demand dictated. Colonial New England towns and villages that ignored laws to maintain classical grammar schools often provided tax monies and private capital to expand access to the more practical branches of education. Post-Revolution Americans had not fallen from educational grace. The seemingly ineffective secondary school legislation of Connecticut and Massachusetts simply reflected shifting priorities. And so Carter misinterpreted the past, Barnard and his allies retold his tales, and history became less a search for truth or understanding than an aid to contemporary reform.

Carter repeatedly argued that the establishment of rural district schools, primary schools in towns or cities, or academies of any kind failed to compensate for the decline of the Latin grammar schools. In 1824, Carter advocated state teacher training-schools. Two years later, in his most famous educational work, *Essays Upon Popular Education*, Carter admitted that the period had witnessed "the rapid progress of knowledge, and the consequent demand for instruction of all kinds," but he wondered who would control this education and shape its direction.[20]

The idea of educational decay persisted in Carter's *Essays*. Once towns had controlled schools, educated rich and poor, and prepared youth for college, teaching posts, and public service generally. New England's schools then slipped and sank. Uninspiring teachers kept thousands of district schools; most were poorly trained, ignorant of the art of teaching and science of instruction, and patently inferior to their predecessors. Academies, too, were unwelcome, pretentious places that siphoned off the support of wealthy parents in towns and villages and that helped "not the poor, but the rich and middling classes of the community." In the academies the rich bathed in "the direct rays of the State's favour" while the poor suffered in their low status, declining institutions.[21]

Carter argued that the private academy had also developed without respect for *its* original mission, which was "to afford instruction in other and higher branches of education" not ordinarily taught in district or town schools. Now the increasingly popular academies, which often taught both elementary and advanced subjects, imperiled the very idea of a common school system, publicly controlled and open to everyone. "Patriotism and philanthropy are dull motives to exertions for the improvement of common schools, compared with parental affection," Carter emphasized. Wealthy parents who supported academies would do little more for free schools than pay their taxes, as those with the "most intelligence and the most leisure" had abandoned the once-cherished common school.[22]

This distorted view of history, predicated upon a mythical decline of public education, appealed to crusaders for reform. Other contemporaries routinely noted the fascination of the citizenry with all manner of education. Even Carter recognized the increased demand for schooling, but his preoccupation with state control blinded him to the era's possible educational achievements. Instead, Carter developed a theory of original intent that used history to explain and justify state control, centralized power, and hostility to academies. He helped nurture a powerful, emerging idea: that academies weakened an otherwise deeply embedded, wisely conceived public system that once served rich and poor admirably. This helped reformers believe that high schools would restore the balance, opening avenues of opportunity for all talented youth.

Drawing upon Carter's writings, an essayist in 1827 helped popularize his version of the past: "While the demand for knowledge, like the demand for everything else, increases rapidly as society advances in opulence and improvement,—the proportional number of teachers for the common schools has been made less, and their requisite qualifications strangely diminished." Carter faded from public memory more quickly than his ideas. In 1868 the Connecticut State Teachers' Association used history to endorse a unified system whose public high schools overshadowed all competitors. "A well-arranged system of public schools," it resolved, "now requires, as truly as it did in colonial times, that the elementary schools should lead to a higher grade of schools, maintained by districts, towns, counties, or neighborhoods,—so that the doors to higher education may be freely open to all who are disposed to enter."[23]

Public school activists distorted the place of district schools and academies in American society between the 1780s and 1840s. These schools were imperfect, diverse, and easily caricatured, but they hardly represented some retreat from a golden age. In their search for political power, reformers obscured the contributions of district schools and academies. Those who hoped after the 1820s to create a system of schools where none existed eagerly embraced the fanciful tales of writers such as James G. Carter. Northern reformers romanticized the schools of colonial America, discounted the achievements of local districts in popularizing elementary education, and downplayed the ability of academies and some district schools to teach some youth the higher branches.

District schools and academies boosted educational enrollments beyond anything imaginable earlier even in the most school-conscious seaboard cities. This zeal for learning impressed many citizens. Indeed, these schools contributed fortuitously to the ultimate shape of the American high school. As Carl F. Kaestle demonstrates, antebellum district schools in the countryside consistently enrolled a higher percentage of school-age children than did city schools, and they became the public schools of rural America. By teaching elementary and occasionally some advanced subjects, they also contributed to the ultimate expansion of secondary school enrollments in the nineteenth century. Ironically, academies, too, helped nourish the growth of public high schools by demonstrating the growing bourgeois demand for the higher English branches.[24]

District schools laid an essential educational base for the higher learning by spreading basic instruction and literacy into many sparsely populated areas. As the population spilled beyond town boundaries, citizens sought self-governance, and the district became the fundamental unit of school organization. Colonies and later states followed emerging social practice and enshrined the district system in law. Legislatures did so in Connecticut in the 1760s, in Massachusetts and Vermont in the 1780s, and in Rhode Island, New Hampshire, New York, and Maine in subsequent decades. School districts soon dotted the territories and young states of the trans-Appalachian West.[25]

School reformers in the 1840s who preferred centralized power naturally favored town over district control. Like other Whigs, Henry Barnard of Connecticut believed that district control and state aid to academies had undermined civic pride and sound educational practice. Connecticut had weakened the laws requiring Latin grammar schools in the late eighteenth century. Demand was so low that only the Hartford and New Haven schools, both feeders to Yale, survived the Revolution, and their fates largely depended upon hefty private endowments, not popular favor. In the 1790s, the legislature approved the establishment of school societies, local governing bodies that reduced town control. Barnard was appalled by the decline of the Latin schools, one of which he had attended, and by the push toward decentralization, which yielded nearly two thousand school districts in his native state by 1839.[26]

The ubiquitous district schools of the North evolved into the common public schools of rural America. Everywhere they offered a relatively inexpensive education that emphasized basic literacy skills in nonclassical, English subjects. Financially they depended upon a mixture of tax dollars and private tuition or other forms of support; most were not completely free. Even older states—including, to Barnard's embarrassment, Connecticut—allowed tuition or "rate bills" until after the Civil War. The Nutmeg State was not unusual. Most district schools were ungraded, governed by lay people and local communities, and oriented around the lower English branches. By the 1820s, a precocious few who thirsted for deeper knowledge occasionally studied algebra, Latin, or another higher branch with a sympathetic teacher. Pursuing a full range of higher studies in these settings was difficult, as advocates of centralized, "union" schools repeatedly emphasized after the 1840s.[27]

Whenever reformers persuaded local schools to consolidate with neighboring districts, the upper levels of the new multiroom union schools often became public "high schools." But before the 1840s, the typical country school was a one-room building that emphasized the lower branches: reading, writing, arithmetic, and, after the 1820s, some geography and history. Daily doses of the Lord's Prayer and the King James Bible supplemented this educational fare. School reformers defended the Protestant tone of these one-room schools, emphasized the precedence of moral training and character building over intellectual goals, and yet condemned the nation's district system as archaic, unprofessional, and too decentralized. And the myth grew among schoolmen that education had deteriorated in the decades after the Revolution, a time of "retrogression."[28]

Professional school people who wanted centralized state authority regarded district-level control as inimical to plans for a uniform system. Organized into ungraded classes taught by nonspecialists, one-room schools were especially ill-suited for the higher learning. In the early twentieth century, a historian of education succinctly captured the prevailing view. "The district system," he asserted, "by its very nature called for the splitting up of administrative functions, a dissipation of financial support, and a diversion of public interest which were entirely antagonistic to the best interests of secondary education."[29]

Antebellum school reformers consistently highlighted the foibles of local school politics in the countryside before professional educators set things straight. They viewed all farmers as reluctant taxpayers and emphasized how local politics shaped too many educational decisions. Most nineteenth-century school leaders, often Whigs or, later, Republicans, rejected the Jeffersonian dictum that decentralized government ruled best. Local self-government was harmful, one educator noted in a history of Massachusetts' schools. "The violence of ebullition is inversely as the size of the pot. Questions involving the fate of nations have been decided with less expenditure of time, less stirring of passions, less vociferation of declamation and denunciation, than the location of a fifteen-by-twenty district schoolhouse." At best, the district school provided only a "scanty" education to anyone.[30]

In reality, the district system was a remarkable initiative and fundamental to the growth of public secondary schools. Neither the federal government nor the Bill of Rights made education or school attendance an inherent right. Yet northern white citizens increasingly sent their children to school beginning in

The Owosso, Michigan, "high school," like many others in the nation, was located on the top floor of the local union school. From *Thirty-Eighth Annual Report of the Superintendent of Public Instruction of the State of Michigan* (Lansing, 1875).

the mid-eighteenth century. The Northwest Ordinance of 1787 modestly stimulated the establishment of schools in newly settled territories; most education funding, however, was local, a mixture of public and private monies. The percentage of children in school continued to increase, especially in the countryside, from the postrevolutionary years to the early 1830s, when the percentage in attendance leveled off.[31]

This was, then, no age of regression. Why more children went to school remains controversial, but the admission of girls to rural district schools certainly contributed to school expansion. Though reformers after the 1820s romanticized town control of public education in the colonial period, they ignored the common exclusion of girls before the 1750s. After Yorktown, however, girls—the future mothers of virtuous citizens—appeared vital to the safety of the republic. District control infuriated school reformers, but local schools educated hundreds of thousands of children—the numbers now boosted by the admission of girls—whose families sought a basic education and sometimes some exposure to the higher branches. These schools did not represent a golden age of American education, but they should not simply be judged by the standards of centralized authority.

Antebellum reformers regarded district schools as a major impediment to quality education and to the expansion of free secondary instruction. Academies, whose countrywide popularity grew after 1776, were deemed equally pernicious. In addition to weakening town control and the illustrious classical schools, leaders in the new nation had presumably undermined progress by encouraging the spread of privately controlled academies, seminaries, and other institutions of higher learning. In truth, just as district schools signified a rising demand for rudimentary education, academies symbolized broad middle- and upper-class demands for something more.

Beginning in the 1820s school reformers dreamed of the day when academies would cease to exist. James G. Carter captured well the growing reform sentiment when he blamed academies for the collapse of the Latin schools (which in fact had died from lack of demand). When Samuel Adams Wells promoted the English Classical School, he remembered his grandfather's admonitions that the evil private sector would drain elite support from Boston's municipal schools. Talented, ambitious boys needed an alternative to Boston Latin, warned Wells, because important taxpayers now sent their sons to "private academies in this vicinity, to acquire that instruction which cannot be obtained at the public seminaries."[32]

Complaints about the private sector grew more shrill in the 1830s. J. Orville Taylor, editor of the New York *Common-School Assistant* between 1836 and 1840, argued that because very few children advanced to the higher studies, the common schools deserved exclusive access to public monies. In his long-forgotten gem, *Satirical Hits on the People's Education* (1839), Taylor defended the district school as the "people's college" and called private schools enemies of the people. Horace Mann, Henry Barnard, and other northern reformers were less sympathetic to district schools, especially their organization and control, but essayists in Mann's *Common School Journal* and in other professional magazines similarly labeled private academies as "pernicious."[33]

Mann's own attacks upon private secondary schools were widely quoted by fellow partisans. When wealthy families embraced private academies, he asserted in 1837, the common system lost vital community support. Echoing Carter's earlier thoughts, Mann believed that wealthy families always set the standard for education. "Reforms ought to be originated and carried forward by the intelligent portion of society, by those who can see most links in the chain of causes and effects," he warned. Private academies, especially those founded by religious denominations, divided communities. If, however, the private sector disappeared, the best people would more generously support the public system, expand educational access, and thus bridge the social divisions now separating American society.[34]

Mann's generation of reformers worked strenuously to undermine the appeal of academies, highlighting their many evil influences. Were academies harmful to the public interest? Or, as some people thought, did they exemplify the age's commitment to enlightenment and learning? If the "rich and middling classes" abandoned private academies, as James G. Carter hoped, would they expect uncommon benefits for certain youth in the common system?

The demand of white middle- and upper-class parents for more secular and specialized education for their sons and daughters nurtured the growth of academies by the mid-eighteenth century. Even progressive cities such as Boston, as Samuel Wells realized, then had a very restricted vision of public schools, leaving the education of girls to the private sector. Even for the most favored white boys, the city's only advanced education was at Boston Latin, despite rising interest in the higher English branches. As a result, pay schools and other private ventures arose in Boston and in inland towns and seaboard cities.

In 1747 Benjamin Franklin had issued what became a famous call for an English academy that taught useful, practical subjects. Students should "be taught *every Thing* that is useful, and *every Thing* that is ornamental: But Art is long, and their Time is short. It is therefore proposed that they learn those Things that are likely to be *most useful* and *most ornamental*, Regard being had to the several Professions for which they are intended." From astronomy to geometry and geography to history, "modern" subjects offered more youths a more useful learning than the dreaded Latin and Greek.[35]

Franklin complained that his ideas were imperfectly translated into practice in Philadelphia, but secular English instruction gained popularity during his lifetime. Private schools offered those who could afford tuition a variety of subjects to enrich children's lives, from polite accomplishments such as dancing to practical subjects such as navigation. With the emergence of a more market-driven society, stimulated further after the Revolution, parents wanted more for their sons than classical education or college—the choice of a privileged few—could offer.

Many citizens unfamiliar with Franklin's writings shared his faith that the "good Education of Youth" led to greater happiness: "Almost all Governments have therefore made it a principal Object of their Attention, to establish and endow with proper Revenues, such Seminaries of Learning, as might supply the succeeding Age with Men qualified to serve the Public with Honour to themselves, and to their Country." And daughters in the new republic, too, now gaining access to district schools, provided an additional market for private seminaries and academies.[36]

Encouraging "Seminaries of Learning" became a common state concern after the Revolution. Just as country district schools expanded, so did academies. In the late eighteenth century, Massachusetts provided academies with grants of land, a policy that some critics said undermined the Latin schools. Other New England states also encouraged the formation of English secondary schools. The Vermont Constitution of 1777 required the establishment of secondary English "Grammar Schools," one per county. Like Massachusetts, Maine and New Hampshire offered land grants to encourage the establishment and incorporation of advanced centers of learning. Rhode Island had no land to give to academies, and Connecticut earmarked its holdings in the Western Reserve for the common schools.[37]

Academies spread throughout the nation, reflecting increased demand for the diffusion of knowledge in general and the higher branches in particular. By the 1820s, Indiana had academies in its southern villages and towns, and along with Iowa it created "County Seminaries"—secondary schools built on free state land that, like other academies, charged tuition. Michigan experimented by establishing lower branches of its university throughout the state to better link with the common schools. Mixed academies and female seminaries also boomed in Illinois and Ohio. Illinois chartered at least 125 academies and seminaries between 1818 and 1848; Ohio incorporated approximately 100 between 1803 and 1840.[38]

Academies were especially noteworthy in the South. With a dispersed rural population, the South was repeatedly condemned by Yankee reformers for failing to build enough free public schools; those that existed were largely for the poor. Southerners nevertheless created numerous private elementary and secondary schools in the antebellum years. Many southern states contributed money from various "Literary Funds" and, as in the North, legislatures provided land grants and occasional cash to encourage and sustain seminaries and academies. There were apparently twenty-four incorporated academies in Alabama and fifty-five in Virginia by the early 1830s. As in the North, female schools proliferated in the Deep South and in the border states.[39]

Formed at a time of rapid social change, this array of schools, which taught the higher branches, was stimulated by the public purse though controlled by individual proprietors or a private board of trustees. Recognizing the variety of schools in his midst, the editor of *The American Almanac and Repository of Useful Knowledge* tried to describe them for readers in 1834. "Academies, grammar schools, high schools, and gymnasiums are terms applied to seminaries which hold an intermediate rank between common schools and college," he wrote, based on information gathered on different kinds of secondary schools across the nation. "Some of these are classical schools, designed chiefly for preparing students for admission to college; others are appropriated to English education; many are a mixed character, having a part of their pupils pursuing the study of the ancient or modern languages, and more of them pursuing English studies."[40]

Estimates of private school attendance were unreliable. One collector of statistics concluded in 1834 that in "the principal towns" of New England "private schools abound; and much more is expended in the large towns upon private than upon the public schools." Henry Barnard said there were over 6,100 incorporated academies in 1855, with enrollments nine times higher than in the colleges. Most academies, however, never sought a charter and thus remained unincorporated. A few served local communities for decades; most were ephemeral. Even progressive Massachusetts did not gather private school statistics until late in the antebellum period, so the number and types of academies remain a mystery.[41]

They were at any rate sufficiently numerous and influential to anger public school leaders, who held academies and district schools responsible for ending better times. The Yankee *North American Review* complained in 1837 that classical education had become dwarfed by the English studies. "We always regret and wonder to hear it said, that the Academies, which have sprung up during the present century, in such numbers, have supplied the want thus created."[42]

Critics had difficulty seeing academies as uniquely suited to a changing society. Academies existed in a world of intensified market relationships, improved communication, and growing interest in the role of science and technology in economic development—and amid political debates over governmental responsibility for social innovation and public welfare. Unlike older European nations, America never endowed many schools. A few elite Latin grammar schools and a handful of academies enjoyed fabulous wealth. These were, however, extremely rare institutions.[43]

After the Revolution, as demand accelerated for nonclassical education for boys and more access for girls, legislators thought it wise to encourage learning. Legislators did not create academies or create the demand but simply responded to public willingness to pay for a new kind of education. School reformers were less interested in understanding than in discrediting the competition. Academies were enormously diverse because they rose and fell with demand, and individual institutions reflected the idiosyncrasies of local teachers and communities of students, never part of a uniform system.

Academies, as they developed after the 1780s, generally had a classical and English stream of studies, but most emphasized the modern branches. A few academies like Phillips Andover or Exeter competed with Boston Latin to be the preferred institution for Boston elites preparing their sons for Harvard. But America's collegiate population was so small that most academies and seminaries had a more practical bent and could not survive by teaching only classical subjects. Unlike Andover and Exeter, most academies lacked endowments. Educational entrepreneurs tried against the odds to make money; if demand weakened, their schools closed.[44]

Some academies were single-sex institutions. Most were coeducational, though they did not necessarily teach men and women together or even the same subjects. Separate men's and women's departments were common, especially in boarding schools, which assured parents of propriety. When Catholics or the more numerous evangelical Protestant organizations founded academies, religion permeated the school's atmosphere. Even husbands and wives unaffiliated with specific denominations who opened small seminaries and academies, whether in the countryside or city, required their pupils to attend a church of their choice every Sunday. School days opened with a prayer and a reading from King James, and the spirit of evangelical Protestantism filled the classroom.[45]

Academies often taught elementary and secondary subjects; after the 1820s, they more typically instructed children older than ten in secondary subjects less easily taught in ungraded district schools. Most academies had one to four teachers who taught—or in their advertisements claimed to teach—a wide range of classes. Lacking a sense of humor about their own institutions, public school leaders were quick to poke fun at the academies for promising the sky. Canaan Academy in Maine in 1814 offered to teach "English, Reading, Writing, Composition and English Grammar, the Greek and Latin Languages, Mathematics comprehending Arithmetic, Euclid's Elements, Plane and Spherical Trigonometry, Gauging, Land Surveying, Algebra, and Geography with the use of Globes." Schools laid wide nets to snare their prey, claimed a literary journal that ridiculed all "the high-sounding and comprehensive" advertisements. The age of educational bunkum had arrived.[46]

Whatever their size, financial base, or promises, academies suited families that could forgo their children's income and afford tuition. A few academies offered some scholarships for poor children through a donor's bequest or occasionally by statute. Most academies, however, taught only those children whose parents could pay the tuition and related expenses. School reformers continually complained that academies taught mostly the rich—which is what critics later said about public high schools. Histories of well-established academies emphasize that they generally served a broad range of middle-class families, who preferred an English over a classical education for their children.

Contemporaries generally believed that academies served the public interest. State governments commonly promoted private enterprise and economic development; indeed, the Whigs and later the Republicans used government to stimulate the private sector. Individual entrepreneurs, local lay groups, and religious denominations all built academies, which continued to grow nationally in the 1820s and 1830s.

Academies widened girls' access to the higher branches, and they made the modern English subjects the heart of secondary education forever. Many classically trained reformers in the 1830s and 1840s lamented the passing of the old Latin schools, but academies simply met a demand local district schools or town schools were unwilling or unable to provide. Academies offered variety, innovation, and whatever parents and their children could afford in the educational marketplace.

States like New York invested money in academies partly to improve the quality of common school teachers, a function of high schools in later decades. Most academies, with or without state aid, trained many teachers of the district schools, whose increased enrollments nurtured demands for still more qualified instructors. A few academies even offered some specialized courses in pedagogy. New York's experiment began in the 1780s, when debates on education in the republic intensified. Pay schools and academies emerged in towns and cities in the Empire State in the eighteenth century, as the merchant classes in particular pressed for something other than Latin for their sons. Changing times demanded new avenues to the future.[47]

In 1784 Governor George Clinton urged the state to help nurture piety, virtue, and enlightenment in "Seminaries of Learning." Benjamin Franklin had earlier touted academies as a potential source of teacher training, for poorer boys especially, and New York subsequently gave land grants to academies to help prepare district school instructors. By 1817 New York had incorporated forty academies, and the number rose over the next two decades. In 1827 the state earmarked money for academies to train prospective teachers in special departments; in the mid-1830s it mandated an academy with a pedagogical division in every senatorial district. Public school leaders in the late 1830s increasingly attacked the private sector and advocated state normal schools, which later eclipsed the academy system. Until then, New York as well as other states supported academies financially to help improve instruction in the common schools.[48]

The academies produced diverse, not uniform, educational experiences. Responding to the vagaries of the marketplace, without a firm grip on state aid, antebellum academies would continue to compete with public high schools in many parts of the country, especially the South. High schools later shared many characteristics of the academies, despite the nasty things reformers said about them. The success of the high school seemed dependent upon the elimination of their rivals. As one partisan understood: "The period [between] 1821 and 1865 is best characterized as a struggle between two institutional ideals. The establishment of the Boston English Classical School marked the beginning; and the decline of the academy marked the end."[49]

America's first specialized education journals appeared in the 1820s and 1830s, and their contributors frequently applauded the rising interest in the higher learning. Although the movement against academies accelerated during these years, most writers regarded increased enrollments in advanced studies as a sign of educational progress. How to undermine the private sector and enhance the position of public high schools soon became a major goal.

The appeal of the higher English branches expanded in the 1820s. In 1826 the *American Journal of Education* praised new private male and female "high schools" in New York City and a public Girls' High School in Boston. Soon it also congratulated the boosters of Pittsfield, Massachusetts, for planning a new boarding school, the "Berkshire High School." "A general sentiment appears to prevail," said one writer, "that a more extensive establishment of what are commonly termed *High Schools* for the instruction of youth is needed, in which all the important branches of education requisite for their advancement in life, in its most useful occupations, shall be thoroughly taught."[50]

Several private "high schools" also opened in New York State, and various towns in the Northeast slowly turned their attention to the issue of establishing public secondary schools. Salem, Massachusetts, opened an alternative to its public Latin school in 1828. Following Boston's lead, it created a free high school for boys interested in the "English studies" but not bound for college. In the same year, America's preeminent moral philosopher, Francis Wayland, urged his townsmen in Providence, Rhode Island, to build a school "of a more elevated character" than an English grammar school "to do honor to the public spirit of the commercial and manufacturing metropolis, but not at all beyond what is demanded by the advanced intelligence of the age."[51]

Pleas to advance the higher learning abounded. Surveying the wide assortment of newly established schools, one writer in 1833 declared: "There is much in the state of education in this country, which is encouraging to the philanthropist and scholar." It was often difficult to fix firm labels on these schools, to call a school public or private, or to distinguish a "high school" from an "academy." In many states, privately controlled incorporated academies charged tuition but received some state aid; district schools often charged rates that in states such as New York produced higher revenues than tax assessments; and all institutions served individuals by educating them and hence in a broad way advanced learning and benefited the public.[52]

The absence of uniformity in the higher learning did not lead most citizens to despair. Since the late eighteenth century, numerous writers had used generalities to describe schools that offered more than grammar-level subjects. The Connecticut school law of 1798, for example, permitted local authorities, when supported by two-thirds of the voters, to create "a School of a higher order, for the common benefit of all the Inhabitants, the object of which shall be to perfect the Youth admitted therein in Reading and Penmanship, to instruct them in the Rudiments of English Grammar, in composition, in Arithmetic and Geography, or, on particular desire, in the Latin and Greek languages, also in the first principles of Religion and Morality, and in general to form them for usefulness and happiness in the various relations of social life." Most district schools then offered reading, writing, and arithmetic; "a school of a higher order" meant anything more advanced. Americans throughout the early 1800s wrote approvingly of schools of a "higher order" that offered an "advanced education" in the "higher branches" in something often called a "high" or "higher school." High was whatever was not low.[53]

Studying the higher branches grew increasingly popular. In 1830 an essay on "High Schools" in an evangelical periodical described "several flourishing institutions" that resembled "German Gymnasia." The following year the same journal published an impressive review of "Academies, High Schools, Gymnasia," without distinguishing one category from another. Yet all of these "classes of institutions," assured one writer, "defuse [sic] the blessings of knowledge through all the ranks of the community."[54]

Distinguishing "high schools" from "academies" was a fetish of common school reformers, who wanted careful lines drawn between "public" and "private" institutions. In frontier Indiana, however, "Marston's Academy" was advertised in 1837 as the "Indianapolis High School." Across the river from Louisville was another private school, "The New Albany High School for Young Gentlemen." In later decades, public secondary schools sometimes had the word "Academy" in their title, further promoting ambiguity. As early as 1819, a correspondent for *Blackwood's Magazine* in Edinburgh visited numerous American private schools and ridiculed the presumptuousness of the typical "academy": "The Americans take a strange delight in high-sounding names, and often satisfy themselves for the want of the thing, by the assumption of the name."[55]

The imprecise terminology so common in the 1820s and 1830s frustrated those who wanted uniform public schools and a common educational vocabulary. In 1838 the indefatigable Henry Barnard used his pen to clarify everything, or so the ambitious young Whig reformer thought: "By a Public or Common High School, is intended a public or common school for the older and more advanced scholars of the community in which the same is located, in a course of instruction adapted to their age, and intellectual and moral wants, and, to some extent, to their future pursuits in life." Budding professionals should recognize a high school on sight, but Barnard's definition described an ideal, not reality. The educational landscape lacked the smooth contours of the Connecticut Yankee's prose.[56]

How to define an "advanced scholar," identify "intellectual and moral wants," and link a course of study with one's "future pursuits" in life dominated contemporary debates. *Most* secondary schools claimed to address these issues best. Barnard's definition was part of a war of words penned to promote a single state-controlled school system. Despite Barnard's vast knowledge about schools, his definition of a public high school inevitably faltered. Hostile to those ubiquitous academies, Barnard knew that public schools lacked much uniformity. He realized that some "public," tax-supported secondary schools were free, while others charged tuition; that some educated boys and girls together, while others practiced rigid segregation; that some existed in large cities with some graded classrooms, while most children studying the higher branches sat a few benches from abecedarians in one-room schools. Was uniformity possible or desirable?

Many ordinary citizens would have found these concerns about definitions or distinctions between private and public institutions odd. Common school reformers, however, sought greater clarity as they advocated a single system of tax-supported schools after the 1840s. Schools had traditionally been funded from diverse sources. Some church-related schools and many academies received public money, including Catholic schools that educated the urban poor. America's oldest school, Boston Latin, had been first aided by private donations and then made secure by the tax man. "There are two public schools in Boston of a higher order, the English High School and the Latin Grammar School," asserted a writer in the *North American Review* in 1837. Both were "higher" public schools for boys, one offering advanced studies "for life," the other mostly for college admission.[57]

Even the English Classical School faced a few name changes before it permanently became the English High School in 1833. In an era of ambiguous labels, English High was technically not a high school by Barnard's definition or Massachusetts law. Contrary to Barnard's description, it was open to "advanced scholars" who could pass an admission test, but it excluded girls. Massachusetts legislation in 1827, which avoided the phrase *high school*, mandated the establishment of English schools of a higher order for both sexes. After the Girls' High School closed in 1828, girls were allowed to study some advanced subjects in the upper grammar grades. Even when a girls' secondary school opened in the early 1850s, it initially offered normal classes, not equivalent academic instruction.[58]

The absence of a single definition of a high school in the 1820s and 1830s provides an important clue about historical change. Editors, newspaper writers, and pamphleteers publicized an assortment of "high" or "higher schools." As one Bostonian recalled, "advanced education was then a matter everywhere in the air," later assuming many institutional forms. There were endless ways to become acquainted with the higher learning, especially if one had money. There were numerous private higher schools, some run for profit, some small, some large, some coeducational, some not, some transitory, some that endured. Here and there fully tax-supported "public" high schools opened in large towns or major cities before the 1840s, but they were still relatively rare and only added to the mix of choices for an interested public.[59]

The creation of public high schools in Philadelphia and Baltimore in the late 1830s encouraged reformers, but public secondary education continued to encounter apathy and even dissent. The frightful depression of 1837 made the opposition especially hostile. Horace Mann, the nation's greatest school reformer, was stung by critics and tried to quash the popular belief that high schools were rich men's schools. His *Common School Journal* lobbied for more public, not private, education, yet he was clearly frustrated when he entered the debate over public high schools in 1839.

Mann actually urged fellow reformers to avoid the phrase "high school." Opponents, he warned, conveniently invoked it as a general term of derision: "Although, intrinsically, there is no more objection to calling a public town school, a high school, than there is to the phrases 'high road,' or 'high water,' or 'high seas,' or 'high' anything else; yet while such a senseless prejudice exists against calling a public school 'high,' it is better to avoid exciting it, than to be defeated by it. I am not compelled to run against a 'high' granite post, because it has been wrongfully placed in the 'high' way." Without a suitable alternative, however, reformers seemed to prefer running into granite. As they bumped their noses and bruised their egos, they understandably feared for their cause. A handful of public high schools did exist by the late 1830s, but for decades children had traveled different roads to the higher learning. A market society, surfacing most dramatically along the eastern seaboard in the eighteenth century, deepened class divisions and generated distinctive educational needs usually met in a wide range of institutions.[60]

That the public would continue to embrace choice seemed likely as market relations spread across newly settled parts of America in the early 1800s. The considerable attacks on monopolies in the 1820s and 1830s complicated the efforts of school reformers and made their ultimate political victories even more impressive. After praising Barnard and Mann for their leadership, the Whig *North American Review* in 1840 sensed that the movement to improve the public schools would accelerate. Activists would try to persuade taxpayers to support both free elementary schools for all white children and high school education for the talented few.[61]

A Republican Crown

A High Public School, located in some
central part of the city, into which our
youth should be gathered by way of promotion from the other Public Schools,
without regard to condition of life, or the
artificial distinctions of society, and with
reference to merit alone, would be the
crowning work of our Free School
System.

—LEVI BISHOP, President of the Board of
Education of Detroit, 1853

America descended into five
long years of economic depression after the Panic of 1837, and leading
reform-minded citizens again debated the relation between education—not
least the higher learning—and the future of the republic. Bourgeois moral-
ists and politicians urged the poorer classes to resist the heresies of Robert
Owen, Fanny Wright, and other radicals who denounced the evils of early
capitalist society. Instead, they demanded social order and personal restraint
as the economy collapsed and produced untold human misery. Mass education
became a political weapon against dangerous ideas, and the higher schools
conferred intellectual and social benefits to certain worthy students.

Edward Everett's oft-cited remark about schools and stability thus appeared
approvingly in the *Ladies' Garland* in 1839. "Education is a better safeguard for
liberty than a standing army," he claimed. "If we retrench the wages of the
schoolmaster, we must raise the wages of the recruiting sergeant." Ideological
disputes over mass education and free high schools always intensified during
recurrent panics and depressions, providing some continuity to reform sentiments in future decades. The comfortable classes agreed that blackboards
were preferable to bayonets.[1]

Since the 1780s, many political leaders had emphasized that republics
throughout history were fragile and evanescent. Most agreed that the nation's
survival depended upon a virtuous and intelligent citizenry. But what did this

mean in a new age? By the 1830s and 1840s, America had become a commercial republic, one in which "free" individuals were more interdependent, tied to the marketplace, and vulnerable to economic downturns via the mysterious workings of the invisible hand. Bourgeois writers, however, spoke ever more feverishly about personal responsibility and the values of Poor Richard—precisely when the individual became less autonomous and independent, when factory hands replaced artisans in the production of shoes, clothes, and other consumer goods. Common schools and high schools promised public safety and social improvement as society encountered startling levels of change.[2]

Bourgeois men's and women's magazines advocated social order as economic depression threatened political stability. *Godey's Lady's Book* told readers that in republics the people made the laws, which required universal compliance. "We never like to hear the rich and poor spoken of in invidious comparison, as though the sufferings of the latter were caused by the former," Mrs. Sarah Josepha Hale editorialized in 1841. "Honest industry, judicious enterprise, and careful management, deserve to succeed, as they generally do in our country, and to stigmatize all who thus obtain wealth as aristocrats and enemies of the poor, is wrong, and may be the source of a fountain of troubled waters which will sweep away what is most beneficial and beautiful in our social fabric." All the barriers to the diffusion of knowledge had been leveled, she argued, and only hard work, application, and achievement separated the rich from the poor.[3]

The Rev. Horace Bushnell was another champion of free secondary schools. Echoing Hale's paeans to progress, this equally famous writer joined with fellow Whigs to promote a free high school in Hartford. Like most reformers, he explained that schools could not eliminate social class divisions, which reflected different levels of individual achievement, but that they could undermine criticisms of a market economy. The widening gap between the social classes, exacerbated during the depression, meant that civic-minded men had little choice but to attack private academies and support a common school system, where talent alone determined success and advancement. In this way the state would offer comfort to the more privileged and opportunity to the worthy poor.

Bushnell claimed in 1841 that "agrarianism and the rising of the masses" threatened Christian values and social order, and men of property and youth seeking advancement desperately needed free high schools. Republicanism could flourish only if towns like Hartford, with neighborhoods increasingly stratified by income and schools governed by autonomous districts, built central high schools for the few exceptionally talented pupils. Society's leaders should not be born to power but should gain it through hard work and achievement. "Republicanism permits distinctions of rank and association, but not separations of rank," he warned, "for separation is non-acquaintance, and that is too close upon the verge of hostility." Said plainly, everyone should attend elementary school, only the best should enter high school, and then only the most capable would become the leaders of society.[4]

Schools were the fairest way to distribute power and influence, according to reformers who accepted the reality of social classes but feared the outbreak of class war. Every individual should take responsibility for earthly success and personal salvation. Common schools, claimed the *North American Review* in 1842, were "eminently democratic in their nature" and "the only great engine for the elevation of the laboring classes." Legislation could not eliminate social inequality, despite the rhetoric of office seekers who promised to level the rich and uplift the poor. "Public schools," on the other hand, "tend to equalize social advantages, because they enable all men to start fair in the race." Every teacher was "a despot himself" but "an efficient laborer in a republican cause."[5]

By the 1840s, many middle-class writers and reformers wanted the higher learning to play a special role in their more class-oriented society. Schools should not criticize the social order or question bourgeois ideas about work, success, or individual responsibility but rather help create productive workers and respectable citizens. Transplanted Yankees who built the public schools of New Orleans, for example, believed that republican values and sound learning counteracted radicalism. "If the rights of person or property are ever invaded, it will be when hordes of ignorant men are spread over the land, ready and willing to do the will of the demagogue."[6]

The idea that schools produced politically safe individuals for the new commercial, increasingly industrialized order nourished the ideological roots of high schools between the 1830s and 1880s. Well-educated people, so the theory went, would defend property, social inequality based upon merit, and proper views of political economy. By cultivating virtue and intelligence, schools made a distinctive contribution during these dangerous times. One southerner, an "anti-Owenite," called for low-cost academies in the 1830s to enable an "aristocracy of talent" to rule the land and undermine socialist agitators. A free-labor advocate in New Hampshire in 1849 shared this goal but preferred free high schools, since "the only qualifications requisite for an admission, are certain intellectual attainments, which may be acquired with as great facility by the enterprising sons of the poor as by those of the rich." Mrs. Hale would have included daughters, too. If the state cultivated the intellect of its brightest youth, property and social order would be secure.[7]

"Educatio Populi Salus Reipublicae"—the education of the people is the safety of the republic. This simple motto formed the cornerstones of a common faith among Yankee school reformers after the 1830s. Educational leaders believed that only the most intelligent people should gain power, whether in business, politics, or the professions. And an array of leaders— from ordinary teachers to wealthy activists—told youth that hard work and application enabled individuals to control their own destiny. When labor agitation erupted in the 1870s, one educator in East Saginaw, Michigan, characteristically called the education of the few in the higher branches wise political economy. "A few splendid scholars, well trained intellects," he wrote, "are worth much more to the community than scores of ordinary pupils."[8]

To enhance their prestige and political legitimacy, northern reformers claimed that their version of republicanism adhered most closely to America's revolutionary past. Ignoring how much they differed from republican theorists of the early national period, they fashioned an ideology congenial with their particular social interests. Reformers best revealed their values and distance from their ancestors when they called the high school the "crown" of the emerging public school system. This common image revealed their support for hierarchy, centralized power, and cultural authority. That republicans of the revolutionary period opposed the centralized power symbolized by the English scepter and crown mattered little as familiar words assumed new meanings in a changing social context.

Between the 1830s and 1880s, common school reformers and high school advocates wove a particular blend of republicanism into the fabric of bourgeois social thought. Certain factions of society doubted that these activists captured the true essence of republicanism, but these dissidents failed to alter the emerging shape of public schools and have been largely forgotten by posterity. Those who triumphed had a particular reading of America's republican past, which they interpreted in the light of changing social conditions and offered as an explanation for their actions.

Zebulon Jones, a school commissioner in Rockingham County, New Hampshire, provided a familiar view in 1851: "Republican institutions are founded in the virtue and intelligence of the people." Such claims emanated from hamlets and major cities that built systems of public schools. Who could disagree with the Michigan school superintendent who believed that the (Federalist) spirit of George Washington was still alive? "American statesmen," he wrote in 1863, "have always asserted the close dependence of free government on the cultivated intelligence and virtue of the people." Oran Faville, Iowa's chief school officer, nodded in agreement and heaped scorn on private academies, because only public high schools truly reflected "the spirit of Republicanism."[9]

The ideology of republicanism remained a mighty force in antebellum and postbellum America but wore many guises. Whatever their party preference, citizens generally accepted Jefferson's claim that ignorant men could not be independent and free. To agree that intelligence and virtue were the basis of republicanism, however, did not mean universal support for the emerging public school system or consensus on other social policies. Thoughtful men and women quarreled over the many forms education and schooling might assume in a new nation; republicanism continued to command wide allegiance but had multiple, sometimes contradictory, meanings; and the modern school systems that the Father of Our Country presumably would have supported represented a particular expression of republican ideology. Indeed, public school systems reflected selective ideas firmly rooted in the historical experiences of northern middle-class reformers, whose republicanism was a special elixir advertised as a common brew.

Republicanism never constituted a single, universally accepted body of ideas. Context meant everything. From the Revolution to the days of the

Robber Barons, people with opposite social and political beliefs bowed before that holy word. Educational reformers in the nineteenth century generally assumed that republicanism found expression in centralized, uniform, tax-supported schools. Their opponents, however, also described themselves as republicans. They envisioned emergent school bureaucracies equally as responsive to the citizenry as King George's court had been in the eighteenth century.

For many patriots of the revolutionary period, republican ideology helped shape resistance against monarchical England. Republicans believed in liberty and independence and condemned the luxurious lifestyles, political decadence, and corruption of the English aristocracy. King George and his slavish ministers exemplified the evils of unrestrained, concentrated power. After the Revolution, republicanism often meant independence, especially political freedom for white men who owned property, and faith in a government of laws and not men that restrained the politically powerful.[10]

The spread of market relations in the countryside and in towns throughout the North undermined most people's economic self-sufficiency. Communities carved from the wilderness became integrated into a more market-oriented economy after the War of 1812. The former Ohio and Indiana Territories soon produced more surplus agricultural products; new towns and cities such as Cleveland, Cincinnati, Chicago, and Indianapolis became processing, marketing, and banking centers; and public institutions arose that prepared children not for independence per se but for living in a more integrated economic system. Gone was the world that had given birth to earlier versions of republicanism, yet the belief persisted among many articulate citizens that republicanism remained central to the American experience.[11]

Many citizens in the 1820s and 1830s continued to associate republicanism with independence and hostility to centralized authority. Most people also accepted the proposition that the safety of the republic rested upon the intelligence and wisdom of the people. But it hardly followed that the state should endorse a full-fledged system of schools, complete with high schools, or that an aristocracy of talent was necessarily superior to an aristocracy of birth or wealth. Moreover, the spread of capitalism produced more distinct social classes and posed new questions about government's role in educating the citizenry.

In 1827, the *United States Review and Literary Gazette*, whose editor understood republicanism in terms of social class and educational opportunity, praised James G. Carter for his attack on academies, support for Latin grammar schools, and call for the return of centralized town control over local tax-supported schools. Academies presumably educated only the rich, while the famed Boston Latin School befriended the poor, who could in theory and sometimes did in fact attend. "Such establishments do infinite honor to the republican feelings of the city and state to which they belong," opined the editor. In 1831, a state official in New York added that republicanism thrived in rural, not urban, schools. One-room country schools welcomed all (white) children, while New York City's free schools in contrast mostly taught the unchurched poor. Writers in the 1780s and 1790s had viewed education, broadly conceived, as basic to a republic. In the 1830s and 1840s, however, certain republicans thought that widely accessible, publicly funded schools were necessary to preserve the nation by promoting opportunity and social harmony.[12]

Public school reformers everywhere agreed with Henry Barnard of Connecticut when he announced in 1840 that the opponents of high schools were "anti-republican" in denying opportunities to the poor. That the children of the revolutionaries of 1776—young men as well as women—had sometimes attended academies hardly impressed him. That working-class families were unlikely to send their children in large numbers to *any* secondary schools was also moot. Barnard simply insisted that true republicans opposed academies and supported free high schools. Countless Whigs in the 1840s similarly criticized those who held alternative perspectives on republicanism or dissenting views on education. A steady stream of arguments flowing from the public school press became a flood during panics or depressions. Reformers assured worried citizens that the safety of the republic depended upon expanding educational opportunities for all social classes, particularly in newly founded high schools.[13]

A few writers offered fascinating criticisms of the Whig view of republicanism and education. One thoughtful dissent appeared in the *Democratic Review* in 1849. An anonymous author asserted that the typical high school educated those who already could attend academies and taught them useless foreign languages. Implying that high schools were college preparatory institutions, he added that Latin was a luxury and its mastery antirepublican. Hence citizens should eliminate public high schools, which were "at variance with republicanism and the spirit of our institutions."[14]

Although many high schools taught foreign languages, including Latin, the vast majority of secondary students were not preparing for college and studied English courses. Ironically, such Jacksonian critics, who glorified the common man, criticized Whigs for being elitists, while Whigs pointed out that high schools taught practical subjects and opened their doors to the poorest students if they were ambitious and talented. Recognizing that the working classes would likely be underrepresented in most secondary schools, some Jacksonians responded by assaulting the class composition of the typical high school class and "aristocratic" learning.

Whig (and later Republican Party) politicians joined with northern school reformers to reshape republicanism for mostly bourgeois ends in a class-oriented society. When accused of fostering elitist institutions, they deftly employed democratic rhetoric, emphasizing the potential of public schools to promote opportunity while castigating academies as defenders of privilege. Liberty, freedom, and other republican values would emanate from public institutions that wore a crown.

"This is the era of public institutions. Graceful philanthropy covers the land with charities. The harlot and the blind, the mute, the madman, the pariah, are taken gently and tenderly by the hand, and their rugged path smoothed for them." So wrote the editor of the *American Whig Review* in 1850. Later generations sometimes wondered whether asylums, penitentiaries, workhouses, and public schools reflected the best of the American spirit. But faith in institutions ran strong among the Whig opposition to Jacksonian Democracy in the antebellum years and among many Republicans when their new party appeared in 1856. Whigs embraced a powerful middle-class ideology of republicanism that influenced educational thought and institutions throughout the century.[15]

A Whig opposition to Jacksonian democracy emerged by the early 1830s that shaped the second American party system. Federalists and anti-Federalists in the early 1800s did not live in a world of democratic sentiment that revered the "common man"; the new parties were not their direct offspring but rather emerged in a different social context. Still, some New England Whigs saw themselves carrying on Federalist traditions, once so strong in Massachusetts and Boston. Federalists had founded America's first public high school, and Samuel Adams Wells, Benjamin Russell, and Lemuel Shaw later became Whigs. When the English Classical School opened in 1821, it represented elite support for a new institution of higher learning, open to talented boys and controlled by a citywide committee. Within a decade, northern Whigs became the primary advocates of universal public school systems, including free high schools.[16]

Leaders of both major parties and opposition splinter groups claimed to best embody the new republican spirit. Writing in a national journal in 1852, one partisan argued that George Washington was "the first Whig." The Whig program, he wrote, varied somewhat from state to state but essentially comprised a coherent set of ideas. Since the late 1820s, Whigs had favored state investment in internal improvements. They believed that new transportation systems from canals to plank roads to railroads required public investment to ensure economic growth. They sponsored protective tariffs and often opposed war and the annexation of foreign territory. Regarding the South's "peculiar institution," some Whigs were antislavery though not always abolitionist. Above all, the writer concluded, the Whigs were strongly pro-Union, unlike certain Southern Democrats.[17]

Nothing better revealed party differences than their stances toward public education. Although Jacksonian Democrats hardly opposed education or common schools, Whigs took the lead in building the public systems. According to the same author, attitudes toward popular education (and free high schools) set Whigs apart from Jacksonians:

> We do not claim that this measure belongs exclusively to the Whigs, but we contend that they have been far more earnest and successful than their opponents in carrying it out. The Whig States throughout the Union are invariably better educated, and

have a better system of common schools than those where the opposition are usually in power. Massachusetts, Connecticut, Rhode Island, and New York, have admirable systems of instruction, while Virginia, Pennsylvania, and every Democratic State, leaves large masses of its people wholly uninstructed. . . . Is this indifference, or is it design? Do they dread a thinking constituency?[18]

Whigs believed in systems, in union, in public investment in children, in schools that best preserved republicanism. "The Whigs look upon education as the firmest support of their party, because without it no popular advancement can take place."[19]

The key idea in Whig republicanism was individual merit. Eighteenth-century writers described self-interest as inimical to republicanism, a threat to the common weal. But expanding market relations nourished a new philosophy of individualism among leaders of the major parties. Both Jacksonian Democrats and Whigs accepted economic inequality as a given, yet they disagreed about its determinants. Men were unequal and deserved unequal rewards, but what was the proper relationship between government and the political economy? Except for a radical fringe, Jacksonians believed that banking systems, heavy government investment in internal improvements, and other state meddling inevitably corrupted the body politic. Centralized power—which, many Jacksonians thought, had been bravely assaulted in 1776—always guaranteed special privileges to some at the expense of the people. Whigs seemed determined to destroy opportunity. Like their opponents, Democrats believed in individual competition in a free market, but they were more suspicious of governmental interference in the struggle for survival and preferment.[20]

As market relations further undermined personal independence, the Whigs intensively argued that the expansion of public schools would help preserve opportunity and individual rights. They called for social harmony and urged laborers to see capital as their friend. Jacksonians, they argued, inflamed class jealousies by their rhetorical assaults on capitalists such as bankers (and Whigs) like Nicholas Biddle. Both parties prized independence and individualism, but Whigs counted on state systems of education to soften class lines. As the gap widened between rich and poor in America's booming towns and cities, Whigs advocated more public schools as an economically wise, Christian, and philanthropic response to this frightening specter.[21]

Reconciling commercial realities with individual merit became a keystone of Whig philosophy and of emerging public school systems. An early expression of Whig thinking appeared in the *North American Review* in 1833. Entitled "Popular Education," the essay applauded the proliferation of public schools, acknowledged the intimate ties between learning and liberty, and equated ignorance with personal slavery. Aware of the pernicious effects of a class society, the writer proposed an education that strengthened property rights and inoculated society from revolution. Education, he argued, would preserve the republic by making class differences palatable, not preventable. "That there must be distinctions in society, we freely admit; but we have a right to demand that these distinctions shall be graduated as nearly as possible to the principles of human nature, and to the claims of individual merit. Let talent laboriously cultivated, let wealth honestly earned, let virtue sacredly cherished, each have its distinction."[22]

Another essayist responded in the pages of this famous New England journal to a "feverish" debate over "emulation," or student competition. Critics (promptly dismissed as fostering indolence) claimed that competition in the classroom and in life became an end in itself; it appealed to the worst aspects of human nature, fostered a sense of superiority, and undermined community. This author, however, embracing the capitalist ethos, believed that the pursuit of personal advancement promoted the public good. Competition encouraged the discipline central to the new economic order, and it had to be taught at home and at school. Otherwise the "hum of industry would soon die away, the plough would stand still in the furrow, the reaper lie down in the field, the loom and the spindle would cease their motion, the stately ship would crumble in the dock, and the restless activity of business would give place to universal lethargy."[23]

Only utopians or unreflective people—the advocates of "Radicalism" and "Agrarianism"—believed that every tree could reach the same height, or that "every blossom wear the same hue," or that every high-achieving individual was selfish and opposed the common good. At its worst, emulation brought discomfort to the losers and created "heart-burnings" and "envy." That was a small price for social progress.[24]

Individual merit soon became enshrined in the ideology of American education. Its recognition promised to prevent class distinctions from becoming immutable, thus safeguarding the republic. Countless educators both famous and forgotten espoused remarkably similar arguments about the place of schools in the social struggle. To those who argued that schools reflected social inequality, John A. Dix, school superintendent of New York state in 1837, responded: "It is neither to be expected nor desired, that social distinctions, which have their origin in differences of talent and industry, should be disturbed; but it is consistent with the preservation of the just rights of property, and it is in the highest degree desirable for the order and well being of society, that the effect of such distinctions should be as far as possible counteracted by throwing open to the widest extent, all the avenues of knowledge."[25]

State superintendents of instruction usually shared Whig values, providing educators with a coherent way to see the world and to appraise their good works. In New Hampshire in 1849, Richard Sutton Rust strongly favored the free high school to help the "enterprising" poor, despite the foot-dragging of local residents who preferred their one-room schools. James P. Wickersham, the well-known Republican laboring in Democratic Pennsylvania, argued in 1867 that "a State cannot afford to lose the wealth of a single great soul, whether God chose to send it into the world in a cottage or in a castle."[26]

Under the severe economic depression of the 1870s, debates raged about high schools from coast to coast and—as in previous periods of social crisis—

bourgeois beliefs on education were reaffirmed. According to Maine's leading educator, the free high school checked "the tendency of the wealthy to become the ruling class through the force of the higher culture which wealth can easily secure, but from which poverty unaided is shut out." A partisan from California similarly emphasized that "the *free High School is a barrier against the establishment of class distinctions in American society*, which, if allowed to grow, are fatal to the interests of a republican government."[27]

Individual merit: the idea became a monotonous refrain throughout the free states. "The children of the affluent ought, for their own sakes, to learn early, before their minds are vitiated with ideas of factitious distinctions, to take their position according to personal merit alone," said one educator from the Bay State at midcentury. Public schools honored only those pupils with the best minds and morals. In 1852 a Cincinnati school official emphasized that "the only passport to the highest honors" at the local high schools was "talent, devotion to study, and submission to all the rules prescribed for their government." Anything else undermined republicanism.[28]

When Cleveland's Whig mayor had agitated for a high school, he announced that the "poorest child, if possessed of talents and application," should have the chance to become the next Franklin. In 1879 the local principal, speaking at the dedication of a new building, updated the language by proclaiming that the high school rewarded merit through "natural selection." Also speaking at the dedication, Peter Zucker, president of the Alumni Association, called his alma mater the "people's college." Tolerant on racial issues, Zucker said that Central High personified "our system of government."

> As these pupils, rich and poor, black and white, sit side by side at their studies, or stand shoulder to shoulder in their recitations, they appear to me to be the very exemplification of our nation, with all its people united, marching forward shoulder to shoulder in the march of progress. It is the boast of our land that here there is no distinction of caste. The great danger of its appearance is in the drawing of any sharply defined lines between the richer and poorer classes, the erasure of those lines, the great leveler of all caste distinctions are our Common and especially our High Schools.[29]

An eerie sense of crisis mixed with confidence characterized much public school discourse. The concerns of famous magazine writers or well-heeled state school superintendents reverberated on the local level, where the real battles emerged over every aspect of educational policy. The high schools reflected a distinctive view of human nature, philosophy of government, and institutional growth, and school people became defensive and sometimes hysterical in the face of criticism. With their tireless reiteration that schools erased social distinctions and loosened economic classes, educators revealed their nervousness about supposedly universal self-evident truths.

Advocates of public high schools often assured the citizenry that property was safe if people were educated properly. Mastering knowledge and cultivating intelligence were not intended to promote free thinking and critical inquiry, the badges of heretics and political radicals. Instead, religious leaders such as Horace Bushnell wanted high schools to train young people in a kind of Christian republicanism, a nonsectarian Protestantism that also protected the free-market economy. Believing that the creation of public schools was "the first, the most sacred duty of a Christian state," the New York City school superintendent similarly asked in 1868: "And has not the general diffusion of sound knowledge, the inculcation of pure morality, the formation of virtuous habits" and so forth rendered "the possession and enjoyment of property more secure, more valuable and certain?"[30]

School reformers promised to slow the hardening of social classes just as it accelerated, and they insisted that labor and capital had a "harmony of interest" just as strikes, lockouts, and labor violence intensified. The bourgeoisie wanted peace as social tensions worsened. Every economic panic produced demands for social harmony and for better education. In the 1870s, for example, a decade of violent industrial conflict, public school spokesmen defended the free market and free school as enthusiastically as state militia protected property and capital.

As criticisms of free secondary schools mounted, the *New England Journal of Education* asserted that high schools were essential to restoring social stability. In 1875 the editor invoked familiar themes: that self-government required well-educated people and that closing high schools meant fewer opportunities for the poor. "If the rich wish to put capital finally into the hands of brute labor, and themselves at the mercy of a communistic mob, let them put down the higher schools." Indeed, opposition to free high schools was "singularly stupid and suicidal." In 1877, the year of the most intense labor-capital violence, a western educator wrote in the *Pacific School and Home Journal* that more than basic education was needed "to deal with the problems of government and finance, land, labor, and capital." The message was clear: "Free education will save us from the horrors of communism." If the talented poor had access to free high schools, radical claptrap would dissipate.[31]

Fears of social discord in the heartland led the editor of the *Indiana School Journal* to employ military metaphors in these rhetorical battles. In several editorials he lambasted opponents, arguing that all societies, even republics, needed leaders—special, right-thinking men—and that the ongoing crisis made the need especially acute. "The State is as much bound to educate its law-makers and its leaders as it is to educate its voters," he warned. "Generals and colonels are as indispensable to an army as are the common soldiers. Hence, in self-protection, the State must encourage higher education."[32]

Did public schools prevent class distinctions from solidifying or reflect them? Whigs thought they had the answer, and in hundreds of communities the bourgeoisie turned social crises into educational problems. They praised individual responsibility and merit in a land where dependency increased. They formed the leadership that tried to keep republican traditions, never monolithic and always facing revision, relevant in changing times. And they ultimately persuaded enough people that centralized, hierarchical institutions represented the fulfillment of republican dreams.

One of the most prominent educational leaders of the late nineteenth century was John D. Philbrick, Connecticut's former school superintendent and a longtime administrator in Boston. In 1885, Philbrick reminded everyone that cities had decisively shaped educational development. Although most Americans still lived in the countryside, he wrote, "the influence of cities in determining the public welfare is out of all proportion beyond the numbers of their population. They are the centers of wealth, culture, science, business enterprise, and social and political influence." Cities were indeed vital, home both to wealth and extreme poverty, science and superstition, business growth and economic depression. Public school systems, including high schools, emerged from a situation of potential chaos through the discipline of Whig politicians and their middle-class allies.[33]

Already by the 1820s and 1830s an identifiable and self-conscious bourgeoisie began to appear in small towns and larger cities. From skilled artisans with more status than manual workers to a wide variety of professionals and business people ranking below the top income and wealth earners, the middle classes were diverse, yet shared certain values. The spread of commercial capitalism had undermined mercantilism in the eighteenth century, and the acceleration of market forces after the War of 1812 transformed the nation's urban social structure. A more integrated economy, stimulated by internal improvements, made cities a central place for social class formation in this rapidly changing world. Various merchants, businessmen, professionals, and skilled workers—integrally bound in different ways to the new economic system—formed a broad band of bourgeois interests.[34]

The urban middle classes gave the impetus to most contemporary reform movements. Most embraced the Whig Party, which thrived especially in urban and rural areas most directly affected by the marketplace. Cincinnati, for example, was a Whig stronghold in an otherwise Democratic area, but many farmers in the hinterland who had moved beyond subsistence or bartering and now sold surplus goods also joined the fold. As Philbrick noted, cities decisively influenced many people beyond their immediate borders. And support for extended education, including high schools, had become an identifiable trait of middle-class culture in antebellum America.[35]

Being middle class expressed itself in many specific ways. Economically segregated neighborhoods became more common in urban areas after the 1820s. Although poverty ruined many lives in colonial towns and cities, neighborhoods had contained a wide range of social groups. As the economic system bred greater social distinctions, those people able and lucky enough to escape manual labor for more remunerative and satisfying work began to separate themselves from the larger community. Compared with manual workers, the middle classes now tended to own more expensive houses with more elaborate furnishings.[36]

Class differences also generated diverse attitudes toward education. A merchant or attorney or skilled worker recognized that apprenticeships, the traditional avenues to male independence, were steadily disappearing in the early 1800s. Many middle-class families now limited family size and used surplus resources to extend the education of some of their children. Initially such sons and daughters paid to attend academies, the only available source of secondary instruction except for self-study or tutoring.

In contrast, later generations attended public high schools, as reformers stressed "the moral danger . . . when young persons are placed at even the best-regulated boarding-schools, where the watchful eyes and constant promptings of loving parents cannot follow to shield them from harm." As the middle classes limited family size, the bonds of affection between parents (especially mother) and child seemed to intensify. While the very rich continued to patronize ever more elite private schools after the 1880s, the middle classes gave their support to the local people's college. Whig writers wrote most of the school textbooks and the new child-rearing manuals that proliferated for bourgeois parents. These primers of propriety urged parents to rule their children through love and affection and to support local public schools.[37]

In a world of deepening class conflicts, middle-class parents searched for order and predictability in their own families and in the larger society. The separation between home and the urban workplace widened, and middle-class mothers assumed more responsibility for raising children while fathers toiled away from the household. High quality local high schools held greater appeal than distant boarding schools in these perilous times. Whig reforms responded to middle-class anxiety that, without the proper discipline, supervision, and self-control, anyone could slip into the poorhouse. In periods of severe economic distress, the respectable classes formed voluntary associations to address various social ills, from intemperance to prostitution, demanding individual regeneration by the fallen through acceptance of personal responsibility. A broad coalition of middle-class reformers hoped that public schools might ameliorate the harsh realities of urban life.[38]

With the greatest concentration of population and visible extremes between rich and poor, urban areas were flash points of social disorder throughout the nineteenth century. But they also became centers of such social innovations as public school systems. In larger cities and smaller towns, the northern middle classes sought to eliminate academies, to centralize town control over districts, and to build an educational system that would provide sound moral and intellectual training from the elementary through the higher branches.

The difficult goal of "popularizing" public education in the 1820s and afterward by incorporating the children of all social classes was never fully achieved. Property taxes from the upper classes helped support the new institutions, and the very rich certainly shared middle-class fears of social conflict. The wealthiest citizens nevertheless rarely patronized urban public schools in the nineteenth century, and attracting the middle classes to a tuition-free school required time and patience. "Public" education in many cities had traditionally meant charity education. Boston did not create tax-supported primary schools for the poor until 1818, three years before it opened America's first high school. Seaport cities including New York, Philadelphia, and Baltimore opened charity schools for the poor between the early 1800s and 1820s, using private donations and public monies.[39]

The Free School Society of New York City, for example, a philanthropic organization of elite Protestants formed in 1805, operated free schools that competed with other private groups to educate and rescue the children of the unchurched poor. Reorganized as the Public School Society in 1825 as it successfully monopolized public monies to charity schools, the organization next tried to build a more inclusive system. Early attempts to open a free high school—to attract the more respectable classes—failed. The Free Academy did not win approval until 1847, but its founders wanted to attract the better classes to the evolving system: "One object of the proposed Free Institution is, to create an additional interest in, and more completely popularize the Common Schools. It is believed that they will be regarded with additional favor, and attended with increased satisfaction, when the pupils and their parents feel that the children who have received their primary education in these schools, can be admitted to all the benefits and advantages furnished by the best endowed college in the state, without any expense whatever."[40]

Some of Philadelphia's poor also attended public charity schools from 1818 until the mid-1830s, when local Whigs and other reformers demanded a more broadly based system. Central High finally opened in 1838, in the midst of a severe economic depression. Whigs viewed this high school as the perfect vehicle to draw all social classes to the system. It became a prestigious institution, awarding collegiate degrees and competing for students with local colleges. Besides passing a rigorous entrance exam in grammar-level subjects, prospective students at Central High had to attend public grammar schools for a specified period of time, enabling the bourgeoisie to enter the system in a slow and highly palatable way. School leaders here as elsewhere correctly guessed that the middle classes would abandon academies if their talented youth received quality instruction in a public high school.[41]

Baltimore's first high school opened in 1839, as local leaders fought the stigmas that tainted the free schools. Commercial and professional elites, often former Federalists and transplanted New England settlers, led the campaign to enhance the status of public education by hiring better-trained teachers, adding graded classrooms, and ultimately building the free secondary school. The process was slow but reflected the republican Whig view that public schools should unite the social classes.[42]

Whigs and middle-class activists led many campaigns for broadly based public schools. In Massachusetts, with its rich history of support for education and schooling, Whig legislators were primarily professionals and merchants who represented towns and areas most affected by commercial change between the 1820s and 1840s. They helped elevate one of their own, Horace Mann, to lasting fame by naming him secretary of the new State

Board of Education in 1837. Like his counterparts elsewhere, Mann understood that the white middle and upper classes would patronize the private sector unless the public system improved and provided something special for their children.[43]

Towns in the thick of commercial development proved congenial to Whig politicians and middle-class reformers. Boston's English High School, created by Federalists, was later nourished by influential Whigs in the 1830s and 1840s. Other northern cities and towns began comprehensive public school systems during these years, but the devastating depression that began in 1837 slowed the pace of reform. But Whigs were persistent, slowly creating more centralized school systems across the North. And the 1840s witnessed more victories for champions of the "people's college."[44]

"When all the children of the more wealthy and influential families are withdrawn from the public school, it ceases, of necessity, to have prominence in the public eye," warned Horace Bushnell in his campaign for a high school in Hartford in 1841. Without an inclusive system of schools, class divisions would worsen as private academies for the rich flourished. The rich had duties to the poor, Bushnell wrote. Think of the joy of helping poor youths attend a first-rate high school, "instructed in elegant learning and science; going home to speak at their simple table, of the great facts of science, to discuss questions and suggest tasteful thoughts. What a light and warmth would this give, in the bosom of a poor family, or in one just rising into character." Then the poor would not "hate those above them, but only . . . emulate them."[45]

It was not that easy. Hartford was divided into three large districts that further subdivided into many smaller ones. That, of course, was how many people viewed republicanism: local, decentralized self-governance. The working-class section of town rejected Bushnell's moralizing, and middle-class reformers agitated full time for several years before winning the day. One partisan, Henry Barnard, recalled that he and fellow Whigs flooded the town with speakers to persuade people to abandon district controls and to accept a centralized institution such as the high school. One businessman even lived for an entire year off his own capital while leading the forces of reform. When Hartford High opened in 1847 and brought a more centralized system in its wake, victory was finally theirs.[46]

The names of the participants and the circumstances surrounding their battles naturally varied from place to place, but Whigs almost always took the institutional offensive. When the Whigs disintegrated and were partially incorporated into the Republican Party in 1856, their successors also propagated bourgeois reform throughout the nation. Many Whig school reformers still alive in the 1850s made an easy transition to the new party. A young legislator in the Prairie State named Abraham Lincoln stoutly defended public education and familiar Whig views of temperance, hard work, and free labor.[47]

High schools throughout the expanding Midwest owed their existence to Whigs and Republicans. Two cities in Ohio, Cleveland and Cincinnati, exemplified Whig influence. A small community in the 1820s, Cleveland boomed after the Erie Canal and Ohio Canal connected it to the world economy via the Great Lakes and the Ohio River. Once a Federalist stronghold, the Western Reserve remained a version of New England transplanted. Academies offered formal education to middle-class youth in the 1820s, but Whigs fought for an inclusive system. A number of free primary schools opened in the 1830s, and George Hoadley, a Whig mayor, campaigned for a high school in the name of republicanism in 1844.[48]

A Yale alumnus, Hoadley was a Yankee attorney and later a prominent judge who had made a fortune as a real estate speculator. His principal ally was Charles Bradburn, son of a Massachusetts cotton manufacturer. Apprenticed at sixteen in the Lowell Machine Shop, Bradburn received a diploma from the Middlesex Mechanics Association and served two years as a journeyman. By the 1840s apprenticeships were mostly archaic: a symbol of bound labor inappropriate to capitalism. After earning his fortune as a Cleveland merchant, Bradburn therefore sought different educational paths for adolescents, and that ultimately meant a high school. Other Whigs rallied behind the cause, and Central High School finally opened in a church basement in 1846. Bradburn's own son attended Central High before becoming a clerk in the family business.[49]

The transformation of Cincinnati's social life in the new century also had huge consequences for education. Its auspicious location on the Ohio River near productive farmlands enabled the town to become a commercial nexus between the free and slave states by the early 1800s. Like many communities, Cincinnati boomed in the 1820s after recovering from the Panic of 1819. Local academies early provided for the education of the respectable classes. When social tensions flared in the late 1820s, however, middle-class reformers sought more common institutions.[50]

These Whigs were not paranoid. No fewer than eleven riots or major civil disturbances occurred in Cincinnati between the late eighteenth century and the 1850s; many were race riots of whites against blacks or abolitionists. With a large southern as well as New England population by the 1830s, Cincinnati was a tinderbox. The percentage of unskilled workers grew steadily in antebellum Cincinnati. Dependency increased, income disparities worsened, and neighborhoods became more defined by social class. Elite Whigs, such as the famous Beecher family, lived in fashionable Walnut Hills, a reflection of the growing class advantages that schools were supposed to ameliorate.[51]

The high school that Cincinnati organized in 1847 was a tribute to Whig reform. Whig school trustees fought consistently for this higher department and against a restrictive view of public education. Wherever they settled in the midwestern states, transplanted Yankee Whigs or Republicans fought the battle for new institutions that promised to alleviate social distress, uplift moral values, raise intellectual achievement, and base life's rewards on individual merit.

Whigs and Republicans campaigned for public school systems and high schools in many Indiana towns in the 1850s, just as places such as Evansville, on the Ohio River, and Indianapolis, an inland crossroads for trade, became more integrated into the national economy. In Indiana's capital city, Calvin Fletcher and other Republicans fought for free schools. A Yankee immigrant active in banking, railroads, farming, and other enterprises, Fletcher believed that temperance and schooling best promoted the public good.[52]

In the southern tier of Ohio, Indiana, and Illinois, Whig and Republican reformers combated southern attitudes toward education and the Democratic opposition. In the 1860s the Republicans of Jacksonville, Illinois, supported a coordinated and integrated system with graded classrooms and a high school, related innovations also demanded by fellow reformers in nearby communities. Whigs and Republicans tended to fare better in the northern sections of these states, but Democrats with a different view of republicanism fought them at many turns.[53]

Being middle class in nineteenth-century cities was not necessarily enviable or painless. Parents invested more of the mother's time in child-rearing and more money on the formal education of adolescents precisely because unpredictable circumstances could mean financial disaster for loved ones. Temperance reformers flooded the city as public drunkenness increased; riots were real enough and caused harm to person and property; and middle-class parents hated the personal and social disorder that ruined lives and their city's fair name. Most urban residents undoubtedly shared this concern for human suffering, but the middle classes proposed some particular solutions. Discipline, self-control, moral values, additional intellectual training: these and more were needed by youth, and Whigs taught many Americans to expect much more than schools could ever deliver.

"The best mode of promoting a nation's welfare, is to improve its morals, encourage industry, and diffuse education," wrote the student editor of Cleveland's high school newspaper, *The School-Boy*, in its inaugural issue in 1847. "This is the true American system, and we want no other." He and other writers in this paper extolled bourgeois values. In a poem by newsboys who hawked the paper, another student presented the model republican:

> The School-Boy has but one brief plan—
> > The public good,
> > It is his mood
> To be an Honest man.
> A man—mark well—no stupid bore,
> To lounge around a tavern door—
> No dandy, with cigar and cane,
> A whiskered chin, and empty brain—
> No bawling Demagogue, to roar
> For office at the People's door—
> No scoffer of all good men to gain:
> To sum up all the ills at once,
> The School-Boy will not be a Dunce![54]

Young men should be independent, intelligent, temperate, well-groomed, and self-disciplined—traits rewarded, though hardly created, at an institution barely two years old.

Safe institutions had wide appeal in the bourgeois world of the nineteenth century. How to identify core republican values and then adapt them to a rapidly changing society was no simple matter. When individuals representing diverse social and political groups debated the meaning of republicanism, they were really trying to comprehend America's past to guide the future in specific ways. What was the legacy of the American Revolution? What did it mean to be independent and free, and how were these qualities shaped by government action, a free market economy, and social institutions?

Just as republicanism had sustained multiple readings in the eighteenth century, later generations debated the legacy of 1776 and the proposed reforms of Whigs and Republicans. The version of republicanism found in America's public schools very much pleased P. A. Siljestrom, a Swedish visitor. While some radical theorists believed class conflict was central to the modern world, Siljestrom praised the American faith in local control and self-government. What fascinated him most was that, although education was a state and local responsibility, not a federal one, most northern systems looked remarkably similar. He discovered that "nothing is more common in America than imitation and repetition, carried so far as even to give the character of monotony to the public institutions, viewed as a whole."[55]

Americans still primarily lived in rural areas, but even country folk could not fully escape the influence of the city and its emerging institutions. The monotonous similarity of schools in district after district, town after town, did not mean that schools everywhere were identical. But Siljestrom had made an important observation: a society facing severe stresses and strains responded in similar ways throughout the free states. New England settlers did not carry a perfect plan of how to educate the young when they traveled West; rather, the battles of the bourgeoisie were fought simultaneously in New England and in the young states beyond the Alleghenies.[56]

Whigs and Republicans in particular aimed to build a system of schools that promised order, predictability, and discipline and that reinforced the values prized in the ideal middle-class Protestant home. As the centers of commercial and later industrial capitalism, cities and towns offered the models of organization, control, and system-building that a rising class of male educators viewed as the epitome of sound practice. Whig politicians such as Horace Mann and Henry Barnard were simply the most prominent of the thousands of activists who labored on behalf of public education. In 1857 one of Michigan's educational leaders affirmed the importance of republican values, expressed so well in places such as the Free Academy of New York City. "Smaller cities, and especially villages with a population of but a few thousand," he acknowledged, "can not, of course, maintain so extended a system of public schools; but they can accomplish essentially the same thing more perfectly, though on a smaller scale." The race for the perfect system began.[57]

The key to reforming public education was the creation of graded classrooms, with the high school at the top of the pyramid. Accomplished most easily (never perfectly) in cities, with their more concentrated populations, graded classrooms constituted one of the major innovations of the nineteenth century and helped make public high schools possible. The eminent New Englander, Francis Adams, described the reform succinctly: "Grading . . . is the arrangement of children of about the same age, and of nearly as may be similar attainments, in separate schools or departments, under separate teachers, so that the kind of instruction and discipline suited to individual scholars may be adapted to the whole class or grade."[58]

The majority of American children in attendance during the nineteenth century sat in ungraded, one-room country schools, filled with students of all ages. It was precisely this sort of decentralized, local form of education that infuriated Adams and most professional educators, whose campaigns to destroy one-room country schools only partially succeeded, but not for lack of effort.

Ideas on grading circulated in the 1820s and fascinated none other than Samuel Adams Wells in Boston. Wells headed a committee that reported on the subject in 1831. He praised graded classrooms as the best strategy to classify schools, stimulate school competition, and promote greater uniformity. With graded classrooms, he wrote, educators could compare schools, identify the best methods of instruction, and thus improve school practice. The reform required changes in school construction, of course, but the educational benefits justified the cost. Proud of his role in creating America's first high school, Wells remembered fondly Boston's earliest advanced scholars, who had struggled with such "diligence" to prepare for admission to the English Classical School. Graded classes would now make a difficult task easier.[59]

Wells' report proved quite prophetic. Throughout the century urban school reformers actively promoted the graded classroom, which became something of a panacea. It promised greater efficiency and coordination, better discipline, and improved instruction by enabling teachers to introduce students gradually to progressively more difficult subjects. It also allowed school principals and superintendents in urban areas to compare test results from different neighborhood schools, to ascertain what went right or wrong and to reward the best teachers. The high school depended upon these efforts to improve the quality of their students, thus strengthening the entire system. Better classification—which gave teachers, principals, and superintendents greater control over the pupils—simultaneously addressed the system's organizational needs and public fears of social disorder.[60]

Reformers expected high schools to ease social tensions and also to improve the education of children who never even entered the institution. That is, many educators believed that competition for admission to the high school would inevitably raise standards in the lower grades. Almost every petition to establish a high school argued that the "people's college" would improve primary and grammar schools. This was true in Chicago, New York, and other cities in the 1840s and elsewhere later.[61]

By setting certain high school admission standards, superintendents in towns and cities could create a more standardized curriculum and hold principals and teachers accountable if their pupils faltered on these exams. That caused much anguish for those whose pupils did poorly, not to mention for the students themselves. But reformers never claimed that graded plans of instruction brought equality: fair competition was the goal. H. D. McCarty, the Kansas state school superintendent, argued in 1872 that climbing the educational ladder to the high school was something special: "Step by step the weary ascent is made; cliff above cliff is gained, till at length, far up in the giddy heights, from a bold projecting rock over-hanging an awful precipice comes the exultant shout 'Excelsior.'" The thin atmosphere even made sober schoolmen very giddy.[62]

The growth of the American high school was dramatic throughout the nineteenth century. From very modest origins—a single institution in 1821—high schools became ever more common on the social landscape. By the 1830s and 1840s in many northern states, Whigs advocated public schools to advance learning and to solve many serious social ills, goals Republicans later shared. Reformers hoped to instill the values of ambition, hard work, delayed gratification, and earnestness in youth, trained to become sober, law-abiding, and respectable adults. They called for personal responsibility with greater intensity just as social conditions drove more individuals to dependency and despair. Reformers insisted that attaining their lofty goals required the widespread establishment of public high schools. George Willey, a Whig activist in Cleveland, expressed a common hope: "To carry out our figure of the pyramid, we would say, that the apex, the crowning feature of our system, least in magnitude, yet surmounting all, is the Central High School."[63]

By the late nineteenth century, public educators really believed that they stood on the shoulders of giants. In many communities, the middle-class reformers who sponsored free mass education and high schools had created a more coordinated and inclusive system. By the mid-1870s, when high school enrollments started to exceed those of private schools in the northern states, most educational leaders agreed with the observer from Oshkosh, Wisconsin, who proudly stated that the local high school was "the crowning glory of our school system."[64]

A particular brand of republicanism had become compatible with centralized authority. Momentously, some middle-class citizens had redefined a key concept in American history; they had infused republicanism with their own particular values and attempted to make them universally accepted. For all their successes, however, public school leaders did not build high schools when they wanted, as they wanted, or with full public acceptance. A minority of citizens remained hostile to high schools. Opposition to their establishment remained common between the 1830s and 1880s, whether in rural areas, small towns and villages, or major cities.

Whigs and Republicans ultimately triumphed, as free high schools became the predominant form of secondary schooling. Some citizens, however, rejected the idea that Whigs and Republicans knew what was best for America. Critics asked many embarrassing questions about the ideology and practice of northern activism as they took their stand against reform.

The Opposition

We are now in the age of "reform." We are
swinging backward toward the alphabet.
Learning to spell is just now the chief end
of man.

Indiana School Journal, 1875

"Without doubt, the School
System of Ohio is passing through, in some localities at least, a fiery ordeal.
There has never been a time when those who are antagonistic to Free Schools
were nerved to as great an extent as now, for its mutilation." Emerson E.
White, superintendent of the Portsmouth schools, thus opened a lively session
at the Ohio State Teachers' Association meeting in 1860. Savoring success, the
"enemies" of public schools everywhere attacked an exposed flank. White predicted dire consequences "if our Public School system in cities and towns is
struck headless."[1]

According to White, educators had to repel the invading forces:

Resolved, That the High School, in its influence on the lower grades of schools, in
securing thorough and systematic instruction, on the part of the teachers, and good
scholarship, regular attendance and exemplary conduct on the part of the scholars,
and in furnishing from its own members well-trained teachers for these schools, is
worth more than its cost, independent of the intrinsic value of its own importance.

Resolved, That the habits and moral integrity of our youth demand that, as far as
possible, the school education be completed under the immediate eye of their parents, and this can only be done by efficient High Schools forming a part of our
Public School System.[2]

Before the audience voted on the resolutions, however, several individuals challenged White's assumptions.

Daniel Shepardson, the principal of Cincinnati's Woodward High School, responded first: "I do not think we are so near the verge of a precipice," he remarked. Despite the closing of Springfield's high school, "the solid men of this great State are not yet insane; they are not inclined to go back to the dark ages." Overall, the future seemed bright. Cincinnati's two high schools, for example, had already educated hundreds of elementary school teachers, one of their many salutary products. Secondary schools elsewhere were also popular. "When you go into a common school, and ask the boys and girls if they are aiming for the High School, how their hands will fly up," Shepardson boasted.[3]

If common sense did not prevail, dollars and cents would. Citizens knew that "there is more money locked up in our schools than in our banks. The educated man is generally the successful man; the intelligent laborer, artisan, or manufacturer, produces the best work, and obtains the best pay." Self-interest was the foundation of political economy, and higher education yielded strong returns. Even though "a few illiterate men" on school boards opposed high schools, they were politically impotent. Shepardson then shared his beatific vision: "I believe that a brighter and more glorious day begins to dawn; that in our larger cities there will be added to the facilities of High Schools, Colleges and Universities."[4]

An educator from Troy was less sanguine. Large and bustling Cincinnati could easily afford high schools. Most people, however, lived on farms or in small villages and towns, and they complained about the high costs of secondary schools: "'Here is the High School, which costs $1,500 or $2,000 a year—are we bound to keep up that school? It is true, we must keep up the education of the young; but are we, as tax-payers, bound to pay so much in order to give so few a classical education?'" Was the high school so impregnable? The defeat at Springfield made even Trojan warriors "tremble."[5]

Other educators joined the animated discussion. A Circleville resident hoped its expensive high school could maintain the support of local businessmen. A Steubenville man favored opening more rural high schools to reduce local rivalries and jealousies. Shepardson might gloat about Cincinnati's good fortune, but as E. D. Kingsley of Columbus warned, the public sometimes viewed free schools as a financial burden, and some taxpayers griped: "'You have no right to put your hands into our pockets and extort money to pay for the education of rich men's boys and girls.'" However misinformed, the public believed that high schools educated only "an aristocracy, and you can't talk them out of it." A colleague from Zanesville sadly agreed.[6]

The tone of the session remained sober despite the uplifting sermon from Cincinnati. One educator, W. D. Henkle of Lebanon, said that educators needed better political sense. If their enemies distorted the truth, the friends of education should become more clever accountants. "I think some of the superintendents have damaged their institutions by publishing the cost of education in their schools," he told the audience. School reports often itemized expenditures, unintentionally providing the opposition with ammunition. "Give the public the figures in the aggregate," Henkle suggested; "don't help them to weapons to be used against us."[7]

No one publicly accused the speaker of unethical or unprofessional behavior. The barbarians were at the gates, and the schoolmen simply prepared for war. Indeed, the state school commissioner, an ordained minister, did not seem troubled by the advice. He told the faithful to defend Ohio's high schools from "Vandalic hands." Soon after "a vote was taken," and Emerson E. White's resolutions passed unanimously.[8]

Educational leaders fought numerous foes throughout the century, some real, others imaginary. Despite their self-confident rhetoric, school activists worried about public support. They succeeded in building more public schools, including high schools, but a stubborn minority of citizens held alternative visions of school and society.[9]

Who were these opponents and how powerful were they? Francis Adams concluded in 1875 that opposition to the high school was "partial in extent and evanescent in character." The principal of the Denver High School wrote that there "never was a system, however good, which had not its opponents, and against which, there were not, at times, reactions among the people." The venerable John D. Philbrick of Boston opined in 1885—after the noisy complaints of the 1870s were muffled—that the high school had survived: "It has struck its roots deep in the American soil, and there is no Vandal arm strong enough to pluck it up."[10]

What seemed obvious in the 1880s was less clear decades before. In the 1830s Horace Mann hardly knew the fate of public schools. Depressions recurred throughout the century, ruining lives and making tax rates seem unbearable. The *Ohio Educational Monthly*, edited and owned by Emerson E. White after 1861, found enemies lurking everywhere.[11]

As late as the 1870s, many state legislatures debated the wisdom and legality of free secondary schools. According to the *Pacific Home and School Journal*, California legislators regularly introduced bills to eliminate them. During the severe depression of 1873 and the ensuing labor wars, prickly critics condemned public schools in general and high schools in particular. The depression had barely hit when the editor of the *Indiana School Journal* described "a feeling of unrest among the tax payers. As yet, this feeling is vague and ill-defined; but soon, unless the high school increases in numbers and efficiency, this vague feeling will crystallize into definite thought . . . ending, perhaps, in the total abolition of the high school."[12]

Across the nation educators claimed that enemies conspired against public high schools. Sometimes the opponents were identified collectively: the very rich, the very poor, private school people (academy leaders and elite college presidents), sectarians (usually Catholics), rural people, southerners, and Democrats. Defenders of the system often failed to name names, preferring these shorthand labels that in local circumstances effectively smeared a particular person's or group's reputation. Like some amphibians, opponents were simply "croakers."[13]

When the voters of Norwich, Connecticut, refused to support a high school in 1856, one activist complained about "ambitious demagogues." The *National Teachers' Monthly* in 1875 described critics as "Knights of Everlasting Retrogression and Double Rectified Intellectual Density." Another observer said the opposition was "confined to a few stingy millionaires, a squad of conceited impracticables, and the self-appointed leaders of political workingmen's associations." Opponents lacked intelligence or had been duped by clever politicians. "Our public schools have received the hearty support of our wisest and best men," wrote a school official from Richmond, Indiana. "None but the selfish and narrow-minded are found among the opposers of public schools, for can the true philanthropist, Christian or patriot deny to any child the opportunity of an education, the privilege of becoming an honored and useful citizen?" The daunting task for the historian is to identify the real targets of these diatribes—effectively identified only as penurious, unwise, unkind, antirepublican, and going to hell.[14]

Reconstructing the lives and motives of the opposition requires lifting this self-serving veil of sneers. Public school leaders, though familiar with criticism, were often thin skinned. A writer in the *Wisconsin Journal of Education* claimed in 1878 that if one looked closely, "he would find that the opponents are more numerous than he suspects, and that, if they could organize, they might make their opposition quite seriously felt." Another writer announced that the "tocsin of war is now sounding; the enemy is marshalling his forces; already they are under marching orders."[15]

Many educators believed that the very rich and the very poor opposed or insufficiently supported public high schools. The aggrandizement of wealth by the few after the Civil War made middle-class citizens both envious and fearful. Building an inclusive system was difficult as society subdivided into more distinct social classes, and the very rich refused to abandon academies. As one writer commented in 1853, the richest parents believed contact with the poor would lead to "moral contamination." As high schools helped eliminate thousands of academies by the 1870s, those that remained often charged very high tuition, serving an ever more exclusive clientele.[16]

Bourgeois activists complained that the very rich never really embraced the cause. Whenever anyone blocked public school expansion, educators such as James P. Wickersham of Pennsylvania charged that "aristocrats" and wealthy property owners were plotting a counterrevolution. One Ohioan did not know which was worse: "wealthy aristocrats" or the "ignorant poor." The former "do not wish their children to be brought into contact with those of laboring men and mechanics." The latter irresponsibly claimed "that the High School exists only for the benefit of the rich, and they loudly exclaim against the injustice of *their* paying taxes for such a purpose, whilst at the same time they have not, and probably never will have a dollar of taxable property in the world."[17]

Were the very rich so unprogressive? Many school people answered in the affirmative despite contrary evidence. In the early 1840s, for example, reformers in Norwich, Connecticut, tried to centralize control over the town's several districts and to create a high school. The Rev. J. P. Gulliver prepared a platform of educational improvements that voters promptly rejected. In 1856, still smarting from the earlier defeat, he recalled that a "few (but only a few) of the heavy tax-payers were the first to smell treason" at the proposal to fund a high school. These "narrow-minded" men and "demagogues" had defeated the referendum by persuading the electorate to oppose "a school for the rich." Selfish men had hindered progress and duped the masses to vote against their own best interests. Gulliver, however, ultimately persuaded thirty-five of the town's richest men to donate a total of eighty-five thousand dollars to endow a free high school. A private board of trustees governed the new tuition-free institution, which was open to all qualified youths.[18]

In Norwich, wealthy philanthropists had saved the day. Town gossips nevertheless spread ugly rumors that the rich had only schemed to help themselves. "There are in every community many, whose passions and prejudices can be easily aroused," Gulliver warned. "They are suspicious of those whom they term the aristocracy. They fear that some cunning plan is on foot to trample upon the people. They think that in some way they are to be deprived of their hard earnings for the benefit of the rich." Happily, "intelligent" citizens knew better. Gulliver snickered that demagogues had better scents than wolves but had failed to catch their prey.[19]

John O. Morris, master of the East Boston High School, sketched a stereotype of the tightwad capitalist in an article in *Education* in 1883. Certain "men of property" were indifferent or opposed to the high school, calling it elitist. Morris described a self-made though ignorant millionaire: "Mr. Anthracite Ironsides." Ironsides began as a blacksmith's apprentice, worked diligently, saved his pennies, started his own business, and soon was a successful capitalist. Shady deals made him "a coal and iron magnate," and after leaving the middle class he became haughty. "He points to his portly figure in the mirror, and says, 'Mr. Ironsides, I congratulate you. You are a truly successful man. Where are your youthful companions, who were in the high school and the college when you were in the blacksmith's shop? Which of them can point to such evidence of practical success as these? Most of them are school-masters, ministers, architects, or engineers, with now and then a "literary feller,"— good fellows, but no capital. I could buy the whole lot with what I made on that last rise in iron.'"[20] The portly pig had had his say.

Middle-class criticisms of America's leading capitalists did not erase the stereotype of the high school as a haven for the rich. This frustrated teachers, principals, and superintendents, whose jobs were at stake and who believed advanced education promoted the public good. The rich undermined the system by their selfishness and allegiance to private schools, and the public incorrectly called the high school a "palace of privilege." Complaints first heard along the eastern seaboard in the 1820s and 1830s later echoed in newly settled communities.[21]

Such criticisms had led Horace Mann to try to rename the *high school* because *high* implied *superior* and *exclusive*. But no one had a better name, and educators knew that a rose was a rose. So they tried to publicize the high school as a grand republican triumph, the salvation of the social order. That merit determined everything was drummed into every listener's head, though some critics remained unregenerate. "A standard argument with those who oppose high schools," said the *Indiana School Journal* in 1878, is that "they are paid for by the taxes of the poor for the benefit of the rich." According to one common argument, because "the poor are compelled to work, only the rich have the leisure to avail themselves of the benefits."[22]

The claim that "high" schools imparted "higher" culture to the privileged classes persisted. Anger boiled over during hard times and still simmered on better days. Schools reportedly educated a few pupils in Latin and algebra while poorer parents struggled to feed, clothe, and house their children. Especially in hard times, advantages for the favored few seemed indefensible. The *Chicago Tribune* reflected popular sentiment in 1878 when it asked "whether it is more important that a large number of persons should learn to read, write, and cipher, or that a smaller number should learn the differential calculus and the catalogue of the ships." Such talk infuriated promoters of higher education, whose institutions were likened to "horse leeches." "Strawberries and grapes can be produced in only small quantities, compared with bulky vegetables," wrote one angry and defensive Minnesotan, "but the intelligent agriculturist does not therefore decide to exclude them from his fields and to devote himself wholly to rutabagas."[23]

Whether to spend money on both strawberries and rutabagas—and if so, in what proportion—was the focus of debates on tax-supported high schools. Whigs and other reformers in the 1830s and 1840s desperately wanted more middle-class youths to patronize the system, but that meant persuading taxpayers to endorse higher branches that few would likely study. The majority supported popular education, but why invest in such thinly attended institutions? Shouldn't those who wanted advanced education pay for it themselves? Teaching every white child reading, writing, arithmetic, some history and geography, and the work ethic and moral precepts was one thing. Latin was another matter.

The teaching of foreign languages, especially the ancient tongues, strengthened the belief that high schools served only the rich. The many anti-immigrant campaigns in the nineteenth century fueled some of the opposition to foreign languages. But more was at work. One anonymous Democrat said that the high school undermined popular democracy by draining resources from the lower schools. "Indeed, the very name of high school indicates inequality, and has been borrowed, like the routine and courses of instruction therein pursued, from the monarchical and aristocratical institutions of Europe." And, asked the writer, should the public "go to the great expense in establishing and maintaining high schools, in order to give the children of well-to-do citizens a refined and classical education?" The answer was no: those seeking the higher learning should pay for it themselves.[24]

This linkage of elite classes, classical education, and the high school was a potent image that opponents of free secondary schools continually fostered. Even non-Democrats registered similar complaints. Ironically, in most communities classical languages actually formed a tiny part of the overall secondary curriculum and were sometimes completely absent. There were two basic reasons: the bourgeoisie favored practical secular education, and general hostility or indifference to classical education made the English studies more popular with students and palatable to taxpayers. Yet the stereotype that the high school was predominantly a place where the aristocratic rich received a classical education endured. Working-class children generally left school early to help support their families, while the privileged few prepared for college.

Hostility toward the higher learning had deep historical roots. Some citizens had long regarded universities as aristocratic, and the extension of the white male franchise in the Jacksonian period intensified populist sentiments. Although only a few Latin grammar schools still existed in the 1820s, disdain for classical learning remained apparent. Latin schools, colleges, and now high schools stood as aristocratic bailiwicks in this age of the common man. Benjamin Franklin and later advocates of English academies had favored a useful education that excluded or minimized classical training, establishing a tradition that continued in most nineteenth-century high schools. The idea that every secondary student was a pampered classics scholar, however persistent, was long outdated.[25]

Attacks on foreign language instruction were politically savvy, a convenient way to assail the pretensions of the higher learning. So few people went to high school or college, and professionals had such a mixed press, that debates over public funding of Latin and Greek or even the modern foreign languages easily stirred civic passions. Some of New England's Latin grammar schools became college preparatory divisions of newly created public high schools, enabling opponents to smear the whole via its unpopular part. High schools, they said, perpetuated aristocratic privilege. The New Haven High School dropped Greek to satisfy the voters in 1866; the language was not reinstated until 1877. Cleveland's high schools did not initially offer classical languages and continued to stress the modern subjects in later years.[26]

Americans from diverse backgrounds generally believed that limited schooling was fine if it did not substitute for hard work, pluck, and a smart deal. Horace Greeley of New York notably dissented from fellow Whigs and Republicans on high schools. He proposed transferring public expenditures on high schools to charity because spending tax dollars on the advantaged while ignoring the impoverished was unseemly and violated "the fundamental Republican maxim of equal advantages and opportunities for all." That New York's all-male Free Academy became a college confirmed his worst fears. A district school alumnus skeptical of the higher and especially classical learning, Greeley had refused the chance to attend a prestigious academy as a young man. Like Mr. Ironsides, he valued self-help over Latin.[27]

Nothing more infuriated middle-class reformers than the complaint that high schools were extravagant, expensive, elite institutions. The bourgeoisie continually argued, though unpersuasively, that the very rich opposed the high school because they wanted to restrict social mobility for the poor. That stance enabled school reformers to see themselves as champions of opportunity for all talented youth. In fact, the leading men of income and wealth likely applauded the avowed goals of the high school: social stability and respect for individual merit. Sometimes the wealthiest members of a community joined forces with middle-class activists to agitate for a high school. Whatever their direct involvement in reforms dominated by less wealthy people, the top wealth holders simply wanted assurances that their property taxes would remain reasonable.

The association of the high school with classical education and rich children endlessly frustrated reformers. In the late 1870s educators still preached to the unconverted, faithfully repeating their sermons. High schools admitted anyone with merit. They reflected republican values, opened opportunities for the poor, and prevented the hardening of class lines. Why, then, did critics still charge that they were "extravagant attachments" to America's common schools?[28]

Perhaps what schoolmen perceived in some groups as a lack of sympathy to the establishment of high schools was in fact indifference to school innovation. Educators, like religious leaders, often missed shades of meaning and saw only the saved or the damned, and it was unlikely that the extremely rich and extremely poor would unite in common cause. Those in the middle strata often wanted to resolve divisive problems in this polarized society. Worried about the extremes, they also feared other individuals less easily defined by their social class, including those who said high schools undermined the "original intent" of the common schools.

Leading educators from the 1830s onward combated this reading of the original purposes of public schooling. When Cincinnati's Whigs advocated a high school, opponents accused them of betraying the common school ideal. Joseph Ray, president of the School Trustees and the renowned author of mathematics textbooks, complained in 1846 that "some persons" wanted the schools to "embrace nothing more than Spelling, Reading, Writing, and as much of Arithmetic as barely enables a person to perform ordinary business transactions." Like so many reformers trying to attract the better classes to the system, Ray wanted a special school to teach "the higher English branches." His critics, however, said every (white) child should have access to the lower branches before taxpayers funded a higher school.[29]

Frederick A. Packard offered a similar criticism. In *The Daily Public School in the United States* (1866), he joined those who opposed the grafting of the higher branches onto the common system. Although many high school opponents were Democrats, Packard was a former Federalist and Whig. He became notorious in the 1840s when, as a book agent and official of the American Sunday School Union, he battled Horace Mann over school textbooks, finding them excessively liberal. An advocate of moderate Protestant values who condemned sectarian instruction in public schools, Mann the Unitarian confronted Packard the Orthodox Calvinist and won. Losing that noisy fight overshadowed other aspects of Packard's educational views, which were in many regards similar to Mann's. In the 1830s and 1840s both favored the usual package of Whig school reforms.[30]

Like many high school critics, Packard avidly supported mass education. Popular schooling best strengthened a republic, he argued, but individuals should finance their own higher education. Packard believed that high schools actually harmed the common system because they were expensive and detracted attention from the masses of children. Too many children received inadequate elementary schooling, especially in the larger towns and cities; their needs, not those of more affluent citizens, deserved greater attention. Ordinary children often had trouble reading a paragraph well, calculating accounts, or writing "an ordinary business letter in a creditable way." The common school—not the high school—was the real "people's college."[31]

Packard, Horace Greeley, and other critics embraced older traditions of self-help and independence. They worried about the fate of the common school in an age of dramatic social change and rapid institution building. These were not selfish people who pinched pennies at children's expense, as activists alleged. They regarded themselves as good citizens, defending common schools as the bulwark of republicanism. Yet they were dismissed as old fogies and croakers.

Public school educators, like most people, were happiest when everyone agreed with them. They cringed at the thought of limiting schools to the common branches. But many people complained about the expansion of the system and the hiring of expensive teachers and principals. Responding to some critics, Ohio's state school superintendent said in 1855 that "common" was a synonym for "open" and that the high school was surely open to talented youths. James P. Wickersham wrote in 1871 that many Pennsylvanians "seem to think that if they have their children taught simply to read, write and cypher, it is enough. Others add to these branches a smattering of geography and grammar, and call their children educated." While "the three R's might do for a man who travelled on horse-back, carrying a flint-lock gun," wrote a Californian in 1878, "they are found wanting in an age of steam and fulminating powder."[32]

Educators who thought themselves progressive continually maligned their sometimes shadowy opponents. With very few exceptions, state and local school officials advocated the expansion of the high school, the elimination of district control over education, and the greater centralization of power. They regarded those who dissented as reactionaries who would condemn modern youth to inferior schools. Many citizens nevertheless believed in local control, in limited education, and in common schools. They idealized an agrarian republic and mythologized self-sufficiency and independence, as commercial realities bred greater dependency and incorporation into a market-driven society.

When reformers and educators pressed state legislators to make the establishment of high schools compulsory, they were frustrated by the slow pace of change. Even Whig and later Republican-dominated legislatures, however, recognized the popularity of decentralized school organization and control in the North. One- and two-room schools predominated in the countryside by midcentury, and towns and cities had ward-based school boards that grew in size over time.

In the 1840s and 1850s northern legislatures helped centralize urban schools by passing laws that allowed contiguous rural districts and autonomous districts within towns to consolidate if voters approved. Many villages and small towns established "union" (or "union graded") schools in the 1850s and 1860s; these two- or three-story buildings replaced smaller neighborhood schools and often housed primary, grammar, and high school "departments." These changes emanated more from local initiative than from distant state capitals.[33]

As a result, the character, organization, and control of rural education frustrated northern school leaders. Schoolmen saw the city, the center of economic change, as an educational laboratory whose best ideas could improve schools everywhere. Legislatures encouraged rural areas to centralize school boards and to build township high schools, but agricultural communities controlled the situation. Developments in Massachusetts illuminated this phenomenon. Since the time of the Puritans, the Bay State had passed memorable legislation requiring the establishment of various schools; colonial school laws were widely ignored, however, fines of recalcitrant towns suspended, and the General Court's voice sometimes muted. Schools remained so dependent upon local taxes in the nineteenth century that community sentiment still mattered. Perhaps this is why antebellum reformers so eagerly embraced an imaginary educational past, one where colonial governments passed wise and effective legislation and the people really valued schooling.

Because so many contemporaries lacked their reformist zeal, Horace Mann and other activists could not predict the fate of free secondary schools. Towns in Massachusetts built high schools by the 1840s, but economic realities delayed action. In 1827 the state passed a law mandating the creation of English secondary schools in towns with several hundred families; twenty-eight of the forty-four towns covered by the law failed to comply in 1840. The reformers had to tread lightly. The depression of 1837 severely weakened the economy, and the legislature suspended all fines for noncompliance between 1840 and 1848.[34]

That the General Court had behaved similarly in previous centuries when citizens ignored grammar school legislation indicated real continuity with the past. The *Common School Journal* stated in 1851 that no legislation was more evaded than the high school law. One-third of Massachusetts' towns ignored the requirement to establish a high school as late as 1866. Mann's successors in office wanted (but never got) the legislature to impose heavy fines on offending communities. Elected officials understood that people would build schools at a different pace than educational leaders wanted. By the mid-1870s most towns complied with the law, as reformers increasingly persuaded local citizens to follow their lead.[35]

Whether in New England or in the Midwest, professional educators complained that "rural" people opposed educational change. Legislatures, dominated by rural constituencies, pushed reform measures more slowly than educators precisely because they had to answer to the electorate. In the 1830s Connecticut allowed contiguous districts to consolidate in town or countryside if two-thirds of the voters approved. The excessively decentralized nature of rural education made reformers such as Henry Barnard apoplectic, and the law also slowed the movement to create the Hartford High School. Barnard preferred to ignore the voters. As New England and midwestern states passed legislation in the 1840s and 1850s to merge adjacent districts, villages and towns established more graded classrooms, which made the creation of formal high schools to crown the system more feasible. Elected officials encouraged these changes but dared not attempt to mandate them.[36]

Legislators in the heavily agricultural Midwest also moved more slowly than reformers wished. Whigs and Republicans led the vanguard of change but made political compromises. Ohio's "Akron Law" in 1849 allowed the creation of graded classes, high schools, more centralized school boards, and consolidated systems, but again this was permissive, not prescriptive, legislation. The real battles of persuasion occurred locally, where reform proceeded at varying rates. Indiana and Illinois approved legislation to create township high schools, centralized institutions for neighboring rural districts, but the laws were dead letters in the 1870s, prompting a frustrated editor to write that cities remained the best hope for high schools.[37]

The high number of signatures required on a petition as well as other legal requirements undermined the creation of township high schools in Iowa. Centralized institutions were simply unpopular. In 1858, Iowa passed a county high school law that produced a grand total of one school, which met a quick and merciful death. A new law in 1870 accomplished even less. "A broader and more extensive course of instruction, open to all, is demanded" in rural Iowa, claimed Alonzo Abernethy, the state leader, in 1876. "Nothing short of a thorough, practical, industrial education will fit our youth to discharge the duties of enlightened citizenship, or give them a fair chance in the ordinary pursuits of life." The legislature, however, seemed to understand better what hog farmers and tillers of the soil wanted for their children. Similarly, legislation in the 1870s for county high schools in Wisconsin, Minnesota, and other states had limited effectiveness.[38]

Seen as an impediment to high school development by professional educators, country people supported basic education but rejected the values of centralization, specialization, and expertise that guided urban-oriented reformers.

As markets penetrated rural America, the values of the city undermined older ways of organizing, controlling, and shaping local schools. Farmers living miles from town, however, would have laughed uproariously if shown the architectural manuals that appeared in the 1860s and 1870s, complete with fancy designs for elaborate country schools. Rural people prized simplicity: country children received their education in one- or two-room ungraded schools throughout most of the century. Some students received tutoring from a sympathetic teacher in an advanced subject such as algebra, and some pursued the "higher branches" before there were formal "high schools." Still, systematic advanced instruction in specialized classes was mostly the province of the city.[39]

Facing the modern age without access to high schools seemed absurd to city-oriented educators. Rural schools were therefore a "problem" whether or not country folk knew it. And so such people as Frederick Packard captured the spirit of many citizens who resisted reform and maintained a modest view of public education. To them the common school generally fit everyday needs; the high school was largely irrelevant. Reformers saw farmers as an impediment to change. Those who insisted on low property taxes and modest one-room schools were as dangerous as the selfish rich and ignorant urban poor. It was unlikely that these drags on social progress would form an alliance to destroy the high school, but country folk irritated professional educators for decades.

School reformers complained about three additional sources of opposition: southerners, private school people, and Democrats. Like rural folk, the very rich, and the very poor, these groups were untrustworthy. Northern bourgeois reformers found southerners particularly reprehensible, for social theorists below the Mason-Dixon line offered a coherent alternative ideology of education that challenged the reformers' most deeply held beliefs.

Southern leaders necessarily viewed education differently. They lived in a society built on the backs of enslaved blacks and free poor whites. The northern ideology of free labor, individual merit, and social mobility through schooling hardly appealed to southern elites. One writer in 1844 doubted that middle- and upper-class southerners would ever abandon their private academies. As he stated in the *Southern Quarterly Review*, rich and poor alike had "pride of wealth and station." Free schools repelled the South's respectable working poor. "Public opinion," he claimed, was "created for the masses by . . . those who move in the higher walks of society,—the opulent, the fashionable, the educated, the powerful"—and it overwhelmingly opposed "common schools" for all white children. Transplanted Yankees in New Orleans and other port cities created some graded schools, high schools, and other bourgeois institutions, but most southerners equated free schools with pauper education.[40]

Southern political leaders, social theorists, and local worthies often rejected the leading assumptions of northern reformers. While Yankees waxed rhapsodic on common schooling as the foundation of the republic, southerners thought free schools were inferior and "absolutely useless." One writer declared in 1849, "We repudiate most religiously the cant of the day which calls on the State to educate the masses in order that they may preserve their liberties." The children of the Teutonic race hardly needed book learning to protect themselves; all southern whites cherished freedom for the master race. Moreover, northern claims that schools would promote social mobility for the poor was a cruel hoax: "The rich and the poor are mutually necessary to each other's well being"; why pretend that poor children, even if educated, would not "be compelled to return to the habits and occupations of poverty?"[41]

Southern intellectuals tired of northern boasts about the wonders of schooling, and southern newspapers, as well as the *Southern Literary Messenger*, *Debow's Review*, and *Southern Planter*, emphasized the shortcomings of the Yankee value system. A Richmond author told curious readers in the 1840s that among Yankees it "has now become a trite maxim, that virtue and intelligence are the only pillars on which republican governments can safely rest, and that every attempt to build up free institutions without them, must ultimately fail."[42]

Although the South was part of a larger capitalistic nation, it had weaker bourgeois values, prized oral skills, and had no need for a labor force infected with delusions of social mobility. Both the North and the South were largely rural, agricultural, and increasingly integrated into the national and Western European economies, but there the similarities ended. The party of Jackson, which emphasized personal liberty, limited government, and local control, was especially powerful in the South.

Even after Appomattox, Reconstruction faltered because a weak federal resolve and indigenous racist forces made reunion painful and incomplete. In 1871 the *Mississippi Educational Journal*, echoing many other southern journals, reported: "Free schools are fiercely denounced as a Republican institution." The editor asked: "Do the enemies of free schools mean to declare, by their opposition, that Education is Republican, and Ignorance Democratic?"[43]

Traditional southern attitudes toward education for whites and blacks did not disappear in the 1870s, when reformers supported the adoption of Yankee school systems. Some high schools opened, yet it took decades before the South invested seriously in a broad system of public instruction. With their more concentrated populations, urban areas again offered the greatest potential for constructing hierarchical systems for white children. Cities such as Richmond and Atlanta and many towns had public high schools for whites, though some charged tuition and offered limited courses; many were starved financially. Citizens in the 1870s and 1880s still fiercely debated the wisdom of public *elementary*, never mind secondary, schools.[44]

Indeed, middle-class white southerners heavily patronized private academies long after the northern bourgeoisie found them unfashionable. In 1874, George L. Osborne, Louisiana's chief school officer, told teachers that "the people are not fully convinced of the necessity [of] high schools." Though this was also true in the North, southern indifference and opposition were far more extreme. Southerners, after all, had fought a bloody war to defend a way of life. The lower southern tier of the Middle West also remained suspicious of Yankee claims about state-financed education long after the fighting stopped.[45]

As in the North, academies had formed the backbone of southern secondary education after the 1780s. To most Yankee reformers, these tuition-supported schools, encouraged by state governments across the nation, were evil. Private schools had the most to fear from a public school monopoly, and northern activists called for their extinction. What was the relationship between private academies and the public schools? In what sense did private schools and their sponsors stand opposed to public education, as northern leaders insisted?

Labeled in the North as elitist, aristocratic, and antirepublican, academies had educated many of the Whig and Republican reformers who later called them harmful to the public good. Many academy alumni even ran their own private schools, then later joined the movement to close them. Only fully public schools, they now said, deserved anyone's support. In 1852 Indiana's state superintendent of public instruction succinctly described the process: "Under the graded system, select and private schools, supported by rates of tuition, become, except in a few places, unnecessary. Gradually they die out, root and branch. The public *free* schools take the whole field to themselves, and keep it." Unable to compete, academies increasingly disappeared across the northern states after the 1850s. "The academies, the former real High Schools of the people, are gradually disappearing from the field," a Maine reformer said approvingly in 1873. "They must now give place to a new order of things."[46]

Were the academies, which helped popularize the higher learning, fierce competitors with the public system? Private schools always faced difficult odds to survive and increasingly retreated not with a bang but a whimper, either disappearing quickly or being incorporated into emerging state systems. Private schools are easily romanticized, products of a smoothly functioning marketplace, where students wisely chose on demand only what suited them, and where only quality instruction existed. In fact, running an academy was often unromantic. Schools fell and rose with demand, markets produced mediocrity as well as quality, and teachers faced an unpredictable fate. Many private masters were itinerants who were uncommitted to education as a serious pursuit and unable, given the low pay and precarious calling, to assemble a reliable staff.

Not organized into any union, guild, or professional association, private schools were vulnerable once free high schools appeared. No doubt many private teachers deeply resented growing state intervention in education, yet many academy sponsors ultimately welcomed it. State intervention destroyed their independence but enabled them to teach in a more stable environment. Incorporated academies, which were in the minority, often received state grants of land, cash, and other favors. Smaller pay schools—usually one-teacher, ephemeral places of learning—never shared in this bounty and quickly disappeared. Reputable academy instructors found employment in the new high schools and and so had no interest in conspiring against the emerging system.[47]

To patronize an academy, especially a distant boarding school, was by mid-century a major affront to northern bourgeois culture. The middle-class family emphasized a particular form of home life, with heightened bonds of affection between children and parents, the mother especially. The phrase "home education" became popular among middle-class activists in the East in the antebellum period and subsequently in developing areas. Send your children to a local public school, under the watchful eye of people you know and trust, argued local school reformers.[48]

Activists added a veiled and sometimes openly anti-Catholic message: boarding schools resembled monasteries and infected youth with deception and vice, and Jesuits and "Romanists" were enemies of the free high school. Supporting an academy was akin to supporting Papists. At the dedication of a new school in 1869 in Petersburg, Virginia, a speaker attacked the "Jesuits, Priests, and Theologians" who opposed public education. Happily, he added, "the time is past, when a Papal Bull can stop human progress."[49]

The earliest public high schools often opened in former academies. This was true in little villages and in major cities, North and South. Barnesville High School in Ohio opened its doors in 1851 in a familiar place: the local academy. Other villages along the middle border—Logansport, Indiana, and Galesburg, Illinois, for example—also rented or purchased former academies. Cincinnati's "Central School" first opened in a church basement and then moved to "Dr. Colton's Classical Academy" until the high school had its own facility. In Maine, wrote one reformer, the "Bath Academy has died, in the peculiar sense that it has injected its vital current into the veins of another institution, and thus passed into a sort of higher life, losing its personal liberty in the new city High School; choosing to live in it, rather than die by it." Skowhegan's Academy also survived thanks to similar vampire tactics.[50]

New York State had one of the nation's largest groups of private schools, and dozens of them were incorporated into the public system by the 1870s. Some state legislatures offered grants to academies if they promised to transfer their property to the local public system. Many willingly did, realizing that surviving in a competitive market was always difficult and now almost impossible. Whether in Illinois or Pennsylvania, or later in Virginia or Georgia, the teachers, curricula, and other features of private schools often reappeared in a new place: a public high school.[51]

Southern towns and cities frequently converted academies into public high schools. In a contentious atmosphere poisoned by anti-Catholicism, Mobile voted in 1852 to make Barton Academy, which private school groups had previously rented, an exclusively public school. The "high school," which charged tuition, occupied the top floor of the building, similar to a union school in the North. The separate Boys' and Girls' High Schools of Savannah, which occasionally charged tuition in the 1870s, were in the former Chatham Academy.[52]

The impression that the private system was everywhere and always hostile to the emerging public school system derived from well-publicized assaults by prominent leaders of certain colleges and universities. The presidents of prestigious private eastern schools attacked the public high schools for encroaching on the academy system (which supplied them students) and for siphoning off teenagers from local colleges. Professor William Graham Sumner of Yale College insisted that state aid enabled weak institutions to survive, thus violating the laws of nature. In the Midwest, a number of college presidents—at Wabash, Hiram, and Knox, for example—accused high schools of low standards, unfair competition, and public waste.[53]

All of this chatter reinforced the idea that the public schools had numerous enemies. Educational journals continually attacked the critics. The hypersensitive *Indiana School Journal* condemned Joseph F. Tuttle, the president of Wabash College, who skewered the high school in a speech in 1879. Tuttle said that high schools offered "a little Latin, a little English, a little mathematics, and a little natural science, with a male or female youth thrown in as a unifier! and we call the attenuated compound a 'Freshman.'"[54]

The president of Harvard College, writing in the *Atlantic Monthly* in 1875, made the most notorious slurs. Like so many northerners, Charles W. Eliot applauded mass education as a public good, but he rejected full public funding for high schools. "Our theory is republican, but our practices in several details are fast becoming communistic," he complained. Soon families would expect free soup from the state, destroying "republican pride, self-respect, and independence."[55]

Eliot feared that the very word "equality" was undergoing a dangerous redefinition. While scholarships for the poor were laudable, parents and not the state should finance secondary instruction:

> The equality upon which modern republicanism is founded is not social equality, or the equality of possessions, or the equality of powers and capacities; but simply the equality of all men before the law. Republican institutions obliterate hereditarian distinctions, level artificial barriers, and make society mobile, so that distinction is more easily won by individual merit and power, and sooner lost through demerit and impotence; but they give free play to the irresistible natural forces which invariably cause the division of every complicated human society into different classes.[56]

Eliot maintained his stance even after critics reminded him that Harvard had received state aid until the 1820s.[57]

Southerners, private school people, occasional Papists: reformers saw these opponents lurking in the shadows. But members of the Democratic Party who opposed high schools in many communities did so in the broad light of day. Emphasizing personal liberty, family responsibility, and market competition, Democrats were generally suspicious of centralized power. As governors or state superintendents of instruction, they complained that high schools drained money from the common schools and created haughty pupils whose parents should have financed their advanced studies.[58]

Some outbursts against the public schools reflected the contingency of Democratic Irish Catholics who hated native Protestant reformers. But hostility to high schools and centralization reflected wider party feeling about the state's role in everyday life. Democrats in the Massachusetts legislature opposed the creation of the State Board of Education. Whigs who were farmers voted with them to eliminate the Board, but Democrats in particular chafed at state intrusiveness in education. In the small-town Midwest they scoffed at the idea of graded classrooms and related reforms. Although some Democrats across the nation ultimately supported the high school, sometimes grudgingly, sometimes enthusiastically, more often than not they irritated Whigs and Republicans with their slurs on school reform.[59]

Charles S. Smart, Democratic state superintendent in Ohio between 1875 and 1878, notably criticized public high schools. He alienated school people in 1877 by emphasizing that Buckeye high schools enrolled 3.5 percent of the total school population but swallowed 10 percent of teacher salaries and accounted for 15 percent of the total value of school property. He called the high school a "palace of extravagance" and said he was "untrammeled by the natural inclination or feeling teachers may possess to increase the significance or importance of their work and profession."[60]

Smart later charged that his predecessors in office had written about public schools uncritically, leaving "the impression that schools . . . are, as nearly as can be, what the public needs, should have, and pays for." Elementary schools, he thought, deserved more attention than high schools, which lacked incentives to improve if academies disappeared. Smart ridiculed the idea that the "people's college" really helped the poor. "The offer of a liberal education to the poor, as well as to the rich, sounds well, but of what worth is a thing offered to those who can not accept it, though they have aid in paying for it?" he asked. "Scarcely a child of those parents who early need the labor of their children attend, or can attend, the high school. . . . To the poor the high school is like the fountain of Tantalus, a mirage that mocks their thirst." Smart so angered Ohio's school leaders that they apparently conspired to deny him additional information on local high schools. Saying high schools should close and that the state should pay the tuition of secondary pupils at academies did not increase his popularity with them.[61]

Democrats elsewhere shared Smart's critical assessment of public high schools. In Cleveland they filed suit against a proposed high school in the 1840s. One of these Democrats was Harvey Rice, who had taught at the Cleveland Academy in the 1820s before studying law. Rice, often called "the father" of Ohio's common schools for his legislative activity on their behalf, thought that public schools should concentrate on the masses of children in the lower grades. A fellow dissenter, Henry Payne, a major figure in city, state, and national politics, believed it was immoral to fund a high school when perhaps two thousand children still lacked access to the lower schools. In 1847, Payne suggested that "provision ought to be made for the erection of new school houses, and the employment of additional teachers, until an opportunity for obtaining a thorough common school education is furnished to every child in the city over four years of age." The lawsuit failed and Whigs rejoiced.[62]

One exception to the rule of Whig and Republican advocacy of high schools and Democratic hostility toward them emerged in New York City. Townsend Harris, a wealthy merchant and Democrat on the Board of Education, drafted the initial proposal for the Free Academy that voters approved in 1847. The Board was heavily Democratic, and the Whig minority initially opposed the institution as a needless expense. Whig party newspapers also criticized the reform.[63]

Eventually, though, a Whig legislature approved the bill to create the high school, and a Whig governor signed it. Prominent local Whigs soon befriended the institution, adopting the more familiar party stance. President E. C. Benedict of the Board of Education, a Whig, later praised the Free Academy, and other Whigs distinguished themselves as teachers and principals. They did not impress their comrade, Horace Greeley, who in 1850 urged the school's elimination, since the state should only help "the step-children of Nature and Fortune, the outcast, the benighted, the brutalized, the homeless, and the miserable."[64]

The Democratic Party also had its skeptics. Mike Walsh, a radical Democrat, state assemblyman, and self-styled spokesman for the working classes, violently opposed the high school. Writing in the *Subterranean*, Walsh accused the rich of both parties of duping the poor. Merchants and professionals exclusively served on the school board, which lacked working-class representatives. Walsh the Democrat agreed with Greeley the Whig that the Free Academy was an aristocratic school and contrary to the public good. After the bill passed in 1847, he stated that both the poor and the rich hoped to benefit from the institution: "Poor, ignorant, half-famishing dupes were induced to vote for it under the silly delusion that their children would get into it, while knaves more cunning and far more wealthy voted for it with the full knowledge that it was to be created solely for their own especial benefit." Walsh threatened to strangle his own son if he aspired to attend.[65]

In most towns and cities Whigs and Republicans and their Democratic foes drew the battle lines more clearly. Local conditions varied, and other strange alliances and permutations likely existed. School activists, however, accurately depicted Democrats as generally unsympathetic to the high school, often reluctant reformers. With some evidence they accused them of aiding and abetting academies and of encouraging alternatives to free secondary schools. Democrats often filed court actions against the creation of high schools— almost always losing. Dissenters in a little village in Michigan heard the bad news in 1874, and a brief look at their struggle offers some final insights on those who opposed progress.

Charles E. Stuart was precisely the sort of man Emerson E. White feared. Born in New York State in 1810, Stuart settled a quarter of a century later in the village of Kalamazoo, Michigan. After reading law, he became an attorney, made a fortune in real estate, and entered politics. Elected to the state house of representatives in the 1840s, he then served two terms in Congress and held a U.S. Senate seat from 1852 to 1859. A man who defended his ideas tenaciously, Stuart was also a Democrat who led a long legal battle against the public high school. To Whigs and Republicans and most school people, he personified the opposition.[66]

Kalamazoo's schools assumed a new shape during Stuart's adult life. In the 1830s and 1840s, autonomous districts controlled the area's schools. In 1851, however, Whigs successfully consolidated the town schools under the leadership of District No. 1, the central and wealthiest district. A number of ward schools existed in the village, and the trustees helped initiate the slow process of providing graded classrooms and a more uniform curriculum. Overcoming some local opposition, like reformers in other Michigan villages and towns in the late 1850s, Kalamazoo's activists built a three-story, consolidated "union" school.[67]

Daniel Putnam became the first superintendent of schools in 1857, and together with the Republican newspaper, the *Kalamazoo Telegraph*, he praised the graded classrooms and an innovation called the high or higher school. Anticipating the opening of the union school, Putnam wanted the top floor reserved for "a respectable number of pupils in the *highest department*." The Republican paper applauded the completion of the expensive new facility in 1858, and it reprinted a circular announcing that the high school would crown the emerging system: "The course of instruction will embrace all the branches usually taught in the best class of male and female academies, viz., an extended English course; Ancient and Modern Languages, Drawing and Painting, Music, &c." School reform had arrived in Kalamazoo, as in hundreds of little places, and even the panic of 1857 did not suppress the hyperbole.[68]

At the dedication of the Union School in February of 1859, dignitaries handed Putnam a Bible and a key to the building. Local newspapers, however, also made veiled comments about the narrow-mindedness of those who opposed the new school. During the next decade, school leaders made every possible argument to win over the opposition: high schools stimulated the lower grades, rewarded merit, offered opportunity to the poor, and welcomed all worthy youth into "Fame's proud temple." The *Telegraph* continued to praise the high school on the top floor of the Union School, but trouble was brewing. At the annual town meeting of 1867, Charles Stuart attacked the high school and the logic of Whig and Republican reform.[69]

Stuart called for the elimination of the free high school: "*Resolved*, That the tuition in our public schools in this district shall be limited to the English branches so far as the expenditure of the public money and money raised by tax for school purposes is concerned; that all tuition in the higher branches shall be at the expense of individuals sending the scholars; and only to resident pupils unless there be room for non-residents after accommodating resident pupils."[70] The Republican-dominated school board ignored him. For the next several years, however, Stuart persisted. When he and friends in 1872 questioned the board's legal right to hire a superintendent, school officials taunted him. The Democratic *Kalamazoo Daily Gazette* reported: "The Board passed a resolution abolishing the office of 'Superintendent' and established a 'first teacher,' with precisely the duties of the present Superintendent."[71]

Stuart remained defiant. At the annual fall meeting he condemned the high school, the superintendent's position, and foreign language instruction. A gifted orator, he again assailed the town leadership. "Under this system," he complained, "you are educating the children of Silas Hubbard [a wealthy resident] at the expense of poor Irishmen, Hollanders, and other people, who have all they can do to obtain a living. They are taxed to educate and prepare for the State University the children of men worth a hundred thousand dollars. I do not say this out of any want of respect for Mr. Hubbard, whom personally I esteem, but to show how unequal are the results of the system." When the board ignored him, Stuart filed a lawsuit with the Circuit Court with two other Democrats, both bankers. When he lost, he appealed to the state supreme court.[72]

To educators across the nation, Stuart epitomized the enemy. He was a rich man and a Democrat, opposed to higher taxes on major property owners like himself. He questioned the wisdom of centralizing control over schools in the hands of more educational experts. With a hatred of classical languages, he was, like earlier Jacksonian Democrats, caricatured as an anti-intellectual. His explicit attempt to limit the schools to the lower branches and to keep the higher learning for those who could afford it supposedly showed his contempt for the poor. When Michigan's highest court affirmed the action of the Circuit Court, educators everywhere applauded the decision.[73]

Stuart's values clashed with a new educational order sweeping across the land. He thought centralization undermined democracy and that foreign languages, high schools, and superintendents were extravagant, aristocratic additions to the common school. Stuart knew that even in the 1870s dozens of children lacked a place at school or were crammed into overcrowded classrooms, so he shuddered when newspapers reported that a superintendent earned $2,000 a year, a high school principal $1,700, but a regular teacher less than $500. That seemed fundamentally immoral, which is why he and others across the nation regularly tried, however unsuccessfully, to destroy what Whigs and Republicans embraced as improvement.[74]

School reformers saw villains everywhere: rural folk, southerners, private school interests, the very rich like Charles Stuart, and the many faceless poor who existed everywhere. Activists who constructed high schools in the northern villages, towns, and cities after the 1840s often confused indifference toward high schools and support for mass instruction over the higher learning with opposition to education itself. Whether in eminent Philadelphia or in obscure Kalamazoo, school reformers ultimately made the high school a secure part of social life, imprinting their own values onto an emerging system.

Although a few high schools were abolished, starved financially, or otherwise impaired during panics and depressions, grand facilities soon appeared in many communities despite the opposition. Among the most distinctive and impressive forms of civic architecture in the nineteenth century, public high schools warded off their enemies and seemed secure. Malcontents such as Charles Stuart faded from history. Whether they labored in beautiful palaces or modest buildings, educators continued to struggle to satisfy the various needs of talented youth.

Cathedrals of Learning

> To dazzle the vulgar eye, and overawe the
> common sense of the people, by splendid
> equipage and stately building, has been
> the main theory of rulers. The system has
> not failed for want of trial.
>
> —AMASA WALKER, *The Science of Wealth:*
> *A Manual of Political Economy* (1866)

> The northerner . . . does not value knowl-
> edge as a pleasure, but only as a means,
> and he is only greedy to seize on its useful
> applications.
>
> —ALEXIS DE TOCQUEVILLE,
> *Democracy in America*

Between the 1820s and 1880s, American educators consistently emphasized that public high schools would promote republican values, reward talent, and thus secure social order and democratic progress. With their enemies defeated though never silenced, reformers knew that victory was theirs by the waning decades of the nineteenth century. Academy enrollments outside the South dropped precipitously as the middle classes increasingly patronized the public schools. Especially in northern towns and cities, high schools became a secure part of the public system, their existence soon taken for granted.

Public high schools originated in the 1820s as an idea in a few men's minds. They gathered the support of numerous male and female reformers and ultimately appealed to a wide variety of middle-class families. The phrase "high school" entered common parlance, yet individual institutions varied remarkably in appearance and in academic substance. Architecturally, some city high schools resembled Gothic cathedrals; in contrast, many rural pupils who studied advanced subjects sat next to abecedarians in drafty one-room schools. Between these extremes was a range of environments. Assuming multiple forms, high schools had gained enough of the public's confidence to survive and sometimes prosper.

High school enrollments in rural areas, towns, and cities continued to grow during the century, and contemporary educators recognized that diversity characterized the higher learning. In 1877, a contributor to *The Cyclopedia of Education* tried to answer the question: what is a high school? He concluded that high schools offered many different courses to both boys and girls in disparate communities, making a simple response difficult. Despite the efforts of leading educators, noted the author, "there is a great want of uniformity in the grade and character of these schools in different states and in different cities of the same grade."[1]

Searching for the essence of nineteenth-century high schools in their many forms requires moving beyond analyses of the social and political contexts in which they arose. What were the major characteristics of high schools in various settings, and how did Whig and Republican values shape their inner workings? The answers are found by examining the schools themselves. An initial exploration of high school architecture and bourgeois theories on learning and knowledge will illuminate what school officials and many educators viewed as the aims of instruction.

Kalamazoo's Republicans savored the taste of victory when the board of education approved the construction of an expensive new high school in 1880. No longer would the local "high school" reside on the third floor of the "union" school. Charles Stuart and his allies bitterly complained about the movement to build a permanent, separate facility, but his storm of protest abated. Five years earlier, with the institution's legal status secure, the state school superintendent had printed a lovely pencil drawing of the "Kalamazoo Union School" in his annual report. When the same sketch appeared two years later, the caption read: "Kalamazoo High School." And in a few years the controversial secondary school had a brand new home.[2]

Impressive public architecture appeared in many northern towns and cities between the 1830s and 1880s, reflecting growing wealth and civic pride. Along with magnificent customhouses and town halls, public high schools often overshadowed less majestic buildings and helped shape urban identity. Indeed, the drawing of Kalamazoo's union school–turned–high school symbolized the essence of educational reform. The local artist sketched well-dressed couples strolling along the paved sidewalk in front of this solid facility. The men sported top hats and canes, while the women wore long, fashionable dresses with matching coats. In the street, two strong horses pulled an open carriage whose well-groomed passengers seemed to enjoy the view and pleasant conversation.

The scene evoked an air of repose. Absent were street urchins or any signs of lower-class life. Present was an imposing facility that epitomized Whig and Republican school reform. The union school represented concerted attempts to classify, order, and educate children in ways unknown to previous generations. Instead of attending school in largely ungraded classes, Kalamazoo's young people increasingly had more age-graded classes and studied a more uniform, sequenced curriculum. The most talented, ambitious youth were beckoned to the height of respectability and achievement: the high school.

The construction of a separate facility in Kalamazoo in the early 1880s continued this long process of institutional development.

The crown of the public schools shined brightly, encouraging talented and studious scholars to seek the higher learning. Although many young people who pursued advanced subjects, whether in academies or free high schools, did so in very modest facilities, some scholars sat in magnificent buildings that caught every critic's eye. The palaces found in some northern urban areas after midcentury, however, set the standard by which professional educators measured progress. Reformers across the nation lobbied for consolidated, centralized, and standardized school systems that included true temples of learning.

School architecture became one of the clearest expressions of bourgeois social values throughout the nineteenth century. The size, shape, and cost of public facilities revealed dominant attitudes about cultural authority, centralized power, and the special role of high schools in the common system. Educators lamented the poor quality of schoolhouses, emphasizing dilapidated one-room country schools and makeshift facilities in booming towns and cities. That citizens built so many imposing secondary schools was particularly notable when taxpayers were at the same time demanding better roads, lighting, sewers, and water systems.

Even well-furnished high schools quickly became cramped when enrollments swelled, and fires indiscriminately consumed both rickety and substantial edifices. In 1872 a member of the Boston School Committee reminded everyone that investing in the young was wise and that architecture revealed much about the character of a society. "The temples of the ancient world and the cathedrals of the middle ages," he asserted, "showed the estimation in which religion was held by their builders." Like a medieval cathedral, the grandest schools betokened deep-seated cultural values.[3]

Every detail concerning high schools was controversial in the nineteenth century, and debates about school buildings and their upkeep were frequently contentious. Just as heretics had once sacked temples and burned cathedrals, contemporary critics ridiculed the new pedagogical palaces. In 1878, Democratic critic Charles S. Smart of Ohio applauded those who sought the higher learning (especially at their own expense) but condemned those who built a "palace of extravagance." Naysayers everywhere criticized the expenditures on union schools and high schools. Malcontents in Kenosha, Wisconsin, called the high school a "Castle," a common slur.[4]

A writer in the *Massachusetts Teacher* in 1873 assailed reckless public spending. Beautiful buildings might impress the eye, but did they enhance learning? "Amid all the splendors of Athens and Rome the masses were ignorant and degraded; the regal magnificence of temples, the beauty of sculptured marbles, and the costly adornings of princely villas, were wholly insufficient to effect the elevation and refinement of the people." Showy facilities, he warned, never compensated for shoddy scholarship. "While we devote all our available means to the erection of beautiful buildings, and make no provision, or almost none, for the great intellectual wants of the school, shall we wonder at the complaint that the girls of our schools care more for dress than learning? and that our boys like any other place quite as well as the school? Why should they not?"[5]

Some schoolmen acknowledged that towns and cities occasionally wasted money on extravagant buildings, especially impolitic during economic panics or depressions, when they attracted unwanted attention. An educator from Fremont admitted in the *Ohio Educational Monthly* in 1878 that some people too eagerly spent the taxpayer's money: "I have feared for years that the vast expenditures in this direction would eventually react against the public-school system." Even the *New-England Journal of Education*, which often printed sketches of high school castles, complained about the new buildings in Cleveland and Providence. "Both, in architectural design, have sacrificed unity and centrality to general ornamentation."[6]

Educators nevertheless proudly defended their high schools. In 1855 superintendent John H. Tice of St. Louis replied to those who wanted plain, functional buildings without elaborate designs or ornamentation. Why, he asked, "are the wings of the butterfly so gaudy, when leathern wings like those of the bat would answer every purpose? Why have the flowers such beautiful tints and such a variety of colors, when one indistinguishable from the soil on which they grow would be just as well?"[7]

From the 1820s onward, reformers recognized that academies would flourish unless public schools found ways to attract the brightest students. While often embroiled in partisan politics, school people emphasized that high schools popularized the highest social and spiritual values, values they regarded as eternal. An appreciation for "beauty" and "good taste," officials in Exeter, New Hampshire, claimed in 1848, motivated those associated with the new high school in District No. 1. These men knew that buildings and not simply books taught important lessons. "The chameleon changes his complexion in accordance with the leaf or limb on which it rests," argued the committee. "So it is with children. Their thoughts take their hue and coloring from the objects which surround them. This is an immutable law of our being. We become assimilated to the objects of our constant contemplation."[8]

Many modest buildings served as high schools, though opponents often ignored them and pointed to the most expensive facilities. Pupils studied algebra or Latin or natural science in thousands of one- and two-room schools with poor heating and ventilation, and others learned the "higher branches" in tiny, overcrowded rooms tucked away in the attics of "union graded schools." Even in northern states, most high school students did not have classes in a specialized building. Massachusetts early underwent urban growth and commercial development and sometimes had separate higher schools in the larger towns, but even these secondary buildings commonly shared their space with the upper grammar grades.[9]

Throughout New England and the Midwest in the 1870s, schoolmen continued to lament the low and unspecialized quality of school design, despite thundering rhetorical assaults from critics. "If the term high school were well defined light would be thrown upon the general question of the worth of such institutions," wrote J. J. Burns, Ohio's chief school officer in 1879 and a student of school architecture. Like colleagues elsewhere, he even tried to clearly define a high school, with mixed results. Burns discovered that some children in the grammar grades occasionally studied some higher subjects. When enough pupils studied the higher branches, advanced classes emerged, followed by separate high school grades.[10]

An Ohio town or village might report having a "high school" when it really had a high school room. "The term high school building is, therefore, about as indefinite as any collection of words can be," Burns wrote. "I have seen a 'high school' which was not as *high* as an ordinary grammar department." Here Burns muddied the waters somewhat by describing the course, not the place, of study. Another year on the job did not yield greater clarity: "One is at a loss to conjecture where, in some places, children learn to read, and write, and count." There were high schools everywhere. Strong "local pride" created this illusion, Burns concluded. "The thing sounds well."[11]

High schools therefore frequently existed only in the collective mind of the community. The loose definition enabled critics, however unfairly or illogically, to lump together "high schools" of all rank and manner, even when the target of their anger was one particular facility rising grandly in the local skies. The enormous costs of fancy high schools—whether in villages, small towns, or major cities—provoked heated political debates at the public lectern and discussions around the kitchen table and cracker barrel. Building impressive high schools attracted "respectable" families to the system—at the cost of attracting considerable negative publicity.

Although most youth lived in small places and studied in modest rooms and buildings, the opposition readily cited examples of architectural excess. Schoolmen were accused of undermining republican simplicity by imitating the behavior of European aristocrats. Those attending palatial institutions would inevitably become vain and corrupt.

Such champions of the new order as Henry Barnard saw things differently. The famous Connecticut Yankee publicized innovative architectural designs, modern systems of heating and ventilation, better furniture, and other specialized appointments. The author of a groundbreaking volume on school architecture in the 1840s, Barnard reached a national audience through his *American Journal of Education* (1855–1882). Architecture, he insisted, shaped moral values, and a well-constructed school decisively influenced "the health, tastes, manners, minds, and morals of each successive generation of children."[12]

The *American Journal of Education* presented readers with sketches and descriptions of Philadelphia's Central High School and other prominent urban secondary schools. Baltimore's Western Public High School for Girls in 1858 was a beautiful Italianate building with imposing corner towers, an arched portico, and other accoutrements. The drawing spoke volumes, indicating that the Baltimore system, which had a second girls' high school as well, had severed its pauper roots. The lot for Western High alone had cost $20,000

According to Henry Barnard, Baltimore's beautiful Western Public High School for Girls—one of two girls' high schools in the city—was "eminently useful in affording to young ladies the opportunity of receiving instruction in the higher branches of education." From *American Journal of Education* 8 (1873).

and the building and furniture another $30,000. Barnard's journal provided models for educators who demanded respectable schools for the respectable classes.[13]

Palatial high schools and disproportionate spending on the higher learning understandably antagonized many citizens. In 1848, Townsend Harris, the leading sponsor of New York City's Free Academy, denied that he favored an elaborate facility for the college bound. He wanted only "to erect a plain, substantial brick edifice, in the style of our present Public Schools. No extravagant expenditure to erect Gothic towers and pinnacles is intended, but a plain, substantial building, intended for *practical purposes*, and not for *architectural display.*"[14]

In the event, practicality and architectural display were combined. The architect for the Free Academy was a rising talent, James Renwick, whose life accomplishments would include Grace Church, St. Patrick's Cathedral, and the "Norman Castle" of the Smithsonian Institution. Ready for students in 1849, the Free Academy was "an imposing four-story edifice with brown stucco adorning red brick walls, red sandstone trimmings, a gabled roof, and graceful Gothic towers." Filled with modern conveniences, Harris's "plain" building was 125 by 80 feet with well-appointed rooms and an auditorium that seated 1,300.[15]

Many established academies and colleges lacked a facility to compare with the Free Academy, or with elaborate high schools going up in other cities. Henry Barnard's hometown of Hartford, Connecticut, built its first high school in 1847 after decades of resistance to centralization. Fires and other circumstances led to the construction of three different high school buildings by 1884. According to *Geer's Hartford Directory*, their total cost was an incredible $483,248.50, a king's ransom. That the total was reported to the last cent showed the pride taken in accommodating Hartford's best.[16]

These spending spasms removed many of the pauper stigmas originally associated with public education in the cities. Philadelphia spent $75,000 to construct a new high school on a $17,000 lot. Cost overruns on Cincinnati's beautiful Hughes High School in 1855 simply led officials to remark that popularizing education was not cheap. San Francisco spent $35,000 on a new high school for girls in 1870; Worcester, Massachusetts, spent $170,000 to house both sexes two years later; and Omaha, Nebraska, expended $200,000. One cornhusker published a print of Omaha High, with its "campus of nearly ten acres, whose market value is probably not less than seventy-five thousand dollars."[17]

Even country towns occasionally spent their monies generously. Yankee Republicans and former Whigs created Illinois' first township high school in Princeton. At the dedication of the $45,000 facility in 1867, a local activist dismissed charges of "extravagance" and assured everyone that "we have carefully considered your financial interests, for your interests and our interests are one." This typically Republican sense of social harmony ignored the basis for protest. Besides raising taxes the school board floated bonds that, according to Democrats, made eastern bankers smile as thousands of dollars of interest payments filled their coffers.[18]

Newspapers, magazines, and professional journals described the latest architectural wonders in great detail, reminding people living in a competitive system of their community's shortcomings. *The School-Boy* of Cleveland, a student-run high school newspaper, complained bitterly in 1847 that its "school" was in a church basement. In 1850 pupils were still "pent up" in "a cellar" and "more neglected than any other in this city." The *Student Gazette* thanked local Whigs for their support but regarded "the treatment of the City toward the teacher and pupil as extremely shabby, inasmuch they have provided so handsomely for the Primary Schools, while they have totally neglected the High School." The *Gazette's* prayers were answered: a $20,000 school was built in 1856, and a Gothic showpiece in 1878 consumed the princely sum of $74,000.[19]

Communities of all sizes jealously described the more progressive nature of their rivals. In 1856 educators in Concord, New Hampshire, asked: why did Portsmouth build such fine schools while the very capital behaved so niggardly? The Indianapolis faithful lamented that its best scholars sat in the "old dilapidated County Seminary." As late as the 1870s, many small towns—from Bridgeport, Connecticut, to Oshkosh, Wisconsin—had "high schools" that were really a few rooms here or there, embarrassing local educators. The La

Crosse high school was a single room for ninety-one pupils but was usually crammed with more. These places all eventually built separate, relatively expensive secondary schools. The dedication of a new town high school stirred local worthies to remember the struggles of an earlier time and their generosity toward the rising generation.[20]

Whigs and Republicans believed in investing public money in education, and the new buildings represented tradition, hierarchy, and political power. Protestant reformers admired medieval churches, which reached to the heavens but remained bound to the worldly influence of church and state. Faced with unprecedented social changes, America lacked the traditional guidance of an established church, and many reformers wanted schools to fill a presumed void in moral authority. The quickening pace of change encouraged many Western nations to create an imagined past, filled with social harmony, Gothic spires and all.

The solid forms, weighty presence, and imposing character of America's most expensive high schools presented an aura of propriety and order in otherwise chaotic cities. The serene images in every illustration and sketch—children playing respectable games, couples walking arm in arm, ladies protected from the sun by parasols, horse-drawn carriages (and no signs of manure)—evoked a sense of propriety and control attractive to various middle-class families and those trying to rise from the depths.[21]

Superintendents spilled considerable ink explaining and defending their actions. Their offices usually housed in the top floor of the high school, a symbol of their lofty position, superintendents juggled their figures and published selective information for public consumption in their annual reports. Sometimes they assumed that they had won the battle and simply praised the town for its munificence and wisdom. However one presented the balance sheet, high schools were expensive, always somewhat controversial and especially so in hard times. As palaces dotted the urban landscape, educators gloated and critics gritted their teeth.

Schoolmen were often evasive about the costs of the higher learning. When confronted with trenchant criticisms, school officials occasionally printed misleading information and half-truths, but even creative accounting could not disguise the facts. Expensive buildings required considerable initial investment and routine maintenance, and relatively dear teachers' salaries exacerbated the economic burden. Only a few superintendents such as William H. Wiley of Terre Haute were self-confident enough to lecture to the opposition: "In accordance with the American idea of regarding almost everything from a financial standpoint, I ask: Does a High School pay? Ours pays splendidly."[22]

Some citizens remained skeptical. When Frederick A. Packard and other common school advocates attacked high schools in the 1850s, they told those interested in the higher branches to pay the bill themselves. Some citizens were likelier to tolerate public high schools that charged tuition, still a common approach in the South though rare in the North by the 1860s.

Expenditures on free secondary schools often angered citizens, North or South. Schoolmen retorted that quality education was never cheap.[23]

School leaders took care to put the best spin on published financial reports. By the early 1840s officials in Philadelphia—Packard's adopted city—could juggle figures to refute the charge that the new high school was a financial drain. In 1841 it cost five dollars to educate the average child in the system but fifty-five dollars for a student at Central High. Officials soon revised the figures downward and claimed that their secondary school cost less than in other cities. In 1846 Principal John S. Hart revised the high school average downward to fifteen dollars, but the figure soon rose again. Efforts to dazzle citizens with the facts only left them dazed.[24]

Everyone understood that the higher branches—with special facilities, more specialized teachers, and more equipment—were expensive. How expensive was somewhat mysterious, though per capita costs were highest for secondary pupils, as critics tirelessly publicized. In the 1850s, towns and cities usually presented the average costs of instruction by three levels: primary, grammar, and high school. The sly educator who told Ohio's teachers to collapse these figures into one average understood the pitfalls of honesty.[25]

According to Cincinnati's officials, it cost an average of eleven dollars to educate a child there in 1855 compared with fifty-two dollars for a secondary pupil. Local critics repeatedly taunted former Whigs and leading Republicans with such embarrassing figures. Rufus King, president of the school trustees, tired of the whining and argued in 1858 that rising costs were regrettable, especially during the current economic panic, but "we may ask whether it be not better—a hundred fold—that those funds be expended for the maintenance of law and order, thus, than by the mace or bayonet." In 1859 the averages ranged from thirty-six dollars for the high school to thirteen for the grammar grades to six for primary school. High schools were expensive, though Cincinnati's schoolmen, who learned the popular tune, bellowed that theirs were cheaper than those in St. Louis, Cleveland, and Chicago.[26]

Like older eastern and many southern cities, Louisville had separate high schools for boys and girls. In 1865, when the average cost of the "ward" schools was ten dollars, educating a scholar at Male High School cost an average of seventy-one dollars, at the Female High, thirty-four dollars. Such expenditures enraged some citizens. In 1879 the *Louisville Monthly Magazine* applauded the tradition of free common schools and pay academies for the higher branches. "We must have high schools, colleges, and universities," the editor admitted, but "local governments should not cripple private enterprise by weak attempts to establish such schools. Let States take care of common schools; private enterprise will do the rest."[27]

Friend and foe alike quoted dollar amounts selectively to advance particular political ends. Between 1848 and 1863, for example, $680,068 was reportedly expended on the Free Academy of New York. The school had 292 graduates during this period, for an average cost per graduate of $2,329. Since most high school students never graduated, this statistic revealed only one measure of financial costs but became tasty food for critics. A southern apologist for slavery joked that if New York's elites really wanted to help the talented poor, they should simply redistribute the expenditures directly to the paupers.[28]

Some northern officials reluctantly charged tuition as late as the 1850s and 1860s. After the Indiana Supreme Court ruled public taxation for schools illegal in 1857, the Indianapolis High School imposed a special student fee until the decision was reversed. Before small towns or villages were fully integrated into a single system, the richer districts often charged tuition to high school pupils from neighboring districts. Appleton, Wisconsin, built its high school in 1876 in the Second District, "the most populous and wealthy portion of the city," and it still charged tuition to other Appletonians three years later. These "rate bills," which soon disappeared in the North, enabled many small high schools to survive tough times.[29]

The devastation of the southern economy during the Civil War and traditional resistance to a socially inclusive public school system even for whites made tuition charges common below the Mason-Dixon line. While fewer northerners wanted to levy fees in the 1870s, many southerners believed in private responsibility for education. Paying tuition signified social respectability, a writer in Charleston, South Carolina, noted in 1841, voicing an attitude that long endured. When the all-male High School of Charleston opened, only orphans received free instruction. The principal told some Connecticut Yankees that "in order not to wound this honest pride, and also, from a conviction that what costs nothing is nothing prized, our city authorities wisely resolved to attach a compensation to the enjoyments of the benefits of the institution."[30]

Fledgling southern high schools charged tuition in the 1870s. Some of these schools were former academies transformed into tax-supported "public" institutions, and financial exigencies reinforced the old practice of charging fees. In 1877 annual high school tuition in Columbus, Georgia, was about twelve dollars, and officials debated whether a three-dollar increase would yield a profit. The books more than balanced when the rate increased; the school educated twelve paupers for free but still showed a credit of $181.50. Economic ills forced other Georgia high schools to charge tuition. Whether in Savannah or farther north in the Carolinas or Virginia, many southerners still believed only the poor should attend schools gratis.[31]

Richard L. Carne, the school superintendent in Alexandria, Virginia, predicted in 1881 that private school traditions would remain strong in the South. Paying the tuition of needy pupils at private academies, he thought, would cost less than constructing and maintaining expensive public high schools. Palaces for the few seemed a "very costly luxury" when so many poor whites and blacks remained unschooled. Such talk always infuriated Yankee reformers, who wanted a free public system that reached from the primary grades to the "people's college" for every white child. Whether described as the hope of the republic, cheaper than academies, more desirable than bayonets or mace, or as an investment in talent for a more complex and conflict-ridden society,

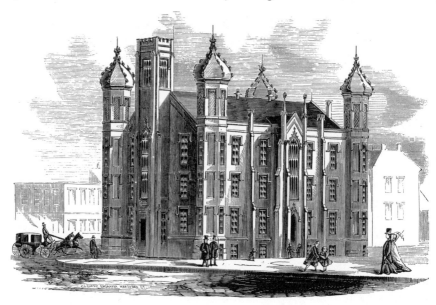

The St. Louis Public High School. From *American Journal of Education* 8 (1873).

reformers thought high schools worth the cost. St. Louis superintendent William T. Harris claimed in 1873 that the high school consumed 10 percent of the local budget but was worth three times as much because it raised standards in the lower grades and educated society's future leaders.[32]

Debates over the costs of building and maintaining impressive high schools erupted everywhere, rising and falling with the prevailing political winds and the economic climate. School leaders emphatically denied that they had built monuments to themselves or castles for the chosen few. Yankee reformers wanted the entire nation to accept the wisdom of free secondary schools, the apex of an elaborate system, open strictly on the basis of personal merit. They urged the middle classes to abandon academies and join the public system.

In many communities, the high school became the most visually impressive educational institution. Indeed, its stately character convinced some citizens that the classics, not a practical education, dominated the course of instruction. The association of secondary schools with colleges, and both with classical education, was a common one, resting upon centuries of European history and memories of Latin grammar schools.

Often accused of extravagance and aristocratic pretensions, reformers and educators in fact consistently endorsed a curriculum that offered a particular blend of practical skills, moral values, and subjects both traditional and—especially—modern. High schools looked like monastic retreats favoring the classics and ancient tongues only to those who confused architectural form with academic substance.

Like church steeples, the most imposing high schools of the nineteenth century reached into the heavens. And like churches, they ministered to a material world filled with happiness and joy, suffering and sorrow. Founded principally by middle-class native Protestants, many fancy high schools borrowed their physical appearance from medieval Catholicism. Reformers were openly or subtly anti-Catholic, almost instinctively equating boarding schools with monasteries; their goal was not to recreate the education of the cloister. They primarily wanted youth to learn a broad range of moral values rooted in Protestantism, as well as practical English subjects, useful knowledge in an expansive market economy.

Recall that all five Bostonians who founded America's first high school in 1821 were Unitarians, including two ministers. Samuel Adams Wells, the wealthy merchant and catalyst for reform, envisioned an alternative to his alma mater, the venerable Latin School, for young males desirous of an advanced but nonclassical education. Most boys aspired neither to the Latin school nor to college, as commercial expansion along the eastern seaboard produced more jobs for young men in "Mercantile" and "Mechanical" pursuits. Wells and his allies advocated a higher school that taught the modern English subjects. History, geography, advanced mathematics, a modern language, and familiarity with English authors: something then found only for a fee at those elitist boarding schools and academies.[33]

Wells had high expectations for the school. It would diffuse knowledge, strengthen the economy, perpetuate the republic, and give "strength and stability to the civil and religious institutions of our Country." Throughout the century, educators publicized a coherent rationale for the American high school that fused moral and civic purpose. Wells had helped establish a nonclassical school, and English High was a monument to his labors. Critics argued, however, that colleges controlled the high school curriculum, which left pupils unfit for the working world. This image frustrated successive generations of schoolmen and persuaded many historians that early high schools stressed college preparation.[34]

Everything school people said about their aims and curricular practices contradicted these critics. When Salem, Massachusetts, built an English High School in 1828, speakers at the dedication ceremony contrasted it with the largely college-preparatory Latin school. Here was a school "in which young men, by an enlarged, regular, and thorough course of English studies, might be fitted to enter at once into the various occupations of men of business."[35]

The message of Samuel Wells and activists in nearby communities echoed across the eastern seaboard. From their modest beginnings in the 1820s and 1830s, high schools always offered a practical education for the non–college bound. In 1834, the Boys' High School of Portland, Maine, promised young men the experience of being "fit . . . for a business life, and of initiating themselves into the abstruse departments of learning." Central High School of Philadelphia had a classical course of study that enrolled a minority of pupils until it merged with the dominant English stream in 1855. Principal Alexander

D. Bache emphasized in 1842, however, that Central High primarily provided "a liberal education for those intended for business life." Bache's great-grandfather was Benjamin Franklin: the doyen of utilitarian education. Franklin would have applauded the focus on the English curriculum and the elimination of the separate classical stream. Central High became the nation's preeminent English secondary school.[36]

Franklin's spirit beckoned schoolmen everywhere. High school alumni would become provident, hardworking, respectable citizens, America's "future Franklins." Memorials on the creation of high schools in Chicago, St. Louis, and other cities and in small towns highlighted the centrality of modern subjects, the reduced significance of classical education, and the intimate ties between the curriculum and business life in a general sense. Middle-class support for the modern branches, largely met in the past by pay schools and academies, accelerated after the 1820s and never wavered in the coming decades.[37]

Public high schools borrowed most of their curricula—with their emphasis on the English branches—from the academies, contributing very little pedagogical innovation. Critics succeeded in planting the falsehood that classical instruction dominated the American high school partly because a small percentage of students in every high school, whatever they studied, aspired to attend college. Moreover, some English curricula included Latin as an optional foreign language, and a few exceptional high schools had a strong, even dominant classical orientation.

Critics called learning the ancient languages antirepublican and aristocratic. They shared the sentiments of Benjamin Rush, who in 1789 questioned the value of classical education: "Do not men use Latin and Greek, as the scuttle-fish emit their ink, on purpose to conceal themselves from an intercourse with the common people?" This dissenting educational spirit soared in some circles in the nineteenth century. High school students (the majority of whom were women) generally did not aim to enter colleges or universities, which only began to admit some females after the Civil War. Very few high schools, if they offered Latin, had courses beyond the first year, and educators in the 1870s claimed that taxpayers would be "mutinous" if anyone suggested teaching Greek. They barely tolerated the occasional class in Latin, noted one cynical writer in 1874, and classical educators faced "the murmurs of lazy boys and utilitarian men."[38]

Devising a coherent English curriculum while also serving the college-bound few was challenging but became easier as colleges and universities increasingly accepted modern subjects for admission. The English course generally dominated. School leaders believed in centralized authority, in a uniform curriculum, and in common standards. Because high schools existed in diverse environments and were sometimes in rooms, wings of buildings, or separate facilities, such uniformity proved impossible, yet the emphasis on modern subjects was a common thread.

Like other contemporary reformers, Henry Barnard strongly endorsed an English education and struggled to devise a thoughtful course of study. In the late 1830s, he defined a high school as a center for advanced scholarship that offered older pupils a curriculum suitable for "their age, and intellectual and moral wants" and in a general way oriented to their life plans. That Barnard reprinted this description in subsequent decades showed that uniformity remained a dream, but he always recognized that a modern school emphasized modern subjects.[39]

To devise a curriculum based on the ages, intellectual and moral wants, or probable vocation of scholars was easier said than done. But a "high" school, Barnard maintained, was a "mockery" if it taught the lower branches or ignored "the wants of the wealthiest and best educated families" patronizing the academies. The talented poor, too, needed access to what the privileged classes could purchase in the marketplace. Specifically, Barnard wanted high schools to teach advanced English courses from bookkeeping to chemistry and "kindred studies." This would both train the mind and acquaint youth with "the varied departments of domestic and inland trade, with foreign commerce, with gardening, agriculture, the manufacturing and domestic arts." High schools—as Barnard envisaged them, at least—were capable of teaching anything.[40]

Barnard nevertheless concluded that high schools would "prepare every young man, whose parents may desire it, for business or for college, and give to every young woman a well disciplined mind, high moral aims, refined tastes, gentle and graceful manners, practical views of her own duties, and those resources of health, thought, conversation, and occupation, which bless alike the highest and lowest station in life." Thus, high schools had a dual role for boys: preparation for business or for college. Women, the majority of students, would benefit from mental discipline, moral training, and bourgeois values; they might also aspire to teach young children. "When such a course is provided and carried out," Barnard believed, "the true idea of the High School will be realized."[41]

Discovering the "true" high school was as simple as finding the Holy Grail. Contemporary educators realized that high schools of every variety and quality existed. One observer in Barnard's Connecticut admitted in 1859 that "various circumstances materially affect the character of different schools called by the same name." Another said in 1865 that "the high schools already established, are very different in character." Hartford High School, for example, had absorbed the former Hopkins Grammar School, which became its classical department and the dominant influence within the institution. Most Connecticut high schools, however, emphasized the modern languages and a "higher English course, for business life."[42]

The diversity of high schools worried many northern educators, in progressive Massachusetts as elsewhere. Once created, the advanced schools that Horace Mann and other Whigs had advocated since the 1830s differed enormously. "At present, 'confusion worse confounded' is the order of the day," wrote one contributor to the *Massachusetts Teacher* in 1859. "In some schools, many branches are pursued that ought to be confined wholly to Grammar schools; in others, the sciences are not admitted at all; while a third adopt them largely, to the exclusion of almost all other branches; others have more of Latin, Greek, and the modern languages, than of our own."[43]

Schoolmen found themselves in situations that in retrospect seem comical. High schools occasionally received some state appropriations before the 1880s, especially when Republicans had power. When Democrats regained control, as in Maine in the late 1870s, they reversed the policy. Whenever educators requested state aid, legislators naturally demanded a clear definition of a high school, which educators could not provide. Speaking at the Indiana State Teachers' Association in 1869, the principal of the Indianapolis High School urged his brethren "to define what a High School is, and then suggest the same to our law-makers" because currently "each town and township fixes its own standard." The *Pennsylvania School Journal* noted in 1877 that the state teachers' association wanted state aid for high schools but also lacked consensus on a definition.[44]

School people sometimes presented the public with incredible or vague explanations about the aims of the American high school. Most emphasized that the course of study at *their* high school was eminently practical, whatever was true elsewhere, and however palatial the facility. A writer in the *Wisconsin Journal of Education* in 1878 covered his tracks by claiming that the high school provided pupils with an education "that shall set the mind free from superstitious notions and vulgar prejudices, enlarge its power of comprehension, give it scope and discipline, cultivate the affections, improve the morals, refine the feelings, impress and illustrate man's relation to man, prepare the recipient of this education to be a good, useful, and honorable member of society, as well as a skilled workman in whatever department of labor he may be called to act his part in life."[45] Every contingency was covered.

Many writers believed high schools fostered republicanism, Christianity, and the economic needs of the individual and state. In 1851 one educational theorist argued that Protestantism, the work ethic, republicanism, and utilitarianism were all compatible and found expression in most secondary schools. Whether you wanted to become polished, practical, or profound, the Male or Female High School was right for you, Louisville's superintendent declared in 1861. Other educators proclaimed that high schools improved the lower grades, centralized authority, trained good teachers, and even undermined communism. More high schools meant more Ben Franklins and fewer jails.[46]

That high schools educated the majority of their pupils in the English, not classical, branches, preparing them for practical pursuits, not for a monastic existence, was a point of pride. A New England school committee captured the spirit: "He who builds good dwelling houses is a public benefactor and a better man than the cloistered student, whose sole claim to notice is that he never trips amid the intricacies of the Greek syntax" or "who partially knows a dead language or two" and "wraps himself in his sheepskin and rests upon his academic honors."[47]

Countless speeches and written reports described the benefits of a practical education, so essential to fulfill the "duties of life." The boys left Boston's English High School well fitted "to go forth into the world, and meet the responsibilities and discharge manfully the duties that devolve upon them." Cleveland's Central High School launched boys and girls alike onto the "sea of life." Duty, self-control, responsibility: values central to a very practical middle-class world. Despite their sometimes ostentatious appearance, high schools everywhere taught useful knowledge and respectable values.[48]

Emma M. McRae, the principal of the Muncie, Indiana, high school in the 1870s, dismissed the idea that high schools made youth vain and pompous. Rather, her school aimed to produce pupils "so impressed with the love of truth, and so imbued with the fullness of life, that noble types of manhood and womanhood be personated in their daily lives." How many young people became "personated" is unknown, but educators concurred that high schools taught practical skills and solid moral values. H. H. Barney, principal of Cincinnati's Central School, the forerunner both to Woodward and Hughes High Schools, anticipated that graduates would "fill every department of honorable enterprise, professional, mercantile, and mechanical. They will attain to positions of influence, and contribute largely to give tone to society."[49]

A few very specialized high schools, such as in Boston or Philadelphia, restricted themselves to the English branches. Boston already had the famed Latin School, and English High addressed a different market. Unusual places such as Hartford High emphasized the classical course, though a quarter of the enrollment was in the English stream. Most graded high schools after midcentury—whether in villages, towns, or cities—allowed boys and girls to select an English or classical course. Pupils voted with their feet. Between 1858 and 1874, approximately 12 percent of Chicago's high school graduates had completed the classical program. When New York's all-male Free Academy opened in 1849, it enrolled 73 percent of its pupils in the "ancient" and 27 percent in the "modern" course. Rough parity between the branches existed by 1856, and the modern subjects grew more popular in the 1860s. Even if pupils elsewhere studied Latin, they were usually enrolled in an English curriculum, reflecting middle-class enthusiasm for useful learning. The high school was eminently practical, frequently leading boys to the counting house and girls to the teaching profession.[50]

Educators understood that the very existence and character of secondary schools revealed the nation's new economic structure. Many workers after the 1820s watched mechanization destroy—almost overnight in certain industries—time-honored crafts and centuries-old traditions of male apprenticeships. Unskilled labor increased across the nation, limiting personal mobility and undermining human dignity, and the gap between rich and poor widened, leading some middle-class commentators to predict an impending social war. When educators said high schools could help combat anarchism and communism, they spoke the language of the middle classes, who sought safe harbors in a turbulent sea.

William T. Harris, no friend to radical political movements, applauded secondary schools for offering educational opportunity to all talented white children. High schools educated and socialized the future "governing classes of the community"—the broad range of respectable men and women whose intellectual skills and moral fiber sustained modern society. Few children went to high school and fewer still graduated, but the "directive power" of those who attended strengthened the social order. As the economy became more specialized, Harris wrote in 1875, society depended upon the "directive intelligence" of those who ran the nation's industries, commanded its militia, and filled government offices. That the major wealth holders needed the high school seems doubtful, for after the 1880s their children patronized ever exclusive private schools. But the message was clear for those with fewer resources: go to high school if possible and increase your odds of entering the economy in a respectable way.[51]

In an age of expansive economic growth, many educators—especially when accused of fostering knowledge for its own sake—emphasized the material advantages of the higher learning. The diffusion of knowledge, many believed, enhanced productivity. Young people faced a world where machines had transformed the nature of work, where science and technology helped conquer the natural environment. Educators argued that high schools prepared boys especially for the world of business and the professions and that the Three R's alone failed to prepare one for modern life.

Without advanced learning, an educator from Lewiston, Maine, wrote in 1880, youth were disadvantaged in the "hot competition of modern life; and the disadvantage is yearly increasing. It is intelligent, skilled workmen that are in demand in every department of industry, at their own price." Never before had "intellectual training" so shaped life's opportunities, for boys as well as for girls. At a time when an increased percentage of young people faced the prospects of unskilled jobs, high school promoters everywhere appealed directly to the economic concerns of middle-class parents.[52]

Whether palaces or modest quarters, high schools aimed to inspire and uplift, to train the minds of young people and furnish them with knowledge. School leaders linked the value of intellectual development to the grim realities of the larger social world, where rich and poor often stood apart. John S. Hart, principal of Philadelphia's Central High School, wrote in 1868 that secondary schools were part of a larger urban police force.

A Presbyterian minister, Hart wanted more schools and churches to help protect property and to impose order and discipline. High schools diffused knowledge and enhanced productivity, adding to personal wealth and national prosperity. "No matter what the cost, the dark holes and alleys must be flooded with the light of truth, before which the owls and bats and vampires of society will be scattered to the winds. A great city without schools," Hart concluded, "would be a hell,—a seething cauldron of vice, impurity, and crime."[53]

To a nation that wanted more Ben Franklins and fewer communists, the high school formed a crucial part of the larger political economy. Schoolmen praised the middle classes for their hard work and moral values, which would

Because of local opposition to building an expensive public high school, reformers in Norwich, Connecticut, had to persuade a number of wealthy residents to donate the money to construct this impressive edifice. From *American Journal of Education* 8 (1873).

yield personal success and inspire poor people to emulate them. Educators embraced the maxims of Poor Richard, trying to help their students to succeed materially without abandoning higher moral purposes. But softening the age's rampant utilitarianism through appeals to the more sublime values expressed in the best school architecture remained a daunting task.

Although thirty-five wealthy residents had donated the money to build and endow the Free Academy of Norwich, Connecticut, citizens honored another man—the inspiring Benjamin Franklin—at the dedication ceremonies in 1856. Mrs. Lydia H. Sigourney, prominent literary figure and writer, offered a fitting tribute to the values that undergirded high schools:

> There's many kinds of stock, they say,
> 　That tempt the speculators;
> But what is safest held, and best,
> 　Might tax the shrewdest natures.
> Sage Franklin said, in earlier days,—
> 　And now the wisest bless him,—
> "What pours his purse into brains,
> 　No man can dispossess him."[54]

Educators regarded training the mind as a wise investment, but did knowledge for its own sake have a place in an increasingly materialistic world?

　Widespread support for useful learning and the diffusion of knowledge enhanced the place of English studies in early American high schools. Calling them centers of classical education was politically effective for critics but factually incorrect. Most educators favored the modern branches; many even shared the wider culture's disdain for or indifference to classical education. While emphatically endorsing the modern subjects, teachers and principals worried that the wondrous growth of the economy promoted materialism and threatened morals and civic virtue.

"The age is rushing on to the utilitarian to the exclusion of the refining," warned Nicholas H. Maguire, principal of the very practical Central High School of Philadelphia in 1865. "Knowledge is estimated by its remunerative value, and not by its intrinsic worth other than its relation to industrial pursuits." Another educator, though, writing in an Illinois teachers' magazine, constantly heard that schools were not practical enough. "I am some times so impatient of the perpetual cry for a practical course of study that I am ready to say No! Let us have nothing practical in the schools; the teachings of life will make men and women practical and prosaic enough! Let us teach them something that they will not otherwise learn!" Was there not more to life than "the sheen of silver, the glitter of gold, or the emerald of greenbacks?"[55]

High school leaders always praised the practical nature of the curriculum but occasionally felt overwhelmed by society's utilitarian demands. Like most Americans unmoved by metaphysics, they nonetheless wanted youth to cherish education for its intrinsic merits and not simply for its cash value. No doubt many parents and educators agreed that moral training, intellectual development, and economic success were compatible. At times, however, some educators passionately insisted that more schooling should produce better and not simply richer citizens. The suggestion that education *only* made men richer and more productive disturbed them.

Daniel Shepardson, the principal of Cincinnati's Woodward High School, wanted pupils to love learning "for its own ennobling and purifying influences." He recognized that middle-class parents worried about their children's fate in a competitive economy that often pitted rich against poor. Shepardson valued hard work, discipline, and academic achievement, but he hoped scholars would seek virtue as well as individual success. "The right kind of education," he wrote in 1860, "makes *men*, not *machines*, works wonders in poverty, introduces a rewarder of merit, and makes a Franklin even more renowned than an Astor." Another midwestern educator added that the "Belknaps" and the "Tweeds" only existed because they lacked "that higher intellectual and moral training" found in free secondary schools.[56]

Calls for an ever more practical curriculum frustrated many school people. The quest for useful learning, of course, inspired secondary activists from the outset. That was the major rationale behind the English Classical School and other new high schools. Henry Barnard and fellow reformers praised free secondary schools for preparing boys for business and the professions and girls for the practical duties of motherhood or teaching. Because school leaders promised to fit youth into a respectable niche in society, taxpayers and critics alike pressed for even closer ties between learning and doing. Like the larger public, educators searched for the correct medium, but they sometimes resisted the utilitarian imperative, for which practicality remained the touchstone.

Educators understood that neither parents nor secondary pupils embraced learning for its intrinsic good. Extended schooling meant the immediate loss of potential wages by the pupils, and high schools, after all, advertised themselves as useful centers of instruction. Critics frequently condemned "esoteric" subjects. "My son is fit for nothing. He knows only a little Latin and Greek," disgruntled Hoosiers reportedly complained in the early 1870s, echoing old criticisms.[57]

"There is a demand for practical studies," wrote the superintendent of the Manchester, New Hampshire, schools in 1874, "but what are regarded as *practical* by one person are not so regarded by another." The concern with practicality partly reflected the anti-Catholic bent of the native bourgeois mind, which saw academies as a lingering form of monasticism housing "cloistered" scholars. More markets and mechanization meant economic expansion, and educators heeded the utilitarian values of the age. William T. Harris noted a demand "for more science and less Latin or Greek, and for a radical extension of the elective system of making up a course of study for each individual."[58]

Pressures intensified to banish the impractical. In 1857 a school board member in Louisville urged the appointment of a professor of natural sciences to the Male High School, for the "dead languages" and "the more abstract mathematics" had "yielded to the imperious requirements of a practical age. Men are no longer educated for a life of useless metaphysical abstractions or for the cloister. Intelligent usefulness is the demand directly made by the spirit of the day." A visitor to the school later applauded its "*useful* rather than *showy*" curriculum, and the high school committee in 1876 encouraged even closer ties between learning and life. The Ohio River, a great commercial artery, still offered untapped riches. "Our sons should be trained to restrain that water and make of Louisville a Manchester or a Lowell." The committee feared not the dark Satanic mills.[59]

Without middle-class support high schools would disappear, and even those educators who recoiled at the thought that they only fit youth for the workaday world could not live in a social vacuum. A few educators said parents often misunderstood what was "practical." Occasionally school officials eloquently defended the higher learning apart from its remunerative rewards. One such defense came from the Acting Visitors who inspected the schools of Meriden, Connecticut, in 1872.

Once all children had mastered the elementary subjects, the Visitors argued, the "higher studies" should help "improve the mind and elevate the taste" and do more than "merely satisfy the lowest demand for practical use, and contribute only to the worldly interests of the pupil." Studying English and classical subjects cultivated thoughtful men and women and not just workers. "It is true that men do not make bargains in Latin or Greek, or talk French in the market, or plough with syllogisms, or compute the value of stocks by the propositions of Euclid, or rake hay with the principles of morals," claimed the Visitors. "Yet the man whose mind has been sharpened, and drilled, and enlarged by such exercises, is not only a wiser and more skillful man in business, but a nobler and better man in his various relations of life." Throughout the nineteenth century, other educators lamented the "coarse materialism" of a culture that prized the glitter of gold over values well formed and lives well lived.[60]

How to be practical while avoiding the cloister was a constant concern. In small towns and major cities, educators feared that they could never make their schools practical enough to satisfy their critics. "It is not all of life to live," said the Exeter, New Hampshire, school committee in 1852. "The process of digestion is not the only nor the highest function of organized existence. We have hearts as well as animal appetites." Indeed, the committee continued, the common criticism that schools taught impractical subjects was unfounded. "We might, however, say with entire truth, that every study, which requires mental exertion, is a practical one." Whatever required application and close study—whether algebra or "low Dutch"—served the " 'working-day' world. The solution of a hard problem in Algebra strengthens and invigorates the mind, just as roast beef does the body."[61]

Indeed, many educators and theorists of "the science of the mind" believed in what became known as faculty psychology. They argued that the brain consisted of separate *faculties* best developed by the diligent study of difficult subjects such as Latin and mathematics. Classics teachers especially embraced this idea and fought the swelling waves of utilitarianism. Instructors of the English branches said that their studies, too, trained the mind. But many Latin teachers doubted that astronomy or English literature matched the intellectual benefits of a classical education.[62]

While some high school pupils and their parents seemed too interested in the cash value of learning, educators emphasized the importance of "mental discipline" or "mental culture" in the classroom and opposed narrowly conceived vocational courses. Education elevated one above animal existence, wrote one northern administrator in 1845; man should seek "the expansion and enjoyment of his moral and intellectual faculties." Chicago's superintendent, William H. Wells, author of an influential guide to school organization and graded classrooms, argued in 1860 that "the highest and most important object of intellectual education, is *mental discipline*, or the power of using the mind to the best advantage." In countless speeches, local reports, and books, educators and officials emphasized mental discipline, academic achievement, and the lasting benefits of rigorous study.[63]

These tensions between intellectual growth and material advance sometimes gave the erroneous impression that schools and families were on a collision course: that educators mostly cared about the minds of their pupils while everyone else cared about money. Teachers expected pupils to complete their homework, prepare for recitations and tests, and sacrifice many freedoms as slaves to the classroom. They bluntly told lazy pupils to stay home. Such de facto expulsion nurtured the idea that the goal of education was mental discipline and ignored the moral purposes of education, the inherently utilitarian focus of an English education, and the truth that few Americans valued learning for its intrinsic worth. Constantly on the defensive, classicists even argued that the ancient languages taught accuracy and clarity and thus enhanced business.

Having "a well disciplined mind" was an important goal of secondary instruction, even for women, wrote Henry Barnard as commissioner of education in Rhode Island in 1846. He immediately added that the schools should also teach "high moral aims" and "practical views." The goal of mental discipline was thus part of a matrix of ideas, all embedded in dominant views of political economy. Fellow reformers in New London, Connecticut, in 1855 claimed that a well-furnished mind enabled pupils to think clearly, analyze well, converse fluently, and calculate accurately, so that boys would be "influential in whatever branch of business they may be engaged." For others, "the union of mental discipline and business utility" was exactly what "a great mercantile and manufacturing community require in their highest scholastic institutions," often the local high school.[64]

Mental training was thus inherently practical and best prepared young people "for life." Indeed, educators were confident that schools capably prepared youth for adult responsibilities and that the addition of narrowly conceived classes would undermine the productivity of future workers. Before the 1880s most educators therefore opposed training high school pupils, at least boys, for specific jobs. Girls, however, were often trained to become teachers, occasionally through normal classes in larger towns and cities. But even they usually received such instruction only in their final school terms.[65]

Schoolmen claimed that all of their instruction produced practical results. Sound academics prepared boys especially for an "active life" in business. Charles A. Dupee, principal of the Chicago High School, nevertheless wrote in 1860 that knowledge from school always lacked immediate application. "The main object is to gain such mental discipline and acumen, such power of analysis and synthesis, as shall be serviceable in all the relations of life, and in whatever employment the individual may engage." As Dupee's counterpart in Dayton, Ohio, later remarked, only "discipline of mind and breadth of culture" would produce workers who spoke, wrote, and reasoned clearly. What could be more practical?[66]

Momentous economic changes had swept the nation since the first high schools opened in the 1820s. Commerce, industry, and technological and scientific advance promised Americans greater material wealth and a higher standard of living. Middle-class families, whose children predominated in high schools, were part of a new class system, and they naturally wanted schools to teach respectable social values and marketable skills. The towering new high schools in many communities reflected the surplus wealth of a rich nation with some respect for the sublime.

Few Americans cherished knowledge for its own sake, and mental discipline or the love of learning was never an end in itself. Palatial buildings reflected a lofty medieval tradition of imagined social unity as well as contemporary wealth; students with well-disciplined minds stored much timeless knowledge and pursued utilitarian ends. The truth of de Tocqueville's observation that the bourgeois northerner did not "value knowledge as a pleasure, but only as a means" saddened some educators, but their jobs rested upon economic growth and the increased value of a school credential.[67]

Training minds and training morals were the twin goals of secondary schools that dotted the urban landscape by the 1880s. Some of the most spectacular high school facilities, drawing on a medieval and Catholic past, projected an illusion that they were monastic institutions, housing future scribes who would conceal knowledge, hide it from the masses, and remain separated from the world. Critics who accused high schools of mostly serving as college preparatory institutions pressured them to become even more useful. In response, some schoolteachers, principals, and administrators worried that materialism made their society coarse and corrupt, that education produced richer people but not better people.

"Each year the cry, 'practical,' grows louder," said a writer who defended classical instruction in the *Indiana School Journal* in 1873. "And what does it mean? Is it grasp of mind, power to think, and disciplined faculties that we are to call 'practical'?" Were the classics impractical? Would Americans blithely "throw aside the experience of 2000 years?" Like many educators then and later, this writer had discovered that Americans valued intellectual life if it seemed a wise investment.[68]

High school advocates promised to provide America with an aristocracy of intellect based upon academic achievement, an alternative to a class system based upon birth or wealth. As educators attempted to train the minds and morals of youth, they relied heavily upon textbooks to convey a coherent understanding of knowledge and its modern uses. Some scholars sat in a rickety country school surrounded by abecedarians, others sat in a well-graded urban palace. But advanced students everywhere faced a world of printed words that tried to shape their minds and values. Even in the dullest of textbooks, dominant values of respectable culture sprang to life.

Knowledge of the Most Worth

Avoid extreams. Never decieve. Knowledge inlarges the mind.

—LINDLEY MURRAY, *Abridgement of
Murray's English Grammar* (1830)

Levellers are generally the dupes of
designning men.

—GOULD BROWN, *The Institutes of English
Grammar* (1853)

"Books are the great store-
house of knowledge, and he who has the habit of using them intelligently has
the key to all human knowledge," claimed an algebraist in 1877. Nineteenth-
century educators often applauded the salutary role of textbooks, which
helped to organize and diffuse knowledge. Standard classroom texts so influenced pedagogy that some critics believed they undermined creative instruction and taught mostly useless facts. Whether friend or foe to sound
education, textbooks remained central to the curriculum.[1]

In ungraded one-room schools, serving beginners and some advanced students, textbooks framed the order of studies, exposing scholars to uniform
subject matter and common values. And when public high schools opened in
the 1820s, textbooks in better-graded institutions systematically taught older
students advanced subjects and the basic tenets of an evolving capitalist
economy. Advanced scholars everywhere knew textbooks as their constant
companions.[2]

The proliferation of elementary and advanced textbooks was part of a larger
publishing revolution that transformed American cultural life by the 1820s.
Technological innovations led to cheaper, mass-produced print, and textbooks
helped define acceptable knowledge and shape instruction. Yankee-based newspapers, magazines, and printed materials flooded a growing national market.
"Books are the true organizers of the future, and the real legislators of the pres-

ent," claimed one Mississippian in *DeBow's Review* in 1857. An apologist for slavery, he called for southern books for southern children. Yankee books, he claimed, were a Trojan horse, hiding abolitionists and other enemies.[3]

Northern educators usually regarded common reading materials as a major educational advance, if not a panacea. Textbooks presumably democratized knowledge, making specialized learning available to everyone. William T. Harris, steadfast friend of the high school, defended these books in 1880 against criticisms that they promoted lifeless instruction. Standard texts, he wrote, made more authoritative knowledge more accessible. They enabled "the bright pupil, even under the worst methods of instruction, to participate, by his own efforts, in the recorded experience and wisdom of mankind," and they also helped "even the dull and stupid, to some extent." Good textbooks promoted good instruction.[4]

Textbooks constituted the heart of formal instruction in the high school, and the expanding market proved lucrative for many publishers, especially in the North. The absence of a powerful national ministry of education or of effective state school bureaucracies meant that publishers and authors dealt directly with thousands of independent school districts. Competing volumes in all subjects struggled for survival and preferment. As hundreds of new titles appeared, some observers predicted chaos in the classroom. Despite this growth and proliferation, a handful of textbooks in every subject dominated the national market.[5]

Textbooks enabled theorists and practitioners alike to try to popularize their ideas about the content of subject matter as well as instructional practice. Today they reveal what was often taught or intended, not necessarily what was learned. Indeed, knowing what students read opens a window onto the special world of knowledge and values embraced in America's high schools.

Textbooks presented the young with a particular reading of the natural and man-made worlds, providing useful knowledge for understanding their place in a dynamic society. Scholars confronted rules for knowing and for living, moral lessons and sound ideas on political economy. School texts also denounced Owenite socialism, feminism, agrarianism, and communitarian philosophies. Because textbooks became so commonplace and were so ideologically selective, nervous southerners understandably warned kinsmen to beware of Yankees bearing gifts.

"There are fortunes made in this city every year from the sale of school books," said one angry secondary student in Cincinnati in 1881. Scholars at Woodward High, like students elsewhere, periodically complained about the high costs of classroom texts, which averaged ten dollars per year by the 1870s. They assailed the "rings" of salesmen who helped make some publishers millionaires and even petitioned school boards to provide free books. In the larger towns and cities, with the most concentrated student populations, selling knowledge squeezed between two covers was very profitable.

Scandals over kickbacks to elected officials occasionally rocked communities as publishers spread their octopus-like arms around the schools.[6]

The authors of high school textbooks were usually not business people, however much they found pleasure and profit in guiding pupils along the correct academic path. Exceptional writers such as J. Dorman Steele, a prolific author of science as well as nonscience texts, earned enough money to retire early and comfortably on his royalties. Most volumes, however, never appeared in a second edition. A few lucky men (and fewer women) skillfully cornered a substantial share of the market. Daring souls attempted a new approach to instruction and often failed; most took safer routes, imitating the standard bearers to enjoy some limited success.[7]

Whether studying in mighty Chicago or modest Muncie, pupils encountered a similar world of intellectual, ideological, and moral values in assigned books. Whatever they actually learned, every high school student knew that Harkness wrote Latin texts, that Ray meant Joseph Ray, the author of a fabulously successful mathematics series, and that Wayland meant readings in political and moral economy.[8]

Subjects were widely equated with authors in the nineteenth century. Town and city school reports often published the names of authors but not the subjects under the "Course of Study." But textbooks reigned supreme. Some writers thus complained in the late 1870s that textbooks largely defined the curriculum and determined instructional practice. Teachers allegedly brutalized their students by forcing them to memorize the innumerable facts contained in their assigned reading. "And what kind of influence can be exerted by a teacher that never goes beyond the narrow scope of the school text-book?" While there was a "legitimate use of text-books," said one writer, a "servile dependence upon them" was very common.[9]

The earliest high school advocates had championed a sequenced, textbook-oriented course of study. When Boston's reformers triumphed in 1821, they organized the curriculum around volumes by particular authors. Towns and cities did likewise for decades to come, even though they increasingly publicized formal curricula that emphasized subjects. Some well-established northern high schools continued to print the authors' names long after they had a well-graded curriculum.[10]

Many schools in the nineteenth century still assigned some English authors, but the spread of nationalism after the 1780s soon enabled native writers to dominate the burgeoning textbook industry. Most authors of elementary and secondary textbooks shared common characteristics. In the early 1800s, many were Federalists who maligned Jeffersonian Republicans as Francophiles, deists, and revolutionaries. After the 1830s, Whigs and later the Republicans controlled the field, not surprising given their central role in promoting school systems.[11]

The most famous authors of high school textbooks were exceptional individuals. They were usually New England-born, Protestant, white men who had attended college or other higher schools. Joseph Ray was college educated, an M.D. and surgeon at the Cincinnati Hospital, and professor of mathematics at Woodward College for nearly two decades; when the institution became a public high school in 1851, he became its principal. Francis Bowen, author of a standard volume on political economy, attended one of Boston's best grammar schools en route to Phillips Exeter and Harvard. He became editor of the Whig *North American Review* in 1843 and later was a Harvard professor.[12]

Bowen fit well in the cavalcade of accomplished people who tried to shape the minds of youth. College professors and presidents probably constituted the majority of successful authors because they had the training and leisure for reflection and writing. President Francis Wayland of Brown University wrote books on political and moral economy that became educational staples. Albert Harkness, who taught Greek at Wayland's school from 1855 to 1892, wrote one book on Greek and eighteen on Latin.[13]

Other leading authors taught in prominent northern academies, colleges, or occasionally in high schools. The scientist Alonzo Gray taught at Phillips Andover. Emma Willard, founder of the Troy Female Seminary, wrote a popular history and a geography text. Indeed, authors often taught for a living, strengthening their common claim that their pedagogical theories were rooted in practice. John S. Hart was among the handful of secondary teachers before the 1880s who wrote widely for a high school and college audience. The author of prominent English-language readers and literature texts, Hart was a teacher and principal at Philadelphia's prestigious Central High School and later a professor at Princeton. Like many textbook writers, he was an ordained minister.[14]

Successful in many aspects of their career, these prominent textbook writers presented young people with a coherent approach to the specialized domains of knowledge that were emerging in the nineteenth century. Usually specialists in particular subjects, these writers held common cultural views toward mankind, gender relations, nature, capital, labor, and America's destiny. They offered pupils a remarkably uniform worldview, whether asking them to solve algebra problems, parse English grammar, or study geography. Though never without their critics, textbooks organized knowledge systematically and helped teach talented youth common intellectual and moral precepts. Those who learned their lessons well, said America's school leaders, would lead lives of respectability and even distinction.

Three years before the opening of Boston's English Classical School, a writer in the *Academician* defended the centrality of Latin and Greek in a "liberal" education. Revolted by the age's sordid materialism, he asked how anyone "can read the works of a Plutarch, a Homer, a Xenophon, a Demosthenes, a Vergil, a Terence, a Tully, a Tacitus, or a Longinus, and not derive improvement both to his heart and understanding?" Unfortunately for him, the equation of liberal education with classical studies continued to erode. Since the late eighteenth century, the middle classes had sought more useful learning and practical skills for their sons and daughters, often in academies that popularized the "English" or modern studies. Textbooks in these new subjects multiplied rapidly in the next century. Indeed, the English studies later found in the high school—the advanced sciences, mathematics, nonclassical languages (including English itself), history, and related subjects—first came to prominence in New England's academies.[15]

The earliest high schools in the 1820s and 1830s set important precedents. Students in the dominant English curriculum sometimes studied one or two years of Latin, Greek attracted very few scholars, and enrollments in classical studies generally remained small. Foreign language instruction tilted toward modernity: expanding trade and cultural contacts made French, German, and Spanish seem especially apposite. The proliferation of textbooks also reflected a rising middle-class preference for chemistry and algebra over Vergil and Ovid. Henry Barnard, himself a prize-winning Latin pupil at Yale, asserted in 1842 that the ideal high school should teach whatever advanced "the pursuits of commerce, trade, manufactures, and the mechanical arts."[16]

Such thinking affirmed the justifications for the earliest high schools, and in postbellum America most classicists realized that practicality and modernity had triumphed. According to the president of Middlebury College, who defended the more classically oriented academies, the typical high school seemed to absorb commercial values "like a sponge," as if governed "by a law of social attraction." A midwestern school superintendent fully concurred in 1876: "In the battle waged between the classicists and the scientists, the victory on all the substantial points has fallen to the latter."[17]

Classicists had never controlled most high schools, though their central role in the Latin grammar school colored the perspective of many educational critics. By midcentury, the larger northern towns and cities had separate high school buildings and a fairly distinct course of study from the grammar grades. And, as in the primary grades, the modern subjects were the rule. Only a tiny percentage of students attended college—boys or girls, before or after the Civil War—limiting the appeal of classical, precollegiate instruction.

The high school curriculum, like the textbooks that gave it form, changed over time in some communities. School committees added and dropped courses here and there and occasionally rearranged their sequence. What stands out between the 1820s and 1870s, however, is the essential continuity in the curriculum. When Boston's all-male English High opened in 1821, it offered mathematics, the sciences, English, history, moral philosophy, and such practical classes as Mensuration and Astronomy. This curriculum shaped the character of high schools forever. When superintendent William H. Wells of Chicago published a model secondary English curriculum in 1862, it differed in the sequence and arrangement of classes, not in the basic kinds of study, long accepted as appropriate.[18]

Science rapidly emerged as central to secondary instruction. First taught in academies, often both to women and men, natural philosophy (mostly physics), physiology, chemistry, botany, and sometimes geology and zoology appeared in the English curriculum after the 1820s. In an expanding nation with bountiful natural resources, citizens eagerly embraced scientific studies as useful knowledge. Predictably, classicists said science promoted materialism; Latin teachers, in turn, were called aristocrats and anachronistic. Horace Greeley, so opposed to free high schools, lamented the absence of science instruction in his district school education. In his autobiography in 1869, he remarked "that such homely sciences as Chemistry, Geology, and Botany were never taught," despite their "inestimable value."[19]

Why were the sciences so valuable? The laws of science helped legitimize a society whose economic system favored growth and man's dominion over nature. Contemporary high school chemistry texts divided their subject into inorganic and organic chemistry, and they all promised a practical education that would reveal the workings of a beneficent God who always blessed a productive people. Edward L. Youmans' *A Class-Book of Chemistry*, which sold nearly 150,000 copies, was perhaps the most popular text at midcentury and was widely imitated by rivals. Like most authors, Youmans emphasized chemistry's "practical and useful applications."[20]

Science offered more than useful knowledge. Educators argued that it also trained the mind, taught logic and reason, and sharpened the powers of observation. Still, Youmans' assertion about the utility of chemistry echoed, and echoed loudly, in most science texts. Astronomers discussed maritime careers for navigators, and geologists applauded the expansion of the extractive industries. *Wells' First Principles of Geology* (1864) began with the usual plea: "Intimately connected as Geology is with the great industrial interests of the country—especially with mining and agriculture—and constituting also an important member of the circle of the sciences, its place as an element in an English educational course is daily becoming more and more recognized." Youmans fully agreed, though chemistry remained the jewel in the high school crown.[21]

A popular public lecturer and later the founder of *Popular Science Monthly*, Youmans attacked the pretensions of the "cloistered" scholar. Chemistry is inherently more valuable than the ancient languages, he wrote, for it teaches "the processes of human industry, connects its operations with our daily experience, involves the conditions of life and death, and throws light upon the sublime plan by which the Creator manages the world." Youmans connected his science with broader views on political economy. Pupils studying metals read that only societies that used iron wore "the emblem of beneficent and intelligent industry." Advanced, superior nations first used iron for basic tools and then for machines. Chemistry taught girls how to bake bread and to cook other food properly and helped farmers increase their annual yields.[22]

Lending support to Protestant temperance crusaders, *A Class-Book of Chemistry* attacked alcohol consumption for its deleterious effects on the reasoning faculties and for leading to debauchery. Youmans added that the only known example of spontaneous combustion was of "spirit-drinkers, and most of them old people who were fat." Youmans always tied his seemingly materialistic subject to the sublime. Understanding scientific laws drew people closer to God, partly by enhancing productivity, and Youmans taught students that life and death, themselves shaped by chemical processes, were part of an endless cycle, as dust was unto dust.[23]

J. Dorman Steele, the author of the most popular series of science textbooks, similarly saw chemistry and all the sciences as practical yet divinely inspired. God placed man on earth to master it, to conquer nature for human happiness and gain. Knowing chemistry enabled individuals to transform the material world, from learning the best way to dye wool to restoring fertility to a barren field. Like many science authors, Steele depicted God as a "Master Workman." "God has no idlers in his world," he wrote. "Each atom has its use. There is not an extra particle in the universe." Like Youmans, Steele believed that life was a "glorious paradox": "*We live only as we die*."[24]

Steele also offered scholars a sense of the beauty of the universe and life's interconnections. "We are but parts of a grand system," he asserted, "and the elements we use are not our own. The water we drink and the food we eat today may have been used a thousand times before, and that by the vilest beggar or the lowest earth-worm." Moreover, all particles assumed a new purpose as they passed from one form to another, inexorably obeying the laws of God: "From us they will pass on their ceaseless round to develop other forms of vegetation and life, whereby the same atom may freeze on arctic snows, bleach on torrid plains, be beauty in the poet's brain, strength in the blacksmith's arm, or beef in the butcher's block. Hamlet must have been somewhat more of a chemist than a madman when he gravely assured the king that 'man may fish with the worm that hath eat of a king, and eat of the fish that hath fed of the worm.'"[25] A U. S. Bureau of Education survey in 1880 on science instruction in towns and cities named Steele's chemistry text the undisputed classroom leader.[26]

In 1884 the Women's Christian Temperance Union officially endorsed a revised version of Steele's *Fourteen Weeks in Human Physiology* (1873) for the public schools. One can easily see why. His physiology texts drew upon chemistry to attack alcohol, tobacco, and drug abuse. The God-given laws of science protected youth, he promised, but only if students mastered chemistry. Contrary to popular opinion, alcohol was not a food, and it was a stimulant, not a depressant. Alcohol also impaired the ability to reason, so it naturally encouraged immoral behavior. "The reason giving way, the animal instincts assume the mastery of the man. The coward shows himself more craven, the braggart more boastful, the bold more daring, and the cruel more brutal." Ultimately the "revel of the drunkard ends in utter insensibility." The association between knowledge and respectable behavior was clear.[27]

The science textbooks generally assigned in public high schools between the 1820s and the 1880s shared the theism, concern with practicality, and heightened faith in man's imminent triumph over nature that Youmans and Steele taught to generations of students. Natural philosophy courses all emphasized practical, useful knowledge, and many authors—who obviously knew their market well—explicitly told prospective readers that theoretical discussions of science would be absent or minimized. According to Alonzo Gray, a leading figure in science, natural philosophy revealed the grand laws of the universe, everywhere demonstrating the omniscient "Power which first brought it into being." Moreover, knowledge of mechanics, hydrostatics, hydraulics, pneumatics, magnetism, optics, electricity, and acoustics revealed the intimate links between Heaven and Earth, as Gray and rival authors claimed. Knowing and doing were intimately bound, as science taught the God-ordained laws of the universe and helped man subdue nature.[28]

Whether in chemistry or natural philosophy classes, students learned that a useful education was hardly a Godless one. Astronomy, geology, and zoology—which disappeared from the curriculum after the 1870s—were occasionally taught in the high school and reinforced the worldview of the related sciences. Astronomy texts might inspire a few students to become navigators or scientists, but the subject had loftier potential: to show students the "wisdom, power, beneficence, and grandeur in the Divine Harmony of the Universe." God was the only monarch permitted in republican America.[29]

Standard geology and zoology textbooks either ignored or rejected Darwin as late as the 1870s, preferring the revealed truths of Genesis to the godless theory of natural selection. James D. Dana's *Manual of Geology*, the standard bearer since its appearance in 1862, affirmed in the third edition nearly two decades later that the Bible was "both true and divine." Countering new theories on evolution, Steele's geology text reminded readers that man was God's greatest creation and that "no gorilla ever took out a patent."[30]

Just as geology taught the truths of Genesis, so did zoological classification, which named man "the lord of the Animal Kingdom." "There are intellectual and moral features, moreover, which place man high above all other animals," wrote Steele in 1877. "The scope of his mind and the possibilities of immortal soul, mark the rank of being who is alone declared to have been created 'in the image of God.'" Though Steele died in 1888, five of his science books and two of his history books remained in print as late as 1928.[31]

Science revealed the mysterious laws of the natural world, helped citizens exploit the riches of a bountiful land, and taught youth to revere God. Only in some distant future would science books suggest the conservation of natural resources or wildlife preservation; in the 1800s science provided keys to unlock the world's hidden riches. Texts routinely described humans as God's special creation, better than the animals beneath them, who existed for man's use. The universe was interconnected, but man mattered most.

As James Dana, the geologist, claimed in 1862, "Man was the first being that was not finished on reaching adult growth, but was provided with powers for indefinite expansion, a will for a life of work, and boundless aspirations to lead to endless improvements." Similarly, a science text in its twentieth printing in 1868 assumed that "chemistry is one of the great agents in the transformation of nature, and its subjection to the wants of man." Such boosterism complemented the larger world of values and knowledge that defined the high school curriculum.[32]

Horace Greeley regretted the absence of science instruction in his youth but shed few tears for algebra. As he remarked in 1869, "I am thankful that Algebra had not yet been thrust into our rural common schools, to knot the brains and squander the time of those who should be learning something of positive and practical utility." Classicists shared his wonder at how quickly algebra, geometry, and trigonometry—a mathematics trio—had staked their claim in the English curriculum. Few people used algebra or geometry in everyday life, wrote one defender of classical instruction in 1888, yet Latin and Greek were often attacked for *their* lack of utility. Another writer questioned both "the utterly extravagant value attached to mathematics" and the pomposity of Latin teachers. In too many colleges, "mathematics is harnessed with the classics, making a double team which annually delivers for graduation hundreds of young men whose hearts are full of vanity and whose heads are full of ignorance."[33]

Whether or not mathematics made people vain and ignorant, algebra, geometry, and trigonometry appeared in the English curricula of the earliest high schools in the 1820s and were never dislodged. The curricular sequence varied, but higher arithmetic, followed by algebra, geometry, and trigonometry was the usual pattern. The key subject was algebra, and relevant textbooks flooded the marketplace. As in other subject areas, a few writers dominated, especially Charles E. Davies, Joseph Ray, and Benjamin Greenleaf. The broad range of middle-class interests that principally supported high schools favored a useful, nonclassical education. Once again, the public system delivered.[34]

The rise of commerce and western exploration revived the study and popularity of arithmetic and mathematics in early modern Europe. Colonial Americans shared this enthusiasm. Private tutors and academies responded to the demand, which increased after the 1780s. Mathematics was essential for surveying, navigation, and construction and in trading, banking, and shipping. Increasingly pulled into a more market-oriented culture, citizens and educators embraced the view that mastery of the higher mathematics was central to a liberal education.[35]

Many educational writers in the 1800s saw the rise of mathematics as Providential. Edward D. Mansfield, like other school activists, claimed that mathematics contributed to the spread of Christian, republican, civilized views about man and society. In *American Education: Its Principles and Elements* (1851), he praised "The Utility of Mathematics," affirming its practicality and secure place in an English curriculum. A nation on the brink of geographical expansion needed mathematics to help build better roads, survey land, construct homes, and otherwise enhance commerce and human enterprise. Once the Indians disappeared, settlers would fill the West, and "in the mines of iron and lead, and copper, gold, and quicksilver, they will need geometry as well as chemistry to aid them in mining and smelting." Engineers would build bridges over wild rivers and streams, fostering western expansion. "And in all of these operations mathematics will be the active agent and kind assistant."[36]

One very kind assistant was *Ray's Algebra*, which appeared in several editions to become one of the nation's most familiar school books. Like some competitors, Ray completed a full series of volumes that extended from the elementary grades through college. He died in 1865, but his books had sold an estimated 120 million copies by the early twentieth century. "The object of the study of mathematics," Ray argued, "is two-fold: the acquisition of useful knowledge, and the cultivation and discipline of the mental powers." According to Ray (and other writers), the French mathematicians were too theoretically minded. He preferred the more practical German and English scholars. In 1852, Ray wrote that algebra "is justly regarded one of the most interesting and useful branches of education, and an acquaintance with it is now sought by all who advance beyond the more common branches."[37]

Practicality was in the eyes of the beholder, but the word was continually evoked in algebra textbooks. Benjamin Greenleaf even called his text *A Practical Treatise on Algebra* (1854). Nearly every mathematics textbook, from "higher arithmetic" through trigonometry, mentioned the utility of the subject. Daniel Fish's *Progressive Higher Arithmetic* (1860) tried "to give the pupil a thoroughly practical and scientific arithmetical education, either for the farm, the workshop, the profession, or for the more difficult operations of the counting-room and of mercantile and commercial life." Children encountered useful knowledge in their "Rays" and "Greenleafs."[38]

Ninth-grade students first reviewed higher arithmetic to ensure their readiness for algebra. Markets often reward conformity, and "competing" texts had remarkably similar content: a progression from simple computation with whole numbers through fractions, decimals, U.S. money, compound numbers, duodecimals, and ratios to square roots and cube roots, and so forth. Students were not simply taught mathematics as they advanced through their lessons. As in science class, they encountered a particular way of thinking about society and its relationship to their studies. Problems in arithmetic and higher mathematics analyzed stocks and bonds, business transactions, foreign exchange, compound interest, and the calculation of wages for a sometimes undependable work force. If they learned their lessons well, pupils entered high school recognizing the intimacies of calculations, commerce, and capitalism.[39]

Most algebra texts progressed from a discussion of rules and definitions through theorems and factoring, algebraic fractions, simple equations, the formation of powers, and quadratic equations to logarithms and more. Authors quarreled over many fine points, but story problems in texts before the 1880s revealed similar social and economic values. Algebra books offered countless exercises about commerce and capitalism, continuing on a higher level the lessons from the lower grades. A problem on simple equations readily became a moral lesson about political economy.[40]

Ebenezer Bailey published one of the earliest algebra textbooks in the early 1830s. The principal of the Young Ladies' High School, a private academy in

Boston, Bailey helped set the standard for how to teach advanced pupils the practical applications of algebra. Bailey and countless successors framed their story problems cognizant that theirs was a class-riddled society. An early chapter on fractions in Bailey's *First Lessons in Algebra* described a citizen giving money to beggars, no doubt a common sight in the Bay City. Problems on "Equations of the First Degree" depicted other kindly men of substance, charitably though discreetly aiding the poor. Other typical problems concerned time, weights, distance, depths, costs, profits, and ages of people. Additional assignments portrayed a society splintered into competing segments. Just as scientists depicted a world in which a monarchical God reigned over republican subjects and men ruled everything else, authors of algebra texts described a stratified social system.[41]

When "gentlemen" appear in *First Lessons* in hypothetical situations requiring algebraic solutions, they are frequently benevolent: "A gentleman gave to two beggars 67 cents, giving to the second 13 cents less than to the first. How many cents did each receive?" When a "laborer" appeared, students were asked how to deduct wages if the person was shiftless. On the same page, students met a "gentleman" resolving everyday problems with his servants; on the next page, he visits "several poor families." The generous man who found 67 cents for two beggars to share—or perhaps another gentleman—later spent $126 for a horse and $4,350 for land for his new house.[42]

In his standard algebra text of 1845, Charles E. Davies caught the spirit of a song for little children called *Contraries:*

> One, two, three,
> Land is not sea,
> Rich is not poor
> Window's no door.[43]

Like other authors preparing hundreds of story problems, Davies thought in "contraries." In back-to-back problems on equations, he presented two tales: a carpenter who earned $1 per day, and a "capitalist" whose annual income was $2,940. The "problem" of the "idle" worker remained a staple in algebra books. Gentlemen seemed forever benevolent and industrious, leaving huge bequests, aiding beggars, making smart investments, or buying horses and carriages. Laborers, in contrast, lacked servants, fine goods, investments, or expensive carriages, perhaps because they were often idlers.[44]

Ray's Algebra offered a typical dilemma in 1848. The assignment was to solve a simple problem. "A laborer was engaged for 30 days. For each day that he worked, he received 25 cents and his boarding; and, for each day that he was idle, he paid 20 cents for his boarding. At the expiration of the time, he received 3 dollars; how many days did he work, and how many days was he idle?" Ray and other authors presented problems that involved young clerks who broke goods in the dry goods store or who quit their jobs and lost their wages. Pity the poor lad who broke 10 percent of the glass vessels he was asked to deliver, thus hurting his employer's profit and his own wallet. Being thoughtless and careless impoverished everyone.[45]

Horatio Nelson Robinson, whose algebra texts appeared in multiple editions, also demonstrated the different worlds inhabited by the rich and the poor. Throughout his 1860 edition, his gentlemen, like Ebenezer Bailey's, generously aided the poor, cared for their families, and purchased fine goods. The workers, too, were recognizable, still breaking goods, violating labor agreements, suffering from idleness, deserving their fate. What was one to think of poor people, met in a text printed during the depression of 1873, who were either so lazy or unintelligent or too proud to meet a generous benefactor at an appointed time for a handout?[46]

Algebra, geometry, and trigonometry grew in importance as citizens tamed the natural world and leaders tried to organize and control a more complicated and stratified economic system. Authors who promised a useful, nontheoretical education in the mathematical sciences realized that high school pupils above all other youth might one day play a special role in society. Alumni would make positive contributions as merchants, entrepreneurs, clerks, industrialists, teachers, commercial farmers, and otherwise respectable citizens. Intellectual and moral training was essential.

God and nation demanded hard work and productivity from everyone. This message informed science books as well as algebraic equations that linked learning and life. A student never met a merchant in a high school textbook who sold shoddy goods, or a usurious banker, or a lazy, greedy, or callous businessman. Although man was lord over creation and lived in an unequal social state, some individuals wasted their time and squandered their opportunities. They ended up poor.

In addition to science and the higher mathematical studies, English, history, geography, and modern foreign languages became central to the higher learning. Just as political and economic values shaped the pedagogy of chemistry and algebra, the common textbooks in these branches also reflected familiar bourgeois ideals. A host of other subjects, often taught for only a single term, supplemented the academic diet of secondary students, including moral science, political economy, and more rarely "Evidences of Christianity."

The growth of English studies testified to the pervasive influence of nationalism upon education after the American Revolution. Benjamin Franklin's dream that modern subjects would supplant classical education in the higher schools materialized. After the 1780s, Noah Webster and other notables labored to unite the nation through a distinctive American language, shorn of regional dialects and slang. Diversity in language use never disappeared, but the growing importance of studying English grammar sounded the death knell to the once-esteemed place of classical education in the higher studies. Academies, district schools, and urban elementary schools promoted the cause of practical education, which high schools further cultivated through the study of English.[47]

English grammar was widely taught in high schools before the 1880s. Rival texts battled for control, but before the 1840s Lindley Murray's various texts overwhelmed all competitors—many of whom pirated his ideas. He ultimately sold approximately one million volumes. A merchant and loyalist, the American-born Murray fled to Britain after the Revolution but remained a potent intellectual and cultural force in the nation's schools. Like many contemporaries, Murray defined English grammar as "the art of speaking and writing the English language with propriety." He divided the subject into four parts: orthography, etymology, syntax, and prosody. Though the idea lost favor after midcentury, Murray and many contemporaries believed that good writing naturally followed the mastery of grammar and precluded preparing compositions at school. In teaching grammar, Murray promoted prevailing ideas about society and good taste.[48]

Murray attended Franklin's famed academy in Philadelphia, and the ghost of Poor Richard hovered over his prose. Murray taught grammar but much more. Like his competitors, he "borrowed" ideas from other authors and used pithy examples to instruct the uninformed. He lifted Franklin's homilies to demonstrate a compound sentence: "Life is short, and art is long." Franklin, who had himself cribbed the aphorism from the ancients, penned this sentence to promote an English education, so it did double duty. Agreement of articles could yield "A Christian, an Infidel . . ." Conjunctions were easy. "*As* virtue *advances so* vice *recedes*"; or "He is healthy *because* he *is* temperate." Teaching orthography provided a special opportunity: "A dutifull child." "A noizy school." "An importunate begger." "Prophane tales." "We must be studeous."[49]

In parsing exercises, the progression of sins followed the progressive difficulty of lessons: "Vice degrades us," to "DISSIMULATION in youth, is the forerunner of perfidy in old age." Lessons on "syntax" were also lessons in morality and political economy. "Idleness and ignorance is the parent of many vices." "Man's happiness or misery are, in a great measure, put into his own hands." There were idlers everywhere. Had Murray been reading algebra texts? The rules of punctuation involved more than mastering commas or periods: "Idleness is the great fomenter of all corruptions in the human heart." Correct the following: "By the unhappy Excesses of Irregular Pleasure in Youth how many amiable Dispositions are corrupted or destroyed How many rising Capacities and Powers are suppressed How many flattering Hopes of Parents and Friends are totally extinguished"[50]

In addition to teaching English grammar, high schools beginning in the 1820s assigned readers of uplifting prose and poetry. Students encountered an array of well-written essays and poems that extolled hard work, discipline, Christianity, and America. "Fly therefore from idleness, as the certain parent both of guilt and ruin," urged the *High School Book* in the 1830s. The Rev. J. L. Blake's popular *High School Reader* (1832) provided excerpts from John Milton, the Puritan poet, and Lyman Beecher, the evangelical Protestant. One poem was entitled "The Folly of Procrastination" by "Young," who rather sounded like Old Ben. Heed the "Importance of Industry" or suffer poverty, and remember that lazy people were "a herd of leeches." "Industry and Prayer" reminded the student that "Time well employed is Satan's deadliest foe: It leaves no opening for the lurking fiend."[51]

A new generation of grammar (and then composition) books after the 1850s softened but hardly eliminated such intense moralizing. George Howland's *A Practical Grammar of the English Language* (1867) warned pupils about vulgar and slovenly behavior, and John S. Hart's innovative *Manual of Composition and Rhetoric* (1870) praised Christianity, charity, hard work, discipline, frugality, honesty, and temperance.[52]

Mastering English enabled the most adept students to become lord and master over a useful body of knowledge. Moreover, grammar and language skills helped in other studies and provided a certain polish and style. Ending sentences with a preposition led to "the want of dignity," warned Professor Hart; using improper constructions showed "bad grace," and failing to alternate harsh and soft sounds in one's prose evoked "an impression of weakness and effeminacy." In addition, feeling comfortable with English gave scholars a certain edge in conversation, and handling words well could have lifelong benefits.[53]

High schools occasionally offered short courses in elocution, another useful skill for boys and for girls planning to become teachers. Rhetoric classes, too, helped students speak clearly, precisely, effectively, elegantly. Avoid slang and choose "*good society*," wrote one rhetorician, for "frequent association with intelligent and cultivated persons" helped nurture a fine vocabulary. "Low companionship, on the other hand, reveals itself in one's choice and use of words."[54]

Literature classes grew in popularity after the 1850s. Access to Shakespeare and Pope helped acquaint future opinion makers with the literary allusions that peppered both prose and oral discourse. Good literature countered the rising though vulgar fascination with novels, so often attacked from the public lectern and even banned from some school libraries. A contemporary nicely captured the challenge in teaching literature: "In such studies, more is caught than taught. The teacher must feel the beauties and communicate the feeling by looks and tones." More American literature appeared on the reading lists after midcentury, joining the familiar British and Western standards. By the 1850s, Sargent's *Standard Speaker* and Cleveland's *Compendium* helped introduce native writers from Edwards to Emerson to the rising generation. Still, the journey from Beowulf to Browning remained the preferred path to erudition.[55]

Grammar lessons, English readers, literature texts, and occasional classes in elocution and rhetoric all gave high school pupils the capacity to use language differently from less privileged citizens and to strengthen their intellectual development. Like English grammar, history and geography appeared in academies by the late eighteenth century and entered various public schools by the 1820s. These subjects also reflected the rising spirit of nationalism and tried to shape the minds and sentiments of youth. Once again, textbooks presented students with a particular understanding of human purpose and destiny.

"In the beginning God created the heavens and the earth," and despite the promise of eternal paradise, man and woman proved unworthy and were "condemned to a life of toil and to the forfeiture of immortality." Thus began a popular world history text, already in its eighth edition in 1849. The *Elements of Universal History* led students through the trials of Cain and Abel, the Flood, Babel, and other turning points in "sacred history." Like "the herb that flourishes best when most trod upon," Christianity spread despite persecution by the early Romans, as "the blood of martyrs" nourished true religion. The fall of Rome led to centuries of barbarism, though lights of hope flickered as the Crusades brought enlightenment to heathens and sinners. Thankfully, Catholicism later collapsed under the weight of its own evil practices, and the Reformation allowed Protestants to move humankind forward. America, peopled largely by the right sort of pious individuals, was a land of destiny, as the growth of its population and commerce signified.[56]

Various Western and world history texts provided similar interpretations. The Rev. J. L. Blake's *Historical Reader* (1837) started out with "The Creation" and "Paradise" while moving toward the sack of Rome and ending with an "Address to the Deity." Samuel G. Goodrich, the prolific author of children's books, also produced volumes on ancient and world history for older pupils. *Modern History, From the Fall of Rome, A.D. 476, to the Present Times* (1847) provided a popular interpretation of world events. Dividing the globe into several geographical regions, Goodrich made history an explicit moral lesson. Asia, he claimed, had not advanced in "the last thousand years." Only when Japan opened its doors to the West or Europeans seized control of India's commerce did progress visit these benighted nations. Arabia, commonly regarded as part of Asia, was the birthplace of Christianity, but Islam almost guaranteed its degeneration.[57]

According to Goodrich, "Mohammed displayed, from his infancy, a reflecting propensity and a fiery imagination. He was generous beyond his fortune, compassionate, susceptible of warm friendship, but abandoned to licentious pleasures." Africa teemed with uncivilized negroes that white missionaries somehow uplifted; the "dark" continent was lucky that outsiders developed and controlled its trade. Europeans, especially in the North and West, constituted the highest form of civilization, since they were largely industrious Protestants, who soon dominated world commerce. Happily for this morality play, Providence dictated that "Anglo-Saxons" settled America and soon spread across the continent. Clearly, "there is no other population on the globe, of equal extent, that enjoys liberty and the means of happiness in an equal degree." The only thorns in this garden of paradise, claimed another text, were the uneducated poor, Catholic immigrants, and the growing "prevalence of *mobs* in our country." Bibles and schools, however, would solve these social ills.[58]

"History," claimed William T. Harris in 1874, "is the revelation of what is potentially in each man." Since the 1820s, public schools had taught children and youth that America was Christian, republican, and the greatest nation on earth. To understand why required understanding the past. History textbooks proliferated. While authors disagreed about particular issues, most agreed upon some fundamental truths about America. Few writers doubted the claims in the *School History of the United States* (1838), which called America "one of the most important territories on the face of the globe, extensive, varied, rich, and salubrious." Had God not smiled upon this "American Israel?" Few writers questioned J. B. Shurtleff's statement in *The Governmental Instructor* (1846) that the "industry, intelligence, Christianity, and enterprise of the early settlers, laid the cornerstone of our present powerful Republic." These hardy pilgrims faced vicious heathens, harsh climates, evil kings, the treachery of Benedict Arnold, and triumphed only through extraordinary struggle and divine guidance.[59]

Other history books followed a familiar thematic format. They applauded the rise of Western exploration, the settling of the colonies, the movement toward independence, and the hallowed victory at Yorktown. Wars—with Indians as well as with the French, Spanish, and English—filled the pages of history readers. Following the Constitution's ratification, the heroic founding fathers united America through their wise leadership, and the eagle soared. No school leader blushed when a writer at midcentury praised history for its "utility," claiming that it revealed the hand of Providence.[60]

One widely adopted volume was Marcius Willson's *History of the United States* (1855). The author of several works, Willson presented familiar interpretations and concluded that the Bible, Western commerce, and republicanism were the wellsprings of modern civilization. The expansion of Western capital and trade in heathen lands around the globe showed God's wisdom. J. Dorman Steele, who popularized science as a school subject, also completed a popular history text in 1871 filled with the usual heroes and villains. Once pupils studied "the wonderful history of their native land, they [would] learn to prize their birthright more highly, and treasure it more carefully." Patriotism was not the last refuge of scoundrels but the aim of historical study.[61]

Nationalism also markedly shaped ideas about geography. The growth in maritime trade and colonial expansion stirred interest in this useful subject. Between the 1780s and 1820s, Jedediah Morse's highly nationalistic texts taught a generation of young people to appreciate the physical grandeur of an expanding republic. Commonly taught in the grammar grades and in high school, geography, like history, was more than an academic subject. It revealed the character of the nation and its place in the world order.

S. Augustus Mitchell, the leading geography textbook writer in the 1840s and 1850s, repeated many familiar patriotic and nationalistic themes, always glorifying America. Mitchell wrote geographies of ancient, world, and American history, reaching hundreds of thousands of readers. As he noted in *A General View of the World*, the "importance and utility of becoming acquainted with the geography of the various parts of the earth, but especially of our own country, must be sufficiently obvious to the understanding of every individual." Knowing geography was a matter of "practical necessity to almost every profession in a civilized community."[62]

Like many contemporary authors and scientists, Mitchell believed that God had established natural laws that, once understood, promoted Christianity. It was "a Christian duty for every rational being to study the order and economy of the visible world." Even though minutia filled the geography texts, most had a fairly clear thesis. Geographers believed that climate decisively influenced man's morals and lifestyles, appearance, and potential. Like many historians, Mitchell emphasized that Asia (Arabia, specifically) gave birth to Christianity; after that continent's decline, Europe became the center of civilization. While inhabiting only a small corner of the globe, Europe had the most "intelligent, enterprising, and industrious" peoples. Their ships controlled distant trading routes, whereas Asians lacked forks and spoons, Africans were ugly and barbarous, and Pacific islanders were far down the human scale.[63]

Numerous authors fought Mitchell in the marketplace, but Arnold Guyot was the standard bearer by the 1860s and 1870s. The Swiss-born writer claimed that geography heavily shaped customs, morals, and overall lifestyles, and he received widespread acclaim with the appearance of *The Earth and Man* in 1849. Guyot espoused what was later called the "white man's burden," urging Caucasians to uplift those living in the torrid or frigid zones. God had placed his best people in the temperate zones, and whites were "the most pure, the most perfect type of humanity." Living in moderate climates, they were industrious, ambitious, and hardworking, destined to civilize the world's backward peoples. Those who read Guyot's description of the "retreating forehead" of the Congo Negro must have indeed wondered about the relationship between geography and goodness, climate and civilization.[64]

High school juniors and seniors before the 1880s often studied a now-archaic-sounding subject called "political economy." In the broadest sense, the entire public school curriculum was an object lesson in this field. Algebra texts assumed the world had certain social relationships; chemistry books affirmed man's dominion over nature; and English classes linked language usage with cultural propriety. Moreover, history and geography books reinforced much of the worldview espoused elsewhere in the curriculum.

Every domain of learning offered intimate knowledge of God's universe. Following divine law led to academic achievement, productivity, and happiness. There were rules for proper sentence construction, formulas for chemical experiments and algebra problems, and ways to distinguish barbaric and civilized nations. All textbooks emphasized the need to learn about the "natural" order. The rise of commercial and industrial capitalism in the West created a chaotic social world, but the higher learning taught students that individuals who suffered or failed were largely responsible for their own fate.

Adam Smith was the modern pioneer of political economy, and nineteenth-century textbooks trumpeted the virtues of free-market capitalism. Francis

Wayland's books were ubiquitous in high school and college classrooms, enjoying wide popularity for many decades. Although popular writers on political economy disagreed violently about such issues as the tariff or the ideas of Malthus, all denounced those who questioned the moral foundations of capitalism. Formal courses in political economy, everyone agreed, taught the "science of wealth," including its nature and distribution. Authors discussed the power of supply and demand and usually supported limited government intervention in the economy. Like Smith, most authors favored some public taxation for education. Otherwise, as one author wrote in 1838, government should not interfere in the "natural order of things."[65]

Political economy textbooks often shared many assumptions about society, including basic values that permeated the entire high school curriculum. Political economists realized, as algebra books suggested, that beggars and poor people were common sights in the land. Although encountering the poor was often unpleasant, the malady was easily explained. A few people were by God's choosing incapacitated, unable to labor. For the able-bodied work was basic to survival and social mobility but usually distasteful, the penalty exacted for Adam's Fall.

Respectable citizens knew better than to give money indiscriminately to poor people. Private charity was noble but unwise if it removed the spur to labor. In *Elements of Political Economy* (1841), Wayland warned that a productive society required productive individuals. Simple laws guided a progressive society: "*Industry* and *Frugality. Virtue* and *Intelligence.* Possessed of these, no nation, with the ordinary blessing of God, can long be poor. Destitute of either of them, whatever be its natural advantages, no nation can ever long be rich."[66]

Laziness, immorality, drinking, bearing too many children: these were the major causes of poverty. To remove the incentive to labor from the strong but shiftless violated a cardinal rule of political economy. "If a man be indolent," wrote Wayland in his text on moral science in 1835, "the best discipline to which he can be subjected is to suffer the evils of penury." Idleness, not a lack of opportunity, destroyed many lives. Radical labor leaders who claimed that rich capitalists oppressed the poor failed to understand the laws of wealth, whereby self-interest always contributed to the common good.[67]

Labor and capital were allies, not enemies. In God's natural order, particularly in bountiful America, the social classes were interdependent and mutually beneficial. Self-interest was common to all God's children, the foundation of a just social order, wrote Francis Bowen in 1870 in *American Political Economy*. Like earlier writers, Bowen argued that the concentration of wealth in the hands of the few enabled the many to benefit from the attendant division of labor. If all wealth were equalized, everyone would be equally destitute. "It is true that men are usually selfish in the pursuit of wealth; but it is a wise and benevolent arrangement of Providence, that even those who are thinking only of their own credit and advantage are led, unconsciously but surely, to benefit others." Adam and Eve's behavior showed that humans were self-centered, but God "turneth their selfishness to good." The invisible hand never rested.[68]

Like other political economists, Bowen believed that poor Americans regularly became wealthy by following the simple but effective laws of political economy: industry, hard work, and saving and investing surplus wealth. God made some men more industrious than others, some wiser than others. "It is the *fixedness*, and not the *inequality*, of fortunes which is to be dreaded; it is the retention of them in the same families throughout many generations, which chills exertion and unnerves the right arm of toil." Cast from paradise, man must labor or starve, though laziness now seemed hereditary, as the sins of the parents visited the young.[69]

Political economists had a clear sense of history. The collapse of feudalism, which had tied most people to a servile social position, and then of mercantilism, which had sanctioned government monopolies, allowed individual talent to reign freely. God blessed America with material abundance. If they worked and saved, today's poor became tomorrow's solid citizens. Knowledge grew more specialized in the nineteenth century, and assigned textbooks offered talented high school scholars a coherent way to understand the world around them. The advanced sciences, mathematics, English studies, history, geography, and other formal study in "political economy" constituted the curricular core of the best-developed town and city high schools. Wherever students tackled the higher branches, they encountered reading material compatible with the bourgeois political interests that founded and supported nineteenth-century high schools.

Students lucky enough to enter well-graded high schools faced three or four different courses per term, all dominated by textbooks. The mastery of books was central to going to high school. One expert on the "laws" of moral science in 1853 warned students that "sensuality, laziness, or a torpid indifference to consequences" often led individuals to become "stupid or doltish." Students who failed to follow certain prescribed laws and learn their lessons well would "properly incur the name of a blockhead. Many a person, with native faculty for much influence and usefulness, allows himself to become a dunce in stupidity from his own sloth and vicious indolence." Immersion in textbooks could prevent this calamity.[70]

Textbooks thus served many crucial functions in the nineteenth century. They set common academic expectations for advanced pupils, who increasingly attended better-graded classrooms in the larger villages and urban areas. Even those pupils studying one or two higher branches in one-room country schools read the standard bearers. Textbooks thus helped create a common curriculum, ordering the course of studies in a familiar way while teaching the rising generation a coherent approach to political economy. Whether faced with the demands of algebra or chemistry, history or geography, or literature or moral science, scholars encountered new forms of specialized knowledge bound in an intellectual framework useful in bourgeois society.

Anyone who attended high school before the 1880s long remembered that some famous authors and their textbooks defined the curriculum. Ray, Wayland, and Steele were as familiar to secondary pupils as McGuffey was to the multitude. Studying remained a solitary activity, which heightened the importance of common reading materials. But students did not train their minds and morals in isolation. They were part of a larger age of improvement, dedicated to preparing respectable citizens and future community leaders.

The creation of free secondary schools brought in its wake a new body of instructors: high school teachers. Although textbooks remained the scholar's constant companion, lay reformers, school officials, parents, and students understood that teachers above all shaped the academic and moral climate of the classroom. Without effective, distinctive teachers, schools could not systematically disseminate useful knowledge to the talented few.

The Business of Teaching

In the early morning of June 7, 1856, a pleasure packet departed from a Cincinnati wharf. Traveling down the Ohio River, it arrived an hour later at a "beautiful grove," where two hundred former pupils, teachers, and trustees of the "Old Central" school enjoyed a picnic and celebration. Everyone reminisced about the short-lived institution, which served as Cincinnati's public high school when it opened in the basement of the German Lutheran Church in 1847. A coeducational school, Old Central helped form the basis of two new high schools, Woodward and Hughes, in 1851, when the city combined its tax dollars with two private bequests. At the reunion, students reminisced of days gone by, and teachers were honored for their esteemed role in school and society.[1]

H. H. Barney, the principal teacher of Old Central, who had become Ohio's chief educational officer, addressed his audience at the appointed moment. Alumni, he said, had led exemplary lives, testifying to the usefulness of public high schools. As the summer sun continued its ascent, Professor Cyrus Knowlton, a former teacher at Central and now the principal at Hughes, also rose to speak. Tall oaks grow from small acorns, said Knowlton, invoking an educational chestnut to applaud the alumni. Knowlton fondly remembered teaching at Central. As in that more famous Eden, Barney had tilled the garden of learning but "could not prosper without a woman," so the memorable Miss Eliza Bush and other teachers had joined the staff. Beautiful new buildings such as Hughes and Woodward pleased the eye, but Knowlton paid homage to the founders of the school, who had made the real contribution to progress in the Queen City. "Like the coral workers of the mighty deep, in silence they built the massive substructure on which rests the whole framework of modern society."[2]

All the speakers highlighted the civic and domestic achievements of the alumni. Lawyers, businessmen, teachers, mechanics, mothers: they were a tribute to the higher learning and to republicanism. Before returning to their packet ship, the honored guests raised their voices and sang "Home, Sweet, Home." The day had been a toast to the virtues of Christianity, respectability, and bourgeois schooling. Old Central had nurtured careers or important new domestic roles for everyone associated with it. Cyrus Knowlton, for example, had even climbed the ranks to become a high school principal.[3]

Knowlton resigned in 1860 to practice law. A decade later he was dead but not forgotten. In 1870 the Hughes alumni published a book that included a eulogy on Knowlton by a former colleague. Born in 1822 in the Green Mountains of New England, Knowlton advanced quickly from teacher to principal. A Brown University graduate, where he learned perhaps too well Francis Wayland's strictures against idleness, he was the son of a cabinet maker, learned the trade himself, but aspired to teach. Married in 1848, he suffered from poor health. Faced with a growing family, he remained a compulsive worker after resigning as principal, perhaps hastening his death at age 48. Knowlton left behind a wife and children, some written reports from his tenure as principal, and some worldly goods. And colleagues and students remembered him in the alumni volume.[4]

Eulogies for noteworthy teachers and principals were common during these years. Urban schools were rapidly becoming impersonal bureaucracies, but the cult of the Christian teacher, middle-class gentleman, and saintly schoolmarm persisted. Bureaucracies paused to remember an exceptional few, both the living and the dead. After a quarter-century of service, the principal of Boston's English High School in 1867 was praised as "a ripe scholar and thorough Christian gentleman." Similarly, one of Hartford's best was described as "a lady of refined culture, and of a high toned, pure, and unselfish character."[5]

Like many male secondary teachers at midcentury, Knowlton was college educated and relatively well paid compared to other instructors. He also fit the stereotype of the Yankee schoolmaster. Demanding and aloof, he criticized Pestalozzi and other romantic educators, emphasizing the importance of medals and prizes to stimulate classroom competition. Like most schoolmen, Knowlton attacked as immoral the reading of novels, ever praising a solid English education for its practicality and intellectual rigor. He supported the still-controversial idea that girls and boys should recite in the same classroom, and he ignored those who called recitation a mortal pedagogical sin.[6]

Knowlton's eulogist aptly wrote that "education, in his theory, comprehended available knowledge, the widest culture, and the complete development of the best character." The heart of learning, however, was memorization, the letter-perfect recitation essential to educational growth. "Many of his pupils will remember, even gratefully, their mortification when a blundering recitation called forth the rebuke: 'Return to your seat, sir, and make yourself acquainted with this subject.' He regarded an exact statement, not only as the best evidence of a knowledge of the subject, but as the best means of incorporating it with the student's own thought." Blunt and direct, he was "an extreme advocate of the 'memoriter method' of recitation."[7]

In the classroom, Knowlton had a "controlling presence," his "countenance . . . stern." His "penetrating eye" terrified some students as he quietly praised some and dramatically corrected others. "If his rebuke was keen and incisive, his approval, though not demonstrative, was pervading and satisfying. It was sunshine in the landscape." "Was he sometimes cold or distant?" asked one of Knowlton's former colleagues. "He was absorbed and anxious, he had not time to cultivate many intimacies."[8]

In countless communities across the North at midcentury, the Cyrus Knowltons and Eliza Bushes of the world labored to develop the minds and morals of the next generation. They strove to identify and reward talent among the student body while simultaneously building suitable careers in the local high school.

Peeling back the layers of image and stereotype that blanket early high school teachers is complicated. Much more is known about teachers' careers than about their personal lives. They received substantial wages compared with elementary and grammar-level teachers, who taught larger classes and more pupils from less privileged backgrounds. Antebellum high school teachers were an elite corps within the common schools, and male instructors were often called "professor," befitting their lofty status.[9]

Some schoolmen worried about the widening gap separating elementary and secondary teachers. In 1853, when Hughes and Woodward High Schools were only two years old, Rufus King, the president of Cincinnati's board of trustees, already sensed a serious problem: the rise of the free secondary schools had left grammar and elementary level teachers feeling less valued. Teaching the masses was the highest moral and democratic duty, but also meant lower pay and status.[10]

Another local official soon complained that elementary teachers—overwhelmingly women—believed that a successful teaching career included promotion to a higher level. Superintendent Andrew J. Rickoff hoped to quell this promotion fever, which resulted from the establishment of favored, specialized positions within the system. Could female teachers have failed to notice that men advanced *their* careers, in Cincinnati and throughout the urban North, by distancing themselves from the youngest children? Knowlton advanced from teacher to principal, Barney moved from teacher to principal to state superintendent, and Rickoff had the highest pay in Cincinnati's schools and did not teach anyone. Becoming a high school teacher became a badge of honor with obvious material advantages.[11]

High school founders initially raided academies in their quest to assemble distinguished teaching staffs. In the 1820s, James G. Carter of Massachusetts bemoaned the collapse of the Latin grammar schools and, he thought, the consequent decline in the quality of public school teachers. The demand for knowledge had increased, he wrote in a national magazine in 1827, but teacher "qualifications" sank lower. An early advocate of state normal schools, Carter realized that academies would continue to prepare most teachers unless public high schools proliferated and destroyed the competition. Similarly, a speaker before the elite, New England-based American Institute of Instruction in 1832 encouraged high school teachers to seek the status of the best professionals.[12]

The pretensions of some secondary teachers angered and amused many contemporaries. Raising the status of some teachers over others improved the system's credibility but weakened morale. "The practice of calling the teachers of every little academy, seminary, or graded school 'professor,' is prejudicial to the highest interests of sound learning," wrote the editor of the *Ohio Educational Monthly* in 1862. "It makes unjust distinctions, and often subjects those who are innocent of any such pretensions, to very great annoyance." A student in the classical, college preparatory Hopkins Grammar School in New Haven, Connecticut, was unimpressed:

> H. G. S. is the happy possessor
> Of an ape they call a professor.
> The unhappy Junior on a flunk's very brink
> Is quickly gobbled in by Darwin's last link.
> Loved by none and hated by all.
> He bears the cognomen of Ely Hall.[13]

Whether missing links or Christian soldiers, professors proliferated, and the pay, status, and respect accorded them and especially principals in hamlets, towns, and cities testified to the growth of a hierarchical system.

Professionalism was not cheap. One observer doubted that high schools cost less to operate than the academies from which they had drawn many of their teachers. Savings on tuition would be offset by rising property taxes. "Teachers, such as they are connected with these public high schools, do not teach for *nothing!*" wrote the principal of the Classical and Mathematical Institute of Newburgh, New York, in 1848. "They cannot be had for a song! Their salaries, perhaps, excel the incomes they themselves received when independent teachers. The combined or concentrated system of public schools cannot be cheap."[14]

Among the best-educated people in any community, academy and then high school teachers enjoyed a high status that increased as elementary enrollments swelled in the nineteenth century. Career paths in public schools opened, for men and occasionally for women, without the hazards of the open market. Men played favored roles, as school trustees, superintendents, and high school teachers and principals. And the uneven quality and insecure status of many contemporary colleges and universities made high school posts relatively attractive.

When the English Classical School opened in 1821, Boston turned to George B. Emerson. The son of a physician, Emerson received a classical education at Harvard, ran an academy after graduation, and returned to his alma mater as a tutor. He turned down a Harvard professorship to accept the high school post. Two years later he resigned to open a girls' academy, a successful venture that lasted for thirty years. In the antebellum period, such fluid career moves—from a college, to a public high school, to a female academy—were not unusual for ambitious men, for the lines between institutions were still permeable.[15]

High school teachers and principals, well educated and usually native white Protestants, often shared the worldviews of Whigs and Republicans. They wanted free secondary schools to identify and reward talent, both for students competing for class honors and for teachers seeking advancement. Exceptionally fortunate teachers, especially men, might become principals, sometimes even superintendents. John D. Philbrick, a Dartmouth alumnus, ran a private academy in 1842, taught at the famed English High, and at age twenty-nine became master of the Quincy School, reportedly the nation's first fully graded grammar school. Then he presided over a state normal school, later became Connecticut's chief school officer, and returned as superintendent of the Boston system in 1856. Unlike academy teachers, who competed on the open market, such men were entrepreneurs within the emerging public system.[16]

Although secondary teachers, men or women, generally taught only for a few years, many individuals less famous than an Emerson or Philbrick had long educational careers. Networks also emerged between particular colleges and local high schools; meriting a job included attending the right college. Throughout the nineteenth century, Harvard educated most of the male masters, submasters, and tutors of Boston's Latin school, English High School, and the girls' secondary school. Yale educated many teachers for Connecticut's larger high schools, including prestigious Hartford High. Many eastern academy and college graduates moved westward, filling positions as teachers and principals until normal schools and state universities forged links with local secondary schools that, in turn, produced students for them.[17]

From the beginning, school promoters expected men to dominate high school instruction. In the 1820s and 1830s, officials tended to hire males as secondary principals or teachers first, adding younger female teachers later as lesser-paid assistants in mixed classes, in separate girls' departments, or in all-female schools. Although eventually the majority of secondary teachers were women, school reformers at first favored them for the lower grades and thought the higher learning should favor men. Most colleges excluded women before the 1860s, and educators wanted teachers with the best academic credentials for the higher branches. Women should primarily teach young children, said Horace Eaton, Vermont's superintendent of common schools in

1849, "while in the higher department, designed for the older and more advanced pupils, a male teacher would be required."[18]

Bourgeois writers throughout the century emphasized that a well-ordered home required separate spheres for men and women. This ideology encouraged distinctive hiring practices. With more opportunities elsewhere in the economy, male teachers in towns and cities increasingly abandoned the primary schools by droves, remaining in the system only if given a lucrative salary and other advantages.

The occasional demands by women for equal pay or opportunities made no impression on those who condemned high schools for being expensive and for advertising their wares as cleverly as the great Barnum. But by the 1820s and 1830s, even cranks realized that most high schools were modest institutions. "The progress of popular education, so-called, does not consist . . . in introducing *high* studies, and a great many of them, into a school having only one or two teachers, and thus make it *high*," noted one critic in the *American Journal of Education* in the 1860s. Like existing academies, the typical high school was only partially graded, enrolling one or two dozen pupils taught by a "principal" teacher and perhaps a lesser-paid assistant.[19]

Frederick A. Packard wondered how secondary teachers taught remedial elementary branches, "fifteen distinct sciences (some of them the most abstruse and difficult that can be named), and three languages besides, all for an average salary of $800." Could normal schools or colleges prepare such teachers adequately? As late as 1863, a teacher at Cleveland's Central High School "taught English Grammar one term, Physical Geography, Natural Philosophy, Chemistry, Geology, Astronomy, Household Science, and one class in Latin" while also providing all the scientific apparatus. The overwhelming majority of high schools had a small and unspecialized staff. Most children lived in rural communities and small towns, whose secondary teachers heard recitations in many different subjects. Few labored in high schools like those in John Philbrick's Boston or John Hart's Philadelphia.[20]

The tendency, however, was toward more specialized teaching and a more uniform curriculum. One former instructor recalled teaching eleven different subjects at the English high school in Providence, Rhode Island, but urban high school teachers gradually became experts in certain subjects. Many towns and cities after the Civil War adopted the "department" system, by which teachers specialized in particular areas. Cyrus Knowlton and his fellow secondary instructors in Cincinnati in the 1850s taught two or three different subjects; by the early 1870s they taught one or two. The principal of Hughes even asserted in 1873 that the teacher "must make himself master of his department. He who professes to do this in all, or even half our High School course, is either an imposter or an ignoramus."[21]

Major cities became the standard bearers for smaller communities. A town whose high school was a room in a union graded school in the 1840s might advertise elaborate courses of study—classes in the "Latin-Scientific," "English," and "Classical" streams. The realities were more modest. As late as 1880, Ohio—regarded as a boom state for the higher learning—had 257 school rooms designated exclusively for secondary instruction and only nine separate high school buildings.[22]

Once academies disappeared, public schools had a relatively closed market and advertised creatively. The Middletown, Connecticut, high school was nearly a quarter of a century old in 1865, led by a male principal with two female assistants. The school offered (at least on paper) three complete courses of study. M. B. Green of the Zumbrota, Minnesota, high school had only one assistant in 1875 but prepared students for college "in all studies except Greek."[23]

By the 1840s and 1850s, a distinct pattern of teacher appointments appeared in the North. In many villages, the high school principal did double duty as the superintendent. Almost always a man, the principal was the highest-paid school employee, responsible for teaching secondary subjects part-time and supervising the other teachers in the system. New Hampshire's state superintendent noted this trend in 1849 when he praised the Portsmouth and Manchester schools. These villages had consolidated contiguous districts and placed the older scholars in a single secondary class. "The infant and primary schools are taught by females, and the grammar and high schools are each under the supervision of a male principal, assisted by several females."[24]

In midwestern states in the 1840s and 1850s, the new union graded schools often had high school departments. A male principal teacher-superintendent usually headed the union schools and hired many women instructors. As a result women were soon in the majority among secondary teachers throughout the urban North. Definitions of what constituted a high school varied widely, but even imperfect statistics indicated women's importance. Ohio claimed fifty-seven "high schools" in 1855, with seventy-one male and sixty-three female teachers. By 1861, women held 42 percent of Hoosier high school teaching positions, and they were 60 percent of New Hampshire's secondary staff by the late 1870s. Like the lower grades, high schools depended upon women who received lower wages than men for comparable work.[25]

Most male teachers in any northern urban system after midcentury taught in the high school, but females were vital to its instructional mission. In 1858 St. Louis High had a male principal and one female and seven male assistants; in 1871 the male principal had seven female and five male assistants. A similar phenomenon prevailed in Cleveland's controversial Central High, like many urban coeducational secondary schools: by 1875 the male principal worked with four male and six female teachers. Three years later, of the 356 teachers in the entire system, only twenty-eight were men, eleven of them in the high school.[26]

In older eastern cities, which often had separate male and female high schools, officials translated the doctrine of different spheres into practice. In New York, only men taught at the all-male Free Academy, which became a college in 1866; a well-paid man headed the normal college and had only male "professors" but female "tutors." Men taught and administered at Philadelphia's Central High School, while the Girls' High and Normal School had a male principal and ten unmarried women teachers in 1862. In 1877 the sixteen teachers at Boston's English High and the thirteen Latin school instructors were men. Except for the male principal at the Girls' High and Normal School, all fifteen teachers there were women. A special committee in 1878 studied trends elsewhere, discovering that Boston's refusal to hire women to teach male secondary students was an anomaly outside the major eastern centers.[27]

What women lost in status and salary they sometimes gained in kind words when they parted this earth. When Miss Margaret G. Abbot, a young assistant at the High School for Girls in Portland, Maine, died in 1857 of a "violent fever," the male principal remembered her finest points: "There were combined in her character many excellences, both intellectual and moral." In 1862 the City of Brotherly Love mourned the untimely death of Miss Mary E. Tazewell, teacher of ancient history, geology, botany, and Latin at the female secondary school. "In her withdrawal," wrote the male principal, "the faculty lose the co-operation of her zealous labors, and the pupils part with one, whose earnest desire for their welfare was manifested on all occasions and whose high moral tone ever exerted upon them its exalted influence." Eulogies for male and female teachers emphasized Christian virtues and duty to school and pupils. Female teachers especially deserved their heavenly rewards, but the route to recognition was fatal.[28]

Female secondary teachers earned more than primary school instructors but always less than men working in the next classroom. However satisfying women found teaching, they made taxpayers even happier by keeping taxes low. Men often left teaching because of greater opportunities in an expanding economy. Women had fewer choices if they left the classroom. Salary differences separated male and female teachers throughout the century. In Chicago in 1856, the schools set the maximum salary at $1,000 for male teachers, $600 for females; a male principal could earn up to $1,500. The pattern was repeated in places large and small. In Madison, Wisconsin, the male principal-superintendent in 1858 earned $1,000, the male teacher $600, the "preceptress" $300. A decade later the male principal in Middletown, Connecticut, earned $1,500, the two female assistants $350 each. In the late 1870s, Bridgeport raised the male principal's salary to $1,800, his female assistants' to $700. Everywhere the title "professor" was through custom reserved for men.[29]

School officials said men commonly had more experience than women, more advanced education, and families to support. Male college graduates dominated the staffs of the older male high schools on the east coast, and trustees gloated about the talented men who competed for these positions. School officials at Philadelphia's Central High gave candidates a three-day examination and posted the names of the winners and losers. The annual reports of other prestigious high schools also reeked of self-importance, listing all the degrees held by their elite pedagogical corps.[30]

College degrees ensured advantages. In the 1870s the Easton, Pennsylvania, high school had three male teachers "of college culture, and two lady graduates of the high school." Male secondary teachers in Chicago in 1878 had only slightly more teaching experience than their female colleagues, but over 55 percent of them (and only 10 percent of the women) had attended college. Nearly half of the women, however, graduated from the city normal school, which replenished the supply when female teachers married, quit, or were fired.[31]

Some citizens argued that the elementary school teachers deserved more money since they taught more pupils. Charles S. Smart, Ohio's commissioner of education, argued in 1878 that high school instructors constituted a minority of the teaching force but consumed disproportionate funds. Of the 23,003 teachers statewide, apparently 711 taught high school, consuming over $436,000 of the total $5 million expended on salaries. Angered by the salaries paid to secondary school teachers, Smart nevertheless ignored the disparities *within* the high school.[32]

By 1880, women teachers had become crucial to the public high school. Large and smaller cities reported the following numbers of high school teachers: twenty women to sixteen men in Chicago, forty to thirty-five in Boston, twenty to eleven in San Francisco, fifteen each in St. Louis, fourteen each in Cincinnati, thirteen each in Cleveland. In cities with separate female high schools, women were concentrated there. Most high school teachers, of course, worked in small communities, where a male principal-teacher often labored with an assistant or two, usually a lesser-paid woman. Rock Island, Illinois, had one male teacher and three females; Logansport, Indiana, and Saginaw, Michigan, each had one male teacher and two female assistants, as did Steubenville, Ohio, and Chester, Pennsylvania. Women labored for less, but labor they did.[33]

Sometimes an enterprising, popular woman in a small community rose from the teaching ranks to become the high school principal. Sandusky, Ohio, gave Emily Patterson a principal's salary of $1,200 in 1876. A former teacher at the school, which previously had male principals, Patterson was assisted by Mary Lambe, who taught mathematics for $900, and Julia Mills, who taught Latin for $800. These three teachers probably taught more subjects than listed in the public record. Although their salaries certainly exceeded the $350 to $400 paid to most female elementary teachers, they earned less than some male grammar school principals. In an age that characterized girls and boys as different elements in God's plan, differences in salaries based on gender seemed normal. It reflected the natural order, just like the laws of science, political economy, history, geography, or other subjects taught at school.[34]

The Emily Pattersons and Mary Lambes were crucial to nineteenth century high schools. The famous educators who left the most written records and who appeared in published histories of local schools were mostly men. The most renowned educators, whether hoping to imitate Henry Barnard or Catharine Beecher, left the classroom speedily to become principals, superintendents, editors of professional journals, and authors of pedagogical primers. But men consistently landed the best-paying posts.[35]

Some male principals and superintendents became famous. Everyone in the leading educational circles equated Alexander D. Bache and John Hart with Philadelphia's Central High School, Horace Webster with New York's Free Academy, William Wells and George Howland with Chicago High, and George B. Emerson and his many esteemed successors with Boston's English High. By the 1840s, as enrollments increased and his institution attracted a steady flow of visitors, Hart sought more release time from teaching at Central High.[36]

Less prominent men admitted that administration was preferable to teaching. When A. P. Stone resigned as principal of the Portland, Maine, high school in 1874 to become a superintendent, he spoke for many, especially women, who could not talk so freely or advance so easily. Though Stone loved the classroom, "the business of continual teaching is very exhausting, and sooner or later literally grinds out the soul and body of those who follow it."[37]

In 1827 the editor of the *North American Review* avidly endorsed popular education but lamented the low quality of the teaching force. While "man" instinctively sought knowledge and improvement, "there is no business in the world so proverbially dull, there is none among us so reluctantly pursued, as the business of learning." In ensuing decades, educators spilled oceans of ink discussing teachers and their failings and how to stimulate student achievement. Contemporaries debated whether graded classrooms promoted more uniformly higher standards or simply more dull uniformity and whether competition raised overall academic excellence or only helped the few.[38]

A minority of educators complained that textbooks shackled the creativity of teachers and students, promoting a pedagogical system that emphasized competition, memorization of facts, and classroom recitation. Thus a weary observer concluded in the *National Teachers Monthly* in 1875 that creative pedagogy was rare, for teachers could not be artists in "our system of cram." Decades of intermittent criticism against the dominance of textbooks and recitations had failed to change common patterns of instruction.[39]

Between the 1820s and 1880s, many educational theorists and practitioners grappled with the ancient problem of how to motivate students to study and whether *emulation*—the desire to excel, or to surpass others—promoted sound pedagogy. Samuel R. Hall warned in 1829 that emulation was a sign of vanity, ambition, and pride. In *Lectures on School-Keeping*, Hall pointed to its pernicious effects among adults in "the race of popularity, office-seeking management and maneuvers, and efforts to elevate one's self by the downfall of others." Was not individual advancement—the pursuit of self-interest—detrimental to republicanism? In 1833 a fellow New Englander noted that graded classrooms, among the most important educational innovations, raised anew questions about the benefits and drawbacks of competition. Understanding "the internal economy of education, or the *proper motives* for study and effort," dominated many educational discussions.[40]

Some private and public high schools in the 1820s used monitorial instruction. Seen as cheap and efficient, the system employed advanced student monitors who instructed groups of children, rewarding the most talented pupils with prizes and praise and humiliating less able students with psychological punishment and demerits. Inspired by Andrew Bell and perfected by Joseph Lancaster, it was common in urban charity schools for the poor in Britain and America in the early 1800s. New York's John Griscom adopted the plan for his private secondary school after seeing it practiced at the Edinburgh, Scotland, High School, a classical grammar school. Other private high schools in the Empire State adopted variants of the Lancasterian plan in the 1820s, though it remained largely associated with charity education, not middle-class schools offering advanced subjects.[41]

In the 1820s, the *American Journal of Education* favorably described the adoption of monitorial instruction in a few public secondary schools, including the Salem, Massachusetts, high school and the Girls' High School in Boston. It survived in the Middletown, Connecticut, high school as late as the 1840s, though its association with the poor and its presumed incompatibility with graded classes led to its demise elsewhere a decade earlier. Most urban high schools had formal classes or groups of students taught by a teacher, not student monitors.[42]

In *Reminiscences of an Old Teacher*, George B. Emerson remembered how he organized the classroom as head of the English Classical School. He grouped his all-male student body into classes on the basis of ability and proficiency demonstrated through recitations, and he gave the strongest students more homework and additional subjects. "I required all to commit to memory, and recite every Saturday, lines from the best English poets," he added, and he spent more time hearing recitations than teaching.[43]

Complaints about emulation were sufficiently loud to cause the Whig *North American Review* to rise to its defense in 1836. It claimed that emulation was basic to political economy in school and society. The "irksome discipline of the recitation-room" built character, essential to adult success. Sound political economy included free competition, the recognition of talent, and respect for the invisible hand. Though pupils who sought honors appeared selfish, private gain inevitably led to the public good. Indeed, "God's present moral government" emphasized the importance of rewarding each individual who practiced "industry and frugality."[44]

Most school officials believed that classroom competition was conducted fairly. The high school flattened social distinctions, wrote Birdsey G. Northrup, secretary of Connecticut's State Board of Education in 1868: "Money and station no where count less than in the recitation-room." But certain theorists and some practitioners condemned the competitive system, sympathizing with the losers. Over a half-century after the event, George B. Emerson painfully recalled the evils of awarding competitive prizes at English High. Like many critics of emulation, Emerson wanted students to work hard and to seek self-improvement, not mastery over others. Following established policy, however, he honored the most talented scholars with medals.[45]

In old age Emerson still remembered one scholar who did not receive a coveted prize: "He never looked kindly upon me from that hour; and whenever, for years after, I met him on the street, he looked away, with a cloud on his face. If I had had one medal more, I would have given it to him. But there were only six to give. I ought to have gone to the [school] committee and insisted upon having another to bestow; but I did not. The poor boy, afterward a somewhat distinguished man, never forgave me,—and I never forgave myself; and I never look back upon the whole matter, I never think of him, but with pain."[46] Although some teachers and principals complained about the worst effects of competition, the majority followed the rules, awarding grades, merits and demerits, and prizes. Only a few high schools—mostly all-female schools on the East Coast—avoided the practice, claiming that emulation harmed women.[47]

Despite periodic criticisms and lamentations, classroom recitations remained basic to public education throughout the century. Most school children attended rural, ungraded one- or two-room buildings, where they progressed through textbooks rather than classes or formal courses of study. Schools had some common activities, including prayers and devotional activities, singing, and spelling bees. Pupils mostly advanced, however, at their own pace, reading and memorizing material from textbooks for recitations. In ungraded settings, older students who studied the higher branches perforce relied heavily upon textbooks.[48]

In larger town and city high schools, students by the 1850s reportedly spent about half of their day in study, half in recitation, sometimes in separate rooms. According to various commentators, students made anywhere from three to seven daily recitations. A male scholar at Pittsburgh's Central High in the late 1860s recalled a daily regimen of morning and evening chapel, one study hour, and four recitations. Age-graded classrooms did not destroy the idea that memorizing knowledge was the hallmark of education.[49]

To the dismay of some educators, didactic teaching methods remained entrenched, whether in academies or public high schools. "Our high schools do not infuse into the mind a love for learning," wrote one observer in the *Ohio Educational Monthly* in 1868. "They simply grind the ax, without producing that breadth of culture which enables men to solve great problems." A high school principal in San Francisco said that teachers were demoralized. "Teachers are ordered to give certain intellectual doses at certain times, in certain ways and in certain quantities alike to all pupils and repeat the dose at stated intervals." Cramming was confused with education, said one educator from Maine in 1880, and the knowledge so gained soon forgotten, vanishing "like Hamlet's ghosts at the approach of dawn."[50]

Unlike rural youth, students in towns and cities memorized and recited in classrooms that were more strictly age-graded. Written assignments became more common, and the appearance of various materials other than textbooks further diversified instruction. But recitation in its many guises remained central to classroom practice.

"Theories of education are plenty," wrote the Rev. Baynard R. Hall, an academy principal in New York State, in 1848. "Every place, noted or obscure, abounds with lecturers on the art of teaching. Sometimes the creatures come in swarms, like the plagues of Egypt." New theories rarely changed old practices. "Some—*many*—do, indeed teach by line and rule, even as a street organist plays music by a crank: the latter reproduces the same tunes, with endless reiteration, till the mechanism wears out; the former do with one mind what is done with another, and by applying the same instruments, and in the same manner! or, they administer books and lessons as quacks do their pills, potions, and panaceas; they are equally pretenders."[51]

Instructional primers frequently condemned this monkey-grinding pedagogy, but their effect on classroom procedures was usually negligible. David P. Page, former principal of the State Normal School in Albany, New York, offered a typical assessment in 1852 in *Theory and Practice of Teaching*. Teachers lectured too often, and too many otherwise passive students competed for grades and prizes. "This practice of lecturing children into imbecility is altogether too frequently practiced," he warned, but his limp suggestion was "that intelligent teachers will pause and inquire before they pursue it further." Most methods books during the next thirty years repeated the advice, offering different ways to conduct a recitation but none to replace it.[52]

Why did individual recitations remain so prevalent? This was the traditional, time-tested way to evaluate students. Recitations—of complicated grammar, vocabulary, and selected prose—had predominated in the Latin grammar school. Private academies also emphasized recitations. Oral skills remained important in the nineteenth century, though urban schools had more written examinations after the 1840s. Leading citizens, too, emphasized that individuals determined their own fate, and the dominant contemporary theory of learning, faculty psychology, assumed that memorizing and reciting difficult material strengthened the mind and demonstrated intellectual progress. What mattered was contained in textbooks, stored in one's mind, and recited to teachers. Little wonder, then, that one pedagogical primer called recitation "the *summa summarium* of teaching."[53]

Primers on how to teach proliferated as academies, common schools, and high schools spread across the northern states. Nearly every primer condemned prizes, immoderate competition, and excessive memorization. David Page's popular primer said that emulation in school led to "*ambition*" later, "such as fired the breast of Napoleon, who sought a throne for himself, though he waded through the blood of millions to obtain it." Pupils lusted more for prizes than for learning, said many writers. "In studying his lesson he thinks of the *prize*. He studies that he may merely *recite* well; for it is a good recitation that wins the prize. He thinks not of duty, or of future usefulness; the *prize* outshines all other objects."[54]

Why study? There were, many writers agreed, good and bad motives. Page doubted that prizes motivated many students because only one or a few could win, and most pupils were realistic about their chances. One should study because it won the approbation of teachers, parents, and society (often in that order), because it was simply good to want to improve, because it was a pleasure to learn. The superintendent of the Danvers, Connecticut, schools, condemned prizes in 1853, agreed with Page's attacks on emulation, and said competition made youth "dishonorable and selfish." After listing the usual catalogue of sins associated with prizes, James P. Wickersham of Pennsylvania concluded that "The Prospect of Heavenly Reward" should ultimately stimulate student scholarship.[55]

Recitations, competition, and emulation nevertheless remained familiar school practices. Pestalozzi fired the imaginations of many educators and some textbook authors after the 1820s, but most teachers and principals endorsed or at least accepted the existing system. Although theorists from Catharine Beecher to Horace Mann attacked competition as insidious, practicing educators saw the world differently. In 1862 William H. Wells of Chicago wrote that a teacher should never make "the daily tasks of his pupil[s] as easy as possible." Theorists condemned prizes; nearly everywhere, however, high-achieving scholars carried away honors on graduation day.[56]

"Scarcely any subject has been more thoroughly discussed than the propriety of resorting to emulation as a school incentive," wrote one observer in 1877. After decades of debate, he said, educators still mostly concluded that children preferred play over study (as adults might favor idleness over work). Work was God's punishment, and study promised educational salvation. Teachers who allowed competition to deteriorate into classroom jealousies and mean-spirited rivalries should curb the worst features of the otherwise sound practice. In 1880 John Swett, principal of the Girls' High and Normal School in San Francisco, admitted that "prizes and gifts" were often abused as classroom "stimulants." Thus "the wise teacher will check the spirit of reckless ambition in the wild race for promotion."[57]

Whether they parsed sentences or studied algebra, chemistry, history, or geography, high school students faced a competitive system of winners and losers. "System, uniformity, discipline, are the great educational watchwords of the day," complained one critic in the *National Teachers' Monthly* in 1875, who believed the textbook-bound, recitation-oriented classroom resembled "Oriental despotism." The majority of educators and citizens, however, heartily disagreed with that conclusion.[58]

A more uniform curriculum, standard textbooks, and graded classrooms in urban areas decisively shaped teaching practices. Common textbooks enabled teachers to compare student performance, and uniform examinations allowed administrators to compare different schools. As in the elementary grades, textbooks helped determine not only *what* was taught but *how* it was taught. Despite recurrent criticisms of pedagogical methods, individual recitation and personal accountability for learning remained commonplace. Innovative pedagogy crept into all levels of contemporary schools, but familiar practices flourished. A glimpse at the pedagogical uses of textbooks in different subject areas and contemporary observations of high school classrooms show what the critics were up against.

Despite efforts within every discipline to loosen the pedagogical lockstep, textbooks codified acceptable knowledge and powerfully shaped instruction. A handful of authors, whether in mathematics or in geography, wanted to weaken the reigning system of pedagogy oriented around passive students whose education consisted of memorizing facts. Because the market for innovation seemed small, however, authors and publishers often imitated the leading texts, which reinforced the emphasis on memorization and recitation instead of possible alternatives.[59]

The English or modern branches remained quite conventional regarding pedagogy. Even the most beautifully written textbooks had hundreds of mind-numbing questions and answers: on the side of the page, on the bottom, embedded in the text, italicized, in bold face, or in small print. Textbooks, whether or not they were illustrated or had pleasant colored images, were ubiquitous in a system that prized conformity and what critics called dull and deadly teaching. Francis Parker, an especially prescient thinker, said in 1883 that the rising appeal of uniform written examinations helped turn teachers into automatons. Emerson E. White—who was no Francis Parker—agreed.[60]

The teaching of English grammar and literature remained a bastion of conservatism. Students memorized the rules of correct usage, vocabulary, and verbatim selections from textbooks, imitating traditional practices once found in the Latin grammar school. One alumnus of a major urban high school recalled that he never wrote a composition as a student, even in the 1870s. And scholars who prepared compositions often presented them aloud to reveal their oratorical as well as grammatical skills.[61]

Authors of grammar and literature textbooks quarreled over how much students should memorize and whether they should recite everything verbatim, but memory work remained powerful after midcentury. As late as the 1870s, literature textbooks emphasized mastering literary "gems" and favorite classics. Ephraim Hunt of the Boston female high school remarked in the *Literature of the English Language* that pupils should memorize particular selections, since they would thereby *"form habits* of expressing [their] own thoughts with greater force and elegance." Authors of rhetoric and composition texts still urged teachers to rely heavily on books and daily recitations. "Encourage the best students to recite verbatim what they can of the matter in fine type," wrote one author in 1878, "but require of the class only the substance, assigning lessons accordingly."[62]

History textbooks, whether covering the world, Western Europe, or America, promoted rote instruction and oral recitation. Because it encompassed all past human experience, history could be a demanding subject. History was full of facts, and students met them at every turn. Marcius Willson's often beautifully written, popular American history text was suffused with rote questions. J. Dorman Steele claimed in a successful American history text in 1871 that the subject was too often dull and boring when it should be inviting and exciting. Yet the publisher and Steele faced a real world with real class-rooms; the ubiquitous rote questions appeared in the back of the book, not at the bottom of the page.[63]

Throughout the century, authors promised the reader more than another catalogue of facts but then broke the promise. Even when authors attacked "the meaningless details of the majority of school histories" in a preface, students could expect reams of minutia. Advanced technology for printing textbooks buttressed orthodox teaching methods. By the 1840s, history books had so many items in boldface, capitals, and italics—the names of important people, lakes and rivers, and military battles—that knowing what to memorize was confusing.[64]

Though history teachers sometimes had maps and globes to supplement the written word, rote recitations abounded. A visitor to Boston's English High remarked in 1855 that "the boys seemed able to recite an unlimited amount of the text book, sometimes in the language of the compiler, and sometimes in their own." In 1863 this visitor was again impressed by how well scholars had mastered the written word. The teacher had them memorize the Constitution, "word for word . . . so thoroughly that were any boy, in reciting a section or article, to make a slight mistake, such as using the definite for the indefinite article, or the reverse, nearly every hand would go up in recognition of it."[65]

Geography instruction was similar. Like many kinds of textbooks before the 1820s, early geography books had a catechismal style of short questions and answers reminiscent of colonial primers. This particular didactic form disappeared, but the chapters of the new geographies still emphasized facts for the memory. Many geography books after the 1820s urged teachers to use maps in the classroom, and commercial houses also sold globes and atlases to accompany written material. This helped diversify instruction, yet teaching aids existed within the bounds of traditional pedagogical assumptions.[66]

The leading geography textbooks emphasized facts and offered countless rote questions and answers. S. Augustus Mitchell's popular texts in the 1840s and 1850s contained hundreds of engravings to help enliven the reading, along with innumerable questions and answers perfect for sing-song drill. Arnold Guyot, whose works superseded Mitchell's, genuflected before Pestalozzi. Critics nevertheless claimed that Guyot's books filled student minds with a surfeit of facts.[67]

Learning grammar meant memorizing elaborate rules of English usage, mastering history meant learning names and dates, and knowing geography meant first memorizing the zones, spheres, and races of man. *Cornell's High School Geography*, published in 1856 by Sarah S. Cornell, illustrated a common pattern. After the standard presentation of topics and definitions, students took a roller coaster ride to lands near and far. On one page the innocents had to locate fifty-one towns and cities on a map of Massachusetts. What the author thought important was often difficult to ascertain because a single page could contain twenty words in capital letters, fair game for recitation or written examinations.[68]

The teaching of mathematics, science, and modern foreign languages had similar characteristics. *Ray's Algebra*, like many imitators, had fifty-two rules and definitions in the space of five pages. Even authors who condemned memorization in their prefaces and called for new approaches to instruction urged students to memorize dozens of rules and definitions before they proceeded. Edward Olney's *Complete School Algebra* (1870) told teachers to ensure "that the RULES be committed to memory, *verbatim*; not, indeed, to be recited as a mere parrot-like performance, but as a means of acquiring the language of the science, and attaining facility in clothing its thoughts in a becoming garb."[69]

Whether students felt fully garbed or naked at recitation time, they encountered algebra textbooks with hundreds of written problems. These books often contained answers (usually without explanations) following the problems or at the back of the book or in special "keys" published expressly for teachers. Seen by many as perfect for strengthening the reasoning faculties, algebra and geometry were condemned by some critics in the 1870s and 1880s for promoting mental gymnastics.[70]

Algebra teachers were commonly accused of "hearing recitations" more than teaching the subject. A rare glimpse of classes in advanced arithmetic and algebra, at the English Classical School in 1823, provides an example of why pedagogical progressives denounced recitations and worried about emulation: "The boys of a class are arranged on their benches with their slates before them. The teacher proposes a question to the whole, and gives sufficient time to solve it. Some individuals are then called upon to give the several steps of the process, and the result. A mistake exposes a boy to lose his place, which is taken by the next one below who has performed the operation correctly. By this means an immense saving of time is made to the instructers [sic] and most of the pupils, and a competition excited which acts on all strongly and constantly."[71]

Although widely credited with strengthening the mind, the higher mathematical sciences were not always taught in exciting ways. After visiting mathematics classes at the Columbus, Ohio, high school in 1877, a school committee concluded: "We believe it is desirable to inspire more enthusiasm in these studies, undertaken as they often are with reluctance from their dryness and difficulty." And the "prevailing text-book in geometry," claimed one dissident, "with its superfluous and mischievous explanations and demonstrations, is the very center and strong-hold of the 'cram' method."[72]

Contemporary science instruction was oriented not toward experimentation but toward textbooks. Mastering astronomy meant memorizing stars and galaxies, chemistry was replete with definitions of elements and scientific equations, and natural philosophy and the other sciences emphasized mental training in practical topics. Science textbooks contained many facts for recitations and questions and answers galore. James M'Intire's popular *New Treatise on Astronomy* (1860) offered this observation on Oblique Ascension: "The Oblique Ascension of a heavenly body is that degree of the equinoctial which rises with the body in an oblique sphere, and is reckoned from the first point of Aries eastward round the globe." The question on the bottom of the page read: "What is the oblique ascension of a body, and from what point reckoned?" The vast majority of questions in every textbook in every field started with "what" rather than "why."[73]

If one could learn to write well by memorizing the rules of grammar, one could also master chemistry or other sciences by studying the subject without performing experiments. Before the Civil War, very few high schools had well-equipped chemistry laboratories. Such materials were costly, and few students in the 1860s and 1870s handled any chemicals or expensive equipment. Teachers usually performed classroom experiments while the student observed and took notes for recitations, examinations, or posterity. Critics noted that "three months of laboratory work will give more real insight into any science than a whole year's study of the printed page," but textbooks dominated before the 1880s.[74]

Elite institutions such as Philadelphia's Central High School owned some unusually expensive scientific equipment. Modest schools purchased a few inexpensive chemicals or rock collections to help enliven instruction. As in the teaching of many subjects, strengthening the memory seemed more important than understanding the subject. Miss S. C. Starrett, a high school teacher in Belfast, Maine, complained in 1880 that students needed "objects" to observe what they encountered in textbooks. Impatient for change, she was discouraged at the prospects: "Go through the schools of the State, gather up all the apparatus, all the illustrative objects anywhere and everywhere afforded, and how small the aggregate, how insignificant to the needs of our thousands of schools. And the more emphatic does the meanness of our collection become when we remember that but a fraction of it can be claimed by schools below the grade of the High."[75]

After the 1820s, the purchase of maps, globes, blackboards, slates, and then paper and pencils meant that textbooks did not stand alone in the classroom. Commercial houses later began selling relatively cheap scientific apparatus, adding to the diversity of many pupils' classroom experiences. Anatomy and physiology teachers in Cincinnati requested the purchase of diagrams and a mannequin in 1870 to replace "a skeleton, which has become somewhat injured by frequent transportation between the two high schools." Philadelphia's Central High School took "object" teaching seriously, possessing the "ear of a bird; ear of a fish; human tongue, greatly enlarged," and an interesting trio of "snail; leech; idiot's brain." Textbooks, however, remained dominant, defining acceptable knowledge and familiar patterns of instruction.[76]

Indeed, many teachers—much like Cyrus Knowlton—were remembered and often praised for their ability to conduct recitations. A Mrs. Reed, who taught German at Chicago High, impressed a visiting committee: "Her quick, nervous manner keeps them on the alert—very little time for brains to be addling during her recitations, and very little sympathy with the 'know, but can't remember' style of pupils." In a eulogy for Samuel Capron, a devout Christian at Hartford High School, a colleague remembered not an automaton but talented instructor: "In conducting a recitation as it is done in the High School, a teacher is obliged to carry on simultaneously a number of distinct trains of thought. Having put a question, he must attend to the answer, assign to it a mathematical value out of ten or twenty possible marks, correct errors, frame the next question, select the next scholar, all at once, keeping meanwhile a general grasp of the subject, and a general hold of the class, and a general eye to the lapse of time, besides minor matters."[77] As elsewhere, Hartford High appropriately had desks and chairs that rested "on iron supporters, firmly screwed to the floor."[78]

By the 1870s, teachers and students in the larger towns and cities in particular encountered a system of education that emphasized routine, predictability, and uniform methods of teaching and evaluation. Common textbooks even allowed some enterprising superintendents to administer examinations to determine the content of children's minds. Critics asked whether any test could measure what really mattered: pupils' development of a love of knowledge, their appreciation of beauty, justice, or moral values. But written examinations continued their ascent, shaping teaching practices. Francis W. Parker claimed in 1883 that written tests were "the greatest obstacle in the way of real teaching. . . . If I am not mistaken," he wrote, "the examinations usually given, simply test the pupil's power of memorizing disconnected facts."[79]

Written end-of-term examinations in urban areas helped determine student promotion, and Parker believed that the testing mania had destroyed any hope for innovative instruction. When he asked teachers why they resisted more diverse pedagogical practices, they replied that they were too busy cramming their students with facts for upcoming tests. "The demand fixed by examiners is for cram, and not for art," Parker emphasized, and the demand seemed inexhaustible.[80]

Throughout the nineteenth century, public schools increasingly prized uniform values and standardized measures of teaching and academic performance. Written examinations challenged the hegemony of oral recitations, as school superintendents in the larger towns and cities relied less on teachers' subjective opinions on student progress and more on common tests. Students who aspired to join the aristocracy of talent in the high school understood that tests and textbooks were their constant companions. This was readily apparent as grammar school graduates with high hopes prepared for their high school admission exam.

Scaling Olympus

"To be received, they must be at least twelve years of age; have a good moral character, certified in writing by the instructers [sic] of the schools which they last attended; and be well versed in Reading, Writing, English Grammar, Modern Geography, the Fundamental Rules of Arithmetic, both simple and compound, Reduction, and Vulgar and Decimal Fractions." So read the rules for admission to Boston's English Classical School in 1825. Beginning in the 1820s, Boston and other port cities based admission to their free high schools on entrance examinations; only the talented few were welcomed into the new cathedrals of learning. Reformers in sleepy villages and bustling cities alike wanted to make the public high school academically respectable and a tribute to republicanism. Admission examinations were the first major hurdle for prospective scholars and remained common in America's urban systems until the end of the century.[1]

Admission tests were a major innovation in the evolution of public school systems. They helped local officials centralize authority, construct a hierarchy of graded schools, and elevate the written word over oral communication. The final tallies enabled educators to inform taxpayers why some but not all children qualified for high school. When the Boston School Committee hired George B. Emerson to head the English Classical School, he was told to prepare a rigorous entrance examination, which among other things would raise academic standards in the grammar schools. Emerson dutifully failed 60 of

135 boys on the admission test. By mandating a tough examination in particular subjects, the school trustees sought sweeping changes in a single stroke: to prove that the public high school was not an inferior but a desirable institution, to create a healthy rivalry among grammar masters, and to build a better-sequenced, hierarchical course of study. This presaged similar thinking and educational practices elsewhere.[2]

Admission examinations epitomized Whig republicanism by emphasizing individual merit. In the language of the day, it was a sign of manliness and independence to face the rigors of competition—even though the majority of secondary pupils during the century were women. At a time when independence was increasingly illusory, when the percentage of unskilled workers rose and class divisions intensified, many opinion makers emphasized more strongly that each individual controlled his or her personal destiny. Impartial entrance tests, they said, allowed poor but talented scholars to enroll in superior schools.[3]

Young children routinely sang about the rules for success and read about the fairness of competition in their schoolbooks. The *School Harp* (1855) offered sweet music to the ears of educators if not to every pupil:

> Our studies may perplex us, be rather hard and dry
> But we can conquer them by magic words, *"I'll try."*
> And the mottoes always bear in mind, "where there's a will there's a way."
> And 'tis the constant drop that wears the hardest rock away.
> Our great men that govern the nation, or smaller stations fill,
> Once worked in school like us, to climb stern science['s] rugged hill,
> Their honors are free for competition, open to us all.
> We'll work for knowledge, for the people may give us a call.[4]

To climb the highest academic hill required perseverance, ambition, and classroom achievement. High school admission exams, among the first systematic attempts to measure academic progress, reflected a passion for certainty and order in an age of market uncertainties and occasional social crisis. This quest for some predictability in human affairs found expression in percentage points, scores, and other numerical signs. One-room schools, with their rule-of-thumb methods of appraising student performance, seemed antiquated in an age of machines and railroads. In school as in society, standard, uniform measures grew more popular.[5]

Contemporary school reports in towns and cities soon bulged with charts and numbers. Like bourgeois merchants checking their books, schoolmen tried to calculate human achievement. Attendance statistics and deportment averages documented punctuality and obedience to authority. Cumulative scores of each grammar school on admission tests, published in local newspapers, sorted out institutions for praise or censure. And individual pupils succeeded or failed.

The ascent of formal written examinations created an educational revolution, though school systems never attained machinelike efficiency. Reformers wanted standard ways to screen applications, but they also promised to identify the best schools, which presumably could transform weaker ones through competition. Tensions arose between competing neighborhoods and the central office, however, and the lower schools continued to differ enormously from each other. Urban schools never became as age-graded as reformers desired. Some citizens also defended the varied achievements of grammar school teachers and principals, who disliked being measured by their ability to prepare high school scholars. The grammar schools, noted one Bostonian in 1872, were really "the academies and colleges of the poor" because few students entered high school. Tests helped identify who merited admission, but critics feared for the reputations of schools and scholars who performed poorly.[6]

Even though some educators by the 1870s believed that the admission tests had become too easy, citizens still likened them to Olympic competition. Mary Bradford, who became a school superintendent, recalled her entrance examination in Kenosha, Wisconsin, in excruciating detail over a half-century later. On September 14, 1869, four boys and nine girls jumped the great hurdle. The minimum passing score was 70; young Mary received a "67¼." "I remember nothing about the examination but recall that I needed some consolation after the results were made known." The school committee met and decided to admit her anyway.[7]

Examiners could have a perverse sense of humor, as Chicago's prospective high school students learned in 1872. Nothing was especially unusual about the subjects in this particular competition: arithmetic, U.S. history, geography, English grammar, and spelling. But the students twice had to write the following passage, as a spelling exercise that they then rewrote to demonstrate their penmanship: "With throbbing hearts we await the result of this examination. We have thus far pursued our course of study with an earnest purpose to excel. If successful, we shall rejoice, and our friends will be made glad. If we fail, we will not suffer discouragement to weigh us down, but will rise to renewed effort. Whatever the issue of this trial, the close of the summer vacation shall find us better prepared than ever before for persistent labor, without which no great success will be achieved. Wearied by this long-continued examination, we cheerfully bid our examiners, Farewell!" In Chicago and other established systems by the 1870s, most candidates scaled Olympus. Whether or not they were amused by the dictation lesson, only 4 of 161 boys and 4 of 228 girls failed to gain an admission card. Some contemporaries grumbled that standards had plummeted.[8]

Oral recitations predominated in schools on all levels, but since the 1820s and 1830s, high school entrance tests had been largely written rather than oral, and so they remained throughout the century. In recognition of the importance of public speaking for men and face-to-face conversation for everyone, examiners occasionally dictated a part of the examination to appraise the ability of pupils to listen and to think under pressure. But the tests were primarily written, for administrators wanted impartial, impersonal assessments.[9]

Entry to the earliest classes of the English Classical School required competence in several grammar school subjects. By the 1840s this meant reading, writing, spelling, English grammar, and basic arithmetic. Numerous towns and cities soon added history and geography to the list, and algebra—a grammar-level subject in some places—occasionally joined the group. The same basic subjects appeared on admission exams in northern towns and cities and in the postbellum South, with the same relative emphasis on written performance. "A large number and variety of experiments have been tried by different boards of examiners," wrote William H. Wells of Chicago in 1862, "and they have almost invariably resulted in the decision that written examinations afford the most reliable test of qualifications, and are on the whole the most just and satisfactory to all parties."[10]

Not everyone could take the admission test. Educators carefully screened requests to take the examination. School boards and teachers of the higher branches wanted special scholars: morally upright, academically talented youth predisposed to submit to more rules and regulations. And, although some parents tried to rush their children through the system, schoolmen wanted pupils young enough to stay but old enough to behave responsibly.

Alexander D. Bache, principal of Philadelphia's esteemed high school, described the familiar admission requirements in 1839. "The requisites for admission might properly include, having attained twelve years of age, and a competent knowledge of reading, writing, especially orthographically, of the rudiments of grammar, and of arithmetic, to include the rules of proportion and of fractions." Prospective candidates also needed a written testimony on their moral character from the head teacher of their last school, whether a public grammar school or an academy. Down the coast in the slave South, the local Board of Supervisors admitted morally upright lads to the High School of Charleston at the age of ten or even younger, provided that they could "spell correctly, read fluently, and [were] acquainted with the four fundamental rules of Arithmetic."[11]

If a grammar school principal believed that a pupil lacked "good moral character," the path to candidacy ended abruptly, though how often this occurred is not clear. Principals also assessed a scholar's academic record, commitment to study, punctuality, and deportment. Intellectual capacity mattered in nineteenth-century high schools, but concern for deportment and attendance showed broader concerns about scholars' moral faculties and character. The model citizens depicted by Whigs and Republicans in political economy textbooks and in advice books were the ideals, though some flesh-and-blood individuals disappointed their elders. Nothing angered educators more than unworthy pupils who gained admission to high school after concealing their moral flaws.[12]

The local grammar school curriculum largely defined the academic subjects

in the admission examination. Some towns emphasized specific textbooks. In
1853 students in Charlestown, Massachusetts, responded to questions drawn
from Willson's U.S. history and from arithmetic books by Colburn and
Greenleaf. The Keene, New Hampshire, high school required "a reasonably
thorough knowledge of Greenleaf's Practical Arithmetic, Quackenbos's Elementary Grammar, History of the United States, and Geography."[13]

Because reformers wanted to popularize the school system and to undermine academies, they often required candidates to attend public schools for a
minimum time period. Educators nevertheless trod lightly. It was impolitic to
lobby for more tax dollars but then exclude the children of important
ratepayers who patronized academies. Yet the schools also needed greater
commitment to the system from those who would benefit from the higher
branches. Because many reasonably affluent parents supported private
schools, local trustees usually set low residency requirements. Cleveland was
an exception, refusing to examine private school alumni in the late 1840s and
early 1850s. More typically, Philadelphia required prospective scholars in the
1840s to attend public schools for at least one year. New York City followed
suit in the 1850s, as did Chicago, Pittsburgh, and other communities.[14]

High school entrance tests thus addressed several concerns simultaneously.
Educators held the carrot of free, high-quality secondary instruction before
families currently supporting private schools. School administrators also used
tests to help centralize their power. They reduced the status of the grammar
grades, whose masters at the upper levels now directed some of their attention
to preparing high school pupils. And, whether they covered specific textbooks
or broader academic material, examinations forced prospective secondary students to master their grammar-level subjects. Local grammar masters or principals had to verify that candidates for the test were morally trustworthy, and
their own reputation increasingly rested on how their alumni fared in a higher
school.

School trustees prepared some of the earliest entrance tests. These community notables—ministers, businessmen, or professionals who were sometimes academy graduates—saw the high school as the pinnacle of academic
achievement and took pride in setting standards. Enthusiasm for this time-
consuming labor dissipated when disgruntled parents and students complained about the test results. Principals and teachers wrote and graded most
of the exams. Laymen on school committees established the minimum admission score but otherwise deferred to the educators. When Cincinnati created
a central school in the late 1840s, one trustee from each ward helped write the
test; as the numbers of applicants grew, administrators devised efficient, if not
universally popular, methods to test and evaluate prospective scholars.[15]

"How delicate and difficult a task it is to decide upon the merits of so many
pupils, in so many studies, and in so limited a time, and do justice to each one,"
wrote one examiner in Cincinnati's *School Friend* in 1850. Cincinnati's pupils
faced a three-day test covering seven subjects. A team of teachers needed an
entire week to evaluate the responses of the 102 candidates. "It is possible,"

commented an exhausted pedagogue, "that some have been admitted, who ought to have been rejected, and some rejected who ought to have been admitted. If such an unfortunate case has occurred, we trust that parents and teachers will not impute it to any improper motive, but rather to the circumstances of the examination, under which it would be strange if mortals should not make a mistake."[16]

Given the ordeal, educators soon shortened the test, and fewer trustees wanted direct involvement. In the mid-1850s five trustees supervised the labors of the staff of Hughes and Woodward High Schools. Here as elsewhere, the examination lasted for three hours. In some large cities by mid-century, secondary teachers graded only the responses in their academic specialties, making the evaluation process more specialized. To draw attention to their work, school officials sometimes appointed prestigious citizens to external examining boards that watched pupils sweat through their tests but let the teachers wade through the responses. As late as 1873, when nearly everyone taking Chicago's examination passed, the test was proctored by "committees composed of gentlemen of much learning and high standing in the community, as well as in literary circles."[17]

No one enjoyed telling pupils they had failed. In villages and towns, where everyone knew the local teachers, elected officials sometimes helped inform candidates of their fate. The High School Committee of Portsmouth, New Hampshire, noted in 1856 that it had recently raised the admission standard. Rejecting candidates was painful yet essential. "No part of the Committee's duty is more unpleasant, and in the discharge no part of that duty are they more likely to be visited with severer censure. It would be much easier and much more pleasant to gratify the candidates and their parents by admitting all who present themselves." But that would lead to "*high* schools only in name," so admission "must be guarded with vigilance."[18]

Teachers, principals, and elected officials cooperated to ensure honesty and fairness in test procedures. Until 1852, after the city hired a superintendent, Boston's still powerful grammar schoolmasters conducted the entrance examination. The test was mostly written, but the masters controlled the content. This was very unusual, an extreme example of local autonomy. Questions inevitably arose about whether different masters used different standards in grading examinations, which ultimately played into the hands of administrators and trustees who wanted to centralize admission procedures.[19]

By the 1840s and 1850s, elaborate rules emanated from the central offices of high school principals and urban superintendents, who thus consolidated their power and, they said, made examinations more objective, impersonal, and fair. Urban educators read each other's published writings and reports and heard the latest ideas at various professional meetings. Soon tests were common enough for examiners to learn from past mistakes.

John Hart, the principal of Philadelphia's Central High School between 1842 and 1859, was widely credited with perfecting the best method of examining high school pupils. Even before Hart became principal, test takers were identified by numbers rather than surnames to ensure anonymity and to help guarantee an "impartial examination." Hart and his staff prepared different sets of tests, and a student never sat near anyone with the same questions. In response to "idle charges and suspicions" that some students gained admission unfairly, Hart replied in 1846 that he supervised candidates carefully; they sat six feet apart. In addition, after the professors graded the tests, some were, most unusually, passed along to colleagues for an independent evaluation. Most of the examination was written, some of it was oral, all of it was tightly monitored.[20]

Tens of thousands of young people took high school admission examinations in the nineteenth century. When pupils failed the Olympic trial, some vilified teachers, principals, and elected officials. A few critics accused the authorities of fixing scores and of insulting worthy pupils. Most citizens, though, even those who opposed tax-supported high schools, regarded those who wrote and graded the tests as honest. Nasty allegations rarely produced evidence to the contrary.[21]

Citizens unhappy with the outcomes of the tests pushed for wider admission to the tax-supported institutions, prompting a few principals and teachers to resign. In 1856 the school committee of Nashville, Tennessee, approved an admission test of one hundred questions and required pupils to attain a minimum score to enroll in certain higher classes. According to J. F. Pearl, the local superintendent, some "indolent and vicious lads" caused a furor after they flunked the test. Pearl took comfort by remarking that the exclusion of the riffraff demonstrated the value of the test, which served as "an effectual barrier to undesirable pupils."[22]

Pearl's assessment was typical of educators before the 1870s: many pupils, especially those of questionable morals, would fail their admission exams. Those who failed presumably were lazy, tardy, stubborn, and thus deserved their fate. Schoolmen disliked intelligent youth of questionable morals, partly out of personal conviction and partly because the public schools desperately sought social respectability. To secure a status higher than rival academies meant that high schools could not open their doors to just anyone.

Promoting students from one grade to another was the most challenging task of educators, claimed a writer in the *Ohio Educational Monthly* in 1865. And young folks knew that passing an entrance exam meant mastering the grammar school curriculum, which was heavily shaped by textbooks. The vast majority of teachers, principals, and elected officials defended the tests as the only fair way to identify worthy and superior students.[23]

Because high schools built upon the work of the lower schools, entrance tests typically emphasized the factual information that pupils had diligently memorized. Francis Parker doubted that becoming educated meant memorizing reams of information, but most contemporaries assumed that the best-educated people were those who knew the most facts, and that understanding subject matter, critically or otherwise, first meant memorizing and mastering it. Some critics said too many teachers behaved like automatons, but school people dismissed this as the talk of dreamers and reckless theorists.[24]

By 1891, however, even the educator Emerson E. White had concluded that excessive testing had harmed public education. Increased reliance upon written examinations had encouraged "narrowed and grooved instruction," "mechanical and rote methods" of teaching, and "cramming and vicious habits of study. Teaching has thus been made the art of preparing wares for the examination market, and supervision the art of applying a lead pencil to examination products, just as the soundness of the earthenware is tested in the pottery by tapping." Insensitive administrators often published ranked lists of neighborhood schools, embarrassing those students who did poorly. Test scores for a small percentage of pupils had become a proxy for academic excellence.[25]

Throughout the century, critics argued that the admission examinations reflected the powerful grip of mechanical teaching in the lower schools. To most educators, however, the tests simply rewarded superior students. Mastering basic information was the essence of learning. Scholars who survived the Olympic trial would soon encounter more didactic pedagogy and more demanding texts, so tests suitably identified the most promising pupils. To call tests the building blocks of a system of cram was irresponsible. Knowing grammar subjects well was a prerequisite to passing an entrance test, and there was no substitute for rigorous study.[26]

Arithmetic questions covered basic material drilled into students in grammar school, and the subject was often reviewed in high school before scholars tackled algebra. Items on the Chicago test in the 1850s were typical: "What is the greatest Common Divisor of 125,350 and 365?" "Add ⅓ square foot and ⅓ foot square," "Give the table of square measure?" "Define the terms 'Promissory Note,' 'Bank Discount,' 'Present Worth,' 'Usury.'" Arithmetic textbooks used story problems with practical and commercial concerns: weights and measures, pounds, interest, conversion of American dollars into British currency, and so forth. Cities as disparate as St. Louis, Pittsburgh, and New York also included introductory algebra problems on the test in the 1850s, but algebra disappeared from the upper grammar grades once high schools stood upon firm ground.[27]

The arithmetic problems were usually short and uncomplicated and addressed basic rules and procedures. Antebellum officials reportedly weighted the arithmetic scores; some scrutinized them more closely than the other subjects. In 1873 the headmaster of the Dorchester, Massachusetts, high school recalled that in admission tests decades before "more importance was attached to arithmetic than to any other branch of instruction. The rank of mathematics in education was like that of charity among the moral virtues." Arithmetic questions often appeared first in the examination, though the practice was not universal.[28]

Arithmetic and the mathematical sciences were valued as inherently useful and in their highest manifestations abstruse, difficult, mysterious, and invaluable for mental discipline. Contemporaries believed that the mastery of arithmetic demonstrated sufficient mental capacity for success in other higher branches. Sometimes particular test problems could tax the most diligent pupils. Imagine the see-saw experience in St. Louis, where pupils in 1855 were asked to "Divide 9.9 by .0225" but also faced the juggernaut of a problem that appears at the head of this chapter.[29]

Arithmetic problems sometimes included local examples to give the tests a regional flavor. Atlanta's entrance examination in 1874 asked: "A cotton speculator sold a lot of cotton for 5 per cent. less than cost, losing thereby $237.50; what was the cost of the cotton?" Young Atlantans faced the usual questions about decimals, percentages, ratios, proportions, and bank discounts, but with a southern twist: "A merchant sent his agent to Richmond with $2375.50 to buy tobacco, after deducting his commission of 2⅛ per cent. What was the amount of his commission, and how many dollars worth of tobacco did he buy?" North or South, calculations and capitalism were best friends.[30]

Most tests covered five or six subjects, including English grammar and spelling. Educators regarded language skills as central to academic success, and tests covered familiar items from English grammar textbooks. Scholars parsed sentences, defined the parts of speech, differentiated regular and irregular verbs, compared adjectives, and occasionally analyzed short passages of prose and poetry. Like secondary English prose readers and composition books, examiners taught literary rules and social propriety. Parse the italicized words: "*He that* would be wise, *must apply* himself *closely*." Correct bad grammar: "I don't want no pencil." "I love no interests but that of truth and virtue." "Grammar learns us to speak proper." Cincinnati's youth in 1856 analyzed the following: "God made him what he is." "I have came home and wrote several times." Was Lindley Murray smiling with approval?[31]

Spelling—what the better educated called orthography—was a hardy perennial on admission tests. Words to spell had to be dictated, breaking the silence at many admission exams. Pupils might face unfamiliar words if high school openings were scarce. The boys of Cincinnati, who were outperformed by the girls, had trouble with certain choices in 1848; 61 percent could spell *refugee* and 56 percent *drawl*, but fewer than 4 percent got *thanatopsis, orgies,* or *ennui*. In Chicago's examination in 1868, pupils had to spell and define words such as *effluvia, inimical,* and *trisyllable* and some easier choices such as *digestion* and *melodies*. Pupils probably heard the word pronounced only once at the examination, so spelling correctly partly reflected good hearing and a clear-throated examiner.[32]

By the 1840s, history and geography were common subjects and thus fair game on entrance tests. Both fields—as taught and as tested—drew upon a deep reservoir of facts. Francis Parker wondered why educators emphasized the memorization of facts over understanding and analysis, particularly when studying history. In 1883 he noted that several years' memorization of historical facts would leave a student's comprehension "as a drop of water to an ocean." But most educators still stressed the mastery of basic knowledge, in history as in other subjects.[33]

To some pupils, history undoubtedly seemed like a bottomless pit of facts. Grammar-level textbooks presented pupils with a thesis about American democracy, destiny, and progress, but facts predominated. Examinations routinely emphasized rote skills. "Give an account of Massosoit." "Describe the settlement of Pennsylvania." "Name the different wars upon this continent previous to the Revolution, with date of commencement of each." Examiners asked who signed what document, when, in what city, in whose presence. They did not ask why the person signed it, its significance, or its import to understanding the past or informing the present. In 1858, Cincinnati's pupils confronted twenty history questions; only two of them referred to causation. High school students typically were asked, "Who discovered Florida, the Pacific Ocean, the Hudson River, the Mississippi, the St. Lawrence, Mexico, North America, South America, the Rio de la Plata?"[34]

Because written history emphasized wars and politics, military battles were ubiquitous test items. One group of students in 1870 had six minutes to respond to the following battery: "Mexican War—Cause, Close, and Leading Effects." "Siege of Vicksburg." "Battle of Gettysburg." That warmed the brain cells for the "Leading Events of Jackson's Administration," "Battle of Pittsburgh Landing," and "Causes of [American] Revolution." After facing a barrage of similar questions, Atlanta's scholars finished with "The principal wars with France—their causes and results."[35]

Parker correctly noted that geography examinations everywhere had similar pedagogical assumptions. Even the most progressive authors filled their textbooks with rote material. St. Louis's scholars might identify the Show-Me State's "principal vegetable products," or pupils in Charleston, Savannah, or Atlanta might recall facts about cotton. But pupils across the country studied definitions of zones, mountain chains, oceans, bays, rivers, streams, and peninsulas, memorized territorial boundaries, identified capitals, learned what rivers flowed in what direction, and tried to differentiate the "characteristics" of the races. Cincinnati's youth in 1859 had to remember "the bounds, divisions, climate, productions, religion, and seven principal cities of Italy," to name the longest rivers in Asia, Africa, and Europe, to list the world's ten highest volcanoes, and to identify the country with a town "whose latitude is about 34 degrees South, and longitude 19 degrees East."[36]

Pupils walked into an entrance test expecting complicated questions: which rivers did a person cross in traveling by train from Butte to Indianapolis en route to Fort Sumter, or what seas entered "the coast of Asia, in their order, commencing at Behring's [sic] strait." Chicago's candidates in 1870 were asked to name which state had the largest population, good harbors, salt deposits, cotton, wheat, copper, sugar, kinds of manufacture, and so forth—all in the space of a single question.[37]

Learning facts was a mainstay of education. The primary and grammar schools socialized pupils to use their minds in a certain way: to gather as many facts as possible and to strengthen the memory. When students entered the examination hall, they were told to "name" events and "describe" lakes and "correct" examples of false syntax. A few critics found this deplorable, but most educators believed time-honored practices produced the best minds.

Grammar-level pupils had read few schoolbooks that encouraged them to ask *why* something was true, had happened, or was noteworthy. The entrance examination provided continuity in the child's formal school experience by reinforcing what naysayers denounced as mechanical thinking. Pupils who entered the "people's college" represented an aristocracy of intellect, as contemporaries understood these words. The minds of the best scholars held the most knowledge of greatest worth.

Entrance examinations remained common until the late nineteenth century. Then graduation from grammar school became the main gateway to the higher branches, a natural development inasmuch as entrance tests drew heavily upon ever more standardized coursework. Through the 1880s, editors and concerned citizens continued to debate the effects of admission tests. For these exams did more than identify who should gain admission to high school. They were also expected to improve academic quality for those whose school days ended in grammar school and never even took the test.

In 1831, Samuel Adams Wells of Boston prepared an insightful report on the relationship between high school entrance examinations and the grading of classrooms. Wells emphasized that "classifying" pupils was a major challenge for urban educators. Notably, the English Classical School offered valuable and practical knowledge for non-college-bound boys, but it also stimulated competition and promoted a more uniform curriculum in the grades below. The new institution, Wells wrote, provided "an incentive to diligence" even for youth not destined for high school.[38]

For the remainder of the century, mainstream educators and lay reformers praised high school admission tests for their salutary influence. Common school reformers in the 1830s and 1840s already believed that these examinations had enormous potential. In 1839, Connecticut's Henry Barnard, the young commissioner of common schools, praised competitive tests as a healthy way to raise academic standards in the grammar schools. Moreover, these tests could help define and limit what was taught in these grades, thereby promoting a better-sequenced, graduated system of instruction. Barnard correctly noted that some upper-grammar-level pupils in various towns and cities pursued the higher branches—an admirable enterprise that, ironically, undermined efforts to build separate high schools.[39]

Early high school advocates everywhere praised admission tests for lifting standards overall and for offering new ways to evaluate pupils, teachers, and the lower schools. The president of Philadelphia's school trustees, Henry Leech, applauded the beneficial results as early as 1842: "Boys who are looking forward to obtain places in the High School, have a powerful incentive to exertion; and teachers whose labors are to be estimated by the qualifications of their pupils, are in like manner stimulated." District trustees now had "the best test of the condition of their schools, in the numbers which they can obtain for admission . . . at the High School." According to the constant refrain, admission tests measured individual merit, but the reputations of teachers and their schools were at stake as well.[40]

Examples abounded of the uncritical faith of schoolmen in the power of the test, which applied the reigning ideals of political economy to the emerging educational system. In the mid-1840s Cincinnati's Whigs labored to centralize and better coordinate the local public schools. In 1846 Joseph Ray, then president of the school trustees, called for the suppression of the higher branches in the upper grammar grades and the implementation of a "rigid" admission examination for advanced study. Ray explained that all of Cincinnati's district schools offered a basic English education. "Besides, in most of the Houses, the higher classes study a popular course of Natural Philosophy and Astronomy, and elementary courses of Algebra and Geometry." Ray and other reformers wanted to restrict these classes to a central institution.[41]

School reformers said tough admission requirements to high school had a "reflex" influence upon the lower grades. Such an "impartial examination" helped improve the entire system, wrote Hartford's Whigs in 1848. The dream of attending and excelling in high school would awaken the best within every child, claimed many northern educators, who pointed to such examples as the expensive new township high school of Princeton, Illinois, dedicated by older Whigs and younger Republicans in festive style in 1867. "Every other school within the six miles square has been helped by the higher school," claimed a female activist. "Every child attending one of these schools has been made ambitious by its influence. Even its high brick walls have been an inspiration to the boys who plow the fields and the girls who look through the kitchen window."[42]

The election of reformers to local school boards accelerated efforts to remove the higher branches from the upper grammar schools. School trustees approved the official course of study, enabling high schools to offer the advanced subjects exclusively, though seizing complete control took time. The high school was a centralized institution open to qualified students throughout a township, village, town, or city. But board members represented particular wards or districts, and elected officials fiercely defended neighborhood prerogatives. In many communities, some advanced studies lingered in the grammar schools, partly a sign of neighborhood resistance, and there algebra, for example, might remain on the entrance test. Indeed, Henry Barnard still listed algebra as a suitable examination subject in 1842.[43]

Removing the advanced studies from the lower grades was controversial. As the system evolved, the curricula became better coordinated, and the primary, grammar, and high school grades came to resemble a ladder of opportunity that narrowed at the top. But the elimination of advanced subjects below the high school meant lost opportunities for pupils unable to advance. Most high school pupils were from the middle and upper classes; thus, removing advanced subjects from grammar schools restricted chances for talented but less advantaged youth to taste the higher learning. Angry Democrats in particular saw the "reform" as discriminating against the poor.

Joseph Ray's Cincinnati illuminated this problem. The Queen City established a central school in 1848 and had two coeducational high schools by the early 1850s. Algebra was on the admission test in 1848, but it had disappeared as a grammar school subject by 1856. The reformers had triumphed. In the process, however, the number of pupils studying algebra in the city's schools declined. In 1854, 513 pupils studied algebra in the entire system; only 220 (43 percent) of them were in high school. Less than 2 percent of the pre-high school pupils took algebra, so the higher branches were hardly part of mass education. But two years later a student had to enter high school to pursue this advanced subject. Algebra disappeared from the examination. The two high schools gained control over the higher branches, and the number of youths studying algebra dropped: in 1870 only 387 pupils studied the subject.[44]

Jacksonian Democrats in the 1830s and 1840s who condemned the building of high schools sometimes argued that each district school should offer the advanced subjects. That seemed preferable to committing scarce resources to an expensive, centralized institution. Whigs and then Republicans disagreed, arguing that high schools should be distinctive and distinguished, with special teachers, equipment, and pupils.

Grammar-grade pupils who studied the higher branches represented a small percentage of enrollments, but enough to give some merit to the proposed Democratic policy. When Boston refused to open a girls' high school in the 1830s and 1840s, the School Committee allowed the female grammar schools to teach some advanced subjects. Indeed, high schools often became possible only when enough pupils in the highest grammar grades demonstrated their capacity for the higher learning. This was true in cities as diverse as Chicago and San Francisco, Cleveland and Dayton.[45]

Reformers soon discovered, moreover, that grammar teachers and masters resented the assumption that schools that produced few high school scholars were inferior. Was an effective school one whose students, even a select number, scored high on an admission test? Neighborhood-oriented educators in villages, towns, and cities struggled against the centralization of power. This defiance of authority, however, was largely limited to rear guard actions. When school boards published ranked lists of grammar school alumni in the local high school, the pressure to conform was huge. Teachers and pupils could not ignore progress.

Reconstructing how grammar school pupils prepared themselves for entrance examinations reveals how scholars and teachers adjusted to change. Admission tests emphasized short questions and answers, facts, and more facts; preparing for them was hard work, but it was simplified by the lower schools' emphasis on memorization and their assignment of textbooks with mostly question-and-answer formats. As some critics tirelessly argued, this structure diminished innovative pedagogical practices, including object teaching. But the tests reflected the realities of instructional practices in elementary and grammar schools, which valued particular forms of knowledge and ways of thinking.

Cultivating the memory was a widely shared goal of instruction, and it was indispensable to pass the entrance test. A former high school pupil in Boston in the 1830s remembered well how his class prepared for public display:

> Before a public examination, there was a general preparation and cramming for the occasion. A very few pages of the book we were to be examined in were marked off and regularly drilled into us day after day; and the boys were so often "taken up" at a particular place during the preparation, that no one could doubt an instant of the exact passage he would be called on to show off in before the "fathers of the town." I very well remember that one boy, having been drilled pretty thoroughly in the declining of "duo," was inadvertently called on to decline "tres," before the assembled wisdom. He faltered, looked toward the master at first completely dumbfounded; then in utter despair faltered out, "That's not my word, sir!"[46]

The boy regained his composure and recited admirably, but the incident highlighted a pitfall of preparing for admission tests.

Cramming became a high art form and part of capitalist enterprise. Entrepreneurial educators prepared formal study guides for entrance tests as well as for the Regents' examinations in New York. Wealthy parents purchased these volumes, which provided sing-song drills in the appropriate subjects. Moreover, well-informed, well-educated parents coached their children, for school boards frequently published the previous year's test to inform the public of what candidates might encounter. Everything conspired to encourage cramming.[47]

Examinations were commonly held in June, so each spring grammar teachers and masters spent considerable time drilling the students—even if only a few of the students ultimately stood for candidacy. The pressure to prepare for the entrance test was intense, a principal of a girls' grammar school in Philadelphia told a visiting educator in 1865. Indeed, the principal "frankly confessed that she was preparing her 'wares for the market'; whatever results the examinations for the high school demand, she must secure, as these constituted the entire measure of her success. We learned that the instruction of the grammar schools is not only narrowed to the limits of these examination tests, but that the highest classes are vigorously crammed for the ordeal—the classes being kept after school, drilled on Saturdays, etc."[48]

This emphasis was hardly unusual. In 1861 the principal of Philadelphia's Girls' High and Normal School said cramming was common and that many students wrote correct answers on information they memorized but did not understand. Superintendent John D. Philbrick of Boston later noted that some grammar masters coached pupils extensively, a practice exacerbated by the policy of printing ranked lists of schools from the most to the least successful.[49]

Despite recurrent criticisms, leading schoolmen since the 1820s had believed that written tests were fair, impersonal, and meritocratic. When Boston conducted citywide grammar school examinations in 1845, separate from the high school admission tests, a School Committee member enthusiastically explained the value of a common written test: "Firstly, because it gives facts, authentic facts, instead of uncertain, varying opinions; it gives facts which, when continued from year to year, become reliable statistics, by which the condition, improvement, or deterioration of our schools can be ascertained or shown." And, he added, the teacher was thereby placed directly "before the public" and held accountable.[50]

School administrators usually applauded efforts to make teachers and students compete for the admission prize, and some educators thought that only fools expected grammar schools to send equal numbers of pupils to high school. Sympathetic observers groped for euphemisms to explain why some schools sent so few pupils. Calling children poor pained the reformers, who were building expensive high schools instead of equalizing opportunities for the majority of children. John Hart of Philadelphia explained that a school "in the midst of a good population" would yield "a large number of aspirants for the high school." Applicants to the Girls' High and Normal School of Boston, said a school official in 1860, came from different neighborhoods; he advocated more nuanced readings of test scores, including considerations of the social "class" background of pupils and their "home advantages." A Chicagoan similarly told readers to interpret test scores carefully, given "the character of the pupils in different districts."[51]

Most grammar school teachers and principals followed their orders, cramming and stuffing as much knowledge as possible to prepare their wares for market. Some refused to send pupils who were likely to fail and depress the school average. Such manipulation forced the Cleveland school board in the early 1850s to require each grammar school to send a minimum number of candidates. In older urban systems along the East Coast, grammar masters fought the forces of centralization for decades, defending their honor and that of their school.[52]

Boston, though its system was hardly representative, illustrated the volatility that the rise of high schools introduced into relations between local grammar masters and the central office. Boston had created English grammar schools in 1789, and grammar masters were still fighting against the champions of high schools after the Civil War.

Boston's grammar masters and teachers enjoyed relatively high status in the antebellum period. The annual enrollment at English High did not reach 150 pupils until 1842 and did not exceed 200 until 1865. During these years school officials routinely called the grammar masters autocratic for deliberately holding students too long in their upper-division classes and restricting the numbers taking the admission test, which they administered until 1852. These masters were proud men whose independence and high status infuriated people, including their chief nemesis, Superintendent John D. Philbrick.[53]

The grammar masters continued to send relatively few students to the admission test in the 1860s and 1870s until the School Committee, egged on by the superintendent, slowly stripped away their power. In 1873 the grammar masters apparently tried a different tack to sabotage the testing, sending a large number of pupils to the admission test, even though few of them planned to attend high school. Those grading the exams had wasted their time. More than 200 pupils who passed the test failed to enroll, claimed Philbrick, who added that "this is owing, no doubt, to the growing custom, among the masters of the Grammar Schools, of advising their graduates to take the examination, even though they may not have decided to become High School pupils."[54]

But masters gradually lost influence, as did grammar school teachers and principals in many towns and cities, as the high school solidified its position. The battles were less dramatic in many newly settled communities than in older, established systems. Still, the battles in Boston graphically highlighted why a noisy minority of critics accused high schools of elitism and of elevating the status of the few above the many.

The machinations in Boston also showed that some students were learning how to manipulate the system for their own benefit. Those who took the entrance exam without any intention of enrolling in high school behaved rationally. They wasted many graders' time by qualifying for the entrance examination, passing the test, but then showing their admission ticket to a prospective employer. Such clever pupils took the schoolmen at their word, that passing the test demonstrated moral worth and intellectual competence. Increasing numbers of children, mostly boys, who passed the examination in many towns and cities never enrolled. The figure hit 25 percent in 1872 in Chicago, leading the superintendent to dryly remark: "Many have no design of pursuing the course when examined for admission." It ranked among the best student pranks, but as usual educators did not find it amusing.[55]

High schools wanted to enroll only the best pupils. They preferred model students likely to succeed and unlikely to embarrass themselves or the institution. Confident that grammar schools had improved significantly, a few educators by the 1870s believed that their alumni, if sufficiently mature, should enroll in high school without passing a test. Some towns and cities allowed grammar school graduates to do so, but examinations remained common.

In well-established systems, an extremely high percentage of pupils passed the tests by the 1860s and 1870s. Some educators interpreted this as a sign that more qualified candidates existed; others perceived a decline in academic quality. A vocal minority of educators fretted that too many unqualified pupils, albeit successful test takers, now entered high school.[56]

In 1883 a principal from New England remarked in *Education* that pupils commonly advanced from the primary to the grammar grades but rarely proceeded further. "Here there seems to be a way-station, a change of cars, quite often many travellers conclude to give up the journey at this point, while those that go on really consider that they are starting on a new journey." Individual grammar schools were diverse way stations, though, and a few of them supplied a disproportionate number of scholars. Schoolmen attacked the consistently low academic performance of certain schools, especially those not in the "best" neighborhoods with the "right" class of people. The burden was on the teacher and the pupil, not the administrator or elected official, to improve performance.[57]

In 1856 the *Acorn*, a student newspaper from Cleveland's West Side High School, boasted of the high entry standards of its school. But unreasonably high standards meant a very small school. When West Side's rival, Central High, had opened in 1848, school officials had filled the classroom by accepting every applicant. When the Middletown, Connecticut, high school opened its doors in 1840, educators rounded up as many suitable nine-year-olds as possible. "The question of the point at which the standard of admission to the High School should be fixed, involves many difficulties, and is one with regard to which your committee cannot profess to be wholly clear in their own minds," claimed the School Committee of Danvers, Massachusetts, three decades later. "We have followed thus far the general principle of keeping the school nearly filled, and thus of securing to its advantages for the largest number possible,—our aim being not to make the best possible school, but to make the school most useful to the children of the town."[58]

Those who built high schools or graded tests generally assumed that accepting all or most applicants indicated low standards. The men of Danvers wanted to fill their school; most educators spoke less openly even as they behaved similarly. The availability of seats varied and directly influenced the admission standard. Individual merit existed in this changing social context. School boards raised and lowered minimum admission scores; teachers and principals adjusted the difficulty of the tests and overall severity of their grading as conditions dictated. Principal Hart of Philadelphia's Central High said in the 1840s that test questions had become "unusually, perhaps unduly, difficult" to keep class numbers low. Finding the right balance—admitting enough strong students to preserve quality without offending too many of those whose children might lower the standard—was never easy.[59]

Educators everywhere worried about defining academic standards, wondering whether they rose or fell, whether tests reasonably predicted future scholarship, and whether pools of candidates varied as much as some teachers believed. Educators tried to create impartial and fair tests, but various social and political realities also shaped testing.

Most educators thought that admitting everyone was unhealthy, weakening competition in the lower grades and embarrassing the high school. Places like Danvers emphasized quantity while acknowledging the need for more quality. Principal George Howland noted in 1862 that because Chicago's high school was almost full, admission that year was unusually difficult. Similarly, when La Crosse, Wisconsin, and other towns built more spacious facilities, standards correspondingly changed. A pupil rejected out of hand one year was worthy the next year. Schoolmen in Petersburg, Virginia, admitted the best pupils available in 1869, knowing that high standards led to an empty building.[60]

In most towns and cities, school boards worked with principals to set the minimum admission score. These scores were raised and lowered according to the situation. The general trend in major cities was to increase the required minimum, but for a variety of reasons pupils still passed the test with increasing frequency. Chicago's candidates needed 53 percent on the test to enter in 1853 and 60 percent the next year. The figure then fluctuated to as high as 74 percent until it was set at 70 percent throughout the 1870s. The percentage of pupils who passed the test increased from 44 percent in 1856 to 56 percent in 1861, and then it continually rose, hitting 99 percent in 1874 and not dropping below 88 percent for the rest of the decade. In New York City the percentage of candidates who passed rose from 49 percent in 1849 to 91 percent at the end of the Civil War, when the Free Academy became a "college" with the same overall curriculum. The percentage admitted to Central High School of Philadelphia fluctuated during its early years but had a range of 70 to 95 percent between 1851 and 1867.[61]

The percentage of students admitted increased for several reasons, though some critics simply said standards had declined. Some communities deliberately admitted as many students as possible simply to help undermine the private sector and to popularize the public schools. More students were also better prepared to pass the examinations. Copies of past examinations circulated freely in published school reports, even as students and teachers were condemned for excessive cramming. More pupils got more correct answers as grammar schools met new expectations by teaching what was tested, and students probably became more accustomed to short-answer written examinations. Political pressures to admit more students also played some part, for complaints about rejections largely came from the very families needed in the system.

Educators realized that the percentage of candidates admitted to high school varied in different communities. Uniform standards were nonexistent. Some cities such as Philadelphia and Boston had a low percentage of pupils in high school compared with other places. But even in those communities educators who wanted more but better scholars feared that too many ill-prepared students entered high school. Superintendent Philbrick, in his war with the grammar masters, said that all youth of "fair capacity" should enroll; yet he complained in the early 1870s about student quality at English High. He noted in 1873 that admission standards fluctuated and that staff turnover produced changes in evaluation. Passing a written test did not guarantee that a pupil entered high school eager to study, listen, and learn. In 1872 the chairman of the School Committee called the Boston Latin schoolboys an unruly "mob," and another observer said that the student body came from "the refuse of other schools. . . . Side by side, boys well prepared, sat near those hardly prepared at all."[62]

A common complaint was that the tests had become too easy or were graded too leniently. Some worried educators blamed parents for pressuring elected officials to depress the standards, as indeed sometimes happened. The minimum standard to pass had often been raised, but school board members may have pressured principals and teachers to grade lightly as applications increased. The principal of St. Louis High, C. F. Childs, admitted that financial problems forced him to lower standards in 1865, but he assured the public that he excluded "the manifestly incompetent, or the incorrigibly lazy." Like other principals and teachers, Childs said some parents were blind to their children's failings and forced school officials to admit the ill-prepared and the immature.[63]

The situation in Cincinnati was typical of a growing city. In the 1840s Joseph Ray insisted on a demanding entrance test, which was reduced from three days to three hours. The minimum score increased from 60 to 70 percent in 1852, when two new high schools opened, and local leaders applauded their influence in elevating scholarship in the lower grades. By 1853, however, the serpent of mediocrity crept into the garden of learning. H. H. Barney, principal of Hughes High School, complained that too many pupils lacked the mental discipline or capacity to master advanced subjects. Such criticisms, rare in the 1850s and 1860s, became familiar in the 1870s.[64]

As high schools grew larger in places such as Cincinnati, some educators fondly remembered the intimacies of smaller schools and intensified their jeremiads accordingly. Hughes High School enrolled 452 pupils in 1876, and principal E. W. Coy wrote that the entering class had "a wide diversity of mental peculiarities": the "bright" and the "plodding," the "studious" and the "idle and indifferent." The ideology of early high schools assumed that quality and quantity were incompatible. Every village, town, and city after the 1820s periodically complained that the standards were too low or had once been high but had seriously declined.[65]

Where political pressures permitted many indifferent students to enroll, quality clearly had declined. But many high schools raised the minimum average for admission, and many more youth passed, having learned that studying, cramming, and coaching worked. School boards forced many principals and teachers to admit pupils who seemed unworthy to the pedagogues, and some educators doubted whether a test was a test if nearly everyone passed. Did Zanesville, Ohio, really have a "high" school in 1858, if the seventeen candidates who faced a combined total of 1,530 questions on the admission exam got only 17 wrong?[66]

Every high school in every decade had students with a range of mental capacities and levels of previous academic achievement. Schools praised their brilliant scholars one year and bemoaned the "clogs" the next. Parents in Portland, Maine, reportedly forced authorities to admit incompetent boys to the English high school in the 1840s. The Concord, New Hampshire, school board in 1857 said that one-third of the high school pupils should not have been admitted. Northerners and southerners alike complained in the 1870s that the unfit everywhere wasted the taxpayer's money and the teacher's time. Hartford's High School admitted 92 percent of its applicants in 1868; the School Visitors in 1875 said that "the examination exercises were not too difficult for the average applicant" and that a more difficult test would undermine the school's original goal of being widely accessible.[67]

Actually, even in 1849, the founders of Hartford High had worried about the "too slender qualifications" of its scholars. Like teachers and principals everywhere, they met students who discouraged them. In 1876 the School Visitors considered dropping the examination and enrolling anyone recommended by a district principal, which would "relieve the mortification and disappointment" of those who failed. But the Visitors, repeating time-tested arguments, ultimately concluded that eliminating the exam would "tend to lessen the ambition, weaken the spirit of emulation, and lower the standard of recitation." To promote nearly everyone to high school would "prove to be a process rather of levelling down, than one calculated to elevate the scholarship and enlarge the acquirements of the pupils, or to improve the public estimate of the school." Entrance tests were imperfect, allowing some unworthy pupils to matriculate. So the trustees accepted "the trite, but true maxim: 'Let well enough alone.'"[68]

High school entrance examinations did more than identify the brightest pupils, even though some with marginal talents still entered the "people's college." Admission tests revealed the kind of minds and intellect prized by public schools before the 1880s. The tests measured factual information, ignored analysis or interpretation, and demonstrated the prevalence of mechanical pedagogy. As high school enrollments increased and young people became adept at tests, people forgot that a range of talents had always existed in the high school and probably always would.[69]

Students could be wonderful scholars or clogs in the machine. Teachers applauded them as paragons of virtue or embarrassments to their old grammar schools. As they advanced to the higher studies, pupils faced more hurdles, more expectations, more decisions about their future. They had scaled Olympus, demonstrating in most instances their moral worth and mental capacity. When they returned to earth, though, it was time for prayers and books: it was time to go to school.

The Choicest Youth

Why cannot New England be dominated,
like Ireland or Spain, by a succession of
brilliant demagogues, each good for a revolution? Because New England, in a
larger degree than any other group of
States, has made that public provision for
the training of the superior middle class of
society, which is the keystone of the arch
in a republic.

—A. D. Mayo, *Talks With Teachers*, 1881

The rising popularity of writ-
ten examinations in academic subjects in the nineteenth century did not mean
a declining concern for the moral and spiritual development of youth. Admission tests covered secular material: the length of rivers, profits and losses, false
syntax, and the major battles of the American Revolution. Educators also
taught pupils that knowledge was inseparable from the higher intelligence
governing the universe and that intellectual and moral growth were inter-
twined. Miss Harriet Vail presented an "Original Hymn" at the dedication of
the new Cleveland High School in 1856 that simultaneously honored God
and praised human talent:

> Let solemn thanks to Heaven arise;
> Our College Dome salutes the skies!
> The country's hope, the choicest youth,
> Shall here be trained for right and truth![1]

School people throughout the nineteenth century wanted to enroll intelligent youth who were spiritually alive. Bible reading, prayers, and religious
hymns opened the school day, whether in academies or high schools. Young
people from God-fearing, Protestant homes found the transition to the moral
world of the high school relatively painless. Contemporaries still worried

about the materialism that saturated American culture, threatening moral development. Even the "choicest youth" who enrolled in high school needed protection from the worst aspects of popular culture and an innate tendency to stray from virtue.[2]

According to many educators, students entering secondary schools faced one of the most dangerous stages of life. Only moral education and diligent study could curb errant tendencies and teach social propriety. Indeed, debates raged after the 1820s about the character and thus the social backgrounds of high school students. Exactly who attended high school? Were students the pampered children of the rich, aristocratic and antirepublican, as some critics alleged? Were pupils often too young and immature to study the higher branches, as many teachers and principals contended?

Academy and high school scholars studied in an atmosphere of evangelical Protestantism. Congregational ministers had founded many of the earliest New England academies in the late eighteenth century, and recurrent waves of evangelical reform produced schools in many newly settled areas. The principals and teachers of academies often required students to attend daily chapel and Sunday worship. Public high schools also emphasized the written word and the higher power. Their principals and teachers, frequently academy alumni, equally valued well-stored minds and healthy souls.[3]

By the time scholars proved their moral worth, passed the entrance test, and entered high school, they well understood the intimate bonds between learning and religion. Readers, spellers, and other textbooks had nonsectarian but religious foundations. School songs before the 1880s socialized the young to love work and hate sloth and to condemn liquor and embrace the Lord. The *Common School Songster* (1843) included "Going to School," of "Teutonic" origins. "Going to School" led to happiness, said the song, and it meant more than studying books:

> Wisdom makes us love
> Him who reigns above,
> Leads to what is good:
> Angels love my ways,
> When I spend my days
> Rightly serving God.[4]

Classroom songs emphasized that "The Bible is [the] Word of God" and that only the virtuous entered "The Pearly Gates of Heaven." "There's Nothing True But Heaven," claimed *The Young Minstrel* (1843). Like textbook authors, the compilers of various "songsters" were native-born Protestants and often temperance reformers, proud of Pilgrims and Puritans and disdainful of Papists and Demon Rum. Songsters implored pupils to "Come Sign the Pledge" and to beware of "King Alcohol," which

> has many forms,
> By which he catches men;
> He is a beast of many horns,
> And ever thus has been.

Young Christian soldiers who sang "The Cold Water Song" seemed primed for chemistry and physiology texts, which attacked alcohol, tobacco, and illicit drugs.[5]

High schools throughout the land were steeped in the precepts of evangelical Protestantism. Bible readings, prayers, and religious songs filled the air. Pupils at the Louisville Female High school opened the day with a song from their own hymnal in the 1860s:

> Gracious God, our Heavenly father,
>   Meet and bless our school, we pray;
> As in humble trust we gather,
>   Teachers, scholars, here to-day,
> Every joy and every blessing
>   From thy bounteous hand we own;
> May thy love, our souls possessing,
>   Draw us nearer to thy throne.
> Weak, imperfect, tempted, erring
>   From thy precepts, Lord, we stray;
> Let thy spirit, from our wandering,
>   Bring us back to virtue's way.[6]

The familiar cadence of a Protestant hymn was unmistakable: one can almost hear the rise and fall of voices united in praise, the spirit wrestling with sin, hopeful of victory.

Writing in the *Indiana School Journal* in 1868, W. A. Bell, principal of the Indianapolis High School, described some common religious rituals. Bell opened his school precisely at 8:45 A.M., though pupils were not marked tardy until 9 o'clock. "The order during the intervening fifteen minutes," Bell noted, "is as perfect as at any other time, except that pupils may speak by *permission*. . . . At exactly nine o'clock the bell strikes, at which signal *all books*, except the singing books, are placed in the desks. When there is perfect silence I proceed to read the morning lesson"—usually some short verses from the King James Bible.[7]

Bell explained that he did not usually read "the historical parts of the Bible, but select such passages only as teach moral and religious truths." Like many public school educators, he opposed "sectarian" instruction. After Bible reading came a prayer of approximately three minutes, during which students rested their heads on their desks. Then came religious songs and special announcements, after which Bell sent tardy students home for written explanations. Finally, the principal instructed pupils to store their singing books and to retrieve their textbooks for their recitations, which began promptly after ten minutes of silent study.[8]

Students in other communities encountered a variety of religious practices. In addition to prayers and religious songs, a visitor to America's oldest high school in 1853 discovered pious Christians in the French class. The French master was quite animated, randomly calling upon students to translate passages from the New Testament. "The teacher was at times vociferous. When a pupil made a mistake he came down upon him like an earthquake, accompanying his sharp reproof with a strong slap of one hand upon the other." The teacher, who taught French and religion simultaneously, left a very positive impression. "If the Boston schools train the intellects of all their scholars in this way, it is nothing wonderful that the merchants of Boston are famed the world over for the vigor and dispatch with which they conduct their business."[9]

An English visitor to the nearby coeducational Salem high school in the 1860s offered additional insights on religious instruction. This school typically opened with singing, various psalm readings (apparently by the teacher), and the Lord's Prayer. Then "one of the boys 'declaims,' or one of the girls reads some piece, usually of poetry, and then the work of the day begins." High school pupils everywhere were taught piety and learning. Mary Bradford of Kenosha, Wisconsin, recalled that her former principal, H. O. Durkee, nicknamed "HOD," "always read a brief passage from the Bible and delivered a short extemporaneous prayer, to both of which pupils gave respectful attention."[10]

These familiar religious practices often embittered sectarian Protestants and many Catholic immigrants, sometimes leading to heated arguments and occasional violence. King James nevertheless remained omnipresent, and nondenominational Protestant values informed songs, texts, and various reading materials. When Alexander D. Bache helped reorganize Philadelphia's Central High School in 1839, he even advocated a course in "Evidences of Christianity," a subject already taught in a few seaboard cities. Pupils at Central High received "Bibles or testaments" which "they read in turn, each one a verse." Sectarian groups complained. Soon only the principal or classroom teachers started the day with a public reading of the Holy Word.[11]

Many high school teachers and principals were evangelical Protestants and Christian activists. Some educational leaders, such as John Hart of Philadelphia, were ordained ministers, ensuring that a religious tone pervaded their schools. "Education and religion are the great agents of mental and moral culture," claimed Hart's counterpart at the local Girls' High and Normal School in 1866. "When they are allowed to exert their proper influence, they banish vice, immorality, and crime from the community. They redeem man from ignorance, bigotry, false pride, and vain glory. They lift him up from the dust by an all-ruling Providence in companionship with the highest intelligence of the universe."[12]

Throughout the century, the "choicest youth" everywhere met teachers and principals concerned with their moral and religious development. George B.

Emerson, the first master of Boston's English High School, asked for God's blessing in morning school prayers in the 1820s. With others he believed that character development superseded academic goals. "I taught as well as I could," he reminisced years later, "but always considered this teaching of little consequence with that of the formation in my pupils of a single and noble character. . . . To be able to speak confidently to the effect of my teaching, I must be able to look into the hearts of my pupils." He liked what he saw: pupils who observed "order," developed "good habits," and showed him "affectionate confidence and respect."[13]

Who went to high school and how well they behaved remained controversial issues. The fate of free secondary schools was uncertain at times in many communities, so the character of pupils was a constant concern. Most educators in the nineteenth century assumed that character development, religiosity, and intellectual achievement were inseparable. Knowledge was always embedded in a moral framework. Explicit instruction in sectarian religion, however, was unusual, and high schools did not become vestibules of Protestant denominations. Classes in "Evidences of Christianity" were rare and in many respects superfluous. Many principals, teachers, and pupils were active Christians, textbooks and songsters were decidedly religious, and nondenominational Protestant prayers and activities remained common.

Broadly Protestant values gave comfort and direction to many families during decades of severe social change. Bourgeois families in particular knew that, more than ever, hard work, application, delayed gratification, and intellectual and moral growth were essential to survival and preferment in this new competitive order, where the individual was supposedly master of the future. By practicing proper behavior and studying useful knowledge, pupils could internalize proper values to help face a new and unsettling social order.

As one important Massachusetts reformer noted in 1859, contemporary society especially needed youth who exercised restraint and self-control. Evil lurked everywhere. Isolating youth in boarding schools shielded them from the evils of the street but also from the uplifting environment of good homes and local institutions. Did this prepare young people to confront and resist sin? "Virtue is not exclusion from the presence of vice," answered George Boutwell, "but it is resistance to vice in its presence." Moreover, "it is not the glory of Christ, or of Christianity, that its Divine Author was without temptation, but that, being tempted, he was without sin."[14]

Hence the middle classes especially needed to send their most talented youth to local public schools, where they would be exposed to temptation but ever shielded by teachers who taught propriety, responsibility, and order. Schools, Boutwell warned, could not make a perfect world from imperfect materials. But the high school above all taught the virtues of independence, struggle, and application. These were things the poor learned perforce but which more pampered youth did not. "We must look at facts as they are," Boutwell concluded. "Some people are poor; I am sorry for them. Some people are rich, and I congratulate them upon their good fortune. But it is not so much of a benefit, after all, as many think. It is worth something in this world, no doubt, to be rich; but what is the result of that condition upon the family first, the school afterwards, and society finally?"[15]

As Boutwell saw it, pupils growing up in reasonably prosperous families who could extend their schooling needed to learn how to compete and strive for improvement, central goals of the high school. In contrast, children of the poor, unlikely to be found in large numbers in secondary schools, already knew how to fight for existence as they and their parents struggled for their daily bread. Ironically, the "choicest youth" most needed public high schools.

Middle-class parents naturally felt anxious about the changes that transformed American culture. The decline of male apprenticeships in the North by the 1820s meant that wage labor grew more common, and markets produced more freedom and individual rights but also more temptation. New England farm boys without land to inherit headed west or for the cities, searching for opportunities and facing temptations all along the way. How to shield respectable youth from the disorder of the city and the lower classes in particular required new strategies of education and socialization.

Understanding who went to high school and why must be understood in this volatile context. Bourgeois men and women, who created countless voluntary associations to advance moral reform, worried about those youth moving to the cities, whether native born or foreign, and feared for the fate of the rising generation, whether boys or girls. Advice manuals for youth, usually written by Whigs or Republicans, proliferated. Growing up seemed increasingly difficult, even for relatively advantaged middle-class children, in need of discipline and self-control.[16]

Helping boys and girls find their way seemed arduous. After the War of 1812 the economy became more complicated, specialized, and nationally integrated through the spread of markets. As barter economies increasingly disappeared, control over one's destiny shifted to more impersonal, distant forces. Religious awakenings—demanding individual responsibility for correct behavior—occurred earliest in western New York, where the Erie Canal heralded a new world of internal improvements. As commercial capitalism spread, linking more tightly the countryside and cities, familiar social patterns and relationships unraveled.

Middle-class native families often responded by emphasizing the importance of personal salvation. They wanted youth to learn the tried and true: piety, individual responsibility, respect for authority, hard work, and the related virtues of Poor Richard. Sunday school and the weekday school provided useful knowledge and the moral ballast to sail safely through uncharted waters. Bourgeois parents believed pupils entering high school were awkwardly positioned: close to their childhood but approaching a dangerous stage of life in an increasingly competitive world.[17]

Advocates of the earliest high schools in the 1820s witnessed the erosion of an older economic order and wanted to provide boys in particular with sound moral values and intellectual training. Samuel Adams Wells of Boston, like subsequent reformers, was troubled by the loose fit between schools and life. He worried about boys who, by age twelve or thirteen, reached "that interesting and critical period" when "character" was shaped, for better or worse. Boston's English grammar schools, largely middle-class institutions, allowed boys to stay until they were fourteen, but Wells wanted the English Classical School to provide the higher branches to them at age twelve. Here as elsewhere, twelve became the minimum entrance age for high schools for many decades.[18]

The growing demand for institutional change soon gained momentum. Wells and other antebellum reformers advocated age-graded classes to improve academic instruction and social order. The bourgeoisie, whose family size shrank noticeably after the 1820s, were especially receptive to gaining more control over the stages of life. Traditionally, Americans had not dissected life into fine age-graded segments, believing instead that maturity came through broad stages. This attitude seemed antiquated and imprecise to those now infatuated with standardized measures.[19]

The majority of children nevertheless reached maturity surrounded by family, neighbors, friends, and classmates from a wide age range. Country schools continued to embrace children and youth of all ages. Faced with the quickening pace of change, urban reformers advocated a better-sequenced curriculum more tightly linked to precise ages and integrated into a hierarchical system. They were unable to build perfect age-graded systems before the 1880s, but written examinations, forced scholastic competitions between grammar schools, and the suppression of the higher branches in the grammar grades nudged urban schools in that direction.[20]

All of these changes resulted from the belief, growing by the 1820s in the advanced centers of economic change, that communities should provide particular opportunities for a small but important group of youth. A particularly troubling age was the period separating the years of about twelve to fourteen, the transition from childhood to youth, and about eighteen to twenty-one, the shift from youth to adulthood. And the rise of more distinctive social classes deepened public awareness of the effects of family background upon schoolgoing. By age twelve, working-class children usually worked to help their families survive. Educators encouraged all talented children to aspire to high school but knew that social realities made that prospect unlikely.

Many citizens regarded puberty as a dangerous period, made more so by the collapse of such traditional controls as male apprenticeships; this perception in turn stimulated concern for the health of the family, the question of coeducation or separate curricula for the sexes, and the growing northern bour-

OPPOSITE: Towns and cities along the eastern seaboard often maintained separate high schools for boys and girls by the middle of the nineteenth century. Here is a photograph of the students at the Boys' High School, Portland, Maine, ca. 1850. Collections of the Maine Historical Society.

geois preference for "home education" in local schools rather than in academies. The period between ages fourteen and twenty were "perilous," wrote a
contributor to the *New-England Journal of Education* in 1880. It was a
"bewitched period . . . when the boy is getting up his beard and the girl
emerges from pantalets into trails." This was the age when "the rampant
master" and "giddy miss" first envisioned their distinctive roles in family life
and society.[21]

In 1877 a contributor to *The Cyclopedia of Education* tried to explain how
modern educators defined age. "Childhood" embraced the period from birth
to seven and was characterized by dependency upon adults and the need to
master the primary subjects; "boyhood" and "girlhood" existed between seven
and fourteen and witnessed further mental and physical development,
including recognition of sexual differences; and "youth" was a period of
increased mental capacity and gradual sexual maturity, inclusive of ages fourteen through twenty-one. During youth young men and women became
"aware of their special duties of life and of the difference in the careers upon
which they are respectively to enter. The time of study is drawing to its close;
the entrance into active life is at hand."[22]

But as George Boutwell had noted, youth was experienced differently by
various social groups. Some youth were poor, learning independence through
experience; those more advantaged needed more schooling to learn how to
compete. Becoming an adult was not a uniformly experienced process.
"Among the lower classes of society," continued the author in *The Cyclopedia*,
"this transition" occurred by age fourteen or earlier, "and the only increase of
knowledge that is accessible to most persons of these classes must be derived
from evening schools, public lectures, and reading." In contrast, the talented
and lucky few studied the higher branches or otherwise prepared for a professional or mercantile career.[23]

Educators wanted to make the passage to adulthood more safe, secure, and
predictable through better-graded classes, a sequenced curriculum, and the
careful screening of high school applicants. Schoolmen shared middle-class
fears of moral degradation and contamination, hoping to teach pupils personal
responsibility and common Christian values. However much the parents of
high school pupils shared these aims, decades passed before even the best-
graded urban high schools successfully enrolled children of the same age in
the same class. For example, Anson Smyth, Ohio's state superintendent in
1858, said in the *Ohio Journal of Education* that too many so-called high schools
enrolled eleven-year-olds. Even though the average age of the pupils was fifteen, Smyth urged local districts to set the minimum admission at fourteen.[24]

Boston's officials early recognized that raising the minimum produced
better-prepared and more mature scholars. In 1826 the Rev. John Pierpont
and like-minded reformers established a High School for Girls. When it was
inundated with applicants, mostly bourgeois scholars from private schools,
officials raised the entrance age from eleven to fourteen. In contrast, the minimum age at the boys' high school was twelve. Mayor Josiah Quincy claimed

that the female secondary school would bankrupt the city because girls had fewer job prospects and thus formed a larger pool of prospective students. Some teaching of the higher branches was allowed at the female grammar schools, after the High School for Girls closed its doors in 1828.

By setting the entrance age higher for girls than for boys, Boston's officials had contained costs and restricted public provision for advanced female education. In most communities for decades to come, the majority of high school pupils were females. Communities usually had the same minimum admission age for both sexes, but girls continued to enroll at a slightly older age than boys. Curiously, few contemporaries discussed this phenomenon. Perhaps girls approaching their early teens had family responsibilities that slowed their progress to the higher grades. Perhaps principals promoted boys more quickly than girls, or girls lacked sufficient access to tutoring or special coaching for the entrance test. Although the age differences were slight—usually a year or so—enrolling older girls did save taxpayers money.[25]

By the 1850s and 1860s, the average age of pupils admitted to northern town and city high schools was about fourteen to fifteen for boys, slightly older for girls. As systems matured and the lower grades became more uniform, the average entrance age increased. In Cleveland, for example, the average age of admission in 1848 was thirteen. By 1872 it increased to more than fifteen, with a few scholars from twelve to twenty admitted. This was not an ungraded, country-style school, however: more than 70 percent of those admitted were ages fifteen to seventeen, the middle years of what contemporaries called youth.[26]

Other city systems followed a similar pattern. In Cincinnati in 1851, the boy's average was thirteen, the girl's fourteen; in 1877 the average was slightly over fifteen, lower for boys, higher for girls. At St. Louis High, opened in 1852, the number of twelve-year-olds was minimal, and the number of thirteen-year-olds admitted, 39 percent in 1860, was negligible a decade later. Chicago High School's average entrance age in 1859 was fifteen years, five months, holding fairly steady in the early 1870s, with the girls slightly older. Similar patterns existed in the older seaboard cities.[27]

Twelve- and thirteen-year-olds increasingly disappeared from high schools as the grammar schools came into line and graded classrooms became more common. In many systems before the 1880s, many more students who were fourteen and older remained in the lower grades than ever entered the high schools. In Cincinnati in 1854, only 7 percent of all thirteen-year-olds enrolled in the system, 16 percent of fourteen-year-olds, 47 percent of fifteen-year-olds, and 42 percent of sixteen-year-olds were in one of the two local high schools; the rest were in the lower grades. All the seventeen-, eighteen-, and nineteen-year-olds still in the system were, however, in high school, as these youths were kept out of the lower grades.[28]

In the larger northern towns and cities with reasonably developed school systems, most twelve-, thirteen-, and even fourteen-year-olds still pursuing their studies were in the lower grades. Educators disliked enrolling children rather than youth. Cities that had had high schools for two decades still complained in the 1870s about the immaturity of some "scholars" whose overzealous parents pushed them through school too quickly.[29]

Towns and cities gradually increased the minimum entrance age from twelve to thirteen and even fourteen after midcentury, typically when the grammar schools became more age-graded, when more youth applied, or when schoolmen simply refused admission to younger pupils. Despite all the complaints about the pupils, most were already older than the minimum because only precocious children could master all the information for the entrance test. By the 1850s and 1860s the majority of pupils admitted were fourteen or fifteen. Those who mastered enough material entered high school from a wide age range even in established northern systems in the 1870s, but "children" became more scarce, and "youth" between fourteen and sixteen predominated.

As schoolmen labored to make schools more hierarchical and age-graded and to make pupils morally upright and academically respectable, they faced a constant barrage of disparagement of their students by critics who were uninterested in the metaphysics of instruction or the appropriate age ranges in an ideal classroom. These citizens complained about the social backgrounds of high school pupils, who were characterized as haughty and aristocratic and enemies of true republicanism.

The Columbian Song Book in 1856 provided children and youth with a pleasant diversion from oral recitations and silent study. Compiled by a leading author of songsters, Asa Fitz of Boston, it included dozens of songs suitable for middle-class homes and respectable schools. One German song assailed "Procrastination." Another had the inviting title, "Begone, Dull Sloth." But the "Village School" best revealed the ethnic character of homogeneous districts still untouched by immigration, and it well represented the central characteristics of high schools.

> Harriet, Mary, Ann, Joanna
> Lizzy, Phebe, Georgianna,
> Mira, Sara, Caro, Hannah,
>   And Pamela are our names;
> We're a band of sisters;
>   And may we thus remain.
> Herbert, Joseph, Lucius, William
> Caleb, John, George, and Clinton,
> Benjamin, Foster, Charles, and Calvin,
>   And Nathaniel are our names;
> We're a band of brothers;
>   And in union may we live.[30]

These were the proverbial Anglo-Saxon, Christian, model names for the native born, whose values permeated nineteenth-century high schools. This hardly made the schools inviting to Pat O'Reilly or Rose Finnerty.

The majority of high school pupils before the 1880s were native born, and they read textbooks that taught familiar ethnic and social ideals. English textbooks were sprinkled with selective allusions. Students corrected misspelled words such as "plum puddin," "beefstake," "sholder of lamb," and "fillett of veel." Rhetoric and composition books applauded the European bourgeoisie, with their "chaste and refined" cultural tastes. Geography and world history textbooks openly applauded the "Anglo-Saxon" origins of America and the spread of Protestant Christianity to Africa, Asia, and other "uncivilized" continents. The Teutons were virtuous; other ethnic and racial groups were inferior. Chemistry and physiology textbooks championed the cold water army, insulting many workers, especially Irish Catholics.[31]

School periodicals, like mainstream men's and women's magazines, praised America's Anglo-Saxon heritage and the evolution of free high schools. Writing in *The Academy*, a journal devoted to secondary education, a professor of pedagogy at the University of Michigan praised the high school in 1887 for taking its place in the nation's social life. Like their counterparts in the English public school, the French lycée, or the German gymnasium, America's high school students epitomized dominant cultural values. "It is a fact of no slight significance that this institution responds to the intellectual needs and aspirations of three such races as the Anglo-Saxon, the Teutonic, and the Latin, the three dominant races of the world." The blood of the Caesars and Germanic warriors coursed through the veins of the best and brightest scholars.[32]

The middle and upper classes in America's towns and cities at mid-century were predominantly white Anglo-Saxon Protestants. Before the 1840s many eastern seaboard cities were still relatively homogeneous, and the defining social characteristic of the high school for many decades was its native bourgeois character. The surnames of the boys at Boston's English High School in 1825 reflected a British heritage: Hall, Thayer, Dean, Smith, Cutter, Quincy, Pierpont, Davenport, and Richardson. Their counterparts at the short-lived High School for Girls in 1826 included Allen and Barker, Cutler and Fairbank, Hale and Hall. As in Britain's public schools, Boston's head teachers were "masters," the assistants "ushers."[33]

Cleveland's student newspaper, *The School-Boy*, edited by nascent Whigs and Republicans, condemned street arabs, immigrants, and tipplers. In "Temperance," H. K. complained in 1849 that the city had "three hundred places where liquor is sold by the glass." Cleveland was becoming "a city of drunkards, and nothing else. Rum is used to feed the political steam engine. . . . If it were not for liquor, the Democratic party about here would not live a moment." The author further claimed that "two-thirds of these foreign voters, Irish and Dutch [that is, Germans], know nothing of the principles of [the] party, and the reason why a great many of them vote the Democratic ticket, is that on that day they can drink and get drunk without its costing them anything."[34]

Among the "choicest youth" in early public high schools were these male scholars
studying science at Cleveland Central High School, ca. 1850. Western Reserve
Historical Society.

After the Free Academy opened in New York, school officials defended the
institution in the late 1840s and 1850s from labor radicals and also from
Horace Greeley, who called it a school for the rich. Educators claimed that
talent was the only ticket for entry. In fact, though those admitted had indeed
passed an admission test, the student body overrepresented the more comfortable classes. "The vast majority of Academy boys were native born Americans, predominantly of Anglo-Saxon, Dutch, or Huguenot descent," wrote
the historian of the school. "There were only a few recently-arrived Irish and
German immigrants, and even fewer Jews, mostly from old New York families." The local "people's college" had a distinctive native cast, as impressive as
its Gothic architecture.[35]

Studies of various high schools before the 1880s reached similar conclusions.
Not a single child of Irish laborers attended the Sommerville, Massachusetts,
high school in the 1850s and early 1860s. Immigrants were less likely than
natives to attend or graduate from high school in Newburyport and other
Massachusetts towns. In the late 1870s, only about 3 percent at the Indianapolis
high school were the children of immigrants. Between 1859 and 1873, approximately 95 percent of the pupils at the St. Louis high school were native born.
Luring the middle and some of the upper classes to the system meant providing
expensive high schools for the native born, who otherwise patronized academies and boarding schools. The native and immigrant poor in many rapidly
growing cities who attended school were often in overcrowded classes in the
lowest grades; sometimes they were turned away altogether.[36]

Secondary pupils came from a broad range of native-born, middle-class, Protestant families. Hyperbolic critics accused high schools of aristocratic pretensions, exaggerating the social distinctions of the student body. The very rich, especially after the 1870s, continued to attend ever more prestigious and exclusive academies. High school pupils usually represented families from the middle sectors of society: the children of merchants; small businessmen and manufacturers, clerks, and various professionals, not "aristocrats." Skilled workers sometimes sent some of their children to high school, and although these master mechanics or elite workers were "labor aristocrats," they were hardly members of a ruling class.[37]

The charge that the high school was only for the rich infuriated school officials. Most secondary pupils were bourgeois, but admission to high school was a personal honor, not a right of any social group. Whigs such as James Carter, Henry Barnard, and Horace Mann had loudly attacked private academies as bastions of aristocratic privilege, but they were often uncomfortable discussing the class backgrounds of high school pupils.

Most school leaders argued that only a student's morals, academic achievement, and potential mattered. An official in Richmond, Virginia, told white youth in 1857 that "patient industry and faithful study will be finally rewarded with the privilege of tuition in the High School." The schoolmen's passion for propriety sometimes led them to patronizing condemnation of the lower classes as immoral. John Hart complained about "wharf-rats" who poisoned the City of Brotherly Love, and William Ruffner of Virginia, like others, censured the "fouler classes."[38]

Advanced scholars recognized their social distinction. Student editors and contributors to Cleveland's *School-Boy* and other newspapers often had a well-developed sense about the social classes. In 1847 the Cleveland pupils published a teacher's essay that attacked the "idle and profane boys" who loitered around the docks, skipped school, ignored curfews, and would become "miserable and wicked men." The following year a student complained about "Rude Boys," who were "running and hooting about the streets, and throwing gravel stones against the store windows, turning over boxes, and doing various sorts of mischief. They had best look out, as we are informed that seven good cowhides have been bought for the purpose of correcting such bad boys." Beating bad boys contrasted sharply with middle-class ideas about child-rearing for the well born. The newspaper praised Christian ethics, punctuality, hard work, and Benjamin Franklin—whose plaster-cast bust greeted students at their school.[39]

The hooligans apparently learned of their notoriety in the *School Boy*, which had a very wide circulation in Cleveland. Another newspaper, the *Students' Gazette*, complained in 1850 that toughs taunted the scholars as they walked to school. "There is a certain class of boys in this city, who make it their business to ridicule the personal appearance of every one under eighteen, who don't happen to have a patch on his knees, or wear his collar a little elevated out of the common order of things." *The Acorn*, representing the West Side High

School, applauded its school and city in 1856: "Cleveland offers to the enterprising business man, or to him seeking a desirable home, advantages superior, we think, to any city in the West." Apparently not everyone embraced these opportunities, since the same issue endorsed a state reform school for the bad boys.[40]

Many citizens after the 1820s debated the vexing question of who went to high school. The Whigs and then the Republicans defended the institution, emphasizing that all qualified children could enroll. Democrats more frequently complained about the effects of centralization, hierarchy, and bureaucracy in school reform. "Who, then, are the scholars in our high schools, and those who comprise the most advanced scholars in the grammar schools?" asked a critic in *The United States Magazine, and Democratic Review* in 1849. "They are the children of our rich or well-to-do citizens, with very few exceptions. That this is so, and must always be the case, is evident from the circumstance, that a vast majority of our citizens, when their children are of an age to be admitted into the high schools, require their assistance in various trades and occupations, or put them out to labor, so as to assist their almost universally straightened circumstances."[41]

By the 1840s, bourgeois writers as well as radical polemicists had spent two decades discussing why the gap between the rich and poor in society had widened. Educators and social reformers accepted wealth and poverty as inevitable features of contemporary life; schools offered useful learning and moral values essential to social order and personal mobility. Educators in the 1820s and 1830s had emphasized the importance of teaching ambition and independence to the poor, fostering their mobility. When the number of paupers increased, the *New-York Mirror* in 1830 called for a House of Industry, not charity or criticisms of the social system. Idleness should be punished, said many mainstream publicists. Reacting to the social dislocations that followed the panic of 1837, the priggish *Lady's Book* attacked the "idle and uneducated poor," adding that "we rarely find a very poor person who has any idea of economy." And the very poor, said every critic, were usually not found in the high school.[42]

When accused of teaching only the better classes, high school principals and teachers responded by citing the example of the poor but worthy student who ultimately wore the high school crown. Educators and administrators applauded the orphan or poor scholar who struggled against the odds, entered the high school, and graduated with distinction. These examples represented some remarkable cases of achievement; they also highlighted what a few individuals achieved rather than the overall nature of the schools, which gave advantages to the already advantaged.

Ordinarily, officials shifted the discussion, sidestepping their most severe critics, by explaining that scholars had fathers or guardians from a range of occupations. In response to Democratic or radical critics, they called the high school the crucible of republicanism, where rich and poor sat side by side in many classrooms.[43]

In the late 1840s the principal of the Female High School in Newburyport, Massachusetts, claimed to have "both extremes under my charge—the child of affluence and the child of low parentage and deep poverty." This assertion may have been true, since this was a girls' school. Within poor families, girls were more likely to attend high school than their brothers, who left school earlier because of parental expectations and the availability of low-skill jobs. Typically, schoolmen contended that the high school knew no social classes but recognized only talent. As the local poet put it at a high school dedication on the Illinois prairie:

> And here shall rich and poor alike,
> Be nurtured for the world's great strife,
> And hence go forth, with earnest hearts.
> To lead the Nation's Upward life.[44]

Questioning the ubiquitous claim that high schools served a social spectrum, foreign observers generally agreed that the middle classes predominated. In time, particularly after high schools were secure and had enrolled more pupils, some native school leaders concurred. The Rev. James Fraser, studying the high school for England's Schools Inquiry Commissions, met many Americans who insisted that all citizens were equal and free; but he saw a different social pattern. "Speaking generally," he wrote, the high schools were "in possession of the great middle class, the artisans, storekeepers, farmers."[45]

As high schools became increasingly secure after midcentury—as legal challenges failed, enrollments grew, and most northern academies disappeared or became public institutions—even some school officials called them middle class. In old age, Henry Barnard admitted that high schools had been created and mostly utilized by the more comfortable classes and had lacked much popular support. A younger generation of educators and reformers more easily defended the high school, now on firmer ground and even visible in the urban South during Reconstruction. When labor strife accelerated in the 1870s, renewing fears of communism and socialism among the propertied classes, school officials emphasized that the high school promoted personal mobility and national security. Foreign observers concurred that the high school strengthened the middle class, the key to social harmony.[46]

Generations of educators and social reformers had praised the merit system as the key to personal mobility and social cohesion in America. Cleveland's school superintendent articulated this point of view in 1884. "A census of the pupils attending a city high school," wrote B. A. Hinsdale, "will reveal the fact that the great majority of said pupils belong to neither the rich nor the poor, properly so called, but to that large class which lies between the two. In fact, the American high school is a sort of middle-class school." This, of course, was why many critics had always opposed the high school.

Growing in confidence, Hinsdale and other educators now more openly affirmed what dissenters and foreign observers had long claimed.[47]

Frederick Packard, a dependable critic of liberal Protestantism and of high schools, worried in 1866 that the poor would thirst for the higher learning despite the inferior quality of their lower schools. Too many children did not even attend school, particularly in the cities. Many who did, he said, still had trouble comprehending basic prose, performing elementary calculations, or writing a simple letter. Let the rich pay the tuition of their own children pursuing the higher learning; most children would never attend high school, and their basic education especially affected the health of the republic. Packard feared that poorer citizens would be mesmerized by the sirens of advanced study. "The argument in favor of high schools in which Latin and Greek are taught, has much popular force," he feared. "The term 'People's Colleges,' suits the ears of a multitude, and the mechanic and day laborer rejoice in the idea of giving their sons 'college learning' at the public expense, so that they shall not be a whit behind the chiefest of those who expend large sums to obtain a university education."[48]

Children of the poorest families and even skilled workers—the so-called labor "aristocracy"—were consistently underrepresented in high schools, as they had been in private academies. Mechanics sent some children to high school after the 1840s, as apprenticeships increasingly evaporated, but day laborers had difficulty following suit. To school people, the presence of some working-class students was proof that high schools were meritocratic, the embodiment of true republicanism.

Packard's prediction to the contrary, economic realities of the nineteenth century meant that if day laborers heard the siren call of higher learning, most still sent their children to work, not to high school. A minority of middle-class youth attended high school before the 1880s, but their family position increased their odds of reaching the upper grammar grades or the higher branches.[49]

Primary and grammar schools remained neighborhood institutions throughout the century. High schools centralized authority and assaulted local prerogatives, but they never equalized opportunities in the lower schools. Neighborhoods in antebellum towns and cities along the eastern seaboard often became increasingly segregated by social class. Irish immigration by the 1840s gave many formerly homogeneous neighborhoods a new ethnic cast. Grammar schools thus served different populations of children, whose parents often needed their income to subsist. Central offices increasingly applied a single standard, a written examination score, to judge neighborhood institutions.

School boards and superintendents compared the performance of the handful of students from different schools in the high school entrance test; they gave other common examinations—also containing rote questions and answers—to appraise the quality of primary and grammar schools. When the scores revealed wide neighborhood disparities, schoolmen did not call for more aid to the poorer schools, the reassignment of the system's superior teachers, or other amelioration. Emulation would in theory raise the standards, though in practice poor ratings simply embarrassed the low-achieving pupils and their teachers.

As towns and cities developed hierarchical systems with the high school as the capstone, certain public grammar schools began to prepare most advanced scholars. Discussing the English High School in 1862, the Boston School Committee noted that "the majority of the pupils admitted to this school have usually been sent from a few of the Grammar Schools, while others have sent but a small number." Although the battles between Boston's high school leaders and grammar masters were legendary, similar tensions arose elsewhere. The public system comprised neighborhood or district schools that varied enormously and never met a common standard.[50]

Between 1845 and 1873, sixteen grammar schools prepared pupils for Boston's English High, but five sent over half of them. Districts becoming immigrant enclaves—such as the Endicott School in the North End, or the Boylston School to the South—contributed few scholars compared with such schools as Brimmer and Dwight, in the near-suburbs with more native-born residents. Similarly, five grammar schools provided 53 percent of the students admitted to the girls' secondary school between its birth in 1852 and 1872. The Latin School also depended on particular schools and middle- and upper-class students for survival in a city receiving thousands of Irish immigrants by midcentury.[51]

Emulation was supposed to equalize opportunities through competition, an educational invisible hand. The social history of high school recruitment told a different story. Throughout the 1840s, Philadelphia's Central High received the majority of its pupils from a handful of schools, an experience repeated in many towns and cities. In Cincinnati's Central School, four of the twelve local district schools in 1851 provided 51 percent of the pupils.[52]

Whether in Cleveland or Hartford, Louisville or New York City, firm links connected the most favored grammar schools with the high school. While presumably one only needed intelligence and industrious habits to enter the high school, coming from the right family and attending the right grammar school seemed beneficial. In many towns originally divided into autonomous districts, residents of the leading districts, often named "District No. 1" or "Center District"—the richest areas, and the catalysts for free secondary schools—continued to send disproportionate numbers of pupils forward.[53]

Although working-class boys attended high school less frequently than their sisters, some contemporaries admired poor, ambitious, talented girls for their pluck. Girls had fewer job opportunities than boys, and elementary teaching positions were often available for high school graduates as primary enrollments expanded. Like the majority of pupils, poorer girls mostly studied the English branches. "A greater number of girls than of boys who attend the high schools are from the poorer classes," noted Charles S. Smart, the Democratic commissioner of Ohio's schools, in 1878. Although he doubted the utility of free high schools for anyone, Smart said the prospect of a teaching position stimulated some poor girls to excel. Like other contemporaries, the Rev. A. I Mayo called the "superior middle classes" the "keystone in the arch of tł republic," but poor girls brought some timber to the structure. "The daugł ters of poor parents receive the advantages of High Schools to a much greatɛ extent than do the sons of the same parents," said R. W. Mitchell, the president of the Memphis school board. Similarly, an official in Sandusky, Ohio, said closing high schools would hurt pupils of "very moderate circumstances. . . . Especially would this be true of those girls of poor parents who are preparing themselves for teaching."[54]

Overall, though, the selective pattern of high school recruitment—drawing upon many grammar schools but especially a few dominated by the native middle classes—meant that the "people's college" largely served the more advantaged citizens. Most high school pupils by midcentury came from the relatively privileged native born. They entered high school from ages twelve to twenty, but most boys were usually fourteen or fifteen and girls slightly older. In rural schools the ages of those who studied the higher branches might vary even more.

By the 1880s, educators were not embarrassed that the high school was "a sort of middle-class school." This was the dream of antebellum educators: to attract the better classes to the system. Public schools were no longer pauper schools. Some high schools even had some poor youth, girls more often than boys. School people could thus proclaim that the high school was a democratic institution that fulfilled the republican goal of recognizing the merit of all (especially white) pupils. Throughout the century, educators tried to avoid answering questions about who went to high school. When accused of running schools for the rich, they highlighted the range of jobs held by the parents of students. According to the schoolmen, their institutions recognized merit and talent, and the middle classes, too, had to pass the entrance test. Though economic classes divided society, schools prevented the hardening of social caste by allowing pupils to compete fairly for survival and preferment.

Those intelligent enough but too poor to attend high school told a different tale about being young, about the less sunny side of growing up. Lucy Larcom, a New England mill girl, attended grammar school for a few months and progressed nicely, aspiring to attend high school. "It was a great delight to me to study," she later recalled in her autobiography, "and at the end of the three months the master told me that I was prepared for the high school. But alas! I could not go. The little money I could earn—one dollar a week, besides the price of my board—was needed in the family, and I must return to the mill. It was a severe disappointment to me, though I did not say so at home." Lucy's mother was disappointed, too, though a neighbor whose daughter was planning to enroll shared the view articulated by George Boutwell. Said the neighbor: "Oh, my girl hasn't any such head-piece as yours has. Your girl doesn't need to go."[55]

After passing their entrance examination to prove their moral worth and intellectual capacity, scholars who did advance faced the high expectations of their elders. The "choicest youth" had scaled Olympus, but at each turn they met demanding teachers and principals, who tried to shape their morals and minds in every way possible.

Good Scholars

Lazy people say, "*Tomorrow*,"
So they always, always borrow,
But they never, never pay;
All that's good tomorrow doing,
All that's ill they're then eschewing,
Great things to do, but not *today*.

"Procrastination,"
in *The Common School Songster* (1843)

Throughout the nineteenth century, educators sought model pupils who would bring respectability to the new secondary schools that dotted the land. Clues about what constituted an ideal scholar surfaced in various cautionary tales, often in school songsters. One memorable air was the saga of "Lazy Bill." Appearing at midcentury in *School Songs for the Million!* "Lazy Bill" taught an important lesson:

There was a young truant,
They call'd him Lazy Bill,
He fled long ago, long ago!
When last I saw him he ran behind the mill—
For to run, sir, he wasn't very slow.
Then place all his books in a row;
Pack up his trinkets for a show,
No more lessons for poor young Bill,
He's gone where all the old truants go.[1]

Truancy led Bill down a darkened path. He became dirty, obstinate, and incorrigible.

Disrespectful of authority, "Lazy Bill" stole a watch, cursed his teachers, and was jailed "in an iron cage."

O, who would be a truant, like wicked Lazy Bill,
And lose all the pleasures of our school!
To loaf about the street, or to hide behind the mill,
Never mind propriety and rule.[2]

Punctuality, deportment, "propriety and rule": these formed the pedagogical creed of common schools and emerging high schools. To disregard these virtues might not lead to an iron cage, but it often meant social disapproval or even expulsion from school.

Teachers had high moral and academic expectations for secondary pupils. Contemporaries emphasized moral education and the Three R's for the majority of schoolchildren, who were in the primary grades. In high school, educators similarly told advanced scholars to worship a holy trinity: attendance, deportment, and scholarship. School officials and teachers saw these three components of student life as mutually reinforcing, shaping classroom culture and the pupils' destiny.[3]

Statistics on punctuality and attendance reveal how regularly and promptly students heeded the morning bell. Deportment demonstrated their capacity to suppress wayward tendencies and to exercise self-restraint. And, finally, scholarship—another potentially contentious issue between home and school, teachers and pupils—addressed the strictly academic side of secondary education. Punctuality, decorum, and study together made good scholars.

To attend school regularly and punctually was a moral imperative, according to many bourgeois writers. Time discipline intensified as commercial activities increased and as small-scale factories appeared in the North. Nature still set a natural rhythm for agrarian life and labor, and country schools followed the seasons more than the clock. But schools in more-developed areas increasingly emphasized the virtue of being on time.[4]

Middle-class writers believed that punctuality cultivated character. In the 1820s and 1830s, reformers directed the message to children in the lowest grades, which had the largest enrollments, as well as to the smaller high school classes. Mrs. Sarah Josepha Hale urged the young to learn the meter of time consciousness. Her popular *School Songbook* in 1834 praised perseverance, industry, and faithful attendance.

Cheerily, cheerily, sound the strain—
Happily, happily met again,
Here we stand—
Who at home has dared to stay?
Who has loitered by the way?
And who for idle play
Do we miss from our band?[5]

Mrs. Hale wanted this sung every Monday morning, the traditional day of rest for male laborers whose weekends included too many draughts.

The preoccupation of principals, teachers, and superintendents with punctuality never diminished. Adults admonished pupils not to dally on the way to school, or mischief would seduce them:

> For Time is ever on the wing,
> And death will come at last,
> Then let us learn each useful thing,
> Before our Youth be past.

It is unclear whether singing "The Truant's Soliloquy" was much fun or very effective; those who needed the song most were presumably absent. Still, occasional latecomers might profit from the aptly titled *Humming Bird*:

> Now hurry to the school, boys,
> While the day is bright,
> Hurry let the work be done,
> And then for play tonight.[6]

Urban school administrators kept detailed (though not always uniform or consistent) attendance records, always linking time consciousness with other desirable traits. Pupils in every school read textbooks inspired by Poor Richard. Authors of advanced mathematics books said precision, standard measures, and clocklike regularity characterized advanced nations. Francis Wayland claimed that punctuality and related traits strengthened the will. Exercises in false syntax in grammar books warned about tardiness, idleness, and moral degeneration. "Tuition is lost on idlers and numbsculs," claimed a popular book first printed in the 1820s. The *High School Reader* (1832) caught the spirit, too: "Be wise to-day, 'tis madness to defer."[7]

After Cincinnati opened its "Central School" in the late 1840s, Principal H. H. Barney sent a letter condemning irregular attendance to every scholar's home. The competitive system, he said, otherwise faltered: "The emulous mind is depressed by the sloth of an irregular attendant; the patience of the Teacher is put to the torture; and the common hope of the School is clipped in its rising." Barney reaffirmed the intimate ties between punctuality, regular attendance, and academic success in 1852. "Our records show most conclusively," he asserted, "that the pupils most irregular in their attendance are, as a general rule, most backward and most delinquent in everything else."[8]

Since the 1820s, report cards had offered a tripartite definition of school achievement. Already in 1825, scholars at Boston's English High School were ranked by merit: "The standing of each individual is determined by his proficiency and good conduct." Apparently "good conduct" referred to punctuality as well as acceptable behavior. In subsequent decades, northern urban educators assumed that attendance (measured against tardiness and/or absence) plus

NAMES.	P. C. Scholarship.	P. C. Attendance.	P. C. Deportment.	Days absent — Junior.	Second.	Third.	Senior.	Four Years.	Times tardy — Junior.	Second.	Third.	Senior.	Four Years.	Discredits — Junior.	Second.	Third.	Senior.	Four Years.	Rank.
1. Allan, Anna	68.7	97.2	95.3		7		7	14							4	1	9	14	44
2. Allen, Eveline	86	97	100			2	3	5											7
3. Ball, David	81.8	93.4	99.3	4		1	6	11	1			4	5				2	2	18
4. Banister, Alice	74.8	97	95.5				1	1				1	1	3	3		2	8	32
5. Bouton, Ada	83.8	88.7	84.7		5		4	9		2		1	3		23	9	14	46	33
6. Boyden, Ida	91.3	100	98.3												4	1		5	1
7. Brand, Dorothea	76.5	95.2	92		10	13	1	24		2	1		3		3	7	14	24	35
8. Brookes, Lizzie E	81.7	98.6	99	3	1		1	5	1		1	1	3		1	1	2	4	14
9. Budd, Louisa O	79.5	90.6	95	14	9	4	14	41						8	9	2	1	20	31
10. Burns, Emma L	85.9	97.6	96	3		3	2	8			3	1	4			10	2	12	10
11. Cassilly, Geo. E	70.2	87.5	67.6		2	2	12	16		1	4		5		37	27	33	97	55
12. Connelly, Mary	76.1	94.8	84				4	4		1		2	3		13		19	32	43
13. Cousland, Barbara	88.3	98.9	99.3			1	1	2		1	1		2			1	1	2	4
14. Cozzens, Ella L	86.1	98.5	100		1	4	2	7											6
15. Dale, Henry	72.1	100	84.7											11	6	12	34	63	46
16. Fairchild, Mary	78.7	94	86		9	4	2	15			6	5	11		2	10	30	42	36
17. Felix, Eugenia	79.6	95.6	93.3	4	3		3	10	4	2		4	10	11	6		3	20	28
18. Fisher, Laura E	80.6	98.5	97	1	1			2	2	4		2	8	3	4		2	9	17
19. Ford, Rochester	81.6	95.8	89.6		9	7		16		1	1	4	6		15	7	9	31	27
20. Gilliam, Geo. T	72.3	85	100				14	14											45
21. Goff, Eva	83.9	99.7	98		1	1		2						3	3	1	1	8	11
22. Hancock, Clara	80.5	91.1	94	7	6		10	23	8	13		9	30	7	6		5	18	29
23. Higdon, Jno. B	73.8	99.7	88.2	1		1		2						9	9	15	14	47	40
24. Hight, Carrie S	77.9	99.6	85.6								1	1		17	13		13	43	34
25. Hoffmann, Charles	79.9	99.4	96.3	3				3		1			1		2		9	11	19
26. Kueffner, Otto	77.7	98	92				1	1								4	12	16	30
27. Kohn, George	67.3	98	86.2		2		3	5						1	10	17	27	55	50
28. Lane, Rose	68.3	89.7	84.7	2	14	22	10	48	1	7	9	1	18	2	26	20	13	61	51
29. Logan, Annie B	78.1	96.7	99.3	2		3	1	6		1	4		5				2	2	21
30. Macbeth, Eugene	68.7	99.9	53						1				1		63	49	29	141	56
31. Martin, Clara E	79.7	93.4	97.2	3	8	6	8	25		2	2	1	5	7	1	2	1	11	24
32. Martin, Joanna A	82.7	98.9	100				1	1				1	1						12
33. Martin, Mary	79.6	98.2	99.6		1	3	1	5		1		1	2		1			1	16
34. Matthews, Annie L	84.8	98.6	99.3			4	1	5		1		1	1		1		1	2	8
35. Matthews, Fannie L	83.5	94.3	98.2	7		1	9	17		1	1		2		4	2	1	7	15
36. McElwain, Sophia J	73.7	94.7	94.7	8	8	6	2	24	5	6	1	3	15	6	5	6	4	21	37
37. Meyer, Claudina	79.1	98.4	95		1		2	3			2	3	1		2	8	5	15	22
38. Mudd, Lulu C	75.7	87	60		5		12	17	2		4	9	15	31	50		39	120	53
39. Peebles, Jessie De E	70.7	97.2	97.7	11			1	12						2	1		4	7	38
40. Riddle, Jennie P	60.2	83	92.5		6		6	12			1	7	8		4		11	15	54
41. Rosenbaum, Ella	77.8	96.6	98				5	5		1		2	3			2	4	6	25
42. Rotteck, Amalia	80.2	99.3	93.3		1			1		4	2		6		14	2	4	20	20
43. Schnuhr, Anna	82.8	98.2	97.6	2			1	3		1		2	3	5	1		1	7	13
44. Scott, Ella M	79	93.3	100		4		11	15	3	1		3	7						23
45. Shaw, James G	72.9	98.7	91.2		2	1		3	1			2	3	6	12	3	7	13	35
46. Sprague, C. C	66.1	100	93.3											5	11		4	20	48
47. Summers, Mary	88.9	98.8	98		1		1	2									6	6	5
48. Starr, Abbie	73.2	91.5	96	6	8	5	4	23	1	3	1	5	10		4	6	6	16	41
49. Tarrants, Lena	84.2	99	99.6		1		1	2			1		1		1			1	9
50. Taussig, Charles	68.7	97.3	92.7	2	2	1		5	1	2	3	6	12	3	1	11	14	29	47
51. Thompson, Ella	79.2	97.5	98		2	8		10			1	2	3			4	2	6	42
52. Walker, Mary	72.4	93.1	83.3		9	6	9	24			1	1	2		16	17	17	50	49
53. Wead, Charles M	81.1	90.3	97			6	7	13			1	2	3			1	5	6	26
54. Willson, Anna	90.2	99.4	100		3			3	1				1						2
55. Wurdemann, Gust. A	63.2	99.2	83.3		3			3							5	13	32	50	52
56. Zobel, Bertha	89.7	96.6	99.6			2	2	4									1	1	3

Ida Boyden stood at the top of the class at St. Louis High School in 1876. Urban school systems frequently published such ranked lists, flattering the successful and showing the range of talents present in every high school. From *Twenty-First Annual Report of the Board of Directors of the St. Louis Public Schools* (St. Louis, 1876).

deportment (denoted by demerits) plus scholarship (also a compound of indicators) determined one's monthly, term, and annual rank.[9]

A few educators criticized the combination of dissimilar quantities into an academic profile. Most, however, accepted the model established by superintendent William H. Wells of Chicago in 1862. Wells borrowed liberally from contemporary educators as he succinctly described the purpose of "school records": "The three essential elements of the records which are designed more particularly to aid the teacher in raising the standard of scholarship and discipline, are *attendance, scholarship,* and *deportment.*"[10]

Educators laboring in the best-graded systems, in union graded schools in northern villages and especially in larger places, proudly enforced rules on punctuality. Moses Woolson, a rock-ribbed New England schoolmaster, was principal of the Girls' High School in Portland, Maine, from 1850 to 1862. He locked the school door once the clock struck nine. An alumna recalled that Woolson's students were never tardy—just absent. In nearly every high school, an absence or late arrival reduced one's class mark and rank. Woolson, who required the most advanced pupils to prepare essays and poems for oral delivery—on Saturday mornings before the entire school—probably enjoyed "Nellie's" essay in 1857. She agreed that "Tardiness" harmed good scholarship.[11]

Even though most high school pupils were relatively privileged, social change dispelled any complacency their parents might have had. Students, they realized, were entering a new world, where economic shifts and more centralized control over the means of production destroyed the familiar outlines of an earlier America. A new kind of education and discipline offered some lucky, hardworking, talented youth with the intellectual and moral sensibilities to survive and prosper.

Scholars who streamed into the expanding secondary schools had not suddenly discovered the intrinsic joys of learning. Rather, certain parents wanted their loved ones to have a competitive edge in an increasingly combative social order. Parents pressured their children to internalize self-discipline, and secondary students often resembled the model pupils depicted in school songs, textbooks, and advice manuals. Prescriptive literature for boys and girls stressed duty, propriety, punctuality, and respect for authority. Harvey Newcomb's *How To Be A Man* (1847) condemned tardiness, smoking, drinking, gambling, "tight-dressing," and loitering on the streets. The companion volume, *How To Be A Lady* (1852) emphasized women's central role in a respectable family and taught bourgeois proprieties on dress, personal demeanor, and respect for teachers and schools.[12]

School officials were proud of their advanced scholars. In contrast, the embarrassment of superintendent Alexander A. Gow of Evansville, Indiana, was evident when he wrote in 1871 that the average daily attendance at the local high school was only 73.6 percent and that the institution had registered 499 cases of tardiness. "In a commercial and manufacturing city like ours," he thought, "it might be supposed that the value of punctuality as an element in success in business would be so well understood and appreciated that it would require no special effort to secure its exercise, even in the high school." The institution enrolled 110 pupils, and it was "rather mortifying to record that with a school averaging 81 pupils there should be nearly 50 cases of tardiness in every four weeks." And, Gow realized, a larger rival such as St. Louis reported more progress.[13]

The St. Louis schools, made famous during the superintendency of William T. Harris (1868–1880), had indeed made remarkable strides. St. Louis High was a paragon of machinelike efficiency. Between 1858 and 1880, the average daily attendance never dropped below 95 percent of total enrollment; it reached its apogee of 97.9 percent in the 1873–74 school year. The inclusion of decimal points reflected the era's fascination with precise measurement as well as the centrality of punctuality in the mission of secondary schools. Harris' reports on the evolution of the local system became famous, and they emphasized how high schools would produce society's future leaders. Being on time helped guarantee success.[14]

Throughout the antebellum and postbellum periods, schoolmasters applauded secondary students for their faithful attendance and punctuality. Statistics in towns and cities revealed that the attendance in St. Louis was not unusual, but educators still complained about the lame excuses of parents and scholars for tardiness or absence. Even though tardiness seemed more annoying than serious, principals such as Robert W. Wright of the Fort Wayne high school worried about any moral lapse. Parents too readily kept students home on sunny days, on rainy days, and for frivolous reasons. Even when youth fulfilled family responsibilities that made them tardy—such as running errands or minding siblings—educators winced.[15]

Statistics in most places revealed something more positive about the match between bourgeois families and schools. In Boston in the 1860s and 1870s, for example, the average daily attendance was 90 percent for the entire system. Elementary pupils—because of their age and susceptibility to illness—had the lowest average attendance, grammar school pupils attended more regularly, and high school scholars were even more conscientious. In 1861, for example, the percentage attending daily was 88.7 percent for the primary schools, 93.6 percent for the grammar grades, and 95.2 percent for the high schools. Again, the pupils chose to attend school and respected basic rules and regulations.[16]

Whether in Atlanta or Denver, Chicago or Boston, high school pupils were largely dutiful and responsible. The principal of Cincinnati's Woodward High School proudly wrote in 1858 that "about half of our number have neither been absent nor tardy one minute, while a very large majority have been unusually faithful and studious." Indeed, in many towns and cities, pupils themselves praised the system for demanding compliance. Writing in the Columbus, Ohio, *School-Boy* in 1851, "Asa" typically included punctuality as one of the main "duties" of his peers.[17]

Student newspapers often supported mainstream values, which helps explain why principals and teachers did not usually censor their journalism

THE ACORN.

Published by the Students of]   DEVOTED TO THE EXPANSION OF MIND.   [the High School (West Side.)

Volume 2.   CLEVELAND, MARCH 15, 1856.   Number 4.

Cowles, Pinkerton & Co., Printers, Leader Office.

EDITOR:
E. P. SHELDON.

EDITRESS:
HATTIE F. FARRAND.

CONTRIBUTORS:
L. J. VOIGT,   M. B. NEWTON,
A. QUINTRELL,   M. E. WARMINGTON,
CHAS. LYMAN,   M. E. THORNE,
C. J. MALLORY,   B. H. COLAHAN,
M. QUINTRELL.

A Picture of Life.

It was a day in midsummer. The scorching rays of the sun scarcely penetrated through the foliage of a large and splendid garden. Shrubs and plants, and flowers of the rarest kind shedding their delicious perfume through the air, adorned the "little paradise." Birds were warbling delightful music, and in the midst of the enchanting scene there played a little child. Scarce four summers had passed over that face of surpassing loveliness. In her tiny fingers she held a bunch of beautiful flowers, among which was a fresh young rosebud, still wet with the dews of the morning. Near the bud was a full blown rose, upon whose velvet cheek glittered a pearly dew drop--perfect emblems of thyself, fair young creature. Those golden ringlets time will change; those large dark eyes disease or age will dim; that round soft cheek will often feel the hot tear of sorrow, and ere thy budding youth has blossomed into womanhood, thou shalt have known disappointment. As I watched the merry child, full of happy fancies, now chasing the winged butterfly from shrub to shrub, then pausing for a moment beside a silvery stream, wherein her fairy form was faithfully reflected, she seemed to change.

* * * * * * * *

Years rolled on. Behold a fair and gentle maiden. Beautiful being! One of earth's fairest objects. Dost thou say that rosebud hath never known sorrow? Gaze deep down into those soft, blue eyes —look at that mourning garb—hear that heavy sigh, drawn forth from the very heart, and say, if thou canst, that she hath never tasted grief! While she was yet in all the innocence of childhood, cruel death came, and with unrelenting hand snatched from her young heart her mother. Very early was she called to mourn, but nobly did she bear up under the bereavement, and lovingly devote all her energies to her broken-hearted father, who gradually revived under her kind and gentle influence. Thus did she grow up, loving and beloved, always doing some good deed. Talented and beautiful, and, above all, truly good, is it any wonder that she was admired by many, loved by all. * * * * * *

It is evening. The stars that gemmed the skies were scarcely brighter than stars which adorned the brilliantly-lighted rooms of a large and splendid mansion in ——. As carriage after carriage rolled up the broad avenue, and landed their precious burdens on the large stone steps, the house was soon filled, and the gorgeously furnished parlors were crowded. Beauty and fashion reigned triumphant. Soft music floated on the perfumed air. Still all seemed anxiously waiting for some unseen object. Suddenly the band strikes up a lively piece, and the queen of the evening appears, leaning on the arm of the one to whom she is about to be united. As she moves gracefully along, every eye is fixed upon her. Cleopatra sailing up the river in her splendid galley, in purple and diamonds, to meet Antony, could not have exceeded her in grace and beauty. In that gay assemblage there were many votaries of fashion and ambition, who looked with jealous eyes on the fair young bride. But the little rosebud of former years, now fully matured, reigns peeress of evening. She is arrayed in a dress of white satin. A veil, fastened about the hair, with a garland of delicate white rosebuds, floats gracefully over her neck and person to the floor. But, fair one, as the roses in thy garland must fade and die, so must thou. The ceremony ended, and the benediction of Heaven invoked, the merry congratulations of friends ensue. Many wishes of long life and happiness to the bride are expressed. Ah! how little do her kind-hearted friends dream that e'en now, closely hidden among the leaves of that rose so fresh and beautiful, a deadly worm lies coiled, which is soon to cause its premature decay.

* * * * * *

Time has flown on rapid wing, and brought again the joyous summer time. It is the season for the singing of birds and the blossoming of roses. In an apartment opening out on a widely-extended lawn, adorned with trees and shrubs and flowers, there lies a youthful sufferer. Beneath her window is a large white rose bush, covered with its delicate blossoms. There is the fresh young bud, the half blown rose, and the expanded flower. They shed their fragrance on the air, and it is wafted to the couch of the invalid. As an unseen spirit does it come to whisper to her soul words of comfort and of peace. Frail and short, even as the rose, has her young life been. But, as the death of the rose, so shall not her death be. The rose withers and dies, never to bloom again in immortal youth and beauty beyond the tomb. Thoughts of the beautiful world whither she is going—of its den and never-fading flowers occupy

her mind, and impart a heavenly lustre to her sweet but pale and emaciated face.— Consumption had long since marked her for its victim, and when the roses on that bush sent forth their dying fragrance, she sweetly breathed out her life, yielding it up in meek submission to her God and Savior.

Fair maiden, sporting amid life's pleasant dreams, learn here this lesson of holy truth.

"Favor is deceitful, and beauty is vain,
But a woman that feareth the Lord, she shall be praised."

M. E. 7.

.................."On the sands of life
Sorrow treads heavily, and leaves a print
Time cannot wash away, while joy sweeps by,
With steps so light and soft, that the next wave
Washes his foot-prints out."

Well may we feel that sorrow is one of the burdens of earth. We have seen its footprints, and deeply felt its power; we have seen stately pride and kingly power humbled by its presence.

Unroll the blood-stained pages of history; there we find the imperishable record of those endowed with the highest intellectual gifts, with power and wealth almost unbounded, who would have willingly dispensed with all these vast possessions, to obtain "sureease of sorrow."

Its foot-prints are deep and lasting, and Time, with its unceasing waves, will never erase them from our, perhaps, too sensitive hearts—for they seem ever awake to every approach of sorrow. But to the good such "tribulation worketh patience, and patience experience, and experience hope," and we feel that we are thus the better fitted for the moral conflicts of life, so that complaint seems unjust.

For a while we may be happy, very happy—but the temptations of earth—the perversities of our hearts make us forget our joys, and when the wrong appears distinctly before us, sorrow again returns. Thus it is with us always—now dark and wide-spread clouds hover long and threatening over us—anon a flickering light shines out, cheering for a moment our shadowed 'path, and all is dark again. Sorrow is deep, crushing—Joy is but for a moment, nor can we grasp it in time to stay its progress, or take firm possession of its pleasure.

M. S. N.

Fashion Incompatible with Intellectual Culture.

Observation has taught us that a well disciplined mind cannot exist in the person of a fashion-seeker. We have not learned to look among the giddy crowds, who throng the fashionable saloons, to find intelligent minds, nor, on the other hand to expect to obtain the latest Parisian fashions from Fame's humble abode. Now what is the cause of this opposition in what seems to be the ruling ob-

jects of human ambition? Is it that nature has been more liberal in bestowing her rich gifts upon some than others, that we observe so wide a difference in the plans which are adopted to obtain a general education?

It is true some are formed with superior personal charms; in others the intellectual faculties predominate; but does it, therefore, follow from this simple fact, that a portion of mankind is to pursue the path of folly, while the rest seek to adorn their minds with those bright jewels of knowledge, which are not tarnished by the lapse of time, and the thief cannot steal or destroy?

All are formed with a natural love for the vanities of earth, and where beauty is added to strengthen this love, there is not opposite moral force enough, to resist this overwhelming power, and thus many are led to sacrifice all their finer feelings at the shrine of fashion, and to look upon the intelligent part of the community as a sort of subordinate, though perhaps indispensible element of society.

Mothers are often misled in the education of their daughters, by thinking that only the physical powers require careful cultivation, and, as a result of this false impression, their daughters are perfected in all the graces—thoroughly skilled in music, dancing, &c., before their neglected minds have become sufficiently developed to enable them to intelligibly pen a note of invitation to one of their dear associates, or, to find pleasure during the long evenings of winter, in perusing the works of distinguished authors.

Fathers sometimes teach their sons as con as they are able to indistinctly articulate the familiar epithet "papa," that the distinction between a gentleman and a man is, that the former promenades the streets in the finest broadcloth, visits some fashionable French barber-shop twice a day— wears his hat gracefully tipped on one side, to expose to view a fine head of hair, and smokes the best cigars. These then are true gentlemen in the estimation of such persons, and every youth is anxious to become as much of a gentleman as possible, and with this kind of examples, he comes far short of the true application of the term.

Were the mind a tangible object, the little neglected points would be observed, and parents, instead of consulting fashionable dress-makers and tailors, as to the most becoming colors and fashions in which to array their sons and daughters, would be advising with intellectual teachers, to ascertain the best mode of adorning the minds of their children, and of removing mental and moral deformities.

H. F. F.

before the 1880s. Still, the papers reflected an important segment of student opinion and were not mouthpieces of officialdom. Extant student diaries and letters similarly revealed the power of time discipline in scholars' everyday lives.

The student newspaper of Cleveland's Central High School, The *School-Boy*, editorialized in favor of punctuality. "K. C." wrote in 1848 that responsible pupils should not have to be annoyed by lazy, tardy pupils; locking the door when school began seemed reasonable. "If we cultivate the habit of punctuality while at school, we shall be apt to be punctual in all things when we grow up to be men," claimed the pupil, sounding like a teacher or principal. "M." claimed that "in business a man should be punctual, for if he is not he will never acquire anything. His friends will despise him." Being on time at school trained the will and reminded future clerks, merchants, businessmen, professionals, and teachers that life on earth was short. "It is well known that all time is precious," wrote another student at Central High. "Our Creator has placed us here in this world, and allotted us a few days only, and therefore we ought to spend them in the most profitable manner."[18]

Diaries kept by pupils showed the power of time consciousness at school. Sometimes compulsive and unusually introspective, these scholars represented what parents and educators generally admired. The head teacher at the Portsmouth, New Hampshire, Girls' High School, a Mr. Nichols, required every pupil to keep a diary. Almira Hubbard Viles, a model student, competed for a prize for the best diary in 1859. Almira's thoughts, however sincere, were recorded within this context.

Like many pupils, Almira, who lived outside the town and boarded some distance from school, understood the need for promptness. Though she often walked to school, one morning she rode in a horse-drawn carriage. Unfortunately, the seat broke, leaving her and a companion looking quite foolish as they dropped to the bottom of the wagon. Some boys playing ball nearby tried to fix the carriage, but the makeshift repair soon came undone. By the time another good Samaritan appeared, the bell was about to toll. "Then I got out and walked," she noted, and "reached the school-room door just as the clock struck nine."[19]

A week later, Almira's great-uncle died. Attending the funeral meant her first absence "in a year and a half." A month later, Almira noted with approval that Mr. Nichols was concerned about increased absences as summer approached: "I think Mr. Nichols made a very fine rule this morning, by which one who is absent cannot make up her lessons or cannot have the marks for them either. I think it will cause some of the girls to be a little more regular in their attendance at school." When her brother from Bangor visited in June, she wanted to stay home but knew that an absence meant demerits and a lower academic mark. She decided to go to school despite preferring her brother's companionship. But this prize student in Mr. Nichols' Latin class still lost points on her report card because she arrived late. Because of her "deficiencies," she understood, "I rather think I shall not stand number one [in Latin] next month."[20]

Other dutiful students noted how attendance and punctuality shaped the rhythms of school life. Alice Devin, a nonresident scholar at the Ann Arbor, Michigan, high school in the early 1870s, told a friend in a letter that study alone did not guarantee success. One evening in September of 1871, she tackled thirty-seven problems in "Olney's" algebra, which she found very difficult, and she worried about upcoming tests and her overall academic performance. "The teacher's [sic] mark closely and are very strict," she thought, "a days [sic] absence, unless confined to your bed by sickness, gives you less for the days [sic] lessons." An older pupil with an active social life, Alice that same day reflected on the prospects of a date, her views on a recent Lyceum lecture, and other social events. Planning one's time—for fun and for study—was basic to an active life.[21]

The most dutiful pupils everywhere huffed and puffed to arrive on time. Punctuality and attendance together often constituted one-third of their class rank. Lizzie Morrisey, who kept a remarkable journal in 1876, attended the Girls' High and Normal School in Boston. She lived in East Boston, some distance from the school, and she often ran the entire length of Newton Street to arrive on time. One June morning she just beat the bell, arriving precisely in time for the "devotional exercises." Lizzie was a serious young woman, a model student in many respects, and she hoped to become a teacher. Being on time and persevering in one's studies was both a moral obligation and a prerequisite to success.[22]

Going to school regularly and punctually was supposed to be a matter of conscience, natural, not coerced. That message prevailed in the teacher-training textbooks read by such pupils as Lizzie Morrisey. But no matter what they read or were told or believed, scholars knew that being tardy or absent led to punishment. Everyday experience was the best teacher: get to school promptly, behave, and study.

Deportment constituted another third of a high school student's scholastic report. Although interpreting good behavior was more subjective than identifying tardiness or absenteeism, educators throughout the nineteenth century enumerated offenses, ranked them, and prescribed various punishments. This was, of course, the great age of bourgeois advice manuals, etiquette books, and guides to proper behavior. Like other bastions of middle-class life, secondary schools everywhere tried to socialize and discipline, offering a safe path to propriety and respectability. High schools arose in a violent culture: where poverty or its specter haunted native-born whites, free blacks, and Irish immigrants and where slavery would not end without fratricide. Even the most talented and morally upright pupils faced a precarious, competitive world.[23]

"A good scholar never mutters nor disobeys his instructors," claimed Roswell C. Smith in a lesson on parsing conjunctions in his textbook, *English Grammar*, originally published in 1831. Parsing adjectives also taught important values: "The intelligent, industrious, obedient, and docile scholar." "Hush! our instructor is at the door," read the lesson on interjections. Songsters warned about "Lazy Bill" and called for proper demeanor:

> Silently! silently!
>> Open and close the school-room door;
> Carefully! carefully!
>> Walk upon the floor!
> Let us, strive to be
>> From disorder ever free;
> Happily! happily!
>> Passing time away.[24]

A closing hymn offered children in the lower grades similar advice:

> When going home, or when we come,
> At morning, noon, or night,
> Let no one play along the way,
> Or do what is not right.[25]

Like academies, from which they borrowed so liberally, high schools wanted to nurture character. After the 1820s, Whig politicians, school leaders, and authors of advice manuals told youth to develop self-discipline and to respect authority. The middle classes increasingly rejected physical punishment for unruly children and youth, at least within their own families, as they embraced a more genteel and liberal Protestantism. They wanted schools and families to teach self-control, inner restraint, and personal responsibility. Prizes and emulation, although condemned in pedagogical primers and speculative writing, became common in schools, reflecting an emergent ethos of individual competition. Report cards reflected these concerns, as adults monitored every scholar's attendance, behavior, and scholarship.[26]

Writing in the Columbus, Ohio, *School-Boy*, in 1851, "Cato" asked his readers a rhetorical question: "What is the situation of a young man about entering upon the stage of active life, without a good character?" The answer: hopeless. The principal of the Nashua, New Hampshire, High School, located in District 3 and educating about eighty students daily, similarly emphasized the close relationship between scholarship and moral development. Surveying the past year's work, he observed: "The scholars have generally been faithfully and patiently studious. [But] unless they have gained mental culture and discipline, and an increase of moral purity and power, the efforts of the teachers have been unavailing."[27]

Teachers and principals wanted students to strengthen their conscience to regulate their own behavior: to become punctual because it was inherently good, to study because it enhanced moral and intellectual values, and to obey rules and regulations because order demanded it and fostered mature behavior. Overall, pupils were cooperative. They mostly behaved, just as they were mostly punctual. Cincinnati's pedagogues must have smiled when a pupil claimed in the *Woodward Bulletin* that "every school is a community governed by certain laws; to disobey these laws brings upon the offender the penalty." To teachers, nurturing character was vital. Because pupils were imperfect, rewards and nonphysical punishments helped maintain classroom decorum and train the rising generation.[28]

Beginning in the 1820s, town and city school systems codified desirable norms of student behavior in printed rules and regulations. These rules never guaranteed total compliance, any more than printed courses of study matched school practices. But they revealed what authorities prized most. From the beginning the English Classical School made "conduct" integral to class rank. Conduct could take many forms. The same behavior elicited varying interpretations, as teachers and aggrieved pupils discovered whenever conflicts arose. However, scholars were not ordinarily ruffians or ne'er-do-wells. Anyone who entered high school before the 1880s had already demonstrated some of the self-discipline and control that Whigs and Republicans proclaimed as the hallmark of the good scholar and responsible adult. Those who worked with children and youth—however optimistic their views of human nature or disdainful of orthodox Calvinism—usually still held a tight rein on pupils. They rewarded good behavior and recorded every infraction.

Schools nearly everywhere forbade scholars from talking without permission, smoking, inappropriate laughter, cursing, disrupting chapel or morning prayer, showing obstinacy, wearing a hat in class, and so forth. Rule 14 for Louisville's Male and Female High Schools offered the following injunctions in 1859: "All running, jumping, loud talking, whistling or sports of any kind, in the rooms or halls of the institution, is *totally forbidden*. In the recitation rooms, perfect silence and earnest attention to his duties, is enjoined upon every student." Chivalry was dead, for boys were also forbidden to carry guns to school.[29]

This emphasis on self-control and personal decorum led to memorable moments, recalled a former student of Moses Woolson. The Dartmouth-educated Woolson, a fervent defender of women's education, ruled Portland's female school as his fief. A moralizing taskmaster who kept his pupils in line, he required his students to learn Latin to demonstrate that women were equal to every intellectual challenge. One admiring pupil vividly remembered a chemistry experiment in which some "ill-smelling" chemicals exploded and set Professor Woolson ablaze. Appropriately "the whole school looked on as quietly as if it was part of the experiment to see the teacher burn." Woolson ruined his coat, received some burns, and was "minus a part of his eye-brows and whiskers." But disorder never erupted under his watchful eye.[30]

Everywhere the goal was self-control, not draconian discipline. The aim of the high school, wrote the School Committee of Concord, New Hampshire, in 1856, was to train boys and girls to become "refined and gentle in deportment, as well as accomplished scholars." By showing "respect and affection" for the pupils, teachers could "arouse whatever is noble and generous in their natures, and . . . inspire in them a love of learning, and a reverence for virtue." Similarly, the transplanted New England educator, John Swett, principal of the elite Female High School of San Francisco, urged teachers on all levels to

Moses Woolson, principal of the Girls'
High School of Portland, Maine,
between 1850 and 1862, required all of
his scholars to learn Latin and championed women's higher education on the
secondary school level. Collections of
the Maine Historical Society.

tailor punishments to the gravity of the offense. In his *Methods of Teaching* (1880) he offered Rule 9: "Do not try to make scholars learn by whipping them for unlearned lessons." Rule 10 also urged restraint: "*Never strike a child on the head.* Never inflict permanent indignities, such as pulling the hair, pulling the ears, slapping the face; for they excite the bitterest resentment, and are seldom forgiven."[31]

Some educators said lower-class boys were the most unruly and thus whipped the most in high schools. They also formed the smallest percentage of secondary pupils, and physical punishment of anyone was rare. Indeed, the image of well-governed bourgeois homes usually colored the perspectives of high school educators. When Cincinnati opened its Central School, officials told teachers to "use every suitable influence to form in their pupils correct moral habits" and to "inculcate upon them the importance of industry, clean-liness, and good manners." Teachers should also appeal "to the honor, good sense, and self respect of the pupils" rather than to engage in "harsh rebuke, vulgar epithets, ill-judged threats, or degrading punishments." Principal Daniel Shepardson said the "discipline" at Woodward High School "has been kind and gentle, but firm and decided." Indeed, at Woodward the cooperation between teachers and pupils "has sweetened our labors, almost annihilated the apparent flight of time, and made our School like a pleasant home pervaded by the most genial influences."[32]

Antebellum and postbellum educators generally opposed corporal punish-ment for high school students. Because pupils were carefully screened for admission, teachers often reported few serious infractions or cases of physical punishment. Even those who taught in charity schools in the 1820s and 1830s had preferred to humiliate rather than hit unruly snipes. By then, the northern bourgeoisie in particular increasingly wanted to socialize youth through love and affection. Reformers nevertheless knew that even children from the best homes could sometimes falter.

The erosion of traditional forms of discipline and the accelerating dangers of the street frightened many parents across the social spectrum though the middle classes left more written evidence of their ideas and practices. Educators who condemned the abuses of corporal punishment rarely banned its use. Few contemporaries defended "flogging, flagellation, caning, whipping, scourging, beating with birch twigs, thongs, the ferule," but even passionate advocates of "moral suasion" reluctantly conceded the teacher's right to inflict physical punishment as a last resort.[33]

Parents, principals, teachers, and officials all desired orderly classrooms. The earliest published rules at Cincinnati's Central School favored a soft pedagogy but also required teachers to keep "a *register* or *black book*" to record delinquent behavior. Teachers identified unwelcome behavior—whether hellish acts of defiance or silly pranks—in such ominous-sounding volumes nearly everywhere. The dark tomes of Nashville and New York City were called the "Book of Discipline." At Philadelphia's Central High School in the 1840s, the boys nicknamed the infamous ledger the "black book."[34]

While most pupils were punctual, respectful of authority, and well behaved, teachers were always on alert. Some individuals were always suspect, and teachers and principals regarded deportment as a badge of character. One absence, one indiscretion, meant a lower rank. As John Hart noted in 1853, "school honors may indeed be but air; yet are they potential in their influence. A high mark may be to its possessor a richer reward than money, a demerit may inflict more pain than stripes." Generally respected by his pupils, Hart was remembered by one for his military demeanor: "As a disciplinarian, ruling by what he did not do or say rather than by speech or action, he was equal to a regular army general." Reverend Hart seemed stern and humorless, a moralist with military manners.[35]

Pupils never forgot a local martinet or pedant. New York City's officials expected the boys at the Free Academy to have "good manners, good morals," and "manly propriety." Principal Horace Webster, a West Point alumnus and former military instructor, was an unflinching, severe man who gave pupils demerits for smiles and grins. When students giggled at a silly remark in chapel, he assumed a military stance and shouted: "Silly ones, grin! Grinners, rise!" Grinners stood at attention at a crack in his office floor that the miscreants dubbed "the Doctor's crack." At every opportunity, scholars heckled Webster, who was assailed by student doggerel and catcalls and amateur ventriloquism.[36]

Principals and teachers spent considerable time appraising student character. High school teachers in towns and cities often met every Saturday morning to discuss their week's successes and failures, agonizing over every disciplinary case, serious or petty. Preventing aberrant behavior was a constant

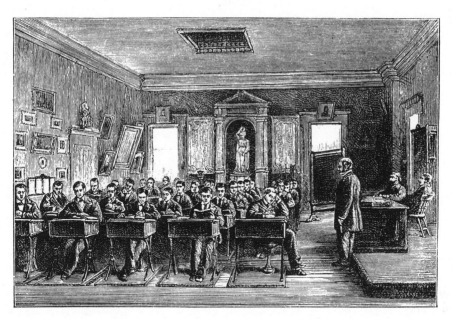

Changes in school architecture on the secondary level were publicized to a wide audience with this sketch of the Boston Latin School, which appeared in 1877 in *Harper's Magazine*. From *Harper's Magazine* 55 (1877).

concern. Daily markings in black books and Saturday faculty meetings were part of a larger effort to maintain educational order.

From the 1820s onward, urban reformers labored to organize graded classrooms, which promised to improve instruction and behavior, even though age grading was never completely implemented. Schoolmen in Boston and elsewhere praised the graded plan for enabling teachers to mold character more easily. Besides refashioning classrooms, innovations in school architecture and furniture also offered additional ways to discipline the young. Urban classrooms became more self-contained, and they usually had bolted-down seats on every grade level throughout the century.[37]

As early as 1832, the boys' high school of Portland, Maine, had individual seats rather than double desks or long-plank seats. This reflected the wider ideology of individual responsibility spreading in a market culture. Pupils studied alone, recited alone, and faced written examinations alone as they competed for academic honors. Double desks still existed in some high schools. By 1869, however, the superintendent of the Savannah schools, W. H. Baker, noted that single desks, while more expensive, were common in the nation's high schools and would soon appear in the local Girls' High School, helping to strengthen self-discipline.[38]

New desks did not guarantee enlightened disciplinary practices. Portland's male high school had single seats, but the master in the 1830s and 1840s still disciplined in traditional ways. Master Libbey reportedly "carried the cowhide under his arm, and honestly used it when needed. Not seldom, in thoughtful mood, he would chew the end of his cowhide, reminding his pupils, as one of them says, of the ruminating possessor thereof." In beating unruly scholars, Master Libbey was an anachronism. Bourgeois notions about nurture and discipline called for more progressive forms of discipline.[39]

In the 1820s, George B. Emerson of the English Classical School established a student court to teach pupils self-control and self-governance. Most teachers before the 1880s, however, assessed demerits for wayward acts. Though boys ordinarily misbehaved more than girls, moral suasion generally seemed to work. Prizes and emulation kept most youthful energies directed toward reaching for the scholastic brass ring, and whipping was unusual in the nation's secondary schools. Parents complained when teachers struck their teenagers, even when physical punishment was legally permissible.[40]

A visitor to Dayton's coeducational high school in 1863 wrote in the *Ohio Educational Monthly* that the pupils were model citizens. "The personal bearing of the scholars was gentlemanly and ladylike, not an instance of boorishness or ill-manners attracting our notice." Still, pupils enjoyed a good prank. At Hartford High in the 1860s and 1870s, pupils taught the water pipes to sing unmelodious tunes, and students giggled as a cat napped undetected on a teacher's bookcase. Clever pupils often planned innocent diversions to break the monotony of the day, but student misbehavior was held to a minimum.[41]

Student diaries reveal how some admittedly atypical pupils valued school deportment. Almira Hubbard Viles agreed with her teacher that noise and idle chatter undermined classroom decorum. Mr. Nichols urged the girls to attend church more regularly to improve their behavior. When he warned pupils not to whisper so much, as spring fever hit the class in 1859, Almira prophesied: "I think this will be quite hard for some of the girls." As the weather warmed and the term dragged on, talking-out-of-turn intensified, and Nichols grew perplexed at the lack of self-restraint. Almira noted that "Mr. Nichols has just invited those who whisper from this time to dine with him—I would not like to be caught talking for I think I should feel cheap going home with him because I have been out of order—it would be a very easy way to get dinner for one who did not expect any at home." She never received a free meal, and the school term closed.[42]

Aspiring to teach, Elizabeth Morrisey of Boston accepted the rules and regulations governing the classroom. Her diary as a normal school pupil reveals that she, too, disliked noisy girls, whether at school or riding the street car. Punctual, studious, and well behaved, Elizabeth also read teacher-training books that emphasized moral suasion over the birch. She and her close friend, Ida, did practice teaching in 1876. On one particular day fate spared her from facing the tensions between theory and practice. Ida "kept school a little while this morning and the children plagued her so she felt like boxing their ears; my children acted splendidly."[43]

Like many high school girls before the 1880s, Carrie Crawford of Louisville also aspired to teach. Her diary covers her junior and senior years—1871 and

1872—at the Female High School, and deportment loomed large in her daily life. Given the formula for determining class rank, Carrie could have become a class valedictorian only through considerable self-restraint. She was a model student and apparently a very agreeable person. A Sunday school teacher, she noted that one professor wanted even better class deportment. Carrie agreed that improving deportment was desirable but grew anxious over tighter restrictions. School was already very competitive, she thought, and how much pressure could young people tolerate? A considerable amount, judging by her own student record. Admittedly unraveled by adult criticism, Carrie wanted to please. She confided to her diary: "Oh, my teachers! How I love them." When she graduated, a teacher applauded her academic achievement and "cheerful and amiable disposition."[44]

Boys were involved in most of the tiny number of suspensions and expulsions in high schools before the 1880s, but female scholars were not always angels. The superintendent of the Nashville, Tennessee, schools caused a furor when he refused to grant diplomas to a few girls who graduated in 1857. In his defense he cited the local rule: "*Diplomas* will be given to those young ladies who complete the *full course* of study, and whose deportment has been *unexceptionable* during their connection with the High School." Deportment remained a vaguer entity than attendance or punctuality, but schoolmen usually assumed that in any dispute they were right and students were wrong.[45]

Adene Williams, who attended Cincinnati's coeducational Hughes High School in the 1860s, respected the rules and regulations and became a teacher. An orphan from a reasonably prosperous family, Adene attended Sunday school, studied hard, and worried about academic success. She nearly always behaved even when she was tempted otherwise. "It was as much as I could do to remain quietly in school today," she recorded in her diary in October of 1865. "I felt like an *untamed Indian*. But we *did* manage to keep up a reasonable degree of order" and fulfill the teachers' expectations. The very next day, however, found Adene furious with Mr. Hotze, who in her opinion unjustly gave her twenty demerits for talking without permission. After she finished her recitation, she openly complained to Hotze, pointing out that the rules specified only ten demerits for her infraction. He replied that twenty caught everyone's attention better. Other students were talking, but he had caught her, and she refused to inform on anyone. The next day everyone in her class had to write an essay. The subject: "Gratitude." She duly recorded her disdain for all "moralizing essays" yet did the assignment.[46]

Students disliked what they saw as injustice, but most complied with the rules. Those who did not were an annoyance and challenged high principles. Even some academically talented boys fulfilled the stereotype of the rude teenager. Charles E. Strattan, studying at the Boston Latin School in the early 1860s, prepped for Harvard but enjoyed causing minor trouble. Francis Gardner, his teacher, was by many reports a gruff, short-tempered, difficult person, admired by many in the community but often feared by the pupils.

"Gardner got off one or two of his rough jokes" was a typical entry in Strattan's diary. If Gardner was sarcastic, his pupil was devilish. "Just before school was out moved lots of desks and made a general row."[47]

Strattan excelled at annoying people. He and a friend attended an English High exhibition that featured an ex-slave: "Nigger spoke, and very well, too. Old woman in front very much troubled by our talking." Gardner called him a liar, which elicited a brief diary entry: "He is a blessed old humbug." Strattan and some friends decorated Daniel Webster's statue and "left it dressed to amuse Gardner, but he was *not* amused." Annoying people was not evidence that Strattan was a mediocre scholar or even disliked his crusty mentor. Before graduation, he and his classmates gave the "old humbug" a farewell gift, and Gardner dutifully tutored the seniors for their college entrance tests. On graduating from Boston Latin in 1862, the somewhat obstreperous Strattan received a medal.[48]

Examples of how a handful of boys preoccupied teachers' meetings emerge in the records of Louisville's Male High School. The school's "Merit Book" in the 1860s and 1870s listed types of deportment problems that faculty discussed each Saturday morning. The staff reprimanded Joseph Woodruff in 1868 for "negligence of Greek & disorderly conduct in the chapel," while others received demerits for skipping class, disobedience, and talking. As punishment, pupils were often forced to write or memorize numerous lines "from Latin, English, or German authors," depending upon their course of study.[49]

Certain pupils were suspended for insolence to their teachers, apologized, were reinstated, then suspended again. Other offenders, though, might be banned from school after a single, albeit egregious, offense. On February 15, 1871, the merit book revealed the "Insubordination of T. Bryan." Mr. Bryan refused to recopy an assignment, tore his original composition to pieces, and was rude to his teacher, calling him a "damned fool." The scholar was expelled immediately, and the "sentence was read out before the school assembled in the chapel."[50]

In early 1872 one lad was expelled "for exploding a torpedo in Professor Butler's room and afterwards telling the principal that he knew nothing of any torpedoes being exploded in the building at all." Others performed catcalls in chapel, rang bells, threw chalk, and otherwise mocked decorum. A Mr. Barries was "arraigned" before the staff in 1876 "for whispering in the chemistry room in distinct violation of his promises to watch his conduct." Professors described infractions in formal legal language: these were "cases" or "trials" that led to "verdicts," "convictions," and "sentences." Young Barries apologized, claiming that "in spite of his better intentions, [he] forgot himself." Before readmission, the contrite young man heard a lecture: "that the professors resp. [sic] are responsible to himself & to the community for this development of his character which has been so far satisfactory—and stated to him that this full[fill]ment of his present promise to be on his guard, shall be in his & their eyes a test of his earnestness & force of character." All for whispering.[51]

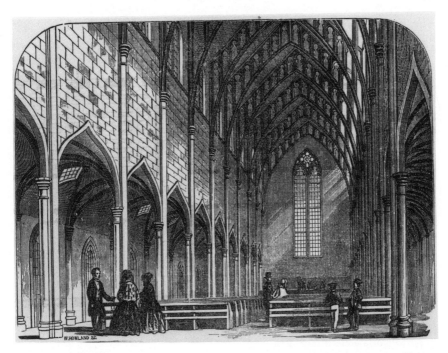

Even ordinarily well-mannered boys at New York's Free Academy sometimes could not resist the opportunity to disrupt chapel services with their catcalls and other student pranks. Only a few elite high schools had formal chapels, though Bible reading was common in secondary schools across the nation in the nineteenth century. From *American Journal of Education* 8 (1873).

Studying was also essential to success. At the Girls' High School of Portland, Maine, scholars knew that teachers regarded study and scholarship as moral virtues. Daily oral recitation grades, monthly and end-of-term written examinations, and marks on homework constituted one-third of one's report card and class rank. As the most advanced scholars at Moses Woolson's school indicated in their Saturday morning essays, poems, and conversations, study and scholarship were integrally bound. One seasoned pupil gave ironic "Advice to the New Scholars" in 1857:

When you go home from school, be sure and carry as large a pile of books as possible, a large dictionary would be grand, and you may also study in the street. This will give you an industrious air and at once show that you belong to the Girls' High School. Read novels to cultivate your sensibilities, follow out all your inclinations, and don't practice any self-denial with regard to staying at home or going to parties as we have found that it won't do any good at all. You will get along just as well if you go, as if you had staid [sic] at home poring over hard lessons.[52]

The pupil's parody exposed the academic expectations of the best high schools.

Other Portland girls offered serious comments as well as spoofs on study and homework. In 1851, "Edith" sang a familiar tune:

> My lesson's missed
> What shall I do
> For oh what shame
> I never knew.
> I am so dull
> And such a fool
> To be sent to this High School.[53]

A decade later another local student drew a pair of pencil sketches that revealed the intimate bonds between bourgeois homes and schools. One sketch showed a student poring over her lessons at her own desk in her private bedroom; another showed her standing next to her school desk and reciting her lesson. These were familiar images to middle-class pupils everywhere. "That awful calamity—a missed lesson, is the cause of many a sigh and many a tear," wrote another young woman, who had been told that a botched recitation indicated a character flaw.[54]

Secondary pupils continually heard that study was analogous to work. To spend one's brief life on earth productively was a Christian virtue and a practical necessity. Standard reading materials, for both children and adults, emphasized the power of study in shaping character and intellect. Respectable journals from the *North American Review* to *The Lady's Book* preached the bourgeois gospel: Providence dictated that hard work yielded good fruits, whereas idleness and drink produced human misery. Advice books said it simply: lazy pupils became poor adults. "He who is neglecting his studies at school, is putting a clog upon himself which will fetter him as long as he lives."[55]

A juvenile and high school singing book offered youth a chant on study:

> How pleasantly the moments,
> In study pass away.
> The hours are too fleeting,
> And far too short the day.

Time was God's invention. He created the world in a fixed number of days, and laziness and tardiness were unchristian. "Begone, Dull Sloth," warned the lyricist in *The Columbian Song Book* (1856):

> For I will work, and I will learn,
> And usefully pass the day,
> And I will think it one of the wisest things
> To drive dull sloth away.

Students frequently sang about the joys of hard work, application, and personal achievement in the competitive schoolroom:

> I love the school; I love its rules;
> I there true pleasure find;
> And in Instruction's glorious race
> I'll leave the dunce behind.[56]

High school textbooks repeatedly told students to prize study and scholarship. Studying formed character by cultivating the work ethic and by effecting the mastery of useful knowledge. Composition and rhetoric books and English readers genuflected before Franklin. "Learning and knowledge must be attained by slow degrees; and are the reward only of dilligence [sic] and patience," warned Lindley Murray in a spelling lesson. Samuel Kirkham's popular English grammar book offered such parsing exercises as "Studious scholars learn many long lessons." Political economy and moral science textbooks said that God rewarded the studious and punished the lazy. Rich or poor lived under the same heaven-inspired rules; "dolts," "blockheads," and "dunces" had sealed their own sad fate. And history and geography textbooks equated Protestantism with the work ethic and Catholic nations with hedonism and laziness.[57]

Even the work ethic could be overdone, however. Most high school teachers and officials expected pupils to study at least two or three hours each evening, including weekends. Occasionally, though, when some citizens believed that rigorous study endangered the health of girls—and sometimes boys—the schools literally forbade homework. Even the no-nonsense, venerable Boston Latin School made homework optional in 1864. At the time the estimated nightly home study was one or two hours, but complaints against overwork forced the school to relent. The chair of the Latin School Committee, Nathaniel B. Shurtleff, explained, "If any parent should prefer that his son should not have any out of school lessons assigned, he can by a written request, have his wishes gratified." But Shurtleff also emphasized that anyone who avoided homework would be ill-prepared for college admission.[58]

Some Bostonians complained after midcentury that excessive study had ruined pupils' health at the Girls' High and Normal School. Girls were often more punctual and better behaved than boys, and their dutiful approach to study, it was argued, had weakened their reproductive systems. Officials responded by restricting girls' homework to two hours daily and limiting school study periods. Criticisms intensified, so homework was abolished in 1862; within two years, however, educators pressed for the return of the two-hour rule to strengthen academic standards. Officials again restricted homework in the 1870s, and the matter was never permanently settled anywhere.[59]

Antihomework campaigns to the contrary, however, schools were places of study, and so were the homes of most secondary students. The sketches by the Portland schoolgirl captured the essence of everyday experience for most bourgeois pupils, male and female. When urban reformers complained loudly enough about the alleged deterioration of women's physical and mental health, homework was banned, only to return as quickly as it disappeared. Sending youth to high school was a sacrifice, even for middle-class parents. Like most educators, parents or guardians believed that the demand for application and study helped define a good school.

After debates flared in San Francisco in the 1860s, the school board limited home study for girls to one hour, boys to two. The local superintendent, however, characteristically said that the cry of too much study was exaggerated and, if occasionally true, a minor ill in an imperfect world. Critics blamed the schools for expecting too much of youth, but teachers and officials said scholars and their parents bore the responsibility for health problems.

"While it is important that the youthful mind should not be over-burdened with too many studies, yet in removing the evil, we must be careful not to run into the opposite extreme," warned San Francisco's superintendent. "If the standard of scholarship is reduced too low, it fails to stimulate the scholars to habits of thoroughness, self-help, and self-reliance." The superintendent then lectured the public on some self-evident truths. "Many of the evils which are charged to the hard study of the school room," he insisted, "are owing to causes over which the teachers have no control. If children mingled less in society, late in the evening, either at home, or at parties and social gatherings, there would be less sickness and incapacity to study in the day time."[60]

From the 1820s through the 1880s, schoolmen in villages, towns, and cities generally dismissed the idea that rigorous schoolwork caused poor health while admitting that, regrettably, some overzealous teachers and precocious pupils lacked restraint. Although high schools expected pupils to work hard and to study, a few hours of evening sacrifice were hardly onerous. At school, pupils usually had four or five classes, where student recitations predominated. Two other class periods usually offered quiet study. The model pupil avoided late evenings, excessive social engagements, novels, bad company, and the evils of the street. M. D. Leggett, superintendent of the Zanesville, Ohio, schools, wrote in 1859 that high schools were special places with high academic expectations. "Those who do not possess sufficient self-denial, to refrain from such pleasures as conflict with their duties, as students, ought to content themselves with the mere rudiments of an English education, and not connect themselves at all with the High School."[61]

Students recognized that the mastery of rote material in textbooks was central to schoolwork. Pupil diaries provide numerous references to reading or studying specific textbooks at home and school. The academic burdens were often heavy. A scholar in Lancaster, Pennsylvania, offered a lament in 1863 that echoed in many quarters of student culture.

> Night sacred to rest, brings me no repose
> For a huge pile of books reaching up to my nose,
> Absorb my whole waking, afflict me in sleep,

And e'en in my dreams most audaciously creep.
My head aches, my side aches, my cheeks have grown pale,
Yet study I must, or certainly fail.[62]

In her "Soliloquy of a School Girl, Just Before Graduation," an alter ego in another town said hurrah to the end of school, which left more time for dances, novels, and frivolity: "How I pity my seatmate who has yet another year to spend in that schoolroom. To be sure she is called a fine scholar and great praise is bestowed upon her by every one, but then what of that."[63]

When accused of assigning excessive homework, high school teachers and principals almost uniformly denied the charge. Pedagogues largely embraced the reigning values of political economy shared by Whigs and Republicans, and even the Democratic opposition acknowledged the importance of hard work and individual application. That individual effort shaped personal destiny permeated the values of the major political parties, schoolbooks, self-help guides, and bourgeois magazines. Just as political economists argued that work, the punishment when man rejected Eden, was distasteful, teachers said hard study was less appealing than play but basic to success and character formation. Asking schools to eliminate homework was like telling farmers to abandon their fields or manufacturers to break their machines. The fear of starvation caused adults to labor, and the prospect of failure caused pupils to study.[64]

High school teachers, principals, and other officials continually defended homework and rigorous study. No one recommended assigning more than a few hours of homework per day, but most adults believed laziness a greater evil than overstudy. That was heard in emerging institutions like Philadelphia's Central High School in the early 1840s and in many high schools after the Civil War. Principal Cyrus Knowlton of Cincinnati's Hughes High School said in 1859 that "propriety in deportment" and "diligence in study" characterized a good school, and if a pupil "neglects his studies, he can be of no service to himself: if he tramples upon the rules, he is a plague to all the others." During Reconstruction, bourgeois Yankee values spread into southern secondary schools. A minister who helped dedicate Charleston's new high school in 1881 blended religion and political economy into a familiar school ethos: "In learning, as in all other things, it is the hand of the diligent that maketh riches."[65]

As more pupils passed entrance examinations and enrollments expanded, educators complained that a significant minority of pupils refused to study once admitted. Just as some pupils were admitted but never enrolled, others matriculated and became "clogs" in the system. Because even one or two years of attendance might give pupils an advantage in the job market, the complaint was somewhat justified: for some pupils matriculation was more important than academic achievement. It was difficult to motivate pupils to study diligently if they did not intend to remain to the junior or senior years.

Unless pupils "have a natural fondness for study, by the time they reach the

High School they are heartily sick of it," claimed one observer in Cleveland in 1866. Some pupils had to work to help support their families, others were sickly or lazy, and still others found homework, recitations, and written examinations less appealing as they grew older. Educators assumed that a high percentage of pupils left school because they found hard work and study distasteful. "Idlers" abounded who had time to read dime novels but not to study. Alexis de Tocqueville observed that the northern bourgeoisie generally "want great success at once, but they want to do it without great efforts." The French aristocrat added: "A middling standard has been established in America for all human knowledge. All minds come near to it, some by raising and some by lowering their standards."[66]

Contemporaries with an intimate knowledge of high schools recognized that academic quality varied enormously in different communities. Some "high schools" were rooms on the top floor of union schools, poorly graded and offering a scanty curriculum. Others admitted pupils unprepared even for meager academic fare, and daunting requirements would have undermined attempts to attract the respectable classes into the public system. Boston's English Classical School grappled early with the problem of classroom standards. In 1823, local schoolmen claimed that "the diligent are not kept back by the indolent, nor the stupid pushed on to what they are incapable of understanding, for the benefit of the intelligent." Nearly a half-century later, a Bostonian could still write that "not every pebble is capable of taking the lustre of the brilliant diamond. . . . This should be constantly borne in mind by committees and educators . . . that all the institutions of learning that capital can build, as High Schools, will be unable to furnish brains for the masses to complete with credit the higher courses of instruction. This is a wise ordering of Providence."[67]

Indeed, early theorists of high schools expected academic standards to vary. Writing as Rhode Island's chief school officer in 1846, Henry Barnard argued that quality would reflect "the standard fixed by the intelligence and intellectual wants of the district." Systems lowered standards to admit pupils to fill vacant seats and tightened them when the building neared capacity. Schoolmen gave admission tests to exclude the unqualified but over time admitted nearly everyone, as the passing rate in many communities soared after midcentury.[68]

Report cards usually counted academic performance—an amalgam of daily oral recitations, monthly tests, and end-of-term exams—as one-third of the final score, but standards fluctuated. The awarding of prizes and honors to stimulate achievement was widespread, except in all-girls' schools. A minority of students, however, simply counted their time, rarely studied, and depressed the class average. Schools and their staff had to compromise, but educators often resented and resisted attempts to open the high school to all.

Whether they hailed from Elyria or Oshkosh, Chicago or Cincinnati, administrators complained about pupils throughout the century. Students cared more about high grades and prizes than knowledge and improvement, said the head of the Woodward High School in 1862. They were pampered and spoiled and often lacked the work ethic, preferring cram over sustained effort. Though officials had gradually raised the minimum age of admission, parents pressured teachers to promote youth too rapidly.

"Many in the High School are certainly beyond their depth," wrote the principal of the Oshkosh high school in 1875. "I find no fault with any one for this. It is natural and pardonable for pupils to desire advancement, for parents to share in their desire, and for teachers to wish as many of their pupils as possible to 'pass grade.'" A scholar from Cincinnati noted an absence of class spirit, as individualism reigned supreme. "A pupil generally cares for his average alone. It does not affect him at all, if the average of the class is low; if he has received the best percents, be they ever so bad, it is immaterial to him whether his class accomplishes anything or not."[69]

Girls on average performed better scholastically than boys in nineteenth-century high schools. Though educators accused some girls of being frivolous and addicted to fashion, female scholars in many towns and cities won the majority of academic prizes in coeducational settings. A comparison of grades awarded to girls and boys at the coeducational Portland, Maine, high school between 1866 and 1880 is typical. In twenty-seven school terms, the boys' average was higher only twice. The girls' advantage was often statistically small but their average was sometimes a half- to a full grade higher.[70]

Whether pupils studied diligently or rarely, study, homework, and the mastery of books inspired considerable student doggerel, poetry, and prose. Scholars complained about missed recitations, failed chemistry experiments, inscrutable algebra problems, and faulty prose. Their voices cracked while reciting, they forgot their textbooks, they prepared the wrong lessons. One schoolgirl in 1852 wondered:

> Poetry in algebra, where does it lie?
> In questions so puzzling and long,
> Is it found in x plus z plus y?
> Is it found when the answers [sic] wrong?

Another young woman, commenting upon the academic rigor of her classes, said everyone found different ways to climb the hill of knowledge. Some accepted the struggle to learn as a "severe necessity"; others enjoyed it like "a dose of castor oil." A half-century after the event, Mary Bradford recounted the horrors of public examinations at the Kenosha, Wisconsin, high school. "How the pupils dreaded those examinations!" The "dignified examiners" and friends and relatives came "to witness the ordeal. Such an examination in physical geography is still clear in my memory. Scared out of my wits, to a degree that rendered doubtful my ability to tell my own name if asked, I blundered on the questions asked me, with the consequent harrowing effects."[71]

Diaries show the place of study in the lives of exceptional scholars. In

Portsmouth, Almira Viles heard a story in the 1850s of a man who went blind because of excessive study. She studied diligently nonetheless. Charles Strattan of Boston Latin, when not annoying others, busily studied and crammed for Harvard's entrance examination. In the fall of 1865, Adene Williams paused while studying in her Cincinnati boarding house to describe a typical day: "Whew! but we *had* a *small* amount of work on our hands today. In addition to our usual work, Latin, chemistry, and Astronomy, I had some *hard* problems which deserved the name and in addition to all this . . . had compositions to write. Subject: 'Humbugs.' Solved some of the problems and then went to work on the composition." She went to bed with a headache, a common complaint of diligent female scholars.[72]

In the 1870s, Alice Devin often commented on study despite her active social life in Ann Arbor. Carrie Crawford of the Louisville Female High School, later a valedictorian, studied continually and got headaches, like many other women who wanted to please their parents, their teachers, and maybe themselves. Elizabeth Morrisey of the Boston High and Normal School was an insatiable reader who studied incessantly. On the weekends she also read library books and attended temperance lectures. Typical references in her diary in 1876 included: "Came home and studied of course" or "studied after dinner." When summer came, she complained: "I could not seem to study at all . . . I'm so tired and sick of it."[73]

Mary Ellen Clarke, a student at the Female High School of Baltimore, studied constantly. Enrolled at the school between 1877 and 1880, she graduated with a 99.3 percent average. She was rarely tardy, attended diligently, and never received a demerit. One year her father wrote on her report card that her record was "very creditable to my daughter & her teachers." Perhaps accustomed to Mary Ellen's near perfection, he signed the card "satisfactory" in February of 1878, when her average was 99.5 percent. In her autograph album in 1878, he said his daughter brought him tears of joy:

> 'Tis that which pious fathers shed
> Upon a duteous daughter's head.[74]

Scholars as "duteous" as Mary Ellen Clarke were the pride of high schools before the 1880s. Some suffered family tragedies, a few boarded apart from their parents, but they took their school responsibilities seriously. They arrived at school punctually, behaved themselves, and mastered the innumerable facts in their ubiquitous textbooks. Training their intellects in often mechanical ways, they recited almost flawlessly when called upon, standing with perfect posture next to their desks. They had beautiful penmanship, used grammar correctly, and performed well on written examinations.

According to their diaries, when pupils returned home after school, many practiced a musical instrument, dined with their parents, and then studied. Some had a home life that matched ideals in prescriptive literature and middle-class magazines. Even those boarding away from home frequently discussed regular visits by parents, siblings, or close relatives. On weekends the most pious and committed Protestants also attended lectures and taught Sunday schools. By the standards of bourgeois homes and schools, they were model individuals and good scholars.[75]

Only a few educators thought the high school academic ranking system odd. In the 1860s the principal of Philadelphia's male high school announced a new academic policy: conduct and scholarship were separated, and only scholarship would determine class rank. Principal George Inman Riché explained that behavior and academic performance were unlike quantities and should not be averaged. "If a student be proficient in scholarship," he wrote, "he is entitled to a clear and unmixed statement of that fact, and to the benefits accruing from it. If his moral character be defective, he is none the less entitled to the credit earned by his application to study." The Philadelphian was hardly suggesting that minds were more important than morals, but this was a radical departure.[76]

Superintendent John D. Philbrick of Boston likewise thought that adding unlike entities was "as irrational as . . . adding the numbers representing the weight and height of a pupil to ascertain the cubical measure of his corporeal figure." Measurement and precision, however, held seductive charms for most contemporary educators. Charts and graphs verified the movement of student populations through different grades and courses. Generals counted their troops, accountants checked their ledgers, and schoolmen ticked off vital statistics on attendance, deportment, and scholarship.[77]

Teachers wanted to provide pupils with the moral tenets and intellectual tools to navigate safely through uncharted waters. They tried to teach values and virtues they regarded as timeless: respect authority, be on time, and strive for personal achievement. Only then could scholars live up to their potential as scholars and then adult citizens. Although the values may have seemed eternal, schoolmen were nevertheless preparing particular youth for a changing economic and social order. The kinds of personal achievement championed in the classroom and glorified in this age of individualism would have horrified citizens before the Revolution. Self-interest became the foundation of a new social order, not something to be feared as a threat to the community.

The moral virtues instilled at school taught talented youth how to succeed by emphasizing the new laws of political economy. Tardiness meant a gray mark on the school record, or lost wages. Misbehavior meant entry in the black book, or social disapproval or punishment. Laziness meant a missed lesson or failed exam, or adult poverty. Teachers combined their assessments of these fragments into a composite of a good scholar, dutifully entering scores on each individual report card awaiting signature from parent or guardian. Assessing the achievements and failures of students remained difficult but common, wherever youth attended school.

Varieties of Experience

We must measure arms with the dominant
class, in Ethics, Mental Philosophy, History, Mathematics, the Languages and
Oratory. We must be their equals in
human knowledge, improvements, and
inventions, and until we are, all schemes
for equalizing the races . . . are nothing
but cob webs, to catch the weak and
delude the weary. It is not enough, then,
that we say—"That all men are created
equal." Kings have smiled at this Democratic gibberish. Our opponents demand a
living example.

JOHN I. GAINES, black teacher and
activist, Cincinnati, 1858

Educators North and South as
late as the 1870s realized that there was really no such thing as *the* American
high school. Compared with the 1820s, there were free high schools aplenty,
but they were hardly cast from a single mold. High school scholars included
those who read one or two advanced subjects in a rural school, those who
enjoyed richer academic fare in a union graded school, and those who imbibed
a full curriculum in America's cities.[1]

As the number of advanced pupils increased across the North after the
1840s and in the urban South after Appomattox, administrators increasingly
gathered basic statistics about various high schools. By the 1870s, when free
secondary education faced intensified criticisms, state superintendents in
Maine and other states collected more information on local institutions. Their
imperfect statistics always reflected particular educational aims and political
goals, as Democrats and Republicans in many states after the Civil War
debated the efficacy of tax-supported secondary education. But despite their
flaws, these studies outlined some of the main characteristics of the nation's
secondary schools by the 1880s.

The high school was an image as well as a place, something different to
superintendents, social reformers, principals, teachers, textbook writers,
authors of pedagogical primers, and pupils. To zealous reformers, the high
school was a great republican experiment, the great hope for poor but worthy

scholars. To many teachers and principals, it was a temporary job or a long-term career. To textbook authors and salesmen, it was a lucrative market. To an exceptional man such as Joseph Ray—a social reformer, high school teacher and principal, and renowned author—the free high school represented all these things simultaneously.[2]

Even though most students were middle class, they never saw the high school through a single lens. Scholars seeking the higher learning faced different educational prospects in a rural area, village, town, or city. Because most "freshmen" in well-graded systems never reached eleventh grade, their perspectives also differed from the minority of pupils who graduated and maybe even aspired to college. Student life also varied for boys and girls, for whites and the tiny percentage of black secondary scholars, and for pupils who attended coeducational schools and those segregated by gender or race. Most pupils studied the English (or modern) curriculum, but separate curricula in normal training or classical education in the larger districts meant added complexity. A poor girl who aspired to become a teacher saw the world differently from a wealthy boy headed for college.

The heightened interest in educational statistics in the nineteenth century never produced great precision, accuracy, or consensus on the exact number of high schools or secondary students. In 1880 a writer in *Education* estimated that America had two thousand high schools, but guesses diverged widely. At midcentury, northern state officials, doubting the accuracy of available statistics, advocated more uniform record keeping. Yet many state officials continued to count grammar school scholars as high school pupils because outside of the larger communities they sometimes studied one or two advanced subjects.[3]

Identifying a high school or a high school student remained difficult. No one could agree whether a high school pupil studied one, two, three, or four advanced subjects, so state and local officials gathered data differently. State officers occasionally employed questionable procedures and unintentionally sent ambiguous requests to the local officials, who failed to file reports or provided unreliable information.

In 1904, William T. Harris, who had long championed high schools, offered his own interpretation of their evolution. In 1850, he believed, 11 high schools in the United States had a two- to four-year curriculum, which he considered the minimum requirement for a secondary school. Using the same measure, he found 44 high schools in 1860, "of which three were in the South." According to Harris, high schools then spread rapidly, numbering 160 in 1870, 800 in 1880, and 2,526 in 1890. And while fewer black than white youth enrolled in secondary schools, the growth of segregated urban high schools in the South after the 1880s reflected this upward spiral.[4]

These estimates would have puzzled many citizens before the 1880s. Things looked different at the grass roots: far more places claimed to have high schools than Harris calculated. Critics in Kalamazoo and elsewhere fought over the "high school"—whether it existed on the top floor of a union building, had a full curriculum, or met certain professional standards.

And if Harris found only 160 high schools in the United States in 1870, Maine's school superintendent counted 143 in his state alone four years later. Between 1855 and 1856, Ohio's high schools leaped in number from 57 to 91, according to state officials; by 1879 the number was 148. What did these numbers mean? What did they reveal about student experiences and the nature of secondary schools before the 1880s? Studying grass-roots developments in Maine, which conducted several investigations of local high schools in the 1870s, provides perspective.[5]

In 1861, Edward P. Weston, the state superintendent, counted many high schools, "so called," in Maine. Most children and youth attended small ungraded schools in rural areas, where taxpayers typically opposed efforts at centralization. Many villages and towns nevertheless offered some postelementary advanced subjects in the upper grammar grades. The school supervisor from Alfred, for example, claimed that "certain higher branches have been taught successfully, to some of the more advanced scholars" in the village's one- and two-room schools: "algebra, natural philosophy, and astronomy."[6]

In the late 1860s and early 1870s, Warren Johnson, a Republican state superintendent and advocate of the English studies, endorsed legislation to convert academies into free public high schools and to advance secondary education in Maine's small "farming towns." In 1873 a Republican-dominated legislature passed a bill that provided some funds for villages and towns to help create high schools. Most existing or new public secondary schools, often former academies, lacked the student demand or resources to justify an extended course of study more common in major cities. Thus they failed to meet the standards conceived by William T. Harris three decades later. Johnson and many contemporaries, however, realized that advanced instruction did not follow a single model, and the statistics gathered on Maine's high schools in 1874 exemplified the diversity common in many states.[7]

Sharing the age's fascination with statistics, Johnson typically used them to embellish his reports. He presented the "Returns of Free High Schools" alphabetically from Abbot to Yarmouth, yet he failed to explain exactly how high schools varied by community size. A seasoned politician, Johnson knew that he lacked the means to impose a common standard, and he hardly needed statistics to know that rural, village, and urban schools differed.[8]

If Maine had 143 high schools in 1874, how much did the "high school" pupils in little Island Falls, medium-sized Yarmouth, or Portland have in common? Following the passage of the high school law, Superintendent Johnson gathered some statistics on local institutions. Table 1 shows some central characteristics of high schools in 1874 along a continuum from the smallest to the largest districts. These averages mask the differences among communities in each category but underscore the disparate experiences of Maine's secondary pupils.[9]

Districts that claimed high schools ranged from Blanchard, which enrolled

TABLE I.
Maine's High Schools, 1874

Total Enrollment in System	No. of High Schools	No. of Pupils	% in High School	Term (Weeks)	Third Reader (%)	Arithmetic (%)	Ancient Language (%)	Modern Language (%)
0-100	4	114	36	12	39	73	2	0
101-199	6	327	36	15	16	84	2	1
200-399	44	3293	26	18	10	83	5	1
400-599	33	3141	20	22	5	71	11	3
600-799	17	2147	18	29	8	82	10	3
800-999	10	976	11	30	8	65	19	10
1000-1499	15	1645	9	27	2	63	16	9
1500-1900	3	287	5	32	0	77	42	16
2000-2499	4	322	4	36	0	31	61	21
2500-2999	2	194	4	40	0	10	56	16
3000-4999	1	80	2	40	0	0	100	0
5000-7999	3	385	2	30	0	46	75	41
8000-	1	401	4	40	0	20	77	38
Totals/ Averages	143	13312	6	23	6	70	17	7
0-999	114	9998	20	21	8	77	9	3
1000-	29	3314	5	31	1	49	41	18

Source: *Twenty-First Annual Report of the State Superintendent of Common Schools* (Augusta, Maine, 1875): 36-43.

69 scholars in its entire school system but claimed 37 high school students, to Portland, which enrolled 10,132 pupils, of whom 401 were high school students. A clear pattern emerges: the smaller the system, the higher the percentage regarded locally as high school pupils. Districts that enrolled fewer than 200 students claimed an average of 36 percent were high school scholars. Blanchard said that 54 percent of its 69 scholars were high school students, and Island Falls said that half of its 82 pupils fit the definition. Small places were proud of their capacity to offer the advanced branches.[10]

A school district's size influenced the percentage of pupils studying high school subjects. As districts increased in size, their schools usually became better graded. As classification improved, pupils counted as advanced students in smaller places were not so regarded in larger districts. Urban areas set minimum admission ages that helped restrict access to secondary classes to youth older than thirteen.

The citizens of Island Falls realized that reformers regarded them as educationally backward. Richer and larger districts like Portland had more specialized teachers, better-graded classes, and separate high school facilities. But all the world was not Portland or Bangor; they were atypical. Those districts enrolling fewer than 800 pupils had 72 percent of Maine's high schools and 68 percent of its secondary pupils. Districts that enrolled 1,500 or more pupils had only 10 percent of the high schools and 13 percent of the advanced scholars.

If the smallest districts had the most high schools and enrolled the highest percentage of secondary pupils, the statistics also had a less flattering side. Pupils in the smallest districts studied the higher branches for the least time. At the extremes, youth in little Blanchard had a ten-week term, compared with forty weeks in Portland. Maine's high schools and advanced scholars were largely in districts with fewer than 1,500 pupils, but these districts often lacked a sufficient tax base and concentration of pupils to support longer school terms. Although larger districts had a smaller percentage of their pupils in high school, scholars in Calais, Bath, Biddeford, Lewiston, and Portland enjoyed longer terms. A handful of smaller communities invested in longer school terms to match the largest districts, but the cost prevented most from doing so.[11]

Other statistics suggest more differences among high schools across the state. Superintendent Johnson asked local officers what their high school pupils studied, but defining a high school subject precisely, including its level of difficulty, remained ambiguous. Johnson specifically asked, for example, whether high school pupils studied the "Third Reader," a grammar-level text. States lacked uniform textbooks, and district officials probably interpreted his question differently, but their responses provide a rough gauge of local practices.

Districts enrolling fewer than 1,500 pupils typically had some high school pupils studying the Third Reader. The average percentage was highest in the smallest districts. In districts enrolling fewer than 100 pupils, 39 percent of the high school pupils on average studied the Third Reader. The percentage declined noticeably to 16 percent for districts between 101 and 199 pupils, and the percentage continued to drop as district size increased.

None of the high school pupils in systems that enrolled more than 1,500 pupils studied the Third Reader. Places such as Portland had better-graded schools and formal admission tests; pupils had to master the Third Reader before applying for the exam. Although a substantial percentage of secondary pupils in the smallest districts read this text, the majority of advanced pupils throughout Maine did *not* study the Third Reader. That is, the majority everywhere had progressed beyond it.

Reformers often criticized small districts, decentralized control, and poorly graded schools and smirked at the so-called "high schools" in rural America. Kinder observers, with a less urban orientation, might have applauded those districts in Maine that enrolled less than 1,500 pupils. With fewer economic resources and relatively short terms, the smaller districts had pushed most of their advanced pupils to master their Third Reader.

Algebra was a bedrock of the urban high school curriculum since the 1820s. Maine's smaller districts, however, still had difficulty offering this advanced subject in the 1870s. A student usually mastered grammar-level arithmetic before tackling algebra, so most pupils still studying the lower subject were not ready for the higher one. Johnson, in fact, inquired about enrollments in arithmetic rather than in algebra. Better-graded systems restricted algebra to the high school, and urban educators generally regarded arithmetic as a grammar-level subject. All but 9 of Maine's 143 high schools, however, taught the lower subject to some of their pupils.

District size remained crucial. For districts enrolling fewer than 1,500 pupils, the percentage on average studying arithmetic fluctuated between 63 percent and 84 percent. Although the trend was irregular, the percentage enrolled in arithmetic continually declined as district size increased. In the larger towns and cities, in Maine as elsewhere, high schools sometimes offered a short refresher course in arithmetic, but most advanced pupils in districts larger than 2,000 students typically studied algebra.[12]

Johnson also gathered information on foreign language courses, adding further insights into differing academic environments in local high schools. Teaching a foreign language required very specialized skills, and only urban districts could attract and afford specially trained teachers. Hence secondary pupils in the largest districts usually had greater access to these subjects.[13]

Contemporaries divided the languages into familiar categories, ancient versus modern. An ancient language was a high-status subject, long associated with the classical grammar school and the preparation of select boys for college. Latin was the staple of the ancient languages, while Greek was a rarity even in America's oldest urban systems. The modern foreign languages, in contrast, had been basic to the English curriculum since the opening of America's first high school in 1821. Antebellum reformers reaffirmed that French, Spanish, or German helped prepare boys for the world of commerce and gave respectable girls a more enriched, higher course of study.[14]

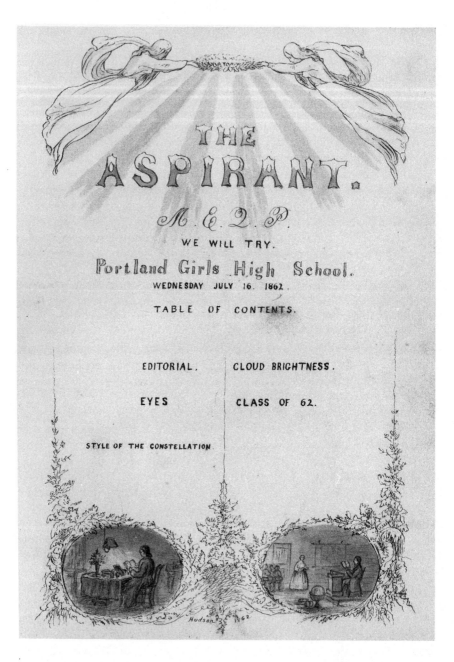

The scholars at Portland's Girls' High School produced student magazines filled with high-quality poems, essays, editorials, and pencil sketches. Collections of the Maine Historical Society.

Superintendent Johnson found that in Maine, districts that enrolled 100 to 599 pupils rarely offered advanced students a foreign language, ancient or modern. On average 2 percent to 11 percent of the pupils in these districts studied an ancient language and less than 4 percent a modern language. Although the trend was uneven, the capacity to offer a foreign language in Maine improved as district size increased. Only in districts larger than 2,000 pupils did the majority of secondary pupils take a foreign language.

Moreover, recall that 87 percent of Maine's high school pupils were in districts with fewer than 1,500 pupils. These scholars did not have specialized teachers, so those pursuing a foreign language had tutorials in mostly ungraded classrooms. In a larger system like Biddeford, on the other hand, all high school students in 1874 took an ancient language, probably Latin. The foreign languages also thrived at Bangor, Lewiston, and Portland. A small number of pupils even took Greek at Portland's coeducational high school, as they had since it opened during the Civil War.[15]

Although the majority of Maine's high school students in 1874 did not study a foreign language, those who did favored a classical tongue, typically Latin. For every category of school district, the ancient languages enrolled a higher percentage than their modern alternatives, even though the vast majority of scholars were in the English stream, preparing for life rather than for college. Again, Latin was a high-status subject, whose mastery, teachers said, trained and disciplined the mind. The hallmark of a classical education since the colonial period, Latin enjoyed the cache of tradition. When Portland opened its Girls' High School in 1852, its no-nonsense principal, Moses Woolson, required every pupil to study Latin to demonstrate women's capacity to master the most abstract subjects. Decades later, female alumni proudly recalled that they had once been Latin scholars at Woolson's school.[16]

Critics had long condemned the foreign languages, especially Latin, as pretentious, aristocratic, and antirepublican. They implied that what transpired at Portland High was typical, though in truth most pupils in Maine did not study *any* foreign language, ancient or modern. Maine's professional educators, of course, believed that Portland, not the little villages, was on the right path. But on the local level citizens often saw things differently.[17]

When Superintendent Johnson asked local officials to describe the higher learning in their districts, he discovered high schools and high school pupils everywhere. Portland was not their polestar. Republican activists often wished that every district had the advantages of a prominent seaport such as Portland, with its specialized high school, well-trained teachers, elaborate entrance examinations, and well-defined curriculum. But small-district contemporaries described their high schools as real enough, even if outsiders discounted some of their achievements.

Efforts to standardize secondary schools foundered on the shoals of localism. To qualify for state funds that helped pay the salaries of secondary school teachers, districts in Maine had to agree to administer an admission test to prospective students, but the provision was toothless: district control was so ingrained in political life that legislators did not allow state officials to prepare the examinations or otherwise set standards.[18]

Like public school activists since the antebellum period, Johnson wanted to make the high school popular but not at the expense of standards. He called for a "*minimum* grade of admission" and offered some guidelines for devising entrance examinations, always treading softly. Johnson knew that upholding standards and making institutions widely accessible were somewhat contradictory. "These schools are intended as the American Free High Schools for the people," he announced in typical Republican fashion in 1873. Yet "the grade of admission," he added, "should not be so high as virtually to exclude the more advanced pupils in the common schools, nor so low as to make them simply 'primary' or common schools of a low grade." Only "the good judgement of the town officers" would determine local standards, which thus varied.[19]

Despite their obvious limitations, the statistics gathered on Maine's high schools in 1874 highlighted this diversity. The smallest districts reported the most high schools and the highest proportion of secondary pupils within a system. Most high school students attended relatively small, often one- or two-teacher schools, which were often poorly graded compared to those in the cities. The largest systems received the most favorable publicity from educational reformers but enrolled the smallest percentage of their total enrollment in high school. Although a larger percentage of pupils in smaller places studied some advanced subjects, they had shorter school terms than their urban cousins. Scholars in the largest towns and cities had a fuller curriculum, more specialized teachers, and more weeks of school.

Most high school instruction therefore occurred in largely ungraded classrooms. Advanced scholars often sat in one- or two-room schools with abecedarians, and they recited from their readers and other advanced books like the youngest pupils. Most of the advanced students in the smaller districts progressed beyond the Third Reader, but they more frequently studied arithmetic than algebra. Only in the larger districts, with the smallest percentage of Maine's secondary students, did most pupils study a foreign language, often Latin.

Johnson's statistics cannot establish exactly when systems reached the threshold to offer a relatively advanced secondary course. Certainly the smallest districts, enrolling fewer than 400 pupils, had the most difficulty offering a full curriculum. Those districts enrolling between 400 and 1,500 pupils, however, showed a marked ability to reduce the proportion of high school pupils still studying the Third Reader and to boost the proportion studying a foreign language. Some had also increased the length of the school term. Yarmouth, for example, had 60 high school pupils, 10 percent of the total enrollment, a thirty-six-week term, every pupil beyond the Third Reader, more than half studying algebra, and almost a quarter learning a foreign language. This sophistication was, however, unusual for a place of this size. Thus urban-oriented reformers typically compared little communities unfavorably with the larger districts, but high schools never conformed to any single standard, as developments in other states demonstrated.[20]

A writer from Savannah, Georgia, complained in 1875 in the *National Teachers Monthly* that southern administrators too often promoted pupils to high school prematurely. This, of course, had been a common complaint in the North before the Civil War. Some southern towns and cities, noted the Georgian, reported that 11 percent of their pupils were in high school, while a well-established northern system like St. Louis's reported only 3 percent. Did a high proportion of pupils in high school signify low standards? Was it sensible to compare advanced scholars from rural areas, villages, towns, and cities? Were there substantial regional differences in the proportion of pupils attending high school before the 1880s?[21]

Throughout the 1870s, defenders and opponents of high schools in the North and South still debated these questions. Unlike William T. Harris decades later, they lacked a coherent definition of a high school or high school student, but state and local statistics describe some broad social patterns. In 1891, Emerson E. White argued that well-graded urban schools resembled a pyramid, a common metaphor. White believed that "about 65 per cent. of the pupils are in the four lower grades, about 30 per cent. in the next four grades, and about 5 per cent. in the four higher grades." The vast majority of pupils, though, including most advanced scholars, still attended ungraded schools.[22]

Social reformers, educators, and critics saw the number of high schools and secondary pupils grow dramatically in the North after the 1840s and in the South during Reconstruction. Some schools founded in the antebellum period doubled or tripled in size by the 1870s, contributing to the sense of rapid growth. Despite the absence of a common definition for a high school or a secondary pupil, friend and foe alike agreed that free secondary schools had become familiar sights. Even state superintendents who doubted the accuracy of many statistics published more figures and reports on school expansion, highlighting the great diversity of student experiences.

By midcentury, northern state superintendents were attempting to describe secondary schools and estimate the proportion of students in the higher branches. Northern states had better-developed school systems than the South throughout the century, enabling a higher proportion of Yankees to attend graded high schools, but as in Maine, the smallest districts had the highest percentage enrolled in high school, while the larger urban systems had a smaller percentage. Ohio's state superintendent, for example, claimed in 1879 that an average of 7 percent of pupils in systems with more than 200 students were in high school, but district size directly influenced the percentage. An average of 17 percent of scholars in the Buckeye state in systems enrolling between 200 and 399 pupils were in high school, compared with a 5 percent average in places with more than 1,000. The 17 percent average for the smaller schools, of course, masked local variations. Felicity happily reported that 58 percent of its pupils were in high school, Chagrin Falls belied its somber name to register 26 percent, and Hicksville had 13 percent. Among larger districts, Zanesville and Columbus registered 6 to 7 percent; Cleveland and Cincinnati reported 4 percent.[23]

A succession of Ohio's superintendents since the 1850s had quarreled over how to interpret enrollment statistics. As late as 1878, the feisty Democratic critic, Charles S. Smart, accused local officials of doctoring the data, yet he felt confident that about 3 percent of all Buckeyes in school studied the higher branches. Definitions of a high school and an advanced pupil varied so much that the precision implied by a number was not always realized. Smart's successor, J. J. Burns, who counted differently, concluded that about 1 percent of all pupils were in high school. As late as 1880, only nine high schools in Ohio occupied separate buildings, mostly in the big cities. Counting the vast majority of advanced pupils who studied in partially graded schools or in one- or two-room schoolhouses remained a somewhat mysterious science.[24]

Many northern officials, employing somewhat different measures, claimed that about 2 to 5 percent of all pupils in their systems were in high school— that is, pursuing several advanced subjects. They tended to discount scholars who studied only one or two advanced subjects but who were regarded locally as high school pupils. Most officials in the 1860s and 1870s agreed that about 5 percent of the pupils in major towns and cities were in high school, an estimate Emerson E. White also advanced for the early 1890s.

Schoolmen before the 1880s also believed that, even though systems overall grew in size, the proportion of advanced scholars stayed reasonably constant. While the experiences of high school pupils varied widely, the proportion of secondary pupils overall remained consistent after midcentury. Only as districts consolidated and placed minimum age limits on high school admission did the percentage of secondary pupils locally decline.

In the Midwest, state officials grappled with the problem of sorting statistics on grammar and high school pupils. Indiana's chief school officer still estimated that fewer than 3 percent of all pupils between 1868 and 1870 were in high school. As in nearby states, the average proportion enrolled differed widely from community to community, determined largely by district size. Among the larger towns and cities in Michigan in 1877, the average percentage enrolled in high school ranged from 4 percent in Detroit to 20 percent in Ann Arbor, whose high school was very unusual since it had many nonresident pupils preparing for entrance to the university.[25]

A Milwaukee educator, speaking before the Wisconsin State Teachers Association in 1874, claimed that, based on his careful reading of available school reports, only 2 percent of all pupils in states carved from the Old Northwest were pursuing a full range of advanced studies. This low percentage, he believed, was a scandal, a denial of America's democratic heritage.[26]

Compared with the North, southern states often reported a smaller percentage of pupils enrolled in public elementary or secondary schools after the Civil War. Hostility to Yankee Reconstruction included fears of classrooms filled with whites and blacks and rich and poor. The depression of the early 1870s compounded the economic difficulties of many southern communities after the Confederate defeat. Even urban public school systems in the region were still in their infancy, largely attended by the poor, while the middle and upper classes continued to support academies.

The South was even more rural than the North, further retarding efforts at improving student classification. William T. Harris rightly saw the appearance of (segregated) high schools in the urban South as part of the overall growth of free secondary schools throughout the nation. The South nevertheless lagged behind. These regional comparisons, of course, may underestimate the extent of southern institution building in its own right, just as northern rural areas seemed backward when assessed by city standards.

Southern school systems also resembled pyramids, smaller in size than their Yankee counterparts but increasingly visible during Reconstruction. A smaller proportion of southern children attended school, and they rarely progressed to the advanced subjects. Moreover, the freedmen had even less opportunity to taste the higher branches, at least in public high schools. Free blacks in the antebellum South had sometimes funded their own clandestine African schools, where some scholars pursued primary and advanced subjects, and the freedmen fought for access to state-supported education. In Mississippi, the state superintendent in 1872 called for "a system of High Schools for both races . . . to perfect our educational structure." Ku Klux Klan vigilantes burned down some freedmen's schools, and the superintendent estimated that 7.6 percent of all white pupils and under 2 percent of blacks enrolled in school studied the higher branches.[27]

Alabama's superintendent reported in 1876 that, despite some unreliable statistics, high school subjects were taught in about 7 percent of the state's school buildings for whites. Not everyone in these particular schools, of course, pursued advanced subjects. Less than 1 percent of blacks had access to the higher branches. The range of opportunities thus differed tremendously: from the typical pupil tackling one or two advanced classes in an ungraded school to a scholar in a better classified system in Montgomery. Moreover, private schools remained the heart of the higher learning and middle-class education throughout the South decades after academies had declined north of Mason-Dixon.[28]

High schools were part of Reconstruction throughout the 1870s. Charleston had long had a college-preparatory tuition high school for white boys and a normal school for white girls, both of which had received state support and taught nonresident pupils. But statewide resistance to free schools remained intense. J. K. Jillson, the state superintendent, in 1875 advocated reforms, including centralized high schools. "The establishment, wherever practicable, of County High Schools," he argued, "would unquestionably be a decided movement in the direction of educational progress, conditioned that they be high schools in *reality* as well as in name." Persuading county residents to approve a required special tax was unlikely. Enrollment figures on the "higher branches" showed that about 2 or 3 percent of the pupils in local systems studied some advanced subjects.[29]

North Carolina and Virginia, like other southern states, still relied upon private academies to supply secondary education to advanced scholars. Fledgling public systems with high schools appeared in the larger towns and cities after the Civil War, but progress in the hinterland remained slow. Between 1876 and 1880, Virginia's state superintendent claimed that approximately 5 percent of all public school pupils studied the "higher branches." For blacks, attending segregated schools, the figure was about 1 percent. Even so, the *Southern Planter and Farmer* opposed even segregated schooling to preserve law and order.[30]

In a celebrated essay, William H. Ruffner, Virginia's superintendent, warned in 1874 that racial integration would destroy the South's public schools. The war had ended slavery, but not the "social inequality" upon which it rested. Pointing to the widespread segregation of free northern blacks, Ruffner urged readers not to confuse Yankee war propaganda with reality. "In order to stimulate opposition to slavery," he wrote, "it was thought proper to exaggerate the doctrines of human liberty, equality, and fraternity, to such an extent, that the negro became the pet of a large class of the people." And despite wartime rhetoric about white generosity, free blacks had always been treated miserably. Separating "the fouler classes" from "decent" citizens was difficult enough, but only anarchists or communists, Ruffner concluded, favored racial integration.[31]

Throughout the 1870s, Ruffner and other southern schoolmen told Yankees that school integration was morally repugnant and politically impossible. "Let intelligent, refined Northern parents consider our situation, and ask themselves what they would do in our situation." Continually highlighting northern hypocrisy, Ruffner nevertheless faced resistance throughout important sectors of southern society that opposed public schools. The *Southern Planter and Farmer* in 1875 condemned the education of freedmen, calling them "sweating animals" suitable only for the fields. Other critics warned against state intervention, which would undermine family responsibility for educational provision.[32]

Despite widespread opposition to education for freedmen, segregated high schools for southern whites and blacks nevertheless opened in some urban areas before the 1880s. Northern missionaries opened high and normal schools for blacks in Charleston and other communities. Agents of the Peabody Fund, Freedmen's Bureau, and other northern philanthropies funded some advanced grammar schools and normal-high schools to help advance the race and to train black teachers, who were restricted to teaching children in segregated schools. Control over the Richmond Colored High and Normal School, in the former Confederate capital and initially funded by the Freedmen's Bureau, shifted to the local school board in 1876. Unlike most normal schools in the North, Richmond's school attracted some male students, who preferred teaching in segregated schools over jobs as unskilled laborers.[33]

Rays of hope glimmered elsewhere. In 1874 J. C. Corbin, the black, Oberlin-educated Arkansas state superintendent, reported "the organization of a white high school in the city of Little Rock, which, early in the present year, sent forth its first class of four graduates, and of a colored high school, which has been in operation during the greater portion of the past year, with fair prospects of success." Corbin and his successors complained about the poor quality of local record keeping; by 1878, however, 1.6 percent of Arkansas' pupils reportedly studied the higher branches.[34]

As Jim Crow spread through the South, blacks necessarily led their own campaigns to fund various schools, enduring discrimination, violence, and defeats for the sake of the occasional victory. Efforts to keep the high schools in New Orleans integrated in the 1870s proved fruitless. In border states and the Deep South, expensive new high schools for whites often opened at a time when even black elementary schools remained in short supply.[35]

After rejecting several petitions by blacks for a "colored" high school, white officials in Augusta, Georgia, finally relented in 1880. They opened a one-teacher school that initially offered the equivalent of eighth-grade classes. Atlanta supported expensive male and female high schools for whites, ignoring black demands until the 1920s. Talented black children, less likely because of poverty and discrimination to attend academies, doggedly pursued expanded educational opportunity. Schools opened under the auspices of Yankee philanthropists, missionaries, public systems, or blacks themselves, furthering the diversity of secondary education.[36]

In the North as in the South, officials knew that only a small percentage of those in school would study the higher branches, but the numbers of secondary pupils continued to grow in America after midcentury. The percentage of Chicago's pupils in high school remained less than 3 percent of the total enrollment. Five percent or fewer attended in Indianapolis, Louisville, Cincinnati, and Cleveland in the 1870s. Cleveland had a few high schools by the mid-1870s, enrolling over seven hundred pupils in 1878 compared with the handful of pupils at old Central High in the early 1850s. Although the numbers of scholars had increased, the percentage enrolled in the higher branches remained fairly constant.[37]

Similarly, Philadelphia's all-male Central High School had undergone many changes since it opened in 1838, but it consistently enrolled only a tiny percentage of the city's pupils. In 1840, Central High School represented less than 0.9 percent of Philadelphia's total school enrollment. The figure was 0.9 percent in 1860 and 0.5 percent in 1880. In 1875, Superintendent Harris of St. Louis estimated that 2 to 5 percent of all pupils in the largest urban systems were in high school. He placed the figure at 2 percent in Chicago, 2.75 percent in St. Louis, and 5 percent in Boston. He correctly added that the percentage enrolled in smaller cities was higher, and in villages and rural areas higher still.[38]

Harris sought an ever clearer definition of a high school as he climbed the bureaucratic ladder. As U. S. Commissioner of Education (1889–1906), he commissioned many quantitative studies and gathered additional statistics about education. Before the 1880s, however, contemporaries realized that high schools in rural, village, and city systems often differed tremendously.

Attending Philadelphia's degree-granting Central High School was qualitatively different from studying a few branches in a coeducational district school in rural Maine or attending a segregated secondary school in the former Confederacy. Girls and black pupils in particular knew that going to school was not the same for everyone.

Recalling her school days of the early 1870s, Mary Bradford reflected upon the "silent influences" of the plaster cast busts of famous people in the assembly room at Kenosha High. Like many graded high schools, her alma mater honored Washington, Franklin, Shakespeare, and Plato. In addition, "there was also the bust of a woman, showing a strong, attractive countenance, not less interesting because no one seemed sure whom it portrayed—some thinking her Sappho, others Mrs. Browning."[39]

Male reformers had created the American high school, but young women remained the majority of its pupils and graduates throughout the nineteenth century. Often superior as a group in academic achievement, female students studied in dissimilar environments, from large single-sex institutions in coastal cities to the small coeducational high schools of rural areas and villages that most pupils attended. Whether inspired by Sappho or Browning, some female scholars complained that educators treated them differently because they were women.

The education of middle-class boys and girls became a heated subject in the 1820s, when Boston's all-male English Classical School opened its doors, and the subject continued to agitate citizens in the 1870s, when debates flared over coeducation. Theorists and practicing educators, lay people and professionals, still disagreed about how to educate girls, guaranteeing a lack of uniformity in female education.[40]

A few writers after the Civil War still claimed that women had inherently less mental capacity. Others believed that their capacity was similar if not identical but that the higher learning weakened women's health and reproductive system. Less debatable was the constant female demand for more higher education. This enthusiasm for advanced instruction, reflected in the rise of female academies and seminaries after the 1780s, had not dissipated in the new century.

Coeducational as well as single-sex academies proliferated in every state. Whether taught along with boys, in separate departments in mixed schools, or in completely separate facilities, female scholars pressed for more schooling. The spread of female seminaries and academies seemed to settle the question of whether middle-class girls would attend secondary school. Whether qualified females should attend public high schools, and what they should study, remained controversial.

The appearance of the first public high schools for boys in places such as Boston and Portland led some citizens to call for equal opportunity for girls. The demand for more secondary education for middle-class youths, including girls, was growing. Women's magazines during the antebellum period touted the higher learning for advancing the cause of republican motherhood, emphasizing that different life spheres for the sexes did not justify inferior education for talented women. According to one common argument, middle-class mothers, whose child-rearing responsibilities increased after the 1820s, needed more schooling, not exclusion from the higher learning, and solid instruction, not dabbling in ornamental branches.[41]

As one bourgeois female reformer argued in 1827, competent mothers needed chemistry as much as embroidery. Chemistry helped in the kitchen, and modern mothers needed more scientific knowledge. While expanding the subjects suitable for both sexes, most reformers carefully explained that enhancing women's education did not undermine patriarchal authority. Because men now worked away from home, mothers had to become more informed. Mainstream magazines carefully espoused separate though expanded spheres for women yet delicately acknowledged male authority. Thus a typical writer in the *Ladies Magazine* in 1828 said that more education made girls better wives and mothers, with this caveat: "Authority over the men . . . must never be usurped, but still, women may, if they will exert their talents, and the opportunities nature has furnished, obtain an influence in society, that will be paramount to authority."[42]

Middle-class publicists generally saw the expansion of women's education as an unalloyed public good. "It is a good sign of the advance of society when attention is paid to the education of women," claimed the *Lady's Book* in 1835. There were foreign languages to master, and scientific experiments to perform. As many writers said, if men received more secondary education, they would inevitably want more knowledgeable wives, who would then become better company for their husbands, and superior mothers, too. Indeed, when the Rev. John Pierpont had advocated a Girls' High School in Boston a decade earlier, he said the school would produce good primary teachers but also "fit wives." Reformers never said boys' advanced education made men "fit husbands."[43]

"It has been gravely asserted that chemistry enough to keep the pot boiling, and geography enough to know the location of all the rooms in her house, is learning sufficient for a woman," complained an author in the *Ladies' Garland* in 1840. But such thinking was "too degrading," she thought, at that late date. More female education, whether in academies or free high schools, had salutary effects: the strengthening of respectable homes, the training of teachers, and the overall diffusion of knowledge. Many citizens debated the merits of single-sex schools or coeducation, but they never doubted education's social significance. In 1879, William Ruffner of Virginia concluded that women had especially benefited from the higher learning. "In the public free schools they have equal advantages, and where public high schools exist they are more favored than they have ever been before."[44]

Academies largely met the demand for advanced female instruction before the 1840s. The responsibility of public schools for women beyond the primary and grammar grades remained somewhat controversial, though in the North generally the tide soon turned in women's favor. Most rural areas and villages educated boys and girls together in the early 1800s. Once they mastered their primary and grammar level texts, ambitious and talented girls as well as boys pursued some higher subjects, usually through individualized instruction. Educators in larger towns and cities, who had more concentrated populations, frequently separated boys and girls into male and female departments or even built separate facilities. In older cities such as Philadelphia, New York, and Boston, talented girls by the 1830s studied some advanced branches in the upper grammar grades, at times decades before the opening of female high schools.[45]

By midcentury, it had become clear that the majority of high school pupils would be girls. Enrollment statistics from individual towns and cities revealed what nearly every educator knew: girls attended and graduated from high school at a higher rate than boys. Boys, wrote many observers, left school earlier to work, though educators believed that laziness and other factors often led to their withdrawal. In larger cities, women formed a high percentage of the total secondary enrollment, partly because of the greater supply for boys of jobs not requiring advanced education. At St. Louis High, women constituted 38 percent of the total enrollment in 1853, 63 percent in 1865, 61 percent in 1875, and 78 percent in 1880. This skewing of the statistics was more common in larger places, but in smaller communities—where most pupils lived—females still approached 55 to 60 percent of high school enrollments after midcentury. In 1890 an estimated 57 percent of secondary pupils and 65 percent of graduates were women.[46]

Women studied the higher branches in an array of settings. Many "coeducational" high schools, like academies, had male and female departments. Large coastal cities in the North and South and major river towns in the border states also had separate male and female high schools; the southern schools often charged some tuition. The rising public sector sometimes resembled the familiar single-sex academies and seminaries, though public high schools were never boarding schools and primarily served local taxpayers. The majority of secondary pupils, like most academy students, were women who studied an English curriculum.

Some female scholars read their books alone in dank rural hovels, others sat in palatial buildings with fine libraries and the latest teaching aids. Some studied Latin in their English curriculum, others substituted history or geography. Although the majority of pupils were in small schools in rural areas and villages, professional male educators focused their attention on the cities, where careers could be made and impressive school bureaucracies constructed. But the expansion of the higher learning everywhere depended upon women students.

Students in public high schools and tuition academies knew that being a woman always made an educational difference. The scholastic performance of women usually equaled or surpassed that of men, and beginning in the early 1840s, the irrepressible Henry Barnard and other Whig reformers praised women's admission to public high schools. In 1846, however, he added that girls needed a "modified" curriculum.[47]

According to Barnard, a boy typically needed a sound English business-oriented education or a classical precollegiate education one, whereas a woman required "a well disciplined mind, high moral aims, and practical views of her own duties, and those resources of health, thought, manners and conversation, which bless alike the highest and lowest stations in life." Barnard and other educators in decades to come continued to endorse a special female curriculum. Small districts, which had the fewest graded classrooms, had the least curricular differentiation and the most students. But the more atypical city schools received the lion's share of public attention.[48]

One controversial issue during the antebellum period was whether academic competition harmed girls, particularly teenagers. The idea that extended schooling endangered women's health, an explosive topic in the 1870s, was hardly new. Principals and teachers in female high schools, located in the older seaboard cities and urban districts in the South and border states, sometimes gloated that, unlike boys' schools, they refused to award prizes to their scholars. They nonetheless kept meticulous records on the grades, deportment, and attendance of female scholars. Moreover, most pupils, especially in the North, attended coeducational secondary schools, where females often won most of the academic prizes.[49]

Contemporaries differed in their appraisal of women's high achievements. Indiana's state school superintendent, W. C. Larrabee, said in 1852 that girls on all levels of education were simply the best pupils. Years of teaching had persuaded him that women ruled the academic roost. "They are more *apt* to learn, more quick in their perceptions, more lively in their apprehension, and fluent in their expression of thought. Nor are they usually deficient in capacity and patience to master the higher branches, and the more difficult and abstruse subjects."[50]

In slight contrast, Daniel Shepardson, an advocate of coeducation and principal of Cincinnati's Woodward High School, noted in 1859 that men and women did about equally well in the "severer branches" such as logic and trigonometry. This neither worried him nor surprised him, for "similar advantages give similar results." If this assessment was true, it did not please everyone. Noting that women at many eastern coeducational schools won most of the prizes in mathematics and classical studies, a foreign visitor feared that tough subjects would make women cool and overly rational, bad traits in a wife.[51]

When Virginia's state superintendent said that women had especially benefited from the growth of high schools, it was not a theory spun from the air. At Chicago High School, women—called "the unmathematical"—were superior students, claimed an examining committee in mathematics in 1872. In Columbus, Ohio, females won all the commencement prizes in 1878. Many people complained that women studied too much and that their successes undermined the boys' self-esteem. But the trend seemed clear. Academies had opened their doors to women, who after tasting the higher branches continued to drink from the fountains of learning in the high school. And women's academic achievements represented only one part of their multifaceted encounters at school.[52]

One major fault line in the larger urban areas was between coeducational and single-sex institutions. All-girl high schools enrolled the smallest number of female scholars, but those in the older seaboard cities received disproportionate publicity. School officials there usually approved high schools for boys first, then built separate schools for girls, often years or even decades later. Boston's English Classical School opened in 1821; a secondary school for girls opened in 1852. Philadelphia's Central High School was established in 1838, followed by a secondary normal school for girls a decade later. The New York Free Academy appeared in 1847, but advanced female scholars remained in the grammar grades or attended academies until 1870, when a permanent normal college opened.[53]

Female high schools in the largest cities sometimes emphasized teacher preparation in the highest grades or in special postgraduate normal classes. This approach narrowed the choice of subject and prepared some of the most talented scholars for elementary teaching posts. Understandably, some scholars felt shortchanged as theories of separate spheres arose. Coeducational high schools also occasionally taught some normal courses to female pupils in their junior or senior years, but separate high schools in the larger cities were especially prone to weave specific teacher preparation courses into the curriculum.[54]

Separate high schools remained common for women in the South before the 1880s, and not simply along the coast. Female high schools existed in the larger towns of the Deep and Upper South as well as in New Orleans and Charleston. After the war, such inland cities as Atlanta, Nashville, Memphis, and Louisville retained separate high schools. Separation, whether in the North or South, often led to unequal treatment, leading some critics to attack the ideology of separate spheres, asking whether it helped elevate women or deny them quality schooling.[55]

Enrollments in female high schools boomed when job openings for elementary teachers were plentiful, but girls in separate facilities occasionally complained that their normal-high schools lacked the full academic orientation of male secondary schools. Women who did not want to become teachers felt slighted. Separation meant an opportunity to discount academic classes. When San Francisco divided its high school into two departments in 1864, it reduced academic course work for women in favor of more normal classes. Feminists and other reformers noted that girls lacked full access to classical education in many cities, an especially gnawing deprivation as colleges opened their doors more widely after the Civil War. Boston's Latin School had become a classical boys' high school, a feeder to Harvard and other colleges, and local activists pilloried school officials until a separate Girls' Latin School opened in 1878.[56]

Female scholars in Louisville, Boston, and other communities knew that separate meant unequal. Louisville's Female High School had inferior science equipment, spent less money on its pupils, and had crowded quarters in the 1860s. This treatment angered Marie B. Radcliffe, a local student. Radcliffe believed that most of her peers aimed to become homemakers, like their mothers, with "the fire-side their only throne." But what about students with other dreams? If some women seemed superficial, she wrote, "the fault rests not in women, but in her education." Radcliffe added that fewer women would be "aimless dreamers" if offered other opportunities. "If in their ranks were seen a physician, a lecturer, a writer, an artist, it cannot be unfeminine, it cannot be wrong, for God gave them their talents, and he doeth all things well."[57]

Such articulate critics downplayed the positive side of attending an all-female school. Though principals were frequently men, female institutions had many talented women teachers, who served as important role models. An accomplished female scholar in Louisville—a future valedictorian and teacher—had a deep crush on Miss Morris, who made her nervous at recitation. "Oh, Miss Morris," the student wrote in her diary, "you have not the faintest idea how much you are in my sleeping and waking thoughts!" Scholars at Portland's female high school edited impressive magazines, which featured the poetic, literary, and scientific achievements of their most talented peers and sometimes stood in praise of sisterhood. Girls elsewhere also produced their own student newspapers.[58]

All-girl schools nurtured powerful emotional bonds between young women, who exchanged personal comments in their ubiquitous "autograph albums." "Albums may be said to be the dip-nets, wherewith young girls catch flattery," wrote a clever scholar in Cleveland's student paper in 1850. Friendship patterns also followed the doctrine of separate spheres. Diaries from female scholars both in coeducational and separate schools showed that girls were closest to other girls, not boys. Young women like Carrie Crawford of Louisville and Lizzie Morrisey of Boston recorded numerous comments, some very critical, about their female friends and instructors. Women pupils often formed strong alumna associations that met decades after their old schools closed.[59]

Critics nevertheless correctly asserted that separation made differential treatment more likely. Coeducation, however, did not guarantee fairness. *Coeducation* was a term, like *high school*, that embraced disparate phenomena. Educating boys and girls together had by midcentury the sanction of most northern schoolmen, who believed that the policy was Christian, economical, and practical. Adam and Eve, despite their mischief, still constituted the first family, said the educators. And the ideal (middle-class) family—with husband and wife, and sons and daughters—was God's model for schools. Separating boys and girls might be suitable for Catholics, but it was anathema in a progressive nation.

Coeducation, insisted its advocates, tamed the rougher instincts of boys and made girls less giddy, naive, and sentimental. Both sexes had equal capacity to

learn, even if they had separate, complementary spheres in life. Clearly, a writer concluded in 1878, in high schools, normal schools, and other institutions of advanced learning, "the tendency is strongly in favor of the coeducation system."[60]

Women were often academically superior as a group, but individual girls in coeducational high schools still had to battle for justice and fair play. Indeed, the idea of attending school together was made to fit the concept of separate spheres. Males and females might study identical subjects, and teachers might view women as very competent or even superior students. But some principals and teachers never let pupils forget that gender mattered. Nearly every aspect of school life reflected the pervasive concern of educators with gender differences. In 1862 a writer in the *North Carolina Journal of Education* accurately noted that "mixed schools" educated boys and girls together but did not necessarily offer identical treatment or the same education.[61]

Northern and midwestern towns and cities by the 1840s commonly built such mixed or coeducational high schools. School leaders in these communities congratulated themselves for progressing beyond the separatist practices of the older cities. William T. Harris of St. Louis became an ardent champion of coeducation, by which he did not mean identical education. In many high schools after midcentury, in the Midwest as well as the East, male and female students entered buildings from separate doors, signifying the importance of gender differentiation.[62]

Midwesterners early debated whether to admit girls to high school and, if so, under what conditions. Cleveland's Central High School initially excluded girls. When Whig reformers secured their admission, the sexes sat in separate rooms. The student newspaper, *The School-Boy*, bragged about the boys' performance at a public examination in 1848. One male writer accused the girls ("dear, faint things") of being timid, for "you could only tell that they were speaking by seeing their lips move." "Kate" responded that the boys confused intelligence with "their own *noisiness* and *self-confidence*. . . . We do not deny the strength of their lungs, for we too have experienced the clamorous effects of it, but we would remind them that sounds are sometimes more *loud* than *musical*." Women here as elsewhere fought diligently for fair representation on the newspaper staff and in other school activities, which were often student initiated but sometimes had faculty sponsors.[63]

In the mid-1850s, Cleveland's female scholars had to demand access to advanced mathematics courses. During both study and recitation hours, they occupied "separate portions of the same room. In passing in and out at recesses, they necessarily pass through the same halls. But we have seen nothing like familiarity between them," wrote a Visiting Committee approv-

OPPOSITE: All-female high schools nurtured deep and long-lasting friendships. Alumnae of Portland's Girls' High School, which merged with the Boys' High School in 1863, assembled again for a reunion, ca. 1890s. Collections of the Maine Historical Society.

ingly. "No interchange of billets is permitted." As late as 1876, Cleveland's superintendent advocated a female high school, which could offer better normal courses for teacher preparation. A separate school meant higher costs, however, and *coeducation* was not easily dislodged from the minds of progressive thinkers. Columbus, Cincinnati, and Indianapolis were among the other cities that provided coeducational institutions. The Midwest and much of the Far West proudly endorsed coeducation, assuring the sexes access to the same building, even to the same overall curriculum, but often providing them divergent experiences.[64]

There were different twists and turns to student life in coeducational high schools. The "Irving Society," formed by Chicago's pupils in 1857, had only male members a decade later. As its name indicated, Cleveland's "Young Men's Literary Association" was not for everyone. The local "Graduate's Literary Society" included both men and women, but it disappeared as the members grew older. Columbus, Ohio, divided its student newspaper in the early 1850s into two parts, one edited by the boys, the other by the girls. Two decades later, however, local female scholars were active in the "Virgil Literary Society," a mixed group that had met in Latin class.[65]

Men dominated as editors on many student newspapers, but women demanded and gained better representation. Cleveland's *School-Boy*, which was run by the men at their coeducational high school, published slurs on the women, who fought back. And when *The Acorn* appeared in 1856 from the new West Side High School, a male and female editor shared literary responsibilities. Hattie Farrand, not a conventional middle-class scholar, immediately denounced women's preoccupation with fashion and called for the liberation of the "toiling millions," especially exploited seamstresses. Elsewhere the feisty Farrands and less controversial pupils fought for more representation and greater respect for women.[66]

Even when women as a group enjoyed equal or superior academic achievement, unequal treatment could encourage relatively privileged citizens to lash out at the less fortunate. In 1873, Miss Sarah Garrett, a teacher in Portsmouth, New Hampshire, complained bitterly at a high school reunion that women's roles had failed to expand beyond motherhood and teaching little children. Colleges, she said, had opened their doors wider, but many men still limited women's opportunities. But instead of attacking the narrowness of the bourgeois men and women who had constructed an ideology of separate spheres, Garrett struck out in other directions. She condemned the "half intoxicated foreigner" who sold a vote that she, a respectable and educated woman, could not secure. Then she asked her audience, "do you place your colored brethren, your naturalized foreigners, on a higher plane than your mothers, your wives and your daughters?"[67]

Although William H. Ruffner of Virginia chided Yankee radicals who advocated racial integration in the South, he remained confident that the northern bourgeoisie would respect propriety and social order. Foreign observers like

Alexis de Tocqueville had documented that free blacks were among the most despised of northern citizens before the Civil War. P. A. Siljestrom of Sweden learned that New York City would not hire a negro to teach whites "were the individual in question even a black Pestalozzi." However much radical Republicans favored integration, most Yankees, like antislavery activists before them, still countenanced the color line. Some northern districts had racially integrated schools, but the region's checkered history of race relations demonstrated that intolerance was a national, not southern, illness.[68]

An essayist in the 1870s who reprinted Ruffner's segregationist comments neatly summed up the situation: "In all the old slave states, and in many of the northern states," he wrote, "the feeling of aversion to, or prejudice against, the negro race is so strong, that the public school system can be made effective only by the establishment of separate schools for colored children; since many white parents would refuse to permit their children to attend schools in which 'the co-education of the races' was carried on." Even newly settled Montana restricted the rights of black children to attend public school. Like free persons of color in the South, before and after the Civil War, northern African-Americans continued their long struggle for equal access to education.[69]

Free black males in the antebellum North had voted heavily for Whigs and then Republicans. These parties had especially supported common schools and high schools, but prejudice among their members against black equality remained strong. Even though antislavery activists by the 1830s had favored free labor and free schools in newly settled states, many midwestern and western states were hostile to blacks. Democratic Party leaders frequently lampooned the Republicans, self-anointed friends of the negro, for passing heavily restrictive black codes in many states. African-Americans faced severe discrimination in housing, health care, jobs, and schools. The radical wing of the Republican Party advocated stronger civil rights legislation and integrated schools after the war. For the majority of northern citizens, however, as Ruffner argued, opposition to slavery did not equal support for racial or social equality.[70]

As in the antebellum period, some northern blacks continued to study the higher branches in an assortment of places: integrated public high schools, missionary schools, and institutions controlled by African-American churches and voluntary associations. The numbers of blacks enrolled were small, and the dearth of good job opportunities suppressed the enthusiasm of many worthy scholars. Midwestern states like Ohio and Indiana had racist education laws, but here as elsewhere Quakers and other humanitarians tried to provide some African-American youth with elementary and secondary education. By midcentury, Quakers operated and controlled some well-known secondary schools in Philadelphia and other northern communities.[71]

Numerous public high schools, when pressured by white abolitionists and black activists, finally admitted some African-Americans. Black scholars were admitted in Boston in the 1850s, in Chicago in the 1860s, and in Philadelphia by the end of the 1870s. Numerous Ohio towns and cities had integrated high schools before the 1880s, though here as elsewhere African-Americans appeared fleetingly in the school records. Chicago reported that it had a "colored" high school pupil in 1863. An official in Connecticut cryptically wrote in 1874 that "colored youth are often seen in High Schools and Academies."[72]

While northerners, especially outside the larger towns and cities, endorsed coeducation, most common school reformers regarded talk of equal or integrated education for blacks as politically unwise. Contemporaries debated the wisdom of building separate high schools for women in the larger urban areas, but few citizens wanted to invest in any sort of black secondary instruction. It was one thing to spend money on the white middle classes, quite another to alienate taxpayers by helping the most despised youth.

Ambitious, talented African-American scholars sought admission to various secondary schools despite this frigid atmosphere. Black communities were often divided into integrationist and separatist factions, adding to the complexity of local politics. Within a decade of the founding of the English Classical School and the ill-fated Girls' High School, some of Boston's blacks petitioned unsuccessfully for their own secondary school; by midcentury other groups had fought successfully for school integration. To provide black teachers for segregated neighborhood schools, New York City opened a Colored Normal School in the 1850s, then permitted a handful of black women to enroll in the Normal College in the 1870s. By then some integrated secondary schools existed in the North, but many on the primary and grammar level remained completely segregated.[73]

The plight of talented black youth in Cincinnati exemplified the limitations of freedom in the North. "It is nonsense to talk of the freedom of the colored race of the United States," wrote the local *Republican* in 1836. "Where does it exist? In the free states it exists in name, but does it exist in reality? Look at the black population of our own city." Freedom sometimes meant the right to starve, turn to crime, or become a beggar, but not to attend schools, find a satisfactory job, or join the militia. In 1829, half of the city's black community was driven from their homes in a race riot. Most never returned.[74]

In subsequent decades, only white philanthropists, Christian missionaries, and abolitionists, as well as African-Americans themselves, ran schools or classes to educate blacks. Cincinnati's economy depended upon trade with the slave South, and rising racial tensions over abolitionism fueled more riots against blacks. The school board considered but then deferred opening a school for "Partially Colored Children" in the early 1840s. Board members contemplating the creation of a high school warned in 1846 that integration would "drive all the white children from the institution, and leave it entirely to the occupation of colored children."[75]

Local blacks depended upon sympathetic whites and their own resourcefulness. A wealthy white minister, philanthropist, and utopian socialist, Hiram Gilmore, opened a school for blacks in 1844 that taught the common and higher branches. Hundreds of blacks, some of whom later enrolled at Oberlin College, attended this school, and alumni included many teachers, ministers, and religious activists. But the school declined for various reasons when the state allowed blacks to attend public schools in 1849. After a series of battles over who should control black education—a white school board or a black one—African-Americans took charge of their own system in 1853. This "colored" board, appointed by the white board until 1856, governed Cincinnati's African public schools until Ohio made separate boards illegal in 1874.[76]

These African schools enjoyed strong community support for the common branches and the higher learning. The abject poverty of black taxpayers meant that their children had poorly equipped buildings—*"dilapidated rat-holes"*—but their passion for education never dissipated. As a white observer said in 1855, "the colored inhabitants of Cincinnati have shared with all its citizens the influence of that respect for education, and for the diffusion of knowledge, which has ever been one of their characteristics." In the mid-1850s, black school officials, board members, and teachers praised their fellow citizens for linking education with the pursuit of a better life. Moreover, some scholars were already studying some of the higher branches—algebra, geometry, and advanced science—in their largely ungraded African schools. The demand for a high school soon grew, as in so many communities across the land.[77]

By 1856, Stephen L. Massey, superintendent of the "colored schools," urged the creation of a separate high school for qualified scholars. John I. Gaines, a veteran black activist, teacher, and clerk of the Colored School Board, similarly claimed that blacks must compete "with the dominant class" by mastering advanced learning. Blacks could become equals only by leaving their mark on society "as painter, poet, sculptor, philosopher, historian, astronomer, divine, or military chieftain." During the Civil War, after Gaines's death, the new clerk of the African-American board asked, "Who can tell how many there are among the rising generation that have minds like that of a Newton, Boyle, Socrates, or a Cicero?" Local whites had two high schools, so why should blacks settle for just elementary schools? In 1866, after some debate, Gaines High School opened its doors, with another activist, Peter H. Clark, as principal.[78]

Like most high schools, the new institution was not located in a separate building. Clark, an alumnus of Gilmore's school, reminisced years later that Gaines High actually offered a superior grammar school education in its early years. Like the white schools, Gaines taught boys and girls in separate departments. When the school opened, it had, in addition to Clark, one male and one female teacher. Its few dozen pupils read such standard secondary textbooks as Ray's *Algebra* and Willard's *History*.

The school was a source of black pride, and Clark ensured that it remained controversial. Like John Gaines, Clark was a former Whig and then a Republican. His grandfather reportedly was the explorer William Clark, who had sired several children with his black mistress. Son of a militant black nationalist, Peter Clark flirted with colonization schemes, became a correspondent to Frederick Douglass' *North Star*, and tried in vain to arm Cincinnati's blacks during the Civil War.[79]

Peter H. Clark, educator and political activist in Cincinnati, devoted his life to expanding opportunities for African-Americans to study the higher branches. From John B. Shotwell, *A History of the Schools of Cincinnati* (Cincinnati: School Life, 1902).

Control over Gaines High School shifted to the white school board in 1874. Until it closed in 1887, however, Gaines was a very important black institution. It educated dozens of future teachers, ministers, and community leaders, who worked not only in Cincinnati's segregated neighborhoods but even in the Jim Crow South. By the late 1870s, Clark, who briefly became a socialist, claimed to have boosted the school's academic quality to match its white competitors, Woodward and Hughes. By 1879, about 4 percent of blacks enrolled in the Cincinnati system were in high school, similar to the percentage for whites. In a controversial move less than a decade later, the white school board fired Clark. He spent the rest of his life as an educator, briefly in the South and then as a teacher in a segregated high school in St. Louis.[80]

Cincinnati's experiment with a black-controlled high school was hardly representative of northern systems. School officials retained separate high schools for females in the older seaboard cities as well as in many southern communities, but dual systems of education for northern blacks did not usually include high schools. The tiny percentage of African-American youth in the North who attended secondary school had to rely upon their own efforts or upon the kindness of strangers, such as white philanthropists, missionaries, or sympathetic school board members.

Cincinnati's black scholars had revealed yet another dimension to the realities of going to high school before the 1880s. Every pupil who attended any secondary school, of whatever quality, was regarded as talented, someone whose claim to respect rested upon individual achievement, not birthright. But the creation of Gaines High School reflected the racial cleavages that separated society at large, even in the land of freedom.

High school pupils constituted a so-called aristocracy of talent, but boys and girls, whites and blacks, rural and urban youth knew that secondary education was not a monolithic phenomenon. Students may have read the same texts and been pressed to conform to ubiquitous school regulations, but a diversity of experiences awaited ambitious and bright scholars from diverse backgrounds living in different kinds of communities. And everywhere teachers and students knew that gender and race continued to affect the lives of even the most talented youth when they left school.

Commencement

The Alumni of Logansport High
School—May they ever be true to their
perceptions of the right, faithful in the discharge of all the obligations imposed upon
them by their position in the world,
whether exalted or obscure, and devoted
to the highest standard of human
endeavor.

"Alumni Banquet," *Logansport Pharos*,
Logansport, Indiana, June 14, 1876

The opening of a branch high
school in Cleveland in the mid-1850s caused students to celebrate. As the
city's population had spread, Central High had become less accessible for west
side residents, so the city fathers approved advanced classes in a neighborhood
grammar school. Like Central High, the new secondary school had a rigorous
entrance examination and a three-year course of study. *The Acorn*, the new student newspaper, could not be happier: "We are now looking forward with
joyful hope to that eventful day when we shall receive our diplomas, and rush
with eager haste into the tumultuous world, to prove our titles to them. What
bright hopes linger around that hour when we shall launch back upon the turbulent waves of the 'sea of life.'" The writer, probably a male student, said talented pupils had reached a turning point by entering high school. "It is the
most important period in our whole life, at least in our *school* life. It is on the
decision of that moment that much of our future career depends."[1]

By midcentury throughout the North, school officials increasingly celebrated the achievements of their high school graduates. Everyone knew that
only a small percentage of the student body ever entered a four-year high
school, never mind graduated. Educators quarreled among themselves for
decades about why so many youth withdrew prematurely from high school. In
well-graded systems, more than half of every class could be expected to depart
before the junior year, and boys left at an especially rapid rate. Why had so few

students graduated? Had the curriculum been too difficult or impractical? Had they been seduced by Mammon? Whatever the answer, the contributor to *The Acorn* made the path to graduation—even in a three- as opposed to a four-year course—appear more natural than was typically experienced.

High school graduation nevertheless became a major public event by the 1850s. Contemporaries interpreted graduation exercises, like the high schools themselves, from diverse perspectives. School officials used graduation ceremonies to elicit public praise for their noble cause; pupils often followed suit but sometimes criticized the limitations of separate spheres; guests in the audience behaved even less predictably; and critics viewed the pomp and circumstance as another reason to condemn free secondary schools. In 1866 the feisty Frederick A. Packard said these celebrations were elitist and antirepublican. "[T]he terms 'commencement,' 'graduates,' 'degrees,' 'diplomas,' 'alumni,' &c., are employed to describe the parties and proceedings that distinguish the close of an academical term," he sarcastically concluded.[2]

The path to graduation was steep, though clear patterns emerged about who would likely stand on the public stage. Commencement celebrations themselves revealed the enduring social tensions surrounding high schools after the Civil War. As academies, especially in the North, disappeared or became public high schools, formal graduation ceremonies gave school leaders and scholars an opportunity to confirm the arrival of a new educational order. The annual ritual also enabled some pupils and noisy critics to debate anew the meaning of the high school. The scholar in Cleveland anxiously awaited graduation day and the subsequent ride on the turbulent waves of "the sea of life." Frederick Packard, however, urged citizens to think critically about the new symbols of local high schools: commencements, graduation exercises, diplomas, even newly formed alumni associations.

In 1885, a scholar in Philadelphia wrote a parody entitled "The Discontented School-Boy." Shakespeare's works had been performed for decades in dance halls and barrooms, and this latter-day Hamlet offered his own soliloquy:

> To leave, or not to leave, that is the question:
> Whether 'tis nobler in the mind to suffer
> The zeroes and notes of outrageous school-life,
> Or to take arms against a sea of troubles,
> And by leaving, end them? To leave, to work—
> And, by working, end the thousand natural
> Headaches, troubles, and dissensions
> That school-life is heir to—'twould be a consummation
> To have no more studies.[3]

The low graduation rates everywhere indicated that leaving school prematurely was more than a dream devoutly to be wished.

Few educators before the 1880s expected many secondary students to graduate, yet the huge class turnover troubled them. Graduation rates varied at
midcentury in well-graded, urban school systems, but approximately 25 percent of those in high school completed a four-year course. Frequently half of
the student body exited by the end of the sophomore year. What going to high
school meant to these pupils provoked much speculation among the friends
and foes of the American high school. The majority of graduates were women,
and schoolmen frequently debated why only a small proportion of men completed their education. Not surprisingly, critics accused the schools of wasting
the taxpayers' dollars to educate the chosen few in the highest grades.[4]

Ever since the first high schools opened in the 1820s, educators and social
commentators had recognized that economic needs forced many pupils, especially boys, to leave school prematurely. The great majority of schoolchildren
left by age twelve and never reached high school. For those who did, mostly
coming from a range of middle-class families, a year or two of advanced study
provided an advantage in the marketplace. A visiting committee from Providence noted in 1828 that Boston's English Classical School admitted from
sixty to eighty boys annually; due to the high demand for clerks, however, only
eight to ten ever completed the three-year course.[5]

Going to high school was often a one- or two-year experience. High schools
resembled a pyramid with a very wide base. A few statistics illustrate the phenomenon. At Cleveland's Central High School in 1862, 51 percent of the
entire high school was in the freshman class, 27 percent were sophomores, 15
percent juniors, and 7 percent seniors.[6]

In the Hartford, Connecticut, coeducational high school, which had a
strong college preparatory course, 46 percent of the students were freshmen,
29 percent sophomores, 14 percent juniors, and 11 percent seniors. Whether
in male, female, or coeducational schools, juniors and seniors were rare. The
Louisville Female High School reported 13 percent of its pupils in the senior
class in 1865, reflecting the longer school-going rate for women. Characteristically, in 1871 a writer in *Scribner's Monthly* wanted more students to stay.
"We only wish our high schools were a little higher, that the course of study
were more extended, so that our children might be induced to remain in them
for a longer period, and might graduate seniors instead of sophomores, as they
are inclined to do."[7]

School officials disagreed about why there were so many "sophomore graduates." Most commentators thought multiple factors explained the phenomenon but that economic considerations predominated. Jobs were basic to
family survival, and even middle-class children left school as soon as possible.
Apprenticeships for boys had disappeared rapidly by the 1820s, as a free-
market economy spread throughout the northern states, undermining bound
or restricted labor for whites. As more commercial and industrial establishments appeared, especially in cities, businessmen created new white-collar
jobs, most of which were secured by young, native-born white males.[8]

High school boys, usually from the native bourgeoisie, became part of the rising cadre of clerks, tellers, salesmen, agents, and lesser accountants. Jobs as clerks were not glamorous and did not usually lead to higher managerial positions, but they offered better pay and status than the numerous unskilled jobs. High schools taught skills and attitudes useful in respectable positions. As an educator from San Francisco claimed, respectable homes taught order and obedience, and society somehow had to encourage more poor children to aspire to attend secondary schools. "The receptivity of a child who has been taught to move, or to stop, when spoken to, must be far greater than that of one whose life has been spent in throwing stones at Chinamen, and building bonfires in the streets."[9]

High school attendance was hardly a prerequisite for boys to secure white-collar positions. Secondary schools, however, taught practical skills and added cultural polish. Mastering advanced mathematics, speaking clearly, and having a legible hand often enhanced the employability of high school pupils in America's burgeoning cities. Reaffirming the utilitarian goals of the English Classical School, Boston's educational patriarchs in 1823 emphasized the need "to fit" the boys "for active life, or qualify them for eminence in private or public stations." The schools did just that, and most boys withdrew from the school as quickly as they felt prepared and a suitable opening appeared. The chairman of the English High School Committee, S. K. Lothrop, remarked in 1856 that a "youth of sixteen is very anxious to get into business—to be doing something for himself. He therefore persuades his parents to let him leave school and go into a store or some active occupation." Hence only about one-quarter of the famous school's entering class graduated.[10]

As the economy expanded and high schools grew after midcentury, urban educators routinely complained that too many pupils rushed to make their way in life. The secretary of Cleveland's school board in 1855 tried to assess the numerous pressures in a male student's life. "A few leave to pursue a preparatory and collegiate course; some because they think their education complete; but most are called away by the demands of business, or the necessity of seeking employment for the sake of its pecuniary awards."[11]

A year later, Superintendent Andrew Freese observed that only about 10 percent of those admitted to Central High School graduated. Male scholars in particular left school in large numbers. "The boys being usually expert arithmeticians and ready penmen," he asserted, "are in request to fill situations in Banking Houses, Railroad Offices, Counting Rooms, &c., and more are ambitious to gain such positions than to reach the end of the course of study and graduate. This is to be regretted." Officials in Concord, Vermont, as elsewhere, complained that boys rarely graduated and that they entered the business world without sufficient knowledge or analytical skills.[12]

Some educators blamed parents, others the students themselves for limiting their education. "'Young America' is too eager to begin to make money," claimed the principal of the Indianapolis High School in 1870, and the "parents are not less at fault in this respect than the boys and girls." Youth foolishly sought jobs when they were still poorly educated. Necessity required some scholars to leave school, admitted another writer, but "the magnetism of the almighty dollar drags more away than poverty."[13]

Girls were not immune from criticism. Even if girls stayed in school longer than boys and predominated on graduation day, many left school without graduating. The minority of students who were poor were typically girls, often aspiring to teach, and poverty likely shaped their decisions to leave early.

In 1853 H. H. Barney, the principal of Cincinnati's Hughes High School, condemned female scholars for leaving school prematurely. But there were many teaching posts in rural areas and growing towns and cities; school was no match for the marketplace. Peter Clark also said that many of his black pupils, males as well as females, left school prematurely to teach. Some officials, upset at the student turnover, berated women for sharing men's concern with material well-being. According to the superintendent of the Fort Wayne, Indiana, schools, too many girls were "allured by the follies of dress and the glittering attractions of society."[14]

Careful to shield teachers and principals from blame, educators shifted responsibility to parents, students, and society generally. As one midwestern school leader emphasized, teachers did everything possible to encourage students to stay in school. Laziness and poor scholarship also drove many pupils away, as only the academically fit survived in high-quality institutions. Commenting on why so many scholars, especially boys, withdrew from Cincinnati's Central School in 1847, H. H. Barney said that they were "either deficient in mental capacity, or too indolent to make the necessary application, or too heedless to appreciate the advantages of the school."[15]

Principals and administrators, defending high standards, agreed that many pupils left because of poor study skills or low achievement. "It is now a settled point," wrote the head of Woodward High School in 1857, "that none but the studious and faithful, can ever hope to graduate." Other educators doubted whether the graduation requirements could be set low enough for those bottom-of-the-barrel scholars who had somehow passed the entrance test. Teachers often evaluated students rigorously as they registered marks on truancy, deportment, and academic merit on report cards. A sophisticated study of Philadelphia's Central High School, which ultimately based class rank exclusively on academic performance, found that grades best predicted whether a boy would graduate from that highly competitive institution.[16]

Most schoolmen shuddered at the suggestion by the Erie, Pennsylvania, superintendent in 1870 that high schools could easily graduate more pupils if they softened their standards. "A common fault of public high schools," said H. S. Jones, is "that they receive a large number and graduate a few. The students, on entering, are subject to a West Point sifting, until most are shaken out at an early stage of the course." High schools were the crown to the school system, he agreed, but their standards were unrealistic. "Let the course and honors be so broad and generous as to crown the weak and the strong according to their several ability." Moreover, he added, "the time has come to discard the old educational maxim, 'that schools are only for those rich in mental gifts.'"[17]

Educators distressed by the high withdrawal rate were not enamored with this alternative and focused on other factors. Some asked whether so many years of hard study, followed by the rigors of the entrance test and quotidian classroom trials, had simply taken their toll. Some wondered whether admission examinations, already viewed by some contemporaries as less rigorous than before, were perhaps too demanding.

Educators debated whether the curriculum was too academic and not practical enough, especially for boys. Others realized that increasing the average age of those admitted to high school, while justified on bureaucratic and pedagogical grounds, had made graduation less likely. Still others concluded that, in a utilitarian world, everyone, boys as well as girls, wanted to work as soon as possible, something over which schools had little control. After all, numerous scholars, especially boys, who passed the entrance test never even enrolled in school but waved their admission ticket before a prospective employer. Everyone hustled to get a better job, and the work ethic simply took different forms. It seemed unrealistic to many parents to send children to school until the age of seventeen or eighteen when they could immediately help support the family and take those arduous but essential first steps toward adulthood.

Everything seemed to militate against ending sophomore graduations. A Hoosier claimed in 1881 that parents often found boys at age thirteen simply "unmanageable." By then the boys "can read some, write a legible hand, cipher a little, and with the practice and sharpening of the faculties which comes from growth and necessity, will be able to reckon their wages and make change in their business transactions. Therefore the home verdict is 'they have had schooling enough,' and they are set to work or allowed to roam at will—a thing very attractive to the average youth." When St. Louis officials after the Civil War studied the problem, they discovered an array of causes. Some pupils had withdrawn but transferred to private schools; others had received poor grades, become ill, gone to work, or simply moved with their family elsewhere. Educators concurred that lazy pupils could not graduate, but they believed many factors explained why the majority never received a diploma.[18]

Throughout the nation, most high school pupils congregated in the first two years of study. Those who advanced were distinctive. "Classes become smaller . . . one member after another quitting school," wrote Sidney H. Owens, principal of the Petersburg, Virginia, white high school in 1871. "Necessity compels one to seek a living by his own exertions; another lacks the mental acumen and patient industry to grasp successfully and to comprehend fully the branches of a higher education." Yet the junior and senior classes, however small, deserved everyone's full attention. These students were special. "During their last term at school," Owens explained, "they are objects of interest to every boy and girl in all the public schools."[19]

As Frederick Packard noted, graduation ceremonies had become common by the middle of the nineteenth century. School officials, though sometimes critical of the scholars' behavior and that of the audience, generally welcomed the annual event. Graduation day enabled them to honor students, teachers, and the community whose taxes made high schools possible.

Commencement rituals drew upon traditions as old as the nation's colleges and academies. The proceedings were usually open to everyone, a policy that made school people somewhat nervous. For students, graduation was above all a day of celebration. A diploma, many said, launched talented youth upon the sea of life. Still, beneath the apparent serenity of commencement were ripples and occasional waves of discontent.

The graduation ritual was a special moment in the life of an institution. It framed the end of a distinctive school experience as momentously as an entrance examination had marked its beginning. Graduation ceremonies were familiar in the high schools of coastal cities in the 1820s and 1830s, but the proliferation of secondary schools after 1850 brought the ceremonies more publicity. Commencement day became more elaborate, the awarding of diplomas more common. In 1885, Boston's John D. Philbrick remarked that by midcentury a host of school-related social activities had grown popular, including awarding diplomas and creating high school alumni associations. "The diploma is commonly framed and conspicuously hung in the home, where it remains a precious memento and a perpetual recommendation of the high school," he noticed. In contrast, Frederick Packard saw only pompous behavior that undermined equality and the values of the common school.[20]

Graduation days were enormously popular occasions, though opinions on their meaning varied. Citizens routinely filled lecture halls to participate in the proceedings, not simply witness them. By the late 1850s, approximately four thousand spectators attended the graduation exercises at Philadelphia's Central High School—and twice that number was turned away. Eight to ten thousand citizens arrived for the event in Cleveland in the 1870s. In small places, too, citizens packed the opera house, church hall, or school auditorium. In Adrian, Michigan, "the opera house, the largest public hall in the city, capable of seating 1,200 persons, [was] always crowded to its utmost capacity, while large numbers [were] obliged to retire for want of standing room."[21]

Thousands waited in line to see a handful of graduates. In 1876, the Kokomo, Indiana, *Saturday Tribune* reported that the opera house hosted "a large, refined, and quite appreciative audience," which came to applaud six graduates. In Shelbyville, near Indianapolis, a thousand people came to hear the graduates: four women and two men. The male and female high schools of Memphis had a joint ceremony, where spectators honored thirteen female and two male graduates. Similarly, white Atlantans in 1873 showed their spirit as they honored, in separate events, eleven scholars from the Girls' High School and five from the Boys' High School.[22]

Female scholars always outnumbered their brothers on the public stage. In

1890 an estimated 65 percent of all graduates were women. Females constituted about 60 percent of Chicago's graduates between the mid-1850s and 1880. In Portland, Maine, 935 students graduated from the coeducational high school between 1864 and 1880, of whom 61 percent were women. In Oshkosh, Wisconsin, only 4 of the 22 graduates in 1875 were men. Because women's ability to speak in public was circumscribed, their predominance posed a difficult problem, at least in theory, on graduation day.[23]

High schools honored the written word, whether in entrance examinations or in classroom textbooks. But this was still an age that valued oratory, public performance, and the diffusion of knowledge. Despite the proliferation of newspapers, cheaper magazines, and books, face-to-face conversation, oratory, and aural entertainment remained integral to daily life. Millions of Americans heard Shakespeare performed in dance halls in Colorado mining towns and in opera houses on Main Street. Community bands entertained countless citizens. Men frequently listened for hours to political debates, as the male franchise broadened during the Jacksonian period. And growing dependence upon textbooks did not end oral recitations, the sine qua non of the classroom.[24]

The doctrine of separate spheres wove its way into graduation day proceedings. A teacher at a classical high school in the 1850s later recounted the usual pattern of commencement exercises. "The young women's productions were always called 'essays,' and never 'orations,' like those of the young men. Although the young men stood on the platform to speak, this was not considered proper for the young women; they read their essays standing on the lowest of the three steps leading to the platform, thus signifying the humbler position to be taken by woman."[25]

Contemporary accounts of graduation confirmed the power of gender differences. Describing the happy event in Cambridge, the *Massachusetts Teacher* in 1851 remarked: "The exercises consisted of speaking by the boys, reading by the young ladies, and singing." The writer added that the women looked "beautiful" but were intimidated by public speaking, no doubt due to inexperience. "One or two read well, however, one remarkably well." Evansville, Indiana, honored its twelve female and four male graduates in 1872. According to the *Indiana School Journal*, by "established usage, the former read essays, and the latter spoke original declamations."[26]

Just as rules regulated, or tried to regulate, student behavior, officials organized graduation ceremonies that became somewhat formulaic. The first graduation exercises for the Girls' High School of Atlanta, held at the Hall of the House of Representatives in 1873, were typical. Joining the graduates on stage were Protestant ministers, school officials, the high school principal, and other dignitaries. When the audience grew quiet, a minister offered a prayer, students read essays and joined in singing, and then the audience heard various speeches by town notables. When a girl finished reading an essay, the audience tossed flowers onto the stage. Near the end of the ceremony, Atlantans heard a "Graduating Hymn," typically an original composition.[27]

Religiosity often filled the air, for singing at church and at school was common:

How wide the pleasing prospect lies!
A fairy realm of boundless skies,
Lies dreaming in the lap of Hope.

O Thou, to whom Creation pays
Eternal Homage! grant us still
Thy loving care in all our ways
And guide us by Thy holy will;
Teach us the wisdom of the skies,
The love, from guile and error free,
By which the spirit gains the prize
Of blissful immortality.[28]

Throughout the ceremony, the audience was expected to applaud at the appropriate moments and to sing on cue. Neither the honored graduates, however, nor the spectators always followed the official script.

Rowdiness and political heterodoxy sometimes visited the event. Although schoolmen wanted conventional, polite readings or declamations from the pupils, and quiet, appreciative behavior from the audience, some well-made plans went awry. Very few students, having reached the public stage after conforming to countless rules and regulations, embarrassed their teachers and principals. Few criticized bourgeois tenets or condemned racism, sexism, or social injustice. Most women graduates praised the cult of true womanhood, not the thunderbolts from Seneca Falls, and they endorsed bourgeois values, not economic or social heresies. In Indianapolis women graduates in 1876 applauded the idea of sacrifice, hard work, and perseverance. The men applauded the self-made man. Occasionally, however, the barriers broke. Final grades recorded, diplomas in hand, a few young people spoke their minds.[29]

The opera house filled quickly in Terre Haute in 1876, and the audience heard some memorable words. *The Saturday Evening Mail* reported that "the audience was not confined to any class of our citizens, for side by side sat and stood the wealthiest men and most elegantly dressed ladies with the swarthy mechanic and ladies in modest attire." Miss Jennie Jackson read a particularly forceful address. She apparently accepted the central values of the local high school, for she proclaimed that "Man is Man and Master of His Fate—a wholesome truth that should be extensively circulated." Miss Belle Cory, however, expressed outrage at prevailing social conditions. According to the local newspaper, "she greatly deplored the indications of the ever-present aristocracy of money, and thought the tendency of the times was to make the rich, richer, the poor, poorer." Whether her teachers or audience judged her on her delivery or on the content of her message is unknown, but the proceedings concluded with all the pupils singing, "Oh! Glorious Lord."[30]

Occasionally brave women used the graduation ceremony as an opportunity to demand respect from fellow students. Indianapolis High School, like most "integrated" institutions, was an unfriendly place for African-Americans after the Civil War. Indiana had very restrictive laws on black education, and even superior black scholars faced a chilly academic climate. Miss Mary Rann attended Indianapolis High in the early 1870s. For four years she suffered vicious, unkind treatment from her peers. "Her white school mates," wrote one contemporary, "would slight her and indulge in rude remarks well calculated to wound her feelings." She persevered and proudly ascended the stage with the white racists on graduation day in June of 1876.[31]

When Mary took her seat with the honored guests, a white classmate refused to sit next to her, according to a news reporter who attended the ceremony. The classmate then relented but "sat with averted face during most of the evening." When Mary Rann read her essay on labor, "she gained the hearts of the audience, and received frequent and enthusiastic applause—while bouquets were showered upon her to such a degree that the young lady who had objected to sitting beside her asked the privilege of holding some of them for her." The audience applauded, forcing the black scholar to reappear at the footlights. "It was truly a great triumph for the young girl, and goes to prove that, after all, color is only skin deep, and confirms the adage, 'Act well your part/Therein true honor lies.'"[32]

Ostentatious students could fulfill the worst fears of school authorities. Schoolmen were extremely sensitive about the select background of students, who sometimes flaunted their social position at commencement. Principals and teachers urged graduates to dress plainly instead of forming a "parade of elaborate and expensive costumes." Wearing lavish clothes opened the door to public criticism. A writer in the *Massachusetts Teacher* complained in 1867 that girls in one community purchased $75 dresses for commencement, an extravagance that might discourage the poor from aspiring to high school. The school trustees in Concord, Vermont, chastised the girls in 1872. The officials did not want to tell the "young ladies" how much to spend or what to wear but cautioned that "no one should attempt a style which is beyond the easy reach of any member of the class, and that the Horatian rule of 'plain in thy neatness' would not be wholly inapplicable to graduation day."[33]

Simplicity was especially welcome in the 1870s, when the nation sank into economic depression. Many insensitive students, however, remained oblivious to criticism. Chicago's superintendent, J. L. Pickard, captured the feelings of many educators in 1875. "Fashion," he said, "has come to require the members of the graduating class to provide expensive costumes, flowers, regulation jewelry and other adornments more befitting ball-room belles than pupils of a public school." The pupils' behavior was shocking. "An expensive dress has made it necessary for the pupils to employ a carriage to take them to and from the Hall where the Commencement Exercises are held. All these operate to discourage the worthy poor, for whom the public schools are designed, from completing their studies in a school whose benefits should be enjoyed by the largest number possible."[34]

Perhaps because women were the most numerous graduates, Pickard and his contemporaries complained more about dresses than men's fancy suits. Still, ostentatious display at a time of high unemployment—and when some Chicago newspapers favored closing the high schools—was clearly impolitic. Schoolmen implored youth who engaged in self-promotion on graduation day to exercise restraint. Boys and girls from comfortable families, however, had long understood that they were special. Moreover, the public praise bestowed upon them seemed to merit distinctive dresses and other apparel. After hearing many complaints about the scholars, a writer in the *National Teachers Monthly* in 1875 told the critics to loosen their ties and let parents applaud the well-decked scholars in the "annual blow-out."[35]

The behavior of spectators also frazzled the nerves of many educators. Most pupils were well-behaved, and the audience was supposed to mind its manners, too. Yet the "annual blow-out" could explode in the faces of those in authority. Certain rituals were welcome. Audiences everywhere tossed flowers on stage after boys delivered their orations and girls read their essays. Even the rancorous debates in Kalamazoo over the high school did not eliminate this hallowed tradition from the age of academies. "At the conclusion of each oration and essay a shower of bouquets were [sic] thrown upon the foot boards," wrote the *Kalamazoo Gazette* in 1872. Noisy, unruly crowds, however, offended the sensibilities of every community's best citizens.[36]

A writer in the *Indiana School Journal* contended that Hoosiers lacked manners. "Who has not been outraged by the 'cat-calls,' 'hisses,' loud talking, and hallooing of rude persons on such occasions, who ought to have been arrested and placed in a calaboose?" Cambridge City had to restrict entry to commencement to the parents or guardians of the graduates. Other towns charged a nickel or a dime for admission to discourage the riffraff.[37]

As in many towns and cities by midcentury, the graduation exercises at Louisville's high schools were immensely popular. Hundreds of citizens could not gain entry to the festivities because of overcrowding, and those admitted were not always compliant. Rowdies remained a problem in the 1860s and 1870s, until ushers refused entry to the "unruly mob," especially "wicked and mischievous youth, and surly, rude men."[38]

In 1878, when the local Female High School graduation shifted from a public hall to the school's chapel, the male mob was replaced by rude women. "There were a number of females," wrote one observer, "who took their stand, for they couldn't or wouldn't take seats in the rear portion of the chapel." "By the constant clatter of the tongues, not withstanding the remonstrances and appeals of Prof. Chase and Vice President Palmer, they managed to drown all sound and prevented the majority of the listeners from hearing most of the exercises. We doubt whether more unruly audiences can be found in attendance anywhere than in these Female High School commencements."[39]

Graduation ceremonies fostered a certain intimacy between the audience and those on stage. Efforts to restrict attendance partially succeeded, but taxpayers still expected open if not free admission. Graduating from high school was an unusual experience, an impressive academic achievement before the

1880s. To parade before the citizenry at the local opera house became a special rite of passage and a moment cherished by scholars.

Graduates usually wrote their own songs, essays, and speeches for commencement. When graduating classes were small, every boy gave an oration or speech, every girl read an essay. As the graduating class size increased, only valedictorians and salutatorians shared in this honor. Sixteen pupils graduated from the Terre Haute, Indiana, high school in 1877. "According to a previous arrangement," the superintendent casually remarked, "the number of essays and orations was limited to nine which together with the music, awarding of diplomas, etc., detained the audience quite long enough." Many schools retained an old tradition, familiar in colleges and academies, whereby a teacher or student composed a poem or song that brought the ceremony to a climax. The metaphors heard at commencement became a bundle of cliches: everyone was beginning life's journey, or was ushered onto a stormy sea, or was about to climb the ladder of life.[40]

Speeches captured the idealism of youth and the evangelical culture of the times: scholars promised to serve mankind, to teach the ignorant, and to minister to the fallen. An occasional oration even rose above the platitudes. In her valedictory address, Lizzie Black, from Milwaukee's Class of '78, assailed the trusts and accused politicians of oppressing the poor. "The wealth of the nation is in the hands of a few individuals, who are accumulating more every day, while the poor are becoming more and more miserable," she proclaimed. "Our men are forgetting that truth, honesty, virtue, and love are far more valuable to the happiness of mankind than extravagant modes of living." She also told women to speak out more in public and to denounce social injustice and corrupt politicians, including the president. Lizzie Black, so full of idealism, became a leading social reformer in Milwaukee. Active in a host of middle-class voluntary associations by the 1890s, she established a settlement house, served on the school board, and was a prominent social activist for decades.[41]

More typical, though, was the "Farewell Song" that Sallie C. Neill, a senior at Louisville's Female High School, wrote for the Class of 1867:

> Softly steps of time are falling,
>   Swiftly speed the hours away,
> Other voices now are calling,
>   We may here no longer stay.
> Here 'mid scenes of joy and pleasure
>   Love has bound us, heart to heart;
> We have sought the priceless treasure —
>   Teachers, schoolmates, now we part.[42]

A school whose graduation crowds were renowned for their boisterousness had sent another class upon the sea of life.

Nineteenth-century Americans had debated every imaginable facet of school policy, so they naturally disagreed about the ultimate value of local high schools. Usually practical-minded in their appraisals, citizens assessed the lives of high school alumni by their deeds, usually by their occupations. Since the 1820s, whether or not they graduated, high school boys often became clerks or bookkeepers while girls became teachers and mothers. And by midcentury critics asked what effects high school graduates had upon the social order.

In 1849, one politico in a major Democratic magazine denounced high school graduates, particularly males, for their elitism. "Most of them in due time become members of the three learned professions and editors of news-papers, a small proportion store-keepers and merchants, and a still smaller, farmers and manufacturers." The writer called professionals antirepublican, "large and expensive consumers" who "produce nothing, and as a whole, set themselves up as an aristocratic section of society." Most male high school graduates, he added, were parasites who likened themselves to "the upper ten percent," filled with "aristocratic notions, and expensive habits," seeking only "to live in style and luxury."[43]

Even professional education journals on rare moments worried about how higher learning affected the quality of life for ordinary citizens. In June of 1879 the editor of the *New-England Journal of Education* examined the tensions between high schools and the common good. "A thousand academical and high schools will send forth, this week, a cloud of graduates," he happily reported. Some of the boys would "swell the over-full current of American professional life," while many of the girls would "join the glorious army of schoolma'ams. . . . But the vast majority of these pupils will fall into the great mid-ocean of American common life. The boys will sell goods, write in counting-rooms, toil in the workshops, sail, or till the earth." Girls, in con-trast, "will chiefly become wives; or in Yankeeland, perchance teachers." Would the whole community, and not just the individual graduates, benefit from the higher learning?[44]

"The test of all high culture," this New Englander believed, "is the willing-ness to put the noblest manhood, the choicest womanhood, into the humblest lot. The great need of America is not more lawyers, ministers, doctors, even teachers. It is a new generation of men of affairs, who shall take into the counting-room and factory a capacity and honesty which ensure an honorable success," working men who would resist the appeal of demagogues, and "a class of women who can make pure, intelligent, refined homes out of mod-erate means, and altogether exalt the life of the Republic." By leading honest, respectable lives, the educated classes could become models of sobriety and good taste, using their learning not to amass riches but, as the editor said else-where, to "ennoble our common American life." Male and female scholars, in their special spheres, had to rise above personal aggrandizement to enrich a common democratic culture.[45]

Like the hostile Democrat or anxious educational professional, many Amer-icans tried to appraise the influence of the high school upon everyday life. Did a high school inevitably create or confirm a higher caste of citizens, under-mining the republican goals that educators advocated? Was it not elitist to "ennoble" life, making alumni a new sort of local nobility? The ostentatious dress at commencement indicated a taste for luxury befitting elite, not ordi-nary, people. Evaluating the position of high school graduates in a democratic culture thus remained controversial and complicated.

One measure proved popular, though it only tangentially addressed the schools' compatibility with republican ideals. School officials by the 1850s increasingly collected statistics on the occupational achievements of alumni. As older high schools expanded their enrollments and many newer institutions opened, countless schools helped shape their self-images by tracing the lives of former scholars. High schools thus began to chronicle their own histories. Alumni associations, common after the 1840s, also strengthened the old school tie.

According to school officials, any reasonable citizen who became familiar with the lives of alumni would see the wisdom of tax-supported higher edu-cation. Schoolmen had little doubt that former students became respectable and honorable members of society. As early as 1846, principal John S. Hart of Philadelphia's Central High School claimed that "the alumni of the High School are already found scattered through the City in almost every walk of useful industry." Indeed, "many of our leading mechanics, manufacturers, merchants, and others, are in the habit of sending to the school whenever they are in want of desirable young men to be trained to business."[46]

The president of the trustees of another all-male school, New York's Free Academy, in 1864 said that "its graduates may be found in the pulpit, in the practice of law and medicine, in engineering and architecture, in commercial pursuits and the education of youth, in the army, and in almost every depart-ment of active and honorable industry." Similarly, Boston's English High School reportedly produced "many of the most able, prominent, honored, and useful" businessmen found in the city.[47]

Pride ran deep in many institutions. Large female high schools, which often had prominent teacher-training curricula, similarly praised their own contri-butions to society: many of their alumna became respectable teachers and honorable mothers. The original justifications for Boston's short-lived High School for Girls in the 1820s remained part of the collective wisdom. Many teachers also hailed from the more numerous coeducational high schools, but single-sex schools naturally drew attention to their own special influence. With elementary-level enrollments rising and teacher turnover rapid, local graduates received special preference in hiring.

By the 1860s, hundreds of alumna of the Girls' High School of Philadelphia were teachers, usually in area schools. Countless women who did not stay until graduation also became teachers. The hope of finding a job as a teacher attracted many girls to high school in the first place, and other desirable posi-tions and prestigious professions were largely closed to them. Atlanta's super-intendent wrote in 1872 that "those who have successfully passed through the entire course of study in the Public Schools, and have graduated with honor, will be the best material from which to select our teachers." The majority who failed to graduate, with or without honor, also swelled the primary teaching force.[48]

The first state normal school appeared in the 1830s, though academies that trained teachers in New York as elsewhere had earlier received some public support. Major cities offered normal curricula within the high school or short postgraduate courses, but most elementary teachers came right from the high school after studying the English branches.

A leading advocate of normal secondary training in Charleston, South Carolina, C. G. Memminger, claimed in 1860 that "no higher good can be bestowed on a community than well educated mothers, capable of training and teaching their own children; and second only to this is the bestowal of a competent body of teachers." Schoolmen wanted "home talent" nurtured at local, tax-supported institutions. As Chicago's superintendent noted in 1854, the high school could help "afford to the City all the advantages of an independent Normal School, and avoid the necessity of relying upon the East for Teachers, by educating its own." Antebellum southerners, fearful of Yankee, pro-abolitionist teachers, agreed completely.[49]

Indiana's superintendent predicted in 1853 that high schools would long serve as an important "nursery of teachers." By training so many talented women for the lower grades, female as well as coeducational high schools provided the system with teachers familiar with local practices. Superintendents could not force ward trustees to hire only the best scholars, but local secondary schools produced a high proportion of elementary teachers in most towns and cities after the 1850s. Many of the female instructors in the countryside were also educated at union graded schools in nearby villages or in better-graded urban schools. In less than a decade the Girls' High and Normal School of Boston produced nearly 300 teachers. By 1863, within Boston itself, 12 high school teachers, 152 grammar teachers (often assistants), and 101 primary teachers hailed from the home institution. In New York, the Normal College graduated nearly 1,600 scholars between 1870 and 1878, of which more than 1,000 taught in the city schools.[50]

Half of Chicago's 300 teachers in 1867 were alumna of the local normal course. Whether in major cities or little towns, high schools became leading teacher-training schools for women. Principal Daniel Shepardson of Woodward High School in Cincinnati, whose institution prepared dozens of teachers for the Queen City, told the trustees in 1862 that "the valedictory was justly awarded to Miss Henrietta Walter, and if her experience as a teacher shall equal her fidelity and success as a scholar, she will eminently deserve your kind remembrance in some future appointment." In Iowa, superintendent Oran Faville wrote that "the graduating class of 1864 of the Davenport High School are all first class teachers." The pattern was repeated in the South as high schools appeared in the larger towns and cities.[51]

Hiring local talent served different social functions. Administrators and ward leaders could use high school attendance or graduation to restrict the number of potential applicants. Female scholars swelled high school enrollments, thus promoting their own employment opportunities. Increased attendance simultaneously advanced the careers of administrators and teachers. And those who appointed teachers had the opportunity to hire scholars who excelled at school and conformed to the system. A growing school population created a large demand for inexpensive instructors, and many female scholars, middle-class and poorer, attended high school with the hopes of landing a respectable job near home. Because so many talented female scholars routinely secured teaching positions, occasionally in their old high schools, educated women were struck hard when the economy soured in the 1870s and jobs became scarce.[52]

School officials at coeducational high schools always highlighted the different pathways of alumni and alumnae. Between 1864 and 1875, 95 women and 26 men graduated from high school in Akron, Ohio. In 1875, 44 percent of the women were teachers, 34 percent were married, and 2 percent were in college; the whereabouts of 20 percent was unknown. Only 3 percent of the men were teaching, about 11 percent were in the professions, 50 percent were in college, and 36 percent were white-collar workers, typically cashiers, clerks, and bookkeepers. In other communities about one-quarter to one-half of male graduates before the 1880s put away their books for a white collar. A smaller percentage typically entered college en route to the professions, while others became merchants, shopkeepers, and small manufacturers. Separate spheres continued to characterize the educated classes after they finished school.[53]

Thus the township high school of Princeton, Illinois, sent boys and girls into the world as they arrived: separately. "Court records show the ability of some, while society acknowledges the leadership of others," wrote a local historian. "Their voices are heard from the rostrum, in the halls of legislature and in the barn yard. Some have attained eminence, others have married pre-eminence." Lena M. Breed, Class of '72, attained her eminence, teaching in Vermont, Illinois, and in Ohio before returning to teach in Princeton in 1884. She poetically described how alumni and alumnae found their way in the world:

> And though in numbers we were few,
> To purpose high we have been true.
> No idlers we: but every one
> Has found some work that should be done.[54]

The majority of women who worked taught in the primary or elementary grades; few taught after marriage. Whether or not they taught, alumnae often became middle-class wives and mothers. As the historian of the Girls' High School of Portland, Maine, remarked in 1888, "the school fitted many young girls for a useful career in life, while others are the wives of our leading citizens."[55]

"Where have they gone?" asked an alumnus in 1883 in *The High School Stu-*

dent, Chicago's student newspaper, who wondered about the fate of the city's best. His poem gave part of the answer:

> Some will go to Greece and Harvard,
> Some to Boston and to Rome,
> Some to Greenland's icy mountains,
> And some will stay at home.[56]

A study of Chicago's graduates from 1859 to 1872 found that the majority of alumnae who worked were teachers, while some men went to college and became professionals. Most males, however, found midrange though respectable work in mercantile houses. Most women graduates did not go to college but, in the language of the day, after teaching subsequently adorned the household as wife and mother.[57]

Everywhere school committees and educators applauded the alumni and alumnae, endorsing the idea that the graduates had distinctive roles to play in life. As early as 1859, the *Massachusetts Teacher* dubbed the alumni of Boston's English High School the "Local Intelligentsia." Hartford High also had very honorable graduates, said the local trustees in 1868. "In a few years the alumni of the High School, male and female will be found to constitute an important part of the controlling mind of the community, either in professional, mechanical or other employments, or in adorning and blessing the circles of domestic life."[58]

High school graduates by midcentury had become more identifiable members of the community. The doctrine of separate spheres effectively denied women access to many occupations and professions, but locally educated alumnae received preferential treatment in securing teaching positions. They also married within their own educated class, thus reinforcing bourgeois values as parents.

Some critics resented the special attention to the "local intelligentsia" or the high school's contribution to the class system. High schools nevertheless survived the criticisms and seemed securely integrated into social life by the 1880s. Free secondary schools became familiar institutions in the North and more common in the urban South later in the century. One increasingly met high school graduates teaching school, selling dry goods, counting money, and settling the neighborhood merchant's accounts.

High school alumni became an important core of middle-class life. The middle classes had larger homes, lived in better neighborhoods, restricted family size, embraced new theories on child-rearing and, most crucial to school reformers, prevented public education from remaining the special province of the poor in America's urban areas. The urban middle classes enabled tax-supported schools to become increasingly public, embracing all social classes, especially whites, into a common system. Moreover, decades of institution building, and the ever-increasing numbers of graduates, led the former scholars to promote their own sense of being special.

"Associations of alumni of the high schools have spread as far and as rapidly as the custom of awarding diplomas," wrote John D. Philbrick in 1885. "These associations hold annual festivals of a mixed literary and social character, beginning with an oration or essays, speeches, and poems, and ending with a promenade concert or a supper and a dance." Though only alumni, and not the public, could join these organizations, they became important cultural symbols, confirming the vitality and desirability of high-quality public institutions.[59]

Alumni associations appeared in the larger cities by the 1840s and 1850s. Philadelphia's Central High School had an Alumni Association, which initially restricted members to four-year graduates, in 1842. By midcentury the group had over seven hundred members, as graduates and nongraduates alike swelled the ranks. Gushing praise by *The Rhode Island Schoolmaster* in 1857 was typical of alumni associations. "Heaven multiply such schools as 'the Philadelphia High School,' with its efficient principal, its able professors and teachers, and its graduates, who number by scores the noble and honored of the land and the sea."[60]

Former students formed other cultural and scientific groups, binding the generations. Alumni associations usually met annually, allowing members to congratulate themselves on their past and current achievements. Through these rituals, the organizations undoubtedly enabled classmates, particularly the men, to discover new job prospects and other ways to advance in the world.

The English High School Association of Boston originated in 1853, open to all former pupils and even to teachers. Like other alumni associations, this group helped link the past with the present. Boston's best raised money to strengthen the school library, and they established a scholarship fund for poorer students. Although it did not initiate annual reunions until 1872, by then the group had donated plaster casts, paintings, and many books to America's oldest English high school. By the 1860s and 1870s, most well-graded high schools in the Midwest and in the Border States formed alumni associations, which cemented personal and social bonds.[61]

A favorite form of alumni association was the literary society. In 1854, the *Pennsylvania School Journal* reported that the pupils of the Lancaster Male High School had formed the Calliopean Literary Society, which met weekly to discuss common readings. Such organizations helped tighten friendships among future leaders in formal alumni organizations. The High School Alumni Association of Oshkosh, Wisconsin, created in 1870, met monthly to discuss literature and to enhance learning. Such frequent meetings, said the superintendent in 1873, ensured that "the great masterpieces of the English language are thoroughly studied and a taste for good reading cultivated which is of incalculable value, especially to recent graduates, to whom the exercises of the society are a continuation of the school course." No Shakespeare in the tavern for these educated citizens.[62]

Less literary in its origins were the "Woodward Guards" of Cincinnati.

These were the male alumni from Woodward High School who had volunteered to fight Johnny Reb; the tattered flag of their Union regiment hung in their old school for many decades. Whether waving the bloody shirt or promoting literary classics, high school graduates formed various associations throughout the North by the 1850s. Most alumni associations from coeducational high schools admitted both sexes, similarly promoting the higher learning and genteel values. Few African-Americans seemed prominent in these organizations, hardly a surprising development given their low enrollment rates and second-class treatment as scholars. And, even as classmates met years after their last school bell tolled, the doctrine of separate gender spheres, so evident in many classrooms and at commencement, remained powerful.[63]

Men dominated some alumni associations even though most of their classmates had been women. Men were freer to behave aggressively, and women, their participation in public life still restricted, often retreated, as mothers, within the family circle. Male graduates often had higher status because of their occupational positions, and membership in fraternal organizations was widespread for men in the late nineteenth century. Women, in contrast, were active in temperance and church groups and joined other female voluntary associations that became increasingly class based after the Civil War. In Princeton, Illinois, every president of the local alumni organization was a male in the 1870s. When women came to alumni meetings and celebrations, they continued to be treated differently: women still read essays, men still lectured.[64]

The minute book of the Alumni Society of the Indianapolis High School duly noted that only those with diplomas could be active members. Annual dues of one dollar, however, were apparently collected from every former student who wanted to join. The group held annual reunions by the late 1860s. Although women, the great majority of the graduates, became class officers, men dominated the organization's presidency throughout the 1870s.

The rules of the association, moreover, stated that, "at the Annual Reunion, in addition to the President's address, there shall be an essay read by a lady alumnus [sic]" and "an oration delivered by a gentleman alumnus." This happened at many of the local reunions, which had readings by women, speeches by men, and usually a mixer and dance. After one "lady essayist," Miss Rosa L. Kahn, spoke on "Popcorn" ("an original one at best," sneered one classmate), there was more music and dancing, which had punctuated the evening at the 1875 reunion. Then the secretary of the Alumni Society "gave the signal and the band broke loose, the dance was called, the Alumni started, and the Moon began to pale and the chickens were crowing before the last of the sheepskin tribe ceased dancing and descended the Hall steps into the outer world."[65]

Reminiscent of commencement, however, rowdies sometimes disrupted the harmony of the sheepskin crowd. Unlike graduation ceremonies, alumni meetings were private affairs. Forty-five alumni arrived for the reunion in 1876. So did a number of unwelcome guests. "Miss K. V. Branham is responsible for nineteen outsiders," said the secretary in the minute book. "She freely distributed the tickets. . . . These were broadcast and the room was filled but few of the Alumni present." In subsequent years alumnae without escorts were allowed to bring only one guest, a policy that cut down on intruders. Calm had returned by the 1878 gathering, which had the usual male orator and a female essayist—and a much happier secretary.[66]

Alumni associations were supposed to breed exclusivity and encourage that old school spirit. Commoners who aimed to crash the party offended those who had worked diligently to win their diploma. Former scholars read essays on popcorn, gave orations on Shakespeare, and danced until dawn. From their school days, however, they appreciated decorum. By the middle of the century, graduates increasingly recognized that they were special. That was why they donned expensive dress for commencement and formed their alumni associations. In the language of the times, they were object lessons in good taste and propriety.

Epilogue

Knowledge and intellect are the two great
forces that rule the world and are the chief
sources of its wealth and power.

Superintendent DANIEL LEACH,
Providence, 1878

By the 1880s, leaders of the
public schools had every right to congratulate themselves. The most serious
opponents of high schools in the North had been silenced. Lawsuits against
the system in Michigan and elsewhere had failed, and courts had affirmed the
right of local districts to create and maintain free high schools. As free secondary schools became more familiar, and as more alumni entered the
economy and helped shape middle-class culture, opponents would be remembered only as skinflints and reactionaries.

Later generations of educators could imagine that the high schools, representing goodness and indigenous democratic forces, had inevitably triumphed
over the opposition. Politically shrewd activists such as Henry Barnard knew
better. Barnard had promoted high schools throughout the century, first in his
native Hartford, then in New England, and then across the nation as head of
the U. S. Bureau of Education and as editor of the world-famous *American
Journal of Education.*

Reflecting upon his active life, Barnard in 1882 openly documented the elite
origins of the American high school. Citizens in the early 1800s, he correctly
noted, enthusiastically supported the teaching of the elementary branches to
all white children. High schools were different. They were "few in number
and of modern origin, . . . not so much the outgrowth of popular feeling, as the
creations of a few intelligent friends of public education, in advance of any

general demand for this class of institution." But these high schools neverthe-less had "increased rapidly" by the 1880s, spreading to nearly every town and city and "almost every village in the land."[1]

Barnard's history lesson on the genesis of the American high school was remarkable. He had waited until the high school was secure before distin-guishing myth from truth, and in old age he quietly but publicly expressed ideas that in his younger days would have aided and abetted the enemy. Most contemporary school leaders spoke vaguely about the democratic roots of public secondary institutions, a theme that later resonated in many histories of education. Barnard, however, knew from firsthand experience that particular social classes had agitated for and benefited from free high schools.

That same year another Yankee reformer, Barnas Sears, told the faithful at the National Education Association meetings that support for the high school was essentially a "political" matter. High school pupils "belong mainly to the great middle class in society, that class which stands between the extremely poor and the extremely rich and holds in check those extremes, between which exist irreconcilable war." Social movements not led by the respectable classes terrified Sears, but the "middle class," he asserted, "is the great conservator of peace and order."[2]

According to school officials and their allies, the future of the high school depended upon its usefulness. A new generation would debate whether the curriculum needed major alterations, whether boys and girls should study dif-ferent subjects, whether more pupils had the capacity to study the higher branches, and whether more scholars could travel the long road to graduation. For now, however, high schools stood triumphant. Only below Mason-Dixon would academies continue to appeal strongly to the bourgeoisie.

A speaker before New England's venerable American Institute of Instruc-tion proclaimed in 1880 that high schools effectively served the larger society. "The State must have officers as well as soldiers," it was often alleged, "and every high school is a miniature West Point, where local leaders are trained." Educated labor, others argued, produced more wealth, and a sophisticated economic order required a small percentage of scholars who had mastered the higher branches. Thus the division of labor in the economy had its corollary in the public schools. The speaker, principal of the New Hampshire Normal School and a former high school master, disliked the tawdry materialism of the age. While the high school taught useful subjects, it had loftier origins and purposes, a spiritual side "born of Christian faith."[3]

Indeed, a handful of Unitarian reformers, having persuaded Boston's town meeting that certain boys needed a special sort of advanced education, had created America's first public high school. Instead of restricting the mission of secondary schools to classical instruction, reformers everywhere established English high schools that offered the ambitious, talented, respectable classes a way to avoid the pitfalls of poverty and vice. Protestants throughout the nation would consistently infuse free secondary schools with an evangelical faith while promoting the cause of practical studies. As the principal told his audience, high schools offered moral training as well as intellectual discipline. Like members of the ministry, high school teachers were civic leaders with moral power: "They divide with the clergy the honor of being known as an untitled nobility."[4]

Calling students the sheepskin crowd and teachers an untitled nobility would continue to rankle some citizens. Evangelical reformers, whether Whigs or Republicans, had continually argued that public education in all its forms supported republican government. Through membership on school committees and voluntary associations, they actively promoted high schools to prepare talented youth for positions of leadership, deemed especially important as commercial and then industrial changes altered the nation's economic system.

As social class differences deepened after the 1820s, mainstream reformers took their stand. They embraced the theories not of agrarians or Owenite socialists but of free-market political economists. The common school was for every white child, but the high school was for the talented few. Class identity intensified, reaffirmed increasingly by the possession of educational credentials, often awarded by local secondary schools.

In the waning decades of the century, educational activists still regarded America as the world's great hope, a land blessed by Providence, where individual initiative determined personal destiny. The untold wealth of the land, highlighted in so many geography and history textbooks, awaited those with the ambition, drive, and intelligence needed to guide enterprise and to direct the labor of others. By recognizing and rewarding individual merit, high schools promoted social order and harmony, defusing the prospects of class warfare by allowing rich and poor alike to compete for academic honors and a favored position in the marketplace.

For decades, Whigs and then Republicans had argued that investing in youth enhanced republicanism and improved society. That most scholars in secondary schools came from fairly comfortable families was regrettable, but all talented youth, especially if they were white, still had opportunities unknown in monarchical Europe. Even the multitude who never attended high schools, it was claimed, benefited from them, for the schools accelerated age-graded instruction, prepared many teachers, and encouraged the poor to excel.

As the opponents fell, as private academies disappeared or became public property, the schoolmen boasted of their good fortune. That was why speakers could act as if the creation of high schools rested not upon economic or political power as much as on Christian faith. Little was ever said about how much high schools really owed to academies, anymore than schoolmen accepted seriously the criticisms of men such as Charles Stuart or Frederick Packard.

Academies, not high schools, had first provided women with access to the higher learning, offering the talented few greater access to an advanced English education and fitting pupils mostly for life, not college. They also trained countless teachers for the common schools of the early republic and for high schools before the 1840s. Public high schools ultimately became free throughout the nation, but they borrowed extensively from their erstwhile opponents. They became the crown of an emerging system of public education. Members of an untitled nobility increasingly prepared talented youth for leadership in a more class-oriented society.

Educational reformers across the nation felt relieved that high schools had overcome their opponents. "'The High School Question,' as it is called, has been greatly agitated in all the cities of this country," wrote a Memphis superintendent in 1880, but "as so far as my information goes, has always been adjudicated in favor of the High School, as the Key-Stone to the Arch, in the edifice of public education."[5]

The *Louisiana Journal of Education* similarly denounced lingering attempts to close free secondary schools. Unlike private academies, high schools remained the republic's best hope, for their fate and that of the middle classes were nearly identical. The high school, claimed a contributor, "affords opportunities for advancement in life, and this tends to harmonize different strata of society, to destroy caste and [the] money aristocracy; and is an important element in the preservation of our free institutions." In a society in which the pampered rich and ignorant poor often behaved immorally and threatened social harmony, the high school remained a bulwark of the republic.[6]

At the dedication of the new secondary school in Providence in 1878, principal George I. Chace highlighted the significance of the bourgeoisie in America's political economy. "Is an enlightened class of producers more essential to the business prosperity of the country, than honest clerks, skillful accountants, capable and trusty agents, and able and sagacious business men and financiers? At whose door lies the responsibility for the great losses and fearful commercial disasters of the last few years, and for the present depressed state of every species of industry?" As far as Chace was concerned, the problem rested not with the well-educated bourgeoisie, who rejected radical notions of leveling, now appealing to some poor people, as well as the irresponsible behavior of economic titans, now rising to power.[7]

"We must look higher up in society for the origin of our business troubles," said the principal.

> Their fruitful source will be found in unwise investments, in incompetent management, in ignorance of the fundamental laws of trade and finance, in wild and reckless speculation, in enterprises not well considered and from the start doomed to failure, in lack of capacity for the organization and conduct of business, in breaches of trust, in failures of character, in defalcations, and misappropriations, in fraud and trickery and dishonesty of all kinds among the better conditioned class—among those who occupy pivotal positions, and control by their movements, to a large extent, the business of the country.[8]

Part of the solution, Chace decided, was the education of a "higher order of men," future high school alumni. "These more advanced institutions of learning are as essential to the public welfare . . . as schools of a lower grade, where the pupils are fitted for the ordinary occupations and duties of life."[9]

At the same dedication, the local superintendent declared that "the only well-founded hope of the future is in our intelligent and upright youth, who are not only soon to fill the important places of honor and trust, to decide the great question of civil and social polity, but who are to initiate and carry forward the financial enterprises that are to develop and promote our future growth." Talented boys and girls each had a role to play in improving society. While boys entered business, girls would instruct the young "in our lower grades," uplifting the poor and rich alike, teaching the virtues of sobriety, application, and emulation. Thus the high school, and public education generally, had become a key part of wise political economy. "Knowledge and intellect," the superintendent insisted, "are the two great forces that rule the world and are the chief sources of its wealth and power." And in America, "the priceless gifts of genius" came "from the cottages of the poor as well as from the palaces of the rich."[10]

In the next century, the idea that America's high schools could expand their mission and clientele, fulfilling democratic ends, became an article of faith among educators. Schoolmen by the early 1900s, advocates of more vocational education for certain students, complained that the high school was too academic, too exclusive, too tied to the preparation of the college bound.

High schools had indeed previously catered to a special group of students, largely from the white middle classes, capable of passing admission tests. But early twentieth-century schoolmen seemed oblivious to basic truths about high schools in the previous century. From their inception in the 1820s, high schools had emphasized the practical side of life, represented in the English studies, and in theory and practice had already moved far away from the traditions of the old-time Latin school.

In more recent decades, the myth of the early college-dominated high school has merged with the idea that high schools had fallen from an Edenic state. Since the Puritans, Americans have bemoaned the failures of the rising generation. A society that until recently embraced the doctrine of human progress also embraced a theory of youth's decline. Critics had charged that education had fallen precipitously when Latin schools disappeared, giving way to the English studies and then high schools; and recent jeremiads emphasize that contemporary secondary schools have drifted from some imagined days of widespread academic excellence.

Those who seek to return to the past might better let sleeping dogs lie. Schools should be understood in their historical context, not simply to decry the shortcomings of education in another time and place. Even educators who passionately embraced early high schools complained about the many shortcomings of their students and the difficulties of getting students to discover the intrinsic joys of learning. And no one at the time imagined that the higher learning was for everyone. Today's perceived educational crises—fears of escalating violence and incivility among students, incompetence among teachers, and the overall collapse of standards—cannot be fixed by simple reference to a supposedly better time when politicians were wise, teachers superior, and pupils above average.

Have Americans prized the life of the mind and free inquiry? Within nineteenth-century high schools, the knowledge and intellect valued by school people were heavily influenced by broad middle-class values. The knowledge contained in ubiquitous textbooks tended to affirm bourgeois notions of propriety, law and order, and separate spheres for men and women, whites and blacks, and native and foreign born. Like the dominant groups that created them, schools generally did not want inquiring minds that questioned certain assumptions about the social order. Individuals were largely responsible for their own fate, said prominent schoolmen, who assumed the system was superior to European aristocratic societies and thus mostly above criticism.

Those who sponsored and then defended early high schools regarded knowledge as something scholars memorized and recited to their teachers. Intellectual development was synonymous with recalling facts in many subjects and dependent upon long hours of study, delayed gratification, and obedience to many rules and regulations at home and at school. Those with the brightest intellects presumably did well on entrance exams and survived the many academic trials that helped define the high school experience.

Throughout the nineteenth century, educators cared about how well students did in their schoolwork, but they emphasized that the best scholars had to be punctual, deferential, and obedient. The minds of scholars always needed strengthening, but within a context that embraced conformity to these norms. Thinking independently could lead pupils down a thorny path. Intellect needed disciplining along safe channels if youth hoped to succeed at school and then survive future challenges after parents or guardians signed that last report card.

When the young scholar at the Girls' High School of Portland referred to her institution as a little "kingdom" in 1863, she had identified the basic social tension within public high schools. The American middle classes remained uneasily poised between rising numbers of poor citizens and the few who grew more powerful and as rich as kings. Countless social observers viewed bourgeois citizens as the only group likely to prevent class warfare. In school dedications, campaign speeches, newspaper editorials, sermons, and primers on political economy, the middle classes were called the keystone of the republic. Their most talented children became the subjects of a remarkable educational kingdom, ruled by those who prized individual merit, the mastery of textbook knowledge, and respectability.

As the young scholar read her essay before her classmates and principal, she invoked familiar themes, more testimony that high schools were centers of academic excellence. She concluded like so many contemporaries that high schools rewarded talent and promoted republican values. "We the scholars are the subjects of higher or lower rank according to our intellectual capacities, for wealth and noble birth are of no consideration. The aristocracy is only in intellect."[11]

Abbreviations

AA	*American Almanac and Repository of Useful Knowledge*
AAE	*American Annals of Education*
AANyHL	*Afro-Americans in New York History and Life*
Aca	*Academician*
Acad	*Academy*
Aco	*Acorn*
AHB	*Atlanta History Bulletin*
AHR	*American Historical Review*
AIa	*Annals of Iowa*
AII	*American Institute of Instruction*
AJE	*American Journal of Education*
AlEJ	*Alabama Educational Journal*
AlHQ	*Alabama Historical Quarterly*
AlR	*Alabama Review*
AP	*American Presbyterians*
AQ	*American Quarterly*
AR	*American Review*
ArHQ	*Arkansas Historical Quarterly*
ArJE	*Arkansas Journal of Education*
AS	*American Studies*
Asp	*Aspirant*
AtM	*Atlantic Monthly*
AWR	*American Whig Review*
BHL	Bentley Historical Society, Michigan Historical Collections, University of Michigan
BM	British Museum

BPL	Boston Public Library
Ca	*Casket*
CaT	*California Teacher*
CCL	College of Charleston Library
ChHS	Chicago Historical Society
CHS	Cincinnati Historical Society
CHSB	*Cincinnati Historical Society Bulletin*
CI	*Curriculum Inquiry*
Con	*Constellation*
ConnCSJAE	*Connecticut Common School Journal and Annals of Education*
ConnHSB	*Connecticut Historical Society Bulletin*
CS	*Common School*
CSJ	*Common School Journal*
DAB	*Dictionary of American Biography*
DR	*DeBow's Review*
ED	*The Educator*
Educ	*Education*
EEPA	*Educational Evaluation and Policy Analysis*
EIHC	*Essex Institute Historical Collections*
EJVa	*Educational Journal of Virginia*
ER	*Educational Review*
FC	Filson Club, Louisville
FCQ	*Filson Club Quarterly*
FI	*Feminist Issues*
FS	*Feminist Studies*
GaHQ	*Georgia Historical Quarterly*
GaR	*Georgia Review*
GL	Guttman Library, Harvard University
HCQ	*History of Childhood Quarterly*
HEJ	*History of Education Journal*
HEQ	*History of Education Quarterly*
HER	*Harvard Educational Review*
HERe	*History of Education Review*
HMN	*Historical Methods Newsletter*
HPE	*History of Political Economy*
HS	*History of Science*
HSE	*High School Exponent*
HSS	*High School Student*
HW	*History Workshop*
IaI	*Iowa Instructor*
IE	*Issues in Education*
IlMM	*Illinois Monthly Magazine*
InMH	*Indiana Magazine of History*
InSJ	*Indiana School Journal*
InSL	Indiana State Library

Is	*Isis*
JAH	*Journal of American History*
JAS	*Journal of American Studies*
JCCA	*Journal of the Cuyahoga County Archives*
JCE	*Journal of Chemical Education*
JCS	*Journal of Curriculum Studies*
JEA	*Journal of Early Adolescence*
JER	*Journal of the Early Republic*
JG	*Journal of Geography*
JHB	*Journal of the History of Biology*
JIH	*Journal of Interdisciplinary History*
JIlSHS	*Journal of the Illinois State Historical Society*
JIlSTA	*Journal of the Illinois State Teachers Association*
JMHES	*Journal of the Midwest History of Education Society*
JMsH	*Journal of Mississippi History*
JNE	*Journal of Negro Education*
JNH	*Journal of Negro History*
JP	*Journal of Psychohistory*
JSH	*Journal of Southern History*
JSoH	*Journal of Social History*
JUH	*Journal of Urban History*
LaH	*Louisiana History*
LaHQ	*Louisiana Historical Quarterly*
LaJE	*Louisiana Journal of Education*
LaS	*Louisiana Studies*
LB	*Lady's Book*
LC	Library of Congress
LG	*Ladies' Garland*
LH	*Labor History*
LM	*Ladies' Magazine*
LMM	*Louisville Monthly Magazine*
MaT	*Massachusetts Teacher*
MdHM	*Maryland Historical Magazine*
MeB	*Maine Bulletin*
MeHS	Maine Historical Society
MeJE	*Maine Journal of Education*
MiEJ	*Michigan Education Journal*
MiH	*Michigan History*
MiT	*Michigan Teacher*
MnT	*Minnesota Teacher*
MoHR	*Missouri Historical Review*
MsEJ	*Mississippi Educational Journal*
NAM	*North American Magazine*
NAR	*North American Review*
NCHR	*North Carolina Historical Review*

NCJE	*North Carolina Journal of Education*
NEAAP	*National Educational Association, Addresses and Proceedings*
NEJE	*New-England Journal of Education*
NEQ	*New England Quarterly*
NHJE	*New Hampshire Journal of Education*
NT	*National Teacher*
NTM	*National Teachers' Monthly*
NYH	*New York History*
NYM	*New-York Mirror*
OH	*Ohio History*
OhAHP	*Ohio Archeological and Historical Publications*
OhEM	*Ohio Educational Monthly*
OhHS	Ohio Historical Society
OhJE	*Ohio Journal of Education*
PaH	*Pennsylvania History*
PaMHB	*Pennsylvania Magazine of History and Biography*
PaSJ	*Pennsylvania School Journal*
PerAH	*Perspectives in American History*
PMaHS	*Proceedings of the Massachusetts Historical Society*
PR	*Presbyterian Review*
PSAHSM	*Public School Advocate and High School Magazine*
PSCHA	*Proceedings of the South Carolina Historical Association*
PSHJ	*Pacific School and Home Journal*
PVtHS	*Proceedings of the Vermont Historical Society*
QCH	*Queen City Heritage*
QR	*Quarterly Register and Journal of the American Education Society*
RER	*Review of Educational Research*
RIEM	*Rhode Island Educational Magazine*
RIH	*Rhode Island History*
RIII	*Rhode Island Institute of Instruction*
RIS	*Rhode Island Schoolmaster*
RKyHS	*Register of the Kentucky Historical Society*
RPUM	*Research Publications of the University of Minnesota*
SAQ	*South Atlantic Quarterly*
SB	*School-Boy*
SCHM	*South Carolina Historical Magazine*
ScR	*School Review*
SF	*School Friend*
SG	*Student's Gazette*
SHSMo	State Historical Society of Missouri
SHSWi	State Historical Society of Wisconsin
SLJ	*Southern Literary Journal*
SLM	*Southern Literary Messenger*
SLMag	*Southern Literary Magazine*

SM	*Scribner's Monthly*
SPF	*Southern Planter and Farmer*
SQR	*Southern Quarterly Review*
SR	*Southern Review*
SS	*School and Society*
SSH	*Social Science History*
SSJ	*Southern School Journal*
SSM	*School Science and Mathematics*
SSt	*Social Studies*
TA	*Teachers' Advocate*
TCR	*Teachers College Record*
TnHQ	*Tennessee Historical Quarterly*
TSLA	Tennessee State Library and Archives
UE	*Urban Education*
USLG	*United States Literary Gazette*
USMDR	*United States Magazine, and Democratic Review*
USRLG	*United States Review and Literary Gazette*
UtEJ	*Utah Education Journal*
VaHS	Virginia Historical Society
VaMHB	*Virginia Magazine of History and Biography*
VaSL	Virginia State Library
VL	*Visible Language*
VtH	*Vermont History*
WB	*Woodward Bulletin*
WHQ	*Western Historical Quarterly*
WiJE	*Wisconsin Journal of Education*
WM	*Western Messenger*
WMM	*Western Monthly Messenger and Literary Journal*
WMQ	*William and Mary Quarterly*
WoS	*Women's Studies*
WoSIF	*Women's Studies International Forum*
WRHS	Western Reserve Historical Society
WTnHSP	*West Tennessee Historical Society Papers*
WVH	*West Virginia History*

Note: State and local school reports are cited in the endnotes in shortened form. For example, *Thirty-Seventh Annual Report of the Controllers of the Public Schools of the First School District of Pennsylvania, Comprising the City and County of Philadelphia* (Philadelphia: Published by Order of the Board of Controllers, 1856), appears as *Philadelphia School Report* (1856).

Notes

Introduction

1. E. J. Hobsbawm, *The Age of Capital, 1848–1875* (London, 1975), 94, sees the American high school as a "democratic triumph."

2. A very rich literature has emerged on the rise of middle-class education and secondary school reform. Some of the best books include R. D. Gidney and W. P. J. Millar, *Inventing Secondary Education: The Rise of the High School in Nineteenth Century Ontario* (Montreal, 1990); Sandra Horvath-Peterson, *Victor Duruy and French Education* (Baton Rouge, 1984); James C. Albisetti, *Secondary School Reform in Imperial Germany* (Princeton, 1983); Margaret E. Bryant, *The London Experience of Secondary Education* (London, 1986); John Roach, *A History of Secondary Education in England, 1800–1870* (New York, 1986); R. D. Anderson, *Education and Opportunity in Victorian Scotland* (Edinburgh, 1983); Maris A. Vinovskis, *The Origins of Public High Schools: A Reexamination of the Beverly High School Controversy* (Madison, 1985); Reed Ueda, *Avenues to Adulthood: The Origins of the High School and Social Mobility in an American Suburb* (Cambridge, 1987); David F. Labaree, *The Making of an American High School: The Credentials Market and the Central High School of Philadelphia, 1838–1939* (New Haven, 1988); and Joel Perlmann, *Ethnic Differences: Schooling and Social Structure Among the Irish, Italians, Jews, and Blacks in an American City, 1880–1935* (Cambridge, 1989). In a comparative study of four nations, Pamela M. Pilbeam notes that formal education, particularly access to secondary schools, helped shape and define a range of middle-class groups in the nineteenth century. See *The Middle Classes in Europe, 1789–1914, France, Germany, Italy, and Russia* (Chicago, 1990), chap. 1 and especially 7.

3. Bernard Bailyn, *Education in the Forming of American Society* (New York, 1960); and Lawrence A. Cremin, *The Wonderful World of Ellwood Patterson Cubberley* (New York, 1965).

4. For an informative, sweeping analysis of research in the field since the early 1960s, see N. Ray Hiner, "History of Education for the 1990s and Beyond: The Case for Academic Imperialism," *HEQ* 30 (Summer 1990): 137–60.

5. Michael B. Katz, *The Irony of Early School Reform: Educational Innovation in Mid-Nineteenth Century Massachusetts* (Cambridge, 1968); Diane Ravitch, *The Revisionists Revised: A Critique of the Radical Attack on the Schools* (New York, 1978); and the response by Walter Feinberg, Harvey Kantor, Michael Katz, and Paul Violas, *Revisionists Respond to Ravitch* (Washington, D. C., 1980).

6. America's first professional historians claimed that, unlike amateur writers, they alone could

reconstruct the past objectively. It became part of the mythic origins of the historical profession. See Peter Novick, *That Noble Dream: The "Objectivity Question" and the American Historical Profession* (Cambridge, 1988). For a civil and enlightening scholarly exchange, see the "Forum" entitled "The Origins of Public High Schools," *HEQ* 27 (Summer 1987): 241–58.

7. "The Kingdom," *Asp* (December 12, 1863): n.p. (MeHS).

Boston's Legacy

1. *A Volume of Records Relating to the Early History of Boston, Containing Boston Town Records, 1814 to 1822* (Boston, 1906), 166–71. On the enduring sense of mission see Darrett B. Rutman, *Winthrop's Boston: A Portrait of a Puritan Town, 1630–1649* (New York, 1965); and J. Anthony Lukas, *Common Ground* (New York, 1986).

2. On the town meeting, read Rutman, *Winthrop's Boston*, 72; Ronald P. Formisano, "Boston, 1800–1840: From Deferential-Participant to Party Politics," in *Boston, 1700–1980: The Evolution of Urban Politics*, ed. Ronald P. Formisano and Constance K. Burns (Westport, Conn., 1984), 34–35; and Edward M. Cook, Jr., *The Fathers of the Towns: Leadership and Community Structure in Eighteenth Century New England* (Baltimore, 1976), 1, 18–19. The English Classical School became the English High School in 1824, reverted to its original name in 1832, and again became the English High School in 1833. See *One Hundred Years of the English High School of Boston* (Boston, 1924), 1–3; *A Volume of Records*, 166–71; and Pauline Holmes, *A Tercentenary History of the Boston Public Latin Grammar School* (Cambridge, 1935), 283, on the recurrent efforts in the nineteenth century to merge the Latin School and English High.

3. William T. Harris, "Public Services of John Dudley Philbrick," in *A Memorial of the Life and Services of John D. Philbrick*, ed. Larkin Dunton (Boston, 1887), 62. On the early 1800s, see Carl F. Kaestle, *Pillars of the Republic: Common Schools and American Society, 1780–1860* (New York, 1983), chap. 3.

4. See especially Robert F. Seybolt, *The Public Schools of Colonial Boston, 1635–1775* (Cambridge, 1935), 1–5; 33; Samuel Eliot Morison, *The Intellectual Life of Colonial New England* (New York, 1956), chap. 3; Carl Bridenbaugh, *Cities in the Wilderness: Urban Life in America, 1625–1742* (New York, 1938), 121–22; James Axtell, *The School Upon a Hill: Education and Society in Colonial New England* (New York, 1974); Lawrence A. Cremin, *American Education: The Colonial Experience, 1607–1783* (New York, 1970), 184; Henry F. Jenks, *Catalogue of the Boston Public Latin School, Established in 1635, with an Historical Sketch* (Boston, 1886), 5–8; and David D. Hall, *Worlds of Wonder, Days of Judgement: Popular Religious Belief in Early New England* (Cambridge, 1990), chap. 1. On the English background, see John Morgan, *Godly Learning: Puritan Attitudes towards Reason, Learning and Education, 1560–1640* (Cambridge, 1986).

5. Winthrop is quoted in Rutman, *Winthrop's Boston*, 7–8.

6. Jon Teaford, "The Transformation of Massachusetts Education, 1670–1780," *HEQ* 10 (Fall 1970): 287–307; Stanley K. Schultz, *The Culture Factory: Boston Public Schools, 1789–1860* (New York, 1973), chap. 1; and Richard P. DuFour, "The Exclusion of Female Students from the Public Secondary Schools of Boston, 1820–1920," Ph.D. diss., Northern Illinois University, 1981, chap. 1.

7. Rutman, *Winthrop's Boston*; and Bernard Bailyn, *The New England Merchants in the Seventeenth Century* (Cambridge, 1955), 17, 105–11.

8. Teaford, "Transformation"; Walter H. Small, "The New England Grammar School, 1635–1700," *ScR* 10 (September 1902): 513–31; Charles H. Judd, "The Historical Development of Secondary Education in America," *ScR* 43 (March 1935): 173–83; Morison, *Intellectual Life*, 71; and especially E. Jennifer Monaghan, "Readers Writing: The Curriculum of the Writing Schools of Eighteenth Century Boston," *VL* 21 (Spring 1987): 167–212. Many boys in the 1700s found positions as clerks in small businesses after learning valuable skills at the writing schools.

9. James A. Henretta, "Economic Development and Social Structure in Colonial Boston," *WMQ* 22 (January 1965): 78–79. G. B. Warden criticizes radical scholarship in "Inequality and Instability in Eighteenth-Century Boston: A Reappraisal," *JIH* 6 (Spring 1976): 585–620.

10. See especially Gary B. Nash, *The Urban Crucible: Social Change, Political Consciousness, and the Origins of the American Revolution* (Cambridge, 1979); and Nash, "The Social Evolution of

Preindustrial American Cities, 1700–1820: Reflections and New Directions," *JUH* 13 (February 1987): 115–45.

11. Schultz, *Culture Factory*, chap. 1; DuFour, "Exclusion of Female Students," chap. 1. On the debates over the "decline" of New England's schools, see Emit Duncan Grizzell, *Origin and Development of the High School in New England Before 1865* (Philadelphia, 1923), chap. 1; Robert Middlekauf, *Ancients and Axioms: Secondary Education in Eighteenth-Century New England* (New York, [c. 1971]); Teaford, "Transformation"; and Clifford K. Shipton, "Secondary Education in the Puritan Colonies," *NEQ* 7 (December 1934): 661.

12. Shipton, "Secondary Education," 658–61; Teaford, "Transformation"; Bridenbaugh, *Cities of the Wilderness*, 280, 442; Morison, *Intellectual Life*, 77–78; and Robert F. Seybolt, *The Private Schools of Colonial Boston* (Cambridge, 1935).

13. Seybolt, *Private Schools*, 11–13, 30.

14. Seybolt, *Private Schools*, 9, 34–55, 88–89; Shipton, "Secondary Education," 659; and Walter Herbert Small, *Early New England Schools* (Boston, 1914), chap. 9.

15. Alexander James Inglis, *The Rise of the High School in Massachusetts* (New York, 1911), chaps. 2 and 3.

16. Morison, in *Intellectual Life*, 9, emphasizes how the doctrine of the calling was "the main reason why puritanism appealed to the rising middle class, the nascent capitalists of the sixteenth and seventeenth centuries." Linda Kerber succinctly analyzes "the rapid spread of commercial capitalism" after the 1760s in "The Revolutionary Generation: Ideology, Politics, and Culture in the Early Republic," in *The New American History*, ed. Eric Foner (Philadelphia, 1990), 33.

17. Samuel Eliot Morison, *The Maritime History of Massachusetts, 1783–1860* (Boston, 1921), 23; and Nash, *The Urban Crucible*, ix, 55–59, 125, and chap. 9.

18. Kaestle, *Pillars*, chap. 1; Schultz, *Culture Factory*, 22–25; Inglis, *Rise of the High School*, chap. 1; George H. Martin, *The Evolution of the Massachusetts Public School System* (New York, 1898), 83–87, 114–15, on hostility to state aid to academies; and Kerber, "Revolutionary Generation," 31–32.

19. Schultz, *Culture Factory*, 12–13; DuFour, "Exclusion of Female Students," 8; Robert A. McCaughey, *Josiah Quincy, 1772–1864: The Last Federalist* (Cambridge, 1974), 96–97; and Allan Kulikoff, "The Progress of Inequality in Revolutionary Boston," *WMQ* 28 (July 1971): 390. Academies often existed in towns with classical grammar schools, showing they could coexist, though Adams and others still saw them as a threat.

20. "The System of Public Education Adopted by the Town of Boston, 15th October 1789," in Jenks, *Catalogue of the Boston Public Latin School*, 287.

21. DuFour, "Exclusion of Female Students," 7–10; and Charles K. Dillaway, "Education, Past and Present," in *The Memorial History of Boston*, ed. Justin Winsor (Boston, 1880), 2: 242.

22. Federalism in Boston and Massachusetts is examined in Harold Kirker and James Kirker, *Bulfinch's Boston, 1787–1817* (New York, 1964); McCaughey, *Josiah Quincy*; Ronald P. Formisano, *The Transformation of Political Culture: Massachusetts Parties, 1790s–1840s* (New York, 1983); and Linda Kerber, *Federalists in Dissent: Imagery and Ideology in Jeffersonian America* (Ithaca, 1970). These Republicans are not to be confused with those belonging to the Republican Party that formed in 1856.

23. Kulikoff, "Progress of Inequality," 376, 396.

24. Peter Dobkin Hall, *The Organization of American Culture, 1700–1900: Private Institutions, Elites, and the Origins of American Nationality* (New York, 1984), 36–38 and chap. 4.

25. Richard D. Brown succinctly examines the legacy of Puritanism to Federalism in *Massachusetts* (New York, 1978), 128.

26. Hall, *Organization of American Culture*; Kirker and Kirker, *Bulfinch's Boston*; and McCaughey, *Josiah Quincy*.

27. On the Boston Unitarians, see Sydney E. Ahlstrom, *A Religious History of the American People* (Garden City, New York, 1975), 1: chap. 24; Ann C. Rose, *Transcendentalism as a Social Movement, 1830–1850* (New Haven, 1981), chap. 1; Conrad Wright, *The Beginnings of Unitarianism in America* (Hamden, Conn., 1976); and Edith F. McCormick, "First Church in Boston Founded in 1630," in *Sketches of Some Historic Churches of Greater Boston* (Boston, 1918), 62–78.

28. McCaughey, *Josiah Quincy*; Kirker and Kirker, *Bulfinch's Boston*, chap. 10; and Hall, *Organization of American Culture.*

29. Carl F. Kaestle, *The Evolution of an Urban School System: New York City, 1750–1850* (Cambridge, 1973); and Kaestle, *Pillars*, chap. 3.

30. William Michael Weber, "Before Horace Mann: Elites and Boston Public Schools, 1800–1822," Ph.D. diss., Harvard University, 1974; and Daniel Calhoun, *The Intelligence of a People* (Princeton, 1973), 56–57, 64.

31. Schultz, *Culture Factory*, 25–26; Weber, "Before Horace Mann," chaps. 4 and 5; and Joseph M. Wightman, *Annals of the Boston Primary School Committee* (Boston, 1860), 11–17.

32. Schultz, *Culture Factory*, 38; Wightman, *Annals*, 11–19; and Weber, "Before Horace Mann," 88–90.

33. Weber, "Before Horace Mann," 93; and Schultz, *Culture Factory*, 33–41.

34. Jenks, *Catalogue of the Boston Public Latin School*, 8; Holmes, *Tercentenary History*, 101–2 and chap. 6. Hezekiah Butterworth enabled all of the town's children to learn about the famous Latin school graduates in *Young Folks' History of Boston* (Boston, 1881), 375–76.

35. James Spear Loring, *The Hundred Boston Orators* (Boston, 1852), vii; and *The Boston Directory* (Boston, 1820), 232.

36. Loraine McMichael Webster, "American Educational Innovators: A Sub-Committee of the Boston School Committee of 1820," Ed.D. diss., Arizona State University, 1970, 3, and the long biographical sketch, chap. 6; and *Boston Directory* (Boston, 1820), 215.

37. Winsor, *Memorial History*, 1: 405, and 3: 377, 480; *DAB*, ed. Dumas Malone (New York, 1934), 7: 586–87; and Kathryn Kish Sklar, *Catharine Beecher: A Study in American Domesticity* (New York, 1973), chap. 2.

38. McCaughey, *Josiah Quincy*, 122–30; DuFour, "Exclusion of Female Students," chap. 2; Webster, "American Educational Innovators," chap. 3; and Rose, *Transcendentalism*, 23–24.

39. Octavius Brooks Frothingham, *Boston Unitarianism, 1820–1850: A Study of the Life and Work of Nathaniel Langdon Frothingham* (New York, 1890), 16–17; Rose, *Transcendentalism*, 229; and *DAB*, ed. Allen Johnson and Dumas Malone (New York, 1931), 4: 43–44.

40. Winsor, *Memorial History*, 3: 476; and Webster, "American Educational Innovators," chap. 4.

41. *DAB*, (1935), 9: 42–43.

42. Leonard W. Levy, *The Law of the Commonwealth and Chief Justice Shaw: The Evolution of American Law, 1830–1860* (New York, 1957), 3 and chap. 1; Loring, *Hundred Boston Orators*, vi; *Boston Directory* (1821), 186, 232, 237; and Webster, "American Educational Innovators," chap. 5.

43. *DAB* (1935), 8: 238–40; and John Bixler Hench, "The Newspaper in a Republic: Boston's 'Centinel and Chronicle,' 1784–1801," Ph.D. diss., Clarke University, 1979, 36–37.

44. William J. Rorabaugh, *The Craft Apprentice: From Franklin to the Machine Age in America* (New York, 1986), 17–20, 22–23, 26; Winsor, *Memorial History*, 3: 617–19; McCaughey, *Josiah Quincy*, 110; Frederic B. Farrar, "Benjamin Russell," in *American Newspaper Journalists, 1690–1872* (Detroit, 1985), 409–14.

45. Hench, "Newspaper in a Republic," 43–47; and Webster, "American Educational Innovators," chap. 7.

46. *Volume of Records*, 168–69. Wells also criticized the proliferation of private schools.

47. *Volume of Records*, 169–71.

48. *The System of Education Pursued at the Free Schools in Boston* (Boston, 1823), 8, 16 (including footnote), and 23 (BPL).

Schools of a Higher Order

1. "School Education," *NAR* 9 (June 1819): 188; and "Reviews," *USLG* 1 (April 1, 1824): 2.

2. "Education," *NYM* 6 (May 9, 1830): 351. On common school reform, see the following: Lawrence A. Cremin, *The American Common School: An Historic Conception* (New York, 1951); Michael B. Katz, *The Irony of Early School Reform: Educational Innovation in Mid-Nineteenth Century Massachusetts* (Cambridge, 1968); Lawrence A. Cremin, *American Education: The National Experience, 1783–1876* (New York, 1980); Carl F. Kaestle and Maris A. Vinovskis, *Education and Social*

Change in Nineteenth-Century Massachusetts (Cambridge, 1980); and especially Carl F. Kaestle, *Pillars of the Republic: Common Schools and American Society, 1780–1860* (New York, 1983).

3. David Montgomery, "The Working Classes of the Pre-Industrial City, 1780–1830," *LH* 9 (Winter 1968): 3–22; James A. Henretta, "Families and Farms: *Mentalité* in Pre-Industrial America," *WMQ* 35 (January 1978): 3–32; Gary B. Nash, "The Social Evolution of Preindustrial Cities, 1700–1820: Reflections and New Directions," *JUH* 13 (February 1987): 115–45; Christopher Clark, "The Household Economy, Market Exchange and the Rise of Capitalism in the Connecticut Valley, 1800–1860," *JSH* 13 (Winter 1979): 169–90; William J. Rorabaugh, *The Craft Apprentice: From Franklin to the Machine Age in America* (New York, 1986); and Bruce Laurie, *Artisans into Workers: Labor in Nineteenth-Century America* (New York, 1989), chaps. 1 and 2.

4. Benjamin Rush, "Thoughts Upon Female Education, Accommodated to the Present State of Society, Manners, and Government in the United States of America," in *Essays on Education in the Early Republic,* ed. Frederick Rudolph (Cambridge, 1965), 27; and especially Kaestle, *Pillars,* 27–28, 84–88, and 121–22.

5. Nash, "Social Evolution", 115–45; Rowland Berthoff, "Independence and Attachment, Virtue and Interest: From Republican Citizen to Free Enterpriser, 1787–1837," in *Uprooted Americans: Essays to Honor Oscar Handlin,* ed. Richard L. Bushman et al. (Boston, 1979), 97–124; Drew R. McCoy, *The Elusive Republic: Political Economy in Jeffersonian America* (Chapel Hill, 1980), chap. 8; and Allan R. Pred, *Urban Growth and the Circulation of Information: The United States System of Cities, 1790–1840* (Cambridge, 1973), 7.

6. *Regulations of the School Committee of the City of Boston* (Boston, 1823), 9 (LC); Michael B. Katz, *Reconstructing American Education* (Cambridge, 1987), chap. 1; Carl F. Kaestle, *The Evolution of an Urban School System: New York, 1750–1850* (Cambridge, 1973); Stanley K. Schultz, *The Culture Factory: Boston Public Schools, 1787–1860* (New York, 1973); and David B. Tyack, *The One Best System: A History of American Urban Education* (Cambridge, 1974).

7. "Reviews," *USLG* 3 (December 1, 1825): 172.

8. "Education," *Ca* 1 (February 1826): 48; and S., "Essay on the True End of Female Education," *Ca* 2 (June 1827): 218.

9. "French, Italian, and German Languages," *NYM* 5 (January 26, 1828): 231.

10. "Talent and Conduct," *LB* 9 (August 1834): 84. On the fluidity of the social system, see "Equality," *LB* 4 (March 1832): 160. Another author attacked "Idleness," *LB* 10 (June 1835): 254; and H., "How to Help the Very Poor," *LB* 20 (April 1840): 163, emphasized that the poor were improvident. Also see "The General Diffusion of Knowledge," *IIMM* 2 (May 1832): 343.

11. J. H. P., "Prospects of the West," *WM* 1 (November 1835): 318–19.

12. Azil., "Old Fashioned Schools," *NYM* 11 (July 13, 1833): 13; and Stephen Simpson, "Education and the Exclusiveness of Knowledge," *NAM* 3 (March 1834): 353.

13. Simpson, "Education," 356.

14. An Examiner, "Condition of Common Schools," *WMM* 3 (March 1835): 166.

15. S. O., "Helps to Education, Not Always Helps," *WM* 1 (July 1836): 832.

16. Kaestle and Vinovskis, *Education and Social Change,* chap. 2; George H. Martin, *The Evolution of the Massachusetts Public School System* (New York, 1898), Lecture 2; and Orwin Bradford Griffen, *The Evolution of the Connecticut State School System* (New York, 1928), chaps. 1–2.

17. Henry F. Barnard, "James G. Carter," *AJE* 5 (September 1858): 407–16.

18. K. B. Hutchinson, "James Gordon Carter, Education Reformer," *NEQ* 16 (September 1943): 376–96; Jonathan C. Messerli, "James G. Carter's Liabilities as a Common School Reformer," *HEQ* 5 (March 1965): 14–25; and Cremin, *American Common School,* 139–51.

19. Carter's articles appeared in *Letters to the Hon. William Prescott, LL.D. on the Free Schools of New England, with Remarks on the Principles of Instruction* (Boston, 1824); and Barnard, "James G. Carter," 408.

20. James G. Carter, *Essays Upon Popular Education* (Boston, 1826), 23.

21. Carter, *Essays,* 28.

22. Carter, *Essays,* 29, 31–32.

23. "Carter's Essays on Popular Education," *USRLG* 1 (February 1827): 351; and "Platform Adopted by the State Teacher's Association of Connecticut in 1868, at Meriden, Connecticut," in

Arthur Raymond Mead, *The Development of Free Schools in the United States: As Illustrated by Connecticut and Michigan* (New York, 1918), 210.

24. Kaestle, *Pillars*, chap. 2.

25. *Kaestle, Pillars*, chap. 2; Kaestle and Vinovskis, *Education and Social Change*, 10; Mead, *The Development of Free Schools*, Part 1; Walter Herbert Small, *Early New England Schools* (Boston, 1914), chap. 2; Ava Harriet Chadbourne, *The Beginnings of Education in Maine* (New York, 1928), 81–82; Clyde G. Fussell, "The Emergence of Public Education as a Function of the State in Vermont," *VtH* 29 (January 1961): 14; and Eugene Alfred Bishop, *The Development of a State School System: New Hampshire* (New York, 1930) chap. 5.

26. Griffen, *The Evolution of the Connecticut State School System*, 1–2; Silas Hertzler, *The Rise of the Public High School in Connecticut* (Baltimore, 1930), chaps. 1–2; J. William Frost, *Connecticut Education in the Revolutionary Era* (Chester, Connecticut, 1974), 15–18; and *Connecticut School Report* (1839), 14–15, 26.

27. On rate bills see "What is Doing in Connecticut for the Improvement of Schools," *Conn CSJAE* 9 (June 1854): 303; and Kaestle, *Pillars*, 149–50.

28. W. T. Harris, "Editor's Preface," in Martin, *Evolution of the Massachusetts Public School System*, x.

29. Alexander James Inglis, *The Rise of the High School in Massachusetts* (New York, 1911), 15.

30. Martin, *Evolution of the Massachusetts Public Schools*, 93, 111.

31. See the informative essays in Paul H. Mattingly and Edward W. Stevens, Jr., eds., ". . . Schools and the Means of Education Shall Forever Be Encouraged": A History of Education in the Old Northwest, 1787–1880* (Athens, Ohio, 1987); and David B. Tyack, Thomas James, and Aaron Benevot, *Law and the Shaping of Public Education, 1785–1954* (Madison, 1987), chaps. 1–3.

32. *A Volume of Records Relating to the Early History of Boston* (Boston, 1906), 169. Most interpretations of the common school movement see the elimination of academies as central to the movement; see Cremin, *American Common School*, 137–42; Kaestle, *Pillars*, 118–20; and Kaestle and Vinovskis, *Education and Social Change*, 33–34.

33. J. Orville Taylor, *Satirical Hits on the People's Education* (New York, 1839), 8, 13; Cremin, *American Common School*, 51, 59; and Paul D. Travers, "John Orville Taylor: A Forgotten Educator," *HEQ* 9 (Spring 1969): 57–63.

34. See Mann's *Massachusetts School Report* (1838), 49–50, 55; (1841), 38–43; and Jonathan Messerli, *Horace Mann: A Biography* (New York, 1972), 286–87.

35. Benjamin Franklin, "Proposals Relating to the Education of Youth in Pennsylvania," in *The Age of the Academies*, ed. Theodore R. Sizer (New York, 1964), 70–71; Robert Middlekauf, *Ancients and Axioms: Secondary Education in Eighteenth-Century New England* (New York, [c. 1971]), 125–27; and Emit Duncan Grizzell, *Origin and Development of the High School in New England Before 1865* (Philadelphia, 1923), 28–29.

36. Franklin, "Proposals," 68; and Elmer Ellsworth Brown, *The Making of Our Middle Schools* (New York, 1902), 189–90.

37. Harriet Webster Marr, *The Old New England Academies Founded Before 1826* (New York, 1959), chaps. 1–3; Edward Deming Andrews, "The County Grammar Schools and Academies of Vermont," *PVtHS* 4 (No. 2, 1936): 121; and Middlekauf, *Ancients and Axioms*, 123–25.

38. Outstanding overviews of the academies include Sizer, *The Age of the Academies*, 1–48; and Lynne Templeton Brickley, " 'Female Academies Are Everywhere Establishing': The Beginnings of Secondary Education for Women in the United States, 1790–1830," qualifying paper, Harvard Graduate School of Education, 1982. Also see Albert Mock, *The Mid-Western Academy Movement: A Comprehensive Study of Indiana Academies, 1810–1900* (n.p., 1949); Clarence Ray Aurner, *History of Education in Iowa* (Iowa City, 1915), 3: chaps. 1–6; Paul E. Belting, *The Development of the Free Public High School in Illinois to 1860* (New York, [c. 1969]), 28; Calvin Olin Davis, *Public Secondary Education* (Chicago, 1917), chaps. 6–7; and R. Carlyle Buley, *The Old Northwest: Pioneer Period, 1815–1840* (Bloomington, Ind., 1950), 2: 338.

39. "Literary Register," *QR* 3 (May 1831): 292; "Educational and Literary Institutions," *QR* 5 (May 1833): 321–22; William G. Clark, "History of Education in Alabama, 1702–1889" (Washington, D.C., 1889); Nita Katherine Pyburn, *The History of the Development of a Single System of Education in*

Florida, 1822–1903 (Tallahassee, 1954); Catherine Clinton, "Equally Their Due: The Education of the Planter Daughter in the Early Republic," *JER* 2 (Spring 1982): 39–60; E. Merton Coulter, "The Ante-Bellum Academy Movement in Georgia," *GaHQ* 5 (December 1921): 11–42; and Malcolm J. Rohrbough, *The Trans-Appalachian Frontier: People, Societies, and Institutions, 1775–1850* (New York, 1978), which has considerable information on academies and private schools.

40. "Individual States," *AA* 5 (1834): 146.

41. Sizer, *Age of the Academies*, 12; and "Individual States," 145.

42. "Article IX," *NAR* 44 (April 1837): 509.

43. *In Horace Mann*, 286, Jonathan Messerli notes that Mann gave legislative support to railroads but opposed state aid to private schools.

44. Robert A. McCaughey, *Josiah Quincy, 1772–1864* (Cambridge, 1974), 12–15; William H. Pease and Jane H. Pease, "Education, Property, and Patrician Persistence in Jacksonian Boston," *NEQ* 53 (June 1980): 147–67, for a discussion of the fashionable Round Hill School; and Caroline Ticknor, ed., *Dr. Holmes' Boston* (Boston, 1915), 21.

45. Daniel W. Kucera, *Church-State Relationships in Education in Illinois* (Washington, D.C., 1955), 28–34. Also see Marr, *Old New England Academies*, Part 2; Richard Gerry Durnin, "New England's Eighteenth-Century Academies: Their Origins and Development to 1850," Ed.D. diss., University of Pennsylvania, 1968; Nicholas D. Colucci, "Connecticut Academies for Females," Ph.D. diss., University of Connecticut, 1969; and Lowell H. Harrison, "Laws of New London Academy, 1802," *FCQ* 49 (October 1975): 342. The principal of the Indianapolis Female Seminary in 1879 took students to church if their parents did not designate a preference. See *Catalogue of the Indianapolis Female Seminary* (Indianapolis, 1879) (InSL).

46. Chadbourne, *Beginnings of Education in Maine*, 98; and "Female Education," *NYM* 13 (January 16, 1836): 231.

47. Walter John Gifford, *Historical Development of the New York State High School System* (Albany, 1922), chap. 1; and Keith Melder, "Ipswich Female Seminary: An Educational Experiment," *EIHC* 120 (October 1984): 223–40, on innovative approaches to teacher training.

48. William Marshall French, "How We Began to Train Teachers in New York," *NYH* 17 (April 1936): 180–91; Samuel S. Randall, *The Common School System of the State of New York* (Troy, 1851), 7–9; George Frederick Miller, *The Academy System of the State of New York* (Albany, 1922), 19, 27, 42, 132–34. Also see the *New York School Report* (1830), 17; (1831), 10–12; (1833), 21; (1834), 17–18; and (1837), 21–24.

49. Grizzell, *Origin and Development*, 274.

50. "Berkshire High School," *AJE* 2 (May 1827): 316, reprinted from the *Recorder*; "Course of Education in the New-York High-School," *AJE* 1 (January 1826): 23–29; "Female High-School of New-York," *AJE* 1 (January 1826): 59–60; and "Boston High-School for Girls," *AJE* 1 (February 1826): 96–105.

51. Gifford, *Historical Development*, 22–25; "Monitorial High School, Geneseo, New York," *AJE* 1 (July 1826): 441; "High School of Edinburgh," *AJE* 2 (December 1827): 745–47; "High School of Buffalo, New York," *AJE* 3 (April 1828): 233–35; "Public High School of Salem," *AJE* 3 (July 1828): 492–93; and Grizzell, *Origin and Development*, 251.

52. "Education and Literary Institutions," *QR* 5 (May 1833): 273. In *Pillars*, 29–30, Kaestle describes the mixed sources of funding of most schools before the 1830s and the futility of applying modern distinctions of "public" and "private" education to early antebellum educational arrangements.

53. "Law of 1798," in Hertzler, *Rise of the Public High School in Connecticut*, 226.

54. "Annual Literary Register for 1830," *QR* 2 (May 1830): 234; and "Literary Register," 292.

55. Mock, *Mid-Western Academy Movement*, 13; and "State of Learning in the United States," *NAR* 9 (September 1819): 241.

56. Barnard reprinted his 1838 definition in "Public High School," *AJE* 3 (March 1857): 185.

57. "Article XI," 508.

58. Durnin, "New England's Eighteenth-Century Academies," 204; and Richard P. DuFour, "The Exclusion of Female Students from the Public Secondary Schools of Boston, 1820–1920," Ed.D. diss., Northern Illinois University, 1981, 120–22.

59. The quotation is from Edward E. Hale, *A New England Boyhood* (New York, 1893), 23.
60. L. N. S., "Letter to the Editor," *CSJ* 1 (December 16, 1839), 381.
61. "Barnard's Report on Common Schools," *NAR* 51 (July 1840): 41.

A Republican Crown

1. "Education," *LG* 2 (1839): 288. On the panic and depression, see Bruce Laurie, *Artisans Into Workers: Labor in Nineteenth-Century America* (New York, 1989), chap. 3.
2. Sean Wilentz provides a succinct overview of scholarship on the antebellum period in "Society, Politics, and the Market Revolution, 1815–1848," in *The New American History*, ed. Eric Foner (Philadelphia, 1990), 73–92. That colonial Americans were completely self-sufficient was a myth, of course, as explained by Jeanne Boydston, *Home and Work: Housework, Wages, and the Ideology of Labor in the Early Republic* (New York, 1990), chap. 1.
3. "Editors' Table," *LB* 22 (January 1841): 47; and "Diffusion of Knowledge," *LB* 23 (November 1841): 206.
4. "Common Schools in Cities," *ConnCSJAE* 4 (December 1, 1841): 12.
5. "College Education," *NAR* 55 (October 1842): 302.
6. "System of Common Schools," *SQR* 6 (October 1844): 475.
7. "Popular Education," *SLJ* 1 (November 1835): 184; and *New Hampshire School Report* (1849), 42–43.
8. *Louisville School Report* (1874), 92; and *Michigan School Report* (1877), 270.
9. *New Hampshire School Report* (1851), 42; *Michigan School Report* (1863), 71; *Iowa School Report* (1865), 23. Similar claims were common in other northern states and in various educational publications; see, for example, "Higher Education," *InSJ* 20 (February 1875): 81–83.
10. There is an enormous, contentious literature on early American republicanism. See especially Joyce Appleby, "Republicanism and Ideology," *AQ* 37 (Fall 1985): 461–73; Joyce Appleby, "Republicanism in Old and New Contexts," *WMQ* 43 (January 1986): 20–34; Linda K. Kerber, "The Republican Ideology of the Revolutionary Generation," *AQ* 37 (Fall 1985): 474–95; Robert E. Stalhope, "Toward a Republican Synthesis: The Emergence of an Understanding of Republicanism in American Historiography," *WMQ* 29 (January 1972): 49–80; Robert E. Stalhope, "Republicanism and Early American Historiography," *WMQ* 39 (April 1982): 334–58; James T. Kloppenberg, "The Virtues of Liberalism: Christianity, Republicanism, and Ethics in Early American Political Discourse," *JAH* 74 (June 1987): 9–33; Bruce Laurie, *Working People of Philadelphia, 1800–1850* (Philadelphia, 1980), 81–82; William G. Shade, "Politics and Parties in Jacksonian America," *PaMHB* 110 (October 1986): 502; and James Oakes, "From Republicanism to Liberalism: Ideological Change and the Crisis of the Old South," *AQ* 37 (Fall 1985): 551–71. Women's role as citizens, as noted previously, increasingly revolved around child-rearing to strengthen the republic.
11. Malcolm J. Rohrbough, *The Trans-Appalachian Frontier: People, Societies, and Institutions, 1775–1850* (New York, 1978), chaps. 3 and 4; Andrew R. L. Cayton, *The Frontier Republic: Ideology and Politics in the Ohio Country, 1780–1825* (Kent, 1986); Joyce Appleby, *Capitalism and a New Social Order: The Republican Vision of the 1790s* (New York, 1984); Drew McCoy, *The Elusive Republic: Political Economy in Jeffersonian America* (Chapel Hill, 1980); Steven Watts, *The Republic Reborn: War and the Making of Liberal America, 1790–1820* (Baltimore, 1987); Cathy Matson and Peter Onuf, "Toward a Republican Empire: Interest and Ideology in Revolutionary America," *AQ* 37 (Fall 1985): 496–531; and, most importantly, Rowland Berthoff, "Independence and Attachment, Virtue and Interest: From Republican Citizen to Free Enterpriser, 1787–1837," in *Uprooted Americans: Essays to Honor Oscar Handlin*, ed. Richard L. Bushman et al. (Boston, 1979), 97–124. On the diverse meanings of republicanism, see Sean Wilentz, *Chants Democratic: New York City and the Rise of the American Working Class, 1788–1850* (New York, 1984), 61.
12. "Carter's Essays on Popular Education," *USRLG* 1 (February 1827): 357; and *New York School Report* (1831): 14–15. These themes are discussed in Lawrence A. Cremin, *The American Common School: An Historic Conception* (New York, 1951); Carl F. Kaestle, *Pillars of the Republic: Common Schools and American Society, 1780–1860* (New York, 1983); and Anne M. Boylan, *Sunday School: The Formation of an American Institution* (New Haven, 1988), chaps. 1–2.

13. *Connecticut School Report* (1840), 35. Also see *Vermont School Report* (1863), 123, 129. Richard Gerry Durnin notes that academies were originally seen as part of a republican spirit ("New England's Eighteenth-Century Incorporated Academies: Their Origin and Development to 1850," Ed.D. diss., University of Pennsylvania, 1968, 147).

14. "Education," *USMDR* 23 (August 1849): 157.

15. "Education," *AWR* 6 (July 1850): 91. Some of the best literature on the Whigs includes Daniel Walker Howe, *The Political Culture of the American Whigs* (Chicago, 1979); Lee Benson, *The Concept of Jacksonian Democracy: New York as a Test Case* (New York, 1964); Ronald P. Formisano's many articles as well as such books as *The Transformation of Political Culture: Massachusetts Parties, 1790s–1840s* (New York, 1983); Richard L. McCormick, *The Party Period and Public Policy: American Politics from the Age of Jackson to the Progressive Era* (New York, 1986); Lawrence Frederick Kohl, *The Politics of Individualism: Parties and the American Character in the Jacksonian Era* (New York, 1989); and Henry L. Watson, *Liberty and Power: The Politics of Jacksonian America* (New York, 1990).

16. Robert J. Haws, "Massachusetts Whigs, 1833–1854," Ph.D. diss., University of Nebraska, 1973, 54–64.

17. "Whig Principle and Its Development," *AR* 9 (January 1852): 124.

18. "Whig Principle and Its Development," 134. In a previously cited essay entitled "Education," the editor argued that there was an increased demand for "knowledge and general judgement" in this period, fueled by increased levels of economic opportunity.

19. "Whig Principle and Its Development," 134.

20. See especially Berthoff, "Independence and Attachment," 97–124; Howe, *Political Culture*, 36–37; Laurie, *Artisans into Workers*, chap. 2; Kohl, *Politics of Individualism*; and Shade, "Parties and Politics in Jacksonian America," 483–507.

21. Themes of class harmony are explored in Howe's *Political Culture* and in Bruce Collins, "The Ideology of the Ante-Bellum Northern Democrats," *AS* 11 (April 1977): 103–21. Edward D. Mansfield linked education, Christianity, and the republic in *American Education, Its Principles and Elements* (New York, 1851), preface and chap. 1, as did S. S. Randall in *First Principles of Popular Education and Public Instruction* (New York, 1868), chaps. 1, 2, 3, and 7; *Ohio School Report* (1838), 7; *Philadelphia School Report* (1839), 10–11; *New Hampshire School Report* (1860), 136, on the town of Exeter; and *Illinois School Report* (1872), 107.

22. "Popular Education," *NAR* 36 (January 1833): 82–83.

23. "The Principle of Emulation," *NAR* 43 (October 1836): 504.

24. "Principle of Emulation," 510–11. As Howe points out in *Political Culture*, 33, discipline was central to the Whig view of the individual and society.

25. *New York School Report* (1837), 24.

26. *New Hampshire School Report* (1849), 42–43; and *Pennsylvania School Report* (1867), xxii.

27. *Maine School Report* (1879), 30; and *California School Report* (1877), 15.

28. *Massachusetts School Report* (1851), 45; and *Cincinnati School Report* (1852), 7. Numerous other educators made this point; see also the *Kansas School Report* (1872), 10–11; and John Ashworth, *"Agrarians" & "Aristocrats": Party Political Ideology in the United States, 1837–1846* (London, 1983), 53.

29. William J. Akers, *Cleveland Schools in the Nineteenth Century* (Cleveland, 1901), 36; *Cleveland School Report* (1879), 87–97. Racial problems worsened locally in the late nineteenth century, according to Kenneth L. Kusmer, *A Ghetto Takes Shape: Black Cleveland, 1870–1930* (Urbana, Ill., 1976), chap. 1.

30. "Common Schools in Cities," 12; and Randall, *First Principles*, 34–36.

31. "Opposition to High Schools," *NEJE* 1 (February 6, 1875): 66; and A. L. Mann, "Are High Schools Entitled to State Support?" *PSHJ* 1 (July 1877): 155.

32. "Higher Education—Danger," *InSJ* 21 (March 1876): 127; "Higher Education," *InSJ* 20 (February 1875): 81–83; "The High School Question," *InSJ* 20 (April 1875): 176–77; "The High School Question—II," *InSJ* 20 (May 1875): 222–24; and "The High School Question—III," *InSJ* 20 (June 1875): 279–80; and *St. Louis School Report* (1878), 48, 55–83.

33. John D. Philbrick, "City School Systems in the United States," U.S. Bureau of Education

(1885), 10; and David B. Tyack, *The One Best System: A History of American Urban Education* (Cambridge, 1974), Parts 1 and 2.

34. The key work is by Stuart M. Blumin, *The Emergence of the Middle Class: Social Experience in the American City, 1760–1900* (Cambridge, 1989). A two-class model is presented in Michael B. Katz et al., *The Social Organization of Early Industrial Capitalism* (Cambridge, 1982).

35. Nancy Jean Rosenbloom, "Cincinnati's Common Schools: The Politics of Reform, 1829–1853," Ph.D. diss., University of Rochester, 1981, chap. 1; Michael B. Katz, *The Irony of Early School Reform: Educational Innovation in Mid-Nineteenth Century Massachusetts* (Cambridge, 1986); and Michael B. Katz, *Reconstructing American Education* (Cambridge, 1989), 21–22.

36. Kenneth T. Jackson, *Crabgrass Frontier: The Suburbanization of the United States* (New York, 1985); Eric H. Monkkonen, *America Becomes Urban: The Development of U.S. Cities and Towns, 1780–1980* (Berkeley, 1988); and Blumin, *Emergence*.

37. William J. Rorabaugh, *The Craft Apprentice: From Franklin to the Machine Age in America* (New York: 1986); Mary P. Ryan, *The Empire of the Mother: American Writing on Domesticity, 1830–1860* (New York, 1985); Bernard Wishy, *The Child and the Republic: The Dawn of Modern American Child Nurture* (Philadelphia, 1968); Karen Halltunen, *Confidence Men and Painted Women: A Study of Middle-Class Culture in America, 1830–1870* (New Haven, 1982); Olivier Zunz, "The Synthesis of Social Change: Reflections on American Social History," in *Reliving the Past: The Worlds of Social History* (Chapel Hill, 1985), 72; and the quotation from James P. Wickersham, *School Economy* (Philadelphia, 1864), 27.

38. Ronald G. Walters, *American Reformers, 1815–1860* (New York, 1978); and Paul Boyer, *Urban Masses and Moral Order in America, 1820–1920* (Cambridge, 1978), 60–61.

39. Kaestle, *Pillars*, chap. 3. Also see Selwyn K. Troen, *The Public and the Schools: Shaping the St. Louis System, 1838–1920* (Columbia, Mo., 1975), 18–19.

40. Quoted in the *Rhode Island School Report* (1847), 224. The best history of the New York City schools is Carl F. Kaestle, *The Evolution of An Urban School System: New York City, 1750–1850* (Cambridge, 1973). Also see Mario Emilio Cosenza, *The Establishment of the College of the City of New York in 1847, Townsend Harris Founder* (New York, 1925).

41. David F. Labaree, *The Making of an American High School: The Credentials Market and the Central High School of Philadelphia, 1838–1939* (New Haven, 1988); David Hogan, "From Contest Mobility to Stratified Credentialing: Merit and Graded Schooling in Philadelphia, 1836–1920," *HERe* 16 (1987): 21–42; Katz, *Reconstructing*, 45; and Franklin Spencer Edmonds, *History of the Central High School of Philadelphia* (Philadelphia, 1902), chap. 2. Most urban high schools had similar residency requirements, and working-class children were often underrepresented even in the upper grammar grades due to economic circumstances.

42. Elmer E. Brown, *The Making of Our Middle Schools* (New York, 1902), 311; and Tina H. Sheller, "The Origins of Public Education in Baltimore, 1825–1829," *HEQ* 22 (Spring 1982): 23–43. The new high school became Baltimore City College in 1851, but local educators opened other high schools to serve the talented few.

43. Howe, *Political Culture*, 13; Watson, *Liberty and Power*, chap. 8; Carl F. Kaestle and Maris Vinovskis, *Education and Social Change in Nineteenth-Century Massachusetts* (New York, 1980), chap. 8; and Katz, *Reconstructing*, 22.

44. Stanley Schultz, *The Culture Factory: Boston Schools, 1789–1860* (New York, 1973); Robert Rich, "'A Wilderness of Whigs': The Wealthy Men of Boston," *JSoH* 4 (Spring 1971): 263–76; and Haws, "Massachusetts Whigs," 64.

45. "Common Schools in Cities," 12.

46. Orwin Bradford Griffen, *The Evolution of the Connecticut State School System* (New York, 1928), chap. 5; and Emit Duncan Grizzell, *Origin and Development of the High School in New England Before 1865* (Philadelphia, 1923), 201–10.

47. In *The Political Culture*, 277, Howe describes the Republican Party as "an intensified version of northern middle-class Whiggery." See also Eric Foner, *Free Soil, Free Labor, Free Men: The Ideology of the Republican Party Before the Civil War* (New York, 1970), 18–23, 39; and Paul E. Belding, *The Development of the Free Public High School in Illinois to 1860* (New York, 1919), chaps. 1, 9, and 11.

48. Edward H. Chapman, *Cleveland: Village to Metropolis* (Cleveland, 1964), chaps. 2–3;

Thomas W. Kremm, "The Rise of the Republican Party in Cleveland, 1848–1860," Ph.D. diss., Kent State University, 1974, 5, chap. 1; and Edward M. Miggins, "The Search for the One Best System: Cleveland Public Schools and Educational Reform, 1836–1920," in *Cleveland: A Tradition of Reform*, ed. David D. Van Tassel and John J. Grabowski (Kent, 1986), 138–39.

49. Andrew Freese, *Early History of the Cleveland Public Schools* (Cleveland, 1876), 32–37; H. L. Warren, "Public Schools of Cleveland," in *Educational History of Ohio*, ed. James J. Burns (Columbus, 1905), 379; James H. Kennedy, *A History of the City of Cleveland* (Cleveland, 1896), 283, 286, 306, and 377; and Miggins, "Search," 138.

50. Rosenbloom, "Cincinnati's Common Schools," 1–19.

51. The social history of Cincinnati is richly documented. See especially Rohrbough, *Trans-Appalachian Frontier*, chap. 4; Irwin F. Flack, "Who Governed Cincinnati? A Comparative Analysis of Government and Social Structure in a Nineteenth Century River City, 1819–1860," Ph.D. diss., University of Pittsburgh, 1977; Patrick A. Folk, "'The Queen City of Mobs': Riots and Community Reactions in Cincinnati, 1788–1848," Ph.D. diss., University of Toledo, 1978; Walter Stix Glazer, "Cincinnati in 1840: A Community Profile," Ph.D. diss., University of Michigan, 1968; Kathryn Kish Sklar, *Catherine Beecher: A Study in American Domesticity* (New Haven, 1973), 112, 129, and 140; and Steven J. Ross, *Workers on the Edge: Work, Leisure, and Politics in Industrializing Cincinnati, 1788–1890* (New York, 1985).

52. Rosenbloom, "Cincinnati's Common Schools," 18–19; James H. Madison, *The Indiana Way: A State History* (Bloomington, 1986), 75–94 and 138; Charles Ross Dean, "The History of the Development of the Public High School in Indiana," M.A. thesis, University of Chicago, 1927, 55; B. R. Sulgrove, *History of Indianapolis and Marion County, Indiana* (Philadelphia, 1884), 417; and Gayle Thornbrough, Dorothy L. Riker, and Paula Corpuz, eds., *The Diary of Calvin Fletcher* (Indianapolis, 1978), 5: xi–xviii, and 6: xix–xvi, 172–73. See March 28, 1853, entry, 5: 47–48.

53. Don Harrison Doyle, *The Social Order of a Frontier Community: Jacksonville, Illinois, 1825–1870* (Urbana, 1978), 203–8; Richard J. Jensen, *Illinois* (New York, 1978), chaps. 1–3; and Daniel W. Kucera, *Church-State Relationships in Education in Illinois* (Washington, D.C., 1955), chap. 3.

54. *SB* 1 (July 16, 1847): 4; and *New-Year Address To the Patrons of "The School-Boy,"* (January 1, 1848), n.p. (WRHS).

55. P. A. Siljestrom, *Educational Institutions of the United States* (London, 1853), 47.

56. Kaestle, *Pillars*, chap. 8. Cf. Kenneth V. Lottich, *New England Transplanted* (Dallas, 1964).

57. Ira Mayhew, *The Means and Ends of Universal Education* (New York, 1857), 386. Also see Tyack, *One Best System*, Part 1.

58. Francis Adams, *The Free School System of the United States* (London, 1875), 199. The Massachusetts reformer George S. Boutwell, like many observers, linked age-grading with the superiority of public over private education in *Thoughts on Educational Topics and Institutions* (Boston, 1859), 196–97. Howard P. Chudakoff examines nineteenth-century developments in age grouping in *How Old Are You? Age Consciousness in American Culture* (Princeton, 1989), chaps. 1–2.

59. *First Report on Grading and Course of Study in the Public Schools* (Boston, 1831), 4; and Schultz, *Culture Factory*, chaps. 4 and 5.

60. The testing mania was condemned by B. A. Hinsdale in "The History of Popular Education on the Western Reserve," *OhAHP* 6 (1898): 55.

61. Hannah Clark, "The Public Schools of Chicago," Ph.D. diss., University of Chicago, 1897, 19; Carl D. Washburn, "The Rise of the High School in Ohio," Ph.D. diss., Ohio State University, 1932, 168; and Cosenza, *College of the City of New York*, 29. Public school officials continually praised the idea of graded classrooms in the nineteenth century.

62. *Kansas School Report* (1872), 11; and Katz, *Reconstructing*, 15.

63. *Cleveland School Report* (1851), 7.

64. *Oshkosh School Report* (1875), 21. Also see T. P. Charlton, "The High School Problem," *InSJ* 21 (August 1876): 370; and the *Indianapolis School Report* (1879), 10.

The Opposition

1. "Discussion at Newark, On High Schools," *OhEM* 9 (August 1860): 243.

2. "Discussion at Newark," 243.

3. "Discussion at Newark," 244–45.

4. "Discussion at Newark," 245. That same year Shepardson compared his school to "a pleasant home" that approached perfection. See the *Cincinnati School Report* (1860), 49.

5. "Discussion at Newark," 245. For more on Springfield, see "Springfield Schools," *OhEM* 13 (December 1864): 396; and "High Schools and Supervision," *OhEM* 15 (February 1866): 57–58.

6. "Discussion at Newark," 245–47.

7. "Discussion at Newark," 247.

8. "Discussion at Newark," 248.

9. Ellwood P. Cubberley offered the schoolman's view of those who opposed public schools in *Public Education in the United States* (Boston, 1919), 120; the enemies were "aristocratic," "conservatives," "politicians of small vision," rural folk, the "ignorant, narrow-minded, and penurious," "taxpayers," "Southern men," and others. Michael B. Katz sparked a revolution in the field when he argued that public schools, including high schools, were "imposed" upon the working classes (*The Irony of Early School Reform: Educational Innovation in Mid-Nineteenth Century Massachusetts* [Cambridge, 1968]), a thesis that has been challenged by Maris A. Vinovskis, *The Origins of Public High Schools: A Reexamination of the Beverly High School Controversy* (Madison, 1985). See also the forum on Vinovskis' volume, "The Origins of Public High Schools," *HEQ* 27 (Summer 1987): 241–58.

10. Francis Adams, *The Free School System of the United States* (London, 1875), 84; *Denver School Report* (1876), 31; and John D. Philbrick, "City School Systems in the United States" (Washington, D.C., 1885), 27.

11. "The High School Question," *OhEM* 15 (July 1866): 227; "Editorial Department," *OhEM* 23 (March 1874): 489–90; "Editorial," *OhEM* 23 (May 1874): 174–75, 179; and "The High School Question," *OhEM* 23 (September 1874): 375–90.

12. A. L. Mann, "Are High Schools Entitled to State Support?" *PSHJ* 1 (July 1877): 155. For further examples see R. M. Wright, "The High School Problem," *InSJ* 18 (June 1873): 214; "Higher Education," *InSJ* 20 (February 1875): 81–83; "The High School Question," *InSJ* 20 (April 1875): 176–77; "Higher Education—Danger," *InSJ* 21 (March 1876): 125–27; and "The High School Question," *InSJ* 21 (May 1876): 220–21.

13. A. J. Youngblood, "An Argument for High Schools," *InSJ* 24 (March 1879): 130.

14. "Norwich Free Academy," *AJE* 2 (December 1856): 665; "High Schools," *NTM* 1 (April 1875): 180; A. D. Mayo, *Talks with Teachers* (Boston, 1881), 76; *La Crosse School Report* (1879), 23, where the superintendent called opponents "educational pygmies"; and *Richmond School Report* (1878), 26–27.

15. B. M. Reynolds, "Should the State Support High Schools?" *WiJE* 8 (May 1878): 200; and R. W. Burton, "Shall the High School Be Organized As Supplementary To the Common School, or As Preparatory to the University or College?" *WiJE* 10 (May 1880): 189.

16. P. A. Siljestrom, *Educational Institutions of the United States* (London, 1853), 176. On elite private institutions, see Edward N. Saveth, "Education of an Elite," *HEQ* 28 (Fall 1988): 367–86.

17. James P. Wickersham, *A History of Education in Pennsylvania* (New York, [c. 1969]), 319; George W. Gear, "The High-School Question," *OhEM* 27 (July 1878): 201–2, adding that the ignorant poor were "quite numerous" in large cities; "A Thought on the High-School Question," *PSHJ* 2 (April 1878): 57; and M. N. Horton, "The High School," *PaSJ* 23 (September 1874): 101–4.

18. "Norwich Free Academy," 665–66. Massachusetts' George Boutwell criticized the inability of Norwich to support a publicly controlled high school in *Thoughts on Educational Topics and Institutions* (Boston, 1859), 155–56.

19. "Norwich Free Academy," 668. For more on the high school, see "Free Academy at Norwich," *AJE* 3 (March 1857), 191–212.

20. John O. Norris, "The High School in Our System of Education," *Educ* 3 (March 1883): 333.

21. That high schools were "extravagant" institutions, palatial in appearance and aristocratic, was a common charge. See *Michigan School Report* (1869), 187; *Ohio School Report* (1877), 47; Mary D. Bradford, *Memoirs of Mary D. Bradford* (Evansville, Wis., 1932), 120; and *Moline, Illinois, School Report* (1880), 16.

22. L. N. S., "Letter to Editor," *CSJ* 1 (December 16, 1839): 381; "The High School Question," *InSJ* 23 (May 1878), 211; and W. A. Bell, "A Few Points on the High School Question," *InSJ* 24 (February 1879): 52.

23. "Reducing the School Expenses," *Chicago Tribune*, March 22, 1878; *Minnesota School Report* (1880), 233.

24. "Education," *USMDR* 25 (August 1849): 149–50, 157–58.

25. Elmer Ellsworth Brown, *The Making of Our Middle Schools* (New York, 1902); and B. Jeannette Burrell and R. H. Eckelberry, "The Free High School in the Post–Civil-War Period," *ScR* 42 (October 1934): 609. In Somerville, Massachusetts, school promoters stereotyped academies as classically oriented, in contrast with the practical English course of study in the high school. See Reed Ueda, *Avenues to Adulthood: The Origins of the High School and Social Mobility in an American Suburb* (Cambridge, 1987), 41.

26. Silas Hertzler, *The Rise of the Public High School in Connecticut* (Baltimore, 1930), 29–34; Andrew Freese, *Early History of the Cleveland Public Schools* (Cleveland, 1876), 39; William J. Akers, *Cleveland Schools in the Nineteenth Century* (Cleveland, 1901), 86; and Carl D. Washburn, "The Rise of the High School in Ohio," Ph.D. diss., Ohio State University, 1932, 241, on local opposition to instruction in the classical languages.

27. Walter John Gifford, *Historical Development of the New York State High School System* (Albany, 1922), 75; Horace Greeley, *Recollections of a Busy Life* (New York, 1869), chap. 5, where he thanks his parents for refusing a benefactor's offer to finance his education; *New York City School Report* (1850), 30; and Jeter Allen Isely, *Horace Greeley and the Republican Party* (New York, 1965), 198.

28. *Ohio School Report* (1878), 70.

29. *Cincinnati School Report* (1846), 5. This common complaint was noted in *Michigan School Report* (1872), 12; Henry Kiddle and Alexander J. Schem, eds., *The Cyclopedia of Education: A Dictionary of Information for the Use of Teachers, School Officers, Parents, and Others* (New York, 1877), 422; Burrell and Eckelberry, "Free Public High School," 606–7; and Richard G. Boone, *Education in the United States: Its History from the Earliest Settlements* (New York, 1894), 340.

30. Frederick A. Packard, *The Daily Public School in the United States* (Philadelphia, 1866); Anne M. Boylan, *Sunday School: The Formation of an American Institution, 1790–1880* (New Haven, 1988), 55–65; and Raymond B. Culver, *Horace Mann and Religion in the Massachusetts Public Schools* (New Haven, 1933), chaps. 5–6.

31. Packard, *Daily Public School*, 11.

32. *Ohio School Report* (1855), 63; *Pennsylvania School Report* (1871), xxvii; and "Suggestions for High School Work," *PSHJ* 2 (March 1878): 36.

33. Orwin Bradford Griffin, *The Evolution of the Connecticut State System* (New York, 1928), chaps. 2 and 6; Paul E. Belting, *The Development of the Free Public High School in Illinois to 1860* (New York, 1919), 178–79; Calvin Olin Davis, *Public Secondary Education* (Chicago, 1917), chaps. 7–8; W. L. Smith, *Historical Sketches of Education in Michigan* (Lansing, 1881), 36–37, 45–49; Eugene Alfred Bishop, *The Development of a State School System: New Hampshire* (New York, 1930), 82; and George Gary Bush, "History of Education in Vermont," United States Bureau of Education Circular of Information No. 4 (1900), 29–34.

34. Alexander James Inglis, *The Rise of the High School in Massachusetts* (New York, 1911), 27–28, 38; and Harriet Webster Marr, *The Old New England Academies Founded Before 1826* (New York, 1959), 289.

35. "Our Common School System, No. VI," *CSJ* 13 (April 15, 1851): 115; *Massachusetts School Report* (1865), 95–96; (1866), 57; Emit Duncan Grizzell, *Origin and Development of the High School in New England Before 1865* (Philadelphia, 1923), 90–91. Inglis, in *Rise of the High School*, disagreed with the official estimates by the state superintendent's office; see especially chap. 3.

36. "First Annual Report of the Board of Commissioners of Common Schools in Connecticut," *ConnCSJAE* 1 (June 1, 1839): 172; Peter J. Harder, "Politics, Efficiency, and Rural Schools in

Connecticut, 1866–1919," *ConnHSB* 44 (April 1979): 52–60; and Brown, *Making of Our Middle Schools*, 302.

37. Edward Alanson Miller, *The History of Educational Legislation in Ohio from 1803 to 1850* (Chicago, 1918), chap. 4; the histories gathered by the Ohio State Centennial Educational Committee, *Historical Sketches of Public Schools in Cities, Villages, and Townships of the State of Ohio* (n.p., 1876); Nelson L. Bossing, "The History of Educational Legislation in Ohio from 1851 to 1925," *ObAHP* 39 (1930): 157; *Illinois School Report* (1872), 105, and (1874), 75; and I. F. Mills, "Are the Country Schools Inferior to the City Schools—If So, Why?" *InSJ* 18 (November 1873): 435–40.

38. *Iowa School Report* (1858), 9–10, 22; (1872), 118; and (1876), 39; Aurelie Edith Zichy, "A History of Public High Schools in Iowa," Ph.D. diss., University of Chicago, 1922, 7, 15–16; S. A. Pease, "The Free High School Law of Wisconsin," *WiJE* 8 (August 1878), 332–33; "The Free School Law—Timid Legislation," *WiJE* 8 (December 1878): 558–60; and *Minnesota School Report* (1880), 234.

39. It is, of course, impossible to cite precise figures on those tutored in advanced studies in the thousands of district schools of the nation in the nineteenth century. Moreover, others taught themselves. "Many a young man has acquired a knowledge of the higher branches by study of books without a teacher," noted G. Dallas Lind, in *Methods of Teaching in Country Schools* (Danville, Ind., 1880), 19. On many of these issues, see E. Wayne Fuller, *The Old Country School: The Story of Rural Education in the Middle West* (Chicago, 1982). On architecture, see Samuel F. Eveleth, *School House Architecture* (New York, 1870); and T. M. Clark, "Rural School Architecture," United States Bureau of Education Circular of Information No. 4 (1880).

40. "System of Common Schools," *SQR* 6 (October 1844): 460, 463; "Education in New Orleans," *DR* 1 (January 1846): 83; Edward Whitfield Fay, "The History of Education in Louisiana," U.S. Bureau of Education Circular No. 1 (1898), 110; Edgar Otto Wood, "A History of the Development of High Schools of Louisiana," M.A. thesis, University of Chicago, 1926, 25–30; Watt L. Black, "Education in the South from 1820 to 1860 with Emphasis on the Growth of Teacher Education," *LaS* 12 (Winter 1973): 617–29; and especially Joseph W. Newman, "Antebellum School Reform in the Port Cities of the Deep South," in *Southern Cities, Southern Schools: Public Education in the Urban South*, ed. David N. Plank and Rick Ginsberg (Westport, Conn., 1990), 17–35.

41. P., "Free School System in South-Carolina," *SQR* 16 (October 1849): 32, 35. "Disguise it as we may," P wrote, "the fact is undeniable, that our common schools are intended for the children of the poor and for no other." Southerners waged a vigorous campaign, often characterized by more talk than action, to replace Yankee schoolbooks with readers, texts, and other materials more sympathetic to slavery and southern history and culture. The controversy can be easily traced in *DeBow's Review* from the 1840s through the late 1850s. Also see Edgar W. Knight, "Some Fallacies Concerning the History of Public Education in the South," *SAQ* 13 (October 1914): 371–81.

42. G. E. D., "Education in Virginia," *SLM* 7 (September 1841): 631; "Instruction in Schools and Colleges," *SQR* 6 (October 1852): 460; Civis, "The Public School in Its Relation to the Negro," *SP* 36 (December 1875): 707–11; and "Southern School-Books," *DR* 13 (September 1852): 258–66.

43. "The Enemies of Free Schools," *MsEJ* 1 (March 1871): 84; "National Education," *MsEJ* 1 (April 1871): 122–24; Ellwood Fischer, "The North and the South," *DR* 7 (October 1849): 312, on southern oral and literary culture, as opposed to interest in Yankee schools; Daniel J. Whitener, "The Republican Party and Public Education in North Carolina, 1867–1900," *NCHR* 37 (July 1860): 382–96; Eric Foner, *Free Soil, Free Labor, Free Men: The Ideology of the Republican Party Before the Civil War* (New York, 1970), chap. 2; Daniel Walker Howe, *The Political Culture of the American Whigs* (Chicago, 1979), 262; and Edward Pessen, "How Different from Each Other Were the Antebellum North and South?" *AHR* 85 (December 1980): 1119–49.

44. W. Stevens claimed that many southerners opposed high schools ("Promotion in Graded Schools," *NTM* 1 [January 1875]: 69). Also see Don H. Doyle, *New Men, New Cities, New South: Atlanta, Nashville, Charleston, Mobile, 1860–1910* (Chapel Hill, 1990); Stephen B. Weeks, "History of Public School Education in Alabama," U.S. Bureau of Education Bulletin No. 12 (1915), 184;

Edward Mayes, "History of Education in Mississippi," U.S. Bureau of Education Circular of Information No. 2 (1899), chap. 15; William Hennington Weathersby, *A History of Educational Legislation in Mississippi from 1798 to 1860* (Chicago, 1921), chap. 6; Dorothy Orr, *A History of Education in Georgia* (Chapel Hill, 1950), 263; *Richmond, Virginia, School Report* (1872), 144; *Atlanta School Report* (1872), 28; and *Augusta, Georgia, School Report* (1877), 22.

45. George L. Osborne, "Should the Public School System Support High Schools?" *WiJE* 4 (March 1874): 101.

46. *Indiana School Report* (1852), 262; and *Maine School Report* (1873), 90. The superintendent of the Madison, Wisconsin, schools noted that every dollar spent on private schools equaled one less dollar for public education; see *Madison School Report* (1856), 8.

47. For an example of a private school critic turned public school employee and defender, see Harold Eugene Davis, *Hinsdale of Hiram: The Life of Burke Aaron Hinsdale, Pioneer Educator, 1837–1900* (Washington, D.C., 1971).

48. *Denver School Report* (1875), 26; *Michigan School Report* (1875), 294; and *Florida School Report* (1870), 9. The all-male, college preparatory, tuition-supported High School of Charleston, South Carolina, also applauded local public schools as superior to secondary boarding schools. See J. L. Dawson and H. W. DeSaussure, *Census of the City of Charleston, South Carolina, for the Year 1848* (Charleston, 1849), 56 (LC).

49. *Petersburg School Report* (1870), 12. "Papistical" opposition to public education was deplored by G., "Fort Wayne and Vicinity," *InSJ* 3 (April 1858), 113.

50. Ohio State Centennial Educational Committee, *Historical Sketches of Public Schools*, 1; *Indiana School Report* (1879), 339; William Lucas Steele, *Galesburg Public Schools: Their History and Work, 1861–1911* (Galesburg, 1911), 39; *Cincinnati School Report* (1848), 22; *Maine School Report* (1860), 38, and (1871), 94; H. B. Weaver, "Legislative Development of the Pennsylvania High Schools," *SS* 23 (February 6, 1926): 159–64; and Grizzell, *Origin and Development*, 137–40.

51. "Editorial Department," *OhEM* 27 (April 1878): 124; George Frederick Miller, *The Academy System of the State of New York* (Albany, 1922), 53; Edward Herring O'Neil, "Private Schools and Public Vision: A History of Academies in Upstate New York, 1800–1860," Ph.D. diss., Syracuse University, 1984; Daniel W. Kucera, *Church-State Relationships in Education in Illinois* (Washington, D.C., 1955), 106; and Raymond P. G. Bowman, "Secondary Education in Virginia, 1870–1938," Ph.D. diss., University of Virginia, 1938, 9.

52. Weeks, "History of Public School Education," chap. 4; Bama Wathan Watson, *The History of Barton Academy* (Mobile, Ala., 1971), chap. 11; Haygood S. Bowden, *Two Hundred Years of Education* (Richmond, 1932), 254–57; *Savannah School Report* (1870), 19, and (1877), 15–16.

53. Burrell and Eckelberry, "Free Public High School," 608–9; B. Jeannette Burrell and R. H. Eckelberry, "The High-School Controversy in the Post–Civil War Period: Time, Places, and Participants," *SR* 42 (May 1934): 338–40; and "Editorial," *OhEM* 27 (June 1878): 191.

54. "Doctor Tuttle vs. High Schools," *InSJ* 24 (March 1879): 120; "The High School Question," *InSJ* 20 (April 1875): 176–77; and D. P. Baldwin, "The Defense of Free High Schools," *InSJ* 24 (July 1879): 294.

55. Charles W. Eliot, "Wise and Unwise Economy in Schools," *AtM* 35 (June 1875): 719.

56. Eliot, "Wise and Unwise Economy," 719.

57. A. D. Mayo, "The Demands of the Coming Century on the American Common School," *NEAAP* (Salem, Ohio, 1876): 24.

58. Burrell and Eckelberry, "High-School Controversy," 337–40. Governors Alonzo Garcelon of Maine and Lucius Robinson of New York, for example, were critical of the high school. Garcelon was originally a Whig, then a Jacksonian Democrat, Free-Soiler, Republican, and, after encountering the Radical Republicans, a Democrat. See "Alonzo Garcelon," in *Biographical Dictionary of the Governors of the United States*, ed. Robert Sobel and John Raimo (Westport, Conn., 1978), 2: 617–18. Lucius Robinson also switched parties, though not as frequently; first he was a Jacksonian, then a Republican, then a Democrat. See his biographical sketch in Sobel and Raimo, *Biographical Dictionary*, 3: 1088.

59. The distinctive worldviews of the Democrats are explored in Jean H. Baker, *Affairs of Party: The Political Culture of Northern Democrats in the Mid-Nineteenth Century* (Ithaca, 1983);

Robert Kelley, *The Cultural Pattern in American Politics: The First Century* (New York, 1979); Lawrence Frederick Kohl, *The Politics of Individualism: Parties and the American Character in the Jacksonian Period* (New York, 1989); Bruce Collins, "The Ideology of the Ante-Bellum Northern Democrats," *AS* 11 (April 1977): 103–21; Carl F. Kaestle and Maris A. Vinovskis, *Education and Social Change in Nineteenth-Century Massachusetts* (Cambridge, 1980), chap. 8; and Henry L. Watson, *Liberty and Power: The Politics of Jacksonian America* (New York, 1990).

60. *Ohio School Report* (1877), 45–46.

61. *Ohio School Report* (1878), 3, 74. Smart asked forty to fifty superintendents from across the state to send him additional information on the local high school; he said about fifteen responded, "a comparatively fair average of school-official promptness and zeal" (74).

62. On Rice, see Elroy McKendree Avery, *A History of Cleveland and Its Environs* (Cleveland, 1918), 1: 557–58, 3: 178; James H. Kennedy, *A History of the City of Cleveland* (Cleveland, 1896), 195; and Samuel P. Orth, *A History of Cleveland, Ohio* (Chicago, 1910), 1: 526–27. On Payne, see William J. Akers, *Cleveland Schools in the Nineteenth Century* (Cleveland, 1901), 46; Kennedy, *History of Cleveland*, 259; and "Henry B. Payne," *The Encyclopedia of Cleveland History*, ed. David D. Van Tassel and John J. Grabowski (Bloomington, Ind., 1987), 758.

63. Analyses include Mario Emilio Cosenza, *The Establishment of the College of the City of New York in 1847, Townsend Harris, Founder* (New York, 1925); S. Willis Rudy, *The College of the City of New York: A History* (New York, 1949); and Jeffrey Mirel, "The Matter of Means: The Campaign and Election for the New York Free Academy, 1846–1847," *JMHES* 9 (1981): 134–55, which documents strong voter support for the Free Academy in the Democratic wards.

64. *New York City School Report* (1850), 31; Mirel, "Matter of Means," 138; and Rudy, *College of the City of New York*, 42, on Benedict. Rudy asserts that Whigs held a slight majority in the legislature and that both Whigs and Democrats split internally on the vote for the Free Academy.

65. Mirel, "Matter of Means," 140; Cosenza, *College of the City of New York*, chap. 9, 212 (quotation); Edward Pessen, "Who Has Power in the Democratic Capitalistic Community? Reflections on Antebellum New York City," *NYH* 58 (April 1977): 129–55; and *Sketches of the Speeches and Writings of Michael Walsh: Including His Poems and Correspondence* (New York, 1843).

66. Archie P. Nevins, "The Kalamazoo Case," *MiH* 44 (March 1960): 94–95; Samuel W. Durant, *History of Kalamazoo County, Michigan* (Philadelphia, 1880), 120; and E. B. Robbins, "High Schools for All," *MiEJ* 17 (November 1939): 220. Much of the history in this concluding section has been reconstructed from articles on education and schooling published in the local rival newspapers, the Republican *Telegraph* (1857–1880) and the Democratic *Gazette* (1862–1876).

67. Durant, *History of Kalamazoo County*, 239–41.

68. "Our Village Schools," *Kalamazoo Telegraph*, November 4, 1857; "Kalamazoo Union School," *Kalamazoo Telegraph*, November 10, 1858; and Daniel Putnam, *Development of Primary and Secondary Education in Michigan* (Ann Arbor, 1904), 86–93.

69. "The Dedication of the Union School," *Kalamazoo Telegraph*, February 2, 1859; "Addresses," *Kalamazoo Telegraph*, February 9, 1859; and "Union School Examination," *Kalamazoo Telegraph*, March 30, 1859.

70. "School Meeting," *Kalamazoo Telegraph*, September 4, 1867.

71. "School Meeting Last Evening," *Kalamazoo Daily Gazette*, August 31, 1872; and "Meeting of the School Board," *Kalamazoo Telegraph*, September 4, 1872.

72. "Meeting of the School Board," *Kalamazoo Telegraph*, September 4, 1872; and "The High School Case," *Kalamazoo Weekly Telegraph*, February 18, 1874.

73. "High Schools," *Kalamazoo Telegraph*, July 29, 1874; E. M. Avery, "Concerning A High-School Course of Study," *OhEM* 27 (September 1878): 292–93; and untitled editorial, *New-England Journal of Education* 3 (January 29, 1876): 54. B. Jeannette Burrell and R. H. Eckelberry demonstrated that *Charles E. Stuart and Others v. School District No. 1 of the Village of Kalamazoo and Others* (1874) was one of a number of court cases against the establishment of the high school, and that in nine successive cases was cited only twice. See "The High-School Question Before the Courts in the Post–Civil-War Period," *ScR* 42 (April 1934): 262–63. Still, to many historians the case was a landmark. See, for example, Cubberley, *Public Education*, 198–99; and Hertzler, *The Rise of the High School*, 31.

74. "Annual School Meeting," *Kalamazoo Telegraph*, September 4, 1872.

Cathedrals of Learning

1. Henry Kiddle and Alexander J. Schem, eds., *The Cyclopedia of Education: A Dictionary of Information for the Use of Teachers, School Officers, Parents, and Others* (New York, 1877), 422; and Maris A. Vinovskis, "Have We Underestimated the Extent of Antebellum High School Attendance?" *HEQ* 28 (Winter 1988): 562.

2. "The Annual School Meeting," *Kalamazoo Daily Telegraph*, July 12, 1880; W. H. Woodhams, "The School Question," *Kalamazoo Daily Telegraph*, July 13, 1880; "Adjourned School Meeting," *Kalamazoo Daily Telegraph*, July 26, 1880; "The High School Again," *Kalamazoo Daily Telegraph*, August 3, 1880; "The School Meeting," *Kalamazoo Daily Telegraph*, August 5, 1880; "The Question of Public Education," *Kalamazoo Daily Telegraph*, August 7, 1880; *Michigan School Report* (1875), 289, and (1877), 288.

3. *Boston School Report* (1872), 29; William W. Cutler III, "Cathedral of Culture: The Schoolhouse in American Educational Thought and Practice Since 1820," *HEQ* 29 (Spring 1989): 1–40; and Lloyd P. Jorgenson, *The State and the Non-Public School, 1825–1925* (Columbia, Mo., 1987).

4. *Ohio School Report* (1877), 47; Mary D. Bradford, *Memoirs of Mary D. Bradford* (Evansville, Wis., 1932), 119–20; and *Michigan School Report* (1869), 187, for criticisms of "our High School palaces"; and David B. Tyack, *The One Best System: A History of American Urban Education* (Cambridge, 1974), 57.

5. A. H. T., "High Schools," *MaT* 26 (June 1873): 197–98.

6. W. W. Ross, "The Public High School," *OhEM* 27 (August 1878): 234; "New High-School House, Providence," *NEJE* 8 (September 26, 1878): 193–94; "New Central High School, Cleveland," *NEJE* 8 (September 26, 1878): 192–94; and untitled editorial, *NEJE* 8 (October 3, 1878): 212.

7. Amasa Walker, *The Science of Wealth: A Manual of Political Economy* (Philadelphia, 1866), 409; and *St. Louis School Report* (1855), 60.

8. *Exeter, New Hampshire, School Report* (1848), 12.

9. For descriptions of modest facilities in ordinary places, see *Minnesota School Report* (1875), 147; G. Dallas Lind, *Methods of Teaching in Country Schools* (Danville, Ind., 1880); and James H. Canfield, *Opportunities of the Rural Population for Higher Education* (Syracuse, 1889). School journals tended to publicize the very expensive, atypical facilities found in the largest cities. Areas with a low density population even had "moving high schools"—teachers who moved from building to building; see *Massachusetts School Report* (1876), 107.

10. See the *Ohio School Report* (1879), 30; and Silas Hertzler, *The Rise of the Public High School in Connecticut* (Baltimore, 1930), 159.

11. *Ohio School Report* (1879), 30–32, and (1880), 33.

12. Henry Barnard, *School Architecture; or Contributions to the Improvement of School-Houses in the United States* (New York, 1848), 56, reprinted by Jean and Robert McClintock as *Henry Barnard's "School Architecture"* (New York, 1970).

13. John S. Hart, "Description of Public High School in Philadelphia," *AJE* 1 (August 1855): 93–102; "System of Public Instruction in St. Louis," *AJE* 1 (March 1856): 348–56; "School Architecture," *AJE* 5 (June 1858): 199–200; "School Architecture," *AJE* 11 (June 1862): 563–612; "School Architecture," *AJE* 13 (September 1863): 611–25; and "School Architecture," *AJE* 13 (December 1863): 818–60.

14. Quotation in Mario Emilio Cosenza, *The Establishment of the College of the City of New York in 1847, Townsend Harris, Founder* (New York, 1925), 197.

15. S. Willis Rudy, *The College of the City of New York: A History* (New York, 1949), 26; A. Emerson Palmer, *The New York Public School: Being a History of Free Education in the City of New York* (New York, 1905), 321; and Calder Roth and Julius Trousdale Sadler, Jr., *The Only Proper Style: Gothic Architecture in America* (Boston, 1975), 34, 68–70.

16. *Geer's Hartford City Directory and Hartford Illustrated: July 1, 1884* (Hartford, 1884), 537.

17. Hart, "Description of Public High School," 95; *The Stranger's Guide in Philadelphia* (Philadelphia, 1862), 79; *Cincinnati School Report* (1855), 5; *San Francisco School Report* (1870), 17–18; "Worcester Classical and English High School," *AJE* 23 (1872): 657; and *Nebraska School Report* (1872), 120–22, and (1873), 342.

18. Richard Alston Metcalf, comp., *A History of Princeton High School* (Princeton, Ill., 1892), 31, 110; and Edward Livingston Carr, "The Development of the Public High School in Illinois from 1860 to 1924," M.A. thesis, University of Chicago, 1925, 43–44. On the backgrounds of the local reformers, see H. C. Bradsby, ed., *History of Bureau County, Illinois* (Chicago, 1885); George B. Harrington, *Past and Present of Bureau County, Illinois* (Chicago, 1906), 80–83; and *The Voters and Tax-Payers of Bureau County, Illinois* (Chicago, 1877), 178–210.

19. "Our School-Room," *SB* 1 (October 22, 1847): 2; W. C., "The High School," *SB* 2 (February 1, 1850): 1, 2; untitled editorial on Cincinnati, *SB* 3 (December 20, 1852): 2; and untitled essay, *SG* 1 (October 26, 1850): 2 (WRHS). Also see Ann M. Giblin, "Factors Affecting Nineteenth-Century Architecture in Cleveland School Buildings," *JCCA* 1 (1981): 32–42.

20. *Concord, New Hampshire, School Report* (1856), 24; (1861), 21; *Indianapolis School Report* (1857), 6; *Bridgeport School Report* (1878), 6, 19; *Oshkosh School Report* (1879), 8–9; and *La Crosse School Report* (1878), 25.

21. On the built environment, see Leland M. Roth, *A Concise History of American Architecture* (New York, 1979), chaps. 4–6.

22. *Terre Haute School Report* (1872), 10; (1878), 23; and *California School Report* (1877), 15.

23. Frederick A. Packard, *The Daily Public School in the United States* (Philadelphia, 1866), 26, 93, and 150.

24. *Philadelphia School Report* (1841), 11; (1842), 12; and (1846), 105.

25. "Discussion at Newark, On High Schools," *OhEM* 9 (August 1860): 247.

26. *Cincinnati School Report* (1855), 5; (1858), 13–14; and (1859), 32.

27. *Louisville School Report* (1865), 8; "Common Schools," *LMM* 1 (1879): 56–58; and "Editorial Department," *LMM* 1 (1879): 469. Few writers complained about the gender gap.

28. *New York City School Report* (1863), 20. Even at the end of the antebellum period, working men rarely earned $1.75 per day, and seasonal employment, layoffs, part-time work, and the like made their lives precarious. One can well imagine, then, how easily opponents could stir opposition to the high costs of fancy buildings and related expenses in maintaining free secondary schools. On working people's wages, see Jeanne Boydston, *Home and Work: Housework, Wages, and the Ideology of Labor in the Early Republic* (New York, 1990), 61–63.

29. "The Results of the Decision of the Supreme Court," *InSJ* 3 (February 1858): 69; Harold Littell, "Development of the City School System of Indiana, 1851–1880," *InMH* 12 (September 1916): 305–11; *Rules, Regulations, and a Revised Course of Study Adopted By the School Board of the Second District of Appleton* (Appleton, 1876), 18–24; and *Appleton School Report* (1879), 52.

30. "High School of Charleston," *ConnCMJAE* 3 (June 1, 1841): 171; J. L. Dawson and H. W. DeSaussure, *Census of the City of Charleston, South Carolina, for the Year 1848* (Charleston, 1849), 56–57; and Eugene Clifford Clark, "A History of the First Hundred Years of the High School of Charleston, 1839–1939," in *Year Book, 1943* (Charleston, 1946), 196, 200, and 232. This school received public funding but charged tuition until 1925.

31. *Columbus, Georgia, School Report* (1878), 29, and (1881), which includes the 1878 report, 5; Raymond P. G. Bowman, "Secondary Education in Virginia, 1870–1886," Ph.D. diss., University of Virginia, 1938, 4–10, on the continuing influence of private schools in the 1870s; *Savannah School Report* (1869), 17, and (1877), 8; and Marie Margaretta Furree, "Development of the Public School System in Savannah and Chatham County," M.A. thesis, University of Georgia, 1933, 95–96. Kentucky and other border states as well as southern states continued to allow rate bills, as noted, for example, in *Kentucky School Report* (1878), 55.

32. *Alexandria, Virginia, School Report* (1881), 30–32; and *St. Louis School Report* (1873), 43.

33. *A Volume of Records Relating to the Early History of Boston, Containing Boston Town Records, 1814–1822* (Boston, 1906), 166–71; and John R. Rooney, "The History of the Modern Subjects in the Secondary Curriculum," Ph.D. diss., Catholic University of America, 1926, 47–53.

34. *A Volume of Records*, 171. See, for example, Arthur G. Powell, Eleanor Farrar, and David K. Cohen, *The Shopping Mall High School: Winners and Losers in the Educational Marketplace* (Boston, 1985), 250, which asserts that in the early 1900s "the old classical course of study had lost its hammerlock on high school work." Also see Diane Ravitch, *The Troubled Crusade: American Education, 1945–1980* (New York, 1983), 10; and John I. Goodlad, *A Place Called School* (New

York, 1984), 9, 151. In fairness to these writers, they were mostly working on twentieth-century topics and thus forced to rely on secondary works for generalization about earlier developments.

35. "Public High School of Salem," *AJE* 3 (July 1828): 492, reprinted from the *Salem Observer* of May 31.

36. *Portland School Report* (1834), 2; *Philadelphia School Report* (1842), 25; A. D. Bache, *Report to the Controllers of the Public Schools, on the Re-Organization of the Central High School of Philadelphia* (Philadelphia, 1839), 14; Franklin Spencer Edmonds, *History of the Central High School of Philadelphia* (Philadelphia, 1902), 43–44, 61; and David F. Labaree, *The Making of an American High School: The Credentials Market and the Central High School of Philadelphia, 1838–1939* (New Haven, 1988), 12–23.

37. William J. Akers, *Cleveland Schools in the Nineteenth Century* (Cleveland, 1901), 36; *Chicago School Report* (1880), 48–66, which discusses the evolution of the high school; *St. Louis School Report* (1854), 337–39; and "System of Public Instruction in St. Louis," 348–56.

38. The quotation by Rush is from Linda K. Kerber's *Federalists in Dissent: Imagery and Ideology in Jeffersonian America* (Ithaca, 1970), 114. Enrollment statistics for the majority of towns and cities demonstrate the preeminent role of the English, nonclassical course of study. On the paucity of Latin instruction beyond the first term or first year, see A. Z., "Need Latin Be Excluded from Our High Schools?" *NEJE* 10 (October 16, 1879): 208. On the "mutinous" taxpayers, see *Indiana School Report* (1870), 37; and R. W. Burton, "Should the High School Be Organized as Supplementary to the Common School, or as Preparatory to the University or College?" *WiJE* 10 (May 1880): 185, where the author quotes William T. Harris of St. Louis on popular hostility to the ancient languages; and James D. Butler, "A Defense of Classical Studies: How Dead Languages Make Live Men," *NEAAP* (1874): 187.

39. Barnard, *School Architecture*, 98. Also see *Connecticut School Report* (1842), 24; "Public High School," *AJE* 3 (March 1857): 185–89; and "School Architecture," *AJE* 11 (June 1862): 570.

40. Barnard, *School Architecture*, 99, 101.

41. Barnard, *School Architecture*, 101.

42. *Connecticut School Report* (1859), 35; (1865), 26–27; Thomas B. Davis, *Chronicles of the Hopkins Grammar School, 1660–1935* (New Haven, 1938); Orwin Bradford Griffen, *The Evolution of the Connecticut State School System* (New York, 1928), chap. 4; and Silas Hertzler, *The Rise of the Public High School*, chaps. 4–5.

43. A. P. S., "Course of Study for High Schools," *MaT* 12 (November 1859): 410; and Chauncey R. Stuntz, "A Course of Study for High Schools," *OhEM* 18 (August 1869): 290–94.

44. W. A. Bell, "Course of Study for High School," *InSJ* 14 (March 1869): 91; and "Discussion: Higher Education," *PaSJ* 26 (September 1877): 90–92.

45. B. M. Reynolds, "Shall the State Support High Schools?" *WiJE* 8 (May 1878): 201.

46. Edward D. Mansfield, *American Education, Its Principles and Elements* (New York, 1851), chaps. 1–3; *Louisville School Report* (1861), 22; and *Connecticut School Report* (1880), 96–104.

47. *Exeter School Report* (1877), 22–23.

48. *Boston School Report* (1855), 74; *Cleveland School Report* (1851), 7; and T. P. Charlton, "The High School Problem," *InSJ* 21 (August 1876): 369.

49. *Muncie School Report* (1876), 14; James Henry Smart, ed., *The Indiana Schools and the Men Who Have Worked in Them* (Cincinnati, 1876), 107; and *Cincinnati School Report* (1853), 37.

50. "Intermediate [Or Upper] Schools," *NEAAP* (1874): 12; Emit Duncan Grizzell, *Origin and Development of the High School in New England Before 1865* (Philadelphia, 1923), 277–79, 359; *Chicago School Report* (1874), 174; and *New York City School Report* (1866), 68.

51. *St. Louis School Report* (1873), 42, and (1875), 79; and William T. Harris, "The Necessity of Free Public High Schools," *NEJE* 11 (January 22, 1880): 53.

52. *Lewiston, Maine, School Report* (1880), 91. On the continual connections made between education and the business world, see *Portland, Maine, School Report* (1834), 2; *New Hampshire School Report* (1856), 76, on Hillsborough County; and the comments from the *Kansas Journal* reprinted in W. W. Grant, "Higher Education," *EJVa* 5 (March 1874): 213–15, arguing that skilled labor was more valuable than unskilled labor to the political economy.

53. John S. Hart, *In the School-Room: Chapters in the Philosophy of Education* (Philadelphia, 1868),

259; Labaree, *Making of an American High School*, 19–21; and Edmonds, *History of the Central High School*, chap. 6.

54. "Norwich Free Academy," *AJE* 2 (December 1856): 670.

55. *Philadelphia School Report* (1865), 227–28; and William L. Pillsbury, "The Course of Study in the High School," *JIISTA* (1869): 75. Also see Michael W. Sedlak, Christopher W. Wheeler, Diana C. Pullin, and Philip A. Cusick, *Selling Students Short: Classroom Bargains and Academic Reform in the American High School* (New York, 1986), 25.

56. *Cincinnati School Report* (1860), 54, in an address where he also hoped graduates would "breast the tide of commercial speculation and political excitement" (50); and "The High School Question," *InSJ* 21 (May 1876): 221.

57. R. M. Wright, "The High School Problem," *InSJ* 18 (June 1873): 214; and R. M. Wright, "The High School Problem—II," *InSJ* 18 (October 1873): 379.

58. *Manchester, New Hampshire, School Report* (1874), 211; and *St. Louis School Report* (1874), 54.

59. *Louisville School Report* (1857), 18, and (1876), 52; and "Editorial—Miscellany," *InSJ* 8 (July 1863): 220.

60. *Meriden, Connecticut, School Report* (1872), 5–6. Baynard R. Hall, *Teaching, A Science: The Teacher, An Artist* (New York, 1848), 52–53, accused advocates of "republicanism" of ignoring the value of classical study. Those who defended the classics often equated "practical" education with materialism.

61. *Exeter, New Hampshire, School Report* (1852), 9.

62. See, for example, W. C. Collar, "The Defects in our High Schools," *MaT* 23 (January 1870): 2; V., "The Study of the Ancient Classics," *RIS* 4 (November 1858): 257–61; *Massachusetts School Report* (1865), 12–13; and *Chicago School Report* (1860), 56, on Latin and mental discipline.

63. *New York State School Report* (1845), 19; *Chicago School Report* (1860), 27; and *Connecticut School Report* (1861), 8.

64. *Rhode Island School Report* (1846), 59; L. B., "Course of Study in the High School of New London," *ConnCSJAE* 10 (June 1855): 289; and *Philadelphia School Report* (1860), 12.

65. In 1871 the St. Louis high school principal complained that the pressure for "practical" education too easily led to demands for narrow vocational studies. See *St. Louis School Report* (1872), 63; and Bernard Edward McClellan, "Education for an Industrial Society: Changing Conceptions of the Role of Public Schooling, 1865–1900," Ph.D. diss., Northwestern University, 1972, chaps. 3–4.

66. *Chicago School Report* (1860), 55; *Cincinnati School Report* (1859), 42–43; and *Dayton School Report* (1877), 24. Some "reformers" in the 1870s urged the establishment of industrial education courses and polytechnical training. This was true even in rural Iowa; see *Iowa School Report* (1876), 40.

67. Alexis de Tocqueville, *Democracy in America* (New York, [c. 1969], rpt. of 12th ed., 1848), 1: 376. He added that northern education reflected all "the good and bad qualities characteristic of the middle classes."

68. Wright, "The High School Problem—II," 379.

Knowledge of the Most Worth

1. "Algebra," in *The Cyclopedia of Education: A Dictionary of Information for the Use of Teachers, School Officers, Parents, and Others*, ed. Henry Kiddle and Alexander J. Schem (New York, 1877), 22. On the "slavish use" of textbooks in the high school, see S. R. Winchell, "The True Function of the High School," *WiJE* 4 (August 1874): 305.

2. The standard interpretation of elementary textbooks is Ruth Miller Elson's *Guardians of Tradition: American Schoolbooks of the Nineteenth Century* (Omaha, 1964). Also see John R. Frisch, "Youth Culture in America, 1790–1865," Ph.D. diss., University of Missouri, 1970, 58–64; Charles Carpenter, *History of American Schoolbooks* (Philadelphia, 1963); John A. Nietz, *Old Textbooks* (Pittsburgh, 1961); and, on children's literature, Bernard Wishy, *The Child and the Republic: The Dawn of Modern American Child Nurture* (Philadelphia, 1968), 61, 74–76.

3. Richard D. Brown, *Knowledge is Power: The Diffusion of Information in Early America*,

1700–1865 (New York, 1989), examines the large-scale changes accompanying the print revolution. On debates North and South, see Ellwood Fischer, "The North and the South," *DR* 7 (October 1849): 312; and C. K. Marshall, "Appendix to Convention Proceedings," *DR* 22 (March 1857): 312. Southern commercial conventions in the 1850s and 1860s urged the establishment of regional normal schools and textbook publishers to counter the influence of Yankee values. Also see Clement Eaton, *The Freedom-of-Thought Struggle in the Old South* (New York, c. 1964), chap. 9; and Carl F. Kaestle, *Pillars of the Republic: Common Schools and American Society, 1780–1860* (New York, 1983), 213–14. Baynard R. Hall thought the proliferation of texts allowed teachers to blame them instead of themselves for poor pedagogy (*Teaching, A Science: The Teacher, An Artist* [New York, 1848], 87–88, 99).

4. William T. Harris, "Text-Books and Their Uses," *Educ* 1 (September 1880): 8. To place Harris' statements in context, many contemporaries called slow learners "block heads."

5. On the power of markets to create selective reading audiences and on differential access to reading materials, see especially Brown, *Knowledge is Power*, 242–43, 275–76; and Ian Westbury, "Textbooks, Textbook Publishers, and the Quality of Schooling," in *Textbooks and Schooling in the United States*, ed. David L. Elliott and Arthur Woodward (Chicago, 1990), 1–22. Also see James D. Watkinson, "Useful Knowledge? Concepts, Values, and Access in American Education, 1776–1840," *HEQ* 30 (Fall 1990): 351–70.

6. "Editorial," *WB* 1 (December 9, 1881): 2 (CHS). According to the *Cleveland School Report* (1876), 113, "The average of necessary expense for text-books, note-books, and other materials, is more than ten dollars per year, a very considerable sum for families of moderate means." A few cities dispensed some free textbooks to some destitute scholars.

7. On Steele's prominence in chemistry, see Paul J. Fay, "The History of Chemistry Teaching in American High Schools," *JCE* 8 (August 1931): 1545. Also read John H. Woodburn and Ellsworth S. Osbourn, *Teaching the Pursuit of Science* (New York, 1965), 193; and Edward J. Larson, "Before the Crusade: Evolution in American Secondary Education Before 1920," *JHB* 20 (Spring 1987): 100.

8. Frank Wigglesworth Clarke, "A Report on the Teaching of Chemistry and Physics in the United States," U.S. Bureau of Education Circular of Information No. 6 (1880), cites an 1880 study of 170 towns and cities, confirming Steele's prominence in the textbook market.

9. "Course of Instruction, or Course of Study," in Kiddle and Schem, *Cyclopedia*, 192.

10. *The System of Education Pursued at the Free Schools in Boston* (Boston, 1823), 16–23 (BPL); *Catalogue of Instructors and Scholars in the English High School* (Boston, 1825), 4 (BPL); *Catalogue of the Bath High School, September, 1867* (Bath, 1867), xiii; *Catalogue of the Lewiston High School* (Lewiston, 1868), 14; and *Catalogue of the Girls' High School, Bangor, Maine, 1860–1865* (Bangor, 1864), 14–15.

11. See sources cited in note 2.

12. Sally H. Wertheim, "Joseph B. Ray," *Biographical Dictionary of American Educators*, ed. John F. Ohles (Westport, Conn., 1978), 3: 1074; and E. S. B., "Francis Bowen," *DAB*, ed. Allen Johnson (New York, 1927), 1: 503–4.

13. "Francis Wayland," *DAB*, ed. Dumas Malone (New York, 1939), 10: 558–60; and "Albert Harkness," *DAB*, ed. Allen Johnson and Dumas Malone (New York, 1936), 4: 265–66.

14. "Alonzo Gray," *A Critical Dictionary of English Literature and British and American Authors*, ed. S. Austin Allibone (Philadelphia, 1858), 1: 723; Nina Baym, "Women and the Republic: Emma Willard's Rhetoric of History," *AQ* 43 (March 1991): 5; and, on Hart, David F. Labaree, *The Making of an American High School: The Credentials Market and the Central High School of Philadelphia, 1838–1939* (New Haven, 1988), 17–19, 72–76. Lloyd P. Jorgenson demonstrates that an incredible number of prominent textbook authors were Protestant ministers (*The State and the Non-Public School, 1825–1925* [Columbia, Mo., 1987], 60–67).

15. "On the Study of the Greek and Latin Languages," *Aca* 1 (September 19, 1818): 61. On the importance of the academies in broadening the secondary curriculum, see John R. Rooney, "The History of the Modern Subjects in the Secondary Curriculum," Ph.D. diss., Catholic University of America, 1926, 47–53; Richard Gerry Durnin, "New England's Eighteenth-Century Incorporated Academies: Their Origin and Development to 1850," Ed.D. diss., University of

Pennsylvania, 1968; Marriet Webster Marr, *The Old New England Academies Founded Before 1828* (New York, 1959), part 4; and Theodore Sizer, ed., *The Age of the Academies* (New York, 1964), 28–30.

16. On modern foreign languages, see Kiddle and Schem, *Cyclopedia*, 792; and *Portland School Report* (1872), 46. Edwin H. Zeydel argues that midwestern high schools gradually came to enroll more pupils in German than French, mostly because the area had many German immigrants ("The Teaching of German in the United States from Colonial Times through World War I," in *Teaching German in America: Prolegomena to a History*, ed. David P. Banseler, Walter F. W. Lohnes, and Valters Nollendorfs [Madison, Wis., 1988], 38). On Barnard see the *Connecticut School Report* (1842), 24; and Edith Nye MacMullen, *In the Cause of True Education: Henry Barnard and Nineteenth-Century School Reform* (New Haven, 1991), 18.

17. Calvin D. Hulbert, *The Academy: Demands for It, and the Conditions of Its Success* (Boston, 1878), 20; and *Dayton School Report* (1876), 109.

18. *Catalogue of Instructors and Scholars*, 1–4; and W. H. Wells, *The Graded School: A Graded Course of Instruction for Public Schools* (New York, 1862), 116–25.

19. Horace Greeley, *Recollections of a Busy Life* (New York, 1869), 56; Deborah Jean Warner, "Science Education for Women in Antebellum America," *Is* 69 (March 1978), 58–67; and Robert V. Bruce, *The Launching of Modern American Science, 1846–1876* (Ithaca, 1987).

20. Edward L. Youmans, *A Class-Book of Chemistry* (New York, 1851), 6; C. A. Brown, "The History of Chemical Education in America Between the Years 1820 and 1870," *JCE* 9 (April 1932): 724; and Bruce, *Launching of Modern American Science*, 96 and 127, on practicality. See also David A. Wells, *Wells's Principles and Applications of Chemistry* (New York, 1858), iii. Contemporaries who favored the subject even worried that its utilitarian value was so obvious that one might ignore its inherent "disciplinary" value for pupils. See Kiddle and Schem, *Cyclopedia*, 125.

21. David A. Wells, *Wells' First Principles of Geology: A Text-Book for Schools, Academies, and Colleges* (New York, 1864), v.

22. "Edward Livingston Youmans," in *DAB*, ed. Dumas Malone (New York, 1936), 10: 615–16; George E. DeBoer, *A History of Ideas in Science Education* (New York, 1991), 4–8; Youmans, *Class-Book*, 6, 15–17, 126, 201–6. In *The Culture Demanded by Modern Life* (New York, 1886), Youmans assailed those who taught "vague metaphysics" or resembled "the refined and elegant scholar, fitted for meditative retirement, in some cloistered seclusion or 'sacred shade,' immersed in the past, and disinclined to meddle with the present" (3, 53).

23. Youmans, *Class-Book*, 331–32, 334.

24. Religious references abounded in science textbooks, for example in Youmans, *Class-Book*, on the "Great Maker of the Universe," 19; John A. Porter, *Principles of Chemistry* (New York, 1868), 4, 63–64; and J. Dorman Steele, *Fourteen Weeks in Chemistry* (New York, 1867), 36–37.

25. Steele, *Fourteen Weeks in Chemistry*, 239–40.

26. Clarke, "A Report on the Teaching of Chemistry and Physics," 15–26; and Fay, "The History of Chemistry Teaching," 1545.

27. Steele, *Fourteen Weeks in Human Physiology* (New York, 1873), 173; and the revised version for the WCTU, *Hygienic Physiology, with Special Reference to the Use of Alcoholic Drinks and Narcotics* (New York, 1884).

28. Horatio N. Robinson, *Elements of Natural Philosophy* (Cincinnati, 1848), iv; Alonzo Gray, *Elements of Natural Philosophy* (New York, 1851), 15–16, 20; David A. Wells, *Wells's Natural Philosophy: For Use of Schools, Academies, and Private Students* (New York, 1857), iii; and J. Dorman Steele, *Fourteen Weeks in Natural Philosophy* (New York, 1872), 13, 38, and 314–15.

29. J. Dorman Steele, *A Fourteen Weeks' Course in Descriptive Astronomy* (New York, 1870), 6; and J. L. Blake, *High School Reader* (Boston, 1832), 61. Colonial ministers had often encouraged the study of astronomy as a way to glorify God's heavens, and one writer in 1851 asserted that astronomy was of great "utility" because it revealed God's handiwork. See Edward D. Mansfield, *American Education, Its Principles and Elements* (New York, 1851), chap. 7, as well as Kiddle and Schem, *Cyclopedia*, 56.

30. James D. Dana, *Manual of Geology* (New York, 1880), 850; Bruce, *Launching of Modern American Science*, 126–27; J. Dorman Steele, *Fourteen Weeks in Popular Geology* (New York, 1870),

7, on "Divine truth," and 251, on gorillas; and Wells, *Wells' First Principles of Geology*, 128–29, on the compatibility between science and Genesis.

31. J. Dorman Steele, *Fourteen Weeks in Zoology* (New York, 1877), 13, 17; "Joel Dorman Steele," in *DAB*, ed. Dumas Malone (New York, 1935), 3: 557; and Bruno Casile, "An Analysis of Zoology Textbooks Available for American Secondary Schools," Ed.D. diss., University of Pittsburgh, 1953, 17–21.

32. Dana, *Manual of Geology*, 578–79; Porter, *Principles of Chemistry*, 2; and Larson, "Before the Crusade," 98–99. On the early modern European background, see Keith Thomas, *Man and the Natural World: Changing Attitudes in England, 1500–1800* (London, 1983); on political economy and natural philosophy, see M. Norton Wise and Crosbie Kent, "Work and Waste: Political Economy and Natural Philosophy in Nineteenth Century Britain," *HS* 27 (1989), 263–301, continued in four parts.

33. Greeley, *Recollections*, 56; William Gardner Hale, *Aims and Methods in Classical Study* (Boston, 1888), 18–19; and Josiah Rhinehart Sypher, *The Art of Teaching School* (Philadelphia, 1872), 27.

34. John Elbert Stout, *The Development of the High-School Curricula in the North Central States from 1860 to 1918* (Chicago, 1921), 45, 56, 75, 111; E. D. M., "Charles Davies," *NTM* 3 (November 1876): 1–4; Floria Cajori, "The Teaching and History of Mathematics in the United States," U.S. Bureau of Education Bulletin No. 3 (1890), 118–20, 294; and Alan R. Osborne and F. Joe Crosswhite, "Forces and Issues Related to Curriculum and Instruction, 7–12," in *A History of Mathematics Education in the United States and Canada* (Washington, D. C., 1970), 157; and Nietz, *Old Textbooks*, 173–78.

35. Patricia Cline Cohen, *A Calculating People: The Spread of Numeracy in Early America* (Chicago, 1982); and David Eugene Smith and Jekuthiel Ginsburg, *A History of Mathematics in America Before 1900* (Chicago, 1934), chaps. 1–2.

36. Mansfield, *American Education*, 133.

37. Nietz, *Old Textbooks*, 177; Joseph Ray, *Ray's Algebra* (Cincinnati, 1848), 3; Ray, *Elements of Algebra, for Colleges, Schools, and Private Students* (Cincinnati, 1852), iii; Horatio Nelson Robinson, *An Elementary Treatise on Algebra: Designed for Schools, Colleges, and Private Students* (Cincinnati, 1846), iii–v; and the various writings of Charles Davies, who translated many important French works and added many practical, commercial problems to his own texts.

38. Benjamin Greenleaf, *A Practical Treatise on Algebra, Designed for the Use of Students in High Schools and Academies* (Boston, 1854), iii; and Daniel W. Fish, *The Progressive Higher Arithmetic, for Schools, Academies, and Mercantile Colleges* (New York, 1860), iii. Edward Brooks stated that most students wanted to use mathematics in everyday life, so he offered his textbook to consumers for its "especially practical" qualities (*The Normal Higher Arithmetic, Designed for Advanced Classes in Common Schools, Normal Schools, High Schools, Academies . . .* [Philadelphia, 1877], vi).

39. See, for example, Fish, *Progressive Higher Arithmetic*, table of contents; Dana Colburn, *Arithmetic and Its Applications; Designed as a Text Book for Common Schools, High Schools, and Academies* (Philadelphia, 1855); Benjamin Greenleaf, *The National Arithmetic* (Boston, 1852), first published twelve years before; and *Ray's Modern Practical Arithmetic, A Revised Edition of Ray's Practical Arithmetic* (New York, 1877). On the commercial orientation of mathematics, see Cohen, *A Calculating People*, 121–27 and 137.

40. This observation is based upon the examination of fifteen algebra textbooks published between the 1820s and 1870s.

41. Ebenezer Bailey, *First Lessons in Algebra* (Boston, 1833), 103. Cohen, *A Calculating People*, 164–65, notes how recognition of the rise of social classes led to more quantification and measurement of this phenomenon.

42. Bailey, *First Lessons*, 115, 128, 129, 131, and 151.

43. "Contraries," in A. N. Johnson and Jason White, *The Young Minstrel* (Boston, 1843), 111.

44. Charles Davies, *Elementary Algebra* (New York, 1845), 88. For comparisons of the worlds of workers and gentlemen, see Elias Loomis, *The Elements of Algebra* (New York, 1851), 22, 23, 25, 28, 30, 34, 35, 252–54; and Greenleaf, *A Practical Treatise*, 80, 83–88.

45. Ray, *Ray's Algebra*, 124, 130. Horatio Nelson Robinson, *New Elementary Algebra; Containing the Rudiments of the Science for Schools and Academies* (New York, 1860), 138, which has several examples of irresponsible workers.

46. Robinson, *New Elementary Algebra*, 138, 310; *Soule's Intermediate, Philosophic Arithmetic* (New Orleans, 1874), 217–18; and D. B. Hagar, *An Elementary Algebra* (Philadelphia, 1873), which contained the standard problems on idle or undependable workers; especially see the example on page 222.

47. Dennis E. Baron, *Grammar and Good Taste: Reforming the American Language* (New Haven, 1982), is indispensable. Also see Rollo LaVerne Lyman, "English Grammar in American Schools Before 1850," U.S. Bureau of Education Bulletin No. 12 (1922); Stephen Nelson Judy, "The Teaching of English Composition in American Secondary Schools, 1850–1893," Ph.D. diss., Northwestern University, 1967, chap. 1; Gene Lawrence Piché, "Revision and Reform in the Secondary School English Curriculum, 1870–1900," Ph.D. diss., University of Minnesota, 1967, chaps. 1–2; and Robert Stanley Whitman, "The Development of the Curriculum in Secondary English to 1960," Ph.D. diss., University of Illinois, 1973, chap. 2. Kenneth Cmiel, in *Democratic Eloquence: The Fight Over Popular Speech in Nineteenth-Century America* (New York, 1990), 186, points to the decline of teaching grammar in some high schools by the 1870s.

48. Baron, *Grammar and Good Taste*, 140–50; Lindley Murray, *Abridgement of Murray's English Grammar* (Peekskill, N.Y., 1830), 9; Lyman, *English Grammar,* 112; and Jorgenson, *State and the Non-Public School,* 63.

49. Murray, *Abridgement*, 49, 53, 55, and 64–65. Contemporaries complained about Murray's plagiarism. See Kiddle and Schem, *Cyclopedia*, 379–80.

50. Murray, *Abridgement*, 85, 91, 99; and Murray, *English Exercises* (Boston, 1819), 132, 134, 142. Many competitors offered similar exercises, mixing language lessons with tutoring in moral and political economy. See, for example, Peter Bullions, *The Principles of English Grammar* (New York, 1846), on "Promiscuous Exercises" in syntax, 134–37. Praise for human industry and criticisms of idleness appeared in "rival" texts: Samuel Kirkham, *English Grammar in Familiar Lectures*, 63d ed. (Baltimore, 1834), 105, 108, 117, 124, 160, 196; Goold Brown, *The Institutes of English Grammar* (New York, 1853, orig. pub. 1823), 24, 30, 155, 182, 194, 206; and Roswell C. Smith, *Smith's English Grammar, On the Productive System* (Richmond, Va., 1864, orig. pub. 1831), 13, 15, 51, and 113.

51. *The High School Book: Being a Selection of Lessons for Reading and Speaking* (New Haven, 1835), 38; Blake, *High School Reader,* 17, 37–39, 101–2, 200–202, 240; and Lindley Murray, *The English Reader* (Poughkeepsie, 1811), 33.

52. George Howland, *A Practical Grammar of the English Language* (Chicago, 1867), 14, 20; and John S. Hart, *A Manual of Composition and Rhetoric* (New York, 1870), 10 and 15. William H. Wells offered similar pieties about hard work, diligence, study, and so forth in his acclaimed volume, *A Grammar of the English Language* (Chicago, 1858), 13, 15, 19, 27, and 108. Franklin's spirit was everywhere; see William Swinton's *A School Manual of English Composition* (New York, 1877), 7.

53. Hart, *Manual*, 99, 104.

54. David J. Hill, *The Elements of Rhetoric and Composition: A Text-Book for Schools and Colleges* (New York, 1878), 26. Propriety also demanded avoiding popular but vulgar words such as *enthused, locomote,* or *bonanza* (28). Despite competing approaches to the study of rhetoric, Kiddle and Schem, in their *Cyclopedia*, 734, could still conclude: "The value of rhetoric, as a branch of study, is to be tested by its practical utility, by what it contributes towards developing clearness, force, and beauty of expression in language." Daniel Walker Howe emphasizes how speaking well was still prized in the antebellum period (*The Political Culture of the American Whigs* [Chicago, 1979], 25–29); and Cmiel, *Democratic Eloquence*, 191, points to the growing interest in "refined" language in school and society in the 1870s and 1880s.

55. Kiddle and Schem, *Cyclopedia*, 79, 277–80; John S. Hart, *A Manual of American Literature: A Text-Book for Schools and Colleges* (Philadelphia, 1873); Judy, "Teaching of English Composition," 60; Albert P. Southwick, *Question Book of American Literature* (Syracuse, 1883), n.p., which emphasized American authors; and the heavily assigned text by Charles D. Cleveland, *A Compendium of*

American Literature, 3d ed. (Philadelphia, 1859), discussed in Peter David Witt, "The Beginnings of the Teaching of Vernacular Literature in the Secondary Schools of Massachusetts," Ed.D. diss., Harvard University, 1968, 139–45.

56. H. White, *Elements of Universal History* (Philadelphia, 1849), 13–15, 154; and Richmal Mangnall, *Historical and Miscellaneous Questions* (New York, 1863), 9. Mangnall's history was in its eighty-fourth London edition and fifth American edition.

57. J. L. Blake, *The Historical Reader* (Rochester, 1837), iii, 9–15; S. G. Goodrich, *A Pictorial History of Greece* (Philadelphia, 1846); S. G. Goodrich, *Modern History, From the Fall of Rome, A.D. 476, to the Present Time* (Louisville, 1847), 50–58, 90–98, 206; and Samuel Whelpley, *A Compend of History, From the Earliest Times . . .*, 8th ed. (New York, 1925), 131–38.

58. Goodrich, *Modern History*, 142, 221–56, 482–83, 543; and S. R. Hall and A. R. Barker, *School History of the United States* (Boston, 1838), 365.

59. *St. Louis School Report* (1874), 70; Hall and Barker, *School History*, 3–4; J. B. Shurtleff, *The Governmental Instructor, Or a Brief and Comprehensive View of the Government of the United States, and of the State Governments, In Easy Lessons, Designed for the Use of Schools*, 4th ed. (New York, 1846), 17, who noted in the preface that history was "useful knowledge."

60. Nietz, *Old Textbooks*, chap. 7; J. Dorman Steele, *Brief History of the United States* (New York, 1871); G. P. Quackenbos, *Illustrated School History of the United States of America* (New York, 1877); William Swinton, *A Condensed School History of the United States* (New York, 1871); Mansfield, *American Education*, chap. 8 (on "utility"); and, on elementary school history and geography textbooks, Elson, *Guardians of Tradition*.

61. Marcius Willson, *History of the United States* (New York, 1855), 372; Stout, *Development of the High-School Curriculum*, 180; and Steele, *Brief History*, vi.

62. S. Augustus Mitchell, *A General View of the World* (Philadelphia, 1847), 3; Nietz, *Old Textbooks*, 229–30; Heber Eliot Rumble, "Early Geography Instruction in America," *SSt* 37 (October 1946): 266–68; and Sidney Rosen, "A Short History of High School Geography," *JG* 56 (December 1967): 405–6.

63. S. Augustus Mitchell, *An Ancient Geography, Classical and Sacred* (Philadelphia, 1860), 11; Mitchell, *General View*, 18, 21–25, 298, 521, 535–36, 691–92; and Sister Marie Leonore Fell, *The Foundations of Nativism in American Textbooks, 1783–1860* (Washington, D.C., 1941), chaps. 8 and 10. On Western superiority and the "classes" of peoples around the world, see Sarah S. Cornell, *Cornell's High School Geography* (New York, 1856), 13; James Monteith and S. T. Frost, *McNally's System of Geography, for Schools, Academies, and Seminaries* (New York, 1866), 7, 118; *Appletons' Elementary Geography* (New York, 1880), 82; *Colton's Common School Geography* (New York, 1868), 16, 30, 88; and *Harper's School Geography* (New York, 1874), 18, 116–18.

64. Arnold Guyot, *The Earth and Man* (Boston, 1849), 11–13, 232, and 237, where he describes the Congo Negro, with "the retreating forehead, the prominent mouth, the thick lips, the flat nose, the wooly head, the strongly developed hind-head," all of which "announce the preponderance of the sensual and physical appetites over the noble faculties of the intellect." On Guyot's influence, see Kiddle and Schem, *Cyclopedia*, 334, 394; Eric Fischer, Robert D. Campbell, and Eldon S. Miller, *A Question of Place: The Development of Geographic Thought* (Arlington, Va., 1967), 357; and Rosen, "Short History," 407–8.

65. Henry Vethake, *The Principles of Political Economy* (Philadelphia, 1838), section entitled "Book Fifth." Also see R. D. Freeman, "Adam Smith, Education, and Laissez-Faire," *HPE* 1 (1969): 173–86; David Horowitz, "Textbook Models of American Economic Growth, 1837–1911," *HPE* 7 (Summer 1975): 227–51; and John E. Waldron, "The Historical Development of American Secondary School Economics Textbooks to 1900," Ph.D. diss., University of Pittsburgh, 1955, 136, 145, 150–51, 155, and 161.

66. Francis Wayland, *The Elements of Political Economy* (Boston, 1841), 152. J. T. Champlin's judgment was typical: "Man has been styled a 'lazy animal,' and with reason. Labor is irksome to him; if it were not, he would value it at nothing, and hence set no price upon its exertion or results" (*Lessons on Political Economy* [New York, 1868], 71). Also see Amasa Walker in *The Science of Wealth: A Manual of Political Economy* (Philadelphia, 1872), 31. On the views of Adam Smith and

classical economists on labor, see Jonathan A. Glickstein, *Concepts of Free Labor in Antebellum America* (New Haven, 1991), 127.

67. Francis Wayland, *The Elements of Moral Science* (Boston, 1835), 376. Warnings about indiscriminate almsgiving to the poor appeared in many political economy texts. Many algebra problems solved in high school, as well as sentences corrected in English grammar classes, warned against encouraging laziness by giving money to those who did not deserve it.

68. Francis Bowen, *American Political Economy* (New York, 1870), 15, 18. "Political economy assumes as its basis in human nature that men in their business affairs are governed by *selfishness*," argued Champlin's *Lessons*, 13–14. One lesson in false syntax in Brown, *The Institutes of English Grammar*, 213, read: "Among every class of people self-interest prevails."

69. Bowen, *American Political Economy*, 107.

70. Laurens P. Hickok, *A System of Moral Science* (Schenectady, 1853), 97–98.

The Business of Teaching

1. *"Old Central School" Re-Union* (Cincinnati, 1856), 5 (CHS); Isaac M. Martin, *History of the Schools of Cincinnati* (Cincinnati, 1900), chaps. 3–4; and *"Old Woodward": A Memorial Relating to Woodward High School, 1831–1836 and Woodward College, 1836–1851* (Cincinnati, 1884).

2. *"Old Central School,"* 19–21, 24–26.

3. *"Old Central School,"* 28–31.

4. *The Annual* (Cincinnati, 1870): 51–60 (CHS).

5. *Boston School Report* (1867), 88; and *Hartford School Report* (1873), 20. Such tributes, common in the nineteenth century, reflected the missionary nature of public school teaching.

6. *Cincinnati School Report* (1854), 43–46; (1855), 89–92; (1856), 70–73; (1857), 119–22; (1858), 49–50; (1859), 41–45; and (1860), 59–67.

7. *The Annual*, 52–53.

8. *The Annual*, 56–58.

9. Atlanta's superintendent proudly announced in 1879 that his secondary instructors were "chosen with reference to their skill, experience, and scholarship" (*Atlanta School Report* [1879], 16). Also see Maris A. Vinovskis, "Trends in Massachusetts Education, 1826–1880," *HEQ* 12 (Winter 1972): 522.

10. *Cincinnati School Report* (1853), 10.

11. *Cincinnati School Report* (1854), 32. Also see Nancy Jean Rosenbloom, "Cincinnati's Common Schools: The Politics of Reform, 1829–1853," Ph.D. diss., University of Rochester, 1981, 187–237; John L. Rury, "Who Became Teachers? The Social Characteristics of Teachers in American History," in *American Teachers: Histories of a Profession at Work*, ed. Donald Warren (New York, 1989), 9–48; Michael W. Sedlak, "'Let Us Go and Buy a School Master': Historical Perspectives on the Hiring of Teachers in the United States, 1750–1980," in Warren, *American Teachers*, 257–90; and Geraldine Joncich Clifford, "Man/Woman/Teacher: Gender, Family and Career in American Educational History," in Warren, *American Teachers*, 293–343.

12. "Carter's Essays on Popular Education," *USRLG* 1 (February 1827): 351; William C. Fowler, "Influence of Academies and High Schools on Common Schools," in *The Introductory Discourse and the Lectures Delivered Before the American Institute of Instruction* (Boston, 1832), 190–91; and Paul H. Mattingly, *The Classless Profession: American Schoolmen of the Nineteenth Century* (New York, 1975).

13. Quoted in Thomas B. Davis, *Chronicles of the Hopkins Grammar School, 1660–1935* (New Haven, 1938), 411; and "Who is a Professor?" *OhEM* 11 (November 1862): 354. An English visitor, the Rev. James Fraser, smirked at the pomposity at New York's Free Academy and Philadelphia's Central High (Schools Inquiry Commissions, *Report . . . On the Common School System of the United States and of the Provinces of Upper and Lower Canada* [London, 1866], 130). Also see P. A. Siljestrom, *Educational Institutions of the United States* (London, 1853), 306; and *Iowa School Report* (1858), 15.

14. The Rev. Baynard R. Hall, *Teaching, A Science: The Teacher, An Artist* (New York, 1848), 222; Emit Duncan Grizzell, *Origin and Development of the High School in New England Before 1865*

(Philadelphia, 1923), 34, on the centrality of academies in preparing high school instructors; and George Frederick Miller, *The Academy System of the State of New York* (Albany, 1922).

15. "George B. Emerson," *AJE* 5 (September 1858): 417–26; Stanley K. Schultz, *The Culture Factory: Boston Public Schools, 1789–1860* (New York, 1973), 59; and Michael B. Katz, *Reconstructing American Education* (Cambridge, 1987), 99–100, who notes that a Boston high school teacher still had higher status than a Harvard mathematics professor in the 1880s.

16. Larkin Dunton, *A Memorial of the Life and Services of John D. Philbrick* (Boston, 1887), 14–27, 31–48. On the ladders of opportunity, see David F. Labaree, "Career Ladders and the Early Public High School Teacher: A Study of Inequality and Opportunity," in Warren, *American Teachers*, 157–89.

17. Pauline Holmes, *A Tercentenary History of the Boston Public Latin School* (Cambridge, 1935), chap. 5; Arthur Wellington Brayley, *Schools and Schoolboys of Old Boston* (Boston, 1894), 97; and Silas Hertzler, *The Rise of the Public High School in Connecticut* (Baltimore, 1930), 164–69.

18. *Vermont School Report* (1849), 9.

19. Charles Hammond, "New England Academies and Classical Schools," *AJE* 16 (September 1866): 424.

20. Frederick A. Packard, *The Daily Public School in the United States* (Philadelphia, 1866), 127–28; and *Cleveland School Report* (1863), 72.

21. Henry Kiddle and A. J. Schem, *The Dictionary of Education and Instruction* (New York, 1881), 218; William A. Mowry, *Recollections of a New England Educator, 1838–1908* (New York, 1908), 109; *Cincinnati School Report* (1853), 44; (1873), 67–68; (1878), 67; and *St. Louis School Report* (1873), 55.

22. *Ohio School Report* (1880), 33–34.

23. *Middletown School Report* (1865), 8, 23; and *Minnesota School Report* (1875), 151.

24. *New Hampshire School Report* (1849), 43.

25. Calvin Olin Davis, *Public Secondary Education* (Chicago, 1917), 186–87; Carl D. Washburn, "The Rise of the High School in Ohio," Ph.D. diss., Ohio State University, 1932, chap. 7; *Ohio School Report* (1855), 5; *Indiana School Report* (1861), 6; and *New Hampshire School Report* (1880), 146–57. See the various statistics in the *New Hampshire School Reports*, 1877–80.

26. *St. Louis School Report* (1858), ix; (1871), ciii. Cleveland's high school principal in 1869 was a man assisted by three men and two women, as noted in the *Cleveland School Report* (1869), 99, compared with the figures in the *Cleveland School Report* (1875), 48; and (1878), 24.

27. *New York City School Report* (1872), 31–32; (1874), 81–83; *Philadelphia School Report* (1862), 182; and *Boston School Report* (1878), 109–11.

28. *Portland School Report* (1857), 6; and *Philadelphia School Report* (1862), 189. On the moral, Christian role of teachers in the classroom and community, see Edward D. Mansfield, *American Education: Its Principles and Elements* (New York, 1851), chaps. 1 and 4; David P. Page, *Theory and Practice of Teaching: Or, The Motives and Methods of Good School-Keeping* (New York, 1852), chap. 2; and John S. Hart, *In the School-Room: Chapters in the Philosophy of Education* (Philadelphia, 1868), 249.

29. *Chicago School Report* (1856), 6–7; *Madison School Report* (1858), 13–16; *Middletown School Report* (1865), 8; *Bridgeport School Report* (1877), 27; and George T. Fleming, *My High School Days* (Pittsburgh, 1904), 21.

30. *Philadelphia School Report* (1846), 221; (1853), 22; Franklin Spencer Edmonds, *History of the Central High School of Philadelphia* (Philadelphia, 1902), 38–41; David F. Labaree, *The Making of an American High School: The Credentials Market and the Central High School of Philadelphia, 1838–1939* (New Haven, 1988), 108–9.

31. *Pennsylvania School Report* (1876), 181; and the information printed in the *Chicago School Report* (1879). I am indebted to Dina Stephens, a graduate research assistant, for her help in analyzing this data.

32. *Ohio School Report* (1878), 77.

33. *Report of the Commissioner of Education for the Year 1880* (Washington, D. C., 1882), table 2, 421–27.

34. *Sandusky School Report* (1860), 22; (1874), 23; and (1876), 17.

35. See Kathryn Kish Sklar, *Catherine Beecher: A Study in Domesticity* (New York, 1973); and the biographies of Barnard previously cited in this study.

36. *Philadelphia School Report* (1846), 84.

37. *Portland School Report* (1874), 3.

38. "Improvement of Common Schools," *NAR* 24 (January 1827): 159–60.

39. G. E. Seymour, "Fetichism in Education," *NTM* 1 (February 1875): 103.

40. Samuel R. Hall, *Lectures on School-Keeping* (Boston, 1829), 111; and "Education and Literary Institutions," *QR* 5 (May 1833): 274.

41. See Carl F. Kaestle, ed., *Joseph Lancaster and the Monitorial School Movement* (New York, 1973), 1–49; David Hogan, "The Market Revolution and Disciplinary Power: Joseph Lancaster and the Psychology of the Early Classroom System," *HEQ* 29 (Fall 1989): 381–417; "Course of Education in the New-York High-School," *AJE* 1 (January 1826): 23–29; John H. Griscom, *Memoir of John Griscom, LL.D.* (New York, 1859), chap. 6; Walter John Gifford, *Historical Development of the New York State High School System* (Albany, 1922), 23–25; and William R. Johnson, "'Chanting Choristers': Simultaneous Recitation in Baltimore's Nineteenth-Century Primary Schools," *HEQ* 34 (Spring 1994): 1–23.

42. "Boston High School for Girls," *AJE* 1 (June 1826): 380–81; "Public High School of Salem," *AJE* 3 (July 1828): 492–93; and Orwin Bradford Griffin, *The Evolution of the Connecticut State School System* (New York, 1928), 109–10.

43. George B. Emerson, *Reminiscences of an Old Teacher* (Boston, 1878), 56, 58. Also see Siljestrom, *Educational Institutions*, 304, on the ubiquitous recitations at the large eastern high schools he visited.

44. "Principle of Emulation," *NAR* 43 (October 1836): 496, 503.

45. *Connecticut School Report* (1868), 126; and Emerson, *Reminiscences*, 54.

46. Emerson, *Reminiscences*, 62.

47. Nancy Green, "Female Education and School Competition," *HEQ* 18 (Summer 1978): 129–42. For a typical response from a girls' high school, read John Swett, *Methods of Teaching: A Hand-Book of Principles, Directions, and Working Models for Common School Teachers* (New York, 1880), 68.

48. G. Dallas Lind, *Methods of Teaching in Country Schools* (Danville, Ind., 1880), 19; and James H. Canfield, *Opportunities of the Rural Population for Higher Education* (Syracuse, 1889), 4, where the author concluded that most schoolgoing youth were still in ungraded rural schools. The percentage varied by region from 80–90 percent in the South to 50–60 percent in the West to 20–30 percent in the Northeast and Middle West.

49. The estimates on the time students spent studying and reciting are based on reading annual school reports for dozens of towns and cities before the 1880s. See, for example, Fraser, *Report . . . on the Common School System*, 132; *Philadelphia School Report* (1849), 130; *St. Louis School Report* (1869), 37; and (1874), 29; and Fleming, *My High School Days*, 13.

50. "Ohio Teachers' Association," *OhEM* 17 (September 1868): 290; *San Francisco School Report* (1875), 297; on New Orleans, *Louisiana School Report* (1874), 355; *Maine School Report* (1880): 82–83; and, on similar pedagogical practices in academies, Richard Gerry Durnin, "New England's Eighteenth-Century Incorporated Academies: Their Origin and Development to 1850," Ed.D. diss., University of Pennsylvania, 1968, 98–99; Nicholas D. Colucci, "Connecticut Academies for Females," Ph.D. diss., University of Connecticut, 1969, 210–20; and Theodore R. Sizer, ed., *The Age of the Academies* (New York, 1964), 29, 39–40.

51. Hall, *Teaching*, 20, 31.

52. Page, *Theory and Practice of Teaching*, 79; and David Cole, "Classical Education," *AJE* 1 (August 1855): 68–69. On memorization, see Josiah Rhinehart Sypher, *The Art of Teaching School* (Philadelphia, 1872), 26; Seymour, "Fetichism," 103; and Albert Plympton Southwick, *A Quiz Book on the Theory and Practice of Teaching* (Logansport, Ind., 1887), 167.

53. John Ogden, *The Art of Teaching* (Cincinnati, 1879), 43, 85. On Latin grammar, see Rollo Laverne Lyman, "English Grammar in American Schools Before 1850," U.S. Bureau of Education Bulletin No. 12 (1922), chaps. 1, 5; and Donald E. Stahl, "The Development of the English Curriculum in the Chicago Public High Schools from 1856 to 1958," Ph.D. diss., Northwestern University, 1960, chap. 3. On the continuing importance of individual recitations, see Edwin C. Hewitt, *A Treatise on Pedagogy* (Cincinnati, 1884), 159–60; J. V. Coombs, *School Management and Methods of Instruction*

(Indianapolis, 1883), 45; George Howland, *Practical Hints for the Teachers of Public Schools* (New York, 1890), chap. 8; and Emerson E. White, *The Elements of Pedagogy* (New York, 1886), 173–90.

54. David Hamilton, "Adam Smith and the Moral Economy of the Classroom System," *JCS* 12 (October–December 1980): 283–89; and Page, *Theory and Practice of Teaching*, 123–24, 129. Spokespersons for early academies, like their high school counterparts, were divided over the value of prizes, but they also generally awarded them. See Harriet Webster Marr, *The Old New England Academies Founded Before 1826* (New York, 1959), chap. 22; and Colucci, "Connecticut Academies," 221–25.

55. Charles Northend, *The Teacher and the Parent: A Treatise Upon Common-School Education; Containing Practical Suggestions to Teachers and Parents* (Boston, 1853), 150; Page, *Theory and Practice*, chap. 8; Amos M. Kellogg, *The New Education: School Management, Practical Guide for the Teacher in the School Room* (New York, 1880), 36–37; and James P. Wickersham, *School Economy* (Philadelphia, 1864), 149.

56. William H. Wells, *The Graded School: A Graded Course of Instruction for Public Schools* (New York, 1862), 145. Also see the criticism by Edwin C. Hewett, *A Treatise on Pedagogy* (Cincinnati, 1884), 211.

57. Henry Kiddle and Alexander J. Schem, eds., *The Cyclopedia of Education: A Dictionary of Information for the Use of Teachers, School Officers, Parents, and Others* (London, 1877), 260; and Swett, *Methods of Teaching*, 68.

58. Seymour, "Fetichism," 104.

59. The best studies of teachers in the period include Barbara Finkelstein, *Governing the Young: Teacher Behavior in Popular Primary Schools in 19th Century United States* (New York, 1989); Carl F. Kaestle, *Pillars of the Republic: Common Schools and American Society, 1780–1860* (New York, 1984), chap. 6; and the relevant essays in Warren, *American Teachers*.

60. Lelia Patridge, comp., *Notes of Talks on Teaching, Given by Francis W. Parker* (New York, 1883), chap. 23; and White, *Elements of Pedagogy*, 148–49, 198–208.

61. Lyman, *English Grammar*, chap. 1; Stahl, "Development of the English Curriculum," chaps. 3, 5; Gene Lawrence Piché, "Revision and Reform in the Secondary School English Curriculum, 1870–1900," Ph.D. diss., University of Minnesota, 1967, 17, 20, 80–81, 92–98, 101; and Dennis E. Baron, *Grammar and Good Taste: Reforming the American Language* (New Haven, 1982), 142. Contemporaries often saw intimate ties between developing reading skills and speaking skills. See Ebenezer Porter, *The Rhetorical Reader* (Andover, 1831), iii, vii; *The High School Book: Being a Selection of Lessons for Reading and Speaking* (New Haven, 1835), 3; Epes Sargent, *The Standard Speaker; Containing Exercises in Prose and Poetry for Declamation in Schools, Academies, Lyceums, Colleges,* 12th ed. (Philadelphia, 1864); and J. C. Zachos, *The High School Speaker: A Collection of Declamations, Poetic Pieces and Dialogues* (Cincinnati, 1868).

62. Ephraim Hunt, *Literature of the English Language; Comprising Representative Selections from the Best Authors* (New York, 1870), iii; and David J. Hill, *The Elements of Rhetoric and Composition: A Text-Book for Schools and Colleges* (New York, 1878), v. See also Charles D. Cleveland, *A Compendium of American Literature*, 3d ed. (Philadelphia, 1859); and John S. Hart, *A Manual of American Literature: A Text-Book for Schools and Colleges* (Philadelphia, 1873).

63. Marcius Willson, *History of the United States* (New York, 1855). In a chapter on South Carolina, Willson wrote: "The pleasant location of 'Oyster Point,' between the rivers Ashley and Cooper, had early attracted the attention of the settlers, and had gained a few inhabitants; and in 1860 the foundation of a new town was laid there, which was called Charleston." Which led to the typical question: "Give an account of the settlement and progress of Charlestown" (161). Also see Joel Dorman Steele, *A Brief History of the United States* (New York, 1871).

64. William Swinton, *A Condensed School History of the United States* (New York, 1871), iii. Also see Agnew O. Roorbach, *The Development of the Social Studies in American Secondary Education Before 1861* (Philadelphia, 1937), 79–82, 92. For a taste of fact-filled textbooks and rote questions, see H. White, *Elements of Universal History* (Philadelphia, 1849); S. G. Goodrich, *A Pictorial History of Greece: Ancient and Modern* (Philadelphia, 1855); and Richmal Mangnall, *Historical and Miscellaneous Questions*, 84th London ed., 5th American ed. (New York, 1863).

65. *Boston School Report* (1855), 75; (1863), 67; and Benjamin Adams Hathaway, *1001 Questions and Answers on the Theory and Practice of Teaching* (Lebanon, Ohio, 1886), 101.

66. W. L. Mayo, *The Development and Status of Secondary School Geography in the United States and Canada* (Ann Arbor, 1965), 1–12; John R. Sahli, "An Analysis of Early American Geography Textbooks from 1784 to 1840," Ph.D. diss., University of Pittsburgh, 1941, chaps. 1, 3, 5; and Ned Culler, "The Development of American Geography Textbooks from 1840 to 1890," Ph.D. diss., University of Pittsburgh, 1945, chaps. 1–3.

67. S. Augustus Mitchell, *A General View of the World* (Philadelphia, 1847), iv; S. Augustus Mitchell, *Mitchell's Geographical Question Book* (Philadelphia, 1852), which contains 139 pages of questions and answers; Arnold Guyot, *Physical Geography* (New York, 1885, orig. pub. 1873); Mayo, *Development and Status*, 15; James Monteith and S. T. Frost, *McNally's System of Geography for Schools, Academies, and Seminaries* (New York, 1866), preface, n.p.; and, another example of presenting beautiful color maps along with scores of rote questions and answers, George W. Fitch and George Woodworth Colton, *Colton and Fitch's Modern School Geography* (New York, 1857).

68. Sarah S. Cornell, *Cornell's High School Geography* (New York, 1856), 50, 64.

69. Joseph Ray, *Ray's Algebra* (Cincinnati, 1848), 25–30; and Edward Olney, *The Complete School Algebra* (New York, 1870), vii. Authors often urged students to memorize dozens of rules and definitions. Daniel W. Fish provided fifty-seven definitions (with even more "sub-definitions") in the space of seven pages; see *The Progressive Higher Arithmetic, for Schools, Academies, and Mercantile Colleges* (New York, 1860), 11–18. Self-proclaimed, bombastic Pestalozzians were often no better, as evidenced in *Soule's Intermediate, Philosophic Arithmetic* (New Orleans, 1874), 9–13.

70. Floria Cajori, "The Teaching and History of Mathematics in the United States," Bureau of Information Bulletin No. 3 (1890), 106, which notes how the ideas of Pestalozzi were more influential in elementary than in high school teaching. Also see Willard Ellsbree, *The American Teacher* (New York, 1939), 233.

71. Kiddle and Schem, *Cyclopedia*, 22; and *The System of Education Pursued at the Free Schools in Boston* (Boston, 1823), 21 (BPL).

72. J. W. MacDonald, *Geometry in the Secondary School* (Boston, 1889), 4, 23–24; *Columbus, Ohio, School Report* (1877), 143; and Alva Walker Stamper, *A History of the Teaching of Elementary Geometry* (New York, 1909), 99–103.

73. James M'Intire, *A New Treatise on Astronomy, and the Use of Globes, for the Use of High Schools and Academies* (New York, 1860), 25. Elias Loomis, in *Elements of Astronomy* (New York, 1869), preface, n.p., noted: "Great care has been taken to render every statement clear and concise, and it is important that the student, in his recitations, should be trained to a similar precision." Also see Frank Wigglesworth Clarke, "A Report on the Teaching of Chemistry and Physics in the United States," U.S. Bureau of Education Circular of Information No. 6 (1880), 15–26; the question-and-answer–oriented volume by the popular J. Dorman Steele, *Manual of Science for Teachers: Including Answers to the Practical Questions and Problems in the Author's Scientific Text Books* (New York, 1870); and Albert P. Southwick, *Question Book of Physics, With Notes, Queries, Etc.* (Syracuse, 1881).

74. Clarke, "Report on the Teaching of Chemistry and Physics," 17; Samuel Ralph Powers, "A History of the Teaching of Chemistry in the Secondary Schools of the United States Previous to 1850," *RPUM* 13 (November 1920): 20–24; Sidney Rosen, "The Rise of High-School Chemistry in America," *JCE* 33 (1956): 628–30; Paul J. Fay, "The History of Chemistry Teaching in American High Schools," *JCE* 8 (August 1931): 1533–62; and John H. Woodburn and Ellsworth S. Osbourn, *Teaching the Pursuit of Science* (New York, 1965), 170.

75. Labaree, *Making of an American High School*, 22; *Chicago School Report* (1868), 118; and *Maine School Report* (1880), 85.

76. Sidney Rosen, "A Short History of High School Geography," *JG* 56 (December 1967): 406; Heber Eliot Rumble, "Early Geography Instruction in America," *SSt* 37 (October 1946): 266–68; Elsbree, *The American Teacher*, 215–28; *Cincinnati School Report* (1870), 110; and *Philadelphia School Report* (1875), 40.

77. *Chicago School Report* (1868), 117; Margaret Blythe, "Samuel M. Capron, The Man and the Teacher," in *Memorial of Samuel Mills Capron*, ed. J. H. Twichell (Hartford, 1874), 41–42.

78. "School Architecture," *AJE* 11 (September 1862): 607.

79. Parker, *Notes of Talks*, 150–51.

80. Parker, *Notes of Talks*, 155; and White, *Elements of Universal History*, 148.

Scaling Olympus

1. *Catalogue of Instructers [sic] and Scholars in the English High School* (Boston, 1825), 3 (BPL).

2. George B. Emerson, *Reminiscences of an Old Teacher* (Boston, 1878), 52; and *Regulations of the School Committee of the City of Boston* (Boston, 1823), 15, 24 (LC). Also see Robert M. W. Travers, *How Research Has Changed American Schools: A History from 1840 to the Present* (Kalamazoo, 1983), chap. 1.

3. Michael B. Katz, *Reconstructing American Education* (Cambridge, 1987), 15–19; Marvin Meyers, *The Jacksonian Persuasion* (Stanford, 1957), chap. 2; and Henry L. Watson, *Liberty and Power: The Politics of Jacksonian America* (New York, 1990), 135. Hartford educators said taking the test was a "manly" activity (*Connecticut School Report* [1877], 192).

4. M. Cotton, "We'll Study On," in E. H. Bascom and M. Cotton, *The School Harp* (Boston, 1855), 14.

5. Margo J. Anderson, *The American Census: A Social History* (New Haven, 1988), chaps. 1–3; and Patricia Cline Cohen, *A Calculating People: The Spread of Numeracy in Early America* (Chicago, 1982).

6. *Boston School Report* (1872), 10–11. Francis H. Underwood, chair of the School Committee, nevertheless criticized the grammar masters for holding pupils back who should have applied for the Latin School or other high schools.

7. David B. Tyack, *The One Best System: A History of American Urban Education* (Cambridge, 1974), 57; and Mary D. Bradford, *Memoirs of Mary D. Bradford* (Evansville, Wis., 1932), 105–6.

8. *Chicago School Report* (1872), 79.

9. On the rising importance of written examinations, see "Examinations," in *The Cyclopedia of Education: A Dictionary of Information for the Use of Teachers, School Officers, Parents, and Others*, ed. Henry Kiddle and Alexander J. Schem (New York, 1877), 288–91; Emerson E. White, "Promotion and Examinations in Graded Schools," U.S. Bureau of Education Circular No. 7 (1891); *Richmond School Report* (1873), 290; and Daniel Calhoun, *The Intelligence of a People* (Princeton, 1973), 61–78, 322–35. On the mixture of oral and written examinations in the 1840s, see Silas Hertzler, *The Rise of the Public High School in Connecticut* (Baltimore, 1930), 51.

10. William H. Wells, *The Graded School: A Graded Course of Instruction For Public Schools; with Copious Practical Directions to Teachers* (New York, 1862), 129.

11. A. D. Bache, *Report to the Controllers of the Public Schools, On the Re-Organization of the Central High School of Philadelphia* (Philadelphia, 1839), 27 (BM); and J. L. Dawson and H. W. DeSaussure, *Census of the City of Charleston, South Carolina, for the Year 1848* (Charleston, 1849), 55–57 (LC).

12. Proof of moral values was everywhere a precondition to admission to the test. See *Public Schools of the City of Boston* (Boston, 1838), 12 (LC), and the verbatim language in the *San Francisco School Report* (1864), 48–49. Also see the *Cincinnati School Report* (1848), 25; the *St. Louis School Report* (1855), 105; and Emit Duncan Grizzell, *Origin and Development of the High School in New England Before 1865* (Philadelphia, 1923), 284.

13. Schools Inquiry Commissions, *Report . . . on the Common School System of the United States and of the Provinces of Upper and Lower Canada* (London, 1866), 130; *Charlestown School Report* (1853), 13; and *Keene School Report* (1870), 107–8.

14. "High School," *SB* 1 (April 28, 1848): 4; untitled editorial, *SB* 3 (March 15, 1850): 2 (WRHS); *Philadelphia School Report* (1846), 194; *New York City Report* (1851), 20; *Chicago School Report* (1860), 83; and George T. Fleming, *My High School Days* (Pittsburgh, 1904), 126.

15. Grizzell, *Origin and Development*, 283; *Cincinnati School Report* (1848), 22; and *Louisville School Report* (1855), 20.

16. "Examination of Candidates for the Central School," *SF* 4 (August 1, 1850): 168; and "Remarks on Examination of Candidates for Admission to the Central School," *SF* 5 (February 1, 1851): 72 (OhHS); and *Cleveland School Report* (1855), 31.

17. *Cincinnati School Report* (1855), 93; and *Chicago School Report* (1872), 21.

18. *New Hampshire School Report* (1856), xl-xli.

19. *Boston School Report* (1864), 160–63.

20. Wells, *A Graded Course,* 125; David F. Labaree, *The Making of an American High School: The Credentials Market and the Central High School of Philadelphia, 1838–1939* (New Haven, 1988), 6, 49; *Philadelphia School Report* (1840), 10, 24; (1846), 196–99; (1869), 38–39; (1876), 43; and (1877), 14. The adoption of a quota system (by geographical district) was adopted in 1867, which horrified those who embraced the idea of personal merit.

21. J. S. R., "Depression of High Schools," *MaT* 8 (May 1855): 138–39, for discussion of the pressure placed upon school committees to admit students, even the very unworthy.

22. "Minutes of the Board of Education, Nashville, Tennessee," (September 6, 1856), 59 (TSLA); and *Nashville School Report* (1857), 5–6. On rumors of test-fixing, see Franklin Spencer Edmonds, *History of the Central High School of Philadelphia* (Philadelphia, 1902), 193.

23. S. A. N., "On Advancing Pupils to Higher Grades," *OhEM* 14 (August 1865): 225–26.

24. Lelia Partridge, *Notes of Talks on Teaching, Given by Francis W. Parker* (New York, 1883), chap. 23.

25. White, *Promotions and Examinations,* 14, 34.

26. An early study of Boston's entrance tests in the early 1850s noted that they emphasized rote skills; see Louis J. Fish, *Examinations Seventy-Five Years Ago and Today: Comparisons and Results of Entrance Examinations to High School* (Yonkers-On-Hudson, 1930), 15; and Calhoun, *Intelligence of a People,* 331–35.

27. *Chicago School Report* (1857), 18; (1868), 123–24; (1872), 77–78; *St. Louis School Report* (1855), 107–8; *New York City School Report* (1853), 39; and Fleming, *My High School Days,* 9, where the author recalls studying algebra in grammar school in Pittsburgh.

28. The comments from the Dorchester principal appear in the *Boston School Report* (1873), 86. Also see the recommendations on the weighting of arithmetic and English grammar in Wells, *Graded School,* 128. Arithmetic appeared first in several of the examinations in Chicago cited above. Also see *St. Louis School Report* (1855), 106–10, which printed arithmetic first and then algebra. Many examiners may have put arithmetic first because the word started with the letter "a," but the subjects were often not in alphabetical order after arithmetic.

29. *St. Louis School Report* (1855), 106.

30. *Atlanta School Report* (1874), 23, and (1878), 24.

31. *Chicago School Report* (1870), 77; *St. Louis School Report* (1855), 109; and *Cincinnati School Report* (1856), 75.

32. *Cincinnati School Report* (1848), 43–44, in which the girls, who were slightly older on average, got 32 percent of the spelling words correct to 25 percent for the boys. Also see the *Cincinnati School Report* (1856), 75; and *Chicago School Report* (1867), 108; (1868), 126. Examiners, so fond of having pupils correcting false syntax, also had them correct misspelled words.

33. Parker, *Notes on Talks,* 151.

34. *Chicago School Report* (1857), 19; (1867), 108; and *Cincinnati School Report* (1858), 91.

35. *Chicago School Report* (1870), 78; and *Atlanta School Report* (1878), 25.

36. Parker, *Notes on Talks,* 151; the *St. Louis School Report* (1855), 110; and *Cincinnati School Report* (1859), 81.

37. *Chicago School Report* (1857), 17–18, and (1870), 77.

38. Samuel Adams Wells, *First Report on Grading and Course of Study in the Public Schools* (Boston, 1831), 4.

39. *Connecticut School Report* (1839), 50.

40. *Philadelphia School Report* (1842), 12.

41. *Cincinnati School Report* (1846), 4–5, 7, 30.

42. *Connecticut School Report* (1848), 124; *Concord School Report* (1857), 28; and I. H. Elliott, "The High School in the Township," in *A History of Princeton High School,* Richard Alston Metcalf, comp. (Princeton, Ill., 1892), 50.

43. *Connecticut School Report* (1842), 24, where Barnard explained that the admission tests in the Nutmeg State might cover "algebra, geometry, Surveying, natural, moral, and mental philosophy, political economy, the history and constitution of Connecticut and the United

States, bookkeeping, composition, and drawing, with reference to its use in various kinds of business."

44. One can trace the enrollments in the *Cincinnati School Report* (1854), n.p.; (1863), 24; and (1870), 141. The six-hundred mark was soon broken as enrollments boomed in the two local high schools in the early 1870s.

45. See the essay by David L. Angus, citing Robert Bain's research on Cleveland, "Conflict, Class, and the Nineteenth-Century Public High School in the Cities of the Midwest, 1845–1900," *CI* 18 (Spring 1988): 12; and Richard P. DuFour, "The Exclusion of Female Students from the Public Secondary Schools of Boston, 1820–1920," Ed.D. diss., Northern Illinois University, 1981, 82–83.

46. Quoted in Louis J. Fish, *One Hundred Years of Examinations in Boston* (Dedham, 1941), 20.

47. See W. H. F. Henry, *The High School Question Book: Questions and Answers Embracing Advanced English Studies Usually Pursued in Public High Schools, Academies, Etc.* (Indianapolis, 1886); Daniel J. Pratt, Assistant Secretary, Regents of the University, *The Regents' Questions* (Syracuse, 1878), which covered the years 1866 to 1878; and the numerous pamphlets published by Albert P. Southwick in the 1880s, part of his "Dime Series." The series provided rote questions and answers in many different subjects. Dime Series No. 1 was *Question Book of Physics, with Notes, Queries, Etc.* (Syracuse, 1881) (LC). Most of the questions in these books promoted cramming for entrance tests to high schools, exit tests, and college entrance examinations.

48. "Public Schools of Philadelphia," *OhEM* 14 (July 1865): 216.

49. *Philadelphia School Report* (1861), 199–200, where the principal complained about the recent policy of testing children on specific pages of grammar textbooks, rather than on general knowledge; *Boston School Report* (1867), 215–16, where Philbrick also called for the end of printing grammar school scores; and the *Massachusetts School Report* (1871), 196.

50. Quoted in Fish, *One Hundred Years*, 23.

51. *Philadelphia School Report* (1853), 137; *Boston School Report* (1860), 37; and *Chicago School Report* (1862), 23–24.

52. *Cleveland School Report* (1855), 31.

53. The statistics are printed in the *Boston School Report* (1872), 192–95.

54. *Boston School Report* (1864), 7, 182–83; (1867), 89–90, 223; (1868), 62–63; (1871), 156–57; and (1873), 185.

55. *Chicago School Report* (1872), 150; *Boston School Report* (1861), 58; (1867), 129, where the chairman of the English High School Committee said boys used their admission ticket "as testimonials of their character, and procure them good situations in counting-rooms and stores"; *Hartford School Report* (1869), 18–19; *Milwaukee School Report* (1869), 45; *New York City School Report* (1875), 34–35; and (1876), 314. Also see Robert C. Serow, "Credentialism and Academic Standards: The Evolution of High School Graduation Requirements," *IE* 4 (Summer 1986): 19–41, on how pupils sought credentials over learning.

56. The principle that the high school should remain selective remained powerful within educational circles in the 1860s and 1870s. See "High Schools," in *Cyclopedia of Education*, 423.

57. John O. Norris, "The High School in Our System of Education," *Educ* 3 (March 1883): 339.

58. "Patrons of Our Public Schools," *Aco* 2 (March 15, 1856): n.p.; Hertzler, *Rise of the Public High School*, 50; and *Massachusetts School Report* (1871), 78.

59. *Philadelphia School Report* (1840), 25; (1841), 29; (1846), 74; (1849), 84; and (1852), 96.

60. *Chicago School Report* (1862), 43; *La Crosse School Report* (1878), 25; (1879), 27; and *Petersburg School Report* (1869), 13.

61. The statistics for Chicago appear in the 1880 annual report; for New York City see its 1866 report; for Philadelphia see Labaree, *Making of an American High School*, 80–81, and the local annual reports.

62. *Boston School Report* (1864), 182; (1872), 23; and (1873), 26.

63. *St. Louis School Report* (1865), 28.

64. *Cincinnati School Report* (1846), 7; (1853), 6–7, 41. Principals by the 1870s often complained about their "lazy and incompetent" pupils and chided the school board for refusing to raise entry standards. See the *Cincinnati School Report* (1872), 44; (1875), 42–43; (1876), 53; and (1877), 52, 64.

65. *Cincinnati School Report* (1876), 50–53.

66. *Zanesville School Report* (1858), 16–17.

67. *Portland School Report* (1844), 10–11; *Concord School Report* (1857), 24; and *Hartford School Report* (1868), 14, and (1875), 29.

68. *Hartford School Report* (1849), 8; and (1876), 25–26.

69. W. A. Bell noted the absence of uniform standards of admission in Indiana in "Course of Study for High School," *InSJ* 14 (March 1869): 91–92.

The Choicest Youth

1. Quoted in Andrew Freese, *Early History of the Cleveland Public Schools* (Cleveland, 1876), 45.

2. The *Lady's Book* and other middle-class journals during the hard times of the 1840s urged schools to check the passions of youth; see "The Necessity of Education," *LB* 23 (September 1841): 119. Also see Daniel Walker Howe, *The Political Culture of the American Whigs* (Chicago, 1979), 27–33; Lawrence Frederick Kohl, *The Politics of Individualism: Parties and the American Character in the Jacksonian Era* (New York, 1989), 70, 123–32, 152–53; Michael B. Katz, *The Irony of Early School Reform: Educational Innovation in Mid-Nineteenth Century Massachusetts* (Cambridge, 1968); and Karen Halttunen, *Confidence Men and Painted Women: A Study of Middle-Class Culture in America, 1830–1870* (New Haven, 1982).

3. On academies, see Nicholas D. Colucci, "Connecticut Academies for Females," Ph.D. diss., University of Connecticut, 1969, chaps. 2–4; Elbert W. Boogher, "Secondary Education in Georgia, 1732–1858," Ph.D. diss., University of Pennsylvania, 1933, 131, chap. 8; Albert Mock, *The Midwestern Academy Movement: A Comprehensive Study of Indiana Academies, 1810–1900* (n.p., 1949), 28–40; and Harriet Webster Marr, *The Old New England Academies Founded Before 1926* (New York, 1959), 3, 124, 210. On the public schools, see Lloyd P. Jorgenson, *The State and the Non-Public Schools, 1825–1925* (Columbia, Mo., 1987).

4. "Going to School," in *The Common School Songster*, comp. George James Webb (Boston, 1843), 49.

5. "Will you Come Sign the Pledge?" and "King Alcohol," in *The Rochester School Song Book*, comp. William T. Merriman (Rochester, 1847), 6, 20; "The Bible the Word of God," in *The School Harp*, comp. E. H. Bascom and M. Cotton (Boston, 1855), 71; "Pearly Gates of Heaven," in *The Humming Bird*, comp. J. W. Dadmun (Boston, 1862), 100–101; "There's Nothing True But Heaven," in *The Young Minstrel*, comp. A. N. Johnson and Jason White (Boston, 1843), 20; "The Drunkard's Bowl" and "The Cold Water Song," in *The American School Hymn Book*, comp. Asa Fitz (Boston, 1854), 122; and "Water is Best," in *The School Harp*, 76–77.

6. *Hymns for the Female High School* (Louisville, 1864), 5 (FC).

7. W. A. Bell, "How I Conduct the Opening Exercises in My School," *InSJ* 13 (January 1868): 21; *Charleston, South Carolina, School Report* (1860), 11, on morning devotions at the Girls' High and Normal School; and "Remarks," in *Louisville School Report* (1860), 13.

8. Bell, "How I Conduct," 22–24.

9. K., "A Visit to the Boston High School," *OhJE* 2 (1853): 384–85.

10. Sophia Jex Blake, *A Visit to Some American Schools and Colleges* (London, 1867), 184; Mary D. Bradford, *Memoirs of Mary D. Bradford* (Evansville, Wis., 1932), 116–17, and the reminiscences of Elizabeth Rowland, *The Girls' High School, Portland, Me., 1850–1863* (n.p., n.d.), 32 (MeHS).

11. A. D. Bache, *Report to the Controllers of the Public Schools, on the Re-Organization of the Central High School of Philadelphia* (Philadelphia, 1839), 15, 19 (BM); and *Philadelphia School Report* (1846), 159.

12. *Philadelphia School Report* (1839), 10–11, on the linkage of Christianity, liberty, and republicanism; (1846), 159, on morning religious exercises and controversies; (1853), 110; (1855), 122, 190; (1866), 265; and Franklin Spencer Edmonds, *History of the Central High School of Philadelphia* (Philadelphia, 1902), 138.

13. George B. Emerson, *Reminiscences of an Old Teacher* (Boston, 1878), 62–63.

14. George S. Boutwell, *Thoughts on Educational Topics and Institutions* (Boston, 1859), 163.

15. Boutwell, *Thoughts*, 159.

16. Allan Stanley Horlick, *Country Boys and Merchant Princes: The Social Control of Young Men in New York* (Lewisburg, Pa., 1975); Bruce Laurie, *Artisans into Workers: Labor in Nineteenth-Century America* (New York, 1989); and William J. Rorabaugh, *The Craft Apprentice: From Franklin to the Machine Age* (New York, 1986).

17. Paul E. Johnson, *A Shopkeeper's Millennium: Society and Revivals in Rochester, New York, 1815–1837* (New York, 1978); and Mary P. Ryan, *Cradle of the Middle Class: The Family in Oneida County, New York, 1790–1865* (New York, 1981).

18. *A Volume of Records Relating to the Early History of Boston, Containing Boston Town Records, 1814 to 1822* (Boston, 1906), 168; and *One Hundred Years of the English High School of Boston* (Boston, 1924), 1–2.

19. Joseph F. Kett, *Rites of Passage: Adolescence in America, 1790 to the Present* (New York, 1977), part 1; Carl F. Kaestle, *Pillars of the Republic: Common Schools and American Society, 1780–1860* (New York, 1983), chaps. 2 and 6; Howard P. Chudakoff, *How Old Are You? Age Consciousness in American Culture* (Princeton, 1989), chaps. 1–2; and Harvey J. Graff, "Early Adolescence in Antebellum America: The Remaking of Growing Up," *JEA* 5 (Winter 1985): 411–17.

20. David L. Angus, Jeffrey E. Mirel, and Maris A. Vinovskis, "Historical Development of Age Stratification in Schooling," *TCR* 90 (Winter 1988): 211–36, on the loose fit between grades and ages before the 1930s and 1940s.

21. "Theory and Practice in Co-Education," *NEJE* 11 (March 11, 1880): 168; and J. C. Zachos, *The High School Speaker* (Cincinnati, 1868), iii, on the significance of ages twelve to sixteen in boys' lives.

22. "Age in Education," in *The Cyclopedia of Education: A Dictionary of Information for the Use of Teachers, School Officers, Parents, and Others*, ed. Henry J. Kiddle and Alexander J. Schem (New York, 1877), 6–8.

23. "Age in Education," 8.

24. Anson Smyth, "Causes of Poor Scholarship in Our Public Schools," *OhJE* 7 (February 1858): 44–46.

25. Richard P. DuFour, "The Exclusion of Female Students from the Public Secondary Schools of Boston, 1820–1920," Ed.D. diss., Northern Illinois University, 1981, chap. 2; Robert A. McCaughey, *Josiah Quincy, 1772–1864: The Last Federalist* (Cambridge, 1974), 122–28; and Alexander James Inglis, *The Rise of the High School in Massachusetts* (New York, 1911), 19–20.

26. "High School," *SB* 1 (April 28, 1848): 4 (WRHS); *Cleveland School Report* (1872), 55.

27. *Cincinnati School Report* (1851), 74; (1878), 76; *St. Louis School Report* (1862), 11; (1872), 75; *Chicago School Report* (1860), 47; and (1873), 172–73. Also see *Philadelphia School Report* (1844), 72; (1847), 103; (1852), 99; (1855), 139; and (1856), 139; and *Boston School Report* (1861), 57, 63; (1863), 74; and (1874), 135–40.

28. *Cincinnati School Report* (1854), 27; (1862), 40; and (1877), 123–24.

29. *Terre Haute School Report* (1875), 29.

30. "Village School," in *The Columbian Song Book*, comp. Asa Fitz (Boston, 1856), part 2: 12, 72.

31. Lindley Murray, *Abridgement of Murray's English Grammar* (Peekskill, N.Y., 1830), 64; and David J. Hill, *The Elements of Rhetoric and Composition: A Text-Book for Schools and Colleges* (New York, 1878), 140–41. See other specific references in the chapter on textbooks.

32. W. H. Payne, "The Functions of the High School," *Acad* 2 (1887): 399. On anti-Catholic, anti-Irish sentiments, read "Idleness," *LB* 10 (June 1835): 254; "Editors' Table," *LB* 26 (May 1843): 249; "I Won't Be a Nun," in *The Public School Singing Book* (Philadelphia, 1848), 17; and *Boston School Report* (1858), 131.

33. On the class composition of cities at midcentury, see Stuart M. Blumin, *The Emergence of the Middle Class: Social Experience in the American City, 1760–1900* (Cambridge, 1989), 252. Also see *Catalogue of Instructers [sic] and Scholars in the English High School* (Boston, 1825), 1–3 (BPL); and *An Account of the High School for Girls, Boston: With a Catalogue of the Scholars* (Boston, 1826), 7 (LC).

34. H. K., "Temperance," *SB* 2 (November 23, 1849): 4.

35. S. Willis Rudy, *The College of the City of New York: A History* (New York, 1949), 68. Compare Carl F. Kaestle, *The Evolution of an Urban System: New York City, 1750–1850* (Cambridge, 1973),

104–9; and Jeffrey Mirel, "The Matter of Means: The Campaign and Election for the New York Free Academy, 1846–1847," *JMHE* 9 (1981): 150.

36. Reed Ueda, *Avenues to Adulthood: The Origins of the High School and Social Mobility in an American Suburb* (Cambridge, 1987), 47; Maris A. Vinovskis, "Have We Underestimated the Extent of Antebellum High School Attendance?" *HEQ* 28 (Winter 1988): 556; *Indianapolis School Report* (1879), 69; Selwyn K. Troen, *The Public and the Schools: Shaping the St. Louis System, 1838–1920* (Columbia, Mo., 1975), on the social class backgrounds of pupils; and the *St. Louis Report* (1873), 72.

37. Edward N. Saveth, "Education of an Elite," *HEQ* 28 (Fall 1988): 367–86; and Kaestle, *Pillars*, 121–22.

38. *Richmond School Report* (1879), 56; John S. Hart, *In the School-Room: Chapters in the Philosophy of Education* (Philadelphia, 1868), 261; and William H. Ruffner, "The Co-Education of the White and Colored Races," *SM* 8 (May 1874): 88. Ruffner said that many respectable whites opposed sending their children to school with poor whites, and that racially mixed schools were unthinkable.

39. A. F., "School-Boy Correspondence," *SB* 1 (November 12, 1847): 3; "Rude Boys," *SB* 1 (March 17, 1848): 2; G., "Habits," *SB* 2 (June 1848): 3; "Time," *SB* 2 (October 1848): 2; "Benjamin Franklin," *SB* 2 (October 1848): 3; "Good and Bad Habits," *SB* 2 (October 19, 1849): 1; "Bad Boys," *SB* 2 (February 1, 1850): 2; H. K., "Profanity," *SB* 2 (February 1, 1850): 2–3; and M. B., "Habit," *SB* 3 (March 15, 1850): 2 (WRHS).

40. Editorial, *SG* 1 (October 26, 1850): n.p.; E. P. S., "Cleveland Water Works," *Aco* 2 (March 15, 1856): n.p.; and, in the same issue, "Educational," n.p. (WRHS).

41. "Education," *USMDR* 25 (August 1849): 157–58.

42. "Industry," *NYM* 5 (April 12, 1828): 315; "Increase of Pauperism," *NYM* 6 (February 7, 1829): 247; "Pauperism," *NYM* 6 (April 18, 1829): 327; "Poverty," *NYM* 6 (May 9, 1829): 351; "Idle People," *NYM* 7 (March 13, 1830): 284–85; Grenville Mellon, "Some Thoughts on Education, No. II," *LB* 15 (October 1837): 167; and H., "How to Help the Very Poor," *LB* 20 (April 1840): 163.

43. David L. Angus, "A Note on the Occupational Backgrounds of Public High School Students Prior to 1940," *JMHES* 9 (1981): 158–83.

44. Richard Alston Metcalf, comp., *A History of Princeton High School* (Princeton, Ill., 1892), 41; and "Public Schools in Cities and Large Villages," *RIII* 1 (June 1 and 15, 1846): 234.

45. James Fraser, Schools Inquiry Commissions, *Report . . . on the Common School System of the United States and of the Provinces of Upper and Lower Canada* (London, 1866), 97; and the description of the report by the French Educational Commissioners in Joseph Cook, "Defense of High Schools," *WiJE* 9 (May 1879): 207–9.

46. "Historical Development of Education," *AJE* 32 (1882): 872.

47. B. A. Hinsdale, *Schools and Studies* (Boston, 1884), 162.

48. Frederick A. Packard, *The Daily Public School in the United States* (Philadelphia, 1866), 126.

49. Rorabaugh, *Craft Apprentice*, 118–19; Laurie, *Artisans Into Workers*, 58–60, 128; and Ueda, *Avenues to Adulthood*, 58, 106, 116.

50. *Boston School Report* (1862), 25. The majority of pupils at Boston's short-lived female high school in the 1820s were private school alumni.

51. *Boston School Report* (1874), 425; Schultz, *Culture Factory*, 286–89. The *Boston School Report* (1862), 50, noted that of 101 pupils admitted to the English High School, 74 percent came from four schools; only 13 pupils came from South Boston and only 7 from East Boston. The local reports in the 1850s and 1860s also noted that a few grammar schools prepared the majority of Latin pupils.

52. *Philadelphia School Report* (1842), 35; (1851), 93–94; (1862), 156–57; and *Cincinnati School Report* (1850), 41.

53. The School Visitors of Hartford noted in 1847 that the local grammar schools were unequal, but the "Center District" still sent the most scholars a decade later. In the 1860s two or three of the leading grammar schools sent 50–75 percent of the pupils (*Hartford School Report* [1849], 18–19; [1857], 17; and [1869], 18). Also see the cumulative statistics for the Cleveland

High School, 1846 through 1862, in *Cleveland School Report* (1863), 79; *Louisville School Report* (1869), 76; and *New York City School Report* (1859), 10; (1866), 65; and (1874), 358–59.

54. *Ohio School Report* (1878), 73; *Memphis School Report* (1876), 8; and *Sandusky School Report* (1878), 13.

55. Lucy Larcom, *A New England Girlhood: Outlined from Memory* (Boston, 1889), 155–56.

Good Scholars

1. "Lazy Bill," in *School Songs for the Million!*, comp. Asa Fitz and J. W. Greene (Boston, 1850), n.p. Other songs in this volume included "Swear Not," the "Idle Scholar's Choice" (sung to "Billy Boy"), "Try, Try, Again," and a song that attacked idleness and extolled the school, "The School-Room," sung to "Old Susanna."

2. Fitz and Green, *School Songs*, n.p. For a survey of music education in primary and secondary schools, see James A. Keene, *A History of Music Education in the United States* (Hanover, N.H., 1982), chap. 9.

3. B. Edward McClellan, *Schools and the Shaping of Character: Moral Education in America, 1607–Present* (Bloomington, Ind., 1992), chaps. 2–3.

4. Carl F. Kaestle, *Pillars of the Republic: Common Schools and American Society, 1780–1860* (New York, 1983), 69–70, on the controversial issue of school discipline. Also see D. D. Raphael, *Adam Smith* (Oxford, 1985), 52, 78–79; and David B. Tyack, *The One Best System: A History of American Urban Education* (Cambridge, 1974), 50–59.

5. Mrs. Sarah Josepha Hale, *The School Songbook* (Boston, 1834), 34. Also see "Industry," *NYM* 5 (April 12, 1828), 315; "Always Too Late," *NYM* 5 (April 28, 1828): 331; and Michael O'Malley, *Keeping Watch: A History of American Time* (New York, 1990), 38–39, 156–58.

6. "Hurry to the School Boys," in *The Humming Bird*, comp. J. W. Dadmun (Boston, 1862), 52; "The Intermission," in *The Public School Singing Book* (Philadelphia, 1848), 49; and "The Truant's Soliloquy," in *The School Harp*, comp. E. H. Bascom and M. Cotton (Boston, 1855), 52.

7. Eli T. Tappan, *Treatise on Plane and Solid Geometry, for Colleges, Schools, and Private Students* (Cincinnati, 1873), 130; Francis Wayland, *The Elements of Intellectual Philosophy* (Boston, [c. 1834]), 128; Goold Brown, *The Institutes of English Grammar* (New York, 1853), 24; J. L. Blake, *High School Reader* (Boston, 1832), 101–2; and Lindley Murray, *The English Reader* (Poughkeepsie, [c. 1832]), 29.

8. *Cincinnati School Report* (1850), 44; and (1852), 98.

9. *Catalogue of Instructers [sic] and Scholars in the English High School* (Boston, 1825), 4 (BPL).

10. William H. Wells, *The Graded School: A Graded Course of Instruction for Public Schools* (New York, 1862), 131.

11. Elizabeth Rowland, *The Girls' High School, Portland, Me., 1850–1863* (n.p., n.d.), 10–11; and Nellie, "Tardiness," *Con* (September 12, 1857), n.p., in the Portland Girls' High School Alumni Association Collection (MeHS). All references to *The Constellation* and *The Aspirant* are from this manuscript collection.

12. Harvey Newcomb, *How To Be A Man: A Book for Boys* (Boston, 1847), chaps. 11–12; and Harvey Newcomb, *How To Be A Lady: A Book for Girls* (Boston, 1852), chap. 13, which emphasized bourgeois family responsibilities.

13. *Evansville School Report* (1871), 26–27.

14. On the history of this city system, see Selwyn K. Troen, *The Public and the Schools: Shaping the St. Louis System, 1838–1920* (Columbia, Mo., 1975); and the cumulative statistics in the *St. Louis School Report* (1881), 102.

15. *Fort Wayne School Report* (1873), 40.

16. *Boston School Report* (1861), 6.

17. *Cincinnati School Report* (1858), 45. *The School-Boy* can be found in the *PSAHSM* 1 (1851). The essay cited was by Asa, "The Duties of School-Boys," 92 (OhHS).

18. K. C., "Punctuality at School," *SB* 1 (January 14, 1848): 3; M., "Punctuality," *SB* 2 (September 1848): 3; K. E. W., "Time," *SB* 2 (October 1848): 2; and O'Malley, *Keeping Watch*, 47–50.

19. Almira Hubbard Viles, *School Journal* (Portsmouth, N.H., 1859), entry for March 31, 1859, n.p. ("Viles-Hosmer Papers, 1814–1948," manuscript collection, Joint Collection, University of

Missouri, Western Historical Manuscript Collection—University of Missouri at Columbia and State Historical Society of Missouri.)

20. Viles, *School Journal*, entries for April 5, 1859; May 10, 1859; and June 30, 1859, n.p.

21. Letter, Alice Devin to Annie J. Moore, September 20, 1871. See the manuscript collection, "Alice Devin Letters, 1870–1872" (Michigan Historical Collections, Bentley Historical Library, University of Michigan).

22. Lizzie Morrisey, *Daily Journal for 1875* (Boston, 1876), entries for January 5, 1876; January 9, 1876; and June 5, 1876, n.p. The title of the journal notwithstanding, the contents cover 1876 (Rare Book Room, BPL).

23. Karen Halttunen, *Confidence Men and Painted Women: A Study of Middle-Class Culture in America, 1830–1870* (New Haven, 1982), 13, 28, 43–51; Joseph F. Kett, *Rites of Passage: Adolescence in America, 1790 to the Present* (New York, 1977), chaps. 4–5; Mary P. Ryan, *The Empire of the Mother: American Writing About Domesticity, 1830–1860* (New York, 1985), 49–56; and John F. Kasson, *Rudeness and Civility: Manners in Nineteenth-Century Urban America* (New York, 1990), 5–7, 34–37, passim.

24. "Morning," in Asa Fitz, *The American School Hymn Book* (Boston, 1854), 110; and Roswell C. Smith, *Smith's English Grammar, on the Productive System* (Richmond, Va., [c. 1864]), 15, 39, 40.

25. "The Intermission," in *The Public School Singing Book*, 49.

26. Bernard Wishy, *The Child and the Republic: The Dawn of Modern American Child Nurture* (Philadelphia, 1968).

27. Cato, "A Good Character," *PSAHSM* 1 (1851): 59; and *Nashua School Report* (1858), 7.

28. See the discussion of moral education in Daniel Walker Howe, *The Political Culture of the American Whigs* (Chicago, 1979); and the editorial, *WB* 1 (December 9, 1881): 2–3.

29. A. Parish, "Appendix," in Charles Northend, *The Teacher's Assistant, Or Hints and Methods in School Discipline and Instruction* (Boston, 1859), 319–24; and *Louisville School Report* (1859), 12–13.

30. Rowland, *The Girls' High School*, 20–21.

31. *Concord School Report* (1856), 25; (1861), 20; and John Swett, *Methods of Teaching: A Hand-Book of Principles, Directions, and Working Models for Common School Teachers* (New York, 1880), 75–76.

32. *Cincinnati School Report* (1848), 26–27; (1858), 45; (1860), 49; and (1876), 54, for comments on the discipline of the poorer children in the high school.

33. "Corporal Punishment," *The Cyclopedia of Education: A Dictionary of Information for the Use of Teachers, School Officers, Parents, and Others*, ed. Henry Kiddle and Alexander J. Schem (New York, 1877), 185; and Carl F. Kaestle, ed., *Joseph Lancaster and the Monitorial Movement* (New York, 1973), 4–9.

34. See, for example, *Cincinnati School Report* (1848), 26; *Philadelphia School Report* (1846), 169–70.

35. *Philadelphia School Report* (1853), 125; and J. Thomas Scarf and Thomas Westcott, *History of Philadelphia* (Philadelphia, 1884), 3: 1930–31. On the perceived ties between deportment and character, also see Thomas B. Davis, *Chronicles of the Hopkins Grammar School, 1660–1935* (New Haven, 1938), 365–66, 382–83.

36. *New York City School Report* (1854), 13; and S. Willis Rudy, *The College of the City of New York: A History* (New York, 1949), 71–72.

37. James Johonnot, *School House* (New York, 1871), 122; and Robert and Jean McClintock's reprint of Henry Barnard's *School Architecture*, from the 1848 edition (New York, 1970), 56.

38. *Portland School Report* (1832), 4; and *Savannah School Report* (1869), 11.

39. Edward Henry Elwell, *The Schools of Portland* (Portland, 1888), 21. For a student parody in verse, read *The Re-Union of '73* (Portsmouth, N.H., 1873), 65.

40. George B. Emerson, *Reminiscences of an Old Teacher* (Boston, 1878), 53, 60. On gender differences generally, see especially E. Anthony Rotundo, "Boy Culture: Middle-Class Boyhood in Nineteenth Century America," in *Meanings for Manhood: Constructions of Masculinity in Victorian America*, ed. Mark C. Carnes and Clyde Griffen (Chicago, 1990), 15–36; and Carroll Smith-Rosenberg, *Disorderly Conduct: Visions of Gender in Victorian America* (New York, 1985), 213.

41. "The Dayton Schools," *OhEM* 12 (March 1863): 91; Margaret Blythe, "Samuel M. Capron,

The Man and the Teacher," in *Memorial of Samuel Mills Capron*, ed. J. H. Twichell (Hartford, 1874), 42–44. Suspensions were rare in many high schools, as shown in *Zanesville School Report* (1859), 14; *Denver School Report* (1874–1880); *St. Louis School Report* (1865), 24; (1873), 64; and, on the separate girls' high schools, *Boston School Report* (1855), 78; *Philadelphia School Report* (1852), 139; and (1855), 190.

42. Viles, *School Journal*, entries for the following dates in 1859: May 30 and June 2, 13, 23, and 28.

43. Morrisey, *Journal*, May 1, 1876.

44. Carrie Lena Crawford Moffitt, *Diary of Carrie Lena Crawford Moffitt, 1871–1898* (n.p., 1871–1898), entry for January 19, 1872; and letter from W. Coleman to Carrie Crawford, n.d. in 1872, in *Album of Remrance [sic], Carrie Lena Crawford Moffitt* (n.p., 1872), n.p. (Manuscript collection, VaSL).

45. *Nashville School Report* (1857), 19.

46. Adene Williams, *Diaries*, 1: October 4, 5, and 6, 1865 (CHS).

47. Charles E. Strattan, *Extracts from the Diary of a Member of the Graduating Class of the Boston Public Latin School, April–July 1862*, entries for April 9, 11, 15, and 19 (Rare Book Room, BPL).

48. Strattan, *Extracts*, entries in 1862 for May 7 and 15, June 3 and 7, and July 2, 11, and 12.

49. "Merit Book," in the "Louisville Male High School Collection," seven volumes (Manuscript Collections, FC). See 2: November 12, 1868; September 10, 1869; November 17, 1869; November 22, 1869; January 28, 1870; and *Louisville School Report* (1872), 18, for rules and regulations on misbehavior.

50. "Merit Book," 2: February 15, 1871.

51. "Merit Book," 2: January 9, 1872; May 3, 1872; April 25, 1873; and May 25, 1876.

52. "Advice to the Scholars," *Asp* (September 5, 1857): n.p.

53. Edith, "Agreable [sic] Sensations on Missing My Lesson," *Con* 1 (September 26, 1851): n.p.

54. See *Asp* (July 16, 1862): n.p.; and "Life in the School Room," *Con* (May 12, 1855): n.p.

55. Helen C. Cross, "Is Poverty Favorable to Genius?" *Ca* 5 (May 1833): 229; "Idleness," *LB* 10 (June 1835): 254; Grenville Mellen, "Some Thoughts on Education, No. II," *LB* 15 (October 1837): 166–68; and John S. C. Abbott, *The School-Boy; or A Guide to Truth and Duty* (Boston, 1839), 10, 13–14, 19.

56. "Hours of Study," in *The Musical Class Book, for the Use of Female Seminaries, High Schools, Adult and Juvenile Singing Schools*, comp. A. N. Johnson (Boston, 1845), 282; "Begone Dull Sloth," in *The Columbian Song Book*, comp. Asa Fitz (Boston, 1856), part 2: 12; and "I Won't Be a Dunce," in *The School Songster*, comp. Asa Fitz (Boston, 1855), 10.

57. Lindley Murray, *English Exercises, Adapted to Murray's English Grammar* (Boston, 1819), 55, 104, a volume that went through dozens of editions; Smith, *Smith's English Grammar*, 58; Samuel Kirkham, *English Grammar in Familiar Lectures*, 63d ed. (Baltimore, 1834), 74, 195; Francis Wayland, *The Elements of Political Economy* (Boston, [c. 1841]), 15, 105–10; Laurens P. Hickok, *A System of Moral Science* (Schenectady, 1853), 97–98; and the various works on history and geography described in the earlier chapter on textbooks.

58. *Boston School Report* (1864), 62.

59. *Boston School Report* (1860), 17, 35–36; (1862), 33; (1863), 80; (1864), 83–84; (1865), 281. In 1873, study was again abolished at the Girls' High and Normal School, but as the excerpts later in the chapter from Elizabeth Morrisey's diary show, the policy was again short-lived.

60. *San Francisco School Report* (1861), 37–38. Also see the *San Francisco School Report* (1869), 57, for recurrent complaints about excessive study at the Boys' High School.

61. *Zanesville School Report* (1859), 15.

62. Quoted in James Mulhern, "A History of Secondary Education in Pennsylvania," Ph.D. diss., University of Pennsylvania, 1933, 585.

63. "Soliloquy of a School Girl, Just Before Graduation," *Con* (October 4, 1862): n.p.

64. See Howe, *Political Culture*, 36–37; and Laurence Frederick Kohl, *The Politics of Individualism: Parties and the American Character in the Jacksonian Era* (New York, 1989).

65. *Philadelphia School Report* (1840), 22, on the need for more home study, affirmed in (1841), 22; (1842), 24; *Cincinnati School Report* (1857), 116, 120; (1859), 37, 44; (1860), 61–62; (1875), 43;

Columbus, Ohio, School Report (1875), 62; and (1879), 108; *St. Louis School Report* (1867), 27; and *High School of Charleston* (Charleston, 1881), 12.

66. See, for example, the typical complaints about pupils in *Cleveland School Report* (1866), 67–68; *Cincinnati School Report* (1862), 45; (1875), 43; and especially (1877), 52–55; Alexis de Tocqueville, *Democracy in America* (New York, [c. 1969], rpt. of 12th ed., 1848), 1: 56; 2: 440.

67. *The System of Education Pursued at the Free Schools in Boston* (Boston, 1823), 18 (BPL); and *Boston School Report* (1869), 19–20.

68. *Rhode Island School Report* (1846), 59.

69. *Oshkosh School Report* (1875), 29; and editorial, *WB* 1 (December 9, 1881): 2.

70. The statistics are from the "Appendix" of a bound volume in the Portland High School Collection (MeHS). Also see, more generally, David Tyack and Elisabeth Hansot, *Learning Together: A History of Coeducation in American Schools* (New Haven, 1990), chaps. 4–6.

71. "Poetry in Algebra," *Asp* 2 (November 20, 1852): n.p.; "Life in the School Room," *Con* (May 12, 1855): n.p.; and Mary D. Bradford, *Memoirs of Mary D. Bradford* (Evansville, Wis., 1932), 118.

72. Viles, *School Journal*, entry for April 19, 1859; and Williams, *Diary*, 1: September 20, 1865; October 5, 1865; and January 4 and 8, 1866.

73. Letters, Alice Devin to Annie J. Moore, April 5, 1871; November 6, 1871; March 2, 1872; and March 20, 1872; and Morrisey, *Daily Journal*, entries for January 5, 6, and 18, 1876; March 20, 1876; April 6, 1876; and June 18, 1876. Also see John L. Rury's examination of student social life in *Education and Women's Work: Female Schooling and the Division of Labor in Urban America, 1870–1930* (Albany, 1991), 77–89.

74. See the report cards in the "Clark Family Papers, 1815–1938," and Mary Ellen Clark (Pollard), *Autograph Album*, and the poem from her father dated March 2, 1878 (VaHS).

75. These generalizations are based on the student diaries cited in this chapter. Middle-class proprieties and musical interests are also highlighted in Stuart M. Blumin, *The Emergence of the Middle Class: Social Experience in the American City, 1760–1900* (New York, 1989). On the importance of the piano in the bourgeois home, also see Paul E. Johnson, *A Shopkeeper's Millennium: Society and Revivals in Rochester, New York, 1815–1837* (New York, 1978), 19; and Kathryn Kish Sklar, *Catherine Beecher: A Study in American Domesticity* (New Haven, 1973), 25.

76. *Philadelphia School Report* (1868), 210.

77. *Boston School Report* (1867), 158.

Varieties of Experience

1. Henry Kiddle and Alexander J. Schem, eds., *The Cyclopedia of Education: A Dictionary of Information for the Use of Teachers, School Officers, Parents, and Others* (New York, 1877), 421–22; and Maris A. Vinovskis, "Have We Underestimated the Extent of Antebellum High School Attendance?" *HEQ* 28 (Winter 1988): 562.

2. Because of the multiple functions of the high school, scholars have frequently highlighted a particular theme to explore in depth, often in case studies. See, for example, the study of meritocracy by David F. Labaree, *The Making of an American High School: The Credentials Market and the Central High School of Philadelphia, 1838–1939* (New Haven, 1988); the focus on politics by Jeffrey Mirel in "The Matter of Means: The Campaign and Election for the New York Free Academy, 1846–1847," *JMHES* 9 (1981): 134–55; or the broad quantitative analysis by Maris Vinovskis, *The Origins of Public High Schools: A Reexamination of the Beverly High School Controversy* (Madison, 1985).

3. James McCosh, "On the Importance of Harmonizing the Action of the Primary, the Secondary, and Collegiate Systems of Education," *Educ* 1 (September 1880): 13, drawing upon the reports of the U.S. Bureau of Education; and Calvin Olin Davis, *Public Secondary Education* (Chicago, 1917), 61, 180–81.

4. William T. Harris, "The Growth of the Public High-School System in the Southern States and a Study of Its Influence," *ER* 27 (March 1904): 259–60. On Harris, see Lawrence A. Cremin, *American Education: The Metropolitan Experience 1876–1980* (New York, 1988), 157–64.

5. *Maine School Report* (1875), 36 (the number of high schools printed here is 142 but should be

143); *Ohio School Report* (1855), 5; (1856), 4; and (1866), 17–18. On the bewilderingly inconsistent ways of gathering statistics, see Nelson L. Bossing, "The History of Educational Legislation in Ohio from 1851 to 1925," *OhAHP* 39 (1930): 158–59.

6. *Maine School Report* (1861), 18, 67, 79; and (1870), 33–35. Helpful historical data also appear in Ava Harriet Chadbourne, *The Beginnings of Education in Maine* (New York, 1928), chaps. 4–5; and in Nelson Dingley Jr., "Free High Schools," *Proceedings of the Maine Pedagogical Society for 1880–1881* (Farmington, 1883), 98–102.

7. *Maine School Report* (1870), 34–36; (1871), 92–94; (1873), 85–104; and (1874), 6–7, 26–38.

8. *Maine School Report* (1875), 36–43.

9. *Maine School Report* (1870), 214; and (1875), 36–43, which contains the statistics for 1874, the basis for this section of the chapter.

10. *Maine School Report* (1875), 38–39.

11. *Maine School Report* (1875), 36–43.

12. Edward Henry Elwood, *The Schools of Portland* (Portland, 1888).

13. Johnson gathered information on English grammar, geography, natural science, and foreign languages. Unfortunately, information on the first three subjects has relatively little value. Since the early antebellum decades, these were grammar-level as well as high school subjects. Publishers printed a variety of competing textbooks, available by the 1840s in a graduated series from the primary grades through high school. Unfortunately, Johnson did not ask local officials to distinguish among different levels of subject matter.

14. Critics of high schools often wrongly accused them of favoring the ancient languages over English subjects. See Archie P. Nevins, "The Kalamazoo Case," *MiH* 44 (March 1960): 91–100; and Hugh Graham, "Significant Aspects of the Kalamazoo Case," *Educ* 52 (October 1931): 100–103.

15. Information on the Greek classes was found in the "Portland High School Collection," Manuscript Collection (MeHS), volume labeled "Appendix." In the 1863–1864 school year, when the boys' and girls' high schools merged, enrollments in the fall semester were 267 in Latin, 33 in French, and 8 in Greek; in 1880 in the fall semester there were 151 in Latin, 113 in French, and 39 in Greek.

16. Newspaper clipping, "The Girls High School at Portland, 1850–1863," *Portland Sunday Telegram* (September 9, 1906); Elizabeth Rowland, *Seventy Years Out of the Portland High School for Girls* (Typescript, 1929), 10; and Elizabeth Rowland, *The Girls' High School, Portland, Me., 1850–1863* (n.p., n.d.), 17 (All MeHS).

17. On the urban biases of school reformers, see David B. Tyack, *The One Best System: A History of American Urban Education* (Cambridge, 1974); and Carl F. Kaestle, *Pillars of the Republic: Common Schools and American Society, 1780–1860* (New York, 1983).

18. *Maine School Report* (1874), 35.

19. *Maine School Report* (1874), 35–36.

20. According to statistics for 1874, eight of the thirty-three schools that had total enrollments of 400–599 pupils, including Yarmouth, had at least thirty-week terms.

21. W. Le C. Stevens, "Promotion in Graded Schools," *NTM* 1 (January 1875): 69–72.

22. Emerson E. White, "Promotions and Examinations in Graded Schools," U.S. Bureau of Education Circular of Information No. 7 (1891), 14.

23. *Ohio School Report* (1880), 118–32.

24. *Ohio School Report* (1878), 64, 74; and (1880), 33–35. Other states reported similar percentages and faced similar problems gathering basic data. See *Pennsylvania School Report* (1874), xxv–xxvii; and *California School Report* (1875), 15; and (1880), 10, 86–87.

25. *Indiana School Report* (1870), 32; *Michigan School Report* (1877), 6, 222, 229–34. See the *Columbus, Ohio, School Report* (1876), 145, for a discussion of midwestern urban high school enrollments.

26. S. R. Winchell, "The True Function of the High School," *WiJE* 4 (August 1874): 304.

27. *Mississippi School Report* (1872), 53, 67–74, and 130; and William Hennington Weathersby, *A History of Educational Legislation in Mississippi from 1798 to 1860* (Chicago, 1921), chap. 6.

28. *Alabama School Report* (1876), 26–28; Stephen B. Weeks, "History of Public School Education in Alabama," U.S. Bureau of Education Bulletin No. 12 (1915), 184; and Jack Nelms, "The

Dallas Academy: Backbone of the Permanent School System of Selma," *AIR* 29 (April 1976): 113–23.

29. *South Carolina School Report* (1875), 482; and (1877), 10–11; and praise for Charleston in (1880), 11. The statistics on South Carolina were neither trustworthy nor complete. On Charleston see Eugene Clifford Clark, "A History of the First Hundred Years of the High School of Charleston," in *Year Book 1943* (Charleston, 1946), 194–247; Nita K. Pyburn, "The Public School System of Charleston before 1860," *SCHM* 61 (April 1960): 86–98; and J. L. Dawson and H. W. DeSaussure, *Census of the City of Charleston, South Carolina, for the Year 1848* (Charleston, 1849), 54–57.

30. On academies see Theodore Sizer, ed., *The Age of the Academies* (New York, 1964), 1–48; George William Paschal, "Baptist Academies in North Carolina," *NCHR* 28 (January 1951): 47–62; and Walter J. Fraser, Jr., "William Henry Ruffner and the Establishment of Virginia's Public School System, 1870–1874," *VaMHB* 79 (July 1971): 269. Statistics on Virginia were compiled from the *Virginia School Report* for the period 1876 to 1880. For whites, the percentage of pupils studying the branches between 1876 and 1880 fluctuated from a high of 5 percent in 1876 to a low of 4.3 percent in 1880; for blacks the figure for the same years fluctuated from a high of 1.3 percent to a low of 0.8 percent. Also see Civis, "The Public School in Its Relation to the Negro," *SPF* 37 (February 1876): 108–16.

31. William H. Ruffner, "The Co-Education of the White and Colored Races," *SM* 2 (May 1874): 86–88.

32. *Virginia School Report* (1874), 153; Civis, "The Public School In Its Relation to the Negro," *SPF* 36 (December 1875): 709, and 37 (January 1876): 35–42; B. Puryear, "A Card from Civis," *SPF* 37 (August 1876): 581; Civis, "Public School," *SPF* 37 (February 1876): 115; and Kathryn A. Pippin, "The Common School Movement in the South, 1840–1860," Ph.D. diss., University of North Carolina, 1977, 117–19.

33. James M. McPherson, *The Struggle for Equality: Abolitionists and the Negro in the Civil War and Reconstruction* (Princeton, 1964), 406; and *Richmond School Report* (1879), 59–61. There are innumerable studies on freedmen's education; one of the most incisive is Ronald E. Butchart, *Northern Schools, Southern Blacks, and Reconstruction: Freedmen's Education, 1862–1875* (Westport, Conn., 1980).

34. *Arkansas School Report* (1874), 21; (1878), 35–37; and (1882), 77; and Clara B. Kenman's criticisms in "Dr. Thomas Smith, Forgotten Man of Arkansas Education," *ArHQ* 20 (Winter 1961): 304–7.

35. See John W. Blassingame, *Black New Orleans, 1860–1880* (Chicago, 1973), 116–22; June O. Patton, "The Black Community of Augusta and the Struggle for Ware High School 1880–1899," in *New Perspectives on Black Educational History*, ed. Vincent P. Franklin and James D. Anderson (Boston, 1978), 50.

36. James D. Anderson, *The Education of Blacks in the South, 1860–1935* (Chapel Hill, 1988), chaps. 1–2, highlights the monumental efforts of the freedmen after the Civil War. This theme was also explored in W. E. B. DuBois, *Black Reconstruction in America 1860–1880* (New York, 1935), chap. 15; *Augusta, Georgia, School Report* (1880), 15; and Paul E. Peterson, *The Politics of School Reform, 1870–1940* (Chicago, 1985), 96–98. On black initiative, see Eric Foner, *Reconstruction: America's Unfinished Revolution, 1863–1877* (New York, 1988), 97–102, passim; and Butchart, *Northern Schools, Southern Blacks*.

37. Thomas W. Gutowski, "The High School as an Adolescent-Raising Institution: An Inner History of Chicago Public Secondary Education, 1856–1940," Ph.D. diss., University of Chicago, 1978, 15; "Miscellany," *InSJ* 20 (August 1875): 391; *Louisville School Report* (1857), 7; (1865), 7; (1870), 117; (1876), 9; *Cincinnati School Report* (1851), 48; (1859), 27; *Ohio School Report* (1880), 35; and *Cleveland School Report* (1852), 6; (1866), 9; and (1876), 77.

38. David F. Labaree, "The People's College: A Sociological Analysis of the Central High School of Philadelphia, 1838–1939," Ph.D. diss., University of Pennsylvania, 1983, 140; and *St. Louis School Report* (1875), 142. The statistics on Philadelphia are for only the Central High School and do not include enrollments for the Girls' High School, which opened in 1848. On Harris see the *St. Louis School Report* (1875), 142.

39. Mary D. Bradford, *Memoirs of Mary D. Bradford* (Evansville, Wis., 1932), 114–16.

40. On coeducation, see David Tyack and Elisabeth Hansot, *Learning Together: A History of Coeducation in American Schools* (New Haven, 1990). On domesticity and middle-class ideology, see Mary P. Ryan, *Cradle of the Middle Class: The Family in Oneida County, New York, 1790–1865* (New York, 1981); Karen Halttunen, *Confidence Men and Painted Women: A Study of Middle-Class Culture in America, 1830–1870* (New Haven, 1982); Carroll Smith-Rosenberg, *Disorderly Conduct: Visions of Gender in Victorian America* (New York, 1985); Christine Stansell, *City of Women: Sex and Class in New York, 1789–1860* (New York, 1986); and Mary P. Ryan, *The Empire of the Mother: American Writing about Domesticity, 1830–1860* (New York, 1985).

41. See Ryan, *Empire*, 34–42, on the rise of middle-class homes and changes in reading materials. In *Disorderly Conduct*, 26, Smith-Rosenberg sees the bourgeois world maturing further by the 1850s and 1860s. Also see Kathryn Kish Sklar, *Catharine Beecher: A Study in American Domesticity* (New York, 1973).

42. S., "Essay on the True End of Female Education," *Ca* 2 (June 1827): 219; and "Education," *LM* 1 (September 1828): 422–23.

43. "Female Education," *LB* 10 (January 1835): 22; and "Education," *LB* 21 (September 1840): 108. On Boston, see Richard P. DuFour, "The Exclusion of Female Students from the Public Secondary Schools of Boston, 1820–1920," Ed.D. diss., Northern Illinois University, 1981, 46, 135; and the documents reprinted in "Girls in the Public Schools of Boston," *AJE* 13 (June 1863): 243–66.

44. L. C., "On Female Education," *LG* 3 (1840): 11; and *Virginia School Report* (1879), 40. Ruffner had already gone on record favoring coeducation. See "The Co-Education of the Sexes," *SM* 2 (September 1871): 519–24.

45. Tyack and Hansot, *Learning Together*, chaps. 1–5.

46. *St. Louis School Report* (1881), 101; and Tyack and Hansot, *Learning Together*, 114.

47. *Rhode Island School Report* (1846), 59.

48. *Rhode Island School Report* (1846), 59. As chief school officer in Connecticut, Barnard also favored separate departments for males and females in high school; see *Connecticut School Report* (1842), 24; and "School Architecture," *AJE* 11 (June 1862): 570.

49. Nancy Green, "Female Education and School Competition; 1820–1850," *HEQ* 18 (Summer 1978): 129–42.

50. *Indiana School Report* (1852), 264.

51. *Cincinnati School Report* (1859), 36; and Schools Inquiry Commissions, *Report . . . on the Common School System of the United States and of the Provinces of Upper and Lower Canada* (London, 1866), 140, 194–95.

52. In "Union School Examination," the *Kalamazoo Telegraph* (March 30, 1859) claimed that the female secondary pupils did the best academic work. Also see *Chicago School Report* (1872), 71; *Columbus, Ohio, School Report* (1878), 91; and John D. Philbrick, "City School Systems in the United States," U.S. Bureau of Education Circular No. 1 (1885), 29. On the harmful effects of emulation on boys, whose egos forced them to quit if they performed poorly, see Charles Northend, *The Teacher and the Parent; A Treatise Upon Common-School Education; Containing Practical Suggestions to Teachers and Parents* (Boston, 1853), 148–49; cf. John Swett, *Methods of Teaching: A Hand-Book of Principles, Directions, and Working Models for Common School Teachers* (New York, 1880), 68, who said prizes and emulation mostly hurt girls.

53. DuFour, "Exclusion of Female Students," 120–32; A. Emerson Palmer, *The New York Public School: Being a History of Free Education in the City of New York* (New York, 1905), 160; and Robert Wayne Clark, "The Genesis of the Philadelphia High School for Girls," Ph.D. diss., Temple University, 1938, 25–26, 41–44. Separate schools in these and other cities changed their names occasionally, as they attempted to change their emphasis from academic to normal training or vice versa.

54. Tyack and Hansot, *Learning Together*, 130; and Kiddle and Schem, *Cyclopedia*, 421–22.

55. Kathleen C. Berkeley, "'The Ladies Want to Bring About Reform in the Public Schools': Public Education and Women's Rights in the Post–Civil War South," *HEQ* 24 (Spring 1984): 45–58; Timothy J. Crimmons, "The Crystal Stair: A Study of the Effects of Class, Race, and Eth-

nicity on Secondary Education in Atlanta, 1872–1925," Ph.D. diss., Emory University, 1972; and David Moss Hilliard, "The Development of Public Education in Memphis, Tennessee, 1848–1945," Ph.D. diss., University of Chicago, 1946, 167–69.

56. *San Francisco School Report* (1864), 28; (1868), 62–67; and (1870), 59, for information on the normal orientation of the female secondary school. For a flavor of the issues at stake in Boston, see Anna C. Brackett, "Girls in the Boston Latin School," *NEJE* 6 (November 8, 1877): 211; "Editorial," *NEJE* 6 (November 22, 1877): 234; John D. Philbrick, "CoEducation of the Sexes in the Boston Latin School," *NEJE* 6 (November 29, 1877): 247; J. G. Davies, "Co-Education," *WiJE* 8 (January 1878): 15–18; and "Co-Education of the Sexes," *InSJ* 23 (January 1878): 31. Also see Patricia M. King, "The Campaign for Higher Education for Women in 19th Century Boston," *PMaHS* 93 (1981): 59–79.

57. *Louisville School Report* (1860), 26–27.

58. *Diary of Carrie Lena Crawford Moffitt, 1871–1898*, entry for January 25, 1872. See the creative work that Portland's female scholars assembled, preserved in the "Portland Girls High School Alumni Association Collection," four volumes, 1851–1863 (MeHS). Also see the sixteen-page pamphlet produced by the Girls' High and Normal School, *The Waif* 1 (January 1867), which includes a sizzling attack upon men's arrogant attitudes toward women's intellect (BPL).

59. *SB* 3 (March 15, 1850): 2. Crawford's previously cited diary is filled with comments on close female classmates. Also see the diary of Lizzie Morrisey of Boston, *Daily Journal for 1875* (BPL). Her diary has numerous references to "Ida," as well as hilarious references to one of her female teachers, Miss Stickney. Extant female autograph albums examined include the following: *Album of Remrance [sic] of Carrie Lena Crawford Moffitt*, 1872 (VaSL); Mary Prentice Freeman, *Autograph Book* (Portland, 1870) (MeHS); and Mary Ellen Clark, *Autograph Album* (Baltimore, 1880) (VaHS). Also see the broadside entitled *Class of '77* for the Girls High School of Boston, announcing a reunion scheduled for June 4, 1927 (BPL).

60. On the sometimes explicit, sometimes implicit, Protestant and nativist slurs on Catholicism, see Ruffner, "The Co-Education of the Sexes," 519–24; "The Co-Education Question," *PSHJ* 1 (January 1878): 425–26; and the *California School Report* (1867), 77. The quotation in the text is from *The Year-Book of Education for 1878*, ed. Henry Kiddle and Alexander J. Schem (New York, 1878), 33.

61. Allen M. Scott, "Mixed Schools," *NCJE* 5 (January 1862): 8.

62. William T. Harris, "The Co-Education of the Sexes," *MsEJ* 1 (February 1872): 396. P. A. Siljestrom, *Educational Institutions of the United States* (London, 1853), 302. Separate entrances at coeducational institutions remained common; see "New High-School House, Providence," *NEJE* 8 (September 26, 1878): 193. The Providence high school also had separate male and female departments.

63. William J. Akers, *Cleveland Schools in the Nineteenth Century* (Cleveland, 1901), 39; Andrew Freese, *Early History of the Cleveland Public Schools* (Cleveland, 1876), 32; "Examination," *SB* 2 (July 1848): 3; and Kate, "For the School-Boy," *SB* 2 (July 1848): 2.

64. "Cleveland Central High School," *OhJE* 5 (April 1856): 110–11; *Cleveland School Report* (1856) 47; and (1876), 84; *Cincinnati School Report* (1838), 5; (1844), 14; and (1860), 67.

65. *Constitution and By-Laws of the Irving Society of the Chicago High School* (Chicago, 1857), 12 (ChHS); *A Brief History of the Young Men's Literary Association, 1863–1866* (Cleveland, 1866), 2 (WRHS); *The Public School Advocate and High School Magazine*, which was published in 1851 and divided into the male *School-Boy* and female *Incentive* (OhHL); *The Graduate's Literary Society, 1855–1856*, vol. 1 (WRHS); and "Minute Book," *Proceedings of the Virgil Literary Society* (Columbus, 1878–1880), 11–14 (OhHL).

66. Hattie F. Farrand, "Fashion Incompatible with Intellectual Culture," and "Soliloquy of a Seamstress," *Aco* 2 (March 15, 1856): 1, 3 (WRHS).

67. *The Re-Union of '73* (Portsmouth, 1873), 75 (LC). While examining women's changing relationship to public space, Mary P. Ryan argues that women in the 1870s often expressed themselves in class terms, often heavily shaped by racism and ethnocentrism. See *Women in Public: Between Banners and Ballots, 1825–1880* (Baltimore, 1980), 55, 162–63.

68. Siljestrom, *Educational Institutions*, 137; and Alexis de Tocqueville, *Democracy in America* (New York, [c. 1969], rpt. of 12th ed., 1848), part 2, chap. 10.

69. Kiddle and Schem, *Cyclopedia*, 157. On free blacks in the antebellum North and South, see Leon Litwack, *North of Slavery: The Negro in the Free States, 1790–1860* (Chicago, 1961); Leonard P. Curry, *The Free Black in Urban America, 1800–1850* (Chicago, 1981); Ira Berlin, *Masters Without Slaves: The Free Negro in the Antebellum South* (New York, 1974); and Ellis O. Knox, "A Historical Sketch of Secondary Education for Negroes," *JNE* 4 (July 1940): 440–53.

70. Daniel Walker Howe, *The Political Culture of the American Whigs* (Chicago, 1979), 17–18, 38–39, 203; V. Jacque Voegeli, *Free But Not Equal: The Midwest and the Negro During the Civil War* (Chicago, 1967); Roger D. Bridges, "Equality Deferred: Civil Rights for Illinois Blacks, 1865–1885," *JIlSHS* 74 (Summer 1981): 95–96; Eugene H. Berwanger, *The Frontier Against Slavery: Western Anti-Negro Prejudice and the Slavery Extension Controversy* (Urbana, 1967); and Eric Foner, *Free Soil, Free Men, Free Labor* (New York, 1970), 281–95.

71. Curry, *Free Black*, chap. 10; Litwack, *North of Slavery*, chap. 4; Voegeli, *Free But Not Equal*, 2; William Louis Lang, "Black Bootstraps: The Abolitionist Educators' Ideology and the Education of the Northern Free Negro, 1828–1860," Ph.D. diss., University of Delaware, 1974, chap. 4; Harry Charles Silcox, "A Comparative Study in School Desegregation: The Boston and Philadelphia Experience," Ph.D. diss., Temple University, 1972, 63–69; and Linda Marie Perkins, "Quaker Beneficence and Black Control: The Institute for Colored Youth, 1852–1903," in *New Perspectives on Black Educational History*, 19–43.

72. *Chicago School Report* (1863), 54; *Connecticut School Report* (1874), 70; and Robert C. Morris, *Reading, 'Riting, and Reconstruction: The Education of Freedmen in the South, 1861–1870* (Chicago, 1976), 114.

73. DuFour, "Exclusion of Female Students," 72; Silcox, "Comparative Study," 138, 223, 263; *New York City School Report* (1855), 3–4; (1875), 333; and Leonard Ernest Erickson, "The Color Line in Ohio Public Schools, 1829–1890," Ph.D. diss., Ohio State University, 1959, 251.

74. The quote from the *Republican* is from Patrick A. Folk, "'The Queen City of Mobs': Riots and Community Reactions in Cincinnati, 1788–1848," Ph.D. diss., University of Toledo, 1978, 149.

75. Berwanger, *Frontier Against Slavery*, 34; *Cincinnati School Report* (1844), 6; (1846), 35; and Curry, *Free Black*, 158–59.

76. Erickson, "Color Line," 207–8; Richard W. Pih, "Negro Self-Improvement Efforts in Ante-Bellum Cincinnati, 1836–1850," *OH* 78 (Summer 1969): 179–85; David L. Calkins, "Black Education in Nineteenth Century Cincinnati," *CHSB* 38 (Summer 1980): 120–21; and David L. Calkins, "Black Education and the 19th Century City: An Institutional Analysis of Cincinnati's Colored Schools, 1850–1887," *CHSB* 33 (Fall 1975): 161–74.

77. *Cincinnati "Colored" School Report* (1855), 8; and John P. Foote, *The Schools of Cincinnati, and Its Vicinity* (Cincinnati, 1855), 94.

78. *Cincinnati "Colored" School Report* (1855), 15–17; (1858), 8; and (1861), 9. The broad outlines of Clark's life have been sketched by many different historians. The most accessible essay is by Philip S. Foner, "Peter H. Clark: Pioneer Black Socialist," in *Essays in Afro-American History* (Philadelphia, 1978), chap. 9.

79. *Cincinnati "Colored" School Report* (1866), 29–30; *Cincinnati School Report* (1877), 117; John B. Shotwell, *A History of the Schools of Cincinnati* (Cincinnati, 1902), 458–59; and Foner, "Peter H. Clark."

80. Shotwell, *History of the Schools*, 459; and *Cincinnati School Report* (1879), 115.

Commencement

1. "Patrons of Our Public Schools," *Aco* 2 (March 15, 1856): 2 (WRHS).

2. Frederick A. Packard, *The Daily Public School in the United States* (Philadelphia, 1866), 126.

3. Quoted in Franklin Spencer Edmonds, *History of the Central High School of Philadelphia* (Philadelphia, 1902), 243.

4. David F. Labaree, *The Making of an American High School: The Credentials Market and the Cen-*

tral High School of Philadelphia, 1838–1939 (New Haven, 1988), 52; Maris A. Vinovskis, "Have We Underestimated the Extent of Antebellum High School Attendance?" *HEQ* 28 (Winter 1988): 555–56; and Reed Ueda, *Avenues to Adulthood: The Origins of the High School and Social Mobility in an American Suburb* (Cambridge, 1987), 106–7.

5. *Providence School Report* (1828), 4.

6. *Cleveland School Report* (1863), 31.

7. *Hartford School Report* (1869), 25; *Louisville School Report* (1865), 71; and "The Co-Education of the Sexes," *SM* 2 (September 1871): 524.

8. See especially Karen Halttunen, *Confidence Men and Painted Women: A Study of Middle-Class Culture in America, 1830–1870* (New Haven, 1982), 12; William J. Rorabaugh, *The Craft Apprentice: From Franklin to the Machine Age in America* (New York, 1986), passim; and, on the rise of white-collar America, Stuart M. Blumin, *The Emergence of the Middle Class: Social Experience in the American City, 1760–1900* (Cambridge, 1989), 76–77, 129, 137, 252, and 267–68.

9. Blumin, *Emergence*, 252, explains that nearly all the clerks in Boston in 1850 were native born. Also see John S. C. Abbott, *The School-Boy; Or a Guide to Truth and Duty* (Boston, 1839), 26–27; and *San Francisco School Report* (1875), 282.

10. *Regulations of the School Committee of the City of Boston* (Boston, 1823), 23 (LC); *Boston School Report* (1856), 44. On white-collar and commercial positions and complaints about high student turnover, see *Boston School Report* (1864), 72; (1867), 89–90; (1871), 66; and (1876), 56–57.

11. *Cleveland School Report* (1855), 5.

12. *Cleveland School Report* (1856), 34; and (1863), 12–13; and *Concord School Report* (1871), 25.

13. *Indianapolis School Report* (1870), 49; and *New Jersey School Report* (1874), 6.

14. *Cincinnati School Report* (1853), 38; (1873), 64, for a similar complaint two decades later; and the situation at the black high school described by Leonard Ernest Erickson, "The Color Line in the Ohio Public Schools, 1829–1890," Ph.D. diss., Ohio State University, 1959, 236. Also see the *Fort Wayne School Report* (1866), 18 and (1873), 36; and "A New Course In the High Schools," *Chicago Tribune* (February 12, 1875): 4, which called for more practical courses in secondary education. Also see *Chicago School Report* (1865), 46.

15. *Cleveland School Report* (1863), 32; and *Cincinnati School Report* (1848), 23–25.

16. *Cincinnati School Report* (1857), 116; and Labaree, *Making of an American High School*, 54–56, who notes how admission at an early age also influenced graduation rates; those admitted early were often academically strong students who were likely to do well at Central High.

17. Quoted in *Pennsylvania School Report* (1870), 246.

18. *Indianapolis School Report* (1881), 59–60; *St. Louis School Report* (1869), 35–36; (1871), 79; and the statistical summaries in (1881), 101.

19. *Petersburg, Virginia, School Report* (1871), 14–15.

20. John D. Philbrick, "City School Systems in the United States," U.S. Bureau of Education Circular of Information No. 1 (1885), 28. Also see Emit Duncan Grizzell, *Origin and Development of the High School in New England Before 1865* (Philadelphia, 1923), 331–34; and, on academy precedents, Harriet Webster Marr, *The Old New England Academies Founded Before 1826* (New York, 1959), chaps. 20, 23.

21. *Philadelphia School Report* (1858), 124; *Cleveland School Report* (1875), 56–57; and *Michigan School Report* (1876), 304.

22. "Kokomo High School," *Kokomo Saturday Tribune* (May 27, 1876): 1; *Shelbyville, Indiana, School Report* (1872), 13–16; *Memphis School Report* (1873), 13; and *Atlanta School Report* (1873), 33.

23. David Tyack and Elisabeth Hansot, *Learning Together: A History of Coeducation in American Schools* (New Haven, 1990), 114; *Chicago School Report* (1880), 54–70; "Portland High School Collection," Manuscript Collection (MeHS), volume labeled "Appendix"; *Dayton School Report* (1876), 106; and *Oshkosh School Report* (1875), 28.

24. See Lawrence W. Levine, *Highbrow/Lowbrow: The Emergence of Cultural Hierarchy in America* (Cambridge, 1988).

25. Edward Hicks Magill, *Sixty-Five Years in the Life of a Teacher, 1841–1906* (Boston, 1907), 59.

26. "Exhibition of the Cambridge High School," *MaT* 4 (October 1851): 293–94; and "High School Commencements," *InSJ* 17 (July 1872): 287.

27. *Atlanta School Report* (1873), 47–48.

28. *Atlanta School Report* (1873), 47–48.

29. "High School Graduates," *Indianapolis Daily News* (June 15, 1876): 3.

30. "There is One Entertainment," *Terre Haute Saturday Evening Mail* (June 24, 1876): 5; and "Graduates," *Terre Haute Evening Gazette* (June 24, 1876): 1.

31. "The Intellectual Triumph of a Young Colored Girl," *Terre Haute Saturday Evening Mail* (June 24, 1876): 2. Also see Judy Jolley Mohraz, *The Separate Problem: Case Studies of Black Education in the North, 1900–1930* (Westport, Conn., 1979), 12–13.

32. "The Intellectual Triumph," 2.

33. *Oshkosh School Report* (1879), 9; "High School Exhibitions," *MaT* 20 (August 1867): 286; and *Concord School Report* (1872), 22.

34. *Chicago School Report* (1875), 147. For other complaints on ostentatious dress, see the *Cincinnati School Report* (1877), 59.

35. "Reducing the School Expenses," *Chicago Tribune* (March 22, 1878): 4; and "Commencement," *NTM* 1 (September 1875): 346.

36. "Graduating Exercises," *Kalamazoo Gazette* (June 22, 1872): 4.

37. "High School Commencements," *InSJ* 25 (July 1880): 362. According to the *Terre Haute School Report* (1878), 23, admission fees were charged for a seat at the local commencement.

38. Newspaper clipping, "Young Girl Graduates," in "Scrapbook No. 1," *Alumni Club* (Louisville Female High School, Manuscript Collection) (FC).

39. "Young Girl Graduates."

40. *Terre Haute School Report* (1878), 23.

41. Lizzie Black, "Graduating Essay" (1878), Lizzie Black Kander Papers, Box 1, Folder 10 (SHSWi); and William J. Reese, *Power and the Promise of School Reform: Grass-Roots Movements During the Progressive Era* (Boston, 1986), 36–37, passim.

42. *Louisville School Report* (1868), 46.

43. "Education," *USMDR* 25 (August 1849): 158.

44. "High Culture and Common Life," *NEJE* 9 (June 26, 1879): 413.

45. "High Culture and Common Life," 413; and "After Graduation," *NEJE* 10 (September 11, 1879): 133.

46. *Philadelphia School Report* (1846), 96.

47. *New York City School Report* (1864), 14; and *Boston School Report* (1869), 34.

48. *Philadelphia School Report* (1867), 273; and *Atlanta School Report* (1872), 30.

49. *Charleston School Report* (1860), 6; "School Architecture," *AJE* 13 (September 1863): 621; and *Chicago School Report* (1854), 12. These arguments were staples in state and local school reports before the 1880s.

50. *Indiana School Report* (1853), 13; *Boston School Report* (1858), 124, 127; (1860), 34; (1861), 23; (1863), 84; and *New York City School Report* (1879), 54.

51. *Chicago School Report* (1867), 12; *Cincinnati School Report* (1862), 38–39; *Iowa School Report* (1865), 23; and Joseph W. Newman, "Antebellum School Reform in the Port Cities of the Deep South," in *Southern Cities, Southern Schools: Public Education in the Urban South*, ed. David N. Plank and Rick Ginsberg (Westport, Conn., 1990), 20–21.

52. Many large cities could not place their female graduates during the depression of the 1870s, and schoolmen blamed ward bosses for hiring relatives or daughters of friends, not the best-qualified pupils, as teachers for the few openings that remained. See the analysis of the problem in the *New York City School Report* (1878), 216; *Boston School Report* (1876), 16, passim; and *Philadelphia School Report* (1879), 31.

53. *Akron School Report* (1876) 48–50. By 1849, male students from Cleveland's Central High School had already secured many jobs as clerks; see *SB* 2 (June 20, 1849): 4. In *Cleveland School Report* (1877), 110–11, the local superintendent said that 50 percent of male graduates became "clerks, salesmen, book-keepers, or merchants," while about 25 percent became "professional men." The *Louisville School Report* (1863), 65, indicated that "among [Louisville Male High School] Alumni are to be found members of all the learned professions; also, bank, brokers', and mercantile clerks, civil engineers, farmers, manufacturers, and merchants."

54. Richard Alston Metcalf, comp., *A History of Princeton High School* (Princeton, Ill., 1892), 82, 96.

55. Edward Henry Elwell, *The Schools of Portland* (Portland, 1888), 23.

56. John R. Patterson, "Where Have They Gone?" *HSS* 1 (May 12, 1883): 7 (ChHS).

57. *Chicago School Report* (1873), 260, passim.

58. "Local Intelligentsia," *MaT* 12 (March 1859): 119; and *Hartford School Report* (1868), 11.

59. Philbrick, "City School Systems," 28.

60. John Trevor Custis, *The Public Schools of Philadelphia* (Philadelphia, 1897), 571; *Philadelphia School Report* (1853), 142; and "Philadelphia High School," *RIS* 3 (July 1857): 136.

61. *One Hundred Years of the English High School of Boston* (Boston, 1924), 23–24; R. C. Waterston, *The English High School Association: Its Origin, Its Purpose, and What It Has Accomplished* (Boston, 1881), 11–25 (BPL); and "The High School Boy," *OhEM* 8 (September 1859): 266. The Latin School also had an alumni association, whose activities are described in the *Boston School Report* (1855), 71, 76.

62. "Calliopean Literary Society," *PaSJ* 2 (March 1854): 272; and *Oshkosh School Report* (1873), 250.

63. On Woodward High School, see especially *Cincinnati School Report* (1861) 42; Isaac M. Martin, *History of the Schools of Cincinnati* (Cincinnati, 1900), 57–60; and John B. Shotwell, *A History of the Schools of Cincinnati* (Cincinnati, 1902), 165. The Woodward principal, Daniel Shepardson, was an avid Unionist.

64. Metcalf, *A History*, 66; *Meanings for Manhood: Constructions of Masculinity in Victorian America*, ed. Mark C. Carnes and Clyde Griffen (Chicago, 1990); and Mary P. Ryan, *Women in Public: Between Banners and Ballots, 1825–1880* (Baltimore, 1990), 155–71.

65. Minute book, "Constitution of the Alumni Society of the Indianapolis High School," 5, 15, 87, Lyndsay Brown Papers (InSL).

66. "Constitution," 97, 121, 125.

Epilogue

1. "Historical Development of Education," *AJE* 32 (1882): 872.

2. Ellwood P. Cubberley, one of the most prominent historians of education in the early twentieth century, claimed that academies were middle-class institutions, whereas the high school was the product of "a new and aggressive democracy"; see *A Brief History of Education* (Boston, 1922), 387; and *Public Education in the United States* (Boston, 1919). See also U.S. Bureau of Education, "Proceedings of the Department of Superintendence of the National Education Association, at its Meeting at Washington, D.C.," Circular of Information No. 2 (1880), 69.

3. H. P. Johnson, "The Spiritual Side of the High-School Question," *Journal of Proceedings*, American Institute of Instruction, 1880, 28–29.

4. Johnson, "Spiritual Side," 31.

5. *Memphis School Report* (1880), 29.

6. "Our Public High Schools," *LaJE* 2 (October 1880): 169–70.

7. *A Brief Sketch of the Establishment of the High School, Providence, Together With the Dedicatory Exercises of the New Building* (Providence, 1878), 49–50.

8. *Brief Sketch*, 50.

9. *Brief Sketch*, 50.

10. *Brief Sketch*, 40–41.

11. "The Kingdom," *Asp* (December 12, 1863): n.p., Portland Girls' High School Alumni Association Collection (MeHS).

Index

ogage avant publication de Bibliothèque et Archives nationales
uébec et Bibliothèque et Archives Canada

le, Paul, 1961-
onciliation travail-bonheur : humaniser l'entreprise, c'est possible et payant
omprend des réf. bibliogr.
3BN 978-2-9811338-5-4

.. Gestion d'entreprise. 2. Potentiel humain (Psychologie). 3. Qualité de la
ʋie au travail. 4. Rentabilité. 5. Gestion d'entreprise – Québec (Province) –
Cas, Études de. I. Titre.

   HD33.D44 2010   658   C2010-940840-3

ʇvision linguistique : Catherine Guin
ɔllaborateur spécial : Henri Marineau
ɪfographie : Isabelle Bossé
ɪise en pages : Infoscan Collette, Québec

ɪditeur :
ɪes Éditions NKS, le vent dans les voiles
38 de la Perdrix, Stoneham G3C 2J5
Tél : 418-572-2208
Courriel : info@editionsnks.ca

ISBN : 978-2-9811338-5-4

Dépôt légal :
2e trimestre 2010
Bibliothèque nationale du Québec
Bibliothèque nationale du Canada
© 2010

Conciliation
Travail - Bonheur

Humaniser l'entreprise, c'est possible et payant !

PAUL DELISLE

Cata
du (

Del
(

R
(

Table des matières

Remerciements

La ligne d'arrivée est là, tout près. C'est ma première expérience à titre d'auteur. Le courage et la détermination, éléments essentiels à la réalisation de ce projet, de ce rêve personnel et professionnel, trouvent leur source dans le support et la présence de précieux amis et collaborateurs.

Merci à France, ma conjointe de vie, pour avoir relu et commenté chaque texte de ce livre. Merci de ton support et de la manifestation de ta confiance concernant ma capacité à mener à terme ce projet. Merci de la tolérance des nombreuses absences d'esprit en période d'écriture de ce manuscrit.

Merci à mes enfants, Andréa et Alexandre, pour leur support et leurs nombreux encouragements.

Merci à mes frères et sœurs pour m'avoir encouragé à poursuivre, pour avoir commenté certaines parties et pour avoir cru à ce projet.

Merci à Henri Marineau, un ancien professeur du Collège des Jésuites. Ce projet a permis à nos itinéraires terrestres de se croiser à nouveau. Merci de votre patience et du généreux partage de votre expérience de vie à titre d'auteur. Merci pour votre oreille attentive aux moments de doutes. Merci d'avoir accepté de signer la préface.

Merci à Louis Garneau, Anne Morisset et Steve Couture pour leur contribution à l'humanisation de la gestion des entreprises. Le

partage de vos expériences permet à tous les intervenants de croire
qu'une saine gestion d'entreprise peut faciliter le bonheur de tous
les intervenants.

Merci à Yves Sévigny, à Guy Lefebvre, à Lise et Jean-Marc
Gagnon, à Marie-Claude Beaudoin, à Pier Antoine Marier et à
Philippe Dorget.

Merci à vous, chers lecteurs et lectrices, pour avoir parcouru
les chapitres de ce livre. Merci d'évoluer vers le bonheur et de faire
en sorte, à votre façon, que la gestion de nos entreprises soit
dorénavant plus humaine.

Préface

Existe-t-il une relation entre une gestion d'entreprise innovatrice respectueuse des principes de base de la croissance personnelle et le succès des entreprises?

Expert en gestion du potentiel humain, l'auteur partage son expérience auprès des entrepreneurs du Québec et explique simplement et concrètement comment mobiliser les troupes, améliorer la rentabilité de nos entreprises et obtenir l'indice organisationnel du bonheur optimal.

Cette approche ne s'apparente en rien à la voie de la facilité. Elle demeure exigeante pour tous les intervenants. Elle est grandement dérangeante en ce sens qu'elle exige une remise en question de nos façons d'être et de faire. C'est le prix à payer pour accéder au podium.

Ce livre s'adresse à tous les gestionnaires d'entreprises, actuels et futurs, soucieux d'adopter des pratiques de gestion innovatrices dans l'objectif premier d'améliorer la rentabilité de leur entreprise. Il contient une mine de renseignements incontournables pour tout individu soucieux de transformer une zone d'inconfort en opportunité de croissance.

Le lecteur sortira enrichi de la découverte de la pertinence de la relation étroite entre la recherche du bonheur, aspiration de tous les êtres humains, et la gestion humaine des entreprises, un idéal fascinant dont la responsabilité appartient à tous les intervenants, collaborateurs et gestionnaires.

Peu importe son lien d'affaires dans l'entreprise, le lecteur sera appelé à devenir un des acteurs principaux de l'écriture de l'histoire à succès du projet entrepreneurial auquel il aura décidé de se consacrer avec passion et persévérance. L'expérience de l'auteur en gestion du potentiel humain lui permet de conclure que le problème ne se situe pas à propos des lacunes quant aux capacités des individus mais plutôt des stratégies défaillantes ne permettant pas aux intervenants de contribuer à l'atteinte des objectifs organisationnels de façon optimale.

Enfin, un auteur qui relève le défi d'expliquer concrètement comment y parvenir dans un livre qui démontre avec audace et sans équivoque la relation étroite entre la recherche du bonheur et la gestion de nos entreprises.

J'ai pris la décision d'apporter ma collaboration à ce livre car j'ai la ferme conviction que nos entreprises ont avantage à respecter les principes de base de la croissance personnelle et de la recherche du bonheur dans l'implantation et l'application des meilleures pratiques d'affaires, une approche que j'ai personnellement développée, tout au cours de ma carrière, en utilisant au maximum le potentiel humain de mes ressources, m'assurant de la sorte de leur contribution optimale à l'essor de l'organisation.

Un ouvrage dérangeant qui provoque une évolution, voire une révolution culturelle et sociale essentielle au mieux-être des individus et des organisations !

Un livre innovateur qui assure la meilleure utilisation de la ressource humaine, en recyclant au maximum cette précieuse denrée, évitant ainsi le gaspillage et les pertes financières inestimables !

Un choix de société incontournable dans un contexte de mondialisation où nous ne pouvons plus nous satisfaire de performances moyennes !

Un défi qui doit être animé d'une passion et d'une détermination teintées d'un sens de l'innovation que l'auteur de ce livre nous invite à suivre avec confiance!

Voilà, à mon sens, pourquoi la lecture de ce livre s'impose!

Henri Marineau
Auteur

Introduction

Destiné aux entrepreneurs du Québec, ce livre veut contribuer à l'évolution des meilleures pratiques d'affaires et de gestion en y intégrant les principes de base de la croissance personnelle et de la recherche du bonheur.

C'est un défi d'envergure mais cet exercice nous semble le moyen par excellence pour donner accès à une information privilégiée sur les meilleures pratiques d'affaires.

De tous les temps, la croissance personnelle et la recherche du bonheur ont été traitées en priorité. Nous observons, cependant, que dans tous les cas, c'est une approche individuelle et volontaire qui est utilisée.

Ainsi, notre débuterons par une définition du mot bonheur. Nous ferons ensuite la synthèse des écoles de pensées reliées à la croissance personnelle et à la recherche du bonheur. Nous démontrerons que cette initiative s'inscrit dans un mouvement mondial de conception du bonheur par des approches scientifiques.

Nous analyserons ensuite la contribution des profils de personnalité à l'amélioration de la gestion du potentiel humain en contexte d'entreprise.

La troisième partie offrira un coffre d'outils pour entrepreneur, incluant les principales pratiques de gestion assurant l'utilisation optimale du potentiel humain et la rentabilité optimale de nos organisations. Les techniques d'utilisation et d'implantation feront l'objet d'explications exhaustives et le retour sur l'investissement sera largement documenté par les méthodes quantitatives et qualitatives.

Enfin, la quatrième partie racontera les histoires à succès de Louis Garneau de Louis Garneau Sports, d'Anne Morisset de Boulevard Lexus Toyota et de Steve Couture de Frima Studio, trois modèles entrepreneuriaux québécois. Nous vous donnerons accès au vécu de ces entrepreneurs en expliquant comment ils réalisent et mesurent une gestion d'entreprise qui optimise l'indice organisationnel du bonheur.

PREMIÈRE PARTIE

Synthèse des écoles de pensées

Cette première partie veut faire la synthèse de quelques écoles de pensées en matière de croissance personnelle, de développement personnel et de recherche du bonheur.

À partir d'une définition du mot bonheur, nous aborderons le bonheur de tranquillité, le bonheur de jouissance (Être), pour terminer avec le bonheur de croissance (Être plus).

CHAPITRE 1

Définition du bonheur

À partir d'une définition tirée d'un dictionnaire, nous aborderons la notion d'indice de bonheur applicable à la société pour discuter cette notion en contexte d'entreprise.

Le dictionnaire de la langue française définit le mot bonheur de la façon suivante : «nom masculin, état heureux de bien-être, chance, hasard favorable.» Parmi les synonymes, il cite : allégresse, avantage, béatitude, bien-être, bienfait, chance, contentement, enivrement, euphorie, extase, félicité, gaieté, joie, ravissement, satisfaction, sérénité et succès.

Pierre Côté, auteur, décide en septembre 2006 d'orienter sa carrière de consultant en marketing et communication au développement de l'indice qu'il a créé et à l'analyse du bonheur sous toutes ces formes. Il exprime que le bonheur est une notion subjective et relative, ce qui rend sa définition et les différents moyens de l'atteindre quasi impossibles à préciser sans d'abord créer le consensus sur certains postulats de base.

Le bonheur, tel que véhiculé par les chercheurs et philosophes contemporains, semble davantage tourné vers l'externe que vers l'interne. Certains prétendent même que le bonheur est réduit à une notion simpliste, matérialiste et quantifiable.

Pierre Côté définit l'indice relatif du bonheur (IRB) comme suit:

« L'IRB, c'est une façon nouvelle d'évaluer qualitativement et quantitativement l'état d'esprit général des populations et de les comparer entre elles. Nous partons du principe que tout être humain recherche, consciemment ou non, une situation qui s'approchera le plus possible de sa vision du bonheur. Cette dernière est variable et s'appuie sur des valeurs, des acquis et des sentiments qui diffèrent d'un individu à un autre. Ce que l'IRB évaluera, ce sont donc l'impression et la perception que les gens ont de leur propre état.

L'utilité de cet indice est de faire du bonheur une variable qui compte lorsque vient le temps de porter un jugement sur une collectivité donnée et d'enrichir les grands débats de société en introduisant un aspect humain et une évaluation différente... Nous croyons qu'au-delà de toutes ces données, il est essentiel de demeurer centré sur l'objectif principal de toute vie, soit celui d'être le plus heureux possible et de l'être le plus longtemps ou le plus souvent possible.[1] »

Stéphane Osmont dans son livre « À la poursuite du bonheur[2] » nous prédit que le XXIe siècle sera celui du bonheur scientifique.

Mais, existe-t-il une relation entre une gestion d'entreprise innovatrice respectueuse des principes de base de la croissance personnelle et le succès des entreprises? À titre de gestionnaires d'entreprises, avons-nous avantage à contribuer à l'atteinte de notre bonheur personnel et collectif?

L'amélioration de l'indice organisationnel du bonheur et de la rentabilité de nos entreprises exige l'humanisation de nos entreprises. Les outils de gestion disponibles et leur méthode d'implantation en entreprise sont détaillés à la troisième partie de ce livre.

---

1. Larousse 3 volumes en couleurs, Larousse, P., 1970
2. À la poursuite du bonheur; Stéphane Osmont; Éditions Albin Michel; 2000, 198 p.

CHAPITRE 2

Bonheur de tranquillité

Le dictionnaire donne la définition suivante au mot stoïcisme : au sens philosophique, doctrine du philosophe grec Zénon dont l'éthique est basée sur la maîtrise de soi, l'entraide entre les hommes et la modération.

Cette doctrine insiste sur la fragilité et la précarité de la condition humaine. Ses pensées s'orientent sur l'immortalité et sur le caractère inexorable du destin. Tous les livres de croissance personnelle qui assurent la richesse à leur penseur sont largement influencés par cette doctrine.

Épictète, autre philosophe de l'école stoïcienne, a fondé sa doctrine morale sur la liberté et sur l'humanisme. Son secret réside dans le travail sur soi. Il est intéressant de constater son influence encore aujourd'hui. C'est probablement une partie de la réponse au questionnement qui tente d'expliquer pourquoi l'investissement en matière de croissance personnelle existe surtout sur une base individuelle et volontaire.

Marc Aurèle est un autre philosophe stoïcien. C'est lui qui introduisit l'étude de l'être humain axée autour de trois « Moi ». Le MOI tel que perçu par les autres, le MOI ou l'image que tu projettes pour les autres, et enfin ton MOI authentique, ce que tu es. Cette conception a eu un effet majeur sur les profils de personnalité, comme nous le verrons plus loin.

Arthur Schopenhauer est un philosophe allemand (1788-1860). Fondateur du pessimisme, il considère que de tous les mondes possibles «notre monde est le pire qui soit». L'idée fait place à la volonté. Elle est le principe fondamental de l'univers, elle est source de vie, source de progrès. C'est cette volonté universelle, dont la conscience individuelle n'est qu'un moment fugitif, qui pousse l'être à se nourrir du désir de bonheur, bonheur inaccessible qui engendre la souffrance et la douleur, l'état naturel de l'homme selon Schopenhauer.

Le pessimisme de Schopenhauer utilise pour assise principale que la souffrance est universelle. Il laisse peu de place au bonheur, fruit d'illusions ou de moments d'évasion, selon lui.

Le bouddhisme est, selon les points de vue traditionnels, une philosophie, une spiritualité ou une religion apparue en Inde au Ve siècle av. J.-C. Il présente un ensemble ramifié de pratiques méditatives, de pratiques éthiques, de théories psychologiques, philosophiques et cosmogoniques, abordées dans la perspective de la libération de l'insatisfaction, du plein épanouissement du potentiel humain, et ce, en relation personnelle avec une intangible et ultime réalité spirituelle. Nous comprenons ici que le thème de l'épanouissement du potentiel humain ne date pas d'aujourd'hui. Malgré cela, il reste beaucoup à faire pour atteindre l'objectif de l'épanouissement personnel et collectif.

La première vérité du bouddhisme stipule que la souffrance est universelle. Seules la sainteté et la sagesse permettent de voir la souffrance cachée dans les choses apparemment agréables alors que le commun des mortels y voit un mélange de souffrance et de joie. Cette école de pensée va jusqu'à considérer que notre richesse et notre bien-être sont issus de l'appauvrissement des autres.

La deuxième vérité considère le désir comme étant la cause du mal et de la souffrance. Ce désir provoque les cycles de la vie et a pour caractéristique d'être omniprésent.

La troisième vérité indique que le remède à la souffrance réside dans l'extinction du désir et dans la prise de conscience que le moi est une illusion. Le but du bouddhisme demeure de détruire l'individualité et de mourir à soi.

Nous ne pouvons pas effleurer le bouddhisme sans parler de Matthieu Ricard, auteur, entre autres, du « Plaidoyer pour le bonheur ». Il affirme que nous aspirons tous au bonheur mais s'interroge sur les moyens de le trouver, le retenir et même le définir. Sa réponse consiste à cesser de chercher le bonheur à l'extérieur de nous, pour apprendre à regarder en nous-mêmes dans une approche plus méditative et altruiste.

Enfin, pour le Dalaï-lama, « le bonheur est le but de l'existence[1] ». Dans son livre « L'art du bonheur », il exprime que le véritable but de la vie est le bonheur et que l'on peut l'atteindre par l'exercice de l'esprit. Pour lui, le bonheur demeure un but réalisable. En s'imposant une certaine discipline intérieure, on peut, selon lui, transformer son attitude, ses conceptions et sa manière d'être dans l'existence. Cette discipline intérieure repose sur une quantité de méthodes. La voie consiste à isoler les facteurs qui mènent au bonheur de ceux qui mènent à la souffrance pour éliminer peu à peu les facteurs de souffrance et cultiver ceux qui conduisent au bonheur. Cette recherche du bonheur se révélera une source de bienfaits, tant pour l'individu, sa famille que pour la société au sens large.

---

1. L'art du bonheur; Sa Sainteté Dalaï-Lama; Éditions Robert Laffont; 1999.

CHAPITRE

Bonheur de plaisir

Après avoir fait la synthèse des philosophies du bonheur de tranquillité, nous nous attarderons à celles qui traitent du plaisir.

L'hédonisme, du grec ancien «plaisir», et du verbe «se réjouir», est une doctrine philosophique selon laquelle la recherche du plaisir et l'évitement du déplaisir constituent des impératifs catégoriques.

Les plaisirs de l'existence, multiples, varient selon les individus et selon leur éducation. Les penseurs hédonistes ont orienté leur vie en fonction de leurs dispositions propres, tout en intégrant des thèmes communs: l'amitié, la tendresse, la sexualité libre, les plaisirs de la table, la conversation, une vie constituée dans la recherche constante des plaisirs et un corps en bonne santé. On peut aussi trouver la noblesse d'âme, le savoir et les sciences en général, la lecture, la pratique des arts et des exercices physiques et le bien social.

Dans le même temps, les douleurs et les déplaisirs à éviter sont les relations conflictuelles et la proximité des personnes sans capacités contractuelles (sans paroles), le rabaissement et l'humilité, la soumission à un ordre imposé, la violence, les privations et les frustrations justifiées par des fables.

Ainsi, il n'y a pas d'hédonisme sans discipline personnelle, sans ascèse, sans connaissance de soi, du monde et des autres.

Épicure rappelle qu'un plaisir excessif actuel doit être évité s'il conduit à une douleur future.

En présence de choix, la théorie des probabilités propose de calculer les espérances mathématiques de gain et d'opter pour le choix qui maximise cette espérance de gain. En théorie de la décision, on distingue le risque de l'incertitude. Le risque désigne une situation dans laquelle les distributions de probabilités sur les résultats existent et sont connues des agents. L'attitude d'un décideur par rapport au risque est cruciale pour comprendre son comportement face à des situations risquées. L'aversion ou la préférence pour le risque est alors déterminant en ce qui concerne le comportement adopté.

Si les situations de risque constituent, dans la vie courante, des situations assez marginales, l'incertitude est en revanche omniprésente. Optimisation et maximalisation sont les deux mots-clés définissant les théories de la prise de décision basées sur la rationalisation, c'est-à-dire les théories définissant les normes logiques et rationnelles que tous les preneurs de décisions sont censés suivre pour que le choix soit celui qui « rapporte » le plus. La théorie de l'utilité espérée est l'approche la plus communément retenue par la théorie de la décision pour décrire les choix risqués.

John Stuart Mill, qui reprit la doctrine utilitariste, reprocha de ne pas avoir donné de hiérarchisation qualitative de la nature des plaisirs. Mais une telle hiérarchisation fait sortir de l'hédonisme pour y introduire d'autres valorisations et d'autres fins comme celle de « vie bonne pour l'homme », qui recherche une valeur du bonheur en plus des plaisirs. Nous retrouvons ici pour la première fois la notion de recherche du bonheur en tant que valeur.

L'hédonisme, comme attitude de vie sociale est un phénomène provoquant un débat profond sur le plan des valeurs et de la morale. L'hédonisme est associé presque automatiquement à l'égoïsme sur le plan individuel et à l'anarchie sur le plan collectif. Cependant il peut être moralement désirable s'il inclut des valeurs qui dépassent notre individualité et qui obligent à le penser dans le rapport à l'autre et dans un débat critique sur les forces du pouvoir.

L'Épicurisme est une école philosophique fondée à Athènes par Épicure en 306 av. J.-C. Elle entrait en concurrence avec l'autre grande pensée de l'époque, le stoïcisme, école philosophique présentée au chapitre 1. L'épicurisme est axé sur la recherche d'un bonheur et d'une sagesse dont le but ultime est l'atteinte de l'ataraxie, une doctrine matérialiste et atomiste.

Son but est d'arriver à un état de bonheur constant, une sérénité de l'esprit, tout en bannissant toute forme de plaisir non utile, prolongé ou non. Il professe que, pour éviter la souffrance, il faut éviter les sources de plaisir qui ne sont ni naturelles ni nécessaires.

Épicure élabore une théorie de la connaissance qui se fonde sur les sens, sur la véracité des sensations qui garantissent seules que nous connaissons la réalité. Il invente également la théorie des prénotions : nous formons en nous des concepts à partir d'expériences répétées. Ces prénotions donnent un point de départ à la réflexion humaine.

- La passion ou affection, évidence du plaisir et de la douleur : le plaisir nous fait connaître une cause de plaisir, et la souffrance, une cause de souffrance. L'agréable et le pénible sont donc des critères de la vérité non seulement de l'état passif, mais aussi de sa cause.

- La sensation ou impression sensible : c'est un état passif de la sensation, né du contact avec les choses et qui nous fait connaître avec certitude la cause active et productrice. Cet état, en effet, par définition, la sensation étant irrationnelle et sans mémoire, ne peut agir par lui-même et modifier ce qui nous touche de l'extérieur.

Pour Épicure il faut se référer au sens premier d'un mot, lié à la prénotion dont il tient son sens. Cette théorie invite à décrire l'origine du langage pour mieux comprendre la connaissance humaine. Selon lui, une juste compréhension de l'univers permet de mener une vie heureuse.

En réalité, il s'agit d'une philosophie d'équilibre, fondée sur l'idée que toute action entraîne à la fois des effets plaisants (positifs) et des effets amenant la souffrance (négatifs). Il s'agit donc pour l'épicurien d'agir sobrement en recherchant les actions amenant l'absence de douleur, d'où doit découler le plaisir négatif de cet état de repos (ataraxie) ; cependant, la pleine conscience de cette ataraxie procure le plaisir suprême et la clef du bonheur, c'est-à-dire connaître ses propres limites. L'excès doit être évité car il apporte la souffrance.

Le plaisir est le bien et les vertus servent d'instruments. La vie selon le plaisir est cependant une vie de prudence, de vertu et de justice.

Cette classification n'est pas séparable d'un art de vivre où les désirs sont l'objet d'un calcul en vue d'atteindre le bonheur. À partir de là, il est naturel de juger bon le plaisir et mauvaise la douleur, puisque tous les êtres cherchent le plaisir. Ce sont nos sentiments qui nous indiquent que le plaisir est désirable. C'est une conscience naturelle et notre constitution fait que nous cherchons le bonheur nécessairement.

En fin de compte, le principe le plus important de la doctrine d'Épicure est de vivre selon la prudence quand on cherche le plaisir. Elle renvoie au quadruple remède : vivre sans peur, avec les plaisirs de l'amitié et de nos souvenirs, en supprimant les fausses croyances sources d'angoisse et les douleurs évitables.

En conclusion de cette pensée, la philosophie est une activité qui rend la vie heureuse.

CHAPITRE

Bonheur de croissance

Le bonheur demeure le but universellement recherché par tout être humain, peu importe son espace temporel, géographique ou culturel. L'humain tend irrémédiablement à être lui-même, au meilleur de lui-même, dans la plénitude de son être.

Nous faisons référence ici au potentiel humain qui offre une infinité de possibilités dans un environnement complexe en perpétuel changement. Alors que l'analyse du potentiel humain pose encore aujourd'hui des problématiques tant en ce qui concerne sa définition que sa mesure, que penser de l'utilisation et de la gestion de ce même potentiel?

Alors que la littérature abonde de recettes pour accéder au bonheur en utilisant des techniques d'une simplicité telle que le sentiment d'être autre chose que heureux nous fait croire à une certaine marginalité, voilà que Stéphane Osmont, dans son livre « À la poursuite du bonheur[1] », ose reconnaître que son impuissance à connaître le succès l'a poussé à rencontrer des sommités de tous les domaines et à affirmer que le XXIe siècle sera celui du bonheur scientifique.

La psychologie, la sociologie, l'économie, la neurobiologie ou la génétique œuvrent toutes aux avancées scientifiques relatives

---

1. Stéphane Osmont; op. cit.; p. 13.

au bonheur, tant en ce qui concerne les indicateurs que les statistiques.

Même l'ONU contribue financièrement depuis plusieurs années à l'indice de progrès véritable. L'indice de développement humain ou IDH est un indice statistique composite, créé par le Programme des Nations Unies pour le développement (PNUD) en 1990, évaluant le niveau de développement humain des pays du monde.

Le concept du développement humain est plus large que ce qu'en décrit l'IDH qui n'en est qu'un indicateur pour évaluer ce qui n'était mesuré auparavant qu'avec imprécision. L'indicateur précédent utilisé, le PIB par habitant, ne donne pas d'information sur le bien-être individuel ou collectif, mais n'évalue que la production économique. Pour le PNUD, le développement est plutôt un processus d'élargissement du choix des gens qu'une simple augmentation du revenu national.

L'IDH est calculé par la moyenne de trois indices quantifiant respectivement :

1. La santé /longévité (mesurées par l'espérance de vie à la naissance), qui permet de mesurer indirectement la satisfaction des besoins matériels essentiels tels que l'accès à une alimentation saine, à l'eau potable, à un logement décent, à une bonne hygiène et aux soins médicaux ;

2. Le savoir ou niveau d'éducation mesuré par le taux d'alphabétisation des adultes (pourcentage des 15 ans et plus sachant écrire et comprendre aisément un texte court et simple traitant de la vie quotidienne) et le taux brut de scolarisation (mesure combinée des taux pour le primaire, le secondaire et le supérieur) lequel traduit la satisfaction des besoins immatériels tels que la capacité à participer aux prises de décision sur le lieu de travail ou dans la société ;

3. Le niveau de vie (logarithme du produit intérieur brut par habitant en parité de pouvoir d'achat), afin d'englober les éléments de la qualité de vie qui ne sont pas décrits par les deux premiers indices tels que la mobilité ou l'accès à la culture.

Mais quels comportements ou attitudes des sociétés et des individus assurent de meilleurs résultats ? Qui sont les principaux intervenants ? Les entrepreneurs du Québec assument-ils une responsabilité pour améliorer les indices de bonheur et de bien-être ?

Une enquête, menée en 2009 par Jobboom/IRB sur les valeurs des québécois face au travail, permet d'identifier le climat de travail, soit la capacité de travailler dans un climat sain et agréable où règnent l'entraide, la solidarité et la transparence, comme la valeur la plus importante. Viennent ensuite l'argent et le plaisir. Il est surprenant de constater que la santé et le bien-être arrivent en neuvième place. Ainsi, la santé et le bien-être demeurent une préoccupation personnelle, et une perception générale n'établit pas de relation directe entre ce bien-être et la gestion de nos entreprises. Pourtant, lorsque vient le temps d'identifier les causes des maladies, le travail accompli et la gestion de l'entreprise sont souvent cités en premier.

L'humain demeurera toujours le premier responsable de son bonheur et de son bien-être. Sa contribution à la société par le travail rémunéré ou non permet de répondre à certains de ses besoins, selon la pyramide de Maslow. Les quatre avenues à explorer susceptibles d'améliorer son état de bonheur et de bien-être s'expriment par le vrai, le beau, le bon, le bien et les relations interpersonnelles.

Ce désir du vrai m'appelle à me réaliser au maximum de mes capacités et possibilités en apaisant mon besoin d'explorer, de connaître et de comprendre. Cet univers de la connaissance est un moyen d'outrepasser ses limites et de s'ouvrir à la totalité de la réalité dans le respect de ce que nous sommes dans notre unicité. C'est une bonne part de notre richesse intérieure qui offre une source de joie profonde.

L'avenue du beau présente l'opportunité de reconnaître la beauté de l'univers sous toutes ses formes en reconnaissant que je fais partie de cet univers. Ainsi, l'être humain est appelé à développer et à raffiner au maximum sa capacité de conscientisation de la grandeur et de la beauté de l'univers qui connaît la seule limite de l'infini. Cette contemplation de la beauté demeure une forme de la plénitude de l'être.

L'être humain vit en société. La qualité de ses interrelations avec les autres affecte l'évaluation qu'il fait de sa richesse intérieure, de sa qualité de vie et de son positionnement en regard du bonheur.

Voilà une des composantes très complexe de la gestion du potentiel humain. Il ne suffit pas de connaître les forces et les faiblesses de chaque intervenant. Dans une conception de synergie d'équipe et de mobilisation des troupes, il faut s'assurer de la complémentarité des compétences, connaissances et expertises pour faciliter la réalisation des objectifs organisationnels. De plus, il faut statuer sur la capacité des intervenants à agir en collaboration. Cette mission demeure impossible et fort coûteuse si nous n'utilisons pas d'outils de gestion. Ce point sera largement documenté dans la deuxième partie de ce livre.

DEUXIÈME PARTIE

Gestion et utilisation du potentiel humain

En première partie de ce livre, nous avons clairement démontré que, de tout temps, le bonheur est primordial pour l'être humain, peu importe les époques et les cultures. En tant que gestionnaire des ressources humaines, le dirigeant d'entreprise est souvent confronté à une gestion souvent plus complexe que celle exigée par les autres ressources.

L'expérience acquise en gestion des ressources humaines en entreprise permet trop souvent de constater un fort degré de découragement en la matière. Les commentaires reçus dénotent une incapacité à mobiliser le personnel pour réaliser le projet de l'entreprise. Il demeure inquiétant de constater le manque ou même l'absence de préparation des entrepreneurs à assumer cette lourde tâche qu'est la gestion des ressources humaines.

Je me souviens avoir accompagné un jeune entrepreneur qui avait fait l'acquisition d'une entreprise de services dans le domaine des télécommunications. Un an après être devenu propriétaire, il me confiait qu'il avait acheté cette entreprise pour se consacrer à sa passion et qu'il prenait soudainement conscience qu'il passait plus de la moitié de son temps à solutionner des problématiques de gestion des ressources humaines alors qu'il n'avait reçu aucune formation en la matière.

Encore récemment, j'étais en contact avec un autre entrepreneur en affaires depuis plus de dix ans. Il me disait qu'il venait de consacrer près de six mois à définir le plan stratégique de croissance et d'acquisitions, incluant les prévisions budgétaires des cinq prochaines années. Je lui exprimais que mon constat principal demeurait que les entrepreneurs œuvrent à autre chose que ce pour quoi ils ont été formés en institution d'enseignement ou à l'école de la vie !

Les meilleures théories en matière de gestion du potentiel humain ont beaucoup à faire et à vivre pour répondre aux besoins des entrepreneurs sous une forme compatible avec leurs véritables besoins.

La conception théorique de l'utilisation optimale du potentiel humain demeure louable si elle assure l'utilisation de chaque intervenant à l'intérieur de ses zones de performance et la capacité de travailler en complémentarité à la réalisation des objectifs organisationnels. En pratique, c'est moins évident. Nos entrepreneurs et gestionnaires, eux-mêmes, œuvrent au meilleur de leurs connaissance pour répondre aux exigences sans cesse grandissantes de la clientèle sans se demander si le défi à relever permettra d'exploiter leur potentiel humain, se consacrant plutôt sans relâche à satisfaire leur raison de vivre, c'est-à-dire le client.

Une gestion du potentiel humain peut-elle s'appliquer différemment pour l'équipe de direction et pour les collaborateurs ? Notre compréhension reste qu'une saine gestion du potentiel humain doit assurer la meilleure contribution des ressources à la réalisation des objectifs organisationnels. Ainsi, toute intervention en gestion du potentiel humain doit contribuer à la réalisation de cet objectif.

L'utilisation des outils de gestion du potentiel humain exige de prendre en considération des facteurs ayant un impact majeur sur la prise de décision. À titre d'exemple, comment ne pas considérer l'importance capitale du caractère familial des PME québécoises ? Notre expérience en entreprise démontre qu'une décision d'embauche ou de dotation est largement influencée par l'existence d'un lien familial. Nous ne sommes pas convaincus que nos entrepreneurs et gestionnaires utilisent des outils de gestion du potentiel humain pour définir les responsabilités des personnes ayant un lien de parenté !

Par contre, nous pouvons nous interroger longuement sur la pertinence des décisions prises en considérant des facteurs autres que ceux généralement reconnus en matière de gestion du potentiel humain. Servent-elles les intérêts de l'entreprise?

Les coûts directs et indirects d'erreurs en matière de gestion du potentiel humain sont énormes si on tient compte des conséquences sur l'entreprise. L'utilisation de la mauvaise personne pour assumer des responsabilités spécifiques provoque directement l'utilisation d'autres personnes pour les assumer. Ces dernières qui consacrent temps et énergie à assumer des responsabilités autres que les leurs négligent leur propre travail. Ainsi, l'erreur à la base se répercute sur l'ensemble de l'organisation, affectant ainsi sa pérennité et empêchant la saisie des nombreuses opportunités d'affaires.

Vous me permettrez deux exemples vécus pour justifier mes propos. Un de mes clients jongle avec une problématique de gestion en contexte familial, ceci depuis cinq ans. Tous les intervenants internes et externes arrivent à la conclusion qu'une décision drastique s'impose. Ce gestionnaire d'entreprise passe la majorité de son temps à gérer des crises et des conflits interpersonnels au sein de l'entreprise. Celle-ci connaît un fort taux de roulement car l'insécurité des employés est palpable. L'autorité de la direction est mise en doute. Les employés se demandent pourquoi ils devraient agir différemment des autres membres de la direction.

Un autre entrepreneur du Québec me confie un jour qu'il avait la preuve qu'un de ses garçons se servait allégrement dans la caisse de la compagnie. Je lui exprime qu'il se doit de résoudre rapidement cette problématique. Mon client me répond, qu'à titre de gardien de l'harmonie familiale, il assumera l'ensemble des frais et qu'il refuse de prendre le risque de créer un conflit familial. Je lui explique alors qu'à titre de gardien de l'unité familiale, il se doit d'agir rapidement car une telle situation risque d'empêcher toute forme de collaboration. Cette démarche a été très éprouvante pour le père et ses deux fils. Toutefois, un an plus tard, un plan de remboursement était déjà en cours de réalisation et nous avions implanté un système de contrôle qui empêchait de se servir directement dans la caisse. Cependant, le père éprouve toujours des difficultés à développer le réflexe naturel de donner la priorité à l'entreprise lors des demandes de support financier.

Dans les faits, quels sont les outils de gestion disponibles pour faciliter la gestion de cette ressource humaine et de son potentiel ? Une multitude de tests psychométriques et de profils de personnalité sont à la disposition des décideurs en matière de recrutement et de dotation. Sont-ils aussi valables les uns que les autres ? Comment les distinguer ? Comment identifier l'outil idéal de sélection qui assure la bonne personne à la bonne place, évitant ainsi des erreurs très coûteuses à l'organisation ?

CHAPITRE

Évaluations psychométriques et profils de personnalité

Dans un premier temps, il faut distinguer les tests psychométriques des profils de personnalité. Les premiers mesurent les aptitudes. Les seconds tentent de prévoir les comportements d'un individu en tenant compte des aspects de sa personnalité et de ses motivations.

L'utilisation des uns ou des autres ou des deux est dictée par l'objectif poursuivi par l'activité d'évaluation. Les critères de sélection d'un outil d'évaluation sont reliés à sa validation scientifique.

La validité demeure le premier critère. La validité désigne la capacité du questionnaire à évaluer ce qu'il est censé évaluer. Cela consiste à retrouver de façon mathématique les dimensions postulées par le concepteur du test. Les inter-corrélations entre les dimensions évaluées doivent faire l'objet d'analyses afin de vérifier la cohérence du questionnaire avec les théories classiques de la psychologie. Des études comparatives doivent aussi être réalisées entre les différents tests afin de mesurer les corrélations entre ceux-ci. Finalement, les tests doivent permettre une auto-évaluation de chacun des facteurs mesurés afin de s'assurer que les résultats des tests correspondent avec la perception que le candidat a de lui-même.

Le second critère concerne la fidélité du test. Il s'agit de vérifier si les différents items utilisés pour évaluer chacun des traits du questionnaire sont cohérents les uns avec les autres. En d'autres mots, on vérifie ici l'homogénéité dans l'évaluation d'un facteur.

La stabilité temporelle, c'est-à-dire que les mesures doivent se maintenir dans le temps, fait aussi l'objet de validations.

Finalement, le critère de sensibilité est utilisé. Un questionnaire est dit sensible s'il permet de distinguer un candidat d'un autre. La mesure des écarts-types pour chacune des échelles utilisées rend compte de la capacité à distinguer les personnes entre elles.

Il doit exister un contrôle serré de validation des réponses. Les réponses acceptables socialement, politiquement correctes ou prévisibles font l'objet d'une attention particulière. Autrement dit, si le test ne permet que l'obtention des réponses souhaitables, nous pouvons nous interroger longuement sur la validité de l'outil. L'humain étant ce qu'il est, les tentatives d'influencer les résultats ou de répondre correctement aux questions en fonction du poste convoité doivent être formellement exprimées dans les rapports.

L'utilisateur de ces outils d'évaluation des aptitudes et attitudes n'a pas à connaître la complexité liée à leur conception, mais il se doit de connaître les indicateurs de validité de ces outils.

Évidemment, le coût d'utilisation a son importance. Nous reprochons aux décideurs de n'utiliser que ce facteur pour arrêter leur choix. À titre d'information, ces outils sont disponibles dans des échelles de prix variant de la gratuité à plusieurs milliers de dollars pour une évaluation complète.

Notre préoccupation concerne les connaissances et expertises essentielles à une bonne utilisation de ces rapports. Cette tâche minutieuse d'interpréter les rapports devrait probablement être réservée à des membres de corporations professionnelles.

Notre vécu professionnel en ce qui a trait à l'utilisation de l'information contenue dans les rapports pose une problématique majeure. En pratique, regardons comment ça se passe. Un entrepreneur ou gestionnaire doit prendre la meilleure décision pour combler un poste. Il a déjà une idée bien arrêtée sur le choix du candidat. Certaines divergences d'opinions existent au sein du comité de sélection. Il demande alors l'opinion d'un expert pour arriver à un consensus. Lorsque les recommandations cadrent avec les perceptions des membres du comité, ça ne pose pas problème, mais c'est rarement le cas.

Alors, les débats s'animent au sein du comité de sélection. «Ça fait dix ans que je le connais, comment pourrais-je croire que l'opinion de quelqu'un de l'extérieur qui ne connaît pas le candidat est plus valable?» Pourtant, l'objectif n'est pas de démontrer que l'évaluation des membres du comité n'a pas de valeur, mais plutôt d'assurer à l'entreprise qu'elle confie des responsabilités spécifiques à la personne la plus apte à les assumer.

Nous reprochons souvent aux concepteurs de ces outils d'évaluation des aptitudes et des attitudes de rédiger des rapports dans un langage différent de celui utilisé par les clients. Ainsi, l'expression d'une facette plus négative d'un profil de personnalité peut entraîner une mauvaise décision. Nous avons été témoins de décisions regrettables basées sur une seule information négative incluse au rapport.

Nous sommes d'avis qu'une décision d'embauche ou de dotation se doit d'utiliser toutes les sources d'informations disponibles : curriculum vitae, références, réalisations antérieures, mises en situation, tests d'aptitudes et d'attitudes et performances des candidats qui ont occupé le poste antérieurement. Toute zone grise doit être éclaircie et toute interrogation doit trouver réponse avant la décision finale.

CHAPITRE 6

Les profils de postes

S'il demeure essentiel de connaître le potentiel humain, son utilisation exige un exercice de réflexion approfondi sur les connaissances, aptitudes et expertises requises pour répondre aux exigences des responsabilités attribuées à un poste donné.

Cet exercice de réflexion doit demeurer centré sur les besoins de l'entreprise au niveau des connaissances, expertises et expériences requises pour combler les attentes reliées au poste et assurer la meilleure contribution à l'atteinte des objectifs organisationnels. Ainsi, en tout premier lieu, nous devons clarifier les responsabilités à déléguer au futur titulaire du poste. Cette façon de faire assure que l'exercice d'embauche ou de dotation est réalisé en fonction de l'entreprise. L'inversion du processus a pour conséquence directe de structurer la délégation de pouvoirs et de responsabilités sur l'expertise des candidats et sur leurs intérêts personnels. L'entreprise se retrouve alors, à court ou moyen terme, avec un constat que l'équipe n'œuvre pas en étroite collaboration à la réalisation d'une mission d'entreprise commune mais que chaque intervenant réalise individuellement ses objectifs personnels et ses propres ambitions professionnelles.

Un principe de gestion reconnu affirme que le tout est plus grand que la somme des parties. Ainsi, l'ensemble des activités reliées à la gestion et à l'utilisation du potentiel humain doit favoriser le travail d'équipe et la complémentarité dans l'effort pour exceller dans l'application de ce principe de gestion.

Le jargon des professionnels en gestion des ressources humaines utilise différents noms pour cet outil de gestion relié aux postes : profil de poste, profil d'emploi, profil de compétences, profil d'expertises. Tous ces noms se réfèrent à un profil des connaissances, expertises et expériences essentielles pour assumer les responsabilités d'un poste.

Tel qu'il est précisé plus haut, les tests psychométriques d'aptitudes et d'attitudes permettent de vérifier l'étroite relation entre le profil recherché et celui du candidat. Le rôle du comité de sélection consiste donc à réaliser l'adéquation entre le profil idéal de poste et les profils des candidats pour retenir celui qui s'y apparente le plus.

Seul le plan théorique assure que l'objectif de trouver un candidat répondant parfaitement aux exigences du profil de poste est réalisable. Sur le plan pratique, différents facteurs expliquent un écart plus ou moins grand entre le profil recherché et celui du candidat retenu. L'incapacité de convaincre le candidat de saisir l'opportunité, la capacité de payer de l'employeur ou l'incompatibilité avec la culture et les valeurs organisationnelles peuvent, entre autres, expliquer l'écart entre le profil recherché et celui du candidat retenu.

CHAPITRE 7

Principes d'implantation et d'utilisation

La connaissance des outils de gestion facilitant la gestion du potentiel humain incluant leurs caractéristiques et méthodes d'utilisation ne suffisent pas. C'est dans l'implantation de ces outils de gestion que l'entrepreneur et le gestionnaire pourront obtenir le retour sur l'investissement et en mesurer l'impact sur les gens et sur l'organisation.

L'utilisation des meilleurs outils de gestion du potentiel humain et l'approbation de la politique de gestion du potentiel humain idéale ne suffisent pas à assurer le succès en la matière et à provoquer les avantages concurrentiels majeurs dont une amélioration sensible et mesurable de la profitabilité de nos entreprises.

Cette politique de gestion du potentiel humain s'inscrit dans une philosophie globale de gestion de l'entreprise. L'ensemble des politiques de gestion sont des vases communicants et ils doivent respecter les mêmes principes de gestion, indicateurs de performance, critères de conformité et contrôles de conformité.

Le fait d'installer une pièce d'origine neuve sur un équipement ne transforme pas cet équipement en modèle de l'année! Le même principe s'applique en gestion d'entreprise. L'innovation dans une des composantes de l'entreprise doit assurer que les systèmes en parallèle demeurent aptes à s'adapter et à contribuer à l'atteinte des objectifs.

De la même façon, même si l'entreprise dispose des spécialistes pour l'implantation de toute politique de gestion ou outil de gestion, la direction avisée et visionnaire devra assurer la capacité de l'ensemble de l'organisation à les appliquer et à les utiliser. Le retour sur l'investissement optimal exige une analyse approfondie de l'impact sur l'ensemble des composantes de l'organisation.

Nous avons largement expliqué au chapitre précédant qu'un écart plus ou moins important peut exister entre le profil idéal pour un poste et celui du candidat sélectionné. L'utilisation de ces outils de gestion exige l'élaboration d'un plan de développement des ressources humaines pour combler cet écart.

Le contexte généralisé de pénuries de main-d'œuvre, ceci malgré un taux de chômage élevé en raison de la récession, exige du temps pour identifier des solutions assurant la disponibilité des compétences et expertises au bon moment. Souvent, l'employeur doit organiser en interne les activités de développement des ressources humaines assurant la disponibilité des compétences et expertises au bon moment. Ce processus prend du temps et exige une planification à moyen et long terme.

Il est illusoire de croire que la responsabilité de réaliser une utilisation optimale du potentiel humain peut se limiter aux décisions d'embauche ou de dotation. Cet objectif exige d'implanter et d'entretenir toutes les pratiques d'affaires, qu'il s'agisse de la gestion de la performance, de la réflexion stratégique ou de la gestion de la rémunération. Il oblige à une application des principes de gestion du potentiel humain à tous les niveaux de l'organisation et dans toutes les politiques, règles et procédures.

L'évaluation ne peut se limiter à un seul individu. La gestion du potentiel humain exige de vérifier et de valider la capacité du candidat à œuvrer en équipe et en étroite collaboration à la réalisation des objectifs organisationnels.

Le questionnement lié à l'identification de la bonne personne pour assumer certaines responsabilités précises en situation de collaboration trouve tout autant sa pertinence dans le choix des partenaires d'affaires, des fournisseurs et même des clients !

Peu importe le lien d'affaires (employés, partenaires, associés, fournisseurs, clients), il se doit de respecter la culture organisationnelle et ses valeurs sans quoi il devient impossible d'agir en complémentarité à la réalisation d'objectifs communs. Le temps, l'argent et les efforts sont investis à la résolution de problèmes interpersonnels qui n'ont pas de lien direct avec la mission de l'entreprise.

Ainsi, lorsque nous interrogeons les entrepreneurs et les gestionnaires sur leur passé et que nous leur demandons ce qu'ils feraient différemment s'ils avaient la possibilité de recommencer, ils insistent souvent sur la grande difficulté à distinguer les gens qui méritent leur confiance de ceux qui ne la méritent pas.

Ces tests d'aptitudes et d'attitudes s'intègrent-ils aux outils de gestion qui peuvent contribuer à l'amélioration de l'indice organisationnel du bonheur? Pourquoi un propriétaire d'entreprise ou un gestionnaire d'entreprise emprunterait-il cette avenue? Quels sont les avantages pour l'entreprise et pour les individus? Comment mesurer le retour sur l'investissement et quels en sont les indicateurs?

Exceller en affaires et générer des profits nous oblige à faire la meilleure utilisation de toutes les ressources à notre disposition. La gestion de la ressource humaine, au même titre que les autres ressources, doit être gérée dans le respect des règles de l'art. Il demeure impossible d'utiliser une ressource si nous n'investissons pas pour en connaître ses caractéristiques, ses propriétés, ses capacités et sa valeur ajoutée.

Ainsi, les évaluations d'aptitudes et d'attitudes nous renseignent sur la probabilité de retour sur l'investissement. Le salaire versé à un employé pour assumer des responsabilités est un investissement qui doit générer un retour. Une absence de préoccupation en ce sens place la compagnie dans des situations défavorables pouvant affecter sa survie-même.

S'il est difficile d'expliquer les raisons pour lesquelles un employeur doit s'assurer de bien connaître son potentiel humain, il demeure intéressant de vérifier dans nos expériences antérieures les coûts directs et indirects de décisions d'embauche et de dotation prises sur des considérations autres que les principes de base en la matière. Notre entreprise gère-t-elle sa ressource humaine de façon proactive ou réactive ? Nos gestionnaires consacrent-ils trop d'énergie aux employés problèmes qui ne cadrent pas avec l'entreprise ? La direction investit-elle dans les comportements et attitudes souhaitables ou s'investit-elle uniquement dans la gestion des cas problèmes ?

Nos dirigeants d'entreprise doivent entretenir une image corporative attrayante. Le vieillissement de la population, les nombreux départs à la retraite et les réorientations de carrière viennent augmenter la demande des employeurs quant à la main-d'œuvre et diminuer l'offre globale. La qualité des candidatures décroît alors considérablement. Les journaux et les sites internet de recrutement diffusent une quantité considérable d'offres d'emploi. Celles-ci attirent les candidats de haut niveau lorsque l'information disponible permet d'établir la relation directe entre le défi offert et les ambitions personnelles et professionnelles des postulants. Les employeurs peuvent avoir l'impression que le pouvoir appartient en majorité aux candidats et que la seule solution demeure de répondre positivement à toutes les conditions posées par eux, qu'il s'agisse du taux de rémunération, du nombre de semaines de vacances par année et d'une disponibilité très limitée en dehors des heures normales de travail. Lorsqu'une situation problématique survient, l'employé peut exprimer une indépendance liée au fait que d'autres opportunités existent ailleurs.

Nous avons vu des candidats ne pas se présenter à des entrevues d'embauche, ne pas se présenter au travail la première journée, quitter leur nouveau travail après quelques heures et même débuter leur nouvel emploi par un congé de maladie. Ces attitudes démontrent que les étapes préalables à l'embauche ne permettaient pas d'établir clairement la compatibilité des candidats avec l'entreprise, ceci en matière de culture et des valeurs organisationnelles.

L'employeur confronté régulièrement à des menaces de quitter l'entreprise de la part des employés doit s'interroger sérieusement sur le sentiment d'appartenance qui le lie à ses employés. L'évaluation de ce sentiment d'appartenance exige une communication continue sur ce sujet et affecte toute personne qui assume des responsabilités de supervision au sein de l'entreprise. Ne pas réagir positivement aux indices montrant que ce sentiment d'appartenance est fragile a certes des conséquences qui ne sont pas nécessairement avantageuses pour l'entreprise. L'obligation de reconnaître l'écart entre la perception des employés et les volontés de l'employeur demeure un exercice exigeant. Par contre, une saine gestion d'entreprise doit s'exercer en demeurant connectée avec les perceptions des collaborateurs sans quoi le lien qui entretient la confiance réciproque devient très fragile.

Chaque partenaire, chaque employé, chaque client assume une responsabilité majeure pour entretenir une image corporative attrayante. Comment chaque intervenant parle-il de l'entreprise en contexte de travail et au dehors ? Lors des activités sociales, par exemple, parle-t-il positivement ou non de l'entreprise, de ses dirigeants et de sa gestion ? Nous observons trop souvent des employés qui profitent des rencontres avec la clientèle pour remettre leur curriculum vitae !

Pourtant, certains employeurs réussissent avec les mêmes individus à les mobiliser et à entretenir un fort degré d'appartenance. Il faut demeurer conscient que c'est la gestion des ressources humaines qui fait la différence.

Ceux qui relèvent le défi et en sortent gagnants investissent temps et argent pour entretenir une relation de qualité avec chaque intervenant. Ils demeurent proactifs et identifient des solutions sur mesure et durables à toute problématique relative au maintien d'un lien de confiance essentiel. Toute accumulation de problèmes irrésolus demeure nuisible et les conséquences augmentent dans le temps. Ainsi, nous parlons ici d'un processus de gestion et d'amélioration continu.

La prochaine partie du livre présentera différents outils de gestion assurant l'implantation et l'utilisation des meilleures pratiques d'affaires. L'adoption de ces outils de gestion n'offre aucune garantie de résultat. Nous savons que le défi majeur demeure d'assurer une bonne utilisation de ces outils et, peu importe l'outil de gestion, son utilisation demeure la responsabilité des ressources humaines. Le succès de nos entreprises et l'amélioration de leur rentabilité financière sont directement liés à la gestion du potentiel humain.

Des pratiques d'affaires mobilisatrices pour l'ensemble des collaborateurs exigent le respect des individus dans leur dimension humaine, soit des individus à la conquête du bonheur qui établissent une relation directe entre leur travail, les responsabilités assumées et leur évolution pour atteindre les sommets quant à leur bien-être et leur qualité de vie.

TROISIÈME PARTIE

Meilleures pratiques d'affaires

CHAPITRE  8

Réflexion stratégique

L'expression « lac-à-l'épaule » désignait cette pratique d'affaires à ses débuts. Dans la langue administrative et familière du Québec, un lac-à-l'épaule est une réunion de planification stratégique, en particulier lorsqu'elle se tient dans un endroit retiré. Le terme peut s'appliquer aussi bien à un parti politique qu'à une entreprise ou à toute autre organisation. Ce terme est né de la réunion du conseil des ministres de Jean Lesage, qui a eu lieu les 4 et 5 septembre 1962 au camp de pêche du Lac à l'Épaule, situé aujourd'hui dans le Parc national de la Jacques-Cartier. Cette réunion, où a été décidée entre autres la nationalisation de l'électricité, est considérée comme un des temps forts de la Révolution tranquille.

L'avantage majeur de cet exercice de réflexion est de se donner du temps pour faire une étude exhaustive de l'entreprise en réunissant l'ensemble des intervenants principaux. C'est l'occasion par excellence de créer une synergie d'équipe, de définir les objectifs stratégiques et d'élaborer les plans d'actions pour les réaliser.

Trop souvent nous constatons que nous nous affairons au quotidien de nos organisations sans garder en perspective les objectifs à réaliser qui en assurent la distinction. C'est comme s'aventurer en forêt sans boussole. Le risque est élevé de se perdre, de tourner en rond et d'être envahi par la panique. Diriger une entreprise sans objectifs stratégiques précis entraîne, trop souvent, un gaspillage d'énergie fort coûteux et des comportements et attitudes incompatibles avec notre mission organisationnelle.

Il demeure impossible de mobiliser l'équipe en vue de la réalisation d'un projet d'entreprise mal défini, tant du point de vue de ses objectifs que de celui des attentes envers chaque intervenant en termes de contribution.

La majorité des entrepreneurs et gestionnaires ont en tête une idée très précise des objectifs à atteindre. Par contre, l'absence d'écrits fait place à des perceptions différentes de la mission organisationnelle. Il demeure difficile pour un intervenant de contribuer à la réalisation d'un objectif qui ne lui est pas expliqué concrètement.

Un exercice de réflexion s'impose si nous percevons un écart entre nos attentes et la contribution réelle des employés, si les messages reçus des collaborateurs démontrent l'absence d'une même compréhension de la mission organisationnelle, si nos collaborateurs transfèrent à la direction des problèmes à régler au lieu de nous proposer des solutions, si une tendance s'installe à chercher des coupables, si des signes démontrent que les employés trouvent que la direction passe son temps à changer d'idée et si nos collaborateurs terminent leurs journées de travail avec l'impression d'avoir travaillé très fort sans avoir toutefois pu consacrer une minute à nos priorités établies.

Pourquoi réalise-t-on un tel exercice? La contribution optimale des ressources humaines à la réalisation du projet d'entreprise exige de le préciser. Un projet de construction commence par le dessin des plans pour passer ensuite à la réalisation des travaux de construction en commençant par les fondations!

Il est remarquable de constater que les individus et les entreprises qui réalisent le plus en peu de temps commencent toujours par élaborer un plan de match précis. De plus, peu importe le domaine d'expertise, on reproche souvent de se lancer dans l'aventure sans préciser les objectifs, les étapes de réalisation et les attentes envers chaque collaborateur. Comment respecter un budget et les délais de réalisation s'ils ne sont pas définis au départ?

L'exercice de réflexion stratégique trace la voie qui mène au succès. Il assure la synergie et la solidarité à l'équipe de direction et de gestion. Il lui permet d'assumer le leadership essentiel à une entreprise efficace et rentable.

L'organisation de cette rencontre exige une planification ayant un impact majeur sur son résultat et sa contribution à la réalisation de la mission organisationnelle. En ce sens, cette rencontre doit être planifiée dans le respect des règles de l'art en matière d'organisation de réunions. L'ordre du jour doit être distribué à l'avance. Les participants doivent pouvoir faire leurs recommandations sur les sujets à intégrer à l'ordre du jour. Un animateur désigné doit assurer le respect de cet ordre du jour et de l'horaire établi. Évidemment, un procès-verbal doit être rédigé pour assurer le suivi de la réalisation des objectifs fixés.

L'animation de cette rencontre s'inscrit dans une approche de recherche de solutions sur mesure, durables et rentables. L'auteur et maître de la communication Anthony Robbins, dans son livre intitulé «Pouvoir illimité[1]», nous dresse une liste de questions génératrices de solutions:

- Qu'est-ce-que ce problème a de formidable?
- Qu'est-ce-qui n'est pas encore parfait?
- Que suis-je prêt à faire pour éviter que cette situation se reproduise?
- Que suis-je prêt à ne plus faire pour éviter que cette situation se reproduise?
- Comment puis-je prendre plaisir à le faire?

La première étape d'une approche ayant pour objectif d'identifier des solutions exige de créer le consensus sur l'identification de la problématique.

---

1. L'éveil de votre puissance intérieure; Anthony Robbins; Le Jour; 1993; page 216

Principes d'utilisation

L'exercice de réflexion stratégique permet de distinguer l'entreprise dans ses composantes suivantes :

La direction générale

- Énoncé de vision et de mission
- Identification des valeurs organisationnelles
- Identification des objectifs stratégiques pour la prochaine année
- Partage des pouvoirs et responsabilités
- Mobilisation à la réalisation du projet d'entreprise
- Plan de communication interne et externe
- Système de gestion de la performance
- Plan d'investissement
- Développement des habiletés de gestion pour la direction générale

---

La gestion des ressources humaines

- Descriptions de tâches
- Gestion de la performance
- Mobilisation à la réalisation du projet d'entreprise
- Identification des besoins de l'entreprise quant aux connaissances, expériences et expertises
- Inventaire du potentiel humain disponible et stratégies pour combler les écarts
- Plan de développement des ressources humaines
- Politique de gestion de la rémunération
- Rémunération et avantages par rapport au secteur d'activité ou à la région
- Politique de recrutement, de dotation et de sélection
- Sondage sur le climat organisationnel

La gestion de la production

- Systèmes de planification de la production
- Mesure du taux actuel d'utilisation et d'efficacité des équipements
- Veille technologique
- Gestion agile
- Contrôle des achats et des inventaires
- Les relations avec les fournisseurs et partenaires respectant nos exigences
- Contrôle de la qualité et mesures correctives
- Propreté des lieux de travail

Le plan de commercialisation

- Définition du marché cible
- Gestion de l'expérience client
- Suivi de l'évolution des besoins de la clientèle
- Diminution du cycle de vente
- Élaboration et révision du plan de commercialisation
- Plan de rémunération de l'équipe de vente
- Rentabilité du plan de commercialisation
- Enquête de satisfaction de la clientèle
- Politique de prix de revient
- Impact de la concurrence
- Positionnement face aux marchés étrangers

Les produits ou services

- L'image corporative, le logo, le design des produits, les prestations de services démontrent notre différence et constituent un avantage concurrentiel
- La différence de nos produits et services s'établit sur des critères facilement identifiables
- Relation entre le développement des produits et services et l'évolution des besoins de la clientèle
- Cycle de vie de nos produits et services connu
- Planification des projets de développement
- Connaissance de la concurrence
- Budget de recherche et de développement
- Traitement des plaintes des clients
- Innovation dans nos façons de faire

Le contrôle financier

- Utilisation de budgets prévisionnels incluant l'analyse des écarts sur une base mensuelle
- Objectifs annuels de rentabilité
- Système de prix de revient
- Système de contrôle interne pour protéger contre la fraude et le gaspillage
- Gestion des assurances
- Comparaison des résultats financiers sectoriels et régionaux
- Relations avec les partenaires financiers
- Utilisation des subventions ou crédits d'impôts

Cet exercice de réflexion stratégique a un effet direct sur la motivation et sur la mobilisation de l'équipe. Les collaborateurs se sentent impliqués, considérés, reconnus. Chaque participant, suite à cette rencontre, s'assure d'une communication efficace assurant la meilleure compréhension, par chaque intervenant de son équipe, des impacts du plan stratégique sur son travail et sur sa contribution à la réalisation des objectifs. Nous comprenons ici la relation étroite qui doit exister entre la planification stratégique et le système de gestion de la performance.

Le retour sur l'investissement en matière de réflexion stratégique exige que l'exercice se traduise en un plan d'action précis intégrant toutes les activités essentielles au maintien des avantages concurrentiels et à l'amélioration des faiblesses identifiées. Un partage des responsabilités et une planification dans le temps assurent une contribution optimale à la réalisation du projet d'entreprise défini lors de la rencontre.

Le meilleur exercice de réflexion stratégique, s'il n'a aucun impact concret sur les façons de faire au quotidien, n'offre pas de valeur ajoutée. C'est là un des principaux défis des équipes de direction et de gestion. La vision de l'entreprise passe ainsi du rêve à la réalité.

La réflexion stratégique se résume à analyser et comprendre le succès de l'organisation et à prendre les dispositions pour améliorer cette recette de succès en continu.

Voilà un outil de gestion qui contribue à l'utilisation optimale du potentiel humain, à la mobilisation et à l'amélioration du degré de responsabilisation de chaque employé.

CHAPITRE 9

Gestion de la performance

Une préoccupation majeure s'inscrit dans les responsabilités des équipes de direction et de gestion de toute organisation. Elle veut mesurer la contribution des ressources humaines à l'atteinte des objectifs organisationnels.

Les systèmes d'évaluation du rendement et de gestion de la performance utilisent, depuis des siècles, des approches basées sur l'organisation du travail et sur des techniques de supervision assurant la mesure et l'optimisation de la contribution des ressources humaines.

Le taylorisme, entre autres, ne considérait que l'organisation du travail et la mesure des temps et mouvements pour augmenter la productivité des ressources humaines en contexte de production. On a reproché à cette méthode de déshumaniser les entreprises et d'utiliser les humains comme des machines. L'ouvrier est réduit à son état brut sans considération de sa valeur ajoutée liée à sa capacité de s'impliquer activement dans l'identification de solutions aux problématiques de production. Ce mode de gestion a fait dire à plusieurs: «Mon patron n'a utilisé que mes bras tout au long de ma carrière alors qu'il aurait pu utiliser ma tête».

Le post-taylorisme défend une organisation du travail qui met en œuvre diverses formes de participation des travailleurs à la prise de décision concernant la production. Nous parlons ici des méthodes de rotation de postes, d'élargissement et d'enrichissement des tâches, de groupes semi-autonomes et de cercles de qualité. La notion de polyvalence permettant à un employé d'occuper plusieurs postes prend alors de plus en plus d'importance.

Quant à la gestion du potentiel humain, cette évolution demeure encore aujourd'hui très significative. L'objectif d'améliorer la productivité des employés par l'organisation de ses méthodes de travail et par la mesure des temps et mouvements fait place à une contribution optimale des ressources humaines par l'utilisation de l'ensemble de leur potentiel.

Outre ces méthodes d'amélioration de la productivité par l'organisation du travail tant en matière de processus que de l'implication des employés à la prise de décision, la mesure du rendement des employés utilise un système d'évaluation.

L'équipe de direction doit alors identifier le meilleur outil pour mesurer la contribution des ressources humaines à la réalisation des objectifs de l'entreprise.

L'expérience vécue en entreprise en matière d'évaluation du rendement permet d'identifier certains pièges reliés à l'implantation de ce système de gestion.

À la base, l'évaluation du rendement des collaborateurs par leur superviseur crée une résistance majeure de la part de tous les intervenants. Les superviseurs, eux-mêmes, s'interrogent fortement sur leur capacité à mesurer la contribution de leurs collaborateurs en toute objectivité. D'ailleurs, mesurer le rendement semble incompatible avec l'objectivité puisqu'il s'agit de porter un jugement sur quelque chose.

Pour ce qui est des collaborateurs, la résistance est reliée à la perception des vrais objectifs poursuivis par ces exercices d'évaluation du rendement. Ils se questionnent sur l'utilisation faite par la direction du contenu des évaluations. Ils demeurent trop souvent avec une perception que ces évaluations permettent de monter un dossier facilitant le congédiement.

Nous pouvons retenir ici que la réalisation des évaluations du rendement fait appel à des connaissances et expertises particulières.

En ce sens, les évaluateurs doivent être formés et encadrés. L'absence de formation et d'encadrement nuit à la crédibilité du processus de gestion de la performance.

Une autre problématique majeure liée au processus d'évaluation du rendement demeure la relation plus ou moins directe existant avec la gestion de la rémunération ou le pourcentage d'augmentation salariale consenti. Le gestionnaire se retrouve avec une préoccupation majeure, celle de respecter les budgets et d'éviter que les coûts de main-d'œuvre connaissent une proportion démesurée. À titre d'exemple, un superviseur entièrement satisfait d'un collaborateur va réviser son évaluation, car il ignore comment communiquer une évaluation positive, et se limiter à une augmentation salariale équivalente à l'augmentation de l'indice des prix à la consommation. Il ne faudrait surtout pas oublier que ses décisions relatives aux augmentations de ses collaborateurs sont un facteur déterminant pour fixer sa propre augmentation !

Les difficultés liées à la réalisation de l'évaluation du rendement peuvent avoir pour effet de décourager tout effort en ce sens. Mais comme le dit Louis Garneau, il ne faut jamais abandonner. Le processus de gestion de la performance offre d'excellentes opportunités de mesurer la contribution des ressources humaines et de valoriser les attitudes et comportements compatibles avec la mission et les valeurs de l'entreprise. Il évite la tolérance largement nuisible à l'efficacité de nos entreprises. En tant que gestionnaires, nous devons saisir chaque opportunité de valoriser les employés et d'encourager les attitudes qui permettent de réaliser notre mission.

Le système idéal de gestion de la performance doit s'intégrer à la gestion globale de l'entreprise. Il mesure l'impact et la contribution des ressources humaines. En ce sens, une communication claire des objectifs organisationnels et des attentes envers chaque intervenant est essentielle.

Plus les objectifs stratégiques de l'organisation sont communiqués clairement, plus les collaborateurs responsables de leur réalisation peuvent définir comment y contribuer. Ces objectifs doivent être communiqués dans un langage compréhensible de l'ensemble des intervenants. Il demeure capital de valider la compréhension des objectifs par l'ensemble des intervenants et la compréhension de leur contribution potentielle. Ainsi, des attentes précises assurent la reconnaissance de la contribution de chacun par l'équipe de direction et par les collaborateurs eux-mêmes.

Un collaborateur qui ressent que le mérite de son travail est attribué à quelqu'un d'autre se retrouve démobilisé et démotivé. Il s'investit alors pour rétablir l'équité dans l'organisation, ce qui nuit passablement à l'esprit d'équipe et influence négativement les autres collaborateurs.

De plus, un tel exercice doit s'inscrire dans un processus d'amélioration continue. Ainsi, tous les efforts doivent être déployés pour élaborer des plans de développement des ressources humaines qui répondent aux besoins de l'organisation et des gens qui y travaillent. Une relation étroite entre les objectifs personnels et ceux de l'organisation assure la meilleure contribution de chaque intervenant. Même un objectif difficilement compatible de conciliation travail-famille doit être respecté.

Ainsi, une jeune femme avait un avenir très prometteur au sein d'une organisation. On la voyait déjà membre de la direction générale et associée. Au moment où elle a annoncé son intention de fonder une famille, le discours de la direction a changé. Au retour de ses congés de maternité, personne ne parlait de son avenir. Aujourd'hui, cette femme a pris la décision de continuer sa brillante carrière sous d'autres cieux.

Concrètement, la mobilisation atteint son apogée lorsque l'individu reconnaît la contribution de son travail à sa perpétuelle recherche du bonheur et à sa croissance personnelle.

Comme pour toute pratique d'affaires, la direction générale demeure l'instance la plus imputable et elle se doit de donner l'exemple. Sur le plan théorique, tout objectif individuel se doit d'être mesurable, quantifiable, réaliste et compatible avec les objectifs stratégiques de l'organisation. La direction de l'entreprise doit être suffisamment responsable pour encadrer et soutenir ses collaborateurs en discutant avec eux des ressources mises à leur disposition pour atteindre les objectifs.

La mobilisation de tous à la réalisation des objectifs exige que chaque collaborateur puisse exprimer le plan d'action qu'il prévoit de réaliser pour relever le défi. Les superviseurs peuvent trouver éprouvant de respecter des stratégies largement différentes des leurs pour réaliser les objectifs. Il n'en demeure pas moins qu'un collaborateur demeure apte à livrer la marchandise s'il réussit à établir un lien étroit entre sa vision du plan de réalisation et l'objectif. Le rôle du superviseur se transforme alors en coach, en aidant naturel à la réalisation de l'objectif dans le respect des individus et de l'entreprise, ceci à l'avantage de tous les intervenants et de l'entreprise.

Ici aussi, le bon sens et la simplicité doivent dicter les comportements à adopter. De fait, chaque événement qui semble vouloir compliquer le processus d'évaluation du rendement doit être ramené à sa plus simple expression. Certains processus de gestion de la performance entretiennent un degré de complexité tellement grand que les utilisateurs s'investissent pour comprendre comment les utiliser. La vigilance est de rigueur pour ne pas perdre de vue les objectifs du processus.

Évaluer le rendement sans tomber dans le piège du jugement sur les individus exige de mesurer la contribution sur des indicateurs de performance ayant fait l'objet d'une entente au départ.

Nous n'insisterons jamais assez sur le caractère continu de ce processus. Nous avons observé trop souvent des évaluations annuelles basées sur la mémoire des événements des dernières semaines. Une évaluation prévoit des rencontres régulières sur les objectifs et les processus d'adaptation aux nouvelles réalités qui se présentent. Des priorités organisationnelles connaissent des changements en cours d'année. Ces changements ne sont pas toujours sous le contrôle de l'entreprise et du superviseur.

La gestion de la performance s'inscrit dans une philosophie de gestion à la recherche constante de solutions, une philosophie qui transforme en opportunité toute difficulté rencontrée. Le lecteur aura compris qu'un système de gestion de la performance qui facilite l'identification d'un coupable n'obtient pas la collaboration des intervenants. L'objectif qui anime les intervenants devient alors de s'assurer que le nom du coupable ne sera pas le sien. La mobilisation d'une équipe demeure mission impossible dans un tel contexte.

Un critère primordial de succès en matière de gestion de la performance demeure la tolérance à l'erreur. Il sera toujours difficile, exigeant et coûteux pour l'équipe de direction de tolérer l'erreur tout en maintenant le lien de confiance avec les collaborateurs. Réaliser cet exploit ne doit quand même pas suggérer aux collaborateurs de ne pas constater les erreurs! Récupérer les erreurs sans miner le degré de confiance personnelle des intervenants demeure délicat. En tant qu'entrepreneur, nous savons que l'expérience s'acquiert par essais et erreurs. L'important est de ne pas répéter la même erreur!

Le rappel historique de véhicules de la part de Toyota est un exemple de compagnie responsable qui ne remet jamais en cause la sécurité. L'expérience est-elle coûteuse? Absolument. Toutefois, l'engagement à offrir des produits sécuritaires va jusque là!

Les actualités économiques informent, presque quotidiennement, sur les généreux bonus versés aux hauts dirigeants même en période de récession et en l'absence de profits des entreprises. Ces réalités, trop souvent observées, comportent des conséquences négatives à une perception d'équité essentielle à la mobilisation de l'ensemble du personnel de l'entreprise.

Un autre danger lié à la gestion de la performance s'exprime par l'entretien de fausses attentes, tant en matière de rémunération que d'évolution de l'employé dans la structure organisationnelle. S'il est humain de considérer l'avantage financier reçu comme un acquis et un dû, il devient tout aussi naturel d'établir une relation entre la réalisation d'un objectif et une promotion.

Certains se souviendront qu'à une certaine période pas si lointaine les employés généraient un revenu plus grand avec l'augmentation de la valeur des actions de leur entreprise qu'avec leur activité professionnelle. Un tel ajustement à la hausse du rythme de vie rend parfois pénible l'obligation de fonctionner avec un budget plus limité.

Le processus de gestion de la performance offre l'opportunité d'obtenir une information privilégiée sur les ambitions professionnelles, sur les attentes de nos collaborateurs envers l'entreprise pour persister dans le processus de croissance personnelle et évoluer vers le bonheur individuel et collectif. En ce sens, les résultats communiqués sur le rendement doivent se traduire aisément en termes de croissance personnelle pour les personnes évaluées.

Cette communication sur le rendement, dans les deux sens, permet de recevoir les suggestions et les recommandations des employés sur tout sujet relié à l'entreprise. Ces éléments sont précieux pour apporter des modifications aux façons de faire dans le respect de l'opinion des principaux concernés. L'impression qu'on ne tient pas compte de notre opinion est très nuisible au degré de mobilisation et entraîne souvent des résistances à la communication.

La gestion du rendement souhaite entretenir une saine collaboration entre les intervenants en intégrant les avantages d'un contexte compétitif de réalisation du travail. La prudence est de rigueur car la compétition peut entraîner des effets très nuisibles. La mesure du rendement incite à le traduire en chiffres, ce qui autorise les comparaisons sur une base individuelle. Les réactions aux résultats de ces comparaisons sont parfois surprenantes et vont à l'encontre des objectifs poursuivis par les systèmes de gestion de la performance.

L'information obtenue grâce à la gestion de la performance peut être utilisée pour mieux connaître les tendances des marchés et les modifications dans les attitudes et comportements des clients. Une diminution du rendement d'un individu ou d'une équipe de travail peut trouver sa cause dans une problématique relative aux individus, mais elle peut aussi révéler des modifications dans les tendances, dans les marchés, ce qui exigera de revoir la stratégie de commercialisation et même la mission de l'organisation.

Ainsi, le système de gestion de la performance est essentiel à la gestion du potentiel humain de l'organisation. Les indicateurs de performance utilisés doivent évaluer toutes les composantes humaines et non seulement la mesure de productivité des machines et équipements. L'évaluation doit couvrir les aptitudes, les attitudes et l'impact global de l'employé sur l'entreprise.

Ce système offre aussi un des moyens à privilégier pour mobiliser l'équipe à la réalisation du projet d'entreprise dans sa distinction et sa spécificité.

CHAPITRE 10

Gestion de la commercialisation

Philippe Dorget et Pier Antoine Marier, coprésidents de K2 Communications Marketing, ont accepté de collaborer au contenu de cette pratique d'affaires.

Au départ, en quoi consiste un plan de commercialisation et quels sont ses objectifs?

La commercialisation se définit comme l'ensemble des techniques mettant en valeur l'entreprise, ses produits ou services, assurant une augmentation significative et rapide des ventes, des revenus et des profits.

L'impact d'un plan de commercialisation efficace se mesure par l'amélioration de la productivité de vente de l'entreprise, soit le nombre de ventes conclues par jour, par semaine, par mois, par année et même par vendeur.

Pour réussir en affaires, il n'est plus suffisant d'avoir la meilleure technologie, les meilleurs produits ou services ni même au meilleur prix. Pour ce faire, l'entreprise doit être plus attrayante, faire connaître sa spécificité et créer sa valeur ajoutée en la démontrant clairement.

Peter Drucker, expert en marketing, affirme que la commercialisation et l'innovation sont les deux seules activités qui attirent des clients et génèrent des profits.

Le retour sur l'investissement en matière de commercialisation se mesure par l'amélioration de la compétitivité, par une diminution du cycle de vente, par le renforcement du positionnement stratégique de l'entreprise, par la réalisation d'un plan et d'activités de ventes générant des résultats rapides, dont l'amélioration de la profitabilité, et par le maintien de la première position dans le peloton. Bref, une commercialisation efficace permet d'atteindre le podium.

La commercialisation assure la complémentarité dans l'effort entre les départements de production de produits ou services et celui des ventes. Voilà un moyen concret et incontournable si nous voulons développer au quotidien une entreprise performante et profitable où chaque département œuvre en complémentarité à la réalisation de la mission de l'entreprise.

Lors d'une intervention en entreprise auprès de tous les représentants de la force de vente de l'entreprise, incluant la direction générale, j'avais reçu pour mandat de définir les problématiques de relations entre les départements dans la réalisation de la mission de cette entreprise. J'ai alors présenté de façon imagée et humoristique ce que les employés communiquaient, concernant leurs relations entre les départements. À titre d'exemple, j'ai imaginé un directeur de production qui s'acharne sur le département des ventes en précisant que le temps est venu de cesser de sur-vendre le produit en engageant l'entreprise dans des promesses irréalisables ! L'équipe de vente, quant à elle, répliquait que la production n'est d'aucune utilité s'il n'y a pas de ventes. Ainsi, la production n'avait qu'à se conformer aux exigences des contrats de ventes. Un participant me fait alors le commentaire suivant : « Je n'étais pas au courant que tu avais participé à nos dernières rencontres entre les ventes et la production ! »

Entretenir une image corporative attrayante demeure la responsabilité de tous les intervenants. Demeurons conscients de l'effet de nos commentaires à l'intérieur comme à l'extérieur de l'entreprise. Les clients, entre autres, identifient facilement la conformité de l'entreprise avec sa mission en fonction des commentaires reçus.

Il demeure possible d'entretenir des relations respectueuses entre les membres des différents départements d'une même entreprise, ce qui ne signifie en rien que c'est simple et naturel. Les équipes de gestion et de direction de l'entreprise doivent s'y impliquer grandement, donner l'exemple, valoriser et encourager les comportements compatibles avec cette philosophie de gestion. Cette approche implique également de ne plus tolérer les comportements et attitudes incompatibles avec ce style de gestion.

La gestion de ces relations interpersonnelles en contexte de travail est un des aspects directement relié à la gestion du potentiel humain. Les équipes de direction et de gestion, en relevant ce défi, saisissent une belle opportunité d'assumer leur leadership et de maintenir les réseaux de communications essentiels. Ces communications doivent respecter les valeurs organisationnelles distinctives. Les perceptions des employés sur les valeurs de transparence, d'équité et de respect demeurent le principal indicateur de la capacité des équipes de direction et de gestion de vivre ces valeurs au quotidien. Une vigilance de tous les instants est requise et ces exercices de communications ont tout avantage à utiliser les perceptions des employés face aux décisions et aux méthodes de gestion de la direction. Cette tâche n'est pas toujours des plus agréables, mais la mobilisation au projet de l'entreprise exige de rejoindre les employés là où ils se situent.

Plusieurs critères permettent de distinguer les meilleurs plans de commercialisation. Un plan de commercialisation efficace se centre sur le client et sa réalité dans toutes ses composantes. Il prévoit un investissement dans l'expérience client, en ce sens qu'il s'assure que l'entreprise évolue dans le respect de ses relations avec ses clients et qu'elle connaît leur évolution en ce qui concerne leurs attentes envers l'entreprise et leurs besoins. Il définit clairement la clientèle cible et les stratégies à utiliser pour la rejoindre dans sa réalité. Il respecte le principe de base en ventes qui nous exhorte à simplifier la vie de nos clients en apportant des solutions innovatrices et sur mesure aux problématiques de la clientèle. Il précise clairement le budget et les ressources nécessaires et assure le meilleur retour sur l'investissement pour l'entreprise et sa clientèle. Il établit les objectifs du plan et les moyens de mesurer leur réussite.

La stratégie de communication élaborée pour réaliser le plan de commercialisation doit indiquer clairement quoi dire, à qui, comment le dire, à quelle fréquence, ainsi que les indicateurs de contrôle de la réussite des objectifs. Le discours de vente crée le besoin, entretient le lien de confiance essentiel à toute relation d'affaires, permet au client une expérience agréable dont il se souviendra, tout en étant attrayant et distinctif. Finalement, le discours de vente permet à chaque intervenant, interne ou externe, de distinguer le positionnement stratégique de l'entreprise par l'utilisation d'un langage simple, précis et compréhensible.

Le processus d'implantation de cet outil de gestion de la commercialisation explique comment mesurer la rentabilité et la profitabilité des produits ou services. Il insiste sur l'importance de la veille et de l'innovation technologique en précisant les activités à réaliser pour atteindre les objectifs.

La commercialisation demeure, avant tout, un exercice d'analyse et de profonde réflexion. Quoiqu'elle soit dirigée par les équipes de direction et de gestion, elle doit favoriser et supporter l'implication de tous les intervenants à la réalisation des objectifs stratégiques de son plan. Seule l'élaboration d'un plan stratégique de commercialisation assure la réussite de ses objectifs et le meilleur retour sur l'investissement. À la limite, tout investissement en matière de commercialisation et de marketing devrait d'abord prévoir l'élaboration de ce plan respectueux de l'entreprise et de sa mission, incluant le partage des pouvoirs et des responsabilités.

Ce plan démontre le caractère exclusif du produit ou du service, sa valeur ajoutée et sa spécificité. De plus, il segmente les marchés et identifie les stratégies pour un rendement optimal.

Le processus de vente doit aussi faire l'objet d'une réflexion approfondie et de l'élaboration de sa stratégie d'implantation. Les étapes du processus sont alors définies, de même que ses points sensibles, le mécanisme de la prise de décision, sans oublier les composantes internes du support à la vente.

L'efficacité de la distribution se doit aussi d'être documentée en identifiant les forces et faiblesses de celle qui existe actuellement au sein de l'entreprise et les solutions durables pour améliorer son efficacité.

Le rapport qualité/prix fait l'objet d'une analyse incluant les recommandations pour l'améliorer et assurer la meilleure compréhension de la clientèle de l'entreprise.

Finalement, l'ensemble des éléments, composantes, et stratégies doit présenter un vécu organisationnel qui démontre son efficacité et sa capacité à contribuer à la réussite des objectifs du plan de commercialisation.

Cette gestion de la commercialisation, élément stratégique essentiel pour réussir en affaires, exige une gestion optimale du potentiel humain. Ici aussi, c'est l'humain qui peut faire la différence dans la réalisation de la stratégie de commercialisation.

Nous n'insisterons jamais assez sur l'impact humain pour relever le défi d'une commercialisation efficace et rentable. Chaque intervenant interne doit connaître les enjeux de la stratégie de commercialisation et posséder les compétences et expertises pour assurer une contribution optimale à la réussite des objectifs.

L'élaboration et la réalisation d'un plan de développement des ressources humaines qui intègrent les exercices de communication, l'identification des rôles et attentes envers chaque intervenant, les activités de formation et de coaching, les indicateurs de performance et les mécanismes d'ajustement, viennent augmenter la probabilité de succès des activités de commercialisation.

Plus encore, l'exigence de bien connaître son client dans ses besoins, ses attentes, ses préférences en matière de service à la clientèle et de contrôle de la qualité, ses exigences envers les produits ou services de l'entreprise et son évaluation de la relation d'affaires, indique qu'une relation cordiale avec le client a droit à la même considération que toute relation d'affaires, incluant la relation entre l'employeur et ses employés.

Nous avons déjà démontré qu'une gestion optimale du potentiel humain exigeait une contribution au bonheur de chaque intervenant. Pour les mêmes raisons, une commercialisation efficace doit assurer une contribution au mieux être des clients. En ce sens, un client heureux permet d'entrevoir des relations d'affaires à moyen et long termes dans un respect mutuel des individus, des cultures et des valeurs organisationnelles. Il ne faut jamais oublier que la loyauté et la fidélité s'inscrivent exclusivement dans le comportement humain.

CHAPITRE 11

Gestion globale de la rémunération

S'il existe un aspect de la relation employeur-employé très encadré sur le plan législatif, c'est bien celui de la gestion de la rémunération. Le Code du Travail, la loi des Normes, la Loi sur l'équité salariale et de nombreux décrets, pour ne nommer que ceux-là, déterminent les règles en matière de gestion de la rémunération.

Une des réactions souvent observées de la part des entrepreneurs est le constat que ces lois viennent augmenter le pouvoir des employés, diminuant d'autant ceux de l'employeur. Ils arrivent même, trop souvent, à la conclusion qu'entretenir une relation harmonieuse dans ce contexte est mission impossible !

La gestion globale de la rémunération demeure une composante majeure du lien employeur-employé. Toutefois, malgré la croyance populaire, il demeure possible de développer et d'appliquer des politiques de gestion de la rémunération respectueuses tout autant des lois que des droits des employeurs.

L'application de cette politique de gestion de la rémunération exige une bonne compréhension de ses enjeux et des lois. Tous les intervenants ayant des responsabilités de supervision d'une équipe de travail sont concernés par la gestion de la rémunération. Nous pouvons interroger longuement la formation et le support qu'ils ont pour assumer cette lourde tâche qui a peu en commun avec leurs connaissances et leurs expertises.

Voici un exemple de difficulté qui illustre très bien notre expérience dans le domaine de la gestion de la rémunération. Un client, en panique, nous fait part qu'un employé-clé vient de l'informer qu'il a reçu une offre ailleurs avec des conditions salariales très avantageuses. Le réflexe premier du dirigeant est de faire une offre égale, ce qui procure l'avantage de garder l'employé au lieu de le laisser partir chez un compétiteur. Selon notre expérience, cette solution a des effets sur l'organisation qui débordent largement l'impact de l'augmentation salariale consentie. Quel est le message reçu par l'ensemble des employés? « Ici, pour avoir une augmentation de salaire, il faut menacer l'employeur de le quitter. Ça marche à tout coup! » L'employeur qui a consenti une augmentation dans ce contexte a créé un précédent. En plus, le même employé pourrait même répéter l'exploit tant et aussi longtemps qu'il n'a pas obtenu entière satisfaction. À la limite, un grand nombre d'employés pourraient utiliser cette stratégie. Or, comment arrêter cette escalade de la masse salariale?

Dernièrement encore, un entrepreneur considérait sérieusement la possibilité de consentir un bonus imposant à un employé que, selon lui, l'entreprise n'avait pas les moyens de perdre. Je l'ai interrogé pour savoir si la rémunération actuelle était compétitive dans son secteur d'activité. Je lui ai aussi demandé s'il y avait des indices quant à une quelconque volonté de l'employé de quitter l'entreprise, tout en l'invitant à une réflexion visant à déterminer si une augmentation de salaire apporterait une solution durable au vrai problème, le cas échéant. Une gestion des ressources humaines utilisant la peur de perdre des employés comme base de décision comporte des conséquences majeures sur les relations avec les employés. Le comportement adopté par les employés demeure dicté par leur perception des principes de gestion de la direction.

Autre exemple: la direction d'une PME du Québec avait pris la décision d'augmenter les responsabilités et le salaire d'une jeune employée, la dernière engagée dans l'entreprise. La réaction générale des employés a été de rencontrer la direction générale pour lui exprimer leur mécontentement estimant que leur contribution à l'entreprise n'était pas reconnue! « Ici, pour être traité équitablement, il suffit de présenter une menace de quitter. Que faites-vous de notre loyauté?» Dans le monde des affaires actuel, le fait de consentir des augmentations à tout le monde sans établir de liens entre les responsabilités assumées et le taux de rémunération semble faire partie de notre culture organisationnelle.

Pourtant, il est du devoir des dirigeants de valoriser les comportements et attitudes compatibles avec l'entreprise et de décourager les autres. Les lois sont là pour encadrer et non pour assurer le respect des intervenants et des organisations. Voici un modèle d'application d'une politique de gestion de la rémunération, respectueuse des lois, des employés et de nos organisations.

Principes de gestion de la rémunération

La politique de gestion de la rémunération exige une excellente compréhension des lois, de leurs objectifs et de leurs méthodes d'application.

À titre d'exemple, la loi sur l'équité salariale a pour objectif d'éliminer toute forme de discrimination des structures de rémunération, basée sur le sexe. Cette loi oblige donc, dans un premier temps, un processus complexe pour vérifier si ce type de discrimination existe actuellement. Dans un deuxième temps, la loi exige de combler ces écarts pour éliminer la discrimination sexiste des structures de rémunération.

Un programme d'équité salariale se veut respectueux du principe de gestion de la rémunération «À travail équivalent, salaire égal», principe qui va beaucoup plus loin que celui-ci: «À travail égal, salaire égal». Le premier principe utilise le poste comme base de comparaison. Le second utilise la valeur de chaque poste, coté en points, comme base de comparaison. Ainsi, tous les postes sont comparés entre eux, ce qui oblige à comparer les salaires des employés de tous les départements de l'entreprise.

Principes d'implantation et d'utilisation

D'autre part, le système de gestion de la rémunération ne peut pas être appliqué en vase clos. Ce système doit, comme toute politique de gestion, s'appliquer dans le contexte de gestion globale de l'entreprise. Un système de gestion de la rémunération doit faciliter la meilleure contribution des ressources humaines à la réalisation des objectifs organisationnels et à l'amélioration de sa profitabilité. Le meilleur système de gestion de la rémunération améliore de façon significative un retour important sur l'investissement.

Il doit exister un lien étroit entre les objectifs établis et le système de gestion de la rémunération. Ces objectifs sont fixés lors de la rencontre de réflexion stratégique, pratique d'affaires présentée au chapitre 8. Le lecteur comprendra ici que la gestion de la rémunération a pour principal objectif de récompenser les acteurs internes, en fonction de leur contribution et de leur valeur ajoutée à la réalisation de la mission organisationnelle. Un lien étroit entre le salaire et la réalisation des objectifs stratégiques se doit d'exister lors de chaque décision relative à la gestion de la rémunération.

Ce même lien étroit existe avec le système de gestion de la performance, pratique d'affaires présentée au chapitre 9. Nous exprimons ici que le système de gestion de la performance n'est que la suite logique qui assure la mobilisation de l'équipe pour la réalisation du projet d'entreprise et la contribution optimale de chacun dans le respect de ses forces et de ses faiblesses.

La contribution de chaque intervenant à la réalisation des objectifs organisationnels a avantage à être très précise, de même que les indices de mesure utilisés pour contrôler cette contribution. Ainsi, les attentes envers chaque intervenant font l'objet d'un consensus, tant sur leur contenu que sur les stratégies à utiliser pour réaliser les objectifs.

L'élaboration et l'application d'une politique de gestion de la rémunération exige des descriptions de tâches précises et actualisées sur le partage des pouvoirs et des responsabilités. L'évaluation des emplois qui mesure en points l'importance de chaque poste se réfère, de fait, à une description détaillée des responsabilités assumées par les titulaires des postes.

Ces descriptions de tâches assurent une structure de rémunération respectueuse de la contribution des titulaires des postes à la réalisation des objectifs organisationnels. Les employés sont alors rémunérés pour ce qu'ils apportent à l'organisation et non pour des raisons subjectives.

Cette approche offre l'avantage d'appuyer l'application de la politique de gestion de la rémunération sur des considérations organisationnelles. Toute décision en la matière, justifiée par d'autres considérations, augmente le risque d'iniquités dans la gestion de la rémunération. Ces décisions placent la direction de l'entreprise en situation très inconfortable pour justifier ses décisions auprès des employés qui s'interrogent et qui contestent, prétextant, souvent à raison, du favoritisme. L'équité du système de gestion de la rémunération demeurera toujours la résultante des perceptions des employés. Les dirigeants demeurent les premiers responsables des perceptions de leurs employés. Ainsi, un plan de communication doit offrir suffisamment d'information pour permettre aux employés de juger de l'équité de la politique de gestion de la rémunération, tant en ce qui concerne son contenu que son application. L'objectif ici n'est pas de transférer à d'autres instances le pouvoir décisionnel en matière de gestion de la rémunération. Il est plutôt de fournir l'information pertinente qui permettra de s'assurer que les messages reçus des employés sont conformes aux objectifs de ces communications. L'équipe de direction qui assume mal cette responsabilité laisse, malheureusement, trop de pouvoirs aux rumeurs sans fondement. Un employé ayant l'impression qu'il n'est pas traité équitablement quant à sa rémunération peut avoir un impact majeur, trop souvent négatif, sur la motivation et sur l'efficacité de toute l'équipe. La résistance d'une chaîne se mesure à son maillon le plus faible.

Vous aurez compris ici l'importance de réinventer les façons de faire en matière de gestion de la rémunération pour s'adapter aux nouvelles réalités des marchés et de la main-d'œuvre. Cette exigence provoque un questionnement continu pour évaluer si la gestion de la rémunération contribue de façon optimale à la réalisation des objectifs organisationnels. Cette gestion s'adapte-t-elle à l'évolution de l'entreprise ? L'innovation essentielle au succès de nos entreprises est-elle intégrée à nos pratiques d'affaires en matière de gestion de la rémunération ?

La rémunération, c'est l'argent versé aux employés en échange d'une prestation de services. L'employé demeurera toujours à la conquête de son mieux-être. Qui ne fait pas un lien étroit entre son salaire et sa qualité de vie ? Les sondages réalisés placent le salaire au troisième rang des priorités des employés en ce qui concerne leur travail. Ainsi, la gestion de la rémunération est une opportunité en or d'offrir aux employés qui souhaitent améliorer leurs revenus, des défis qui assurent une plus grande contribution à la réalisation des objectifs de l'entreprise. Cette approche exige évidemment une délégation des responsabilités compatible avec le potentiel humain, tout en contribuant à diminuer la pression sur l'organisation et à améliorer le degré d'implication des employés.

En résumé, une saine politique de gestion de la rémunération peut s'avérer un autre outil de gestion qui contribuera de façon significative à l'amélioration de l'indice organisationnel du bonheur.

CHAPITRE 12

Structure organisationnelle de la relève

Théoriquement, la fonction «ressources humaines» inclut la disponibilité des connaissances, expériences et expertises essentielles pour assurer une contribution optimale du potentiel humain à la réalisation des objectifs organisationnels. En d'autres termes, la bonne personne, à la bonne place, au bon moment.

Il est déjà très exigeant pour l'organisation de se doter des outils de gestion assurant la réalisation de la raison d'être de la fonction «ressources humaines». Les exercices d'embauche et de dotation drainent une énergie considérable.

Quoique facilement explicable, une pratique de gestion qui se limite à une vision à court terme ne respecte en rien les principes relatifs à l'intégration des pratiques d'affaires à une vision à moyen et long termes. Ces pratiques d'affaires ne peuvent contribuer à la réalisation d'objectifs à moyen et long termes indéfinis.

Le chapitre 8 a clairement démontré l'importance d'identifier les connaissances, compétences et expertises requises pour réaliser les objectifs organisationnels. L'employeur se retrouve, très souvent, dans l'obligation de développer dans l'entreprise ce potentiel humain. Pour ce faire, la planification est de rigueur car une période de temps plus ou moins longue peut être nécessaire et surtout fort utile.

Cette approche s'inscrit dans un comportement proactif qui assure la pérennité du projet d'entreprise. Par contre, l'attitude réactive invite à identifier des solutions au fur et à mesure que les besoins, sinon les urgences, surgissent, et implique plusieurs délais non souhaitables dans la réalisation de l'adéquation entre le potentiel requis et celui effectivement disponible.

Le chapitre 9 sur la gestion de la performance fait mention de l'importance de l'organigramme et de plans de développement des ressources humaines compatibles avec les aspirations des employés et les besoins de l'organisation.

La structure organisationnelle de la relève définit la structure appropriée à mettre en place pour réaliser les objectifs à moyen et long termes. L'exercice de réflexion trouve son meilleur retour sur l'investissement lorsque nous associons aux différents postes les individus qui les occuperont.

Les partenaires financiers exigent cette structure organisationnelle pour autoriser le financement. Pourtant, trop peu d'entrepreneurs et de gestionnaires reconnaissent la valeur ajoutée de cet exercice.

Le principal avantage demeure la capacité pour l'organisation de gérer des carrières en faisant profiter les employés de toutes les opportunités de satisfaire leurs ambitions professionnelles sans avoir à rechercher des défis ailleurs. C'est là un ingrédient essentiel pour nourrir le sentiment d'appartenance des employés, pour les motiver et les mobiliser. Le lecteur comprendra ici l'impact majeur sur l'attrait de l'entreprise pour les candidats externes.

Le réflexe naturel de demander à l'équipe une collaboration exceptionnelle pour combler tous les besoins humains reliés aux absences, aux vacances et aux mandats spéciaux entraîne un sentiment d'exploitation chez les employés, une impression que l'employeur est redevable et une augmentation sensible du stress qui peut, à la limite, augmenter les statistiques d'absences pour détresse psychologique. Rappelons-nous que chaque délégation de travail en dehors des charges normales de travail entraîne un investissement d'énergie peu compatible avec les zones de performance. De plus, les responsabilités normales s'en trouvent pénalisées en ce sens que le temps consacré à d'autres tâches ne peut plus respecter l'entente prévue lors de l'identification des objectifs individuels.

L'exercice, au premier degré, exige de faire l'analyse de nos façons de faire actuelles pour remplacer les employés absents. Lorsqu'un collaborateur part en vacances annuelles, que se passe-t-il? Son bureau s'encombre anormalement. Son superviseur assume la plus grande part du travail. Nous exigeons de nos collaborateurs qu'ils demeurent disponibles pour les urgences. Ces périodes d'absences prévisibles offrent de belles opportunités de vérifier la capacité d'autres intervenants à assumer en tout ou en partie de nouvelles responsabilités. S'il existe un réel danger de créer de fausses attentes, il y a aussi la reconnaissance que l'évolution de l'entreprise exige la contribution d'autres personnes.

D'un autre point de vue, l'exercice permet de planifier le partage des responsabilités en cas de congés de maladie, de maternité, parentaux. Il évite les crises lors de l'annonce du départ d'un employé clé. Il permet même de ne pas affecter lourdement l'organisation lorsque le pire arrive, par exemple le décès prématuré d'un collaborateur. Ainsi, il protège l'entreprise de la dépendance trop grande envers certains individus, ce qui oblige souvent à prendre des décisions qui remettent en question l'équité de traitement par l'ensemble des employés.

À titre d'exemple, le président d'une PME québécoise décède prématurément à moins de cinquante ans. Sa conjointe, qui s'occupait strictement des finances et de la comptabilité, le remplace à la barre de l'entreprise. En l'absence de mandat d'inaptitude et d'assurances, il demeure impossible de se donner la marge de manœuvre pour absorber le coup. Les termes des relations avec les clients, fournisseurs et partenaires ne sont pas confinés aux dossiers. Malgré la meilleure volonté du monde, cette entreprise ferme un an plus tard.

La structure organisationnelle de la relève se présente comme un outil de gestion qui ouvre la porte à des ententes prenant en considération les particularités de la main-d'œuvre, telles le vieillissement de la population active et le retour au travail de retraités sur des horaires allégés. Cette option offre l'avantage de se donner le temps de transférer à d'autres les connaissances et expertises acquises au fil des années. Les employés des nouvelles générations attachent une importance plus grande à la qualité de vie et à la conciliation travail-famille. L'utilisation réduite des aînés permet souvent de répondre aux nouvelles exigences de ces générations.

En conclusion, la structure organisationnelle de la relève est un levier indispensable qui offre un puissant outil de gestion du potentiel humain pouvant contribuer largement au bonheur de tous et à l'amélioration de la rentabilité de nos entreprises et de nos organisations.

CHAPITRE 13

Agilité organisationnelle

Les méthodes agiles

À l'origine, les méthodes agiles sont des procédures de conception de logiciels plus pragmatiques. Elles impliquent le client au maximum en permettant une grande réactivité à ses demandes. Elles visent la satisfaction réelle des besoins du client. Les méthodes Scrum et XP sont les plus connues en France.

Scrum est une méthode agile pour la gestion de projets de développement de logiciels. Elle a été conçue pour améliorer la productivité dans les équipes. Elle peut théoriquement s'appliquer à n'importe quel contexte ou à un groupe de personnes qui travaillent ensemble pour atteindre un but commun.

L'autre méthode agile de gestion de projet informatique XP ("Extreme Programming") s'adapte aux équipes réduites avec des besoins changeants. Cette méthode tente de réconcilier l'humain avec la productivité. C'est un mécanisme pour faciliter le changement social, une voie d'amélioration, un style de développement et une discipline de développement d'applications informatiques.

Son but principal est de réduire les coûts du changement. XP rend le projet plus flexible et ouvert au changement par l'introduction de valeurs de base, de principes et de pratiques. Ses valeurs sont la communication, la simplicité, le feedback, le courage et le respect, lesquelles sont toutes reliées à l'aspect humain de l'organisation.

Cette méthode agile ciblait, au départ, le développement d'une application informatique. Elle a toutefois provoqué un mouvement plus large de management connu sous le nom de processus d'amélioration continue de la qualité.

Amélioration continue de la qualité

Ce processus prône quatre valeurs fondamentales. La première concerne les personnes et leurs interactions plutôt que les processus et les outils, partant du principe qu'une équipe soudée qui communique vaut mieux que des experts fonctionnant de manière isolée. La deuxième donne la priorité à la fonctionnalité de l'application. La documentation technique offre une aide précieuse, sans être le but ultime. Une documentation précise assure le transfert des compétences au sein de l'équipe. La communication y contribue largement. Les deux autres valeurs, intimement reliées, considèrent la collaboration et l'adaptation au changement. La relation avec le client s'établit davantage sur la collaboration que sur la négociation qui suggère un rapport de force et de pouvoir. L'adaptation au changement, quant à elle, offre la flexibilité essentielle au respect des demandes du client en constante évolution.

Ces valeurs exigent l'adhésion et la conformité à certains principes. La priorité demeure la satisfaction du client. L'adaptation au changement exige de diminuer la résistance naturelle au changement. Les livraisons se réalisent dans les plus courts délais. Les activités quotidiennes démontrent la collaboration de l'ensemble des intervenants. La motivation des individus doit se maintenir à son niveau optimal par un support constant, par la manifestation d'une confiance en la capacité de réussir et l'expression d'encouragements en continu. L'excellence technique et la qualité de la conception font l'objet d'une attention soutenue et continue, incluant les adaptations pour assurer la conformité aux standards. Les pratiques et décisions se conforment à la règle de la simplicité, c'est-à-dire ramener en continu les éléments à leur plus simple expression. L'autonomie des équipes de travail garantit leur efficacité. Les façons de faire font l'objet d'un questionnement continu pour identifier les moyens à prendre pour s'améliorer, le cas échéant.

Ainsi, ce processus se distingue par une approche basée essentiellement sur la motivation et l'implication des ressources humaines. L'agilité représente alors la composante majeure d'un management qui confie la résolution de la complexité au personnel d'exécution. C'est l'utilisation optimale du potentiel humain par le maintien d'un fort degré de motivation et de mobilisation. Cette approche prône aussi des façons de faire réinventées dans un contexte de consensus au sein des équipes de travail.

En pratique, l'agilité se matérialise par une orientation service-qualité et par l'adaptation au changement. Elle utilise pour fondement la motivation des ressources humaines, l'usage intensif des nouvelles technologies et des processus réinventés en continu. La compréhension de cette pratique de gestion par l'ensemble des ressources humaines et leur adhésion à ses façons de faire représentent les enjeux essentiels pour assurer l'agilité organisationnelle.

Il existe alors un lien étroit entre la gestion du potentiel humain et l'agilité organisationnelle. Ses orientations, l'utilisation des nouvelles technologies et la réinvention des processus exigent la contribution optimale du potentiel humain.

Les projets d'optimisation continue des processus demeurent de puissants moyens d'obtenir des avantages concurrentiels au meilleur coût. Ces projets, bien gérés et déployés, assurent la contribution optimale de chaque secteur de l'entreprise à la réalisation de la mission organisationnelle.

Pour IBM, par exemple, l'agilité organisationnelle est sa capacité technique d'intégrer en continu et harmonieusement le changement des aspects vitaux de sa survie et de son succès.

Microsoft, quant à lui, utilise l'agilité organisationnelle pour apporter des solutions en rapport avec les attentes des marchés et des clients.

Allan Afuah, auteur, a écrit dans Innovation Management : "Strategies, Implementation, and Profits" que «pour gérer et développer au mieux son capital humain, l'entreprise agile doit maîtriser quatre processus prioritaires : l'identification des écarts entre les compétences stratégiques et l'état actuel de ses ressources ; le développement de son portefeuille de compétences actuelles, en combinant les différents leviers existants (formation, gestion des connaissances, coaching, etc.); l'optimisation de l'utilisation des ressources et leur mobilisation au sein d'unités d'appartenance forte; l'utilisation des outils de rétribution et de préservation des ressources critiques. »

Olivier Badot, professeur à ESCP en Europe, écrit dans son livre intitulé «Théorie de l'entreprise agile» que « Les hommes et les femmes de l'entreprise agile, par leur connaissance intime des clients et de l'environnement, par leur savoir-faire en permanence affûté, par leur imagination et par les initiatives qu'ils sont autorisés à prendre pour satisfaire de façon originale le client, deviennent alors la principale source de différenciation et de performance commerciale de l'entreprise. La recherche d'agilité pourra alors atteindre le niveau le plus élevé d'implication des ressources : l'entreprenariat. »

William Edwards Deming

L'impact de l'agilité organisationnelle sur le management demeure encore aujourd'hui très grand. Mr. William Edwards Deming, mathématicien et philosophe, a considérablement influencé l'économie mondiale pendant la seconde moitié du XXᵉ siècle. Ses théories sur le management ont transformé les façons de faire du commerce et de l'industrie. Sa pensée trace la route à tous ceux qui veulent établir un management efficace dans le respect de la dignité humaine.

Deming est considéré comme le fondateur du mouvement pour la qualité. Sa pensée, par contre, s'étend largement au-delà des méthodes de la qualité. Il propose un nouveau modèle de société où la compétition fait place à la coopération, dans le respect des valeurs humaines et la préservation des ressources de la planète. Il fut l'un des artisans de la réussite de l'économie japonaise.

Deming a diagnostiqué sept maladies mortelles pour les organisations :

- Manque de constance dans la planification d'un produit ou d'un service.
- Excès d'importance accordée aux profits à court-terme.
- Excès d'importance accordée à l'évaluation par la performance, à l'avancement au mérite, au tableau d'honneur de la performance.
- Excès de mobilité du management : le papillonnage de poste en poste.
- Pilotage de l'entreprise par les seuls chiffres apparents, sans considération pour les chiffres qui sont inconnus ou non connaissables. Au-delà d'une critique des outils de pilotage (indicateurs et tableaux de bord), Deming remet en cause l'inertie des responsables d'entreprises dans leurs choix d'indicateurs. Il plaide en faveur d'un esprit de recherche d'efficacité plutôt que de l'application d'une méthode préétablie et définitive.
- Coûts médicaux élevés.
- Coûts excessifs de la protection juridique (notamment la provision).

Deming définit une sous-catégorie d'obstacles au bon fonctionnement de l'entreprise :

- Négliger la planification à long terme.
- Compter sur la technologie pour résoudre les problèmes.
- Chercher des exemples à suivre plutôt que de développer des solutions.
- L'utilisation à outrance d'excuses pour justifier les décisions de la direction.

Il offre une solution sur mesure pour enrayer la maladie et éviter qu'elle se propage. Elle prévoit la mise en place d'un système de connaissance profonde, la surveillance du bon fonctionnement de l'organisation en quatorze points essentiels et l'implantation d'une démarche PDCA (Plan Do Check Act).

La première étape de cette démarche (Plan) invite à une conception claire de ce qu'on veut réaliser et à une planification précise de la réalisation. La deuxième (Do) concerne la mise en œuvre de la planification, en commençant de préférence à une petite échelle. La troisième (Check) vérifie si les nouvelles idées mises en œuvre satisfont les attentes par des retours sur les expériences et l'élaboration de bilans. La dernière (Act) est la validation ou le rejet des nouvelles idées par l'expérimentation dans des conditions différentes.

Deming a formalisé les clés de la performance d'une organisation en 14 points :

- Garantir la continuité de l'action définie en vue de l'amélioration des produits et des services, dans le but de devenir compétitif, de poursuivre son activité et de créer de l'emploi.
- Adopter une nouvelle philosophie de coopération (gagnant-gagnant) dans laquelle tout le monde gagne et la mettre en pratique en l'enseignant aux employés, aux clients et aux fournisseurs.
- Cesser de dépendre des échantillonnages pour atteindre la qualité. Améliorer le processus et bâtir, en premier lieu, la qualité dans le produit lui-même.
- Mettre fin aux pratiques de choix d'activités sur la seule base des prix. Minimiser durablement le coût total. S'orienter vers un fournisseur unique pour une dépense donnée, basée sur une relation durable fondée sur la loyauté et la confiance.
- Améliorer constamment et durablement le système de production, de service et de planification. Cette approche assurera une meilleure qualité et une productivité conduisant à une diminution constante des coûts.
- Instituer la formation au développement des compétences.
- Adopter et instaurer le leadership pour le management des personnes, en reconnaissant leurs savoir-faire, leurs capacités et leurs aspirations respectifs. La finalité du leadership devrait être d'aider les personnes et les équipements à réaliser un meilleur travail. Le leadership de l'équipe managériale nécessite une révision, de même que la participation des collaborateurs.
- Écarter la peur et construire une confiance de sorte que tout le monde puisse travailler efficacement.
- Briser les barrières entre les différents services. Abolir la compétition et construire un système de coopération gagnant-gagnant au sein de l'organisation. Les acteurs de la recherche, de la conception, des ventes et de la production doivent travailler en équipe pour anticiper les problèmes de réalisation ou de d'utilisation du produit ou du service.
- Éliminer les slogans, les exhortations et les objectifs visant le zéro-défaut et des niveaux de productivité plus élevés. De tels mots d'ordre ont pour seul effet de créer des relations d'adversité puisque la majeure partie des causes d'une basse qualité et d'une faible productivité réside dans le système et demeure hors de portée des employés.
- Éliminer la quantification des buts, les quotas numériques, le management par objectif.
- Supprimer les obstacles qui privent les personnes de leur enthousiasme au travail.
- Instaurer un programme énergique d'éducation et d'amélioration personnelle, mettant ainsi fin à l'évaluation annuelle ou à l'avancement au mérite, lesquelles favorisent la compétition et les conflits internes.
- Mettre tout le personnel à l'œuvre pour accomplir la transformation de l'organisation, laquelle doit impliquer tous les employés.

Les travaux de Deming véhiculent l'idée du changement. L'ensemble de ses propositions et recommandations exhorte à un type de leadership essentiel au management de nos organisations.

Le leader efficace favorise, encourage et réalise le changement dans un contexte de détermination, d'endurance et d'amélioration continue. Il innove. Il vainc la résistance naturelle au changement pour les intervenants confortables et sécurisés dans le système actuel. Il entretient les réseaux de communication pour mobiliser son personnel à l'implantation du changement et de l'innovation.

Erwan Burel, manager consultant formateur, dirigeant de Haute Performance conseil formation accompagnement, exprime : « Ce ne sont pas les théories, les méthodes ou les outils qui sont au cœur de la performance mais l'esprit qui les anime. Cet état d'esprit est celui du leader qui, porté par des intuitions, imagine et conçoit de nouvelles manières de penser, de décider et d'agir. »

La connaissance approfondie est essentielle aux gestionnaires pour assumer leurs responsabilités efficacement. Elle implique la compréhension globale de l'organisation. Elle assure la complémentarité à la réalisation de la mission organisationnelle. Elle appuie chaque décision sur l'observation de la variabilité selon les lois de distribution statistique. Elle quantifie le coût acceptable pour chaque amélioration de la qualité. Elle valide la compréhension des processus par sa conformité aux lois statistiques auxquelles ils sont soumis. Finalement, elle fait preuve de psychologie par la considération des facteurs humains qui déterminent les responsabilités qu'acceptent d'assumer les individus. Parmi ces facteurs humains, il est primordial de reconnaître l'importance des valeurs, des principes et des facteurs de motivation.

Le Système Toyota

L'œuvre de Deming a largement influencé les concepteurs du système de production de Toyota. Ce système est souvent considéré comme l'un des plus performants au monde. Il regroupe plusieurs concepts dont le juste-à-temps, le kaizen, le zéro défaut, l'esprit d'équipe et le kanban.

Le système Toyota fait partie des systèmes de contrôle de la qualité. Les professionnels utilisent le nom de "Lean Manufacturing".

Ces systèmes utilisent trois piliers : la qualité totale, le juste-à-temps et le respect des autres. Comme nous l'avons vu, Deming a développé des techniques de contrôle de la qualité basées sur l'analyse statistique. Plus encore, il a inventé toute une philosophie de gestion ayant pour objectif l'optimisation systématique de la qualité. Les quatorze points de Deming, énoncés plus haut, résument les principes du concept de la qualité totale. Le juste-à-temps ou JAT est une technique de production basée sur l'élimination des sept types de gaspillages que sont : les excès de production, les attentes et les queues, le transport, les stocks, les mouvements inutiles, les opérations inutiles et les défauts de fabrication. À la base, le concept JAT exige que la production soit la résultante d'une commande d'un client. Le respect des autres, quant à lui, suppose que les employés sont conscients de l'importance de leur travail et qu'ils contribuent aux efforts d'amélioration de la production. Ils collaborent aux activités d'identification de solutions et proposent des solutions. La qualité concerne chaque intervenant. Ce respect exige de l'équipe de direction de faciliter les communications, d'entretenir une relation de confiance, de promouvoir les activités de formation et de développement, de valoriser les attitudes et les comportements compatibles avec la philosophie de gestion, de prendre en considération les recommandations même s'il est exigeant de remettre en question les façons de faire et de gérer, de tolérer l'erreur dans un contexte de recherche de solution et de réaliser une vision d'entreprise à moyen et long termes.

Le Système Toyota utilise quatorze principes de base, tirés du livre "The Toyota Way" de Jeffrey K. Liker. En traduction libre, ils s'expriment ainsi :

- Appuyer la prise de décision sur une philosophie de gestion à long terme, en acceptant les conséquences financières à court terme
- Créer et implanter des processus qui permettent de mettre les problèmes en évidence rapidement (flux continu)
- Utiliser le flux tiré (produire sur commande seulement) pour éviter la surproduction
- Lisser la production, c'est-à-dire minimiser les variations trop importantes qui affectent la quantité et la qualité
- Intégrer à la culture le réflexe naturel d'arrêter la production dès l'émergence d'un problème, de façon à produire de la qualité du premier coup
- Standardiser le travail dans le but d'établir la base de l'amélioration continue et de l'implication des collaborateurs
- Utiliser le management visuel afin qu'aucun problème ne soit caché
- Ne mettre au service du personnel et des processus de production que des technologies éprouvées
- Développer des leaders qui connaissent parfaitement le travail, et qui incarnent la philosophie de l'entreprise
- Développer des collaborateurs et des équipes de travail exceptionnels qui embrassent la philosophie de l'organisation
- Respecter son réseau étendu de partenaires et de fournisseurs en les encourageant et en les aidant à s'améliorer
- Aller soi-même sur le terrain pour comprendre en profondeur la situation
- Prendre des décisions lentement, par consensus, en considérant toutes les options possibles. Appliquer rapidement les solutions retenues
- Devenir une organisation qui apprend à travers la réflexion, l'expérience et l'amélioration continue.

Les résultats du système de production Toyota sont spectaculaires. En 1987, le temps de mise en marché d'un nouveau modèle se réalisait en 46 mois, alors que ses concurrents américains et européens avaient besoin de 60 mois, tout en utilisant moins d'ingénieurs et avec beaucoup moins de défauts. Cette même mise en marché d'un nouveau modèle est maintenant réalisée en 18 mois. Toyota prévoit de réaliser l'exploit en 12 mois, d'ici 5 ans. Les enquêtes qualité réalisées en 2007 révèlent, au chapitre de la fiabilité, qu'au bout de 5 ans, les problèmes rencontrés par les clients par 100 véhicules est de 35 pour Toyota, 70 pour Ford, 85 pour GM, et 95 pour Volkswagen. Toyota s'est hissée ainsi au premier rang mondial devant GM.

Toyota a mis plus de cinquante ans à tirer de réels bénéfices de ses efforts et assure de n'être pas au bout de sa quête de l'excellence. Le rappel historique de 2010 des véhicules en fait foi. À ce

sujet, je m'explique difficilement la couverture médiatique de l'événement. Elle a parlé abondamment du nombre de véhicules rappelés,
en ayant soin de préciser les pays concernés. Elle affirmait qu'il
s'agissait là d'un dur coup à la réputation de Toyota. Je demeure sur
l'impression que le professionnalisme des médias exige une information complète, c'est-à-dire l'exposé de l'ensemble des réactions
possibles à la nouvelle. Je me permets d'exprimer ma réaction à ce
fameux rappel historique, réaction largement influencée par l'expert
en gestion du potentiel humain. Tout en reconnaissant l'impact
majeur de cette nouvelle sur le lien de confiance entre Toyota et son
client, j'ai apprécié, qu'enfin, une compagnie d'envergure internationale soit suffisamment responsable pour prendre les mesures
correctives assurant l'élimination définitive de cette faille majeure
à la réputation de fiabilité et de sécurité de ses produits. La mission
organisationnelle de Toyota a dicté les décisions démontrant sa détermination à maintenir sa position de tête. En aucun temps la direction
n'a quantifié l'impact négatif sur les résultats financiers et le coût
de l'opération. Voilà, à mon avis, un exemple d'attitudes compatibles
avec la mission de l'organisation!

Système de management de la qualité (SMQ)

Le but du système de management de la qualité est de garantir
l'assurance de la qualité du produit ou du service et d'accroître la
satisfaction de la clientèle.

Ce système exige un fort degré d'engagement de la direction
à l'implication de l'ensemble des ressources humaines et à des relations d'affaires constructives avec l'ensemble des intervenants
(clients, fournisseurs, partenaires, actionnaires, institutions, etc.).

Ainsi, les concepteurs demeurent à l'écoute du client afin
de créer un produit ou un service répondant précisément à ses
besoins. Pour ce faire, l'accent est mis sur la maîtrise des compétences, sur l'optimisation de l'utilisation des ressources par une
plus grande implication du personnel et une amélioration continue
des processus.

Le SMQ fait donc partie de l'ensemble des outils de gestion mis à la disposition des gestionnaires. Bien au-delà de la conformité à un processus ou à une politique, le SMQ considère le client comme le patron à satisfaire. Sa mise en œuvre consiste en l'application de la roue de Deming expliquée plus haut.

On reproche aux normes traditionnelles des systèmes de management de la qualité de ne pas tenir compte du contexte. Le concept de qualité totale vient remédier à cette situation en intégrant les impacts sur l'environnement, sur les fournisseurs, et sur l'hygiène et la sécurité au travail. Les enjeux du développement durable (risques globaux, changements climatiques, etc.) sont maintenant partie intégrante des systèmes de management de la qualité.

Le SMQ procure des avantages concurrentiels majeurs, qu'il s'agisse de l'amélioration de la rentabilité, de la création de valeur ajoutée ou de l'existence d'une plus grande stabilité.

La clé du succès : Le facteur humain

Les méthodes de management et de gestion de la production tirent leur efficience de la compréhension qu'en ont les utilisateurs et de leur mobilisation à les appliquer en continu. Son efficacité n'appartient pas aux différentes méthodes de qualité assurant sa mise en œuvre au plan opérationnel, mais plutôt à des facteurs humains. Les principes de sobriété, d'apprentissage pour une amélioration continue, de pro-activité et de solidarité des acteurs doivent être respectés et appliqués. Ainsi, l'application de ces méthodes assure le meilleur retour sur l'investissement si elle contribue à la réalisation de la vision et de la mission organisationnelles. Ces outils de gestion ont été largement documentés au chapitre 8.

L'attitude managériale constitue le cœur de l'agilité organisationnelle et l'exigence fondamentale à son succès. Les gestionnaires, en collaboration avec l'ensemble des intervenants internes et externes, doivent maîtriser les techniques d'analyses de problèmes et d'identification de solutions durables et sur mesure. De plus, ces solutions s'appliquent dans le respect de la culture organisationnelle et des individus. Les principes et les valeurs inhérents au processus doivent également être respectés. En un mot, l'agilité organisationnelle exige de développer un réflexe naturel de transformer toute difficulté en opportunité d'affaires par l'utilisation du potentiel humain de l'organisation.

Une des valeurs de l'agilité organisationnelle est d'éliminer toute forme de gaspillage au sein de l'organisation. En matière de gestion du potentiel humain, cette volonté d'éliminer le gaspillage exige d'en reconnaître les causes, de quantifier ses impacts négatifs sur les plans financiers et démotivants et d'identifier les solutions durables.

À ce sujet, quels sont les éléments source de gaspillage en matière de gestion du potentiel humain ? Une analyse honnête exige de reconnaître que chaque délégation de responsabilités incompatible avec les zones de performance des individus et des équipes de travail contribue à un gaspillage suscitant un impact négatif majeur. De fait, confier une responsabilité à quelqu'un inapte à réaliser le travail empêche la réalisation des objectifs organisationnels. L'impact sur la motivation est dramatique. Avons-nous un processus de contrôle de la qualité relié au partage des pouvoirs et responsabilités au sein de l'organisation ? Nos organigrammes et descriptions de tâches demeurent-ils à jour en continu ? Mesurons-nous l'impact des mauvaises décisions ? Finalement, où sont les stratégies organisationnelles pour assurer que les erreurs du passé ne se reproduiront pas dans l'avenir ? La réponse à ces questions réside dans l'application de l'agilité organisationnelle. Pour ce faire, les décisions en matière d'embauche et de dotation doivent faire l'objet d'un consensus au sein d'un comité réunissant tous les intervenants concernés.

L'agilité organisationnelle, tout comme l'organisation, demeure en constante évolution, en perpétuelle adaptation au changement. C'est l'occasion par excellence d'assumer le leadership essentiel à l'augmentation de la capacité à gérer et à implanter le changement.

L'objectif ultime de l'agilité organisationnelle demeure l'augmentation de la performance économique de l'organisation par la mobilisation de tous les intervenants. Cette performance globale et durable exige des entités œuvrant en complémentarité à la réalisation de la mission organisationnelle.

Ainsi, l'efficacité de tout système repose sur l'adéquation entre la vision et la mission organisationnelles et la mission de vie et les valeurs des individus qui y travaillent. Reconnaître l'individu comme levier fondamental de la performance globale exige une compréhension exhaustive de la motivation, laquelle est essentielle à la mobilisation. C'est la clé de la réussite en matière de gestion du potentiel humain. Un employé mobilisé demeure celui qui établit un lien étroit entre ses responsabilités et la réalisation de ses ambitions personnelles et professionnelles. Le sentiment de réaliser sa mission de vie, dans le respect de ses valeurs et de ses façons de faire, garantit la meilleure contribution de la personne humaine.

En pratique, la mobilisation doit être mesurée, en ce sens que l'entreprise doit connaître et communiquer ses critères en matière de gestion du potentiel humain. Les indicateurs les plus utilisés actuellement sont le taux de roulement de la main-d'œuvre, le taux d'absentéisme et les statistiques en santé et sécurité. Il reste beaucoup de travail à faire pour identifier les causes de ces indicateurs et pour documenter l'indice organisationnel du bonheur. Une question fondamentale s'impose : ces indicateurs tiennent-ils compte de l'indice de bonheur de chaque intervenant ?

L'agilité organisationnelle crée une pression énorme sur les équipes de direction et de gestion dont le rôle primordial est d'assumer un leadership efficace sur les performances des organisations et sur leur rentabilité. Ces éléments essentiels doivent aussi faire l'objet d'un contrôle continu et d'une mesure adéquate. L'opinion des personnes concernées est vitale et précieuse. À quand remonte notre dernier sondage de satisfaction auprès des employés, des clients et même des partenaires ?

Les résultats financiers des entreprises les plus performantes témoignent d'une mobilisation optimale des ressources humaines. Force nous est de constater qu'un employé heureux réalise plus et mieux. L'agilité organisationnelle nous offre l'opportunité d'exceller en gestion du potentiel humain. Elle exige un investissement majeur dans le bonheur de chaque intervenant : employés, clients, fournisseurs et partenaires. C'est le prix à payer pour entretenir des liens d'affaires solides et durables. C'est l'autoroute qui assure l'efficacité des employés et la fidélisation de la clientèle. Bref, plus l'individu se réalise dans son travail et ailleurs, plus il est mobilisé !

Consolidation d'équipe par l'action et le jeu

Ce chapitre a été écrit grâce à la précieuse collaboration d'Yves Sévigny, auteur et conférencier, de Formation ACTE Défi Aventure.

L'apprentissage par simulation et par le jeu est une technique innovatrice qui a pris son essor depuis une quinzaine d'années dans différents pays à travers le monde. L'apprentissage utilisant les techniques traditionnelles offre, certes, de nombreux avantages, mais on se questionne sur son impact et ses retombées dans le temps. De fait, tout exercice de formation se réfère encore aujourd'hui à la formation académique. Les participants manifestent une résistance énorme en exprimant leurs appréhensions à se retrouver sur les bancs de l'école.

Plusieurs études, à travers le monde, concluent que, généralement, on retient :

- 10 % de ce qu'on lit ;
- 20 % de ce qu'on entend ;
- 30 % de ce qu'on voit ;
- 50 % de ce qu'on voit et entend ;
- 80 % de ce qu'on dit ;
- 90 % de ce qu'on fait.

La réponse à la question de la durée de rétention dans le temps fait encore l'objet de discussions. La technique d'apprentissage par simulation et par le jeu veut provoquer une évolution dans les méthodes d'apprentissage, de transfert de connaissances et de façons de faire. Elle veut surtout améliorer la durée de rétention des notions acquises.

Cette nouvelle technique d'apprentissage utilise une approche différente pour assurer le transfert de connaissances en contexte organisationnel. L'expérience, au départ, se vit en pleine nature, n'ayant aucune affinité avec le contexte normal de travail. Ce dépaysement ou l'absence des repères habituels offre l'avantage aux participants d'agir dans le respect de leur individualité sans références aux structures organisationnelles. Les statuts reliés aux responsabilités assumées en contexte de travail influencent fortement les relations interpersonnelles, spécifiquement en raison des pouvoirs qu'ils confèrent. De plus, les individus, eux-mêmes, adoptent des attitudes et comportements largement influencés par leur perception du modèle à utiliser pour atteindre leurs objectifs.

Le concept, à la base, en matière de gestion du potentiel humain, veut tracer les profils de personnalité des individus par l'utilisation de techniques innovatrices, pour réaliser l'adéquation entre le potentiel humain disponible et la contribution à la réalisation des objectifs organisationnels.

Un tel concept s'est largement inspiré du Programme de leadership. Il privilégie l'apprentissage par des activités facilement applicables au contexte organisationnel. Il favorise la croissance personnelle et professionnelle des participants par le perfectionnement autogéré. Il rehausse les qualités de chef des participants en identifiant leurs forces et leurs faiblesses telles qu'elles sont perçues par eux-mêmes et par les autres. Il vise à l'amélioration de la productivité des participants par une meilleure conciliation de leur vie professionnelle et personnelle.

Le participant voit une amélioration de sa capacité à composer avec les difficultés qui se présentent en continu et, par le fait même, augmente sa capacité à intégrer le changement. Son degré d'assurance et de confiance augmente pour assumer un leadership compatible avec son potentiel. Il maîtrise les outils et processus susceptibles d'améliorer son leadership. Son degré de motivation est augmenté par une prise de conscience de sa capacité à atteindre ses objectifs professionnels et personnels. Il sort de l'expérience enrichi d'une meilleure connaissance de lui-même et de ses besoins en matière de perfectionnement. Finalement, le superviseur possède une information fiable pour former des équipes aptes à agir en complémentarité et pour encadrer efficacement ses collaborateurs.

Ces expériences, en forêt spécifiquement, ont pour objectif de développer l'esprit d'équipe, le leadership, les aptitudes en communication, l'esprit d'analyse et d'augmenter la connaissance qu'a le participant de lui-même.

Cette approche innovatrice veut propulser le développement du potentiel humain par l'identification de talents souvent insoupçonnés, les contextes traditionnels de travail n'offrant pas l'opportunité de les démontrer. Il n'y a plus de place pour discuter des capacités des individus à influencer le groupe et à contribuer à la réussite des résultats puisque l'observation du participant le démontre clairement. C'est ce que nous appelons l'intégration des connaissances théoriques.

Ces expériences doivent être réalisées sous la supervision d'une équipe d'experts aptes à récupérer les réactions des individus rapidement. Il n'est pas rare que des réactions de panique s'expriment dans ce monde de l'inconnu, source d'insécurité profonde. Ces situations peuvent engendrer des volontés d'abandonner, des constats d'échec, des conclusions sur l'incapacité d'un participant à poursuivre l'expérience et, pire encore, à tenter d'imposer à un autre participant notre évaluation des capacités des autres. Ainsi, il est primordial que l'équipe d'animation puisse intervenir adéquatement sur le champ pour dénouer les impasses.

En situation d'inconfort majeur, il est tout à fait humain de tenter de faire porter le blâme sur les autres. C'est dans ces situations que le groupe doit être respecté dans ses façons de faire et que les individus ont l'opportunité de s'impliquer dans le respect de ce qu'ils sont pour récupérer la problématique. L'équipe d'animation a le défi constant de s'assurer que les expériences vécues demeurent positives, autant pour les individus que pour le groupe.

Les différentes activités et expériences explorent quatre composantes majeures de la gestion des entreprises : la communication, le leadership, l'esprit d'analyse et le travail d'équipe. Elles peuvent faciliter l'intégration de nouveaux gestionnaires par une compréhension rapide des modes de fonctionnement de l'organisation et l'identification de la contribution potentielle de chaque membre de l'organisation. Elles améliorent la communication au sein des équipes de travail et entre celles-ci, favorisant ainsi la complémentarité dans la réalisation de la mission organisationnelle. Elles assurent une délégation des responsabilités et des pouvoirs compatible avec les forces de chaque membre de l'organisation. Elles valident la compatibilité entre les valeurs personnelles et organisationnelles. Elles offrent l'opportunité à chaque participant de faire ressortir les talents et les compétences que les contextes traditionnels n'avaient pas permis de reconnaître jusqu'alors. Elles favorisent l'émergence d'idées innovatrices. Elles assurent une compréhension commune de la mission organisationnelle et de la contribution attendue de chaque membre. Elles augmentent la motivation, la mobilisation et le sentiment d'appartenance. Elles valident la capacité des candidats pressentis pour assumer de nouvelles responsabilités. Elle démystifie la barrière des générations et les perceptions. Finalement, elles intègrent à la gestion des entreprises les processus d'intégration et de développement personnel.

Pour toutes ces raisons, cette expérience retiendra l'attention des gestionnaires d'entreprise à la recherche de nouvelles façons d'améliorer leur gestion du potentiel humain, de même que l'efficacité et la rentabilité de l'entreprise, en favorisant une contribution optimale de chacun à la réalisation de sa mission dans l'entreprise. Cette technique représente une excellente opportunité de valoriser la créativité, l'innovation et de découvrir les moyens d'intégrer ces forces à la gestion de l'entreprise.

Tous les ingrédients permettant de créer une révolution dans les stratégies proposées aux entreprises pour favoriser leur croissance sont maintenant réunis. Voici une façon originale d'améliorer la capacité d'adaptation au changement des organisations, élément déterminant de leur succès en contexte de constante évolution. Cette technique d'apprentissage est l'occasion idéale pour améliorer les aspects de l'entreprise où interviennent les différentes composantes de la dynamique de groupe.

Le retour sur l'investissement optimal exige l'expression par les participants de leur compréhension et de leur appréciation de l'expérience, des difficultés rencontrées, de leurs découvertes et des apprentissages réalisés, tant aux plans personnels qu'organisationnels.

Voici ce que les participants retiennent, entre autres, de cette expérience unique : elle facilite l'intégration de nouveaux gestionnaires en diminuant sa durée ; elle améliore la communication inter-équipes ; elle suscite une implication totale des participants ; elle consolide l'équipe ; le partage des pouvoirs et des responsabilités respecte davantage les forces de chaque membre de l'équipe ; elle mobilise les troupes ; elle assure l'identification précise des valeurs et des objectifs et l'adhésion des participants à ceux-ci ; elle ouvre la porte à l'innovation ; elle renforce le lien entre les missions personnelles et organisationnelles ; elle facilite les relations entre les générations ; elle nourrit le sentiment d'appartenance ; elle favorise l'exploration de nouvelles avenues et solutions.

Par la suite, il restera à l'équipe de direction et de gestion à développer et à appliquer les stratégies qui assurent l'utilisation optimale du potentiel humain, c'est-à-dire à définir les moyens d'utiliser les compétences et expertises découvertes pour qu'elles contribuent efficacement à la réalisation des objectifs de l'entreprise.

Cette pratique d'affaires innovatrice représente un puissant outil de mobilisation par sa contribution particulière et unique à l'identification du potentiel de chaque membre de l'équipe. Elle permet de soutenir la réalisation des objectifs de l'équipe tout en respectant les objectifs individuels. Elle offre l'avantage d'obtenir une information précieuse sur les capacités individuelles, en complémentarité avec celles obtenues par les autres outils de gestion du potentiel humain.

CHAPITRE 15

Planification de la relève entrepreneuriale

La problématique de la relève entrepreneuriale s'inscrit dans les enjeux les plus critiques pour l'avenir du Québec. Le temps presse. Dans notre économie largement dépendante de la PME, le temps de la conscientisation des propriétaires dirigeants actuels à l'importance de planifier le projet de relève appartient au passé.

Il y a cinq ans maintenant que des statistiques indiquaient qu'un entrepreneur sur deux prendrait sa retraite dans les dix prochaines années. De surcroît, la réalisation d'un projet de relève exige entre trois et dix ans.

Les propriétaires et les dirigeants actuels demeurent les premiers responsables de leur conscientisation des enjeux majeurs du projet de relève entrepreneuriale ayant un impact déterminant sur l'avenir de leur entreprise. Malgré la grande complexité de ce projet, ils doivent relever le défi d'assurer la pérennité de leur entreprise dans la perspective où ils ne seront plus à la tête de leur entreprise.

La Fondation de l'Entrepreneurship a réalisé, en février 2009, un sondage important qui a permis de mesurer l'indice entrepreneurial québécois. Les résultats de ce sondage sont critiques. Le plus important sondage jamais réalisé sur l'entreprenariat québécois détruit le mythe du Québec entrepreneurial. Pourtant, l'entrepreneuriat est l'oxygène du système économique. Les principales conclusions de ce sondage précisent que :

- Presque deux fois moins d'expériences entrepreneuriales ont été réalisées au Québec comparativement au reste du Canada
- Autant de gens ont fermé une entreprise au Québec qu'ailleurs
- La même volonté d'entreprendre existe au Québec
- Au Québec, 56 % des entrepreneurs se sont mis en création d'une entreprise pour la première fois et 83 % étaient âgés de 18 à 35 ans
- Les entreprises au Québec ont une moins longue durée de vie
- Les entrepreneurs québécois ne possèdent pas autant de capacités et de compétences essentielles à la création d'une entreprise. Les forces de l'entrepreneuriat québécois sont la persévérance, le goût du risque et le leadership. Ses faiblesses sont une trop grande orientation vers l'argent, une vision à court terme et un manque de connaissances.

Ces conclusions permettent même d'identifier une problématique culturelle caractérisée par une peur viscérale de l'échec. De plus, il existe au Québec un sous-investissement chronique dans l'entrepreneuriat, ce qui signifie que nous négligeons de préparer la relève à agir comme de futurs entrepreneurs. L'apprentissage de l'entrepreneuriat des fondateurs s'est réalisé sur le terrain par essais et erreurs. Cette technique de formation est de loin celle qui exige le plus de temps et qui est la plus coûteuse. Le défi qui attend les entrepreneurs de demain ne possède pas l'avantage de l'apprentissage sur le tas. L'entreprise a déjà atteint un rythme de croisière qui exige de ses dirigeants qu'ils soient aptes à gérer le jour même où ces responsabilités leurs sont confiées.

Enjeux

Les premiers moments de réflexion sur la continuité de l'entreprise amènent un flot de questions : Qui est susceptible d'assurer la relève ou est intéressé par l'entreprise ? Quel est le moment opportun ?

Comment allons-nous procéder? À quel prix? Vont-ils me payer? Quel sera mon rôle? Vont-ils m'imposer ce que je ne veux pas? Que puis-je faire pour assurer le succès de l'opération? Vont-ils respecter mes volontés? Sont-ils dignes de confiance? L'harmonie familiale est-elle en danger? Qu'adviendra-t-il si ça ne fonctionne pas? Comment être équitable dans ce processus?

Selon une candidate pressentie pour la future équipe de direction et de gestion, toutes ces questions demeurent sans réponse au premier abord. Elle reproche aux entrepreneurs et dirigeants actuels de refuser de trouver des réponses, laissant ainsi cette lourde responsabilité au cycle naturel des choses. Pourtant, ils ont bâti leur entreprise sur la confiance et le désir de réussir. Elle s'explique difficilement que ces ingrédients de succès demeurent inutilisés pour assurer l'avenir de l'entreprise.

Des statistiques inquiétantes

De récentes études canadiennes ont révélé que plus d'un dirigeant sur deux prendra sa retraite dans les dix prochaines années. En conséquence,

- 1,2 billions de dollars en biens d'entreprises sont appelés à changer de mains d'ici 2010, soit le plus important roulement de nature économique depuis des générations (MPE, 2005)
- 70% des entreprises ne survivent pas à la deuxième génération et 90%, à la troisième (Grisé et Plante, 2005)
- 90% des entreprises au Québec sont des PME et génèrent 85% des nouveaux emplois

Les statistiques les plus optimistes indiquent qu'un projet de relève sur deux fonctionne. Nous nous intéressons à la problématique de la relève entrepreneuriale au Québec depuis plus de cinq ans.

La solution unique et innovatrice que nous proposons a été développée à partir d'une question adressée aux entrepreneurs du Québec. Cette question avait pour objectif de préciser le comportement adopté par l'entrepreneur lorsqu'il pense à assurer la continuité de son entreprise. Les entrepreneurs ont exprimé à peu de choses près la même réponse: «Le quotidien de l'entreprise est déjà très

exigeant, nous n'avons pas le temps de nous préoccuper de l'avenir!»
Nous avons insisté en précisant que certains événements, comme
l'état de santé et la diminution de la capacité de travailler, entraînaient
l'urgence de penser à la relève. À ce moment, leur réflexe naturel
est de contacter leur conseiller financier, leur comptable, leur fis-
caliste, leur notaire, leur évaluateur d'entreprise et toute personne
œuvrant dans un secteur d'activités connexe. Nous demeurons
conscients de l'importance de se référer à ces professionnels. Par
contre, nous n'aurions pas ces statistiques alarmantes si la solution
se situait à ce niveau.

Alors, quelle est la différence entre un projet de relève qui
fonctionne et les autres? Existe-t-il un moyen de s'assurer de faire
partie des statistiques positives?

Nous avons réalisé plus de trois cents interventions à travers
le Québec au cours des cinq dernières années. Toutes ces entreprises
s'inscrivent dans les statistiques positives, ce qui signifie que nous
avons identifié des solutions sur mesure pour chacun d'eux afin
d'assurer le succès du plan de relève. L'ensemble des activités
décrites plus haut se réfèrent à un des aspects du transfert d'entreprise, soit le transfert de propriété. L'autre aspect du transfert, malheureusement trop souvent négligé, concerne le transfert de direction
et de gestion.

Cet aspect, le transfert de direction et de gestion, consiste à
identifier les personnes qui assumeront les responsabilités de gestion
et de supervision de l'entreprise lorsque les dirigeants actuels seront
passés à autre chose. Les statistiques précisent que les entrepreneurs
investissent en moyenne 80 000 heures pour amener leur entreprise
à un niveau de rentabilité qui lui assure un avenir. Il demeure surprenant qu'ils hésitent, dans ce contexte, à consacrer quelques heures
à la planification du projet de relève entrepreneurial! Pour la majorité
des entrepreneurs, la valeur de l'entreprise représente leur fonds de
pension. Ainsi, pour assurer le retour sur l'investissement principal
de toute leur vie active, l'entreprise doit continuer à opérer en
générant les profits essentiels.

La planification et la réalisation de ce projet de relève entrepreneuriale offrent les meilleures garanties de succès lorsque les

principes de gestion du potentiel humain, largement documentés dans ce livre, sont respectés.

La solution OPERH

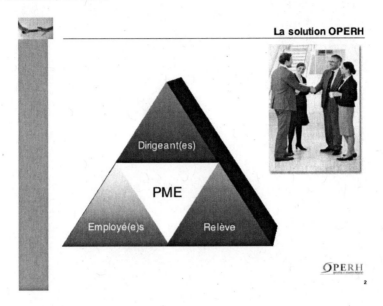

L'ensemble de la réflexion essentielle à la planification du projet de relève doit être réalisée en fonction de l'objectif principal : assurer la pérennité de l'entreprise. Ainsi, l'entreprise est au cœur des décisions de chaque élément du plan de relève. Cette étape de vie de toute entreprise constitue un des plus gros changements à planifier et à gérer. Tous les humains, à l'intérieur comme à l'extérieur, sont concernés, qu'il s'agisse des dirigeants actuels, des candidats pressentis pour la relève, des employés, des fournisseurs, des partenaires d'affaires ou des clients.

Ainsi, la solution à la problématique de la relève entrepreneuriale au Québec se situe au niveau des aspects humains de l'entreprise. Seule, la ressource humaine peut intégrer tous les aspects de ce changement majeur qui a pour effet de faire vivre de l'insécurité à tous les acteurs impliqués.

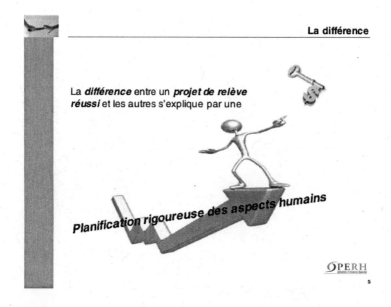

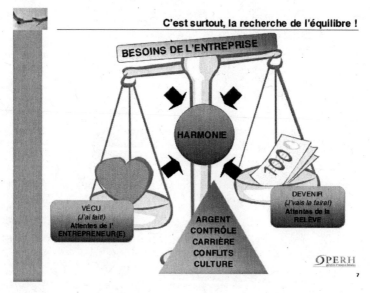

Ce schéma présente toute la complexité d'un projet de relève entrepreneuriale. Ce projet existe pour l'entreprise. L'objectif premier demeure d'assurer sa pérennité. D'un côté, il y a l'entrepreneur ou les entrepreneurs qui ont amené l'entreprise là où elle se situe actuellement. Il(s) a (ont) des attentes précises en ce qui concerne le projet de relève. De l'autre, il y a les candidats pressentis pour la relève qui eux aussi ont des attentes. Sont-elles les mêmes? Pire encore, sont-elles compatibles?

Voilà certains commentaires intéressants reçus des entrepreneurs : L'entrepreneur actuel s'interroge fortement sur la capacité de la relève à réussir en affaires alors qu'elle n'est pas prête à en payer le prix. «Je n'aurais jamais réussi en affaires si j'avais fermé en milieu d'après-midi pour aller chercher les petits à la garderie, si je n'avais pas donné la priorité à l'entreprise à tous les instants! Comment peuvent-ils espérer réussir en affaires alors que leur bien-être personnel prime sur l'entreprise?» Les candidats pressentis pour la relève s'expriment ainsi, quant à eux : «Les façons de faire et de diriger de la direction actuelle sont très discutables et n'ont pas évolué. Passe-moi les commandes de cette entreprise et tu vas voir que ça va marcher! Est-il absolument nécessaire de consacrer tous les aspects de sa vie pour la réussite de l'entreprise?»

Évidemment, nous voulons préserver l'harmonie tout au cours de ce processus en tenant compte que la PME québécoise est en majorité familiale. Les facteurs comme l'argent, le contrôle, la carrière, les conflits interpersonnels latents et la culture organisationnelle peuvent rendre difficile, pour ne pas dire impossible, ce maintien de l'harmonie. Une candidate, impliquée activement dans la planification du projet de relève de son entreprise, insiste sur le caractère trop souvent superficiel de cette harmonie. Elle soupçonne même que la peur de dire les vraies choses amène, trop souvent, les gens à garder le silence, entretenant ainsi une harmonie illusoire.

L'argent demeure un facteur de comparaison entre les individus. Nous avons été témoins de plusieurs membres d'équipes de direction ayant décidé de s'octroyer un salaire égal et largement en bas du marché pour des postes à ce niveau de responsabilités, peu importent les responsabilités assumées, le temps que l'entreprise soit payée. Cette solution a entraîné des conflits majeurs en raison des comparaisons effectuées par les conjoints, ce qui a miné le lien de confiance entre les membres de l'équipe de direction. Un autre élément ayant posé problème est l'implication dans l'entreprise, mesurée en nombres d'heures par semaine. En fonction d'autres priorités que l'entreprise, il est très rare que la somme de travail soit partagée également entre les individus. Lorsque vient le temps du partage des bénéfices, les frustrations reliées à l'implication en nombre d'heures donnent lieu à des conflits parfois très difficiles à gérer.

Le contrôle ou le partage des pouvoirs pose aussi problème. À titre d'exemple, une équipe de direction d'une entreprise avait pris la décision de se partager la propriété et les pouvoirs à parts égales entre les trois individus. Cette décision a littéralement paralysé la prise de décision. Difficile de mener un bateau avec trois personnes à la barre ! Un an plus tard, ils devaient réinvestir une somme d'argent très substantielle et élaborer un plan de redressement de l'entreprise.

Les ambitions professionnelles des membres de l'équipe de direction peuvent aussi être nuisibles à l'harmonie. Cette situation survient lorsque le partage des responsabilités ne tient pas compte de l'adéquation entre les besoins de l'entreprise et ceux des individus. Nous avons été témoins de missions d'entreprises transformées drastiquement en fonction des habiletés et ambitions professionnelles des membres de l'équipe de direction. Ces manques de respect à la mission organisationnelle entraînent un degré de risque de l'opération largement plus élevé.

L'exercice de réflexion concernant l'entrepreneur est dirigé sur trois aspects distincts : entrepreneurial, familial et personnel. Que les candidats pressentis pour la relève aient un lien familial ou non, il y a toujours un volet familial dont il faut tenir compte dans la planification du projet de relève.

Les principaux défis de l'entrepreneur actuel sont reliés à un apprivoisement graduel à l'idée de structurer la continuité de son entreprise, même en son absence. Les aspects psychologiques reliés à cette nouvelle étape de vie nécessitent de planifier l'utilisation de son temps et de définir des projets d'avenir. Enfin, l'entrepreneur disposera du temps nécessaire pour se consacrer à ses autres passions !

Le plus grand héritage qu'un entrepreneur puisse laisser à la relève est de transférer les connaissances et expertises essentielles pour continuer d'appliquer la recette qui explique le succès de l'organisation. Il peut contribuer à l'identification des ingrédients de ce succès et développer des stratégies qui assureront l'utilisation future de ces mêmes ingrédients.

Il est aussi un des principaux acteurs qui puisse assurer que la période de cohabitation inter-générationnelle se vive de façon harmonieuse et respectueuse.

Le questionnement relatif à l'environnement interne concerne l'état du personnel de l'entreprise, la situation financière, les systèmes et outils de gestion en place et ses forces et faiblesses. Le volet de l'environnement externe situe l'entreprise dans son marché, la positionne en regard de la concurrence, définit sa distinction et ses avantages concurrentiels.

La culture organisationnelle doit être analysée en profondeur, ceci en vérifiant les outils de gestion en place qui la supportent. Nous pouvons parler ici de la vision, de la mission et des valeurs organisationnelles. Nous devons aussi définir clairement les relations d'affaires et les principes de gestion qui entretiennent ces valeurs dans le temps.

Ce questionnement relatif à l'entreprise assure une planification de la relève entrepreneuriale répondant à ses exigences et respectueuse de sa distinction largement responsable de son positionnement concurrentiel.

Attardons-nous maintenant à la relève. Les volets organisationnel, personnel et professionnel font partie intégrante de la réflexion. Les candidats pressentis pour la relève doivent clarifier leur intérêt et leurs motivations à relever le défi. Ils sont appelés à préciser la valeur ajoutée de leur candidature pour assurer le succès du plan. L'expression de leur vision de l'entreprise permet d'assurer la compatibilité de cette vision avec celle de l'entreprise pour la future équipe de direction et de gestion. Nous attachons une importance capitale à la disponibilité de toutes les connaissances, compétences et expertises requises pour la réalisation des objectifs stratégiques. Finalement, nous validons la capacité de chaque membre de la future équipe de gestion à œuvrer en complémentarité.

Nous nous assurons que les ambitions professionnelles des individus sont compatibles avec les défis offerts par l'entreprise.

Nous validons également la capacité à agir dans le respect de la mission et des valeurs organisationnelles.

Nous insistons sur le défi d'envergure d'établir des liens de confiance avec chaque intervenant, interne ou externe.

Ces candidats à la relève ont peu de références quant aux exigences d'un poste de gestion et de supervision. En effet, le fait d'avoir été témoins pendant une longue période des agissements et décisions de l'équipe de gestion en place ne rend pas automatiquement aptes à assumer ce type de responsabilités.

Les principaux défis de ces candidats pressentis pour la relève demeurent de s'impliquer activement dans la planification du projet de relève et de profiter de cette période de transition pour démontrer leurs capacités à remplacer les dirigeants actuels. Ils doivent prendre progressivement leur place comme dirigeants et leaders.

Valeur ajoutée de l'intervention en relève entrepreneuriale

- Compréhension du succès de l'entreprise
- Transfert des compétences et expertises en matière de gestion
- Planification du futur de l'entreprise
- Utilisation des meilleures pratiques de gestion
- Compréhension des enjeux stratégiques de gestion
- Gestion optimale du potentiel humain de l'organisation
- Définition d'une stratégie gagnante de gestion du changement
- Maintien de l'harmonie organisationnelle
- Définition d'une vision et d'une mission communes
- Identification des besoins de l'entreprise pour assurer sa continuité

Cette intervention offre l'avantage d'un double retour sur l'investissement. La réflexion sur l'organisation, sa distinction, son succès et les outils de gestion améliorent simultanément les façons de faire de l'entreprise, la communication au sein de l'équipe de direction et la mobilisation à la réalisation des objectifs organisationnels.

L'entrepreneur qui décide de donner la priorité à son projet de relève et de s'y impliquer activement a l'avantage de sécuriser l'ensemble des intervenants internes et externes dans une opération suffisamment délicate en elle-même et qui se doit de limiter les conséquences négatives. Il s'assure de laisser en héritage à son entreprise son savoir-faire, un élément déterminant de son succès. Il vérifie l'existence d'une vision, d'une mission, de valeurs organisationnelles et d'objectifs stratégiques respectueux de l'entreprise, de sa culture et des attentes de la direction, actuelle et future. Il mesure la capacité de la relève à perpétuer et améliorer la recette du succès. Il contrôle ce changement majeur relié à cette étape de vie de son entreprise. Il se donne les moyens pour faire en sorte que le futur permette de réaliser les objectifs du plan de relève. Il assure le retour sur l'investissement en étant payé pour son entreprise. Enfin, il s'assure d'avoir les bons joueurs à la bonne place, aptes à agir en complémentarité pour répondre à toutes les exigences de l'entreprise.

Bref, il relève avec audace et détermination ce qui risque d'être son plus grand défi avant de céder sa place !

Ce chapitre ne serait pas complet sans partager avec vous une expérience personnelle et professionnelle particulièrement significative en matière de relève entrepreneuriale.

L'été 2009, ma fille Andréa, étudiante en gestion – programme DEC-BAC, a travaillé pour OPERH. Toutes les expériences vécues témoignaient des problématiques reliées à une cohabitation inter-générationnelle harmonieuse en contexte de relève entrepreneuriale. Son mandat était de documenter le sujet en exprimant clairement les caractéristiques de la génération Y, d'identifier les enjeux de la cohabitation inter-générationnelle et de faire ressortir précisément les attentes de sa génération envers les employeurs.

Au départ, je croyais fermement que l'expérience serait particulièrement significative pour sa carrière professionnelle. J'étais à cent lieues d'imaginer la complexité de cette collaboration dans le contexte d'un père ayant des responsabilités d'autorité sur sa propre fille. Je ne me doutais pas que cette expérience me permettrait de comprendre les réactions vives de certains entrepreneurs face à leurs propres enfants.

Aujourd'hui, cette expérience nourrit de beaux moments et des souvenirs significatifs. Nous sommes maintenant aptes à en rire, mais je vous mentirais si je vous disais que la gamme d'émotions vécues a toujours été source de joie, d'humour et de rires. À certaines heures, le consultant s'interrogeait fortement pour expliquer son incapacité à réaliser lui-même ce qu'il demandait à ses clients !

Je me souviens, entre autres, qu'à deux semaines de la fin du projet, Andréa me posait encore des questions de précision sur le mandat, ce qui me mettait bien souvent en grande insécurité. J'exigeais depuis le tout début un plan d'action à réaliser, idéalement en ordre chronologique. Comment réaliser quelque chose sans plan de match ? Ce plan, je ne l'ai pas encore.

Un autre événement s'est avéré fort significatif. Andréa me transmet un texte de quelques pages. À la vitesse de l'éclair, je lui transmets mes commentaires. En fait, j'avais réécrit complètement son document dans le respect de son contenu et de ses idées. Je ressentais tout à fait normal que mon expérience me permette d'organiser sa présentation dans un format compatible avec la réalité des entrepreneurs.

Sa réaction fut vive et instantanée. « Je ne sais pas pourquoi tu me demandes des choses, alors que tu prends plaisir à les refaire. En fait, tu as toujours été comme ça, tu as toujours considéré tout ce que je fais comme nul et sans valeur. » Je venais de comprendre pourquoi mes clients n'arrivent pas à dissocier entreprise et famille !

Je vous présente ici un résumé du rapport qu'elle m'a remis à la fin du projet.

En substance, âgée de 20 à 30 ans, cette génération présente un rapport différent au travail. « Elle ne serait pas dans une logique de performance, mais d'épanouissement »
Jean-Emmanuel Ray

Caractéristiques de la génération Y

- Elle entretient une vision différente de l'entreprise
- Débrouillarde
- Elle refuse de perdre sa vie à la gagner
- Seuls l'action et le résultat comptent
- La structure hiérarchique, les politiques et les procédures ne dictent pas ses attitudes et ses comportements
- Impatiente
- Utilisatrice de toutes les nouvelles technologies, dont Internet
- Génération de contacts et de réseaux
- Grande capacité d'adaptation
- Fort désir d'apprendre de ses expériences, en apprentissage continu
- Conciliation travail famille prioritaire
- Besoin de comprendre le sens que revêt son travail dans l'organisation
- Elle aime bénéficier d'une certaine liberté d'action
- Équilibre entre la vie professionnelle et personnelle très importante
- Scolarisée, l'éducation étant un processus pouvant s'échelonner sur une vie
- La loyauté envers l'employeur ne s'exprime pas par l'obligation de travailler au même endroit toute la durée de sa vie active
- Elle possède une culture de mondialisation, dans le respect des différences
- Elle est exigeante et consciente de sa valeur
- Créative et innovatrice
- Volonté de gravir les échelons au pas de course
- Recherche du plaisir dans le travail, d'un rythme et de résultats rapides, d'un emploi stimulant
- Besoin de coaching, recherche d'un mentor et non d'un supérieur, intention d'avancer seule et d'avoir quelqu'un sur qui compter si ça ne fonctionne pas
- L'apprentissage et le développement des compétences sont essentiels
- Elle tient plus à l'élargissement de ses responsabilités et au développement de ses compétences qu'aux promotions
- Elle demande à être consultée de façon quasi systématique sur tout ce qui la concerne
- Elle magasine ses emplois comme les plus vieux magasinent leurs voitures : elle pose des questions, compare, en veut pour son argent
- Elle est à la recherche de conditions optimales pour son développement et son épanouissement personnel et professionnel
- Elle n'aime pas être noyée dans la masse, elle souhaite être reconnue
- Elle recherche une meilleure qualité de vie, en conciliant travail et intérêt personnel
- Elle pense à court terme et est très mobile

> Cette génération a le sens de l'engagement.
> « Elle sait être passionnée et s'impliquer
> sur une mission qui fait sens »
>
> Charlotte Duda,
> Présidente nationale de
> l'Association Nationale des DRH.

Contexte historique

- Les parents des Y se sont investis grandement dans leur travail
- Beaucoup d'entre eux ont vu leurs parents demeurer fidèles à leur employeur durant de longues années avant d'être congédiés sans préavis
- Ce contexte a eu pour résultat de désillusionner les jeunes face aux institutions et de les obliger à se prendre en main de façon autonome
- Plusieurs d'entre eux ont souffert, étant jeunes, de l'absence de repères, de leurs proches
- Comme leurs parents leur achetaient tout, ils sont habitués à tout obtenir, sans effort
- Leurs parents travaillant soixante heures par semaine, ils en ont souffert directement et ne veulent pas reproduire ce modèle.

> Et elle va vite, cette génération, au point,
> souvent, de brûler les étapes. « Depuis
> qu'elle est née, on lui dit que le changement,
> c'est bien »
>
> Jean-Emmanuel Ray

QUATRIÈME PARTIE

Modèles entrepreneuriaux québécois

CHAPITRE 16

Louis Garneau de Louis Garneau Sports

Louis Garneau incarne un modèle entrepreneurial québécois. Sa gestion d'entreprise respecte-t-elle les principes de base de la croissance personnelle et de la conquête du bonheur ?

Une simple lecture de sa biographie « Ne jamais abandonner… ! » écrite par Henri Marineau, permet d'identifier clairement les ingrédients qui expliquent les succès passé, actuel et futur de l'homme et de l'entrepreneur.

Louis Garneau, l'individu

D'abord, Louis Garneau se distingue en tant qu'individu. Le respect occupe une place de choix dans sa vie. Que l'on parle du respect des valeurs familiales, culturelles et patrimoniales ou d'un être fondamentalement humain qui respecte les individus même en contexte d'affaires. « Ce qui me préoccupe essentiellement, c'est le respect des hommes et des femmes, l'attention particulière que je tente de leur donner, certaines valeurs d'où émane une confiance fragile qui, tel un arbre, pousse très lentement mais, peut rapidement être coupée[1] ».

---

1. Ne jamais abandonner Louis Garneau ; Henri Marineau ; Louis Garneau Sports ; 2006 ; page 211

Mais quelles sont les qualités de Louis Garneau ? Nous devons reconnaître sa simplicité, son accessibilité, sa passion de tous les instants, sa vision, sa générosité, son leadership, son intuition, sa capacité à rêver, son acharnement, sa persévérance, sa grande énergie, son besoin de se surpasser, sa spiritualité, son talent artistique, son humilité et sa joie de vivre.

Louis Garneau affirme l'importance de la famille, de ses ancêtres à ses enfants. «La famille représente, au plus profond de mon âme, l'essentiel de ma vie, la substantifique moelle, mon apaisant équilibre[2].»

Il crée un lien étroit entre l'amour, l'amitié et la loyauté. «Nos amis sont les pierres précieuses de notre couronne de bien-être.[3]»

Y-a-t-il place au doute et au tiraillement dans la vie de Louis Garneau ? Que l'on parle de la décision de quitter la compétition, de celle de vendre ou de conserver son entreprise ou de celles concernant l'utilisation de son talent au plan professionnel, Louis Garneau reconnaît être souvent tiraillé dans ces moments de choix et de décisions. Il exprime même qu'il s'interroge souvent sur les motifs qui l'ont incité à opter pour un choix de vie si exigeant.

Louis Garneau, l'artiste

Le sens artistique de Louis Garneau a été déterminant dans l'ensemble de ses choix de vie et de ses réalisations. Nous devons nous arrêter quelques instants sur cet aspect intimement relié à la gestion et à l'utilisation du potentiel humain. De fait, un principe de base en gestion du potentiel humain exige de reconnaître ce potentiel et de décider comment nous allons l'utiliser pour contribuer à la réalisation de nos objectifs.

J'ai fait le choix définitif d'être artiste... Les atmosphères, les lieux que l'on crée deviennent ce qu'on veut devenir[4]...

---

2. Henri Marineau ; op. cit. ; page 238
3. Henri Marineau ; op. cit. ; page 240
4. Henri Marineau ; op. cit. ; page 98

Louis Garneau, l'athlète

Il retient du milieu de la compétition sportive le sens de la victoire, le besoin de se surpasser, les stratégies de la performance, la gestion de la peur, le développement des mécanismes de défense et des réflexes instinctifs, la rigueur, la détermination et l'instinct de survie.

Il associe une grande partie de sa discipline personnelle, sa résistance phénoménale et sa capacité à rebondir dans les périodes difficiles à ses expériences dans l'univers du cyclisme. C'est dans le sport qu'il a appris le leadership.

Louis Garneau, l'entrepreneur

Louis Garneau a décidé de joindre les rangs des bâtisseurs du Québec. Pour ce faire, il n'a fait que transposer ses qualités de cycliste à son entreprise. D'ailleurs, il dirige son entreprise à l'image d'un capitaine de route en cyclisme. Il donne espoir à son équipe. Il assure la synergie dans l'équipe. Il matérialise la complémentarité dans l'effort pour atteindre le podium en équipe, ceci aux jours meilleurs comme aux périodes plus sombres. Il se donne le rôle de motiver les troupes, de les informer de ses projets pour les mobiliser et fait valoir les avantages de la persévérance. Bref, il demeure stratégique, visionnaire et il assure le consensus au sein de l'équipe.

Il reconnaît humblement que la réalisation d'un rêve entrepreneurial comporte ses moments de doutes, d'inquiétudes sur sa capacité à réussir. Vous savez, ces moments d'insomnie et de tourmentes... L'antidote qu'il utilise demeure la persévérance, la détermination, une volonté à toute épreuve. D'ailleurs plusieurs entrepreneurs reconnaissent que la direction d'une entreprise exige d'apprendre à vivre avec le doute et l'inconfort.

Au chapitre de la gestion du potentiel humain, Louis Garneau demeure un adepte des structures administratives légères, souples et avec le minimum de niveaux hiérarchiques. Il s'assure d'une

délégation de pouvoirs et responsabilités respectueuse des zones de
performance de chacun des membres de l'équipe.

> En affaires comme en marketing, il faut à tout prix éviter
> d'appliquer des recettes toutes faites et plutôt utiliser le gros
> bon sens de façon intelligente.[5]

Louis Garneau définit le marketing comme étant la capacité
à imaginer des concepts pour réaliser l'objectif ultime de l'entreprise,
soit le pont entre les produits et la vente sans laquelle l'entreprise
n'a pas sa raison d'être. Dans ce contexte, nous devons reconnaître
que le changement demeure omniprésent. Même si le changement
définit sa règle d'or, il précise qu'il doit s'implanter dans le respect
des traditions établies et de la culture organisationnelle. C'est là une
condition à la progression de nos entreprises.

Ainsi, l'indicateur par excellence de la santé de nos organisations s'établit dans la mesure de la capacité d'adaptation. Celle-ci
n'appartient en rien aux équipements, aux processus et aux techniques mais plutôt à la ressource humaine ; la seule apte à gérer et
à intégrer le changement dans le respect de cycles naturels. Cette
responsabilité ultime des équipes de direction et de gestion de provoquer les changements souhaitables en adoptant les mécanismes
de souplesse essentiels au respect des individus et de l'organisation
fait la différence entre les meilleurs gestionnaires et les autres.

Louis Garneau affirme que la santé de l'économie passe par
l'innovation, le véritable moteur qui conduit à la réussite. Ici aussi,
reconnaissons que la seule ressource ayant la capacité d'innover est
l'humain. Cette innovation doit se réaliser et se matérialiser dans le
respect de la culture organisationnelle et de sa planification stratégique. En fait, toutes les parties de l'organisation doivent œuvrer en
parfaite complémentarité à la réalisation d'une mission commune
et partagée. Les états financiers présentent l'information essentielle
pour quantifier la performance de l'entreprise en matière de gestion
de l'innovation, spécifiquement en ce qui concerne le contrôle du
prix de revient.

---

5. Henri Marineau ; op. cit. ; page 159

Pour Louis Garneau, «plus le président motive ses employés, plus ils se passionnent pour leur travail et plus ils sont en mesure d'apporter de nouvelles idées[6]». Le lien entre leadership, passion, innovation et entrepreneuriat s'établit ici naturellement. Mes expériences en consultation en entreprises me permettent, encore aujourd'hui, de reconnaître l'écart majeur entre un principe de gestion et son application au quotidien. Il est alarmant de constater que la réceptivité aux nouvelles idées des collaborateurs demeure filtrée par la compatibilité entre les suggestions et la vision de la direction! Pour que l'innovation demeure la pierre angulaire des éléments distinctifs de nos organisations, il est essentiel de se doter de pratiques d'affaires respectueuses des idées qui surgissent de tous les intervenants, même si celles-ci remettent en cause nos façons de faire et de gérer.

Louis Garneau reconnaît que la voie empruntée n'est pas celle de la facilité. Il a appris de ses erreurs comme les autres. Il n'a pas sacrifié la survie de l'entreprise pour répondre naturellement à un besoin de démontrer qu'il avait raison. Il fait la différence entre gagner et avoir raison. Pour lui, tout problème a une solution. D'ailleurs, Bernard Lemaire de Cascades abonde dans le même sens en exprimant: «En affaires, la réussite est possible si, à l'exemple de notre père, nous mettons tout en œuvre pour trouver une solution à un problème».

Louis Garneau précise que ces solutions se trouvent le plus souvent dans l'univers de la simplicité.

Pour Louis Garneau, le pouvoir demeure un moyen de relever des défis et non une fin en soi. Et le service à la clientèle est un art et une philosophie. Notre service à la clientèle se doit d'être réinventé en continu pour assurer son adaptation à l'évolution des marchés et des besoins des clients.

À la question: «Quels indicateurs mesurent l'indice organisationnel du bonheur?», il répond qu'ils appartiennent au monde des émotions. Des indices existent dans l'humeur des collaborateurs, dans les sourires et dans l'expression d'une fierté d'appartenir à

---

6. Henri Marineau; op. cit.; page 162

l'équipe. Le taux de roulement mesure la loyauté des employés envers l'entreprise. Un taux de roulement anormalement élevé peut signifier que les employés adhèrent à d'autres causes pour réaliser leurs ambitions professionnelles et pour relever de nouveaux défis.

Louis Garneau affirme qu'une gestion d'entreprise a pour principal objectif de faire naître le bonheur pour les collaborateurs, partenaires et clients.

Lors du passage de la flamme olympique à Québec, Louis Garneau l'a transportée. Il avait arrêté sa production pour permettre à tous les employés de participer à cet événement. Lors de son allocution qui a suivi, il a exprimé que le succès de Louis Garneau Sports dépendait des employés. Il a même exprimé que s'il est rendu là comme individu, c'est grâce à eux !

Nous ne pouvons passer sous silence cette reconnaissance de tous les instants envers ses parents qui l'ont toujours supporté sur le plan financier ainsi qu'en investissant cinq ans sans rémunération pour lui permettre de réaliser son rêve entrepreneurial. Son père exprime ouvertement qu'à certaines heures, le risque supporté par Louis dépassait largement sa propre capacité. « Une chance que sa mère était là, cette beauceronne dans l'âme pour lui avancer certaines sommes en me le cachant ! » Que dire de la contribution de Monique, son épouse, qui, pendant plusieurs années, a permis au couple de vivre avec son salaire d'infirmière tout en passant le reste de son temps à l'entreprise. Ces gens ont eu une implication qui dépasse largement le temps et l'argent, ils ont supporté Louis aux moments heureux et surtout aux heures plus sombres. Ils n'ont jamais retiré leur confiance. Ils ont fait la même chose pour le supporter et l'encourager comme cycliste de compétition.

L'auteur insiste sur la contribution humaine au succès Louis Garneau. Sans enlever quelque mérite que ce soit à ce modèle entrepreneurial québécois, nous pouvons nous interroger longuement à savoir si Louis Garneau aurait atteint ce niveau de dépassement de lui-même en compétition comme en affaires sans ce soutien de ses proches.

Ainsi, Louis Garneau a fracassé les records car il a été supporté et supervisé d'une façon qui l'obligeait au dépassement, au courage, à la détermination et à ne jamais abandonner. Le lecteur reconnaîtra qu'il existe des méthodes de gestion qui incitent au dépassement. Cet exemple nous indique des moyens concrets à la disposition des gestionnaires pour mobiliser à la réalisation du projet d'entreprise.

Ce support exige aussi un respect des intervenants à tous les instants. Il faut investir en communication. Des messages clairs doivent être formulés pour permettre aux collaborateurs de reconnaître leur contribution à la réalisation des objectifs. Ici, Louis Garneau insiste sur le fait que cette reconnaissance n'est pas strictement financière et monétaire. Il faut expliquer et expliquer encore et encore le pourquoi des choses. Cette information privilégiée nourrit le sentiment d'appartenance et enlève toute emprise aux rumeurs.

L'indicateur par excellence d'une gestion d'entreprise qui permet aux employés de s'investir dans le succès de l'entreprise demeure les états financiers et les performances de l'entreprise par rapport aux autres œuvrant dans le même secteur d'activité.

CHAPITRE 17

Anne Morisset de Boulevard Lexus Toyota

Dans un élan de grande générosité, Anne Morisset a accepté de collaborer à l'écriture de mon livre. Elle s'interrogeait grandement sur le pourquoi de ma demande envers elle. Cette collaboration n'aurait pas été possible sans le dévouement et la disponibilité de Patrice Ouellet, directeur général.

Raconter l'histoire à succès d'Anne Morisset sans parler de ses origines, de son père Louis, demeure mission impossible. La philosophie de gestion de Louis Morisset (1932-2006) s'exprime ainsi : «Nous avons construit en valorisant les forces de notre équipe et en surpassant les attentes de notre patron, c'est-à-dire le client. Notre philosophie consiste à être à l'écoute de nos clients afin de leur assurer une entière satisfaction. L'écouter et le comprendre constituent le véritable gage de succès pour notre entreprise.»

En 2001, Louis Morisset, ex-président fondateur de Ste-Foy Toyota et de Boulevard Lexus Toyota, passe définitivement le flambeau à sa fille Anne. Elle devient alors l'une des très rares femmes présidentes de concessions de voitures au pays. Elle possède la même passion que son père et son grand-père pour l'automobile.

Les valeurs actuelles et passées des dirigeants de Boulevard Lexus Toyota demeurent le respect, la qualité, la transparence et l'engagement. Leur but se définit ainsi : «Assurer à tous nos invités clients une expérience exceptionnelle à chaque visite.» Ils se sont engagés à offrir à leur clientèle des produits exceptionnels, ainsi qu'un service remarquable et attentionné. Avec sa nouvelle puissance, Boulevard Lexus Toyota offre encore plus de services et de choix que jamais! Désormais, plus de gens pourront rouler encore plus loin, plus longtemps, sans soucis et sans tracas. C'est ça, mettre l'incontournable puissance au service de sa clientèle!

Les dirigeants de Boulevard Lexus Toyota œuvre dans le respect de cette philosophie de gestion axée sur le client en valorisant l'équipe. Elle recherche avant tout la bonne attitude. Qui ne la recherche pas? Mais comment relève-t-on ce défi? Anne Morisset et son équipe utilisent depuis plusieurs années un outil de gestion du potentiel humain qui consiste à identifier les caractéristiques de personnalité essentielles pour assumer les responsabilités spécifiques de chaque poste. Chaque employé évolue alors dans ses zones de performance.

La direction s'assure aussi que les individus qui composent l'équipe demeurent aptes à travailler en complémentarité à l'atteinte des objectifs organisationnels.

L'équipe Boulevard Lexus Toyota exprime qu'une saine gestion du potentiel humain exige de travailler les zones de force et de pallier les faiblesses.

Est-ce dispendieux d'appliquer cette philosophie de la satisfaction de la clientèle dans le contexte où le client a toujours raison? L'équipe Boulevard Lexus Toyota répond qu'il n'est pas arrivé qu'un client exige quelque chose qui dépasse la capacité de l'organisation à le satisfaire! Cette approche nécessite une grande écoute et une volonté à toute épreuve de réaliser au quotidien la satisfaction de la clientèle.

Pour exceller en affaires, l'équipe Boulevard Lexus Toyota donne l'exemple. Elle investit sur le client et sur les employés. Elle œuvre dans le moment présent en réalisant maintenant dans le respect de sa philosophie de gestion. Elle se ramène continuellement à la réalité client: l'achat d'une automobile demeure stressant pour le client. Boulevard Toyota rend cette expérience agréable malgré tout.

Toyota est l'inventeur du "lean management". Cette méthode de gestion s'appuie sur des principes de base qui exigent de produire la qualité du premier coup par l'utilisation optimale de toutes les ressources, ce qui évite le gaspillage en diminuant les coûts de production des produits et services.

Cette école de gestion est largement documentée et communiquée. Comment se fait-il que si peu d'entrepreneurs réussissent à l'appliquer? L'équipe Boulevard Lexus Toyota répond qu'un maximum de cinq pour cent des entrepreneurs est apte à implanter et appliquer ces principes de gestion!

Boulevard Lexus Toyota utilise une matrice de gestion à cinq composantes: bonne personne à la bonne place, application du bon processus, entraînement sur mesure, plan de rémunération mobilisateur et motivant, et support de l'équipe de direction et de gestion. Ces cinq composantes interpellent la même ressource: la ressource humaine!

Dans l'application de cette matrice de gestion, Boulevard Lexus Toyota a dû développer et raffiner des réseaux de communication bidirectionnels qui assurent que les messages transmis provoquent les réactions souhaitées quant aux attitudes et comportements de l'ensemble des intervenants. Il serait illusoire de croire que l'ensemble des messages des intervenants est facile à recevoir. Lorsque ces messages s'avèrent dérangeants, la preuve est faite que l'objectif de la communication n'est pas atteint. Il faut alors revenir à la base, se centrer sur le client, sur notre mission et appliquer les règles de base de la simplicité et du bon sens pour identifier une solution durable et sur mesure. Ainsi, la direction reconnaît qu'une communication efficace exige d'aller chercher les objections, de clarifier les objectifs en les traduisant en langage significatif pour chaque intervenant, une condition essentielle pour obtenir la collaboration et la mobilisation de chacun. L'employé doit s'approprier l'objectif et reconnaître sa contribution potentielle à sa réalisation. C'est là une définition sur mesure de ce qui doit être réalisé pour assumer le leadership d'une équipe de direction.

Les chiffres parlent d'eux- mêmes!

Boulevard Lexus Toyota gère par département, par centre de profit. Ils investissent dans la formation des employés plus de quatre fois la moyenne de l'industrie canadienne ! Est-il surprenant qu'ils soient aussi les plus rentables et les meilleurs au Canada ? Les indicateurs du retour sur l'investissement demeurent : roulement de personnel quasi inexistant, satisfaction de la clientèle et rendement financier. Le sourire constant des collaborateurs et clients démontre clairement le degré de satisfaction.

L'équipe Boulevard Lexus Toyota insiste pour exprimer que les équipes les plus performantes réalisent les objectifs les plus élevés. Elle arrive à mobiliser les troupes à un point tel que chaque membre de l'équipe agit comme s'il était propriétaire de l'entreprise.

Ainsi, Boulevard Lexus Toyota réussit à se démarquer malgré la concurrence féroce, les marges bénéficiaires limitées, les difficultés liées au recrutement, un rétrécissement de la différence entre les meilleurs et les autres et l'apparition de nouveaux joueurs autrefois peu significatifs sur le marché.

L'équipe Boulevard Lexus Toyota conclut en disant que le président de Toyota, M. Toyoda, petit-fils du fondateur, demeure un visionnaire adepte des structures organisationnelles légères.

Boulevard Lexus Toyota reconnaît que son succès dépend en grande partie d'une même passion qui animait Louis Morisset et qui anime encore aujourd'hui Anne Morisset.

CHAPITRE 18

Steve Couture de Frima Studio

La collaboration de Steve Couture, président de Frima Studio nous permet d'enrichir ce livre d'un vécu entrepreneurial hors du commun.

Fondée en 2003, Frima Studio est une entreprise de Québec qui développe des jeux vidéo sur de multiples plateformes. Sa clientèle est constituée des plus importantes compagnies de divertissement au monde, telles que Disney, Warner et Sony.

Le nombre d'employés est passé de 20 à 250 en 5 ans. Plus de 85 % de ses employés appartiennent à la génération Y. Pendant cette même période, Frima Studio a connu une explosion de son chiffre d'affaires de 5 000 %, ce qui en fait la compagnie ayant connu la plus forte croissance au Québec et la 10e au Canada en 2009 selon le magazine l'Actualité.

La jeune entreprise de jeu vidéo œuvre dans une industrie mondiale très exigeante. Cette industrie de passionnés, qui appartient au monde de la créativité, de l'imaginaire et du divertissement, oblige les dirigeants d'entreprises à sans cesse repousser les limites afin de demeurer les meilleurs.

Steve Couture, lui-même un passionné, apprécie le mariage entre une belle folie créative et un goût pour la technologie. Pour lui, un entrepreneur doit être créatif, avoir le goût du risque et une détermination à toute épreuve.

Très impliqué dans la formation de la relève, M. Couture a développé une nouvelle concentration en multimédia et jeux vidéos à l'Université Laval où il a enseigné pendant huit ans. Il a aussi mis sur pied un programme de formation en jeux vidéos dans un collège privé en plus de contribuer au collectif « Ma carrière en jeux » et à la fondation de l'École Nationale de Divertissement Interactif. Pour lui, la diffusion du savoir technologique dans la société est essentielle.

Sa plus grande fierté est d'avoir participé à bâtir une équipe créative qui développe des produits de grande qualité pour divertir les enfants et les joueurs occasionnels du monde.

L'objectif de Frima Studio est de créer une entreprise qui sera un jour une icône dans le divertissement numérique sur la scène internationale et ce, tout en continuant d'opérer à Québec.

Ce modèle entrepreneurial québécois percutant impose une évolution majeure quant à la gestion du potentiel humain. Les dirigeants de l'entreprise ont compris que le défi de l'industrie du jeu vidéo est constitué de créativité, de passion, d'invention et d'imaginaire. Le succès de Frima, malgré son petit nombre d'années d'existence, appartient au génie créateur et inventif de ses ressources humaines.

Frima mise sur la jeunesse. Il fait des miracles et réalise l'impossible avec des jeunes, génération pourtant reconnue pour donner des maux de tête aux entrepreneurs et gestionnaires. Une analyse d'experts nous oblige à reconnaître que les qualités associées à la créativité, à l'imaginaire et à la nouvelle technologie appartiennent justement à cette nouvelle génération ! La génération Y offre, de loin, le plus fort potentiel en innovation, technologie et adaptation au changement. En ce sens, cette génération demeure celle qui a le plus d'affinités avec les besoins du secteur d'activités de Frima.

Frima Studio offre, en ce sens, des défis professionnels et un environnement de travail sur mesure pour répondre aux exigences de cette génération. Les Y veulent des emplois leur permettant d'exploiter leurs grandes capacités créatrices dans un monde où le résultat de leur travail est le fruit de l'innovation. Ils se réalisent mieux et davantage quand leurs responsabilités permettent d'agir comme pionniers. Les Y exigent aussi un fort degré d'implication à la prise de décision et à la réalisation.

Le lien employeur-employé doit être empreint d'un respect des individus. Nous pourrions discuter longuement sur la définition du mot «respect» par cette génération Y. Des différences majeures existent avec les générations précédentes pour qui le respect était associé à la conformité aux règles établies. Pensons seulement aux nombreux jugements qui considèrent les gens de cette génération comme des enfants-rois, incapables de respecter quelque forme d'autorité que ce soit.

L'équipe de direction de Frima agit comme pionnière en matière de gestion des ressources humaines. Notre compréhension est qu'il semble plus simple de définir des systèmes de gestion adaptés aux caractéristiques de cette génération Y que d'investir dans l'adaptation de systèmes ayant été conçus pour d'autres géné-rations, des différences majeures rendant quasi impossible d'adapter ces systèmes.

Les pierres angulaires de ces systèmes de gestion, éléments peu négociables, connaissent des différences fondamentales. La génération Y ne respecte pas les individus en fonction d'un respect imposé par une structure hiérarchique. Ces jeunes ne veulent pas d'un patron conventionnel mais d'un coach qui les implique et les respecte. Leurs exigences créent une pression énorme sur nos orga-nisations. On peut parler ici de la flexibilité des horaires de travail, de l'importance accordée à la qualité de vie et des exigences sala-riales élevées. Par contre, refuser de s'adapter à la main-d'œuvre disponible dans notre contexte de vieillissement de la population et de diminution de l'offre de travail peut affecter la pérennité même de nos entreprises.

Face à ce constat, les équipes de direction et de gestion de Frima s'appliquent à développer des systèmes très innovateurs pour répondre aux exigences de la génération Y. Les références au passé et aux systèmes existants ne sont pas d'une grande utilité si nous nous fions aux résultats obtenus auprès de cette génération Y. La mobilisation des employés à la réalisation de la mission de l'entreprise exige des solutions innovatrices qui permettent aux employés d'actualiser leur vision du travail, c'est-à-dire un moyen d'accomplissement et une opportunité de démontrer leur capacité à réaliser des choses. Ces solutions sur mesure diminuent largement l'impact de la résistance au changement.

Frima a l'avantage de ne pas avoir à modifier des systèmes de gestion qui assurent une cohabitation harmonieuse entre les générations en contexte de travail. De plus, la compatibilité entre les valeurs organisationnelles et celles des gens qui y travaillent s'établit naturellement. Ainsi, Frima offre un milieu de travail et des défis très attirants pour la main-d'œuvre qu'elle courtise. En ce sens, elle attire les talents essentiels à son succès.

L'obligation de créer et d'inventer constamment a amené Frima à implanter un système de valorisation de la créativité. Des idées de jeux originaux soumises par des employés font l'objet d'une évaluation par un comité de sélection. Les employés dont le projet a été retenu par le comité sont libérés une demi-journée par semaine pour développer leur jeu. Une fois le projet avancé, la direction juge de la pertinence de mettre en marché ce jeu. Si le projet franchit cette étape, la mise en marché est assurée par Frima et un pourcentage des profits est redistribué aux employés ayant imaginé et créé la propriété intellectuelle. L'objectif est de faciliter la réalisation des projets soumis par les employés, car, trop souvent, ces projets demeurent au stade des idées.

Le système de gestion de la performance implanté chez Frima mérite une attention particulière. Il s'agit d'un système de pointage attribué aux équipes de travail selon des critères précis. Les points accumulés peuvent être utilisés pour toute dépense susceptible d'améliorer la qualité de vie des employés, tels que des forfaits au restaurant, des travaux de peinture ou de rénovation, du gardiennage pour les enfants ou un chef à domicile. En plus des avantages sociaux conventionnels, Frima innove en offrant une foule d'avantages hors du commun à son personnel : fruits frais à leur disposition tous les matins, salles de jeux, massage sur les lieux de travail et le ramassage par autobus payé par l'employeur.

L'équipe de direction demeure convaincue que ces investisse-
ments dans le bien-être de ses employés font toute la différence. Les
employés sont fiers d'appartenir à l'équipe et ils démontrent leur
appréciation par un meilleur rendement. Le taux de roulement du
personnel et le chiffre d'affaires par employé le démontrent clairement. À la base, le principe reconnaît qu'un employé heureux dans
sa vie personnelle est un employé plus efficace. L'important est
d'avoir du plaisir au travail. Frima représente la preuve indéniable
qu'une entreprise avec des employés heureux réalise de meilleures
performances.

Steve Couture affirme que le plus important, c'est la ressource
humaine. Il va plus loin: « Si Frima n'avait pas besoin de ses
ressources humaines, je n'aurais pas d'affaire là ».

Il assume lui-même la responsabilité de s'assurer de l'adhésion
de ses employés aux valeurs organisationnelles en faisant en sorte
qu'elles demeurent vivantes au quotidien de l'entreprise et permettent
à Frima de se distinguer. Ainsi, M. Couture organise, deux fois par
année, une rencontre générale avec tout le personnel afin de lui
parler des projets, des nouveautés et des orientations de Frima pour
les prochains mois. Teintées d'humour et de contenu interactif
(vidéos, jeux, tirages de prix, etc.), ces rencontres permettent aux
employés de se sentir impliqués et de connaître la réalité de l'entreprise avec beaucoup de transparence. Il se fait aussi un plaisir de
participer régulièrement aux activités sociales de l'entreprise afin
d'échanger avec le personnel dans un contexte plus informel.

Ce climat de travail mobilisateur se fonde sur une stratégie
de communication active au sein de l'entreprise en multipliant les
rencontres des équipes de travail et en saisissant toutes les opportunités d'améliorer les produits par l'utilisation des idées de chaque
membre de l'entreprise. En plus de ces rencontres et de plusieurs
activités sociales informelles, l'équipe de Frima bénéficie d'un
journal interne qui donne les dernières nouvelles de l'entreprise et
des gens qui y travaillent.

Steve Couture et son équipe provoquent sans contredit une
évolution majeure, voire même une révolution, en matière de gestion
des ressources humaines. Ils influencent positivement leur milieu

et la société. Fidèles à leur mission d'entreprise, ils démontrent qu'une gestion des ressources humaines peut être réinventée. Les outils utilisés sont constitués de passion, de détermination, de vision et d'équilibre personnel. De par sa nature, l'industrie du divertissement provoque l'amélioration de la qualité de vie de tous les clients et utilisateurs. Frima démontre que cette amélioration de la qualité de vie doit d'abord prendre ses racines au sein des employés de l'entreprise.

Conclusion

L'objectif premier de ce livre demeure de démontrer la relation étroite entre la recherche du bonheur, la croissance personnelle et la gestion de nos entreprises. Il veut provoquer une évolution vers des pratiques d'affaires innovatrices et respectueuses des principes de base de la croissance personnelle et de la recherche du bonheur. Il affirme qu'une gestion d'entreprise contributive au bonheur de tous les intervenants, internes et externes, assure une nette amélioration de la rentabilité des entreprises et organisations.

L'humanisation de nos entreprises demeure une composante clé de leur succès et le moyen concret d'améliorer l'indice du bonheur de chaque intervenant.

La première partie fait la démonstration que ce livre s'inscrit dans un mouvement mondial. L'ONU contribue financièrement à l'indice de progrès véritable. L'indice de développement humain (IDH) a été créé par le Programme des Nations Unies pour le Développement (PNUD). Ce mouvement mondial permet même d'affirmer que le XXIe siècle sera celui du bonheur scientifique. De fait, nous voulons quantifier le bonheur et permettre de comparer les sociétés entre elles.

La synthèse des écoles de pensées amène inévitablement au constat suivant : l'humain demeure, depuis ses origines, à la recherche du bonheur.

La deuxième partie démontre la contribution des profils de personnalités et des profils de postes à la gestion du potentiel humain. Les commentaires reçus de la part des entrepreneurs dénotent une grande difficulté à mobiliser le personnel pour réaliser le projet de l'entreprise. Il demeure inquiétant de constater le manque ou même l'absence de préparation des entrepreneurs à assumer cette lourde tâche qu'est la gestion des ressources humaines. L'auteur s'explique difficilement que les entrepreneurs œuvrent à autre chose que ce pour quoi ils ont été formés en institution d'enseignement ou à l'école de la vie !

Une saine gestion du potentiel humain assure la meilleure contribution des ressources à la réalisation des objectifs organisationnels. Ainsi, toute intervention en gestion du potentiel humain doit contribuer à la réalisation de cet objectif. Toutefois, les outils de gestion du potentiel humain doivent prendre en considération les caractéristiques des utilisateurs. L'auteur insiste, à ce sujet, sur l'obligation de considérer l'importance capitale du caractère familial des PME québécoises.

Les décisions en matière de gestion du potentiel humain, utilisant des fondements autres que ceux généralement reconnus en la matière, ne servent pas les intérêts de l'entreprise et des gens qui y travaillent.

S'il demeure essentiel de connaître le potentiel humain, son utilisation exige un exercice de réflexion approfondi sur les connaissances, aptitudes et expertises requises pour répondre aux exigences des responsabilités attribuées à un poste donné. Cet exercice de réflexion doit demeurer centré sur les besoins de l'entreprise quant aux connaissances, expertises et expériences requises pour combler les attentes reliées au poste et assurer la meilleure contribution à l'atteinte des objectifs organisationnels.

Un principe de gestion reconnu affirme que le tout est plus grand que la somme des parties. Ainsi, l'ensemble des activités reliées à la gestion et à l'utilisation du potentiel humain doit favoriser le travail d'équipe et la complémentarité dans l'effort pour exceller dans l'application de ce principe de gestion.

L'utilisation des meilleurs outils de gestion du potentiel humain et l'approbation de la politique de gestion du potentiel humain idéale ne suffisent pas à assurer le succès en la matière et à provoquer les avantages concurrentiels majeurs, entre autres, l'amélioration sensible et mesurable de la profitabilité de nos entreprises.

Cette politique de gestion du potentiel humain s'inscrit dans une philosophie globale de gestion de l'entreprise. L'ensemble des politiques de gestion sont des vases communicants et ils doivent respecter les mêmes principes de gestion, indicateurs de performance et critères de conformité.

L'innovation, dans une des composantes de l'entreprise, doit assurer que les systèmes en parallèle demeurent aptes à s'adapter et à contribuer à l'atteinte des objectifs. Même si l'entreprise dispose de spécialistes pour l'implantation de toute politique de gestion ou outil de gestion, la direction avisée et visionnaire devra assurer la capacité de l'ensemble de l'organisation à les appliquer et à les utiliser. Le retour sur l'investissement optimal exige une analyse approfondie de l'impact sur l'ensemble des composantes de l'organisation.

Souvent, l'employeur doit organiser à l'intérieur de l'entreprise les activités de développement des ressources humaines assurant la disponibilité des compétences et expertises au bon moment. Ce processus prend du temps et exige une planification à moyen et long terme.

La gestion du potentiel humain exige de vérifier et de valider la capacité du candidat à œuvrer en équipe et en étroite collaboration à la réalisation des objectifs organisationnels.

Le questionnement, lié à l'identification de la bonne personne pour assumer certaines responsabilités précises en contexte de collaboration, trouve tout autant sa pertinence dans le choix des partenaires d'affaires, des fournisseurs et même des clients !

L'auteur affirme que, peu importe le lien d'affaires (employés, partenaires, associés, fournisseurs, clients), il se doit de respecter la culture organisationnelle et ses valeurs sans quoi il devient impossible d'agir en complémentarité à la réalisation d'objectifs communs.

Il demeure impossible d'utiliser une ressource si nous n'investissons pas pour en connaître ses caractéristiques, ses propriétés, ses capacités et sa valeur ajoutée. Ainsi, les évaluations d'aptitudes et d'attitudes nous renseignent sur la probabilité de retour sur l'investissement.

Les dirigeants d'entreprises doivent entretenir une image corporative attrayante. Ainsi, l'employeur confronté sur une base régulière à des menaces de quitter l'entreprise de la part des employés doit s'interroger sérieusement sur le sentiment d'appartenance qui le lie avec ses employés. Par contre, chaque partenaire, chaque employé, chaque client assume une responsabilité majeure pour entretenir une image corporative attrayante.

Une saine gestion d'entreprise doit s'exercer en demeurant connectée sur les perceptions des collaborateurs, sans quoi le lien qui entretient la confiance réciproque devient très fragile. Nous parlons ici d'un processus de gestion et d'amélioration continu.

Le succès de nos entreprises et l'amélioration de leur rentabilité financière sont directement liés à la gestion du potentiel humain.

Des pratiques d'affaires mobilisatrices pour l'ensemble des collaborateurs exigent le respect des individus dans leur dimension humaine, c'est-à-dire des individus à la conquête du bonheur qui établissent une relation directe entre leur travail, les responsabilités assumées et leur évolution pour atteindre les sommets au niveau de leur bien-être et de leur qualité de vie.

La troisième partie analyse les pratiques d'affaires susceptibles de contribuer à une meilleure gestion du potentiel humain, soit la réflexion stratégique, la gestion de la performance, la gestion de la commercialisation, la gestion globale de la rémunération, la structure organisationnelle de la relève, l'agilité organisationnelle, la planification de la relève entrepreneuriale et la consolidation d'équipe par l'action et le jeu.

Une pratique d'affaires efficace qui contribue à la réalisation de la mission organisationnelle ne réside pas dans sa conception mais bien dans son utilisation. Celle-ci se doit de respecter les règles de l'art en matière de gestion du potentiel humain.

En premier lieu, rappelons-nous que la seule ressource apte à faire une bonne utilisation d'une pratique d'affaires demeure la ressource humaine. Comme le précise l'agilité organisationnelle, la valeur ajoutée ne se situe pas dans les processus mais bien dans l'utilisation qu'on en fait.

Une pratique d'affaires se doit de s'intégrer harmonieusement à l'ensemble de l'entreprise et agir en complémentarité avec les autres. Bref, elle doit faciliter l'atteinte des objectifs des autres pratiques. Toute pratique d'affaires, quelle qu'elle soit, ne peut atteindre qu'une vision limitée de l'organisation. Par conséquent, une vision globale de l'organisation doit supporter chaque pratique d'affaires.

L'équipe de direction demeure l'actrice principale de l'implantation d'une pratique d'affaires. D'ailleurs, c'est l'entité la plus imputable. Toute pratique d'affaires représente un changement dans les façons de faire. Elle doit donc être supportée par une stratégie de gestion et d'implantation du changement. Elle doit aussi prévoir des séances de formation aux personnes concernées pour assurer une même compréhension de sa portée et de ses enjeux. Les employés doivent comprendre l'importance de collaborer à l'implantation et à l'application de cette pratique, transférant ainsi aux utilisateurs les connaissances et expertises essentielles à la meilleure utilisation de l'outil de gestion.

L'implantation d'une pratique d'affaires exige de la rigueur, de la constance, de la détermination et une souplesse essentielle pour s'adapter en continu aux changements organisationnels et aux modifications des autres pratiques d'affaires. Il demeure impossible de tolérer des comportements et attitudes irrespectueux des pratiques d'affaires, s'assurant ainsi de la crédibilité de la pratique d'affaires et de la collaboration des utilisateurs.

Une bonne stratégie de communication représente un élément essentiel de l'implantation d'une pratique d'affaires. Elle assure que les intervenants concernés comprennent l'information sur l'application de la pratique. Cette validation devrait se faire en continu et l'acceptation de son rôle de leadership par l'équipe de direction exige une réaction rapide à toute information reçue relative à des difficultés rencontrées par l'application d'une pratique d'affaires ou par l'existence de comportements ou attitudes non respectueux de celle-ci.

Nous n'insisterons jamais assez sur l'importance de faire les choses une par une et dans le bon ordre. Rappelons-nous également que la force d'une chaîne se mesure à son maillon le plus faible. Plus la stratégie d'implantation est précise, plus la pratique d'affaires sera efficace et assurera, par le fait même, une amélioration de la rentabilité de l'entreprise.

Enfin, l'efficacité et la pertinence d'une pratique d'affaires se mesurent par sa contribution à la réalisation des objectifs et de la mission organisationnels. L'implantation d'une pratique d'affaires doit assurer l'existence de réflexes naturels qui favorisent la complémentarité dans l'effort et la mobilisation à la réalisation de la mission organisationnelle.

La dernière partie de ce livre partage le vécu de modèles entrepreneuriaux québécois : Louis Garneau, Anne Morisset et Steve Couture, en illustrant clairement comment ces entrepreneurs obtiennent l'indice organisationnel du bonheur optimal.

La principale contribution de Louis Garneau en matière de gestion du potentiel humain réside dans le fait que le succès en affaires exige l'utilisation de tout le potentiel humain de l'organisation en appuyant son succès d'entrepreneur sur l'actualisation de son propre potentiel humain en tant qu'individu, artiste et athlète.

Il insiste sur le respect des valeurs familiales, culturelles et patrimoniales, une attitude qu'il transpose chez toute personne, même dans le contexte d'affaires. En ce sens, il a atteint le podium en affaires en appliquant une gestion d'entreprise respectueuse de l'univers de la compétition sportive.

Louis Garneau a décidé de joindre les rangs des bâtisseurs du Québec. Pour ce faire, il n'a fait que transposer ses qualités de cycliste à son entreprise. Il assure la synergie dans l'équipe en matérialisant la complémentarité dans l'effort pour atteindre le podium. Il se donne le rôle de motiver les troupes, de les informer de ses projets pour les mobiliser et fait valoir les avantages de la persévérance. Bref, il demeure stratégique et visionnaire tout en assurant le consensus au sein de l'équipe. Il reconnaît toute l'importance de la capacité d'adaptation et d'innovation en continu. .

En fait, aux yeux de Louis Garneau, toutes les parties de l'organisation doivent œuvrer en parfaite complémentarité à la réalisation de la mission commune et partagée de son entreprise.

Le modèle Louis Garneau ne présente pas la voie de la facilité. Toutefois, pour lui, tout problème a une solution, laquelle appartient au monde de la simplicité.

Le service à la clientèle est un art et une philosophie. Louis Garneau a fracassé les records car il a été supporté et supervisé, dès sa jeunesse, d'une façon qui l'obligeait au dépassement, au courage, à la détermination et à ne jamais abandonner.

Finalement, pour Louis Garneau, la réussite des entrepreneurs est étroitement liée au plaisir qu'ils éprouvent à exercer leur travail.

Anne Morisset, présidente de Boulevard Lexus Toyota, contribue aussi à l'évolution de la gestion du potentiel humain. Sa principale contribution en ce sens demeure la démonstration que le succès en affaires exige le respect de la philosophie de gestion, de la culture et des valeurs organisationnelles. Sa philosophie de gestion veut valoriser les forces de son équipe et surpasser les attentes du client.

Sa gestion, largement influencée par le Système Toyota, fait la preuve que la différence ne se situe pas dans la connaissance des meilleures pratiques d'affaires mais bien dans leur application quotidienne en contexte d'amélioration continue.

La gestion des ressources humaines respecte les principes de base de la gestion du potentiel humain. L'équipe de direction investit sur le client et sur les employés et se ramène constamment à la réalité client.

Anne Morisset insiste sur l'importance d'une communication franche et d'une réaction rapide aux informations reçues des intervenants internes et externes. Les solutions retenues et appliquées sont empreintes de simplicité et de bon sens. La mobilisation exige une communication utilisant un langage significatif pour chaque intervenant.

L'équipe de direction croit que les équipes les plus performantes réalisent les objectifs les plus élevés. Finalement, au regard d'Anne Morisset, le succès en affaires exige qu'une même passion soit transmise à tous les intervenants concernés.

La contribution de Steve Couture, président de Frima Studio, à l'évolution des pratiques d'affaires en gestion du potentiel humain est certes reliée à son rôle de pionnier dans la définition et l'implantation des pratiques de gestion des ressources humaines compatibles avec l'environnement technologique et la très grande proportion de son personnel qui appartient à la génération Y. Cette entreprise, qui a connu la plus forte croissance au Québec et la dixième au Canada en 2009, œuvre au sein d'une industrie jeune et passionnée, laquelle appartient au monde de la créativité, de l'imaginaire et du divertissement.

L'équipe de direction de Frima Studio investit constamment dans le développement et la formation. En conséquence, la qualité des produits s'appuie sur une équipe créative et efficace dont le succès appartient au génie créateur et inventif de ses ressources humaines.

Frima Studio offre une parfaite compatibilité entre sa mission organisationnelle et les objectifs personnels et professionnels de ses employés. Pour y parvenir, l'équipe de direction offre un environnement de travail sur mesure. Les défis offerts répondent aux aspirations et attentes des employés tout en privilégiant le respect de chacun.

Chez Frima Studio, la cohabitation harmonieuse entre les générations dans le contexte du travail est une réalité vécue au quotidien. Des programmes de valorisation de la créativité et de gestion de la performance innovateurs assurent la mobilisation de chaque intervenant.

Voilà un modèle à imiter qui démontre sans contredit que Frima Studio met l'accent sur la ressource humaine. L'implication des employés est soutenue par une communication constante, incluant des rencontres formelles et informelles avec tous les employés. De plus, l'équipe de direction saisit toutes les opportunités d'améliorer les produits par l'utilisation des idées reçues des employés.

En conclusion, on peut affirmer que Steve Couture et son équipe influencent leur milieu et même la société en provoquant constamment l'amélioration de la qualité de vie de tous les intervenants internes et externes.

En terminant, je vous livre certains commentaires relatifs à la gestion du potentiel humain.

La passion, composante essentielle du bonheur individuel et collectif, demeure l'indicateur par excellence d'une gestion du potentiel humain efficace. Les meilleures pratiques d'affaires en matière de gestion du potentiel humain doivent incarner cette passion au sein de l'entreprise. Elles la génèrent, la créent et la communiquent à l'ensemble des intervenants internes et externes. Cet élément distinctif de l'organisation demeure palpable et perceptible à tout instant !

Ce livre donne une signification renouvelée à la contribution de la gestion des ressources humaines axée sur l'amélioration de la rentabilité de nos entreprises. L'ensemble des intervenants qui assument des responsabilités de supervision des ressources humaines, incluant les professionnels en GRH, auraient avantage à s'en inspirer de façon à contribuer davantage à la réalisation de la mission organisationnelle. Nous demeurons les individus les plus aptes à définir notre contribution optimale à l'entreprise puisque la gestion du potentiel humain fait partie de nos expertises. Prenons notre place, assumons le leadership essentiel et saisissons toutes les opportunités d'améliorer l'indice organisationnel du bonheur. Voilà en quoi consiste l'humanisation de la gestion de nos entreprises.

L'indice organisationnel de bonheur optimal exige la réalisation de l'adéquation entre les objectifs personnels des individus qui y travaillent et la mission de l'organisation. Ce défi demeure très exigeant pour les individus et pour l'organisation mais c'est le prix à payer pour atteindre le podium. Je vous suggère fortement d'écrire votre mission de vie et de définir le plus clairement possible vos objectifs personnels. Vous pourrez alors évaluer la complémentarité avec la mission organisationnelle de l'entreprise où vous travaillez.

Permettez-moi une comparaison entre l'évolution humaine et la gestion du potentiel humain. L'être humain, en évolution, reconnaît d'abord l'immensité de l'univers dans lequel il vit. Par la suite, il se reconnaît comme partie intégrante de cet univers. En matière de gestion du potentiel humain et de recherche du bonheur, l'individu conçoit d'abord l'entreprise dans sa globalité. Ses aspirations lui permettent, ensuite, de visualiser la réalisation de la mission organisationnelle. De cette façon, l'individu reconnaît sa contribution réelle à la réalisation de la mission organisationnelle, dans le respect de sa propre mission de vie.

Voilà la garantie de la mobilisation et de la motivation des ressources humaines. C'est ça, une gestion d'entreprise qui mène au bonheur de tous les intervenants !

Je souhaite ardemment, pour ne pas dire passionnément, que cette lecture contribue à votre bonheur. Puisse-t-elle vous transmettre le courage et la détermination pour réaliser les activités personnelles et professionnelles qui contribuent à votre bonheur personnel et collectif !

Je vous remercie de me communiquer votre appréciation et vos commentaires, contribuant ainsi largement à mon bonheur ! Mon adresse courriel est : delislepaul@operh.ca.

Bibliographie

Deming, W. Edwards, *Du nouveau en économie*, Économica, Paris, 202 p.

Heurtault, Christelle, *Le livre du bonheur Des citations à méditer et des défis à réaliser pour être heureux*, Grancher, Paris, 2004.

Keeley, Brian, *Le capital humain Comment le savoir détermine notre vie*, Éditions OCDE, Paris, 2007, 159 p.

Marineau, Henri, *« Ne jamais abandonner... ! » Louis Garneau*, Louis Garneau Sports Inc., Québec, 2006, 309 p.

OHNO, Taiichi, *Toyota production system: beyond largescale production*, Lavoisier, 144 p.

Osmont, Stéphane, *À la poursuite du bonheur*, Éditions Albin Michel, Paris, 2009, 197 p.

Ricard, Matthieu, *Plaidoyer pour le bonheur*, NiL éditions, Paris, 2003, 380 p.

Robbins, Anthony, *L'éveil de votre puissance intérieure*, Le Jour Éditeur, Montréal, 1993, 568 p.

Sévigny, Yves, *Le défi de la joie: 21 façons de retrouver et d'entretenir la joie au quotidien*, Le Dauphin Blanc, Québec, 2006, 361 p.

Tardif, Marie-Josée, *La leçon de Sitar ou L'art de vibrer de toutes ses cordes*, Éditions du Roseau, Montréal, 2007, 235 p.

Au sujet de l'auteur

Paul Delisle, expert en gestion du potentiel humain, offre le coaching aux entrepreneurs et gestionnaires pour l'intégration de pratiques d'affaires et de gestion respectueuses des principes de base de la croissance personnelle et de la recherche du bonheur. Il contribue ainsi à l'humanisation des entreprises et au bonheur individuel et collectif.

Pour toute information ou pour contacter l'auteur :

Paul Delisle
836, Kennedy
Scott (Québec) G0S 3G0
Tél. : (418) 780-6587
delislepaul@operh.ca